DESIGN AND MARKETING OF NEW PRODUCTS

DESIGN AND MARKETING OF NEW PRODUCTS

Second Edition

Glen L. Urban

Alfred P. Sloan School of Management
Massachusetts Institute of Technology

John R. Hauser

Alfred P. Sloan School of Management
Massachusetts Institute of Technology

PRENTICE HALL, Englewood Cliffs, New Jersey 07632

Library of Congress Cataloging-in-Publication Data

Urban, Glen L.
    Design and marketing of new products / Glen L. Urban, John R.
  Hauser.—[Rev. ed.]
      p. cm.
    Includes bibliographical references and index.
    ISBN 0-13-201567-6
    1. New products.   2. Design, Industrial—United States.
  I. Hauser, John R.   II. Title.
  HF5415.15.U7   1993
  658.5'75—dc20   93-7240
                                                                CIP

Editorial production supervision and interior design: Alan Dalgleish
Acquisitions editor: Sandra Steiner
Cover design: Karen Salzbach
Prepress buyer: Trudy Pisciotti
Manufacturing buyer: Patrice Fraccio

Printed in the United States of America

10   9   8   7   6   5   4   3   2   1

ISBN   0-13-201567-6

Prentice-Hall International (UK) Limited, *London*
Prentice-Hall of Australia Pty. Limited, *Sydney*
Prentice-Hall Canada Inc., *Toronto*
Prentice-Hall Hispanoamericana, S.A., *Mexico*
Prentice-Hall of India Private Limited, *New Delhi*
Prentice-Hall of Japan, Inc., *Tokyo*
Simon & Schuster Asia Pte. Ltd., *Singapore*
Editora Prentice-Hall do Brasil, Ltda., *Rio de Janeiro*

Dedication from Glen L. Urban

to

my mother with deep appreciation.

Dedication from John R. Hauser

Su meile mano žmonai Marijai. Ne užmirštami ir mano brangūs sūnūs—Marius, Aleksas, ir Rolandas.

In memory of my parents, Jesse and Florence, and to my brother, Rowland, and his family.

Brief Contents

Contents

Chapter 13   Designing for Quality

Chapter 15   Advertising and Product Testing   424

Chapter 16   Pretest Market Forecasting   449

Preface

The first edition of *Design and Marketing New Products* was published in 1980 and, although we did publish an undergraduate and updated version in 1987 with Nikhilesh Dholakia (titled *Essentials of New Product Development*), a second edition of the original text has been long overdue.

This revision began in 1989. Because new-product development has changed dramatically in the 1980s, we found that to be up-to-date over 75 percent of the book became new material. New-product development has widened to include global issues, marketing strategy and cross-functional interfaces, quality and customer satisfaction, and new techniques that are relevant across a range of industries. As a result the book now addresses the world as the market; it is written in all sections with a global perspective. New-product development is based firmly in the strategy of the first and includes the marketing, manufacturing, finance, engineering, and R&D functions. A new chapter has been added on quality ("Designing for Quality"—Chapter 13) and the total-quality point-of-view now permeates the text. All the methods of market research and modeling have been updated for the significant advances in the marketing-science field. Applications are described in consumer and industrial, products and services, and frequently-purchased and durable goods. New real-world examples are added to demonstrate the best level of practice in each problem situation.

To make room for these new content areas while maintaining an effective level of accessibility to our readers, we have become less encyclopedic in our references. We rely on excellent review articles that have been published in the last ten years and choose those references that help us discuss and illustrate our mission of defining a successful process for developing new products in the world of the 1990's and beyond. In 1980 many of the details of new-product development methods were available only in the technical marketing literature, thus we felt a need for technical appendices to collect these methods in one place. In 1992 these techniques are widely used and referenced. The technical appendices are no longer necessary for all readers[1]. We still retain the belief that good analysis is essential for new-product success, but in this edition we concentrate more on the managerial use of the analysis than the mathematical details of the techniques themselves. (We do include references to the technology of the analyses.)

The net result of the changes is an updated, comprehensive guide to new-product success in the 1990's where globalization, rapidly changing technology and social change is causing firms to adopt a strategic perspective with an integrated focus on total quality and on the customer.

TARGET AUDIENCE

One primary audience for this book is the marketing major who has taken the basic marketing management course and is looking for an in-depth exposure to new-product development. Another audience is those students in technology management, strategy, or engineering design who want to understand today's customer-driven innovation strategy.

While the 1980 version was written as a textbook, we were gratified to see that many practitioners and marketing-research professionals found it useful. New product directors, R&D managers, product managers, marketing research staffs, and consultants should find this book useful in defining a successful new product. In the global competition between Europe, the Americas, and the Far East innovation increasingly is the competitive advantage. We believe that managers in all countries will find this text useful.

OUTLINE

The text begins with a discussion of innovation strategy and is the followed by five sections each representing a major phase in the new-product-develop-

---

[1] A compendium of the appendices is available from Prentice-Hall upon request.

ment process: 1) Opportunity Identification, 2) Designing New Products, 3) Testing Products, 4) Introduction and 5) Managing the Life Cycle. In the real world the process is not rigid nor necessarily sequential—we adopt this paradigm to allow an orderly pedagogy. We close with a discussion of how to implement the new-product process, and with a view of the future of new-product decision-making in the 1990's continuing into the 21st century.

ACKNOWLEDGMENTS

We have many people to thank for their help and support in the second edition. At MIT our colleagues (Thomas Allen, Gabriel Bitran, Wujin Chu, Don Clausing, Arnoldo Hax, France Leclerc, John Little, Robert Pindyck, Drazen Prelec, Bill Qualls, Ed Roberts, Richard Schmalensee, Lester Thurow, Eric Von Hipple, Roy Welsh, and Birger Wernerfelt) and at other universities (Frank Bass, Bob Dolan, Marcel Corstjens, Josh Eliashberg, Pete Fader, Abbie Griffin, Peter Farquhar, Claes Fornell, Paul Green, Jim Hess, John Hulland, Gurumurthy Kalyanaram, Hotaka Katahira, Jim Lattin, Ted Levitt, Gary Lilien, Len Lodish, Vijay Mahajan, Don Morrison, Scott Neslin, Mike Pessemier, John Roberts, Bill Robinson, Subrata Sen, Allan Shocker, Steve Shugan, Al Silk, Hermann Simon, V. Srinivasan, Rick Staelin, Sudharshan, Alice Tybout, Bruce Weinberg, and Jerry Wind) were important in thinking. Practicing managers and consultants who helped us maintain a high level of relevance include Vince Barabba, Jim Barlow, Carol Berning, Roberta Chicos, Steve Cohen, Tom Cook, John Dables, John DeVries, Mary Jo Fisher, Steve Gaskin, Lou Goldish, Scott Halstead, Lee Haydon, Karl Irons, Marc Itzkowitz, Costa Joannidis, Joe Kasabula, Jerry Katz, Bob Klein, Mel Klein, Michael Kusnic, Sheung Li, Corinne Maginnis, Sean McNamara, Sharon Munger, Dave Newhouse, Joe O'Leary, Matt O'Mara, Bill Roth, Leigh Shanny, Steve Snyder, and Ken Wisniewski. At Prentice Hall the editorial staff (Jennifer Young, Sandra Steiner and Cathi Profitko) were effective and professional. Critical typing and editorial support were provided by Patti Shaughnessy and Polly Slade. To all these people we say, "Thank you!"

DESIGN AND MARKETING OF NEW PRODUCTS

1

Introduction to New-Product Development

New products are crucial to successful growth and increased profits in many organizations. Consider the following examples.

- In 1910 the dominant mode of urban transportation was the streetcar railway. It provided fast, reliable, inexpensive transportation for our nation's cities. Its growth seemed assured. Population was expanding, our cities were becoming more interdependent, and there would always be a need for urban movement. But when Henry Ford provided a more flexible and personal transit option at a slightly higher cost, consumers purchased his new product, and the automotive industry was born.

    Today transportation continues to evolve both within and between cities. The global auto market is diverse providing more than 300 models to span consumer needs. There are, for example, "econoboxes" for low-cost operation, luxury cars for prestige, room, and comfort, minivans for families, sports cars (both high-end and low-end) for excitement, and four-wheel-drive vehicles for rugged outdoor lifestyles. The invention of the airplane further changed the role of the car. In many countries airlines have replaced cars, trains, and buses for travel between distant cities. Airplanes also allowed innovation in document and package delivery by the emergence of overnight carriers such as Federal Express and United Parcel Services, which have gained sales at the expense of government mail services. At the same time conventional mail services are being increasingly replaced by facsimile transfer (FAX) and portable cellular phones that are changing the way we communicate worldwide. Rapid technological change has changed the ways in which we travel and interact and created whole new industries.

- In the 1940s and 1950s International Business Machines (IBM) recognized the need for rapid, accurate processing of business related information and captured most of the market. But in 1957 Digital Equipment Corporation (DEC) developed a rugged, specialized, low-cost minicomputer to meet the needs of a new segment of this market. This innovation resulted in the multibillion-dollar minicomputer market. DEC earned a dominant share in that rapidly growing market and triggered entries by firms such as Data General, Sun Micro Systems, International Computers Limited (ICL), Bull, IBM, and others in what became the workstation market.

  In the 1980s, in a small shop Steven Jobs and Stephen Wozniak began to build personal computers (PCs) and then launched Apple Computer, Inc. Apple Computers now have a significant market share and a loyal following among certain segments of the population, but IBM, with an entrepreneurial division, was able to introduce their own and capture a large share of the market. Later, Compaq recognized a need for transportable, reliable computers and gained the third position in the marketplace. Today Hewlett-Packard, NEC, Toshiba, DEC, Wang, Dell, Zenith, Zeos, Northgate, and others offer a variety of computers and printers for the office and the home.

- In the $2 billion shampoo market, leading marketers resort to extremely well-researched segmentation and positioning strategies. For example, in the 1970s, S. C. Johnson and Sons identified oiliness as a major hair-care problem and introduced Agree Creme Rinse to "stop the greasies." Gillette, recognizing that oiliness was mainly a problem for the 12- to 24-year age group, introduced For Oily Hair Only shampoo. For the 18- to 49-year age group, the problem was replenishing natural oil in hair lost with age, styling, and chemical treatment. In the 1980s Gillette introduced the Mink Difference shampoo, containing mink oil, for the older market and for the younger segment, Silkience, a self-adjusting shampoo that provided differential conditioning, depending on the hair type of the user.

  Today firms are still innovating as the population ages and social conventions and work habits change. There is constant shifting with new hair-care products introduced each year. To stay competitive firms must continue to innovate and design new products that meet the perceived needs of consumers.

- In medical electronics the radiation hazard of X-rays prompted research for new safer and more effective diagnostic equipment. General Electric (GE) achieved a major breakthrough with its computerized tomography (CT) body scanner. This scanner vastly reduced the time and exposure needed to conduct a scanning. In fact, the demand was so great for the scanners that many states introduced regulation that required hospitals to demonstrate need before purchasing a scanner.

  GE continued to innovate successfully by commercializing a new diagnostic machine based on nuclear magnetic resonance. This machine can produce an image without radiation or ultrasound. At GE, positron emission tomography (PET) technologies are now being developed for heart and brain imaging. Although GE has competition from Siemens and others, its innovation has earned it $3 billion a year in sales in the medical imaging market.

These anecdotes are but a small sample of the potential rewards for firms who recognize customer needs, successfully introduce new products, and creatively manage them over their life cycles. This book equips you with an understanding of the managerial strategies and techniques necessary to identify markets, create ideas, understand customer needs, design and produce quality goods and services, position products and services vis-à-vis competition, develop new-product marketing plans, test new-product strategies, and introduce successful new products. We aim to give you an understanding of the underlying concepts, a managerial perspective, and an operating ability to develop and introduce new products and manage them within a sound portfolio of existing products.

INNOVATION IS IMPORTANT—BUT RISKY

The development of new products is rewarding and necessary to maintain a healthy organization. For example, in a survey of 700 firms (60% industrial, 20% consumer durables, and 20% consumer nondurables) Booz, Allen, and Hamilton, Inc. (1982) found that over a five-year period new products accounted for 28% of these companies' growth. In a similar survey, primarily of industrial firms, the Conference Board (Duerr 1986) found that 35% of current revenue was derived from products that were not on the market 10 years previously. In a 1990 study sponsored by the Marketing Science Institute researchers found that 25% of current sales were derived from new products introduced in the last three years (Wind, Mahajan, and Bayless 1990).

Basic marketing theory states that a product undergoes a product life cycle of introduction, growth, maturity, and finally decline. In the maturity or decline phase it is imperative that an organization take an active role to (1) expand the product line and extend the life cycle, (2) redesign the product to maintain superiority, or (3) develop a new product to maintain revenue. If new products are not developed, sales and profits decline as competition increases, technology and markets change, or innovation by other firms make existing products obsolete. An organization cannot afford to ignore innovation if it wants to grow and prosper.

Although there are rewards to successful innovation and penalties for failing to innovate, the introduction of new products can be risky. Henry Ford led the way in developing the automobile market, but Ford Motor Company in the 1950s introduced the Edsel and lost more than $100 million. General Motors was forced to abandon its Wankel Rotary engine, although over $100 million had been invested in the project. Bowmar was the pioneering firm in the market for hand-held calculators, but it failed and terminated operations. DuPont's Corfam substitute for leather resulted in hundreds of millions of dollars in losses. General Mills lost millions of dollars on the introduction of a line of snacks called Bugles, Daisies, and Butterflies. Gillette lost millions on a facial cleansing cream called Happy Face. Xerox invented the personal computer in 1973 (three years before Jobs and Wozniak started) but failed to commercialize the "Alto," which represented a brilliant technical success. Osborne was the first firm to offer a portable personal computer but went bankrupt in the early 1980s. IBM stopped producing the PC Jr. in 1985 because of low sales achievement. Exxon lost hundreds of millions of dollars on its ill fated forays into office information systems and high-tech electric motors. RJR Nabisco lost more than $250 million on "Premier" smokeless cigarettes. Federal Express lost more than $190 million on Zap Mail. Polaroid wrote off $68 million on inventory alone for "Polarvision" instant movies and probably incurred total losses of twice that amount on the project.

New-product failure rates are substantial, and the cost of failure is large. Booz, Allen, and Hamilton (1982) found that the failure rate of new products actually introduced in the market remained in the 33% to 35% range between 1963 and 1981. Crawford (1979) concluded that about 20% to 25% of industrial and 30% to 35% of consumer products fail. The Association of National Advertisers (1984), based on responses from 138 firms (74% packaged goods, 12% consumer durables, 12% industrial, and 9% services), found that 27% of product line extensions failed; 31% of new brands introduced in categories where the company already had a product failed; and 46% of the new products that were introduced to new categories failed. These risks of failure given that a product is introduced to the market are only the tip of the iceberg—many projects fail before launch and result in the loss of considerable time, talent, and funds. Innovation is a high-risk activity and getting riskier as the life of successful new products gets shorter and as technological changes render products obsolete at faster rates.

New-product development is also costly. Large investments in research and development (R&D), engineering, marketing research, marketing development, and testing are made before the product is introduced. Because many products do not make it from idea to the market, much of this investment is made on products that never return revenue. For example, Booz, Allen, and Hamilton (1982) found that only one of seven new-product ideas are carried to the commercialization phase. This means that the successful product must not only return its unique development cost, but cover the costs of the other six products that received attention but were not introduced. Booz, Allen, and Hamilton (1982) report that 46% of the resources spent on new products are allocated to products that fail in the market or earlier in the process.

The high failure rates and the high costs make new product development risky. But new product development can be managed so that the risks are minimized and the profit maximized.

PRODUCT DEVELOPMENT CAN BE MANAGED

Success depends on many factors—the extent to which the product satisfies customers' perceived needs, the relative advantages vis-à-vis competition, the propensity of competitors to defend their market, the size and the growth rate of the target segment, whether or not the firm is a pioneer in the market or a follower, the cost and engineering advantages in producing the product, the creativity of the marketing plan, and so on (we discuss these determinants fully in chapter 3). Some of these factors are under the control of the firm; others require information about the market, competitors, engineering capabilities, or potential customers. Still others are less controllable, but represent risk that can be considered and managed.

One approach is simply to bring products to market one after another in the hopes that they might succeed. Another strategy is to take a systematic approach from the inception of an idea to the decision to reposition or terminate an old product. An organization can act to address critical success factors rather than let circumstances dictate the fate of its products.

A key notion is to understand the voice of the customer in terms of perceived needs and to establish a relationship between this customer input and how products are designed, produced, and managed. Products sell because customers find them to be superior, of higher value, or distinctive. Products succeed because a firm can deliver these perceived benefits more effectively and efficiently than competition. One task of product management is to uncover what makes a product superior, of higher value, or distinctive and to deliver it to the customer better than competition. If such customer needs can be identified and designed into new products and marketing programs the firm will succeed.

Success also requires that the target market segment be sufficiently large and that competition be manageable. Thus we identify and target a segment of the market before the critical activity of designing and producing a product or service that delivers benefit to customers.

Neither customer needs nor competition are static. Tastes fluctuate, technology changes, competitors innovate, markets saturate or evolve—new-product strategy cannot be static. This process can and should be managed. In chapter 2 we discuss new product managerial strategies and in chapter 3 we present a conceptual framework for managing the process. But before we discuss how to manage new product development we set the stage by discussing some initiation forces—forces that help us understand the context in which we manage the process.

INITIATING FACTORS

Good managers are continually aware of the marketing system and the environment that affects their organizations. Several of these factors initiate a need for new products. Among these factors are financial goals, sales growth, competitive position, product life cycle, technology, globalization, regulation, material costs, inventions, demographic and lifestyle changes, customer requests, supplier initiatives, and alliances.

Financial Goals

The pressure to achieve financial goals of profit, market share, or revenue —and the resulting impact on stock price—can initiate new product development. For example, in the Booz, Allen, and Hamilton (1982) study, managers predicted that 40% of their firms' profits over the next five years would come from new products. The telephone companies after the breakup of the Bell System faced profitability pressures when earnings stabilized, deregulation opened the market to competition, and demand became saturated with an average of more than one telephone per household. This triggered the search for new services to meet the desired growth in dividends. Services such as electronic mail, telemarketing, teleconferencing, electronic yellow pages, and cellular phones are examples of new products that attempt to renew growth and establish increased profits.

New-product activity is linked intimately to financial planning. The need for sound earnings growth is one of the most important forces impelling new-product development.

Sales and Market Share Growth

Growth in sales is an important goal for many corporations. Japanese consumer electronic firms have introduced a stream of new products to maintain sales growth. This allowed a dominant share position to be established and, through incremental development and experience, cost advantages were achieved. This strategy of achieving long-term profitability through sales and share growth is now being used effectively by Korean and other Asian firms.

Building a strong share position requires focus on a small set of markets rather than scattered attention to many markets. New products become the chief means of market share growth in a focused market strategy. Product innovation and lower costs are critical success factors in a share-based market strategy.

Although sales growth is a long-term goal, profitability cannot be neglected in the short term. For example, Gillette terminated its efforts to introduce pocket calculators and digital watches because, although they represented sales growth, they did not meet profitability standards.

Competitive Actions

The standing of an organization relative to its competitors is a strong motivational force. In some industries, such as autos, market share changes of as little as 1% are critical to profitability.

When competitors introduce new products, firms in the market react. For example, General Foods' entry of Maxim was the first freeze-dried instant coffee. This put Nestlé under considerable pressure. Nestlé responded with Taster's Choice freeze-dried instant coffee and soon dominated Maxim in many markets because it developed an improved product. Similarly, the introduction of Fiberall, a sugar-free bulk laxative by S. C. Johnson, spurred G. D. Searle, the market leader with their Metamucil brand, to counter with their own sugar-free product.[1] IBM—a late comer in the PC market—responded to Apple's innovation and was able to obtain more than a 25% share of the market in two years.

---

[1] Metamucil is now a Proctor and Gamble brand.

Any indication of an unfavorable competitive position provides a strong incentive for change. In the 1950s, the Soviet satellite, Sputnik, was the competitive indicator that spurred the United States to develop the space program that placed a man on the moon. Japanese auto competition forced U.S. auto manufacturers to develop new products to regain lost share.

Life Cycle

Products often follow a life cycle (i.e., introduction, growth, maturity, and decline) so as the product moves from maturity to decline, profits may fall. To regain profitability, the organization directs its effort toward rejuvenating the product or replacing it with a new product that fulfills customers' needs better. For example, when Alka Seltzer unit sales began to fall, Miles Laboratories significantly increased its new product efforts introducing Alka-2 chewable antacid and Flintstone vitamins for children. Bristol-Myers found their markets for consumer packaged goods reaching maturation, and in the 1980s changed its focus to ethical pharmaceuticals and its name to Bristol-Myers Squib through an acquisition.

A decline in sales might not be permanent. The motion picture industry declined in the 1960s and the 1970s but began a new life cycle in the 1980s. The pattern of "recycle" was found to be common in a study of 258 ethical drugs (Cox 1967). Du Pont was able to keep nylon in a growth phase for more than 20 years by expanding uses and applications through new products, ranging from stockings to cloth, tire cord, sweaters, and carpets. Managers may be able to revive or replace a product whose sales are sagging by opening new markets, improving the product, or repositioning it.

Technology

One of the factors accounting for the decline of some products is the rapid change in technology. Computer memory and logic "chips" are becoming faster and more powerful with each generation. For example, many faculty members now have more memory and power on their PCs than was available on their university's mainframe computer 20 years ago. These changes in the basic technology of memory or logical operations are opening up many new markets besides computers including complex video games (Nintendo), "smart" appliances, electronic controls, robotics, laser printers, FAX devices, and even automobiles. There are also related industries such as the software necessary to use the hardware, equipment to test the chips, retail stores to sell the products, and services based on the new products.

Technological change puts extreme pressures on organizations to innovate or decline. For those that create new products the rewards are high (e.g, Apple Computers). Those that rely on existing products and do not react to new capabilities will soon find their customers leaving to purchase competitive offerings. Biogenetics has the potential to revolutionize the pharmaceutical industry. In packaged goods Simplesse is a fat substitute made by blending protein from eggs and milk that may open whole new categories of low fat foods similarly to the way aspartame changed the market for sweeteners. In commercial construction the advent of a rubber-membrane roofing material is rapidly replacing asphalt and gravel as the material of choice in flat or gently sloping roofs. In banking, telecommunication and artificial intelligence systems are changing the nature of competition for financial services.

Globalization

The advent of increased global trade has put two strong forces on firms to develop new products. The first is the competitive threat raised by the ability of foreign firms to enter traditional markets for the firm, and the second is in the opportunities offered by the world in terms of new markets that were not previously attacked by the firm. Motorola has taken the opportunity to sell its cellular phones and pagers in Japan and is in fact a leading supplier in that market. Likewise IBM has a $9 billion business in Japan. Although Gillette is a very successful player world wide, in Japan Shick outsells Gillette by 4 to 1 because of early entry and the use of an aggressive local Japanese marketing campaigns.

The unification of Europe and the dismantling of its trade barriers will pose many opportunities to European firms as they face larger markets but also many threats as they find more competition. Reunification of Germany and the collapse of the iron curtain raises many opportunities in eastern Europe, the Baltics, and the Commonwealth of Independent States. Successful multinational companies in the future will have to be ready to introduce new products in Europe, Japan, the United States, and the reminder of the world. New-product development will become an important part of an organization's global business strategy.

Regulation

In many cases new government regulations or deregulation causes firms to consider new products. Auto companies have had to reduce pollutants and increase gasoline mileage of cars. These regulations led American automobile companies to develop new downsized models and to introduce many technological improvements in their cars. Regulations on emission controls have led to new water based solvents and paints for manufacturing. Hazardous waste handling has emerged as a new growing market as environmental regulation and consciousness has increased.

Airline deregulation led to no-frill airline services. A vigorous shakeout occurred and only the few innovative and efficient airlines survived—low-cost fare capabilities and quality of service became survival factors. Financial services markets are increasingly becoming open worldwide. Deregulation of brokerage commissions led to discount plans by firms such as Fidelity Investments and to enhanced-services packages such as Merrill Lynch's cash management account, which includes check writing, interest payment, credit card, and improved reporting. Credit cards are now offered by AT&T as well as banks. Banks such as Citibank, Deutche Bank, and National Westminster Bank are offering a full range of financial services on a global basis. Deregulation of pharmaceuticals led to the use of ethical drugs in the over-the-counter market (OTC). For example, new pain relievers based on ibuprofen and hydrocortisone skin care products have been introduced into the OTC market.

Material Costs and Availability

As raw material costs and availability change, products must be revised or dropped. In 1976–77 coffee prices more than doubled. This led General Foods to introduce a new brand called Mellow Roast blended from instant coffee and roasted grain. The increase in gasoline prices and foreign competition were tremendous forces on the auto industry to develop small cars. Brazil launched an ambitious, but perhaps ill-timed, program of conversion to gasohol (gasoline/alcohol mixture) when petroleum became scarce and prices looked like they would double or triple in the 1970s and early 1980s. General Electric spent more than $500 million to develop an energy-efficient prop jet engine called the "unducted fan" engine. Unexpectedly, real prices of gasoline dropped so that in the late 1980s the real price was at the 1970 level; GE did not successfully commercialize its engine. This rapid fluctuation in oil also put continued pressure on automobile makers to innovate by returning to "muscle cars," large luxury cars, and sports cars. In 1991 the war in Iraq set off another speculation cycle in oil prices.

Changes in customer awareness of materials can also have an effect. In the late 1980s the recognition that oat bran had an impact on cholesterol led to many new foods from cereal to bread to beer. When it became known that aspirin could have drastic side effects on children, the children's market switched from aspirin-based products to acetaminophen-based products almost overnight.

Invention

The invention of the Polaroid instant camera is a dramatic example of the potential of a new product. A study of new technology-based enterprises in the Boston area indicated that 160 new companies had been formed by past employees of Massachusetts Institute of Technology's (MIT's) research labs (Roberts and Wainer 1968). Their inventions created new opportunities. Some inventions result in entrepreneurial firms being formed. These firms may grow or present acquisition opportunities for established companies. In biogenetics many of the startup firms have been acquired by larger pharmaceutical companies. Other inventions result in licensing opportunities.

Demographic and Lifestyle Changes

The post–World War II baby boom brought about rapid growth in baby products, then came the "youth" culture, the overflowing colleges, and then a very tight housing market. But as rapidly as the youth growth came, it abated as the demographics of the developed countries' population continued to shift. As the average age increases, some industries will benefit (pharmaceutical producers and health care providers), whereas others (tobacco products and soft-drink manufacturers) may suffer. Both Coca-Cola and Pepsico, Inc., have launched several diet and decaffeinated drinks for the maturing diet-conscious population.

Lifestyle also generates consumption changes. Large numbers of divorces and low population growth have led to smaller families resulting in a demand for condominiums, smaller washer/dryers, gourmet frozen dinners, and so on. As the fraction of women working outside the home increased, time became more valuable and services gained in volume. More than one-third of all meals in the United States are now eaten outside the home. In the 1990s many women are postponing child bearing and the rate of births in the 35 to 39-year age group has doubled in the last 10 years. Health consciousness has led to increases in sports equipment and "healthy" foods. Running shoes became a $2 billion per year industry. Environmental sensitivity is increasing and the advent of "green" parties in Europe may affect consumption patterns as well as political directions.

Customer Requests

A source of many new products—particularly in high-tech and other industrial markets—is customer requests. For example, in the market for scientific instruments for gas chromatography and spectrometry, 80% of the major innovations in performance were the result of users who had a need to fill and build a prototype of what they needed. The manufacturer then produced and sold the new instrument. Similar patterns were found in other technical areas such as process machinery (von Hippel 1978).

Supplier Initiatives and Reactions

Suppliers can also be a force in innovation. Alcoa designed an aluminum trailer and promoted it to manufacturers. Bakelite Company was prepared to supply vinyl bottles and containers, but in the 1940s it could not interest major manufacturers such as Armstrong Cork. It had to develop a vinyl floor tile with a small company called Delaware Products in 1946 and thereby created a new market. In the 1980s Tetrapak, the Swiss packaging company, succeeded in persuading U.S. beverage manufacturers to introduce aseptic containers—"drink boxes." In the 1990s their drink boxes became available in a variety of sizes to meet the needs of different age groups.

Distribution channel members are becoming more important in marketing. It is more difficult to sell new products to retailers, and some are demanding "stocking allowances" to put a new product on the shelf for even a few months. This means manufacturers will have to be more selective in product introductions, and be prepared to have retailer and distributor preferences reflected in their new product and service systems. In some cases the distribution channel is introducing its own private brands. Competition in the distribution channel may result in less control by manufacturers and a more difficult environment for product introduction.

Alliances

Combining skills with other firms in an alliance is becoming an increasingly common strategy. This can initiate new product development by reacting to an offer to become part of an alliance or by promoting an alliance. For example, General Motors and Toyota combined in the NUMI venture to produce small cars in America. Ford owns 25% of Mazda, GE and SENECA jointly manufacture jet engines in Europe and the Airbus is a pan-European effort. These alliances lead to opportunities to serve better the target market needs. Sometimes combinations of firms are forced. The "takeover" abruptly can affect new product strategy by closing some markets and opening others. Air France acquired both UTA and Air Inter to become the largest airline in Europe. If a firm "goes private" and is taken over by its managers, it has high incentive to cut costs and grow; new products gain high priority but may suffer from resource limitations.

Future of Initiating Forces

There are many pressures to innovate. In this section we highlight a few of these pressures so that you can anticipate them rather than simply react to them. By understanding the variety of forces that encourage innovation you can appreciate some of the time pressures in new product development. We believe that these initiating forces will continue to be strong. In particular,

- Forces in the financial markets are keeping pressure on sales growth, profitability, and share prices.
- Within markets, competition is tough and increasingly global in scope.
- Organizations continue to seek new markets and new opportunities outside their traditional businesses as they search for focused profit opportunities.
- Life cycles are becoming shorter, and markets are becoming mature and saturated with product offerings.
- The pace of technological change will increase, and companies (and countries) are increasingly aggressive in supporting high-technology, growth-oriented businesses.
- Social and political change are accelerating. Demographics and consumer attitudes and lifestyles are continuing to change rapidly.
- Buyers are becoming more sophisticated in their decision making and active in demanding products to solve their problems.
- Distribution channel members are gaining power.
- New materials are becoming available, and old materials are being restricted as environmental regulation and consciousness grows.
- Alliances are being used increasingly as a strategic tool in planning overall corporate success.

If these trends in the underlying initiating factors continue, we will see more new product development activity in the future. The role of the new-product development manager will become increasingly critical to the success of the firm.

The task of the new-product manager is to find and develop major new products such that the potential rewards are large, but the risks of failure are kept to an acceptable level. This textbook provides the basic concepts and the tools to make the job of innovation and product management more understandable and controllable.

SEVEN NEW-PRODUCT CHALLENGES

Throughout the text we illustrate techniques with examples. Here are a few examples you might want to think about as you begin to consider new-product development strategy.

Pain-relievers. Figure 1.1 shows 20 brands selected from more than 30 pain relievers on the market. The brands clearly vary. What benefits do consumers buy? Are there any opportunities? How would you innovate?

Health care delivery. If you wanted to innovate in the health care services field, what services would you provide? How would you compete with existing medical services (hospitals and health maintenance organizations [HMO's])? How would you forecast acceptance and financial implications?

Video telephone. The idea of a picturephone has been around for decades, but it has not become a household convenience. How does a video telephone compete with regular telephones, cellular phones, FAX devices, and even personal visits? What benefits must be delivered in a cost-effective manner to attract customers?

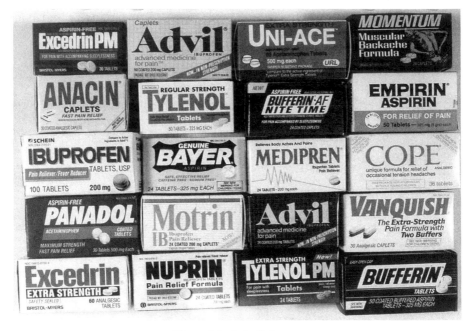

Figure 1.1 Pain Relievers

Luxury sports car. The Buick division of General Motors is known for large, luxury cars. Would consumers accept a luxury, two-seated sports car that has Buick comfort features, softer ride, more room, and easier handling? Would a high-tech "computer-screen" dashboard help or hinder sales? What marketing plan would you need?

Software for computer-aided design. Your firm is one of the leading firms marketing software for computer-aided design (CAD). Competitors are innovating, but so are your customers. You suspect that some leading-edge customers have already modified your software to adapt it to their special needs. How do you find out about these innovations? Can other customers use them? Should you incorporate these innovations in your next generation of software?

Coolers. In the past picnic baskets were the dominate food-carrying device. Today it is coolers. Can you design and market a better cooler? What features would it have? How would you balance durability and increased manufacturing cost?

Management schools. Suppose that you were asked by the dean of a management school to develop a new program or set of programs to satisfy better students and potential students, faculty, and recruiters. How would you identify needs? How would you prioritize markets? Would you change existing programs? Would you introduce new programs? What would be the implications for all of the constituencies involved?

GOALS OF THE TEXT

Our goal is to help you learn how to manage existing products more effectively and how to develop and market new products and services. After completing this book we expect that you will be able to

1. Select a new-product strategy that matches the needs of your organization and set up a disciplined procedure for new-product development and product management.
2. Define target market opportunities and create high-potential ideas.
3. Understand customer needs, structure them, and prioritize the needs to define clearly the benefits and values that your product will deliver when you position it against competition in your target market segment.
4. Integrate marketing, engineering, R&D, and production to design a high-quality product that satisfies customer needs and delivers value.

5. Evaluate the purchase potential of a new product and select a marketing mix. Forecast sales before market launch based on testing of the product and the marketing plan.
6. Launch the product and manage the product into and through the maturity phase of its life cycle.
7. Organize and innovate the new-product development and product-management process.
8. Know the role of analytical support tools (market research and models) in new-product development: when to use them, their limitations and advantages, and the appropriate level of sophistication at each stage in the process.

We expect that the concepts and techniques discussed in the following chapters will help you become a better manager. The ideas in this book will help you improve the performance of your organization whether it be consumer or industrial, public or private, large or small, national or global, or producing durable goods, frequently purchased goods, and services. Some of the concepts presented are generic; others must be modified for each application. Together, however, they should lead to greater profitability and less risk.

REVIEW QUESTIONS

1.1. What is a new product? Why are new products important?
1.2. Why should firms innovate given the risky nature of innovation?
1.3. Select a well-publicized and successful new product introduced last year. What seem to be the main factors accounting for its success? Identify any initiating factors that led to the new product.
1.4. Can you think of a major new product that failed or was withdrawn from the market in the last few years? What factors led to its failure? Could these have been avoided? How?
1.5. Select one of the seven new-product challenges discussed in this chapter. How would you address that challenge?
1.6. Discuss the initiating factors in the following industries during the next decade:

     a. Computers   e. Food products
     b. Automobiles   f. Financial services
     c. Health care   g. Telecommunication
     d. Education   h. Plastic materials

PART ONE

Innovation Strategy

2

New-Product Strategies

The potential rewards and risks from developing successful new products are high, and many factors can impel organizations to consider new product development activities. Although some organizations may survive by trying one product after another in the market until success is achieved, there is a better way. Most organizations find it more profitable to approach new-product development with an effective managerial strategy that is likely to achieve success, but at the same time minimize costs and risk. We begin with a discussion of potential new-product strategies, indicate when they are appropriate, and argue for the need to have a strategy that integrates the functions of marketing, R&D, production, and finance.

Today's organizations face a variety of circumstances, some call for innovation from scratch (new markets and totally new products), and some call for a rapid defensive response that might include imitating a competitor's innovation. To manage in this situation you need to understand the range of strategies that are possible including innovative versus imitative, offensive versus defensive, entrepreneurial versus organizational, and internal versus external development. A good strategy includes a portfolio of product development strategies that are balanced to the demands of the situations the corporation faces.

In this chapter we outline the range of new-product strategies available. Our purpose is to encourage you to consider the breadth of strategic response and to understand the forces that favor different strategies. If we succeed, then, as you learn the concepts and methods of subsequent chapters, you can put them into the perspective of overall development strategies and understand which concepts relate to which market and organizational situations.

RELATIONSHIP TO CORPORATE STRATEGY

Corporate strategy is a framework that gives an organization its overall directions and impels it to action. The strategy formulation process begins with a systematic diagnosis of the threats and opportunities in the environment, an inventorying of the organization's strengths and weaknesses, and an understanding of the key phenomena underlying demand and competition (see Urban and Star 1991, for a complete review of this topic). Then goals, programs, plans, and budgets are formulated to build on the organization's competitive advantages and market opportunities. Finally tactics and control mechanisms are put in place to achieve the goals.

New-product strategy is one part of the overall corporate strategy. It is a means to implement an organization's corporate overall strategy. This means that a new-product strategy depends on the organization's capabilities and its environment. Here are some of the questions that reflect the interface between corporate and new-product strategy. What are we good at? Where are we vulnerable? Why have we succeeded in the past? Where are our major products in their life cycles? What is the forecast for material costs and availability? What technological changes can we expect? How can we tap into areas of our expertise? What actions will the government take that will affect us? What can we expect from our competitors, and what are their strengths and weaknesses? What consumption changes can we exploit? What products and markets must be defended to maintain the corporate image? How much does our organization depend on growth? Does the organization have experience in certain channels of distribution? Can synergies with existing products be exploited in terms of materials, production lines, advertising, brand equity, or promotion? These questions lead us to face the underlying issues: What business are we in, and what are our goals?

The goals that result from a corporate strategy should reflect the nature of the organization, and they should be realistic. For example,

A large publicly traded firm	Ten percent growth in earnings per share, 20% increase in sales, no new product to be considered with less than $10 million per year in revenues representing at least 4% of a market
A small growing firm	Fifty percent growth achieved through a volume of less than $2 million per year and less than 1% of the total market, but 25% in targeted market segments
A public transit service	Reverse the decline in ridership over five years and reduce the deficit by 5% per annum

If these goals are set realistically, they become benchmarks with which to evaluate markets and products. For example, a large publicly traded data-services firm might avoid entering into consulting businesses with heavy dependence on personal relationships and high marginal costs, whereas a small, growing consulting firm might actively seek such business. Throughout the product-development process there are several go/no go decision points where the organization evaluates its progress and decides whether to invest further in a market or a product. If the goals are set carefully and quantified, then these go/no go decisions reflect corporate strategy. If the goals are not set carefully, there is a real danger that any results of go/no go evaluations will be justified post hoc and resources will be allocated to development efforts that do not advance corporate goals.

Given the goal structure and an understanding of our strengths and weakness as well as the overall corporate strategy, we are now in a position to consider alternative innovation strategies.

ALTERNATIVE PRODUCT DEVELOPMENT STRATEGIES

The organization can choose from a range of alternative strategies. One of the basic strategic decisions is whether to be *reactive* or *proactive*. A reactive product strategy is based on dealing with the initiating pressures as they occur, whereas a proactive strategy would explicitly allocate resources to preempt undesirable future events and achieve goals. For example, a reactive view of the competition is to wait until the competition introduces a product and copy it if it is successful, whereas a proactive strategy would be based on preempting competition by being first on the market with a product competitors would find difficult to match or improve.

Each strategy is appropriate under certain conditions. We begin with examples of each strategy and then indicate when each is appropriate. Table 2.1 identifies several reactive and proactive strategies.

Reactive Strategies

A *defensive* strategy protects the profitability of existing products by countering competitive new products. For example, when Datril entered the analgesic market with a position of "the same ingredients as Tylenol, but less-expensive" (Johnson & Johnson), the makers of Tylenol, responded with an effective strategy based on a reduced price, aggressive promotion, and an emphasis on the goodwill built up by years of doctors' recommendations. When Ziplock bags challenged the market leaders, they responded with improved products to limit Ziplock's encroachment on their shares. Some defensive strategies are primarily marketing mix responses—advertising, promotion, or price, whereas some strategies include counteroffensives of new flankers and new products. For example, once Tylenol countered Datril's attack, they launched Tylenol Extra-Strength to establish their brand among consumers who demanded a more effective pain reliever.

An *imitative* strategy is based on quickly copying a new product before its maker is assured of being successful. This imitator or "me too" strategy is common practice in the fashion and design industries for clothes, furniture, and small appliances. For example, once Cuisinart demonstrated that a market existed for expensive food processors, many of the major appliance companies followed with products that imitated Cuisinart. This strategy made sense for them as an expansion of a product line; they could exploit their expertise in the channel, in production, and in marketing. It stopped further erosion in sales as consumers switched from mixers and blenders to food processors. In another example in Japan, once Asahi demonstrated a market for "dry" beer, Kirin, Suntory, and others were forced to develop their own dry beers in an attempt to maintain sales. (Kirin later regained sales with

TABLE 2.1 New Product Strategies

Reactive Strategies	Proactive Strategies
Defensive	Research and development
Imitative	Marketing
Second but better	Entrepreneurial
Responsive	Acquisition
	Alliances

Ichiban, a beer based on a new brewing technology.) When Kirin attacked the U.S. market with their dry beer Anheuser-Busch responded with Michelob Dry and then Bud Dry. Kirin achieved very small sales in the U.S. compared with Michelob and Budweiser Dry.

A more sophisticated strategy to react to competition is the *second-but-better* strategy. In this case the firm does not just copy the competitive product, but identifies ways to improve the product and its positioning. For example, once VisiCalc dominated the market for an electronic spreadsheet, but Lotus 1-2-3 was able to develop and market an electronic spreadsheet (integrated with some graphical and database capabilities) that users found more attractive. Multimate was a very early word processor program, but WordPerfect overtook it in sales by improving on the concept in terms of ease of use, power, and compatibility. A second-but-better strategy might not attack a new product head on but rather identify a niche where it can provide unique benefits. For example, Microsoft's Excel spreadsheet program gained share from Lotus among certain users by providing a superior graphical user interface, flexibility, efficiency, and compatibility to Apple computers. In the early 1990s Lotus had the dominant share of IBM-compatible machines, and Excel has the dominate share among Apple's MacIntosh users. The market battle continues as users move to graphical user interfaces (GUIs).

The final reactive strategy is termed *responsive*, which means purposively reacting to customers' requests. For example, because scientific instruments users often modify and improve the equipment they use, manufacturers can identify new opportunities (and new designs) by facilitating the information flow from users. Such a strategy implies an emphasis on applications engineering and manufacturing. Similarly, an office furniture manufacturer can identify new ideas by observing how customers modify their furniture, for example, to create work stations for computers and printers. Responsive strategies are also used by manufacturers in a chain of distribution in which some other channel member is dominant. Teflon cookware was developed in response to customer requests which in turn were encouraged by the material supplier, Du Pont.

Proactive Strategies

Organizations can be proactive and initiate change. A proactive aerospace company does preemptive R&D and product development. It might take its work to the government and suggest a request for proposal be written around this need. There is some evidence that many companies practice this strategy. Some claim the only condition under which they would bid in a request for proposal is if they had done substantial research before the request. We have had similar experience in obtaining outside funding for academic research (i.e., that we are in a much better position to propose on a grant on the basis of internally funded pilot research). Many successful universities and consulting firms follow this proactive strategy.

The proactive strategy of an organization may be based on a $R \ \& \ D$ effort to develop technically superior products. Some companies have been notably successful. IBM, Hewlett-Packard, and Microsoft are examples of organizations that devote considerable energies to the potential of technological innovation. In 1990 IBM spent almost $5 billion on R&D, Hewlett-Packard spent more than $1.3 billion, and Microsoft spent more than $180 million. The figures represent 7.1%, 10.3%, and 15.3% of sales for each company, respectively (*Business Week*, October 25, 1991).

A firm can also be proactive in identifying customer needs and developing products that provide the benefits to satisfy those needs. Such strategies require that the organization devote energies to understanding the input from the customer; this can include market research, the process of talking to users, and rotation of personnel so that they have contact with the customer. Proctor and Gamble, General Foods, McDonald's, and most consumer product companies use this customer-based philosophy.

Another proactive form of product development is *entrepreneurial.* A special person—an entrepreneur—has an idea and makes it happen by building venture enthusiasm and generating resources. Many high-technology firms in California's Silicon Valley or Boston's Route 128 were started in this way. Even some large companies have tried to use this strategy. At 3M (Minnesota Manufacturing and Mining) a separate new venture division was established where entrepreneurs can take a leave from their regular job to work on their ventures (see Roberts 1991).

Acquisition can be an effective strategy for growth and financial success. In this case other firms are purchased with products new to the acquiring firm and perhaps the market. Raytheon has been notably successful with this strategy in the electronics field. Microwave Associates grew from a $50 million defense contractor to a $500 million company called MA/COM by the acquisition of more than 16 companies. The acquisitions provide an integrated system capability in communications. The Dexter Corporation grew over 10 years by a factor of five in the sales of industrial plastics and coatings by acquiring firms that filled out their product line in specialty materials market segments.

Acquisitions are formal alliances initiated by legally combining two organizations. Increasingly firms are using less rigid forms of cooperation to put together a new product portfolio of skills that lead to success in the market. These may be joint ventures such as the General Motors (GM) and Toyota cooperation (called NUMI) to produce small cars for the U.S. market. In this venture GM gained access to Toyota's skill in manufacturing and quality control, and Toyota gained access to the U.S. market. Similarly Rover and Honda combined in Europe to produce the Sterling.

Not all alliances are joint ventures. Alliances also may be structured as R&D consortia such as the effort by U.S. manufacturers to build new integrated circuit technologies in a venture called SEMITECH. Similarly, European joint efforts in multinational technology development projects like EURICA are large and significant.

Alliances need not be limited to manufacturers or service providers. They can include suppliers or distributors or even customers. Explicitly partnering with customers puts the firm in close touch with the market needs. For example, IBM is partnering with USAA—an insurance company that pioneered in image processing—so that it can leverage from this customer's innovation to build better software and systems for transmitting and manipulating images.

Alliances are designed to bring together the pool of skills in technology, marketing, production, finance, and geographical experience so that the alliance members can be competitive in the market and achieve their goals. Such alliances provide opportunities to the initiating firm to gain skill at lower costs. The participants gain the opportunity to grow without bearing the full risk of market development.

REACTIVE VERSUS PROACTIVE STRATEGIES

To select the appropriate strategy we must understand the situations that affect this decision. Thus we review the concepts of growth opportunities, the probable protection for innovation, the scale of the market, the strength of the competition, and the organization's position in the production/distribution system. These issues illustrate the types of considerations that go into an organization's decision to select a particular type of product development strategy.

Growth Opportunities

We normally think of new product activities as introducing a new product to a new market. An example is a shopping cart with a video screen that broadcasts ads and issues coupons to the consumer as they walk down the aisles of a grocery store. This is a new product creating a new market for point-of-purchase marketing. But this is only one of four possible strategies for growth. Figure 2.1 describes four strategies based on whether the products and markets are existing or new.

The first cell describes opportunity as growth through existing products

	Existing products	New products
Existing markets	1. Market penetration.	3. Market penetration.
New markets	2. Product development	4. Diversification

Figure 2.1   Opportunities Matrix (Ansoff 1957)

and markets. This strategy is one of market penetration and is characterized as developing a high market share in existing markets with the existing products (cell 1). This growth strategy is not based on innovation in products as much as in selling and promotion. Kentucky Fried Chicken has bucked the trend of proliferation in the varieties of fast foods and instead concentrated on chicken with the theme, "We do chicken right." Market focus is becoming increasingly important to firms and total quality programs are increasing. We expect that many firms will return to their home bases before venturing out into new areas.

In many of today's markets, saturation occurs so frequently that firms are increasingly looking toward the new markets. Cell 2 represents the strategy of taking existing products and entering new markets. Heinz has positioned their vinegar product to clean automatic coffee makers "naturally." Arm and Hammer baking soda has been touted as a refrigerator deodorant, drain freshener, kitty-litter deodorizer, dentifrice, and so on. Morgan Stanley, Goldman Sachs, and Solomon Brothers have taken their specialty investment skills to Japan and made significant inroads against the large trading houses such as Numura Securities.

The usual new-product development strategy is to attack existing markets with new products (cell 3). This strategy is consistent with the notion of "building on our strength" and expanding in areas of our skill and knowledge in distribution and production. Many of the examples in this book will fall in this category. For example, McDonald's introduced Chicken McNuggets, McRib sandwiches, salads, and McLean Burgers to expand its menu and widen its product line. Digital Equipment has innovated successfully in its minicomputer and workstation market for more than 15 years to build to more than 10 billion in sales worldwide, but faces the challenges of moving its products to the desktop.

Some companies may choose to diversify into new markets with new products (cell 4). McDonald's entered the breakfast market with longer hours and a line of breakfast items to make further use of their facilities and to attract a new line of business. Although diversification can be successful, Exxon, a leading petroleum company, lost big when it attempted to create a new division to develop products for the rapidly growing "office of the future" market. Financial diversification is decreasing and acquisitions today usually have a strategic synergy as well as potential financial reward potential. If the new market is a strategic opportunity and is consistent with the organization's designated competitive advantage, the use of diversification into new markets can help achieve the organization's goals.

The choice of market opportunity is an important decision that affects the strategic response. If existing products and markets are to be the primary growth vehicles (cell 1), the organization must be superior in production and distribution, and growth-rate aspirations should not be too high. In this case product development would be used to defend the existing products by reacting to competitive and environmental pressures.

However, if the organization wants growth or has a policy of innovating, and has skill in R&D and marketing, a proactive strategy would have potential to help meet its overall organization. Proactive strategies based on R&D and marketing lead to new products and new markets.

Protection for Innovation

Another major factor in selecting between reactive and proactive strategies is the amount of protection a new product can obtain. If the product can be patented, the innovating organization can be more assured that its developmental investment will be returned. Although patents are becoming more difficult to defend, Polaroid's patents have stood up well and have helped preserve its profits. (In 1991 it won a major lawsuit against Kodak.) Protection may be granted by the market when the first firm introduces a good product and achieves a predominant position. For example, although Burger King and Burger Chef and others have copied McDonald's food franchising operation, McDonald's is still the biggest chain, is very profitable, and continues to grow. Systematic research in frequently purchased consumer brands has indicated an enduring market share reward to pioneering brands. The second brand in a market with a product comparable with the first and with comparable marketing effort will get a share that is only about 71% of that obtained by the pioneer (Urban, Carter, Gaskin, and Mucha 1986). In industrial products similar rewards for pioneering have been discovered (Robinson and Fornell 1985, and Robinson 1988a).

In other product categories such as small appliances, a first-in product can be quickly copied, and the innovator has only a short period of competitive advantage. For example, six months after the first electric knife was introduced, more than 10 brands were on the market. Thus, firms that can achieve good protection should be proactive, whereas those that cannot may be better off in a reactive mode.

Scale of Market

Market size and margins can affect the choice of development strategy. In large markets with economies of scale or experience in production, distribution, or marketing, a proactive first-in innovation may establish market dominance and give the firm an advantageous position. Conversely, in markets that have neither the volume nor the margins, a firm may not be able to return its investment in product development—especially if there are high overhead costs. A reactive strategy might be better. For example, special production machines and instruments may represent such small sales potential that the best strategy for a manufacturer is to wait and be responsive to customer requests. Similarly, in the case of teflon, each cookware manufacturer faced such a small market that the best strategy was to wait until the material supplier (Du Pont) invested in promoting the innovation.

Competition

The competitive environment may be critical to selecting a strategic posture. It may make a reactive strategy of imitation feasible and necessary. If the time necessary to copy is short, there are few entry costs, the innovation is not protected by patents, and the organization can achieve quickly economies of scale, this may be appropriate. The relative size of the competitors is also important. A small firm may be particularly vulnerable to competitive reaction and thus must be preemptive in its innovation plans. Similarly a large firm may be proactive to protect its lead. For example in appliances, although imitation is common, Black and Decker allocates substantial resources to design new appliances.

Position in Production/Distribution System

In some situations one firm in the chain of distribution may be proactive, with the others reacting to that firm's innovation. In many industrial markets the supplier of the materials or even the final user may develop the product. ALCOA invented the aluminum truck trailer and then sold it to the trucking industry by showing that less weight in the trailer structure meant more payload that would pay back the higher initial investment costs. In consumer industries the producer is the usual innovator, but powerful retailers will often specify innovative products and then have other firms produce them. For example, Sears' Craftsman line of tools is well respected and commands a premium price.

Whether or not a firm is proactive depends on the stance of other firms in the distribution channel and on its relative power within that channel.

Some firms actually gain power as well as profits by innovation in distribution. For example, Haines Corp. was simply another apparel producer until it introduced L'eggs, a distinctively packaged panty hose, through innovative distribution in supermarkets and drugstores. It is now a dominant force in the multibillion-dollar women's hosiery market.

Synthesis and Recommendations

Depending on the circumstances of the market, an organization will choose either a reactive or a proactive development strategy. In particular, *reactive strategies* may be best in situations that

- Require concentration on existing products or markets
- Can achieve little protection for innovation
- Are in markets too small to recover development costs
- Are in danger of being overwhelmed by competitive imitation
- Are in distribution chains dominated by another innovator

For such situations, innovation may be too large a risk.

Other situations will favor *proactive strategies*. These are situations that

- Require rapid sales growth
- Mean entering new markets
- Provide high volumes or margins
- Offer a capability of achieving patent or market protection
- Supply resources and time necessary to develop new products
- Block competition from rapidly entering with a second-but-better strategy
- Provide reasonable power in the distribution channel

In such situations an organization can achieve success and reduce risk through proactive strategies.

Even if a firm selects a proactive strategy, it is likely at some times to find itself under the conditions that favor a reactive strategy. For example, a customer may come to you with a need or an idea for a product that you had not thought of in a market you had not previously targeted. This may require a responsive strategy that leads to new markets for further proactive development. Another common situation is that even though your firm is innovating in a market, you may be "blind-sided" by a competitor or technological change. In these cases you need to react quickly to defend your market. In reality any proactive strategy needs a reactive strategy companion for unexpected situations. In these cases the reactive strategy must sense changes in the market, competition, or technology; evaluate them; and specify fast-action responses. This means the firm must have competitive intelligence so they can prevent surprises by learning about them before they occur. The reactive strategy must also have an action team that can mobilize the organization's resources quickly to minimize losses, and the firm can return to its base strategy of proactive new-product development. In this book we will concentrate most of our attention on proactive strategies, but we will return to reactive companion strategies in chapter 21—Customizing the New-Product Development Process. We will see that many of the components of a proactive strategy can be used in an effective defensive program.

MARKETING AND RESEARCH/DEVELOPMENT—COOPERATION

A proactive strategy means taking an active role in the development of new products and markets. This active role can concentrate on technology (R&D), on the customer (marketing), or both.

R & D is an important activity. In 1990 private organizations in the United States spent almost $70 billion on R&D—on average about 3.4% of total sales and 46.8% of total profits (*Business Week*, Special Issue, October 25, 1990). For example, General Motors, IBM, Ford, AT&T, Du Pont, Digital Equipment, General Electric, Eastman Kodak, Hewlett-Packard, and Dow Chemical each spent more than $1 billion. Similar spending occurs in European and Japanese firms. For example, the top 74 companies in Japan spent more than $27 billion, and the top 19 companies in Germany spent more than $14 billion. These amounts do not include government sponsored R&D such as the Defense Department in the United States or MITI in Japan.

In a comparison of company performance in 1987 with R&D spending from 1983 through 1986, *Business Week* (Special Issue, June 15, 1989) reports a significant correlation between R&D spending per employee and return on assets. Although there are issues of causality (firms with successful products may decide to spend heavily), the results are provocative and suggest a careful R&D analysis (Holak, Parry, and Song 1991).

The major portion of R&D is spent on specific product development. Gerstenfeld, in a 1970 survey of the R&D directions of 170 large industrial companies, found more than 75% of the R&D expenditures in these firms was allocated to the development of new products. (Table 2.2 shows the percentage by industry.) In a study of the chemical, drug, petroleum, and electronic industries, Mansfield et al. (1971) found that 70% of R&D expenditures was on product development.

TABLE 2.2   R&D Expenditures for New-Product Development in Various
Industries

Industry	Companies in Sample	Percentage of R&D
Electrical equipment	28	79%
Chemicals and pharmaceuticals	34	82
Instruments	16	88
Machinery and computers	19	68
Aircraft	6	84
Foods	7	100

Adapted from Gerstenfeld (1970).

To evaluate the effectiveness of this spending, numerous researchers have traced the source of technological innovations that were successful in the marketplace. More than 2,000 products spanning 100 industries and several countries have been studied[1] to determine the relative role of marketing and R&D. The methodologies varied, but two observations are clear.

- Sixty to eighty percent of successful products have been in response to market demands and needs (e.g., see Table 2.3).
- Sales improvements are more likely for marketing or customer-originated ideas (e.g., see Table 2.4).

Together, these observations suggest that both R&D and marketing (a customer orientation) lead to success in new product development. But there is also evidence that neither R&D nor marketing can go it alone. For example, in a study of 16 new-product development projects, Dougherty (1989) found that successful products came in situations where marketing and R&D cooperated and communicated on all aspects of business plans, customer needs, and technological capabilities. She found also that in the failed products there was little cooperation and communication on at least one of these aspects.

Her results are typical. Table 2.5 summarizes some of the scientific evidence that supports the hypothesis that cooperation is important. Note that in some cases the research is based on surveys of 200 to 300 firms, whereas in other cases it is based on more in-depth analyses.

Roberts (1989) has studied the evolution of successful high-tech firms and found a critical factor in the successful ones is an orientation toward

[1] Little (1959); Carter and Williams (1957); Enos (1962); Hamburg (1963); Jewkes et al. (1970); Langrish (1971); Mansfield (1968); Miller (1971); Myers and Marquis (1969); Mueller (1962); Illinois Institute of Technology (1968); Robertson et al. (1972); Tannenbaum et al. (1966); Utterback (1971).

TABLE 2.3 Product Innovations Resulting from Market Needs and Technological Opportunities

Type of Innovation (Sample Size)	Market or Product Needs	Technical Opportunities
British firms (137)	73%	27%
Winners' Industrial Research Award (108)	69	31
Weapons systems (710)	61	34
British innovators (84)	66	34
Computers, railways, housing (439)	78	22
Materials (10)	90	10
Instruments (32)	75	25
Other (303)	77	23

Adapted from Utterback (1974, p. 622).

marketing. In a study of 21 greater Boston high-tech firms that had survived over five years and had sales of more than $5 million, a market-oriented transformation (importance of marketing, market-oriented control of new products, and new market-oriented chief executive officers [CEOs]) characterized the high performers. In another similar study of 114 technology based firms (Roberts, 1990b), he found an evolution in surviving firms towards marketing with less emphasis on engineering. At the project level in 26 computer-related companies based on 262 projects, he found the best opportunities for rapid growth come from building an internal critical mass of engineering talent in a focused technological area and products targeted for a focused set of customer needs that were sold to gradually broadening groups of end users through single channels of sales and distribution (Roberts and Meyer 1991).

The importance of market orientation has been found in more mundane industries. Narver and Slater (1990) found in a commodity product business such as lumber and building supplies that, based on 140 products, there was a substantial positive effect of market orientation on profit.

A good new-product strategy requires an effective integration of mar-

TABLE 2.4 Commercial Outcome for Chemical Laboratories

Source of Idea	Increase in Sales Caused by Innovation			
	None	Small	Medium	Large
Projects laboratory	66%	17%	17%	0%
Marketing	58	14	14	14
Customer	33	33	13	20

Adapted from Meadows (1968, pp. 105–119).

TABLE 2.5 Examples of the Scientific Evidence that Suggests that Communication among Marketing and R&D Enhances New-Product Success

Researchers	Sample	Type of Firm	Evidence (Partial List)
Cooper (1983)	58 projects	Industrial	Projects that balance marketing and R&D inputs have a higher rate of success.
Cooper (1984)	122 firms	Electronic, heavy equipment, chemicals, materials	Management strategies that balance marketing and R&D have a greater percentage of new product successes and greater percentage of their sales coming from new products.
Cooper and de Brentani (1991)	106 projects	Financial services	Synergy (e.g., fit with the firms expertise, management skills, and market research resources) was the primary correlate of success. (Correlation = 0.45.)
Cooper and Kleinschmidt (1987)	125 firms 203 projects	Manufacturing	Market synergy and technological synergy are both significantly related to success.
Dougherty (1987)	5 firms 16 projects	Industrial, consumer, and services	More communication and communication on *all* relevant topics separated successful projects from unsuccessful projects.
de Brentani (1989)	115 firms 276 projects	Financial services, management services, transportation, communication	Sales, market share, and reduced costs are correlated with communication between functions. (Correlation with sales and market share = 0.38, correlation with reduced cost = 0.29.)
Gupta, Raj, and Wilemon (1985)	167 firms 107 R&D managers 109 marketing managers	High technology	Lack of communication was listed as the primary barrier to achieving integration among marketing and R&D.
Hise, O'Neal, Parasuraman, and Mc-Neal (1990)	252 marketing vice-presidents	Large manufacturing firms	High level of joint effort in new product design is a significant factor in determining success. This is true for both industrial and consumer good companies.
Moenaert and Souder (1990)	Literature review	Products and services	Integration of functions is positively related to innovative success.
Pelz and Andrews (1966)	1311 scientists and engineers	Scientists and engineers	Positive relationships between the amount of interaction and performance.
Pinto and Pinto (1990)	72 hospital teams 262 team members	Health services	Strong relationship between cross-functional cooperation and the success (perceived task outcomes and psychosocial outcomes) of the project. (Correlation = 0.71.)
Souder (1988)	56 firms 289 projects	Consumer and industrial	The greater the harmony between marketing and R&D, the greater the likelihood of success.
Takeuchi and Nonaka (1986)	6 projects United States and Japan	Consumer and industrial	Cross-fertilization and self-organizing teams led to success.

(Griffin and Hauser 1992)

keting and R&D. Marketing identifies and assesses customer needs; R&D and engineering develop the means to meet these needs. R&D develops new technological levels of performance that enable new customer benefits to be created. Working together marketing, engineering, and R&D can bring the organization's capabilities to bear on developing products that deliver benefits that meet or exceed customer needs. Technology alone is not enough (Clark 1989 and Gomery 1989); customer needs and technology must be integrated if success is to be achieved.

Professor Donald Marquis of MIT's R&D management group says,

> Recognition of demand is a more frequent factor in successful innovation than recognition of technical potential. It seems to me, therefore, that management ought to concentrate on any and all ways of analyzing such demands and needs. For example, more effective communication should be established among specialists in sales, marketing, production, and R&D to see that such opportunities are not overlooked. (Marquis 1969)

R&D researcher Edwin Mansfield of the Wharton Business School says:

> R&D isn't worth anything alone, it has got to be coupled with the market. The innovative firms are not necessarily the ones that produce the best technological output, but the ones that know what is marketable. (*Business Week*, June 8, 1976)

In an article based on studying 80 technology-intensive companies, Gupta and Wilemon (1988) begin by saying,

> It is essential for technology-intensive companies to integrate their R&D and marketing functions if their products are to meet the needs of the market.

However, Souder (1988) cautions that

> R&D and marketing personnel depend on each other for the creation of new product innovations. Yet R&D and marketing departments have frequent misunderstandings and conflicts.

Thus, the incentive for cooperation is strong. But it will not happen without being encouraged so we need a process and organizational structure to promote effective interactions (see chapters 5 and 20 for more discussion of this issue).

CROSS FUNCTIONAL INTEGRATION IN NEW-PRODUCT STRATEGY

The success of a new-product strategy depends on more than integration of marketing and R&D. Production and financial activities must also be put together with them in a coordinated set of resources, skills, perspectives, and activities. Figure 2.2 depicts the interrelations. Production means manufacturing in the product company and generation of the service capability in a service company (e.g., the software for the SABRE software system that led American Airlines to great success or the information processing capability that allows American Express to offer the Optima card). Finance reflects the resource base and the consideration of financing those resources to maximize stockholder wealth.

The arrows in Figure 2.2 indicate the major interactions. As we have noted marketing must give R&D correct need input and R&D must design a product to fit customer's needs. But R&D must also design a product that can be manufactured at high-quality levels and low cost. This "design for manufacturing" is increasingly important. Similarly R&D and engineering must work to innovate the process of manufacturing as well as design new products. Both product *and* process must be state of the art for a firm to be competitive in the global market of the 21st century. If the product cannot be built at a cost level, and therefore price level, and quality level that customers demand, marketing will not be able to sell it no matter how innovative the technology is. Finance interacts with R&D, manufacturing, and marketing when financial

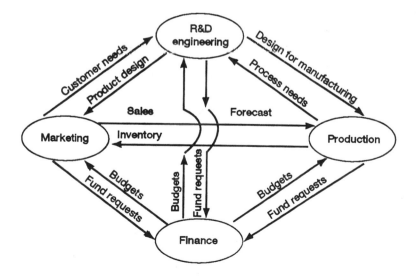

Figure 2.2   Cross-Functional Integration

resources are needed. If not enough is spent on R&D, the firm's core technologies cannot be maintained; if not enough is invested in current production process technology, the products will not meet global quality standards; and if not enough is spent on marketing, customer needs may be misread, forecasting may be deficient, and the launch intensity may be insufficient to capture a dominant position in the target markets. However, funds are often in short supply or expensive, so financial decisions must be integrated with the R&D, production, and marketing strategies so that the resources can be allocated to maximize the long-run return on the funds invested in new-product development.

During the interaction of the functions in product development, marketing input will be most important in the beginning of the development and in the launch phase of the product development. In the beginning marketing has the responsibility of representing the customer in the design process. In the end marketing sells, advertises, promotes, distributes, and services the product. R&D is most important in the early phases of development and decreases in activity as launch nears. Production is the reverse with increasing activity as launch approaches. After launch, marketing and manufacturing are dominant, but all three functions work together to produce continuous improvement in the design, manufacturing, and marketing of the product. Finance is involved at a uniform pace as commitments of funds are made and controlled. However, we must keep in mind that the boundries between the functions are not sharp. Many of the tasks and actions represent shared responsibilities and common decisions. All the functions need to work together for the product to be successful.

The integration of functions requires careful communication and a recognition of changing role of each function over the development cycle. In the next chapter we present a development process that provides information to marketing, manufacturing, finance, and R&D so that the right decisions can be made at the right time to develop successful products. We provide the concepts and the methods to understand the customer, identify products that meet customer needs, and translate those inputs into successful products and services.

REVIEW QUESTIONS

2.1. What are the roles of marketing and R&D in the new product development process? How should responsibility and authority be delegated between these two areas? Should R&D focus on basic research or specific applied projects?

2.2. Mr. Hardy Cell, a manager with Widgets, Inc., has a view of the consumer that is not totally unique. Mr. Cell says, "Consumers are fickle. They don't know what they want! New Products are necessary only because consumers quickly become bored with old products. Consumers should be treated as if they were children. They must be told what they should buy! Advertise anything, and it will sell. If your product sales are falling, tell people the product is new and improved. That's all you need to do.''

    a. Are Mr. Cell's remarks consistent with the empirical evidence presented in the chapter?

    b. Why might some managers support Mr. Cell's position?

    c. Could Mr. Cell's remarks be interpreted as representing a proactive new product strategy? A reactive strategy?

2.3. Discuss the advantages and disadvantages of each of the reactive and the proactive strategies.

2.4. Consider two firms competing in the same market. Would it ever be reasonable for one to adopt a proactive strategy while another adopts a reactive strategy? If not, why not? If so, under what conditions?

2.5. Discuss means by which you might encourage the cooperation among R&D and marketing. What barriers would you have to overcome? How would you integrate production with marketing and R&D?

3

Proactive New-Product Development Process

In the last chapter we stressed the need for a careful selection of an overall strategy. In this chapter we presume that a proactive strategy is being pursued and outline a series of steps that will lead to market success given this strategy. (In chapter 21 we will return to reactive strategies). We describe here a new-product development process and see how it builds on the correlates of success and avoids the pitfalls in new products. We close the chapter by examining the cost, time, and risk attributes of the process and how to get to market faster.

A good proactive new-product development process must control risks, because management is responsible for performance and must minimize the risk of major loss. But caution can be carried to extremes if a "no" decision is always made; there will be no market failure, but also no new products, sales, or profits. The tradeoffs of risk and return are difficult because successful products are in large part the results of creative cooperation of R&D, marketing, engineering, and production. Without guidance, minimization of risk will also minimize creativity. New products must be developed in an environment that allows innovation to flourish. At the same time, the risk inherent in any new venture must be controlled.

Developing a disciplined and creative atmosphere is not an easy task. Organizations are not creative by nature. They have been developed to manage ongoing businesses. Even in new-product development, organizations often spend too much time on routine operational aspects rather than concentrating on developing the idea to its fullest potential. To counter this tendency and to make new-product development a priority, programmed activity, management must institute specific processes and systems to manage creativity and foster innovation. Successful organizations manage the future, others are managed by the present and overwhelmed by the future.

In this chapter we present a new-product development decision process as a sequential set of activities. This allows us to cover each aspect of the process in depth by providing the management concepts and analytical techniques necessary to minimize risks and maximize creativity. In practice the decision process is reasonably sequential in the sense that some steps usually precede others, but successful organizations customize the process to their needs and their capabilities. Furthermore, as new information is obtained (new technologies, new competitors, improved customer research, etc.) the organizations often iterate key steps to improve the product and its marketing strategy.

A DECISION PROCESS

Given that the organization wants to practice a proactive innovation strategy and already has developed an overall corporate strategy, we recommend a five-step decision process for new product development.

1. Opportunity identification
2. Design
3. Testing
4. Introduction
5. Life-cycle management

Figure 3.1 depicts these phases. The arrows indicate a sequential process, but in fact the activities can become quite complex with iterations through each step and interactions among the steps.

To illustrate the process, suppose that we are managing a fishing fleet and fish-processing operation. Suppose that while casting our nets for basic fish such as cod, sole, haddock, and bluefish, we also net many squid (Figure 3.2). The new-product challenge is to develop a squid-based product that has mass appeal to the American market. The market is already well developed in

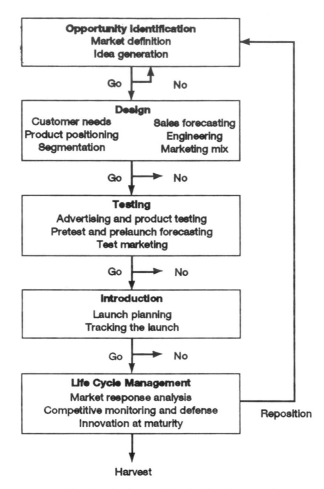

Figure 3.1 New-Product-and-Service Development Process

Japan, South America, and Europe, but North Americans are reluctant to eat squid in part because of images inspired by the giant killer squid in *Twenty Thousand Leagues under The Sea* and the general appearance of tentacles.

Opportunity identification is the definition of the best market to enter and the generation of ideas that could be the basis for entry. For example, in the case of squid, opportunity identification might go beyond the sales of fresh squid and identify the frozen prepared food (grocery) market as high potential and generate a variety of new concepts describing frozen squid dinners. If an attractive opportunity is identified, the design phase is initiated, and if not, further effort is made to find ideas and markets.

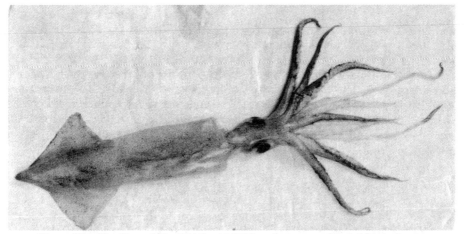

Figure 3.2   The Case of Plentiful Squid (Although consumption is high in Japan and many European countries, American consumers have negative attitudes toward squid as a food.)

Design includes converting the ideas into a physical and psychological entity through engineering, advertising, and marketing. For example, the frozen squid concepts are refined so that they are likely to fulfill a consumer need or desire. Then an actual product (frozen dinner) and an advertising and promotion campaign are designed. In the design phase, these products and strategies are evaluated and refined based on customer measurements until they are ready for final testing. In some cases, when the product is evaluated as less than superior, a "no" decision will be made, and effort will be directed toward other markets and designs.

If a good design is found, *testing* begins. This testing includes testing of the product itself, but also the advertising and introductory strategy. It can include test markets if enough product can be produced, but in many cases consumer-based laboratory simulations of the buying process serve as pretest market analysis of the product and advertising. In high-cost durable goods such as automobiles the only options are pretest and prelaunch forecasting systems.

For example, testing of a squid product might begin with taste tests of the product and audience tests of the advertising. If these are successful, the combination is tested in a simulated store environment. In this way much of the risk has been absorbed before the firm invests in an expensive, large-scale test market.

If final testing is successful, the product is launched. *Introduction* is the difficult task of "making the product happen" in the market. Production and marketing plans have to be coordinated and the new-product design tested for manufacturability. Process improvements are identified to improve the product or lower its cost. The launch is monitored carefully to detect early warning signals and, if necessary, identify improvements in the launch implementation.

If the launch is successful, the product becomes established and the process of *life-cycle management* begins. This last step is critical to ensure the profits that are the reward for the risk taking and creative effort undertaken in developing the new product. A well-designed product and marketing strategy then continues the reward phase of its life cycle, but with periodic product and strategy improvements to maintain maximum profitability. The organization monitors the product to identify these strategic actions, and to identify if and when the product enters the decline stage of its life cycle. At that point, a decision is made to harvest the product, revitalize the product, or reposition it for new markets. We now consider each of these phases in more depth, emphasizing the strategic focus of each and considering more general consumer, industrial, and service marketing as well as our squid example.

Opportunity Identification

At the opportunity identification phase, effort is made to find *markets* that are growing, profitable, and vulnerable. This requires capability to forecast global demand and technology. Opportunity identification includes approaches that describe a market in terms of its structures and its component segments. This step identifies opportunities that match the strengths and capabilities of the innovative organization.

With an understanding of the market and technological potential, the next task is to generate creative ideas to tap this potential. By understanding idea sources and creative group processes, the organization generates ideas that integrate the specific engineering, R&D, production, and marketing inputs. The ideas are in the form of high potential concepts that may ultimately become successful products. The output should be many new ideas that are substantially different from existing products. The ideas should stretch the realm of feasibility and be targeted carefully to match the strategic opportunity.

Design

In the design phase, these new ideas are evaluated and refined to produce a product with physical *and* psychological attributes that indicate a high probability of success in the market. Creative R&D and development engineering occur in this phase as well as the identification of a strategic positioning and marketing plan for the new product.

The first lesson in the design phase is that it is necessary. Perhaps the most common mistake that students and managers make is to become too quickly overzealous about a particular new-product idea. Everyone has his own favorite ideas about what is needed. But today's markets are becoming more and more competitive, the risks of failure are greater, and the consequences more costly. Some organizations still find it deceptively easy to bring one product after another into test market until finally a "winner" is found. But disciplined new-product design techniques identify the failures at a much lower cost to the firm while increasing the ultimate profit from the successes.

These design techniques identify and exploit needs within the overall market identified in the opportunity identification phase of the process. The design effort begins with the newly generated ideas, selects the ideas with the greatest potential, and refines them to fulfill market needs. A key concept here is that preliminary technical and market ideas, no matter how good, change and evolve as the result of iterative cycles of evaluation refinement.

This idea of an iterative process may seem abstract, so let us take an example. Figure 3.3 gives two concept descriptions, a seafood entry made from squid and a squid chowder concept. These concept descriptions were presented to consumers for their reaction. Based on consumer reaction the new-product team refined the concepts to emphasize nutrition. First, a picture was included in the description of "Calamarios" (Figure 3.4). Next, the physical product was developed and advertising was created and tested. Figure 3.5 shows the label for the "Sclam" Chowder can. Product and advertising were subjected to further consumer measurement and analysis until the product and its marketing mix were ready for pretest or test market.

The actual number of iterations in the development process steps would depend on the product. For example a new automobile may move from a concept, to a computer-generated hologram, to a fiberglass mockup, to a not-drivable prototype, to a drivable prototype, to a preproduction model. Each iteration provides better information, refines the product concept, and moves it closer to a marketable product.

Services and industrial goods also pass through iterative stages that come closer and closer to what will be presented in an actual test. For example, a banking service may pass from concept description to brochures and testimonials to pilot services for selected customers. In industrial products, the iteration may be from concept to prototype to pilot production output with sales support materials.

In the section of this book that is devoted to design, we describe techniques to identify, structure, and prioritize customer needs so that the new-product design reflects the "voice of the customer." That is, we want to hear what customers want and their tradeoffs. We then provide procedures to position the product vis-à-vis competition and to target it to the appropriate segment(s) of customers. Sales forecasting techniques provide evaluations

CALAMARIOS

CALAMARIOS* are a new and different seafood product made from tender, boneless, North Atlantic squid. The smooth white body (mantle) of the squid is thoroughly cleaned, cut into thin, bite-sized rings, then frozen to seal in their flavor. To cook CALAMARIOS, simply remove them from the package and boil them for only eight minutes. They are then ready to be used in a variety of recipes.

For example, CALAMARIOS can be combined with noodles, cheese, tomatoes, and onions to make "Baked CALAMARIO Cacciatore." Or, CALAMARIOS can be marinated in olive oil, lemon juice, mint, and garlic and served as a tasty squid salad. CALAMARIOS also are the prime ingredient for "Calamari en Casserole" and "Squid Italienne." You may simply want to steam CALAMARIOS, lightly season them with garlic, and serve dipped in melted butter. This dish brings out the fine flavor of squid. A complete CALAMARIOS recipe book will be available free of charge at your supermarket.

CALAMARIOS are both nutritious and economical. Squid, like other seafoods, is an excellent source of protein. CALAMARIOS can be found at your supermarket priced at $1.10 per pound. Each pound you buy is completely cleaned and waste-free.

Because of their convenient versatility, ample nutrition, and competitive price, we hope you will want to make CALAMARIOS a regular item on your shopping list.

*CALAMARI is the Italian word for squid.

Figure 3.3a   Squid Concept Alternative 1

based on product concepts, prototypes, and so on as the product moves closer to launch. Finally, we provide formats to integrate engineering, production, and marketing mix decisions to "optimize" a new-product strategy.

Testing

A carefully designed product has great potential, but its success is never assured. Thus, a product passes from design into testing.

Testing begins with separate testing of the components of the overall strategy. For example, a Sclam Chowder (Figure 3.5) might be taste-tested with a target group of consumers. The taste tests might vary the ingredients (clams, squid, broth, spices, etc.), and consumers might be asked to try the product after it is prepared in several different ways to simulate the likely

---

SCLAM CHOWDER

SCLAM CHOWDER is a delicious new seafood soup made from choice New England clams and tasty, young, boneless North Atlantic squid. Small pieces of clam are combined with bite-sized strips of squid and boiled in salted water until they are soft and tender. Sautéed onions, carrots, and celery are then added together with thick, wholesome cream, a dash of white pepper, and sprinkling of fresh parsley. The entire mixture is then cooked to perfection, bringing out a fine, natural taste that will make this chowder a favorite in your household.

SCLAM CHOWDER is available canned in your supermarket. To prepare, simply combine SCLAM CHOWDER with 1½ cups of milk in a saucepan, and bring to a boil over a hot stove. After the chowder has reached a boil, simmer for 5 minutes and then serve. One can makes 2–3 servings of this hearty, robust seafood treat. Considering its ample nutrition and delicious taste, SCLAM CHOWDER is quite a bargain at 39¢ per can.

Both clams and squid are high in protein, so high in fact that SCLAM CHOWDER makes a healthy meal in itself, perfect for lunches as well as with dinner. Instead of adding milk, some will want to add ⅓ cup of sour cream, and use liquid chowder as an exquisite sauce to be served on rice, topped with grated Parmesan cheese.

However you choose to serve it, you will find SCLAM CHOWDER a tasty, nutritious, and economical seafood dish.

Figure 3.3b   Squid Concept Alternative II

preparation procedures in the home. In parallel with the taste tests an advertising campaign might be tested by asking consumers to view a "new" television pilot in which Sclam Chowder advertisements have been inserted. The test might measure reaction to the message as well as the impact of the advertisements on intent to purchase.

Once the components of the strategy are refined, they are tested together. In packaged goods (food products, health and beauty aids, etc.) laboratory pretest markets provide an accurate test of the combined product/marketing strategy. For example, 500 consumers might be recruited from shopping malls in four cities, brought to a central location, and asked to view several advertisements, one of which is for Sclam Chowder. After some diagnostic measures they would be allowed to purchase in a simulated store. Observation of their purchases and analysis of the diagnostic information gives an accurate forecast of sales potential as well as suggestions for improving the product and the marketing. The advantages of pretest markets are

Figure 3.4   The Calamarios Concept

that they are relatively inexpensive and allow the full strategy to be tested without alerting competitors.

The need for pretest market research is especially evident in industries where test marketing is not possible. For example, in automobiles or heavy industrial equipment, it is almost as expensive to develop a production facility capable of producing enough goods for a test market as it would be to develop a full-scale production facility. However, customers can be exposed to proto-

Sclam Chowder

-a delicious blend of
squid & clams

Figure 3.5   Rough Design for Sclam Chowder Label

Ingredients: Squid, Clams, Milk, Water, Potatoes, Onion, Seasonings.

types and their reactions measured. By simulating sales stimuli such as advertising messages, word-of-mouth recommendations, dealer visits, and sales messages, a prelaunch forecasting laboratory can give accurate estimates of sales potential. In services, simulated tests may identify major needs for improvements and prevent costly pilot test programs.

Test marketing of consumer packaged goods is perhaps the most visible step in new-product testing. A test market is a controlled, scaled-down version of a national (or international) introduction. By placing the product before consumers in an environment that tests the full marketing mix, including the channels of distribution, the new-product team can observe and fine-tune a launch plan before investing in a full-scale launch. Although a go/no go decision is often an output of a test market, a manager's diagnostic information is extremely important. The team monitors customer response as well as the company's production and distribution systems. A careful test market can evaluate every building block of the marketing strategy. It can identify improvements in advertising, promotion, pricing, distribution, and even in the product itself. A well-structured market test leads to a profit maximizing strategy for full-scale rollout.

For example, a test market for sclam chowder (see Figure 3.5) might be a local introduction in two cities, say Pittsfield, Massachusetts, and Eugene, Oregon. One result might be a go decision based on a projected national share of 10% to 12%. But equally important might be diagnostic information that indicates product and strategy improvements which could increase projected share to 14% to 16% and increase projected profits by $4 million. Among these improvements might be (1) a repositioning in advertising to emphasize smoothness, (2) more aggressive promotions to retailers to obtain special displays in retail outlets, and (3) increased distribution of price-off coupons.

Introduction

Once a product has been tested, it is ready to be introduced. If the firm anticipates rapid competitive entry, it will want to introduce the product quickly and establish a firm position in the market. But if the firm feels that it has a significant lead on its competitors, or if it does not have capital to support full-scale introduction, or if there is still some risk involved in the projected customer response, it may introduce the product on a market-by-market basis or what is called a "rollout."

For example, it is practically impossible to patent the works of an electric can opener. Once the idea is proved, many firms will enter rapidly and capture sales from the innovating firm. In this case, the innovating firm should enter rapidly throughout the target market so that it can establish a strong defensible position. Conversely, a cold medicine may not be patentable, but its formulation of ingredients can be protected, and its image and distribution network take time to imitate. If a firm views the cold remedy product as high risk or it does not have the capital for full-scale introduction, it may begin its national campaign by a (U.S.) regional introduction west of the Rockies and then "roll out" to the rest of the country. Another advantage of a rollout strategy is that improvements can be made in the manufacturing process to reduce costs and gain a competitive advantage. Similarly, a firm may roll out from one country to the next or make a global launch.

During this introduction, whether it be rapid entry or rollout, the firm must monitor and manage the marketing strategy. Even the most carefully designed and tested product can run into trouble in a national introduction. Variations in customer tastes over time or across regions, unanticipated competitive reaction, troublesome channels of distribution, or even crises like a material shortage or product quality problems can all act to undermine the success of the full-scale introduction. Thus, in full-scale introduction, we use techniques to monitor the relevant aspects of the introduction so that the organization can quickly identify and react to any problems or opportunities that occur. These techniques fine-tune a product and marketing strategy (advertising, promotion, sales effort, price, distribution strategies, etc.) to ensure that the new product establishes itself as a productive component of the organization's product line.

Life-Cycle Management

After years of effort and millions of dollars of expenditure, the product is now successfully launched into the market. The profit rewards for this effort now must be returned to justify the risk and investment of developing the new product. Maximizing profit requires an effective decision support system. Precise calibration of market response through statistical analysis, experimentation, and management science models can help managers increase profits for the product. Price, advertising, sales effort, and promotion strategies require change to improve profitability as the product moves through the mature phase of the life cycle.

New competitors enter and defensive strategies must be formulated as a product matures. A firm whose product is under competitive assault has to answer questions such as:

- Should we change our price?
- Should we modify our advertising copy or our advertising budget?
- Should we reposition our product for a different set of customers?

- Should we improve our product or expand the product line?
- Should we change our distribution system by emphasizing different distribution channels?

To maintain profitability in the short run and in the long run we must be ready to address each of these questions and to act quickly to adjust a product and marketing strategy. In the section of this book devoted to life-cycle management we provide analysis techniques to set defensive strategies.

At the end of the mature phase, either the product must be repositioned through product innovation, or managed through its decline phase to harvest its remaining profit potential. If it is to be rejuvenated, the new-product development process is repeated to find the best target market and design to revitalize the product's life cycle. Often in today's markets continuing innovation is necessary for success and the process becomes an ongoing one. For example Honda replaced its existing car models almost three times in the period of 1981 to 1988 and introduced new models as well (Sheriff 1988). The development of new products is continuing innovation and learning. The innovation process does not end; it is a constant process of improving all aspects of the product.

TEXTBOOK PROCESS VERSUS REALITY

We have defined a structured approach to the new-product development process. Some organizations have analogous processes written down on paper, but our experience in the last 25 years suggests that there is temptation to deviate from a disciplined process.

Violations of the Process

Here are a few stylized modes of operation that do not reflect the proposed five step process.

- *Who's got a new idea today?* Despite the structured process on paper, many organizations operate on this totally spontaneous and undisciplined approach. This process is not characterized by an organized search, but rather somebody in marketing comes up with an idea. The idea is implemented with a minimum of testing and evaluation and is often not aligned with the overall market strategy.
- *Here's a new technical discovery.* This is characterized by a firm with an extremely strong R & D department, or in an industry that is techno-

logically oriented. The problem with this approach is that the concept can have very little meaning to the customer despite the technical brilliance of the idea. Recall from the last chapter that 60% to 80% of successful technical innovations in many fields have been in response to market needs and demands rather than in response to new scientific or technological advances.

- *Me too.* Although the organization possesses an aggressive development policy, the organization has very few ideas and therefore is forced to copy competitors' new products and follows them into the marketplace. The problem is the copying organization enters with a parity product that at best produces marginal profits. The times that "me too" makes sense is if the firm can produce a better product or produce it with less cost.

- *Let's run it up the flag pole and see who salutes it.* A systematic generation of many ideas that are not well thought out or well screened before heavy technical, production, and marketing investments.

- *We've got to do something fast.* Sales are down, and we need some help by the end of this year. This reflects short-run pressures that will result in high risks and low levels of innovation. Often minor product-line extensions are rushed to market. Even though there is a development process, the organization does not have the discipline to wait until the major new products come out. This reaction also occurs when the process has failed to give a continuing flow of results that meet the firm's growth needs.

Abuses of the Process

Although violations of the process are bad, we have seen many organizational abuses that are worse. Here are four specific and real examples of the abuse of the new-product development process.

A leading food producer had developed in its test kitchen Pizza Spins (frozen pizza 4 inches in diameter that you cook in the toaster). With the push from an aggressive brand manager it was determined to go national without test market because a company only needs "1% of the snack market." However, the question should not have been how to get 1%, but how to get even one customer to try the product and make a repeat purchase. The trial appeal was limited and frequency of purchase low so that after following the brand manager's advice, the firm ended up with an inventory equal to 60 years of sales at the initial sales level. The testing stage should not have been bypassed.

A leading academic institution was responsible for developing a new transportation system that used minivans to pick up people at their homes after they phoned in a request to take them to their destination. Most of the attention focused on the computer scheduling of the buses and the operational process. It was only after several millions of dollars were spent that it was recognized that customer response was not understood. The implementors did not know how the product's benefits were perceived and how consumers made their decisions. The service was not successful. It had not been carefully designed from the consumers' viewpoint as a superior transportation alternative that deserved consumer patronage, even though the "production" through computer scheduling was brilliant.

In the test market of a scrubbing pad made of plastic and foam with cleanser, the new-product brand manager went to the test cities and personally installed large special displays in all stores. Then he "tested" two ads at once and thereby doubled the advertising pressure. Next, he conducted his own "research" study by personally standing next to the store shelf displaying his brand and then asking people if they had heard of his product. He returned to the office to report 80% awareness and 30% market share in the first two weeks. These actions were not sustainable in a national launch and destroyed the projectability of the test market.

A top of the line luxury car of a major auto manufacturer was downsized by engineering to meet requirements for fuel efficiency with little customer input to guide the redesign. The downsized car looked so similar to another midsized car of the firm that the managing director got into the old midsized car instead of the new model by mistake at an auto preview. Despite research and opinion by some that a disaster was looming, the organization introduced the new model. Sales fell to one half of the old levels instead of doubling as hoped. Dealers and the company suffered losses. Customers left the franchise and managers were replaced. The car was subsequently redesigned and lengthened but sales recovered only modestly.

These examples may sound extreme, but they happened in "sophisticated" organizations with clearly defined processes. The personal career interests of individuals can destroy even the best processes, even if the individuals are enthusiastic supporters of the project.

The Process As It Sometimes Can Occur

The new product director of a major firm once presented the charts shown in Figure 3.6. The process on the left is similar to the one proposed in this book, but the one on the right is how he saw the process actually working in his organization. Although this was meant to be humorous, he said that it was all too real!

The lessons from these examples are that the process is important, but

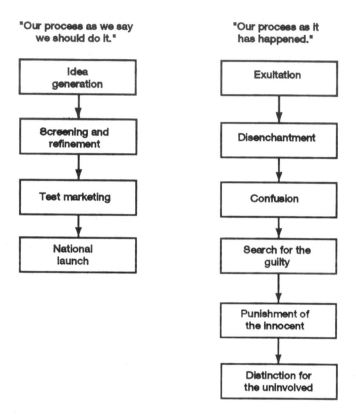

"Our process as we say   "Our process as it
we should do it."   has happened."

Idea generation	Exultation
Screening and refinement	Disenchantment
Test marketing	Confusion
National launch	Search for the guilty
	Punishment of the innocent
	Distinction for the uninvolved

Figure 3.6 New-Product Development Processes—Plans versus Reality

to make it real requires managerial discipline and control. Enthusiasm must be maintained, but discipline enforced. In the case of the cleaning pads, the brand manager was not fired. He was commended on his energy, but presented with the need for accurate forecasts. In the end the product failed because of low repeat rates and increased competitive reaction from the existing brands.

Iteration and Complexity

Before we begin our chapter-by-chapter consideration of proposed process, let us reemphasize once again at this point that in the real world our simple five-step prescriptive process simplifies substantially the activity schedules that occur in development. In practice many of the activities of the phases will be going on simultaneously, and interaction will be common. Cross-communication will occur and continuous innovation will take place in a not so clearly defined process. In fact if the process is used as a rule book, creativity may decline and enthusiasm lost.

Successful new-product development requires creative input and analytical discipline. The process we propose when applied with flexibility maximizes creative input in the stages of idea generation, design refinement, revision after testing, and profit management. Analytical discipline is used to minimize risks in the phases of design evaluation, pretesting, test-market forecasting, controlling the national launch, and transition to maturity. The tools and perspective of a disciplined new-product process allow you to implement effective and efficient new-product strategies in a flexible process customized to your organization.

To help you understand better how to succeed, we examine some correlates of success. We then present a list of the reasons why products fail. By anticipating these pitfalls and by using the new-product process to avoid them you can minimize risk and maximize the potential for reward. After reviewing how to avoid failure, we then examine the implications of being too conservative and too concerned with avoiding failure.

CORRELATES OF SUCCESS

There have been several published studies of new-product success. Among the most famous are reports by Booz, Allen, and Hamilton (1982) and the Conference Board (Duerr 1986) and published articles by Cooper and Kleinschmidt (1987), and de Brentani (1989). Table 3.1 summarizes these studies by listing 13 correlates of success as cited by one or more of the four research programs. We discuss each of these and indicate how the new-product development process builds on the success factor.

Perhaps the strongest indicator of success was *match to customer needs*. This goal is addressed throughout the new-product process in Figure 3.1. In opportunity identification the target group of customers is defined carefully and ideas generated to address their needs. These ideas are refined in the design phase by collecting data on customer needs and focusing technology to address those needs. The testing, launch, and life-cycle management phases monitor the delivery of benefits to fulfill customer needs and improve the product and its marketing to assure that delivery. Similarly, the process addresses *high value to the customer* by identifying the customer's priorities and designing the product to deliver priority benefits at a price which provides high value. Techniques such as perceptual maps, value maps, and preference analyses each focus technology on priority benefits (these will be discussed in chapters 8 to 10).

Innovation is addressed in idea generation (opportunity identification) and by competitive analyses (design), and *technological superiority* is addressed

TABLE 3.1 Correlates of New Product Success

Correlate of Success	Booz, Allen, and Hamilton	de Brentani	Cooper and Kleinschmidt	Duerr
Match customer needs	√	√	√	
High value to customer		√	√	
Innovative		√	√	
Technical superiority	√		√	
Screened on growth potential, etc.		√	√	√
Favorable competitive environment	√			
Fit internal company strengths	√	√	√	√
Communication among functions		√	√	
Top management support	√		√	√
Enthusiastic champion				√
New-product organization	√			√
Use new-product process	√		√	√
Avoid unnecessary risk		√	√	

Adapted from Booz, Allen, and Hamilton (1982), de Brentani (1989), Cooper and Kleinschmidt (1987), and Duerr (1986).

by identifying gaps in the market (perceptual mapping, design) and coordinating marketing, R&D, and engineering (e.g., total quality procedures, design). Superior products that match customer needs and deliver value are the keys to success. In the 1990s quality will be a necessary requirement for success. Clark and Fujimoto (1991) studied the auto industry globally and found that total product quality was critical to attracting and satisfying customers. Building quality products requires qualified engineers and marketers. R&D excellence (e.g., superior quality and reliability, competent engineering, good project management) and technical performance were found by Zirger and Maidique (1990) as the most important discriminants between success and failure in new electronic products.

Issues such as *screened on growth potential, favorable competitive environment,* and *fit to internal company strengths* are each addressed early in the identification of opportunities and modified through design, testing, and launch. Focus in developmental strategy is important because core expertise in specified technologies and markets can lead to success. E. B. Roberts (1990a) reports that the 3M corporation in their in-house ventures experienced 67% success in markets related to their current business when they developed a unique technology versus 25% success in unrelated markets with a unique technology (they achieved 0% success with in unrelated markets and non-unique technologies; 25% success was found in related markets with non-unique technologies).

Communication among functions is an issue that begins when interfunctional teams agree on opportunities and participate in the integration of their functions to design a product that uses state-of-the-art capabilities to deliver priority customer benefits. *Top management support, enthusiastic champion,* and *an effective new-product organization* are infrastructures that make the formal decision process work (these are addressed later in this book when we turn to organizational issues in chapter 20).

Use of the new product process is a success reason cited by three of the research studies. Indeed, in a separate study of 195 industrial firms, Hise, O'Neal, McNeal, and Parasuraman (1989), find that more up-front activities a firm undertakes (i.e., opportunity identification and design) the higher the success rate for new products. Firms that use only a few up-front methods (one or two) had but a 29% success rate, whereas firms that used a full set of up-front activities (6+) had a 73% success rate for their new products. Clark and Fujimoto (1991) indicate that productivity in the development process (e.g., engineering hours for new design, materials used for prototype construction) is important because it lowers costs and allows an organization to produce more new products with a fixed set of resources. A process with efficient up-front design and testing improves the odds for success and profit.

The final reason listed in Table 3.1 is *avoid unnecessary risk.* We now amplify this topic by addressing reasons why new products fail and by reviewing how the new-product process avoids such pitfalls.

One emerging correlate of success not cited in the studies reported in Table 3.1 is "time to market." That is the time from initiation of the project to successful launch. This is sometimes called "cycle time," and it is important in industries where life cycles are short and frequent innovation must fit a moving window of technological or market performance. Clark and Fujimoto (1991) find this as a critical success factor in the worldwide auto market. Cycle time is also critical in fast moving technologies (e.g., integrated circuits, computer workstations) because delay can mean a loss of competitive position or even missing an opportunity all together. Faster cycle times are often associated with increased sales growth (Gomory 1989) and improved global competitiveness. We discuss methods to reduce the time to market later in this chapter.

WHY PRODUCTS FAIL AND HOW TO AVOID SUCH FAILURES

We know many products fail (see data in chapter one), but very few systematic studies have been carried out to diagnose *why* products have failed. This may be due in part to a "don't look back attitude" in organizations, but also it is difficult to untangle what happened and pinpoint the causes of failure. Based on research studies[1] and our own experience, we have identified at least 17 reasons for new product failure. In Table 3.2 we outline these reasons and indicate how the proactive new-product development process provides safeguards to reduce the risk of these failures.

To achieve success each of these pitfalls must be avoided. It is a formidable task to avoid all the pitfalls, but it must be done. Any one pitfall can result in the failure of the effort. The new-product development process in Figure 3.1 helps to avoid these pitfalls by providing disciplined checkpoints at each stage of development. Each pitfall is considered and addressed in one or more phases of the development process. For example, the market definition stage of opportunity identification checks the market for sales and volume potential thus avoiding the trap of *market too small* and this is rechecked at the testing phase. The opportunity identification also is the place to systematically assess the match of the product to the company's skills.

In the design phase of the process, a careful consideration of potential customer benefits, technological expertise, and the identification of a unique competitive positioning avoids the pitfalls of *not new/not different, no real benefit*, and *poor positioning*. Overall process design avoids being late in the market (we discuss specific methods of shortening the time to market below). The testing phase measures channel support avoiding the trap of forecasting errors and inadequate support from the channel. Good launch planning and control minimizes the damages from competitive response and changes in customer tastes.

Avoiding being "blind-sided" by technology takes vigilance in all phases of the development program. Many firms stay too long with old technologies. For example, Henderson and Clark (1990) and Henderson (1990) found in the industry for photolithographic alignment machinery used in manufacturing integrated circuits that systematically the leadership changed as each previous leader failed to recognize technology shifts that led to new generations of equipment. Organizations must develop methods to prevent being myopic in terms of radical as well as incremental technology shifts that change the relationships between the core components of a system. Monitoring and organizational learning are necessary particularly in the mature phase of the life cycle when new technologies can induce new-product life cycles.

The phase of life-cycle management also must assure that follow on service is excellent and continuing innovation and improvement responds to

---

[1] Angelus (1969); Booz, Allen, and Hamilton (1971); Briscoe (1973); Cooper (1975); Crawford (1977); Davidson (1976); Rothwell et al., (1974).

TABLE 3.2 New Product Failures: Reasons and Safeguards

Failure Reason	Elaboration	Suggested Safeguard
Market too small	Insufficient demand for this type of product.	Market is defined and rough potential estimated in opportunity identification. Demand forecasts in design and in testing.
Poor match for the company	Company capabilities do not match the requirements for producing and marketing the product.	In opportunity identification the company's capabilities are matched to the strategic plan. This is then tested in prelaunch, pretest, and test markets.
Not new/not different	A poor idea that really offers nothing new to the customer. The technology may be new, but the benefit to consumers is not evident.	Creative and systematic idea generation in opportunity identification. Product designed with a focus on the customer. Product and position tested before launch.
No real benefit	Product does not offer better performance vis-à-vis customer needs. Under investment in core technologies.	In design, a strategic benefit position is identified and the product engineered to deliver these benefits. R&D designs real product performance improvements. Product tests with customers assure adequate benefit delivery.
Poor positioning vs. competition	Perceived benefits from the product are dominated by a mix of competitive products. Low value.	The use of perceptual mapping, value mapping, and preference analysis identifies gaps in the market relative to competitive products.
Inadequate support from the channel of distribution	Product fails to generate expected channel support. Demonstrations not provided if needed. Product not available to customers. After-purchase service not available.	The channel is considered in opportunity identification. Service delivery is part of the product design. The channel reaction is monitored in testing and in launch.
Forecasting error	Excess production due to overestimation of sales. Opportunities are lost because of underestimation of sales and low production and marketing.	Systematic methods in design, pretest, and testing phases of the process improve earlier forecasts as the product and marketing strategy near completion.
Poor timing	Enter too late in market. Cycle time too long. Miss window of technology or market opportunity.	Design process to get to market fast. Monitor changes. Tradeoff risks of Go or delay.

TABLE 3.2 (Continued)   New Product Failures: Reasons and Safeguards

Failure Reason	Elaboration	Suggested Safeguard
Competitive response	Competitors respond quickly before the product can achieve a success in the market. Price and promotion. Competitors copy design and improve it.	Strategic positioning vis-à-vis competition. Consideration of competitive response in design, pricing, and marketing plans. "What-if" scenarios. Monitoring of tests and launch. Move aggressively to establish first in market advantages.
Major shifts in technology	"Blind-sided" by radical change in technology. Stay with old technology too long.	Monitor new technologies. Look for new benefits they can produce. Continuing education for R&D. Have a contingency plan for shifts.
Changes in customers' tastes	Substantial shift in customer preference before product achieves market penetration.	Frequent monitoring and updating of customer preferences in the design, testing, and launch phases.
Changes in environmental constraints	Drastic change in some key factor such as economic conditions or material costs.	Analysis of environmental constraints in opportunity identification. Monitoring in testing and launch. Adaptability in design.
Poor repeat purchase or no diffusion of sales	Customers buy the product in the beginning, but sales never reach potential.	Trial and repeat, and diffusion measured in design phase and monitored in testing and launch. Product designed to deliver real benefits. Advertising matched to product's benefits delivery.
Poor after-sales service	Product complex or not reliable and service not delivered.	Service considered as an explicit designed in benefit. Monitored in testing and launch.
Insufficient return on investment	Poor profit relative to investment (e.g., poor sales or excessive costs).	Careful selection of markets, forecasting of demand, design of product for low-cost production. Value maps facilitate profit maximization.
Lack of coordination in functions	R&D develops a product that does not meet customer needs. Marketing identifies benefits that cannot be delivered. Design changes make production difficult.	New-product process is used to coordinate marketing, R&D, engineering, and production. The input from the customer drives the design.

TABLE 3.2 (*Continued*)   New Product Failures: Reasons and Safeguards

Failure Reason	Elaboration	Suggested Safeguard
Organizational problems	Conflicts between marketing, R&D, and production. Inadequate communication of key aspects of design and marketing.	Careful attention to communication and explicit programs to coordinate with quality design programs. Management involvement and review at various stages of the process. Careful go/no go decisions with objective criteria.

changes in the environment, market, technology, and competitors. *Poor repeat purchases* is avoided by design activities that provide the benefits they promise and testing to assure a wide market is interested in the innovation.

Before the process can avoid the pitfalls, it must be used. Although it seems only too logical to use such a process, organizational coordination is often lacking between functions, and the development team faces many pressures that cause them to accelerate the process and spend too little time and energy on the early phases of the process. In some cases the risks owing to acceleration are justified; in some cases they are not. We balance these trade-offs in the design, testing, and launch phases. The organizational pitfalls were demonstrated in the abuses and violations of the system cited above and the need for coordination cited in the previous chapter. This topic is considered in chapter 20.

SUCCESS RATES AND THE GENERATION OF NEW BUSINESS

Tables 3.1 and 3.2 suggest that the new-product process must exploit new-product successes and avoid new-product failure. But do these tables tell the whole story? After all, one way to succeed is to keep trying, to bring product after product to the market in the hopes that, by luck, one will succeed. Of course such a process may not be very profitable. Conversely, one way to avoid failure is to never try. A no decision is always safe in the sense that the product cannot be observed to be a failure, but of course an opportunity may be missed and the organization may be risking its long-run viability. What we would like to do is to achieve a balance between avoiding risk altogether and controlling risk while seeking to succeed.

A scientific study that addressed this issue was undertaken by Cooper in 1984. In that study, published in two articles (Cooper 1984a and 1984b), he examined 122 organizations relative to 19 strategy dimensions. He found that there were roughly five types of strategies.

1. *Technology driven* in which firms banked on their technological sophistication

2. *Focused, but technologically weak* in which firms had a strong marketing orientation and looked for products with differential advantages, but were weak on technological capabilities and were not very offensive oriented

3. *High budget, shotgun* in which firms spend heavily on R&D, entered new markets of high potential and high competitiveness with a premium-priced product, but had little focus in programs or products, little production-technology synergy, and spent little on marketing research

4. *Low budget, conservative* in which firms had high synergies among production, technology, and marketing and had high product focus, but were somewhat weak on technology, spent little on R&D, and introduced products without advantages on quality or customer impact

5. *Marketing and technology integrated* in which firms were technologically sophisticated and marketing oriented with focus on products and programs, introducing products with differential advantages on quality and customer impact to high potential markets that they could dominate

The relative success of these strategies is graphed in Figure 3.7. Note that one way to avoid failure is to be conservative and take few risks, but that strategy of *low budget, conservative* also leads to little success. A *technology-driven* firm does achieve successes because much of its sales comes from new products, but it also suffers many failures, failures that could divert resources and reduce profitability. The *high-budget, shotgun* and the *focused but weak-technology* strategies do poorly on both success rate and sales. The one strategy that appears to be a consistent winner is the strategy that *integrates marketing and technology* by focusing on the customer and delivering benefits with state-of-the-art technology. In other words, the firms that focus their energies, integrate functions, and do not neglect any aspect of the challenge are the ones that succeed while avoiding failure. The new-product process is a means to achieve this effective integration.

We now turn our attention to the costs, time, risks, and expected benefits of each phase of the development process

COST, TIME, RISK, AND EXPECTED BENEFIT IN NEW-PRODUCT DEVELOPMENT

Once an organization selects a proactive strategy, it must allocate its resources (time, money, personnel) to projects and to stages of the new-product de-

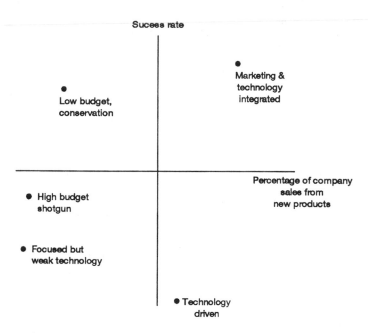

Sucess rate

● Marketing & technology integrated

● Low budget, conservation

Percentage of company sales from new products

● High budget shotgun

● Focused but weak technology

● Technology driven

Figure 3.7   Comparison of New-Product Strategies on the Percent of Sales and on the Percent of Projects that were Successful (Adapted from Cooper 1984)

velopment process. Given the inherent uncertainty in any creative effort, we do not advocate an allocation of fixed budgets to each phase of the development process, but, rather, we advocate a flexible strategy in which specific goals or benchmarks are established. Without such goals it is deceptively easy to justify any outcome of opportunity identification, design, or testing and to advance a probable failure.

Even with a series of go/no go decision points, an organization needs to know what to expect in terms of cost, time, and risk. To provide guidelines we review average costs, time, and risks, recognizing that these averages vary considerably from organization to organization. Because the new-product process is iterative, one-time costs do not tell the whole story. For example, every time we undertake a formal opportunity identification we may not find an idea that passes the go/no go decision point for advancement to the design phase. Suppose that only half of the time we pass the decision point. Then, on average, we must undertake opportunity identification twice to identify an opportunity that is of sufficient potential to pass the decision point. On average, we may need to pass through each phase of the process many times to achieve our goal—a successful new product. Thus, after we review average costs, time, and risk, we use that information to illustrate how

TABLE 3.3 Typical Costs of Product Development for Consumer-Packaged
Goods and Industrial Chemicals

	Costs for Consumer Packaged Goods ($)		Costs for Industrial Chemicals ($)	
	Typical	Range	Typical	Range
Opportunity identification	200	100–500	100	0–200
Design	400	200–1,500	1,300	100–2,800
Testing	2,000	100–6,000	600	200–1,000
Total development	2,600	400–8,000	2,000	300–4,000
Introduction	10,000	5,000–50,000	2,700	800–9,000
Total investment	12,600	6,300–68,000	4,700	1,100–13,000

to forecast the average number of passes through each phase of the process
and the expected cost of each phase.

Cost

We begin by considering the cost of passing a single product through
each of the various phases of development. New product development can
be expensive even in consumer packaged goods. For example, Hallmark
spent almost $4 million developing its "Little Gallery" line of cards and Bic
spent $600 thousand developing a disposable razor concept. As expensive as
is development cost, the cost of a new product launch is larger. Although
Gillette spent $1.2 million developing Ultramax shampoo, they spent $19
million on its launch. S. C. Johnson spent $30 million launching Agree
shampoo and R. J. Reynolds spent $40 million in an attempt to launch Real
cigarettes.

Costs vary dramatically by industry. A new jet engine may cost more than
$1 billion dollars to develop in contrast to the million-dollar requirements of
packaged goods. A new auto program may cost $4 billion. Table 3.3 provides
one more detailed comparison of the differences. It compares typical costs for
consumer packaged goods and for industrial chemicals. The estimates for the
packaged goods are based on our experience in this industry. The costs for
the industrial chemicals are based on Mansfield and Rapoport (1975), updated to 1987 dollars[2]. Variances are large, but Table 3.3 does indicate the

---

[2]Mansfield and Rapoport (1975) report their costs in different categories. We classify
about 15% of their applied research cost to opportunity identification and the rest to design.
Their specification costs are allocated to design and the prototype/pilot plant is allocated to
testing. Tooling, manufacturing facilities, manufacturing startup, and marketing startup are all
allocated to launch. All estimates are rounded to the nearest $100,000 for simplicity of exposition.

substantial investments that are involved. Furthermore, the major part of the investment for both categories of products occurs in introduction—*after* the product is developed. The overall ranges reported are specified to include two-thirds of the projects so some lie outside the range. For example, Gillette's development of the Sensor razor cost $310 million of which $75 million was for R&D, $125 million for capital investment, and $110 million for advertising and promotion (*Business Week*, 1990). The variances are large, but the table gives one a feeling of typical projects.

Data is also available from the Booz, Allen, and Hamilton (1982) study cited earlier. The average costs (in 1987 dollars) based on this study were $700 thousand for opportunity identification, $4.1 million for design, $2.6 million for testing, and $5.9 million for introduction.[3] (Recall that this study is based on 60% industrial, 20% consumer durables, and 20% consumer non-durables.)

Although there is not much data on the costs of new services, their costs are similar in many ways. Because of the nature of services it is important to get experience with providing the service to develop procedures and protocols for maximum benefit delivery. In general, services require fewer funds to be allocated to design and more to in-the-field pilot-testing programs and implementation. American Express's introduction of the "Optima" card entailed significant investments in the computer-processing capability and a substantial launch budget. Cellular phone services required large investments in the infrastructure for transmission, careful research expenditures to forecast demand and price response, and millions to market the ideas and meet competitive pressures.

Overall, it is clear that new-product development requires a major commitment of resources and that most funds are at risk in the final testing and introduction phases. Managerially, this suggests that (1) the time when many creative ideas are to be encouraged is early in design of the product when less investment is at risk, and (2) it is important to eliminate failures early before they lead to a major loss in investment.

Time

The timing of investment can be as important as the magnitude of the investment. Too long a development process can result in lost opportunities, whereas too short a process can ignore key issues and result in failure. Unfortunately, the time required to develop a product is difficult to estimate in advance. It depends on creative breakthroughs and getting the product and marketing strategy right before continuing in the process.

[3] The data were updated based on the 82–87 Consumer Price Index (117.7) and assigned to the categories in Figure 3.1.

For example, although some products like the first Polaroid Land Cameras and Wisk laundry detergent moved to the market in one or two years, many products like penicillin, Bendix washer/dryers, and Maxim coffee took 10 years or more (Adler 1966). Other examples include Crest (10 years), Minute Maid frozen orange juice (2 years), GE electric toothbrushes (3-4 years), Krilium soil conditioner (12½ years), and xerography (15 years). Gillette's Sensor razor took 13 years from project initiation to market launch. New auto development programs have traditionally taken 5 to 6 years to get to market, but recently these times have been shortened to 3 to 4 years with the advent of worldwide competition and improved procedures. Some products are delayed waiting for physical product improvement, whereas others waited until a market could be found. Some of these delays are the result of careful, purposive development of the idea, whereas others were simply organizational time lags.

Table 3.4 reports the average time used in each phase for the chemical innovations represented in Table 3.3. Clearly, the majority of time is allocated to development (applied research specification, and prototype development). The average total time in chemicals, machinery, and electronics is 51 months and the average time in the pharmaceutical industry is 60 months (Mansfield et al., 1971).

Our experience in the consumer package goods market is expressed in Table 3.5 for the case in which no major R&D breakthrough is required. Two and one-half years is a reasonable estimate of the average time, if a product is successful at each phase. Although "me too" or minor variations of products that are product line extensions may be rushed to market in a few months, 18 months is a very fast schedule for a significant new product. If substantial R&D work is required, at least one to two years should be added to the estimate.

Organizations must manage this process by ensuring that sufficient time

TABLE 3.4 Average Percentage of Total Time Elapsed in Various Stages of Innovation Activities

Stage	Average Percentage of Total Elapsed Time	Range on % (± SD)[b]
Applied research	62.0%	34–90
Specification	34.6	7–63
Prototype/pilot plant	35.0	13–57
Tool and manufacturing	21.9	4–40
Manufacturing startup	7.8	2–14
Overlap in phases[a]	59.1	10–108

[a]Overlap is the sum of the months of overlap divided by the total time.
[b]SD=standard deviation.

TABLE 3.5   Estimated Time Required for Development of New Consumer Products

	Average Time Span (Months)	Range (± SD)
Opportunity identification		
Design	5	4–8
Testing	6	2–15
Pretest market	3	2–5
Test market	9	6–12
Introduction setup	4	2–6
Total time	27	18–35

is allocated to each phase, but that abnormal delays do not occur for non-productive reasons. The best way to do this is to be receptive to sources of ideas and to encourage their careful development and evaluation, but to keep a strategic focus on the time to market and the benefits that can be gained by fast, careful progress.

Tables 3.3 to 3.5 give cost and time estimates if each phase is successful. But new products are risky; it is likely that phases will need to be repeated thus increasing both the cost and the time. We return later in this chapter to estimate the expected cost and the expected time to achieve a success, but first we attempt to quantify the risk.

Risk

We have identified some of the overall market failure rates for new products in chapter 1 and identified some of the reasons for failure previously. In this section we look at the component risk factors that occur at each phase of the development process.

The risks of industrial products have been studied by Mansfield and Wagner (1975). Table 3.6a indicates conditional probabilities of success at each phase and the total probability of success. These are averages; there is considerable variation in these probabilities. For example, while the average probability for technical completion is .57, Mansfield and Wagner found it to be as low as .32 for drug innovations and as high as .73 for electronics innovations.

In analyzing the reasons for lack of technical competition, Mansfield et al. found in an intensive study of three labs that 62% of the technical projects that were terminated were stopped because of poor commercial prospects rather than technical problems. Gerstenfeld (1971) similarly found that 52% of the failed R&D projects were failures for nontechnical reasons.

TABLE 3.6a Likelihood of Technical Completion, Commercialization, and Economic Success of New Industrial Products

Probability of Technical Completion	Probabiltiy of Commercialization Given Technical Completion	Probability of Economic Success Given Commercialization	Overall Probability of Success
57%	× 65%	× 74%	= 27%

Adapted from Mansfield and Wagner (1975).

TABLE 3.6b Likelihood of Success for Design, Testing, and Introduction

Probability of Successful Design	Probability of Successful Test Given Design	Probability of Market Success Given Successful Pretest or Test	Overall Probability of Success
57%	× 70%	× 65%	= 26%

Adapted from Elrod and Kelman (1987).

Table 3.6b reports estimates from a study by Elrod and Kelman (1987). Estimates in the same ranges are reported by Nielsen (1982), Stanton (1967), Buzzell and Nourse (1967), Rothwell et al. (1974, p. 50), and Cadbury (1975, p. 98). Although not identical, these estimates are in the ranges reported by Mansfield and Wagner.

Table 3.6 does not report the risks for opportunity identification, but Elrod and Kelman estimate that about 50% of the opportunity identification projects that are attempted produce opportunities of sufficient potential that the process is advanced to the design phase. Adding this consideration implies that only about one in seven (13%) of the projects begun in opportunity identification lead to a successfully launched product.

New-product development is indeed risky at all phases of development. This risk, coupled with the tremendous investment in time and money, implies that for the continued health of an organization this process must be managed carefully. We now use these estimates of cost, time, and risk to consider the *expected* costs of new-product development and to suggest a management philosophy to control these costs.

Expected Cost and Time

Suppose that on average 50% of the time you attempt to identify an opportunity, you do so. Then, on average, you will have to undertake two projects (2 = 1/0.50) to identify an opportunity successfully. But this risk propagates. If the design phase yields a successful design half the time, then, on average, two opportunities must enter the design phase for one success. But to get those two opportunities you need to undertake four (2× 2) projects.

But not all designs pass the testing phase and not all successfully tested products lead to market successes. At each phase we recognize that there is attrition in the number of projects advanced to the next phase. To quantify this attrition, we use the data in Table 3.6b. Multiplying through we see that the likelihood of complete success is 13% at the beginning of opportunity identification (50% × 57% × 70% × 65%), 26% at the beginning of design (57% × 70% × 65%), 46% at the beginning of testing (70% × 65%), and 65% at the beginning of launch. Thus, to get that magic success, we need more than seven opportunity identification projects (1.0/0.13), four design projects (1.0/0.26), two testing projects (1.0/0.46), and one+ launches (1.0/0.65).

Thus, the *expected* costs will be more than the $12.6 million for consumer packaged goods and $4.7 million for industrial chemicals that are given in Table 3.3. The expected costs must reflect the fact that each phase of the process, especially the early phases, must be undertaken more than once to average one success. Table 3.7 reflects this concept by applying the risk percentages in Table 3.6b to average costs reported by Booz, Allen, and Hamilton (1982). (The Booz, Allen, and Hamilton study includes a mix of consumer and industrial products and a mix of frequently purchased and durable products.)

The expected costs (column 4) vary from the costs per phase (column 2). Many opportunity identification projects must be undertaken, but they are not expensive. Conversely, only a few launches are undertaken, but each launch is costly. Indeed Table 3.7 suggests that more than half of the total cost of a success is spent up-front on identifying opportunities and designing the product. Thus, the success must pay back not just its cost, but the costs of the failures at each phase—$35.9 million not just $13.3 million.

TABLE 3.7   Example of the Calculation of the Expected Cost of Each Phase of the Development Process

	Cost for Phase	Likelihood of Success in Phase	Expected Cost	Proportion of Total Expected Cost
Opportunity identification	$ 700	50%	$ 5,400	15%
Design	4,100	57	15,800	44
Testing	2,600	70	5,700	16
Introduction	5,900	65	9,000	25
Total	$13,300	13%	$35,900	100%

Cost in 1987 dollars from Booz, Allen, and Hamilton (1982); likelihood of success from Elrod and Kelman (1987).

Table 3.8 applies the same concepts to the expected time to get a success. Note that if one were to undertake projects sequentially, beginning a new project only when the current project falters, the expected time to success climbs from a modest two + years (27 months in Table 3.5) to almost eight years (94 months in Table 3.8).

EXPECTED BENEFIT OF UP-FRONT INVESTMENT

Skipping Phases in the Process

Table 3.7 suggests that the expected cost of investing in the full development process is substantial. Faced with this investment, firms are often tempted to "save" costs by skipping phases. Does this really save costs? To examine this question we take a simple example. We use the estimates of costs for consumer goods given in Table 3.3, but we simplify the probabilities to make the concept clear. We assume a 50% chance of passing introduction, a 50% chance of passing testing, and a 40% chance of passing design (while avoiding opportunity identification). Overall this gives us a 10% (40% × 50% × 50%) of passing a product straight through. These numbers are not out of line with those in Tables 3.6 to 3.8.

Suppose we decide to "save" development costs by skipping design and testing. Then instead of facing the expected cost of the development process, we will bring, on average, 10 products to market to get a single success. Because introduction is expensive, it will cost us $100 million, on average, to develop a successful new product (Table 3.9).

Faced with this tremendous expected expense, we decide that it might

TABLE 3.8 Expected Time of Development for Frequently Purchased Consumer Products if the Phases of the Development Process are Undertaken Sequentially

	Average Time per Phase (months)	Likelihood of Success in Phase	Expected Time-in Phase (months)
Opportunity identification	5	50%	39
Design	6	57	23
Testing	12[a]	70	26
Introduction setup	4	65	6
Total	27		94

[a] Here we have merged test market and pretest market for illustration. In actual projects, a product is advanced to test market only if it passes pretest market, but this complicates the calculations.

TABLE 3.9 Example Comparison of Alternative Strategies for Using or Skipping Phases of the Development Process

	Save Development Costs (Design and Testing)			
	Example Cost	Likelihood of Success	Expected Attempts	Expected Cost
Introduction	$10,000	10%	10	$100,000

	Save Design Costs			
	Example Cost	Likelihood of Success	Expected Attempts	Expected Cost
Test market	2,000	20%	10	$20,000
Introduction	10,000	50	2	20,000
Total		10%		$40,000

	Save Opportunity Identification Costs			
	Example Cost	Likelihood of Success	Expected Attempts	Expected Cost
Design	$400	40%	10	$4,000
Test market	$2,000	50	4	8,000
Introduction	10,000	50	2	20,000
Total		10%		$32,000

be a good idea to test products before launching them. To "save" some costs we still skip the design phase. As shown in Table 3.9, the idea of testing before launch reduces the expected costs to $40 million—a savings of $60 million. Not bad! Perhaps we should rethink the effects of skipping design?

Table 3.9 suggests that we save another $8 million. The "costs" of design and testing seem a bargain indeed.

Lowering Expected Costs by Spending More Funds Early in the Process

What is happening in Table 3.9 is simple. Up-front costs are very noticeable because many projects fail and because there is often little tangible profit until much later. But up-front investments pay back handsomely. An up-front strategy means that you take your risks when less is at stake. By the time you get to gamble with the really big investments (testing and launch) you have reduced your risks substantially.

Of course there are other benefits to up-front investment. If opportunity identification is successful, the market should be better understood and the

TABLE 3.10 Example Computation of Expected Costs for Full Development Process

	Expected Costs for Full Development Process			
	Example Cost	Likelihood of Success	Expected Attempts	Expected Cost
Opportunity identification	$200	60%	8+	$1,700
Design	400	80	5	2,000
Test market	2,000	50	4	8,000
Introduction	10,000	50	2	20,000
Total		12		31,7000

design process should be able to develop a product that delivers benefits more effectively. Thus, the net likelihood of success of two phases (opportunity identification and design) should be improved over what could be obtained from just one (design). For example, there might be only a 60% chance of passing opportunity identification, but a successful opportunity might increase the overall likelihood from 40% to 48%. (This would imply an 80% chance of passing design; 48% = 60% × 80%.) Such a possibility is illustrated in Table 3.10.[4]

Of course all of these calculations look only at the cost side. If the intermediate steps improve the product so that its expected profitability increases, the advantages of up-front development are even more substantial.

Fortunately there is some evidence that organizations are recognizing the value of up-front investment, evidence that they are not following a shotgun approach (see Figure 3.7), but rather following a focused, integrated approach. In 1971 Booz, Allen, and Hamilton reported that firms generated, on average, 58 ideas for every success. Eleven years later, in a similar report (Booz, Allen, and Hamilton 1982), they reported that this number had been reduced to a much more efficient 7 ideas for every success. In other words, some means have been developed to generate ideas with high potential and with less chance of failure. Further evidence is provided by Moore (1987) who found in interviews with senior managers at 25 large industrial companies that large percentages reported up-front attention to strategically based idea search (85%), preliminary marketing research (75%), initial screening (75%), business analysis (95%), and testing products with potential customers (70%). Feldman and Page (1984), and Cooper and Kleinschmidt (1986) found similarly large percentages.

---

[4]If you run through Table 3.10 with no change in the probabilities the total cost remains $32 million. Thus even in this case, there is no net expected cost to the additional phase of the development process.

Advantage of a New-Product Development Program versus One-Shot Projects

When we calculated the expected time for a success it grew from a little over two years (27 months) to almost 8 years (94 months)—a substantial increase. But new-product projects need not be undertaken sequentially. It is quite feasible to undertake several different opportunity identification, design, or testing projects simultaneously. If this is done, then the average time to completion of at least one success can come close to the 27 months in Table 3.5.

Not only is this reduction in time significant, but an ongoing program of parallel projects means that potential successes will be in the pipeline and that, periodically, successes will be achieved. Such successes will provide the funds for further new-product development and avoid the temptation for crash programs that pay off in neither expected cost, expected time, nor expected benefits.

The difference between the time for a single pass through the process and the expected time it takes for a success also has implications for the tenure of new-product managers. If a new manager is hired or promoted, it is unfair to expect too rapid a success. In fact, if too much pressure is placed on managers, they will take unnecessary risks as illustrated by Table 3.9. One indication that organizations are recognizing this issue is that the tenure of new-product managers increased from an average of two and one-half years in 1967 to an average of eight years in 1981 (Booz, Allen, and Hamilton 1982).

REDUCING THE TIME TO MARKET

The preceding sections argue that up-front work should not be sacrificed and that a program of different but concurrent projects should be underway to be sure that a stream of successful innovation results for the organization. However, if the time to market a project can be shortened without changing the probabilities of success at each phase, rewards can be gained by reaching the market sooner and gaining profits before competition appears. In this section we outline eight component activities of a program to shorten the time from project initiation to market. This time is known as the cycle time for innovation.

1. *Get the slack out of the system.* The first approach to shortening the development cycle without raising risks is to get the "slack" out of each phase. This is the obvious step, because often organizations have added procedures that are not required. Remove unnecessary hierarchical re-

view steps, bureaucratic procedures, and people who do not share the common objective of moving an idea ahead and taking reasonable risks. This can be approached by first describing the actual steps undertaken for past projects and examining if each was needed or how it could be expedited. A new-product project manager can often take the lead in reviewing the steps he or she will have to undertake before initiation of the program and then negotiating with top management to streamline the process for fast and accurate decision making.

Each phase in the process is not necessarily sequential. For example preliminary design work can be initiated even before the opportunity identification phase is complete based on early indications of potential. Forecasting with customers can be begun before the design is complete based on rough prototypes. Creating the launch advertising can be begun based on positive initial consumer testing. Figure 3.8 shows, for an average consumer packaged good, the time for sequential process from Table 3.4 and a process with overlap. Sequentially 27 months is required and the launch is in September 1996. With overlapping design and opportunity identification (2 months), pretest forecasting and design (1 month), pretest forecasting and test marketing (1 month), and test market and launch planning (2 months), the launch occurs 6 months earlier in March 1996. If these overlaps do not compromise the product or represent additional risk, a very major market advantage may be gained.

Figure 3.9 gives actual phase times and overlaps for the worldwide

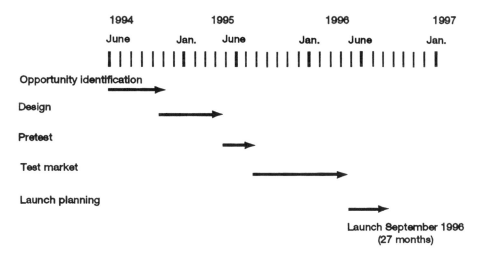

Figure 3.8a   Process for Packaged Goods with No Overlap

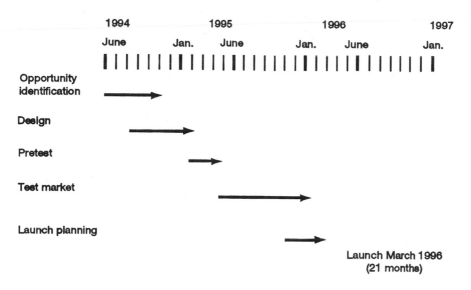

Figure 3.8b   Process for Packaged Goods with Overlap

auto industry (Clark and Fujimoto 1991). Note that the Japanese average is 43 months from start to launch, whereas the United States and Europe average 62 and 63 months. The Japanese process has shorter phases *and* more overlap. Overlap must be managed; more communication, a tolerance for ambiguity, and rapid recycling of work based on new assumptions is required across a multidisciplinary team.

2. *Use technology to shorten steps.* New technologies in engineering design and marketing testing can help shorten the cycle time. CAD and computer-aided manufacturing (CAM) simulation computer software systems make engineers more productive. They also speed up the transfer from engineering to manufacturing. For example, new CAD/CAM systems for designing printer circuit boards allow engineers to sketch the design (number of layers, layout) based on simulations of manufacturing cost and reliability. This results in an explicit "design for manufacturing" link. The software then does the draftsman's work of detailed geometric layout, integrated circuit (IC) placement, and programming of numerically controlled tools for manufacturing the board and inserting ICs. These kinds of capabilities can shorten dramatically the time to design and manufacture a product as well as improve the design. Some experts feel that with such systems prototype testing may be eliminated and "zero testing" of designs for functionality will be required. Therefore a step in the engineering process would be completely eliminated.

As cited earlier new marketing technologies in premarket testing can

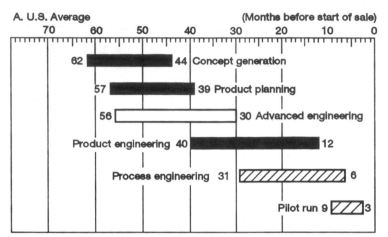

A. U.S. Average   (Months before start of sale)

Note: Average lead of 6 U.S. projects.

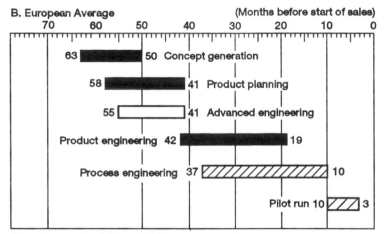

B. European Average   (Months before start of sales)

Note: Average lead time of 11 European projects.

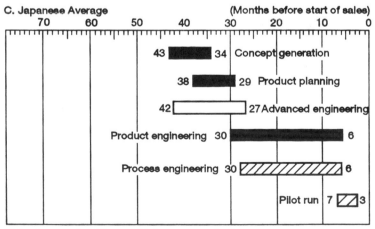

C. Japanese Average   (Months before start of sales)

Note: Average lead time of 12 Japanese projects.

Figure 3.9 Average Project Schedule by Stages (Clark and Fujimoto 1991, p. 78)

shorten the time for testing. The trend is toward systems that will replace test market without loss of accuracy. Pretest market techniques for package goods are spreading to consumer durables, services, and industrial products (see chapter 16 for a review of the state of the art in this area). If the test market is not eliminated, at least it can be shortened by accelerating the trial phase and using the test market to measure frequency of purchase and repeat purchasing which cannot be measured as reliably in pretest market procedures. Test marketing would then be used to test advertising and promotion rather than just to forecast sales. New procedures that electronically target individual homes for specific television ads allow a fast and effective reading of consumer response.

3. *Customer input early to prevent redesign.* One common cause for delay in the development process is the need to revise the product design because of negative customer feedback on the final product. American auto makers find that engineering costs increase as the market launch date approaches. The opposite should be true when engineering has good market information. Indeed, there is some evidence that Japanese manufacturers use customer input to reduce engineering time and costs (Hauser and Clausing 1988, p. 64). The process becomes faster with closer integration of marketing and engineering. Getting customer input early and frequently checking with them as the process proceeds prevents surprises. Similar input comes from the distribution channel members. The marketing research techniques we describe in this book are designed to get accurate customer input early. In the up-front work such procedures pay off in better designs and prevent delays because of redesign.

4. *Inventory up-front marketing and engineering projects.* A substantial amount of time is spent on up-front opportunity identification, advanced engineering, and early market quantification, but the cost is not great relative to the total project investment. It is possible to conduct a number of up-front studies and have them "on the shelf" and ready to go when the firm has the resources to execute them, or when the market or technology window opens. A good example is the Mazda Miata. The car got to market in three years, but work had actually begun seven years before. The up-front work was completed, and the car waited for more than a year until Mazda had a new flexible manufacturing facility in place that could produce efficiently a volume of 50,000 units or less. When this facility was imminent, Mazda implemented a go decision and got to market fast. The up-front work included testing with customers and engineering design. The car was targeted to fill the gap that opened when the traditional British sports cars left the market (e.g., Triumph Spitfire, MG). Mazda found that the sound of such a car was critical to drivers

and reengineered the cylinder heads to achieve the sound (that could not be replicated by mufflers) that customers wanted. The positioning and design work was done before the go commitment. A strategy of having three or four up-front marketing and engineering projects on the shelf does entail additional cost because all the projects may not go, and those that do may need a fast update for changing market conditions. But the time to market could be reduced substantially. In markets where lead time rewards are great this could be a worthwhile strategy.

5. *Flexible manufacturing.* Having flexibility in the manufacturing facility can shorten the time necessary to implement a go decision because a new facility does not have to be built. As cited earlier, Mazda now has the ability to produce 250,000 units in one plant, but these units can be five different models with volumes of 50,000 units each. This gives the capability to revise and innovate designs and bring out new models fast. It also allows the market to be more finely segmented and to be targeted specifically with models customized to customer needs. The costs of production are higher in a flexible manufacturing system, but reducing the time to market and the ability to reach small target groups with customized designs may generate more rewards than costs.

6. *Alliances.* Forming partnerships and joint ventures can reduce the time to market by bringing more resources to bear on the project and by tapping into skills already existing in other organizations. For example, Polaroid in the United States might join with Philips in Europe to produce an electronic camera instead of inventing the electronic technology themselves. Polaroid knows chemistry and optics but could get to market faster if it did not have to build the basic electronic technologies.

   Another possible alliance is with suppliers. Ford could partner with Du Pont on paint and GE on plastics and thereby use Ford engineering to concentrate on frames and power-train design. Ford could let Du Pont handle the finish and GE the plastic body panel technology. Reducing the number of suppliers and making them partners in the effort instead of price competitors for prespecified work also can lead to a bigger development team and incentives for preemptive research by suppliers that allow innovation to be formulated and produced faster.

7. *Skip a step in the process (occasionally).* Eliminating a step from the development process can allow a firm to get to market faster. For example, test market could be eliminated to save time. As we indicated earlier, this is probably not a wise action in the long run because it increases risk and expected costs, but sometimes short-run pressures force an organization to take more risk. For example, if you find out that the competitor is simultaneously developing a similar product and the rewards for being first on the market are great, eliminating test market and increasing the

scope of the pretest marketing forecasting may yield a better payoff of the project. In this case the firm would monitor the national launch carefully so the marketing and product could be improved adaptively during the growth phase of the life cycle. P&G had this situation in its Duncan Hines soft cookies. They stayed in test market while their competitors (Keebler and Nabisco) went national and gained a dominant share. Although the discipline of the test market was commendable, the delay in getting to market caused them to lose market leadership in the new-product category. Although the process should not be compromised in general, there may be conditions that demand a high-risk profile to reach the market before competitors.

SUMMARY

This chapter has introduced a new-product development process based on opportunity identification, design, testing, introduction, and life-cycle management. This development process is designed to encourage creativity and to reduce risk. Disciplined use of the process enables new-product teams to develop products that deliver benefits to customers in a manner that builds on the correlates of success and avoids many of the pitfalls that have led other products to fail.

The new-product development process places emphasis on the early phases and on evaluation and refinement throughout the development program. Up-front investment avoids expensive failures while enhancing the likelihood and the magnitude of success. The process cannot eliminate risk, but it can manage that risk, lead to savings in expected time and cost, and identify highly profitable new products.

The eight methods of getting to market fast indicate the need to balance discipline and good design with agility and quick action. Competition in new products is based on how well a product can meet customer needs and deliver value with quality products, as well as how fast this can be done. The new-product development process must be fast, effective, and efficient.

REVIEW QUESTIONS

3.1. Outline and describe briefly the basic steps in the new-product development process.

3.2. Develop a new squid concept alternative not given in this chapter.

3.3. What is the difference between a test market and a pretest market?

3.4. The Weave Gotit-2 Company has a simple new product strategy. They wait until a competitor launches a successful new product and then they copy it. In this way, they invest nothing in research, nothing in developing new markets, and nothing in product testing. The company has a steady stream of new products, which, in many cases, perform as well as the competitive products.

    a. Why might a company adopt such a philosophy?

    b. What are the pitfalls of such a strategy? Will it lead to long-run profitability?

    c. Are there any circumstances in which such a strategy makes sense?

3.5. Can a new product be profitable and still be classified as unsuccessful?

3.6. Consider some recent new product failures. Speculate why these new products were unsuccessful.

3.7. How can the cost of transforming a specific new product idea into a successful new product be estimated?

3.8. Why does the average total time in developing a new product vary from industry to industry?

3.9. Explain intuitively why up-front research is often so valuable.

3.10. Calculate the expected cost for the following new-product development process.

	Cost per Phase	Likelihood of Success	Expected Cost
Introduction	$20 MM	20%	?
Testing	2 MM	40	?
Introduction	20 MM	50	?
Total			?
Design	.2 MM	70	?
Testing	2 MM	80	?
Introduction	20 MM		?
Total			?
Opportunity identification		60	?
Design	.1 MM	80	?
Testing	.2 MM	70	?
Introduction	2 MM	80	?
Total	20 MM		?

3.11. Which methods of shortening the time to market would be best when applied to:

    a. Personal computers?

    b. Credit cards?

    c. New plastic composites for aircraft?

    d. New snack foods?

    e. Jet engines?

PART TWO

Opportunity Identification

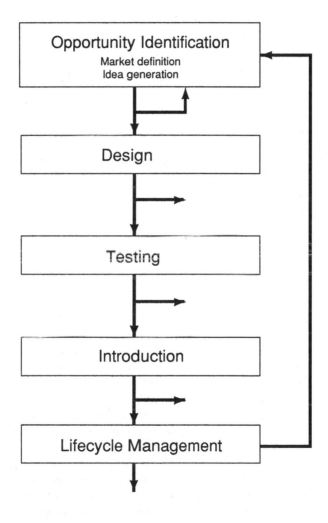

4

Market Definition and Entry Strategy

After an organization has adopted a proactive approach to new-product development, the first step in implementing it is to identify areas of opportunity. This effort is divided into two steps. In the first step, markets and their associated technologies are defined and opportunities within them are assessed. Then specific ideas are generated to tap the potential of these markets and the firm's competitive advantages. When this opportunity identification phase is complete, design work begins based on evaluation and refinement of the idea as a physical and psychological entity that delivers benefits to customers.

This chapter describes market definition and entry strategy. We begin with a discussion of managerial criteria to evaluate alternative markets and then give a simple procedure to combine these criteria and their compatibility to the firm in an overall evaluation of market opportunities. This weighing procedure gives managers a method to screen many potential markets by eliminating undesirable markets and identifying a few high-potential markets. Because the detailed investigation depends on how the market is defined, we discuss alternative bases for segmentation and methods for specifying market boundaries. Finally, we set priorities and select the best market(s) segments to enter.

DESIRABLE CHARACTERISTICS OF MARKETS

Success is likely in markets that have high sales potential, can be entered early, are competitively attractive, can generate economies of scale, require small investments for large rewards, and are low risk. These general criteria are shown in Table 4.1 along with some of the specific measures of a market's performance with respect to these criteria.

Growth Potential

Market potential is measured by the size of the market in dollar sales and the growth rate of the market. While size is important, growth potential is a key to identifying a new opportunity. It is possible to find a successful product opportunity in a stable market, however, sales will have to be taken directly from competitors. Usually this is more difficult than getting a share of the growth in a market. A growing market is also one where prices and margins are higher and therefore more desirable. For example, in a study of 68 new ethical pharmaceutical products, market growth was found to have a significant effect on ability of the firm to earn a high market share for the new brand (Gatignon, Weitz, and Bansal, 1990).

TABLE 4.1   Desirable Characteristics of Markets

General Characteristic	Measure
Growth potential	Size of market Life cycle
Early entry	Order of entry Product and marketing advantage
Economies of scale	Cumulative sales volume Learning
Competitive attractiveness	Share of market potential Rivalry intensity
Investment	Investment in dollars, technology and managerial talent
Reward	Profits ROI
Risk	Stability Probability of losses

Market Sizing.   To assess the growth potential of a market, a forecast and an understanding of the position of the market in its life cycle are required. Various government agencies, trade associations, and syndicated data services provide information on total market sales. Standard Industrial Classification (SIC) data is commonly used in industrial products. In consumer goods, store audit suppliers (e.g., Information Resources Inc. and A. C. Nielsen) can be used. In durable industries, numerous specialized data services exist to supply data to predict market growth rates. Some of these services are listed in chapter 7.

Market Growth Models.   With a database on the market size we can use life-cycle models to forecast the future growth. Bass (1969) has developed a model that is useful in predicting the future sales of a product class based on the past sales history of the products. For example, Table 4.2 shows the actual and predicted peak sales volume and timing for 21 markets that range across industrial, consumer, durable, and services. The actual times to reach peak sales are long (median is seven years). The peaks predicted by the model match the actual data, and there is reasonable agreement between the actual and predicted sales magnitudes. Statistical measures also support the model's descriptive adequacy.

The model is based on the assumption that the probability rate of initial purchase at a given time is a linear function of the total number of previous buyers. Initially, the probability rate would depend on innovators, but would increase over time as the number of past buyers increases. Mathematically, this model implies that the rate of purchases is equal to an initial value due to innovators plus a term that reflects the impact of the word of mouth influence process. This latter term is equal to a constant times the fraction of customers who have already purchased the product.

In equation form this model is given by:

$$P(t) = p(0) + q[Y(t\text{-}1)/m] \tag{4.1}$$

where $P(t)$ = probability of purchase (rate) given that no purchase has been made,

$p(0)$ = initial probability of (rate) adoption

$Y(t-1)$ = total number of people who have bought by the end of period t–1
m = the total number of potential buyers of the product
q = a diffusion rate parameter to be estimated

This equation model is a social interaction process that exerts more pressure for adoption as more people adopt.

TABLE 4.2 Predicted versus Actual Time and Magnitude of Sale Peak

Product/Technology	Predicted Time of Peak (No. of Years)	Actual Time of Peak (No. of Years)	Predicted Magnitude of Peak (Units)	Actual Magnitude of Peak (Units)
Boat trailers	9.8	10	205,240	206,000
Color television, Retail	6.0	8	5,733,400	5,490,000
Color television, manf.	5.8	7	6,637,800	5,981,000
Holiday Inns	10.9	11	131.6	141
Howard Johnson Motel	9.0	11	38.6	48
Howard Johnson, Hoiday Inn, and Ramada Inn	9.8	11	202.6	216
McDonald's, 1955–65	6.1	6	119.7	113
Continuous bleach range	3.2	4	16.7	18
Rapid bleach process	4.1	4	7.2	7
Conversion, 70% H_2O_2 delivery system	3.3	4	48.5	50
Hybrid corn	3.1	4	24.5	23
Home freezers	11.6	13	1,200,000	1,200,000
Black and white television	7.8	7	7,500,000	7,800,000
Water softeners	8.9	9	500,000	500,000
Room air conditioners	8.6	7	1,800,000	1,700,000
Clothes dryers	8.1	7	1,500,000	1,500,000
Power lawnmowers	10.3	11	4,000,000	4,200,000
Electric bed coverings	14.9	14	4,800,000	4,500,000
Automatic coffee makers	9.0	10	4,800,000	4,900,000
Steam irons	6.8	7	5,500,000	5,900,000
Record players	4.8	5	3,800,000	3,700,000

Adapted from Bass (1969, p. 221) and Nevers (1972, p. 88).

The sales in each period, $S(t)$, are the number of people who have not yet purchased times the probability of their purchase. In equation form,

$$S(t)=[m-Y(t-1)]P(t) \qquad (4.2)$$

Substituting equation 4.1 in 4.2 and collecting terms gives

$$S(t)=p(0)\,m+[q-p(0)]\,Y(t-1) - \left(\frac{q}{m}\right)Y(t-1)^2 \qquad (4.3)$$

Interpreting equation 4.3 we see that the market sales will first grow because of the effect of innovators and favorable word of mouth and then decline as the market saturates. The decline results because as more people purchase a product in the market, fewer people are left to purchase the product in the future.

The shape of this function is similar to the life cycle. Figure 4.1 compares the actual history of clothes dryer sales with the sales levels predicted with equation 4.3. In durable products, the model predicts the life of initial sales. The model does not represent replacement after the product wears out. The model helps establish the initial growth rates for a category and hence the attractiveness to new-product entry.

It is important to recognize that the use of this model in market definition is for the growth rate of a *market* not a specific *product*. We introduce models in chapters 12 and 16 that forecast demand for the new product. Although other time-series methods (Box and Jenkins 1970; Nelson 1973) could be used to forecast sales of a product class, the model in equation 4.3 is attractive because its shape is similar to the life cycle of a market and it has a behavioral foundation in the theory of diffusion of innovation.

The original Bass model has been extended and applied in more than 100 publications (see Mahajan, Muller, and Bass 1990 for a review of the literature. See Chatterjee and Eliashberg 1990, and Horsky 1990 for recent extensions). These applications give us ranges for the parameters $p(0)$ and q. Typically $p(0)$ is .04, and q is typically .3 (lower values for consumer durables than for industrial products, higher in Europe than in the United States) (see Schmittlein and Mahajan 1982; Srinivasan and Mason 1986; Sultan, Farley, and Lehmann 1990; and Montgomery and Srinivasan 1989). Forecasting can be based on these typical values or be estimated directly from early time series or cross-country category data by statistical procedures (see Schmittlein and Mahajan 1982; Lenk and Rao 1990; Gatignon, Eliashberg, and Robertson 1989; and Oliver 1987).

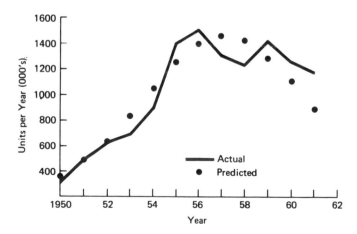

Figure 4.1　Actual and Predicted Sales for Clothes Dryers (Bass 1969, p. 224)

Use of Models to Forecast Growth.   The available growth models are effective in predicting life-cycle growth when six or seven years of data are available in the category. Alternatively, an analogy can be drawn to a market where the parameters ($p(0)$, q, and m) are known. In these cases the use of a growth model is superior to naive straight-line extension of past sales. However, one should be sure to understand the determinants of the curve and be sure the assumptions of the model are met before the forecasts are adopted. (We return to life-cycle considerations in chapter 19.)

Most of the life-cycle forecasting research has been done on consumer durables and industrial products, but recently the models have been extended to capture the effects of successive generations of technological innovations (Norton and Bass 1992, and Mahajan and Muller 1990). If a market is completely new and in an industry where the model has not been applied, either judgment will have to be used or a market research study executed to estimate the market potential (see chapters 12 and 16). At the opportunity identification stage judgment is used and then research conducted only if the potential warrants continuation.

Early Entry

All else being equal there are rewards for being first into the market if the new product is successful. For example, in a study of 82 brands in 24 categories of frequently purchased consumer products, Urban, Carter, Gaskin, and Mucha (1986) found significant rewards accruing to successful pioneering brands. They compared the share that brands achieved with (1) the order in which they entered the market, (2) the relative spending on advertising, and a surrogate measure for the unadjusted preference of the new brands. After correcting for the advertising and preference effects they found the early-entry advantage can be sustained. For example, in a two-brand market with each brand having equivalent preferences and advertising levels, the first entrant is likely to capture 59% of the market compared with the second entrant's 41%. Table 4.3 lists the projected shares for the first, second, third, fourth, fifth, and sixth entrants in one, two, three, four, five, and six brand markets.

The Urban et. al. (1986) study has been supported by a variety of analyses. For example, Biggadike (1976) found that firms that claimed to be pioneers had, on average, a dominant 40% of the market. Although this advantage declined after four years, they did remain higher than the average shares in the categories. Robinson and Fornell (1985) found that pioneers had, on average, 29% of the market, early followers 17%, and late entrants 12%. Analogous data for 1209 SBUs suggested that the average shares were 29% for pioneers, 21% for followers, and 15% for late entrants (Robinson 1988b).

TABLE 4.3 Market Shares and Order of Entry in Packaged Goods

Entry Order of Brand	First	Second	Third	Fourth	Fifth	Sixth
One	100%					
Two	59	41%				
Three	44	31	25%			
Four	36	25	21	18%		
Five	31	22	18	16	14%	
Six	28	19	16	14	12	11%

There are several potential explanations for the pioneering advantage including positioning, the ability to exploit economies of scale, brand consideration, and cognitive structure.

Positioning.   If the pioneer understands the market and has the ability to do so, the best initial position will be to deliver the product that satisfies the needs of most customers. For example, suppose that products in a hypothetical market can be characterized by the customer needs of "effectiveness" and "ease of use." Suppose further that most customers prefer a product that is moderately good on both effectiveness and ease of use to a product that excels on one dimension but not the other. Faced with these conditions and the ability to design a product that trades off effectiveness and ease of use, the first entrant will choose to position for most customers.

Faced with the first entrant's decision, the second and subsequent entrants can either fight for the "center" of the market (and some will) or choose niches by serving the "effectiveness" or the "ease-of-use" segments of the market. Because these are smaller niches, the second entrant will have a lower share. These niches will also be attractive because, by positioning away from the first entrant, there will be less competition allowing both entrants to maintain higher prices. This effect is quite strong and can be shown to occur even if customers are equally distributed in their tastes among the benefit dimensions (see Hauser 1988).

Entry Barriers.   In some cases there will be sufficient economies of scale such that the first entrant can erect entry barriers. For example, Swatch watches invested heavily in advertising and a fashion image spending disproportionally more than more the large Japanese watch makers. In doing so, they made it extremely difficult for subsequent entrants to match their spending (on a per-share basis) and thus made it difficult for subsequent entrants to erode sales in Swatch's fashion segment. Besides the ability to exploit economies of scale, early entrants might find it feasible to become low-cost producers by experimenting with production and process improvements. With such experience they can maintain cost advantages relative to later entrants.

Brand Consideration.   Suppose that a customer purchases a product and finds that that product fulfills the customer's needs. Even if a second entrant promises to be better than the first product, the customer may not switch. There is a chance that the second product may not live up to its claims, and there is a chance that the benefits the second product offers may not match the tradeoffs the customer is willing to make. Thus, the second product must not only be better, but sufficiently better to justify the risk that the customer incurs in using the new product rather than the pioneering product. This means that the second entrant must either offer more benefits, offer a lower price, or settle for a smaller share than the first entrant (see Schmalensee 1982).

Another form of this pioneering advantage is brand consideration. Before customers purchase a brand, they must consider it. If the product they are now using "works," they will be less likely to seek information on new brands and less likely to consider those brands for potential purchase. For example, Hauser and Wernerfelt (1990, p. 402) and Roberts and Lattin (1991) derive the pioneering rewards in Table 4.3 based on empirically observed brand consideration.

Cognitive Advantages.   The organization of information in long-term memory controls the accessibility and availability of that information in decision making. If the first entrant creates a node and becomes an exemplar for the product category then information about competing products may be referenced through comparison to the exemplar. Memory access will evoke the exemplar first, producing a competitive advantage (see, e.g., Carpenter and Nakamoto 1989).

These positioning, entry barrier, brand consideration, and cognitive advantages are strong and provide first entrants with marketing advantages that can be exploited. Thus, markets in which such pioneering advantages are possible are attractive candidates. Conversely, if another firm already has exploited such pioneering advantages, then the market may be less attractive.

Experience Curve

Cumulative sales volume is important because of the presence of the potential to improve production in many industries. This potential can be described by the "experience curve." This curve indicates that for many manufacturing industries the unit cost of producing and distributing a product declines at a constant rate for each doubling of the cumulative sales by the firm. Such learning phenomena represent opportunities for low cost competitive advantages (see Devinney [1987], and Adler and Clark [1991], for a discussion of learning effects).

Figure 4.2 shows an experience curve for an industrial chemical (polyvinyl chloride). As volume increased, price dropped. (Here the market price is taken as an indicator of unobservable costs.) In the early phases this reduction was small, but after large volumes were achieved rapid cost reductions occurred. As volume doubled from 5 billion to 10 billion pounds, price dropped approximately 50%. When such experience curves exist, scale of operation is critical to product success.

Few systematic statistical studies of experience curves have been reported and most curves have been drawn from simple cost plots and judgment. One rigorous paper by Stobaugh and Townsend (1975) studied 82 petrochemical companies and found significant price reductions associated with cumulative volume, economies of scale, and other factors such as standards, and competition. Thirty-five percent of the reductions were due to experience. This indicates the importance of scale but also its need to be combined with other factors in understanding the potential for low costs.

Figure 4.3 shows another experience curve; this one for Ford automobiles (Abernathy and Wayne 1974). After introduction of the Model T, costs dropped 15% for every doubling of sales from 1908 to 1925. This was associated with standardization and innovation in the production process, vertical integration, labor specialization, and better bargaining power over input material costs. This type of curve is common in manufacturing based industries.

Care should be taken in planning for the cost reduction that the experience curve offers. Ford's history demonstrates one danger. The Model T

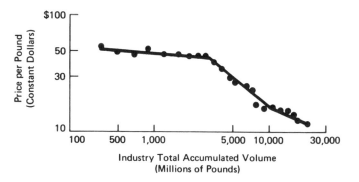

Figure 4.2 Polyvinyl Chloride Price Curve, 1946–68 (The Boston Consulting Group 1970, p. 85).

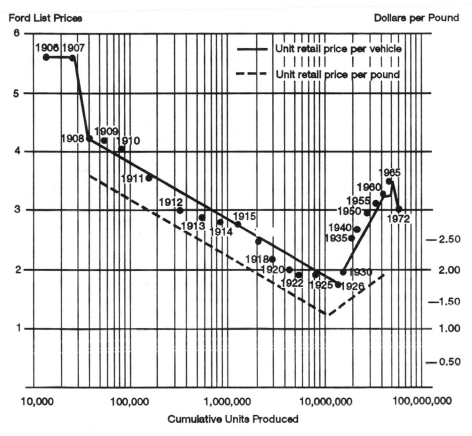

Figure 4.3   The Ford Experience Curve in 1958 Constant Dollars (Abernathy and
Wayne, 1974, p. 112)

enjoyed rapid cost reduction, but GM took away Ford's market share through
greater performance and better capability.

The new competitive environment was reflected in the 1950–72 period
where costs (list price and price per pound) increased as designs were improved and models underwent annual changes. Although Ford redesigned its
car, the company did not regain its initial position. The experience curve
existed, but consumer preferences for comfort, power, and luxury dominated
price as a determinant of market share. The experience curve is an important
phenomenon, but it is not an automatic one. It results from aggressive company actions to take advantage of the potential manufacturing efficiencies
that may result from early entry into a market.

Advantages in cumulative production can be gained from dominant share positions as well as early entry. If the experience curve exists, high market share in a large market is a good way to move to lower unit costs. Large share in a market gives a firm relative strength and dominance in that market and hence control over strategy in the market. With this strength comes a flexibility of action that can lead to increased profitability. For example, Buzzell, Gale, and Sultan (1975) analyzed 600 businesses based on data collected in the PIMS project. They found that rate of return on investment was positively correlated to market share. On average, they found that a difference of 10 percentage points in market share was accompanied by a difference of about 5 points in pretax return on investment. Businesses with market shares more than 36% earned a rate of return on investment three times those with less than 7% market share. However, these results must be interpreted cautiously because of several statistical concerns (see Jacobson 1988, and Jacobson and Aaker 1985, for details). Both scale economies and market share potential are attractive properties of a market. Strategically, this is important because it would imply concentrating resources in a few markets to increase volume and decrease costs. The highest priority would be directed toward a share in a growing market of high potential where early entry is possible. The lowest priority would be markets in which the share potential is low, sales are stable, many competitors are now in the market, and total market volume is low.

Competitive Attractiveness

Although a market is growing, has few entrants, and is subject to economies of scale, it may not be a good opportunity if the competitive environment is hostile and a strong share position cannot be obtained. Some vulnerability to product improvement should be evident. For example, in calculators, Frieden (the leading manufacturer of mechanical calculators in the 1950–65 period) was very vulnerable to exploitation by the new electronic technology. In contrast, although the large computer systems market had a high growth rate in the 1970s, IBM showed little vulnerability due to strength in business applications. In the scientific market, IBM was vulnerable to the workstation technology exploited by DEC and Sun Microsystems. (However, IBM suffered in the 1990s when large computer sales declined.)

In some cases, vulnerability is so high that even a stable category can be attractive. Jergen's dominated the hand lotion market, but were vulnerable to Chesbrough-Ponds' Vaseline Intensive Care Lotion. "Sleepy" markets in which sales are stable and innovation has been absent can represent an attractive opportunity if they are penetrated effectively. In the mature U.S. auto market, domestic producers were vulnerable to higher quality and fuel efficient cars produced in Japan and Europe in the 1980s. Data service suppliers such as A. C. Nielsen Inc. had very high market shares in the early 1980s based on hand-collected store audit data but were vulnerable to new UPC data technology based services offered by Information Resources Inc. in the late 1980s.

Competitive attractiveness is reflected in the competitive aggressiveness of a market as well as its vulnerability. If entry is likely to precipitate a price war and strong retaliatory actions from existing competitors, the market will be less attractive. For example the airline industry has a record of frequent price wars. A firm would not find such a competitive environment attractive unless it had a differential advantage that would allow it to succeed in such an environment.

Investment

The more investment required by a market for entry and penetration, the less attractive it is. For a given level of sales volume, a larger financial investment makes a market potentially less profitable. Furthermore, the stakes are higher and a failure is more devastating to an organization. Besides direct financial investment, an organization must consider the allocation of its other scarce resources such as managerial talent, capital equipment, and laboratory resources, which represent an indirect financial investment.

Reward

Large investments in themselves are not unattractive if they lead to high returns on investment. For example, a large organization may see a market requiring $500 million of investment as attractive if it can return 20% on that investment. Similarly, an organization may reject a market with a low investment requirement if it cannot achieve a good return on that investment—especially if the administrative overhead of entering a market makes the profit insufficient. For example, one major package goods firm will not enter a market unless gross volume is greater than $10 million and payback less than three years. Thus, profitability must be considered rather than sales volume or investment alone.

Large investment entry costs may act as barriers to discourage competitive entry and as a result could lead to long-term profitability. Those who pay the entry costs may find a more stable price environment in their market. Organizations with competitive strength such as excellent financial resources or good channels of distribution or a line of complementary goods or advantageous geographical location, may be well advised to consider markets with high entry costs.

Risk

A final consideration of market selection is risk. Markets characterized by uncertainty are less attractive. If demand is unknown or subject to rapid and large fluctuation the resulting risk of new product failure is high. For example, if we want to consider the market for alternative fuel vehicles (e.g., electric, propane, CNG) we would be much less certain about its size and composition than if we considered the midsized sedan market for gasoline powered cars. Uncertainty can also be evident in supply of key raw materials or their prices. Competitive risk is also important to consider. We discussed the level of this factor under competitive attractiveness, but here we would weigh in our considerations our certainty in predicting the competitive environment. The more certain we are of the demand, cost, and competitive aspects of a market the more attractive it becomes.

An organization must examine a market for characteristics of risk. Judgmental estimates or historic observations of the probability of failure and the variance in payback can be used to evaluate the risk of a given market. We would prefer markets with low risk all else equal, but again as in other factors if we have advantages relative to our competitors in dealing with risk, we may find a risky market attractive. Others will not be as likely to enter, and we will have a competitive advantage if they do enter.

MARKET PROFILE ANALYSIS

The seven criteria discussed previously are used to evaluate the desirability of a particular market. It is rare that a market will dominate all others on all criteria. An organization must have some procedure by which to select markets based on these conflicting objectives.

There are numerous sophisticated techniques based on formal decision analysis (Raiffa 1968; Keeney and Raiffa 1976), but these sophisticated techniques are time consuming and require reasonably accurate estimates of the various measures of market desirability. Such techniques are appropriate later in new-product development when more precise estimates are feasible. At this stage we use a procedure that allows us to screen rapidly many potential markets to obtain a reduced set for further analysis. This smaller set is then subjected to closer scrutiny and more detailed investigation.

The technique appropriate to the data availability and magnitude of alternative markets that must be evaluated is "market profile analysis." The technique is applied in three steps: (1) enumerate and weigh the market selection criteria for your organization, (2) rate each market on each criterion, (3) calculate the overall weighted sum of the ratings for each market,

(4) evaluate the ratings to identify the market with the best opportunities for continued investigation. Those with very low ratings are eliminated.

Enumerate and Weigh Criteria

The first step in a market profile analysis is to generate the criteria that are important in a given organization. This is done by managerial discussion and interaction to specify the important factors in the words of the organization's management. This list becomes a mental checklist for market evaluation. The generation of a consensus on this list is an important activity because it integrates divergent viewpoints and begins to build communication links between key management interests in the company.

Table 4.4 lists a set of factors for a typical organization. In this list, they are grouped according to the seven market characteristics cited in Table 4.4. An additional set of criteria reflect the match between the market and the organization's abilities. If the organization does not have a required capability, it must be willing and able to acquire it before a market can be viewed as attractive.

There are many possible enumerations of factors. Although many lists can be found, each organization should go through the exercise of developing its own list or customizing existing lists of factors. This is particularly true in the matching of markets to organizational capabilities. These matching criteria encompass many unique aspects of an organization such as its technological base, distribution system, and supply advantages.

One aspect that will characterize technologically based companies is the match of the market to the organization's technological capabilities. It is common in such companies to define core technologies and core markets. Table 4.5 shows the Dexter Corporation's (a \$1 billion/year specialty material company) technology and market interactions. Good market opportunities are ones that fit within the priority markets but use the core technologies for the firm. Even if a market had good growth, few competitors, scale possibilities, competitive attractiveness, low investment requirements, high profit potential, and low risk, it would not be identified as an opportunity for new-product development unless one of the firm's core technologies was used. This matching of technology and market focus in this firm is very important in screening new-product development projects and developing competitive technological advantages in focused markets.

Weighing

Weighing the factors in terms of their importance is a necessary step to converting the checklist into a market profile analysis. First, the major head-

TABLE 4.4 Some Factors to Be Considered in Market Profile Analysis

Market Characteristics	
Growth Potential	Investment
Size of market	Investment required
Growth rate of sales	Raw material availability
Life cycle	Technological advancement necessary
Early Entry	Reward
Order of entry	Margin size
Advantages to users	Competitiveness of pricing structure
Time to become established	Return on investment
Economy of Scale	Risk
Potential for dominant cumulative sales	Stability
volume	Probability of competitive retaliation
Significance of experience curve	Chances of failure
	Patent protection
Competitive Attractiveness	Rate of technological change
Vulnerability of competition	Possibility of adverse regulation
Share potential for product	
Rivalry intensity	

Match to Organization's Capabilities
Match to core technological skills
Have financial resources required
Match to physical distribution system
Match to marketing capabilities
Use existing sales force
Probability of technical completion
Ability to service product
Compatibility to other products
Management skills and experience for this market
Past work done in this market
Overlap with current material supply channels

ings are assigned a relative weight, and then the heading weight is divided among the component parts. For example, management might decide that 70% of the weight should be on market characteristics and 30% on the matching to organizational capabilities. Further, they may see the seven market characteristics as equally important or 10% weight. This is continued until each factor has a weight established for it. For convenience, the sum of the weights for each factor should equal 100%. This process of weighing criteria is a valuable exercise for the organization in terms of structuring and setting market priorities.

Occasionally a factor is so important that it must be satisfied before a market can be considered. Such "elimination" criteria are considered by

TABLE 4.5 Dexter Corporation Core Technologies
and Priority Markets

	Priority Markets					
Core Technologies	Aerospace	Automotive	Electronics	Food Packaging	Industrial Assembly & Finishing	Medical
Plastic compounding	X	X				
Surface finishing adhesion		X	X	X		
Composite structuring	X	X			X	
Long fiber/wet laid paper				X	X	X
Biotechnology						X

X = Current product entries

eliminating all markets that do not meet the criteria and then evaluating the remaining markets with the remaining factors and weights. For example, an industrial company might, by policy, decide not to enter a frequently purchased consumer market under any conditions. In this case, all frequently purchased consumer markets are removed from the list of potential markets and the others are considered. Another example carried over from the discussion of criteria in technological industries is the failure of a market to match a core technology of the company.

This judgmental weighing can be improved by technical methods if the factors are independent (Freimer and Simon 1967). Our experience has been that most of the gain from weighing is due to discussion among managers that directs attention to various markets and assures a systematic first look at them. Many of the factors are not independent; a factor that appears to make a market unattractive may actually make it attractive if it matches a firm capability that can be converted into a competitive advantage (Wernerfelt and Montgomery 1986). For example, high investment and risk are generally unattractive, but if the firm has ample funds and can minimize the risk by linking to unique manufacturing, technological, or distribution advantages, the market may be attractive. Similarly if a market is characterized by aggressive competitors, it might still be attractive if the firm has a proprietary technology that can deliver unique benefits in that market. We do not recommend rigid analytical or statistical approaches at this early phase of market considerations. In later phases where more and better data are available we suggest the use of several analytical methods.

Ratings

Given the preceding caveats, it is still worthwhile to rate judgmentally
each alternative market opportunity on each factor. The rating can be done
with a 5-point scale relative to an average existing market for the firm (Figure
4.4). Here a factor such as size of market is rated relative to the size of the
firm's existing market. If the new market is equal to existing markets, it is
rated zero, and if it is much bigger, it is rated +2. Each factor is rated after
management clearly articulates what is meant specifically by "better," "much
better," "average," "worse," and "much worse" for each factor (see O'Meara
1961, for an alternate set of specific scales). Each market under consideration
is rated on each scale.

Overall Evaluation

The next task is to combine the ratings, identify the market with the best
overall appeal, and eliminate undesirable markets. This is done judgmentally
by examining the profile of ratings on each factor for alternative markets.
Discussion in a meeting of heads of production, marketing, finance, R&D,
and engineering is very useful in generating a consensus on the best set of
markets.

In some cases, this process is aided by calculating an average overall
score for each market by multiplying the rating on each factor by that factor's
importance and adding these (weight × rates) for each factor. The markets
with the highest scores are most desirable. Those with a low score are eliminated and resources are not directed at them. Although this linear weighing
may be overly simplistic because of interactions, it provides a useful first cut.
If the management group confirms the qualitative judgments, the highest
scoring markets are considered further and priorities are set among the opportunities that are acceptable.

Overall evaluation scores are an aid to managerial decisions rather than
a substitute for such decisions. The decisions on weights and ratings are
important because they help quantify managerial judgments, but often man-

Factor X	−2	−1	0	+1	+2
	Much Worse	Worse	Equal to average markets we now are in	Better	Much Better

Figure 4.4.   Rating Scale for Factors

agers become concerned about this technique because they think that the market priorities are very sensitive to the selection of weights. One approach is to try a few alternative weightings or rating schemes to determine how sensitive the priorities are to the chosen procedure. In most cases, management will find that over a variety of weightings and rating schemes some markets are always rejected, whereas some markets always pass the screen. Managers can then reexamine the markets sensitive to the selection of evaluation procedures.

If a formal rating and weighing system is used, the firm should keep records of individual judgments. These judgments are then compared to actual results in markets where products are entered. This comparison will indicate biases in the ratings of certain individuals or by the representatives of specific functional areas. For example, it may be found that marketing consistently overestimates its ability to capture a large market share. Although these biases could be corrected by revising the ratings, the most important purpose of the comparison is to enable the individual evaluators to make more accurate future comparisons. Efforts should be made at each phase of the new-product process to learn systematically by comparison of judgments and reality.

The output of the overall evaluation is a set of high potential markets worth further investigation plus a preliminary set of priorities to guide that investigation. However, before we are ready to define our entry strategies we must examine more closely what we mean by a "market," and how to define its segments and boundaries.

MARKET DEFINITION

The previous section has described criteria and an evaluation procedure for *a* market. But what is *a* market? Is our "market" for autos, or for small autos, or for small domestic autos, or for small domestic two-door autos, or for small domestic two-door four-cylinder autos? Or do we define our market as fulfilling the need for economical transportation to and from work in an urban area? Is our market comprised of customers aged 18 to 29 with income greater than $20,000, or do we define our segment as young professional college graduates renting apartments in major metropolitan areas?

One critical issue in market definition is the measures we use to specify our market. Is the market defined based on the products that compete with each other, customer needs, demographics, attitudes, or other criteria? What is the best way to segment the market to identify market opportunities for new products?

Once we decide on the criterion measure for market definition, the exact limiting of the market is critical in specifying the size of a new-product opportunity. If a new battery powered car is going to compete only within the market for small domestic four-cylinder commuting cars, then a 5% share may not be large enough to justify technical development. If, however, it would compete within the market for all small economy autos, a 5% share would represent a significant opportunity.

It is desirable to have a large share of a big market, but it is possible to build a business based on a small overall share if that small share reflects a high penetration in some market segment. Rarely is it profitable to have a product with a low share in all segments.

Another key aspect of market definition relates to the new product's relationship to existing products of the firm. If the new product will be in the same market as an existing product, cannibalization may result. Ideally, the organization would like to have a product line that spans the total set of opportunities, but has little overlap and self-competition. With more than 300 auto models available, many car manufacturers may find that it is difficult to find a market niche that does not overlap with cars it already produces. When product lines have too much duplication market definition is useful in eliminating products as well as adding new products. We would like one entry in each target segment.

In proactive new-product design, management must be very purposive in defining the boundaries of the market they are entering. In this section we first look at the possible bases for defining our market and suggest a hierarchical approach to segmentation that captures the richness of the various criteria that can describe customers. After briefly outlining the methods used to derive segment definitions we discuss market selection and prioritization.

Bases for Defining Markets

There is no one best or correct way to define market segments and boundaries. Although statistics can sometimes be helpful, in the end it is a managerial judgement that is needed. We propose several criteria that are used for segmentation and for the definition of markets. We suggest when each is most appropriate. Each reflects a different way to look at the market; new product managers must examine each of them to see which is the most relevant for their businesses.

Demographics

Demographic segmentation can be a surrogate for market definition if characteristics such as sex, age, marital status, family size, age of children, income, occupation, geographical location, mobility, home ownership, education, and nationality are related to customer needs, information acquisition, or purchasing behavior. For example, suppose that families with young children are interested in safer cars, then such families might be a target for an automobile brand positioned as "safe." Soft-drink manufacturers, for example, believe that younger people like a sweeter taste. This was an underlying reason for the introduction of New Coke and Cherry Coke. When such demographic variables are good surrogates for customer preferences, they provide a straightforward and easy to implement source of customer segmentation.

Demographic segmentation can also identify future opportunities. In the next 30 years, the fastest-growing age segment will be the older than age 55 group, which is forecasted to increase more than 50% (from 20.9% of the population in 1990 to 30.9 percent in 2020). Because people are living longer, have healthier lives, and have higher levels of discretionary income, the older than age 55 segment will provide major opportunities to many firms.

In industrial markets, commonly used demographic variables are size of company (sales volume or number of employees), SIC code business designation, number of manufacturing plants, geographic location, and years of operation. It is common in industrial markets to designate large companies as national accounts and service them with special teams, while selling to smaller accounts through distributors or wholesalers. Priorities for personal selling are often defined by demographics. Government-owned hospitals, for example, had faster adoption rates of CT head and body scanners (Wind, Robertson, and Fraser 1982). Large hospitals have the highest ultimate penetration rate, but small hospitals reach ultimate penetration levels sooner. Therefore, though the first priority for a manufacturer of these scanners would be large government-owned hospitals, small hospitals that are qualified as potential adopters may also deserve immediate attention because of the possibility of quick sales results.

Attitudes

Attitudes provide another means to segment customers. For example, consumers who have different beliefs with respect to social issues (e.g., religion, politics, work, drugs, women's rights) or personal interests (e.g., family, home, job, food, self-achievement, health, clubs, friends, shopping) may have different purchasing behavior or preferences. Customers might even have different attitudes toward product attitudes (e.g., "the highest-quality product is usually the best long-run buy"). The stress on the work ethic in Miller beer advertising ("It's Miller time" after a tough day's work) is an example of successful use of a consumer attitude and its link to consumption.

As an example of attitude segmentation, consider Table 4.6, which describes three sets of attitudes toward using computers. In each case, the atti-

TABLE 4.6 Possible Attitude Segmentation of the Home Word
Processor Market

I hate computers!
- 1.0 years of college
- $25,000 in income
- Shop at a discount store
- Own manual typewriter
- Buy typewriters
- Dislike change
- Politically conservative
- Feel comfortable
- Want children to go to college
- Ease of use important

Computers have to do the job with no hassle!
- 2.5 years of college
- $40,000 in income
- Shop at department or discount stores
- Buy word processors or computers
- Own electric typewriter
- Adopt technology if proven
- Politically liberal
- Want to succeed
- Want children to go to college
- Easy to learn and easy to use important

I love to work with a PC!
- 4 years of college
- $45,000 in income
- Shop at computer stores
- Buy computers
- Own a PC
- Like change
- Independent voters
- Strive for success
- Want children to excel in college and graduate school
- Power and speed important

tudes are linked to demographic variables as well as preferences (ease of use, ease of learning, power, and speed). Importantly, it also appears that the likelihood of considering the purchase of a home word processor[1] varies among the segments. The computer rejecters are unlikely to consider it. The second segment, the functional adopters would consider it seriously if it were

---

[1] A home word processor is a stand-alone machine that includes a CRT screen and a printer and has built-in software for the word processing tasks. We return to this case in chapter 14.

proven to be useful, easy to learn and easy to use. Finally, the third segment, the computer literates, already own a PC (and likely word-processing software), but might consider a home word processor for a son or daughter at college or graduate school.

Preferences with Respect to Product Benefits

Customers vary in their preferences for product benefits. For example, some laundry consumers are concerned with the whitest whites and the cleanest colors—they will purchase a powerful laundry detergent. Others are concerned with the environment and will tradeoff power for an environmentally safe product. Still others will be concerned with detergents that are safe for fabrics, or that are easy to carry home and to store at home. For example, when Kao identified that a significant segment of the Japanese consumers went to the store often, carried detergents home by bicycle or by foot, and stored the detergents in small rooms, they developed a highly concentrated product, Attack, that proved to earn a dominant share in the market.

Benefit segmentation is also important in industrial products. For example, some shipping companies, say Waterford Crystal, are extremely concerned with breakage and are willing to pay dearly for packaging materials that minimize damage. Conversely, other companies ship products that are less subject to breakage and would be willing to use less expensive materials if they were sufficient to deliver the product intact.

Price Sensitivity

Customers who need a premium product and are willing to pay for it may represent a possible segment. Similarly there are markets for midrange and bargain products.

Decision Rules

Customers can be grouped based on similarities and differences in decision-making processes. For example, in industrial marketing, this could result in buyers of copiers and FAX machines being segmented into one group in which the administrative officer is dominant, and another in which users, administrative officers, and purchasing agents are all heavily involved.

Usage

Usage behavior can be an indicator of different customer needs. For example, heavy users may need special service and require products with

greater reliability and robustness than casual users. In many markets, the top
20% of customers in usage account for 80% of sales volume.

When a product has several possible uses, segmentation as a function of
use may be appropriate. It might, for example, make sense to market differently to customers for preengineered steel buildings used for schools, auto
dealerships, and barns.

Product Form

Consider the physical product structure for dog food products: (1)
canned—all meat, (2) canned—mixed meat and grain, (3) dry, and (4)
semimoist forms of product, and the attitudes of owners who (1) feel their
dog is a member of the family, (2) have a dog for work purposes (guarding
or hunting), and (3) have a dog but really do not want it (reluctant owners).
Table 4.7 shows the relationship of product from to psychological attitudes.
An X indicates the segment that uses the product form most often. In this
example, the all-meat and semimoist markets are primarily for those who love
their family dog. There may be an opportunity for a new product for this
segment positioned as "TV Dinners" for your dog.

Competitive Products

A final indicator of a market definition is a comparison of which products compete with one another. If we can find a set of existing products that
form a tightly defined competitive set then, by studying those products, the
benefits they offer customers, and the customers who use the products, we
might be able to identify opportunities for improvement. Consider shaving
cream. Some shaving creams come out from the can in the form of a foam,
whereas others come out from the can in the form of a gel. Some are scented,
whereas others are not. Some are bargain brands, and others are premium

TABLE 4.7 Dog Food Usage Example

Product Form	Family Dog	Work Dog	Reluctant Owners
Canned/all meat	X		
Canned/mix			X
Dry		X	
Semimoist	X		

brands. We might wonder if any of these three cuts of the shaving-cream market can be considered a submarket.

We define a submarket as by a set of products such that if a customer's preferred product is not available then the customer would rather switch to another product in the submarket than purchase a product not in the submarket. For example, by observing shaving-cream consumers we might find that foam consumers prefer to switch to another foam than switch to a gel with the same brand name and scent. If this were the case, we would call the foam (and the gel) markets submarkets. We could then zero in on products within the submarket and learn why they now succeed to design a product that will succeed in competition with those products.

Multiple Perspectives

In opportunity identification we seek to restrict the market to provide a practical target for development. If the market is defined too broadly, say "drinks," then the new-product development team has a difficult time in evaluating the market, selecting target customers, understanding competition, and uncovering what is necessary to succeed in the market. Conversely, if the market is defined too narrowly, say "uncarbonated cherry-flavored drinks sold in 6-ounce containers to children between ages 5 and 10," then the new-product development team is certain to find the market too small and will miss opportunities. The methods of demographics, attitudes, preferences for benefits, usage, product form, and competitive products each give a perspective on how the market might be defined. It is up to the new-product team to use these methods and make the final decision balancing breadth with focus.

Naturally, the six methods of market definition are related. For example, Table 4.6 (word-processor attitude segments) defines the word-processor market by attitude toward computers. But Table 4.6 also demonstrates that these attitude segments are related to demographic segments (income, years of college), competitive-product segments (purchasing of typewriters and PCs), benefit segments (tradeoffs among ease of use, ease of learning, speed, and power), and usage segments (word processing at home and at college). In many ways it depends on how you look at the market. In the end it is important that the new-product team select a market-definition method with which they are comfortable and use that method responsively to define the market for further analysis. As the new-product process proceeds from market definition to idea generation to design, the team must be prepared to modify the definition and consider other perspectives on the market.

METHODS FOR MARKET DEFINITION AND SEGMENTATION

There are many analytic techniques with which to define markets. We review two of the most common: cluster analysis and substitution among products. In cluster analysis the basic philosophy is to find a group of customers who, with respect to some set of characteristics, are similar within groups but different among groups. In product-substitution methods the basic philosophy is to find a set of products that are substitutes for one another. The specific algorithms and interpretations for these techniques vary, but the underlying philosophies are common.

Cluster Analysis

Clusters of customers are formed by matching those who have similar responses to the questions asked. For example, two consumers might be grouped together if they have similar ages, incomes, years of education, and attitudes. Usually, similarity between consumers is based on a formula such as a weighted sum of the squared differences between the answers the consumers give to the questions. In general, clustering methods choose clusters of consumers such that consumers within a cluster are similar and such that consumers in one cluster are dissimilar from consumers in other clusters. The output can take the form of a hierarchical tree or an assignment of consumers to distinct groups. Clustering is still an art, and there are a variety of methods with which to group consumers. For details on the potential formulas, methods to make scales, clustering techniques, and statistics to determine the appropriate number of clusters comparable, see Green, Tull, and Albaum (1988, p. 577–595).

We illustrate the use of cluster analysis with a system, called PRIZM,[2] which is used widely. PRIZM begins by clustering a reduced set of 1,000 possible demographic measures. The basic unit of analysis is Zip Code areas rather than individual consumers. Each Zip Code represents a row of the data matrix; demographic attributes define the columns. PRIZM develops cluster solutions and provides a profile of demographic attributes for each cluster. Table 4.8 shows an example: Cluster 28—"Blue Blood Estates."

As Table 4.8 indicates the families who live in the set of zip codes that are in cluster 28 are more likely to have professional or managerial careers: 51.2% in this cluster versus 22.7% in the U.S. population. PRIZM computesan index (51.2%/22.7% = 222% to indicate the relative concentration of that demographic variable in cluster 28. The cluster profile also reflects higher incomes, education, home ownership, likelihood of being middle age, and

---

[2] A trademark of Claritas Corporation.

TABLE 4.8 PRIZM Cluster No. 28—Blue Blood Estates

Key Demographic Indicators

	U.S.	% Composition Cluster	Index
Occupations			
Professional/managerial	22.7	51.2	226
All other white-collar	30.3	32.0	106
Blue-collar	31.2	9.1	29
Service	12.9	6.9	54
Farming/forestry/fishing	2.9	0.8	27
Household Income			
Less than $5,000	13.2	3.2	24
$5,000–$14,999	31.2	9.9	32
$15,000–$24,999	26.6	13.6	51
$25,000–$34,999	15.7	14.8	94
$35,000–$49,999	8.7	20.4	236
$50,000+	4.6	38.1	829
Educational Levels			
Some high school or less	33.5	7.9	24
4 years high school	34.6	20.0	58
1–3 yrs. college	15.7	21.4	137
4+ yrs. college	16.2	50.7	313
Housing Characteristics			
Owner-occupied	64.5	83.2	129
Renter-occupied	35.5	16.8	47
Single-unit	71.2	87.1	122
2–9 units	13.8	5.7	41
10+ units	10.1	6.8	67
Mobile units	5.0	0.4	8

	U.S.	% Composition Cluster	Index
Age Distribution			
Under 18 yrs.	28.1	27.5	98
18–34 yrs.	29.6	20.4	69
35–54 yrs.	21.4	30.9	144
55–64 yrs.	9.6	12.0	125
65+ yrs.	11.3	9.2	81
Race/Ethnic Origins			
Black	11.7	1.3	11
Oriental	0.9	2.5	272
Hispanic	6.4	2.4	38
Foreign born	6.2	10.2	163
Household Size			
One person	22.7	14.1	62
Two persons	31.3	32.4	103
Three or four persons	32.8	39.0	119
Five or more persons	13.2	14.5	110

Base Population Counts—1980 Census

	Count	% of U.S.
Households	494,852	0.6
Population	1,486,743	0.7
Adults	1,078,179	0.7
Adult males	515,617	0.7
Adult females	562,562	0.7
Median household income	$41,094	n/a
Median home value	$145,975	n/a

(Claritas Corporation, Alexandria, Virginia; reprinted with permission)

average household size. Although cluster 28 represents only .7% of the U.S. population, it would be critical if we were selling luxury goods.

Cluster analysis can also be applied to attitudinal data as was illustrated in Table 4.6. One of the best-known commercial applications of attitudinal clustering is called VALS.[3] VALS is based on attitudes toward issues such as the importance of work, the effectiveness of free enterprise, concentration of power, women's role, strength of religious belief, personality ("I like to be outrageous" or "I prefer a quiet evening at home to a party"), and satisfaction with life. An analysis of 800 such measures across 2,713 consumers produced nine clusters that were labeled: survivor, sustainer, belonger, emulator, achiever, I-Am-Me, experiential, socially conscious, and integrated.

According to VALS survivors and sustainers are need-driven. They are just hanging on in what they see as a hostile world. Belongers, emulators, and achievers are outerdirected. Achievers are action oriented, work within the system, and enjoy good living. Emulators want to make it big but have not yet. Belongers are conservative, middle-majority individuals. Experientials and socially conscious people are inner directed, with the experientials trying what life has to offer, and the socially conscious dominated by social responsibility. The integrated groups combine the best of inner- and outer-directed attitudes.

Table 4.9 illustrates a third example of cluster analysis by listing four groups of stomach remedy users (Wells, 1975). This table is based on a cluster analysis of 80 product-specific items. The clusters are then described based on symptom frequency, benefits provided by brands, attitudes toward treatment, beliefs about ailments, and personality. By defining a market based on the symptom profiles in Table 4.9, the new-product development can design a stomach remedy that meets the needs of that segment.

Substitution among Products

If we know which products compete with one another, then we can use that information to uncover opportunities and design a product that is superior to existing products (in that market) with respect to fulfilling customer needs. Alternatively, by understanding the limits of existing products we might be able to develop an entirely new product form and open a new "market."

Some marketing analysts have worked with direct consumer judgments of product substitutability in use. For example, in the manufacture of a small electric motor and drive system, aluminum, steel, and plastic gears may be possible substitutes. If they are substitutes, they are competing for the same market and could be defined as a market opportunity set. In autos, aluminum, steel, and plastic are competing in component part market for bumpers and

---

[3] A trademark of the Stanford Research Institute, Inc.

TABLE 4.9 Psychographic Segmentation of Stomach Remedy Market

The Severe Sufferers

The Severe Sufferers are the extreme group on the potency side of the market. They tend to be young, have children, and be well educated. They are irritable and anxious people, and believe that they suffer more severely than others. They take the ailment seriously, fuss about it, pamper themselves, and keep trying new and different products in search of greater potency. A most advanced product with new ingredients best satisfies their need for potency and fast relief, and ties in with their psychosomatic beliefs.

The Active Medicators

The Active Medicators are on the same side of the motivational spectrum. They are typically modern suburbanites with average income and education. They are emotionally well adjusted to the demands of their active lives. They have learned to cope by adopting the contemporary beliefs of seeking help for every ill, and use remedies to relieve even minor signs of ailments and every ache and pain. In a modern product they seek restoration of their condition and energy, mental recovery, and a lift for their active lives. They are influenced by a brand's reputation and by how well it is advertised. They tend to develop strong brand loyalties.

The Hypochondriacs

The Hypochondriacs are on the opposite side of the motivational spectrum. They tend to be older, not as well educated, and women. They have conservative attitudes toward medication and a deep concern over health. They see possible dangers in frequent use of remedies, are concerned over side effects, and afraid of remedies with new ingredients and extra potency. To cope with these concerns, they are strongly oriented toward medical authority, seeking guidance in treatment and what products they should use. They hold rigid beliefs about the ailment, and are disciplined in the products they use and how frequently they use them. They want a simple, single-purpose remedy that is safe and free from side effects and backed by doctors or a reputable company.

The Practicalists

The Practicalists are in the extreme position on this side of the motivational spectrum. They tend to be older, well educated, emotionally the most stable, and least concerned over their ailment or the dangers of remedies. They accept the ailment and its discomforts as part of life, without fuss and pampering. They use a remedy as a last resort, and just to relieve the particular symptom. They seek simple products whose efficacy is well proved, and are skeptical of complicated modern remedies with new ingredients and multiple functions.

(Wells 1975, p. 203; reprinted with permission from the *Journal of Marketing Research* published by the American Marketing Association.)

body and trim panels. If we were examining the recreation market for new-product opportunities, television would compete with movies as well as spectator sports such as football games if consumers judged them as substitutes for the use of recreation time. A car may be competitive with a vacation or children's tuition if the dollars are allocated out of the same budget so that only the priority items can be undertaken when income is constrained (see Hauser and Urban 1986).

Substitution in Use.   The degree of substitution in uses can be studied analytically (Belk, 1975). Stefflre (1972) has proposed that consumers should generate the possible uses for a set of products and then specify all possible products that could be appropriate for each use. The resulting matrix of uses by products may be analyzed statistically to group similar products and use combinations. In one study, Stefflre analyzed 52 proprietary medicines for 52 medical conditions to define "markets" by clusters of products used to treat similar conditions. Other researchers have extended the measurement and statistical methods of this approach of defining markets by substitution in use (Day, Shocker, and Srivastava 1979; Srivastava, Leone, and Shocker 1981; Shocker, Stewart, and Zahorik 1990; and Bucklin and Srinivasan 1991).

Processing Sequence.   Another method of defining substitution is to observe the sequence of issues considered and decisions made by consumers (Bettman 1971, Tversky and Sattath 1979, Hauser 1986a). For example, Figure 4.5 depicts a hypothetical hierarchy to describe the market for light industrial structures. This hierarchy breaks the market by material, roof structure, and span. If this were the true representation of the market, consumers would first decide among material, then structure, then span. Products would be more substitutable if they were in the same branch of the hierarchical tree.

To test this hierarchy, we determine if buyers first chose between wood, concrete or steel and then selected within a material type. If, in these interviews, we find that since some buyers use an architect, we would have to understand the architect's decision sequence in designing the building. This

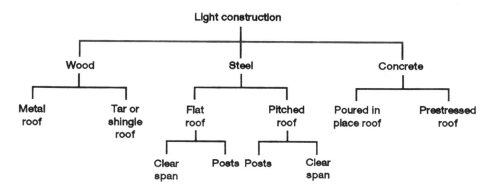

Figure 4.5   Hypothetical Hierarchical Description of Light Industry Construction

kind of research yields an in-depth understanding of the consumer choice problem. The resulting hierarchical decision network is important information. Unfortunately the decision sequence approach is very difficult to execute in the field with current techniques of measurement and analysis. Individuals can be assessed, but aggregation of total markets is difficult.

Product Switching.   Another method is to observe or measure directly which products substitute for one another. For example, one can ask customers (1) what brands they would consider and then (2) what their first-choice product would be. In response to questioning or by means of a simulated buying opportunity, respondents indicate the likelihood of purchasing each of the considered products on any purchase occasion or which products they would buy if their first choice were not available.

We then define candidate sets of competing products—these candidate sets can be defined based on form (ground vs. instant coffee), usage occasion (brands used in the morning versus brands used at dinner), or any other grouping that seems to make sense. We then test to see whether the candidate segmentation of products makes sense. The criterion for evaluating set of products is that if a consumer's chosen product is removed from consideration then that consumer is more likely to choose another product in the segment than would be predicted by market share alone. (Market share is the null model of no segmentation. If consumers choose in proportion to market share, then it does not matter what product had been chosen previously.)

If, for example, we were testing a segmentation of caffeinated versus decaffeinated coffee, we would assign customers to the segment that contains their most preferred brand, and then calculate the probability that they would choose another product in that segment if they were forced to switch. If the probability of staying in the segment were higher than the market share of the segment, the hypothesized segmentation scheme would be supported. If it was low or if an alternate segmentation scheme was significantly better (e.g., ground versus instant coffee), the original segmentation scheme would be rejected.[4]

Figure 4.6 shows a hierarchy for coffee that first divides coffee into ground and instant. Instant coffee is divided into caffeinated and decaffeinated brands and then each of these into freeze dried and regular varieties. For each of the five branches a perceptual map is used to describe the relative positions of brands on the dimensions of "taste" (fresh, full-bodied, rich) and "mildness" (not bitter, does not upset stomach). Spaces in these maps

---

[4] For statistical tests and descriptions of alternative measures of switching including first choice, rank order preference, consideration-set membership, and logit switching probabilities, see Urban, Johnson, and Hauser 1984.)

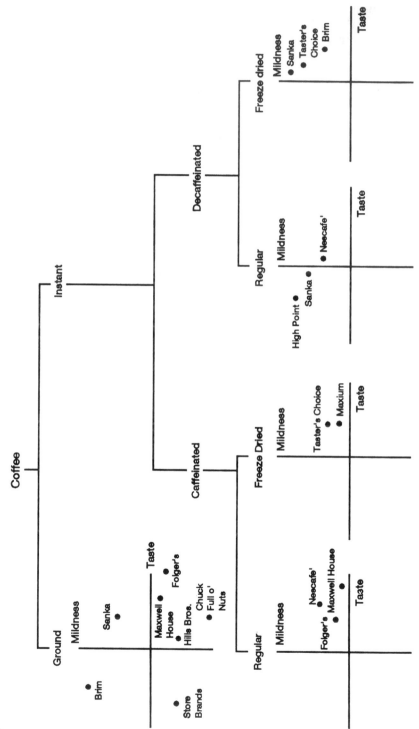

Figure 4.6 Hierarchical Definition of the Coffee Market with Perceptual Maps in Each Submarket (Urban Johnson and Brudnick 1981)

where no brands exist are possible entry opportunities (see chapters 9 to 11 for a detailed consideration of perceptual mapping).

Product Consideration.   An important factor in competitive-product segmentation is how customers process information when they perceive a hierarchical segmentation in the market. If they consider only brands that are in a specific branch of the hierarchy, then either the opportunity is restricted to only the acceptable brands. The new-product team must design the product and communication actions to encourage consumers to categorize the product into an attractive branch in the hierarchy.

For example, suppose you were an auto company designing a two-seat sports car and you found the categorization results shown in Figure 4.7. In Figure 4.7 there are five overall groups with two subdivided further. Consideration sets tend to be restricted to one of the groups (or subcategories). The

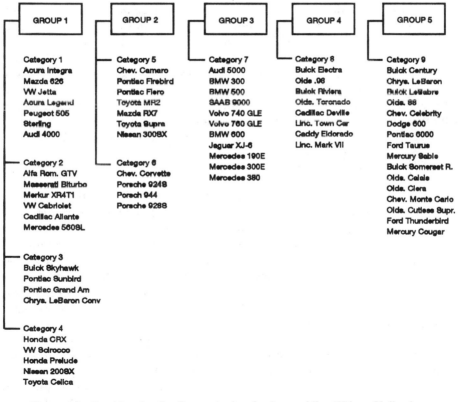

Figure 4.7 Consideration-Set Categorization for Automobiles (Urban, Hulland, and Weinberg 1993)

new-product design question becomes: Where should you target your car, and how can you be sure that it will be categorized in that branch by consumers? If we can determine the characteristics (e.g., country of origin, luxury, power, price, psychological image, etc.) that lead consumers to classify a car in a branch by market research study or judgment, then we can design our car for favorable consideration.

The branch size determines the size of the market opportunity. The early design concepts can be tested to assure that the car is categorized as competitive with the target vehicle segment.

MARKET SELECTION

The outcome of the market definition activity is the identification of a primary basis of segmentation, an understanding of which customers are in the target segment, a description of those customers, their basic needs, and their buying habits, and a knowledge of the products which now compete in that segment.

The market definition provides the structure in which the market profile analysis is conducted. This market profile analysis is used to screen the potential market opportunities from a large number (say 20 to 30 across various markets or segments) down to a relatively few (say 3 to 4). Analysis of the remaining candidate markets is done more analytically for these markets to identify the market boundaries and target consumers. This information then is used to set priorities explicitly and to select the one or two best markets. These "best" markets then pass to the idea generation phase.

Managerial Strategies

An important strategic concept is that when market priorities are set, the new product is part of the firm's complete product portfolio. The status of the set of current products must be understood before resources are allocated to a new product in a given market. It is important to recognize at this point that an addition to the firm's portfolio can be either a single product or a new-product line. For example, a new product for Campbell's Soups was the line of "Soup for One." The initial introduction included more than one flavor (Golden Chicken and Noodles, Old World Vegetable, etc.) and was later extended with additional flavors.

One approach to assessing the product portfolio is to array the firm's offerings in terms of market attractiveness and the strength of the competitive advantage the firm has in the market (see Day, 1986, pp. 193–216, for detailed procedure). Market attractiveness reflects many of the factors we identified in profile analysis (growth rate, early entry, economies of scale, profitability, and risk). Competitive advantage reflects the sustainable benefits we can deliver uniquely to our customers (e.g., technology, distribution, raw material, service, market share, and customer loyalty based advantages). It is based on the core competencies of our firm. The concept of the portfolio evaluation is to array our current business on a grid of market attractiveness and competitive advantage as shown in Figure 4.8. We would like to be in markets that are attractive and where we have a sustainable competitive advantage. If we are not, we can expend resources to gain competitive advantage and move to the upper left of the grid. Or we can enter new markets that are attractive and where we have a competitive advantage.

Setting Priorities

Priorities should reflect the concepts of market attractiveness and potential competitive advantage. Our initial profile analysis allows us to screen

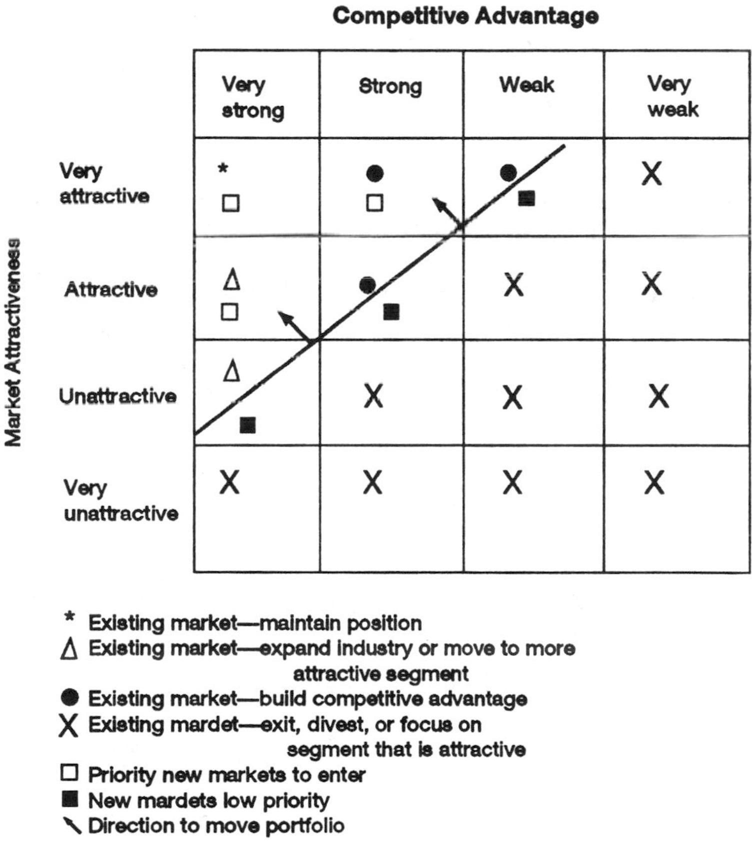

Competitive Advantage

	Very strong	Strong	Weak	Very weak
Very attractive	* □	● □	● ■	X
Attractive	Δ □	● ■	X	X
Unattractive	Δ ■	X	X	X
Very unattractive	X	X	X	X

Market Attractiveness (vertical axis label)

* Existing market—maintain position
Δ Existing market—expand industry or move to more
       attractive segment
● Existing market—build competitive advantage
X Existing mardet—exit, divest, or focus on
       segment that is attractive
□ Priority new markets to enter
■ New mardets low priority
\ Direction to move portfolio

Figure 4.8   Market Entry Opportunities and the Existing Portfolio

markets that obviously are not attractive, that do not match our current skills, or for which we do not have the technological feasibility for creating a competitive advantage. Next, we use more-detailed analyses to update estimates for the surviving markets. That is, we update our estimate of growth potential, early entry, scale, competitive attractiveness, investment requirements, reward, and risk, which were described earlier in this chapter (see Table 4.4).

Each target segment in the market is quantified by its size, growth rate, and competitive vulnerability. This potential is compared with the investment required for entry and the profit margins in each part of the market. For example, in the coffee market defined earlier (see Figure 4.6), ground and regular instant coffee types were the largest markets. They were judged to be vulnerable because the perceptual maps showed gaps that could be exploited by a mild (not bitter) and good tasting (fresh, full bodied, rich) coffee. The estimated share potential could produce a 15% return on the investment of $10 to $20 million required to develop and market a new brand. Only these parts of the coffee market are judged to have opportunities for new-product development given the current market structure. Opportunities would be different for each company in the market and depend on the competitive advantages underlying their product portfolio.

To illustrate this, look at some of the firms in the coffee market and analyze their coverage and duplication in terms of the hierarchical market definition. Table 4.10 shows the offerings of General Foods, Nestlé, Procter and Gamble, and Hills Brothers in the 1980s. General Foods has good coverage, but there appears to be a potential duplication between Brim and Sanka. General Foods may be wise to consider further research to see if Brim and Sanka compete. If this is true, dropping Brim and investing those resources in Sanka or other new products would be appropriate. The opportu-

TABLE 4.10 Coverage and Duplication of Products of Selected Manufacturers

Manufacturer	Ground	Caffeinated Instant		Decaffenated Instant	
		Regular	Freeze Dried	Regular	Freeze Dried
General Foods	Maxwell House Brim Sanka Yuban	Maxwell House Yuban	Maxim	Sanka	Brim Sanka
Nestlé		Nescafé	Taster's Choice	Nescafé	Taster's Choice
Procter & Gamble	Folger's	Folger's			
Hills Bros.	Hills Bros.	Hills Bros.			

nities for General Foods to introduce a new brand may not be attractive because a new ground or instant regular caffeinated coffee would cannibalize their existing brands. The new-product effort at General Foods might be better directed toward creating a new market branch with a major product innovation, rather than adding brands to the existing product segments. Nestlé appears to have an opportunity to add a ground coffee and, indeed, after this study Nestlé acquired Hills Brothers. In 1991 Nestlé had over 13% of the U.S. ground coffee market. Procter and Gamble is tapping two major opportunities. It should not add other instant types unless they have an innovative feature that assures a high probability of becoming the dominant brand in those markets.

Other companies that have the necessary $20 million for investment and required marketing, production, and distribution skills could consider the opportunity for a new ground coffee. This evaluation would be weighed against the other market opportunities that pass the firm's initial market profile analysis. For example, the potential of a ground or instant caffeinated coffee might be evaluated relative to frozen dinners and chocolate snacks. The return on investment (ROI), and the factors of the market profile analysis would be used to prioritize those market opportunities and select the most attractive market for new-product development effort.

The coffee example represents a frequently purchased consumer product, but similar methods are applied to consumer durables, industrial products, and services. An example of hierarchical definition of an industrial market was shown in Figure 4.5 for building construction. Consumer durables or services are described similarly. The measure used to define these hierarchical trees is buyers' preferences for alternatives. Such measures are obtained at a reasonable cost by market research surveys.

Although almost any market could be entered by a major innovation, firms should prioritize their effort and aim at those markets with the most attractive risk-return profiles. It is easier and less risky to develop a product to fill a need in an established market than to create a new market, but the rewards may be less. A firm would be unwise only to consider clearly established opportunities. Some of the biggest new-product successes have been in areas where no previous product existed. For example, Xerox created the plain paper product segment in copiers. Computervision pioneered in CAD/CAM systems, Digital Equipment created the minicomputer product, Sun Micro Systems invented the desktop workstation segment in data processing, and American Express created travelers checks. In the history of the coffee market segmentation, Maxim created the freeze dried branch in the hierarchical tree we used to describe the market. It may be possible to again revolutionize the coffee category by creating a branch for full brewed coffee sold in plastic cups for microwave heating.

We recommend that if a clear opportunity exists and matches your capabilities, you seriously consider exploiting it. However, also devote resources to markets that are subject to a revolutionary approach based on creating new-product segments or markets. If the potential return is judged to be high enough to compensate for the high risk, consider these markets for entry. Even if you take the revolutionary approach, it is important to understand the market you will innovate. Do a market definition study to get a base line for the development effort. If your approach is not revolutionary, be sure to understand the existing market before you enter it or you may find after several failures that it is not a market you should be attempting to enter in the first place.

Profits estimated by projections of sales volume, penetration, and unit margin must be compared with the investment. Chapter 3 presented the expected costs of developing a successful consumer or industrial product. The ratio of the projected, discounted profit to the investment or the calculated rate of return on investment can be used to specify the most attractive market opportunities. Priority for new-product development should be given to products with large sales potential and good risk/return profiles. A portfolio of high-risk/high-return and low-risk/low-return product/markets should be designated. Figure 4.9 shows a hypothetical tradeoff of risk and return, and selection of a portfolio of market entry opportunities. The tradeoff line could be drawn judgmentally or specified analytically.

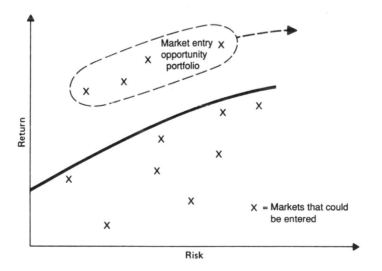

Figure 4.9 Hypothetical Risk-Return Tradeoff

SUMMARY

It is crucial to new-product success that a product category is selected that rewards the innovating organization. Market definition is that process which examines a breadth of markets to determine those that are most attractive. This process, summarized in Figure 4.10, directs resources at the markets of greatest potential while minimizing resources invested in high-risk and low-yield markets.

The first step is market profile analysis in which all markets are evaluated on the criteria of growth potential, early entry, economies of scale, competitive attractiveness, investment, reward, and risk, and match to the organization's capabilities. Criteria weights are established and an overall evaluation is made. The result of this screening process is to eliminate poor markets and concentrate on a few highly attractive markets.

Next, these few markets are analyzed to define the boundaries of the market and to identify the target consumers in depth. These analyses are synthesized to define more exactly the target markets and the vulnerability to entry.

Finally, this information is used along with an assessment of growth rates, profitability, return on investment, and risk to set priorities for further investigation. This market selection analysis yields a portfolio of market opportunities that are highly attractive for the organization's new-product development effort.

REVIEW QUESTIONS

4.1. Can a product compete in more than one market? How should entry strategies be altered if this situation can occur?

4.2. Why should managers start new-product development projects by studying consumers rather than engineering designs?

4.3. Why might businesses with large market shares be able to exert more control over their markets than businesses with smaller market shares? Is it possible a large market share might be an effect rather than a cause?

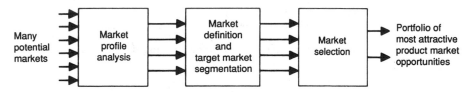

Figure 4.10 Summary of Market Definition

4.4. Suppose a very strong "experience curve" effect is observed in a particular market. Under what conditions would this effect encourage market entry? Hinder market entry?

4.5. How might a company measure the potential reward from entering a particular market?

4.6. What criteria might a small law firm use when deciding which legal services to offer?

4.7. Determining the importance weights of different market selection criteria is a critical activity. In what way might the selection of these weights help promote communication among managers responsible for new-product development?

4.8. When rating new markets how might managers be given the incentive to provide unbiased ratings?

4.9. For a company adopting a proactive new-product strategy the traditional methods for market definition might not be the best approach. Why?

4.10. Compare the different methods of defining a market. Discuss the advantages and disadvantages of each.

4.11. Why is market definition important? How could proper market definition affect the actions of a multiproduct company?

4.12. Perk-a-cup Coffee Company is thinking of launching a new brand of coffee which tastes like orange juice. Mr. Kava, the company's chief marketing executive, believes a great potential exists for this new product based on the size of the beverage market. How could proper use of market segmentation help focus on this brand's ultimate market?

4.13. What are the criteria for market segmentation listed in the text? What are the advantages and disadvantages of employing each criterion?

4.14. Consider the classification of products by market attractiveness and competitive advantage as discussed in the chapter. Why might a company have products in unattractive markets with weak competitive advantages? What should be done about this situation?

4.15. Policy Insurance Company is considering the development of several new financial policies. Their chief statistician, Alan Gorithm, estimated the parameters of Bass's diffusion model for two potential markets. The results follow:

$$\text{Market 1: } S(t) = 2.2484 + .476Y(t-1) - .0048728\ Y^2(t-1)$$
$$\text{Market 2: } S(t) = 2.0500 + .011Y(t-1) - .0001024\ Y^2(t-1)$$

where $S(t)$ = sales (1,000s) in period t
$Y(t-1)$ = total people who have ever bought by end of period $t-1$

What insight do these parameters provide concerning the desirability of entering each of the markets?

5

Idea Generation

In the last chapter we learned how to define and prioritize market opportunities. Now we must find creative ideas that generate value for customers in these markets so we can tap the potential of the identified opportunities. New products are, by their very nature, innovations and these innovations result from creative insight and free thinking. Such creativity is crucial to success. This chapter explicitly deals with techniques for the enhancement and management of creativity in opportunity identification. The creative ideas that are generated are not the final product, that will be determined iteratively throughout the development process, but these ideas do form a basis for further investigation and a set of starting points for design innovation.

Although it may be possible to find creative insights in a vacuum, it is more productive to couple creativity with information from various sources such as R&D, engineering, production, and marketing. We begin with a discussion of how to tap various idea sources and then describe several methods for idea generation. The emphasis is on the creation of major innovations, and new-product concepts that may expand existing markets or develop new markets. The final section discusses idea management by setting guidelines to screen initial ideas and discusses the appropriate number of ideas to advance to the design phase of the development process. Figure 5.1 describes the flow of idea source identification through idea generation and screening. The output of idea generation is a set of exciting product ideas that are targeted toward strategic market opportunities. These may be concepts, completed initial designs of a product, or a prototype product. The form of the idea depends upon the source. Technology may yield concepts while alliances or acquisitions may yield prototype products or even a new operating business. In the design phase of development we evaluate the market potential of the ideas, refine the product concepts and prototypes, and convert them into the reality of quality products that customers find superior to competitive alternatives. In this chapter we complete the opportunity identification phase by idea generation; in the following chapter we consider design efforts based on the output of market definition and idea generation effort.

IDEA SOURCES

New-product activities start from several alternative initiating forces such as new market needs, technological change, new materials or supply availabilities, inventions and patents, and competitors' actions. These forces may also act as sources of ideas, but to be effective the organization should look at all potential idea sources, not just the initiation source. For example, a competitor may introduce a new product and thus force your organization to innovate. Although there is pressure to respond with a "me too" or second-but-better alternative, more effective ideas might come from a complete examination of market needs and recent technological developments. In a proactive new- product development strategy, idea sources should be carefully

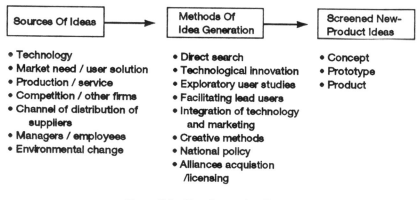

Figure 5.1   Idea Generation Process

studied and products developed before competitors enter. To tap these idea sources we first understand their underlying structure and then use methods of idea generation to find the potential.

Technology

New technologies present new opportunities to meet consumer needs and fill needs that were previously latent. For example, computer technology has opened up the information age. Progress in integrated circuits and software have allowed the computer to be an all pervasive in our society. Costs have dropped amazingly in the last 25 years—if the cost of a Rolls Royce had dropped at the same rate per unit of performance as computers, it would cost only pennies to buy today. Cost reductions and performance increases have spawned new products and opened up new markets at a staggering rate— main frames, minicomputers, PCs, workstations, and supercomputers. CAD/ CAM systems are used routinely by engineers; we are approaching the time when every engineer will have a computer on their desks. Computer technology has been backed by advances in telecommunication that have created information systems that have changed fundamentally the way businesses operate. The banking system has been globalized by this technology; the survivors in the 1990s in this industry will be heavily dependent on computer and telecommunication technology. American Airlines created a competitive advantage with its Sabre system, and American Express used its computer systems to differentiate itself by generating premium services and creating new services.

Biotechnology is creating new markets as expensive existing drugs are synthesized. Genetic engineering and advances in chemistry and biology are creating new drugs for treatment of hypertension, cancer, and AIDS. These technologies have driven the pharmaceutical industry to record levels of growth and profitability.

Materials science has generated new technologies that have resulted in major new products such as composite airplanes, carbon fiber sail boats, plastic auto bodies, and super conductors. These materials allow firms to meet their customers needs better than old products.

Although internal R&D and engineering are valuable sources of technological ideas, external sources should not be overlooked. Contacting inventors and searching for patents may present new ideas for consideration. External consulting companies may have a portfolio of ideas that can be reviewed. The sources of new technology should be viewed globally because it is likely that Japan and the Far East, North America, and Europe will all be committing major resources to technical innovation.

Market Needs and User Solutions

The recognition of technology as a major idea source is crucial to success, but customer needs and user solutions are equally important as a source of ideas. One of the bases for a proactive strategy is a customer-oriented philosophy of seeking to understand customer needs and desires. Chapter 2 demonstrated that 60% to 80% of the successful technologically-based products have their idea source in the recognition of market needs and demands. The financial return from market-based products tends to be higher. Because new products achieve final success through sales and profit, the consideration of market needs seems to be the most obvious source of ideas. However, many organizations do not allocate their idea generation resources to this area in proportion to its potential returns.

The power of the market in generating product opportunities has been identified in several industrial product classes. Table 5.1 shows the proportion of user developed major improvements in the market for scientific instruments. In this study 81% of the improvements were developed by users (von Hippel 1988).

Table 5.2 summarizes the role of the consumer of industrial products in generating successful ideas in several other industries and Figure 5.2 shows this information graphically. These studies illustrate the major role of consumers in product innovation. Not only do consumers represent a source of potential needs, but they often provide solutions to these needs. In some cases a user may have solved a problem that your organization is only beginning to address with a major R&D project. Users do not always innovate, but if they have a problem and it is economic for them to solve it through innovation they will do so. Even if they do not solve the problem they are a valuable source of input with respect to their needs.

TABLE 5.1 Source of Innovation for Scientific Instruments

Major Improvement Innovations	% User Developed	Innovations Developed by			
		User	Manufacturer	NA	Total
Gas chromatograph	82%	9	2	0	11
Nuclear magnetic resonance spectrometer	79	11	3	0	14
Ultraviolet spectrophotometer	100	5	0	0	5
Transmission electron microscope	79	11	3	0	14
Total	81%	36	8	0	44

Adapted from Von Hippel (1988, p. 15)

TABLE 5.2 Frequency with which Manufacturers Initiated Work on an Industrial Innovation in Response to a Customer Request

Study	Nature of Innovations and Sample Selection Criteria	No.	Data Available Regarding Presence of Customer Requests
A. Studies of Industrial Products			
Meadows	All projects initiated during a two-year period in "Chem Lab B"—Lab of a chemical company with $100–300 million in annual sales in "industrial intermediates."	29	9 of 17 (53%) commercially successful product ideas were from customers.
Peplow	All "creative" projects carried out during a six-year period by an R&D group concerned with plant process, equipment and technique innovations.	94	30 of 48 (62%) successfully implemented projects were initiated in response to direct customer request.
von Hippel	Semiconductor and electronic subassembly manufacturing equipment: first of type used in commercial production (n=7); major improvements (n=22); minor improvements (n=20).	49	Source of initiative for manufacture of equipment developed by users (n=29) examined. Source clearly identified as customer request in 21% of cases. In 46% of cases frequent customer-manufacturer interaction made source of initiative unclear.
Berger	All engineering polymers developed in U.S. after 1955 with >10 million pounds produced in 1975.	5	No project-initiating request from customers found.
Boyden	Chemical additives for plastics: all plasticizers and UV stabilizers developed post-W.W. II for use with four major polymers.	16	No project-initiating request from customers found.
Utterback	All scientific instrument innovations manufactured by Mass. firms which won "IR-100 Awards," 1963–1968 (n=15); sample of other instruments produced by same firms (n=17).	32	75% initiated in response to "need input." When need input originated outside product manufacturer (57%), source was "most often" customer.
Robinson et al.	Sample of standard and non-standard industrial products purchased by three firms.	NA	Customers recognize need, define functional requirements and specific goods and services needed *before contacting suppliers.*
B. Studies of Research-Engineering Interaction			
Isenson (*Project Hindsight*)	R&D accomplishments judged key to successful development of 20 weapons systems	710	85% initiated in response to description of problem by application-engineering group.
Materials Advisory Board	Materials innovations "believed to be the result of research-engineering interaction."	10	In "almost all" cases the individual with a well-defined need initiated the communications with the basic researchers.

From von Hippel (1978, p. 38); reprinted with permission.

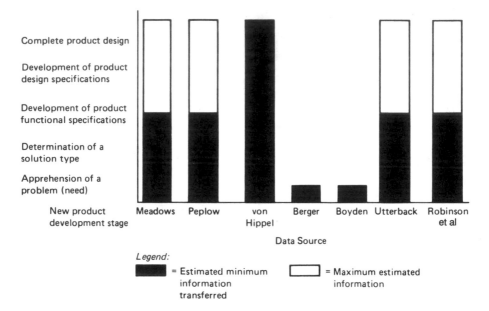

Complete product design

Development of product
design specifications

Development of product
functional specifications

Determination of a
solution type

Apprehension of a
problem (need)

New product   Meadows Peplow   von   Berger   Boyden Utterback Robinson
development stage   Hippel   et al

Data Source

Legend:

■ = Estimated minimum   □ = Maximum estimated
     information   information
     transferred

Figure 5.2 New-Product Development Data Supplied by Customers to Manufacturers (adapted from von Hippel 1978, p. 43)

There is a growing body of literature to suggest that users are active in the innovation process, not just recipients of new products. In customer products, customer needs and user solutions also are likely to be an important source of ideas. Although it is less likely that a consumer will come to a manufacturer with a complete idea, they may have developed solutions that are a valuable basis for a new product. For example women's use of eggs along with their shampoos, to give more body to the hair, was the solution adopted in the protein shampoo market. USAA (a leading insurance company) first implemented an image processing system. IBM initially rejected USAA's idea, and only after it was proved did they partner with USAA to develop future innovations in image processing and attempt to build a business in this area.

Some firms have not been enthusiastic about the receipt of user ideas because these suggestions present legal liabilities for the organization (Crawford 1975). For example, if an unsolicited idea is not handled properly, a subsequent product developed independently in the organization may be claimed by the suggestor. Some firms find so many legal difficulties that they reject all consumer new product suggestions. Crawford found in a survey of 166 companies that 12.6% rejected all outside consumer suggestions, 67.5 used legally dangerous procedures of evaluation, and 19.9% of companies considered the ideas by legally sound procedures.

For example, for a period of time a major consumer products firm had a policy to reject ideas unless they were patented. This means rejecting almost all unsolicited customer input on new products. Their policy on unsolicited ideas included:

> Suggestions relating to advertising, to new uses, and to new products. Although the firm recognized that the policy would eliminate large numbers of excellent ideas, they believed that the legal risks were much more substantial than the benefits they would receive.

> We have seen other firms that place such a premium on avoiding explicit customer input that they avoid testing new concepts with consumers. In some cases, simple ideas that "turn the corner" are overlooked because such customer input is not sought.

Rejecting all customer ideas may lead to overlooking many good ideas and profit opportunities. A legal mentality can stifle creativity and lead to rejecting a significant source of ideas. Although legal problems are present in accepting ideas, they may be addressed effectively by the use of a legal waiver and careful process to handle the receipt of and a response to suggestions. We suggest consideration of accepting customer ideas after the organization has set up a sound procedure based on minimizing the legal risks and maximizing the potential benefits of tapping user innovation as a source of high-potential ideas.

Production and Service

Production is often neglected as a source of innovation. For example, in the studies by Myers and Marquis (1969), 20% of the successful new technological products had their idea source in production.

In project hindsight, Isenson (1969) studied 20 military weapons systems and found that in 85% of the major technological developments, application engineering groups originally described the problem. The problem solving skills of production engineers applied to the needs of the market produces an important source of new ideas. User innovation is often found in process engineering at the customers' site. Products like pultrusion machines (fiber-reinforced plastic pulled through a die) and machines to insert integrated circuits on a printed circuit board are examples where production engineers pushed the products to new limits of performance (von Hippel, 1988). This source of ideas is likely to increase as more attention worldwide is being placed on process versus product engineering.

Service and guarantee experience also can be the source of new products. The records of service identify product needs and gaps in quality. Customer calls in phone services or hot lines indicate not only short run problems, but reflect longer run unmet needs. Repairs made to meet guarantees may reflect new uses where the product is subject to limitations. Instead of voiding warranties when a user modifies a machine to run beyond its recommended performance parameters (e.g., speed or tolerances) the manufacturer may find new ideas for product modification.

Competitors and Other Firms

The reason for competitors' success and knowledge about their developmental strategies are important inputs to idea generation. Even if a firm is a proactive leader in an industry, it must be ready to defend against competitors by preempting such innovation or improving on competitive firms' new products.

Noncompetitive firms in other industries may also be the source of new product ideas. Often innovation flows from one industry to another. For example, software for composition of newspapers was carried over to desktop publishing. Fastener systems in aircraft reflect new opportunities for steel fabrication of buildings. Plastic tent poles suggest ideas for plastic window frames.

Often looking internationally can bring a fresh viewpoint to an industry. The Body Shop uses natural shampoo and cosmetic products based on native formulations from many developing parts of the world. Acetaminophen was popular in England as a pain reliever long before Tylenol (an acetaminophen-based product) became a commercial success in the United States. In Canada "aspirin" is a brand name, whereas in the United States it is a generic ingredient. French grapes became the foundation of the California wine industry; Dry beer and Ultra laundry detergent were invented in Japan.

Channels of Distribution and Suppliers

We tend to think of manufacturers as the major source of innovation, but many times the locus of innovation is elsewhere. DuPont invented Teflon cook ware, which benefited cookware manufacturers as well as DuPont. Suppliers of chemicals and materials are often a source of new ideas for manufacturers. ALCOA wanted to pioneer the idea of aluminum truck trailers for heavy-duty hauling of fill, but manufacturers were reluctant. ALCOA had to build its own demonstration trailers and have truckers use them before truck manufacturers would buy the material. In a study of the market for electric wire termination machines it was found that 83% of the innovations for machines that cut wires and attach terminals to the end were not developed by the machinery manufacturing specialists companies, but rather by the major connector suppliers (von Hippel, 1988, p. 38).

Channel of distribution members are also a source of ideas. Discussions with the butchers in grocery stores led Mrs. Budd's Foods to develop a fresh meat pie that would increase the margins for the fresh meat section of the store. The concept was new, and entry was much easier than trying to market a frozen meat pie where the freezer space was already overdemanded. Channel members introduce their own brands to fill their needs or a perceived need in the final customer market. Understanding the needs and decision rules of the channel of distribution can stimulate new product ideas. Channel members are becoming more powerful in many industries and they are a critical link in selling and servicing products. Video Cart[1] (a video advertising screen attached to a shopping cart in a store that broadcasts advertisements as the cart is pushed down the aisle) reflects manufacturers needs for advertisements at point of purchase and retailers desire to control more of the media resources.

Management and Employees

The creative potential of an organization is high. Managers and employees who are not directly involved in the new products effort may have valuable ideas and insights. This internal source of innovation augments the creative efforts of the development team. Ideas may come from all functions in the organization. A creative, open, and learning organizational culture is a fertile source of ideas.

Environmental Changes

Demographic, economic, and political changes suggest many ideas for services. The trend of both parents working outside the home has led ConAgra to introduce new "Kids Cuisine" microwavable meals that children can prepare when their parents are not home. Kraft introduced "fat-free" ice cream and McDonald's a "91% Fat Free" hamburger in response to a growing health consciousness.

Industrial companies face many new opportunities as regulations for clean air and clean water are enforced. If any product that is now solvent-based (e.g., paints, coating on the inside of cans, adhesives) can be formulated around a water base, a market opportunity can be created. Minimum mileage standards for cars lead to new engine and material opportunities that reduce the weight of a car.

---

[1] Video Cart is a registered trademark of Information Resources, Inc.

Political change such as the reunification of Germany and the opening of the eastern block countries suggests many new markets and idea fields. Deregulation of ethical pharmaceuticals has opened up opportunities for new OTC drugs such as Advil and Nuprin based on the previously prescription-ingredient ibuprofen.

These are only some of the ideas that have resulted from the changes in social, economic, and political phenomena. Identifying these trends can be rewarding.

METHODS OF GENERATING IDEAS

The previous section listed some of the potential idea sources. To achieve success, an organization must be prepared to use fully these idea sources. Methods to generate ideas can be as simple as setting up information channels that are sensitive to idea sources or as sophisticated as using creative group methods and market research (see Figure 5.1).

Some creative ideas come directly from the environment; all an organization must do is to be sensitive to the ideas sources and conduct a direct search of opportunities. Other ideas require technology forecasting or exploratory consumer studies. Still others come by combining needs and technology through lead user analysis. Many ideas can come from individual effort or from creative group methods that use group dynamics to encourage imagination. National initiatives to support industries such as MITI in Japan may be a source of new products; alliances or acquisitions can bring more developed ideas to the firm quickly. Although an organization could rely on only one method, the best approach is to use several idea generation methods, covering all the sources of potential ideas.

The goal of idea generation is to create a large number of very different ideas. The more ideas generated in this step, the more likely one or two of those will pass the screening tests in the idea management phase. More ideas will progress toward the design phase of the development process and, ultimately, be a big success in the market.

Direct Search

To tap effectively external idea sources, it is useful to allocate people to basic information collection. In many organizations (e.g., IBM, Lanier, Johnson & Johnson) top management is expected to spend one day per week in direct customer contact to learn about needs and opportunities to serve customers better. A small staff to study trends in markets based on census data and industry reports and secondary data found in libraries can be a good supplement to face-to-face executive contact. Competitive activity can be monitored by a feedback system which reports a competitor's sales practices, distribution, and new products. For example, some consumer products firms "read" a competitor's new product test markets. In some industrial companies, special employees travel to all the relevant trade shows to learn as much as possible about the competitors' new products. In others, the sales force reports on competitive new products and the needs of members of the channel of distribution.

Search efforts can investigate acquisitions and thereby obtain product experience and development skills. For example, organizations hire lawyers or assign a company person to search for acquisitions or patents that may be of interest to the firm in penetrating a target market. Even such simple actions as a systematic analysis of complaints and warranty cards may identify problems that reflect a new product opportunity. These are but a few of the activities that should be conducted in a particular organization's target market.

Technological Innovation

Exploiting technology for new ideas requires a well-managed and creative R&D group. The group must share and get relevant information, make correct technological forecasts, target its effort towards strategic markets, and function effectively as a creative team with other functions in the organization.

Technical Information Flow.   If technological ideas are to be generated, the most recent and relevant technical information must be in the hands of the project group charged with developing a new product within the specified market. This means that information channels within the R&D laboratory and between technical areas of capability within the company must be functioning. Also, technical material from outside the firm must find its way to the developers.

External sources of technology are important. Mansfield et al. (1971, p.178) found that for pharmaceuticals 54% of the major innovations between 1935 and 1962 were based on discoveries made outside the firm. Similarly, in the development of numerically controlled machine tools manufacturing firms have been heavily dependent on technology that was not present in their own firms.

Although the external sources are important, information within the firm should not be neglected. Marquis (1969) found that in 41% of the innovations he studied, the key innovative information resulted from the person's own training and experience. This implies there is a considerable pool of talent for generating ideas if channels of communication are developed.

A key phenomenon in R&D communication has been identified by Allen (1977). He found that only a few individuals were connected to outside information sources and that these individuals acted as "gatekeepers" for their colleagues. They obtained, screened, and transmitted information. Figure 5.3 shows a typical information flow network. New information brought by individual one is transmitted to three other gatekeepers and reaches its eventual users through their contact with the gatekeeper network. The gatekeepers read journals more extensively and have more personal contacts outside the organization (Allen, 1977, pp. 146–147). They have a reputation for technical competence; others rely on personal contact with gatekeepers for information. To use this information source effectively, gatekeepers should be identified, rewarded, and supported. This facilitates their exposure to technological information and does not obstruct the interpersonal network used to diffuse the information in the lab.

The personal nature of information exchange can be increased by transfers of personnel within the company's divisions. In a large chemical lab, it was found that transferring persons provided an effective communication link back to their old divisions for one to one and one-half years (Kanno, 1968). Of course this use of transfers for information flow must be balanced against any potential detrimental effects of the transfer on the original project output.

In addition to the use of the gatekeeper network and personal contacts, physical layout is important for improving communication. Figure 5.4 shows the probability of communication between R&D lab personnel as a function of the distance between them. This is based on Allen's study of communica-

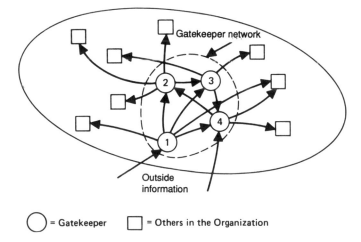

Figure 5.3   The Functioning of the Gatekeeper Network (Allen 1977, p. 162)

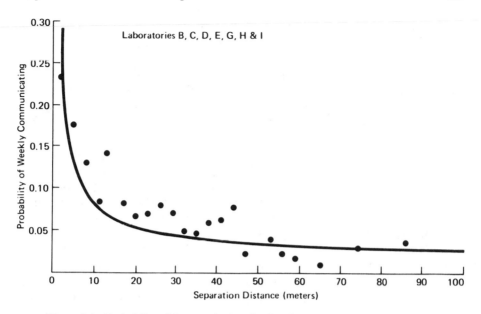

Figure 5.4   Probability of Communication in a Week as a Function of the Distance Separating Pairs of People (Allen 1977, p. 239)

tion contacts in seven research labs (aerospace, universities, chemical, computer, and agriculture fields). The amazing fact about this curve is how fast and far it drops. After a separation of 30 feet, the probability of communication in a week is less than one-third of its maximum. It is approximately .05 at 65 feet. These findings imply that physical layout is important if communication is to be improved. People should have offices as close as possible, and meetings should be arranged to bring people into personal contact. Experimentation has shown communication can be increased by changing architecture to reduce distances (Allen 1977).

Recent work has reinforced these findings. George and Allen (1989) examined communication among people within the same building and among people in different buildings. They found that there was little communication between buildings. In fact there was little communication between people on different floors in the same building. Further, they found that there was little communication across organizational sections and departments (in fact there is less communication across organizational sections than across buildings). Without effective communication across R&D facilities and between organizational units (e.g., marketing, engineering, production), idea generation will be restricted. Communication is clustered around specific locations and organizational units. New-product teams can attempt to bridge these communication barriers by frequent meetings, electronic networking, video conferencing, or "electronic windows" (large television screens that connect social spaces in individual facilities).

Technological Forecasting.   Action to improve communication flows is important to exploring the potential of technological ideas. Another method of locating areas of potential is through technological forecasting. The most common approaches to technological forecasting are based on trend extrapolation and on expert judgments.

Figure 5.5 shows the trend of random access memory (RAM) capacity over time. The vertical scale is logarithmic in factors of four; each unit represents four times the previous storage capacity. This implies dramatic expansion of capacity from 1973 to 1980 when the memory ship capacity went up by a factor of 256 (4^4 power) from 1,000 bytes of memory to 256,000 bytes of memory. In 1985 IBM announced the 1-megabyte chip (1,024,000) and in 1987 announced the 4-megabyte Dynamic RAM. NEC leapfrogged the 4-megabyte chip and was able to announce a 16-megabyte chip at the same time as IBM announced its 4-megabyte Dynamic RAM. In 1990 Hitachi announced a working prototype 64-megabyte chip. A linear extrapolation of this recent trend would imply a 1-gigabyte chip (1,024,000,000) in 1993 or 1994. Clearly any firm manufacturing integrated circuits must plan for products based on this trend. It is important to note that the graph shows announcement dates for working prototypes and not production or availability dates. It was two to three years from announcement to shipment for the 1- and 4-megabyte chips and four years for the 16-megabyte chip. Based on these lags, the delivery of the gigabyte chip is likely in 1996–98.

As memory capacity increases, memory costs of computers are approaching almost zero per bit. This would indicate a major opportunity for firms that develop computer software as well as those who manufacture chips. The new capacity and cost suggests new ideas for software. Software programming becomes a larger share of computer budgets. Along with trends toward massively parallel processing computation, software for operating systems and applications will be very different in the future.

Examining trend data for costs and productivity can be useful in identifying ideas. Various statistical methods are available to project these trends. Most are curve-fitting procedures based on extrapolation (e.g., Ayers 1969, pp. 94–140). More elaborate dynamic models that include the effects of R&D resource allocation on technological progress and specialized models for military purposes have been developed (E. B. Roberts, 1969; Sigford and Parvin 1965). These methods must be used with care, however. Trends may not continue and extrapolation without understanding the underlying technological drivers is dangerous. For example, consider our DRAM trend. Before extrapolation of the recent trend line of 1985–91 it is useful to examine the

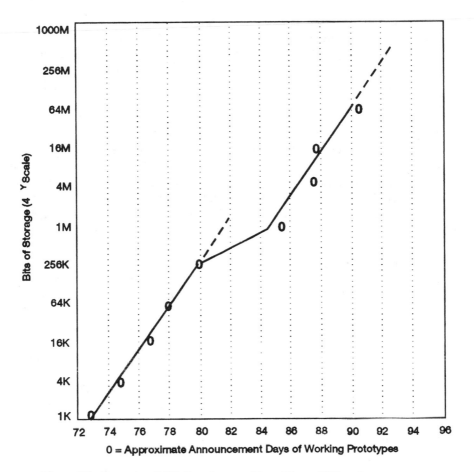

Figure 5.5   Increasing RAM Capacity over Time (Noyce 1977 and company announcements)
IBM—1 megabyte (August 1985)
IBM—4 megabytes (February 25, 1987)
NTT—16 megabytes (February 25, 1987)
Hitachi—64 megabytes (June 8, 1990)

1973–1980 trend. You will note that this trend did not continue smoothly. The progress of the chip capacity past the 256K level had to wait until the "alpha particle problem" could be solved (low level radiation emission adversely affected the new denser chips). It is tempting to extend the 1986 to 1991 trend line, but one must realize that the 64- to 256-megabyte chips require a new lithography technology (electron beam or X-ray) to define the circuit line on the chip. A 256-megabyte chip would have circuit lines only a few hundred atoms wide! In addition shielding and cooling challenges would be faced as density increases. Hitachi used electron beam lithography in its 64-megabyte chip. If its technology sets the new standard for circuit line width, further progress may follow along the trend line. Clearly technological forecasting is more than straight line extrapolation, but considering R&D opinions along with past data should help an organization diagnose technological ideas and opportunities.

Often it is useful to examine and extrapolate the costs of two or more related technologies (Quinn 1967). For example, a large British chemical producer found a way to shatter used tires after they had been frozen by liquid nitrogen and then salvage the steel belting. Initially this process was not economically feasible, but the firm monitored the trend. After 10 years the price of steel had risen and the price of nitrogen had decreased so that this process became practical and could be introduced. Costs of tunneling have reduced so much that this technology can now replace bridges and elevated highways in many applications.

Technological forecasting requires careful projection and monitoring of trends. Even if the curve projections are wrong, they indicate opportunities which can be monitored to determine the appropriate time for a technologically based innovation. There is often ample warning before a technology achieves economic impact. Effort should be directed at diagnosing technological change.

Although trend extrapolation is an important approach to technological forecasting, the prediction of some future events are better handled by other means. For example, will nuclear power become widely available to Third World Countries by 2000? The answer to this question affects the types of products that will be feasible in these countries. Another example would be the possibility of manufacturing drugs in space. If this is practical, a whole range of ideas may be generated and regarded as feasible.

Forecasting long range and discrete technological events is often done by the use of expert judgment. Summaries of potential technological developments are generated and then expert opinions on the likelihood of them occurring are collected by "Delphi forecasting." In the Delphi approach, each expert in the group anonymously judges the likelihood and then opinion feedback and other data is reported to the group before new estimates are made. The process is repeated until a group agreement is obtained for the estimates. Figure 5.6 shows a flowchart for Delphi forecasting. About 15 to 20 experts are used as a panel. They provide inputs of a questionnaire after relevant outside data is provided. After the first estimates, statistical results of the forecasts are fed back to the experts. Usually, after three to five rounds, these estimates converge.

Some good results have been obtained by this method. For example, in an application to the construction industry, Delphi forecasting predicted sales

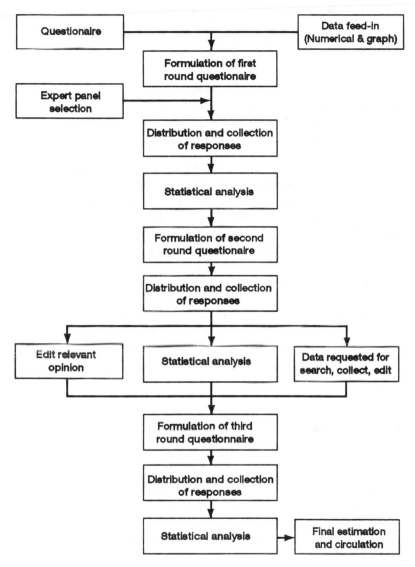

Figure 5.6 Flowchart of Delphi Forecasting (Basu and Schoeder 1977, p. 26)

within 3.3 percent for each of two years. This was better than previous errors of 20 percent and other forecasts generated by regressions and exponential smoothing.

There are some limitations to the method. In experiments with Delphi forecasting where the true answers were known (statistical almanac), convergence was towards the initial group median rather than the true value (Dalkey, 1969). Few tests of comparative forecasting accuracy have been reported. Delphi forecasting must be treated with caution, but expert opinion and re-estimation can help clarify the issues in predicting technological change.

Both technological trend extrapolation and the Delphi methods are subject to error, but it is important to allocate effort systematically to understand the movements in technology and their implications for new-product idea generation. Even if an organization expends effort only to monitor rather than predict technological trends, this information proves valuable in the new-product development process. Invoking a systematic process is sure to result in a dialogue that will build a common base for viewing the future. This may be the greatest benefit of the Delphi and trend methods because technological bets in the end are made based on this understanding.

Although the preceding examples of technological forecasting are primarily for industrial products, they are also applicable to consumer products where such breakthroughs as sugar and fat substitutes, communication bandwidth in the home, biogenetics, and electronic imaging are important to products such as ice cream, movies, OTC drugs, and cameras.

We have emphasized at several points in this book that technology cannot be viewed alone, but must be linked to market needs in the firm's strategically targeted markets if it is to be successful. We now concentrate on market and need input and then suggest methods for integration of market and technology inputs so that innovative ideas that have market potential can be identified.

Exploratory Customer Studies

Because market needs reflect a high potential source of ideas, the closer and earlier the new product developers get to the consumer the better. Observing how people buy and use the product can be done initially by casual observation or introspection of one's own behavior. Although this is useful, care must be taken not to generate fixed opinions based on these ad hoc observations; the observations may not be based on a representative sample of consumers.

A widely used method of gaining a knowledge of consumers is through focused group discussions or what are termed "focus groups" (Calder, 1977). The group is usually made up of 8 to 10 users of the product. It may be housewives talking about hand lotion, corporate controllers talking about the purchase of computers, patients talking about hospital services, or automotive platform engineers talking about new plastics. The group is brought to a central location and the members are usually compensated by $50 to $200 for

1 to 2 hours of their time (in cash or in kind compensation such as source books for industrial buyers). A moderator conducts the discussion. The session is taped and it is not uncommon to have a one-way mirror so that company personnel can observe the discussion; today remote transmission of live video of the session to the sponsor's company can be done with the sponsor being able to control the camera scan and zoom. Discussants are informed of these observations or recordings and almost always find them acceptable. The process of running a good group discussion requires experience; many professional services are available to conduct such groups. However, it is possible to run your own group. Usually the discussion begins with each person making comments on how they use or when they last bought the product under discussion. Likes and dislikes can be enumerated. In some sessions concepts of new products are presented and evaluated. In these discussions it is important for the leader to maintain control and make sure everyone has a chance to speak. At the same time, interaction should be encouraged, because group dynamics can help consumers verbalize their latent feelings. Allowing respondents to write down their reactions to the concept and then sharing them in the group is often a useful structure.

The purpose of focus groups is to learn customers' opinions, semantic structure, usage patterns, attitudes, and buying processes. This exploratory work generates many insights, but even if three or four groups are run, the results can only be suggestive. The work is qualitative, not quantitative. Insight and hypotheses are generated, not final conclusions.

A great advantage of a focus group is that it allows an early contact with users and provides an in-depth feeling for the products now in the target market. Consider a group discussion on hand lotion. Before the session, 10 people were casually waiting with their hands on the table or in view. Within 5 seconds after the moderator announced that the discussion was about hand lotion, all hands had been placed under the table or out of sight and the women's faces became tense. Discussion revealed considerable guilt and shame about the condition of their hands. Further exploration revealed anger that they are expected to have soft hands, but in many cases they must do abusive work such as washing dishes in detergents, cleaning floors, or other work around the home while others who do not share in these tasks and have soft hands. Although this discussion did not directly generate a specific new product, it produced much insight into the product needs; eventually it led to a concept called "Hand Guard," which was designed to protect hands during dish washing and other activities.

While focus groups are used most commonly for consumer products, they can and have been used in developing services (e.g., health, transportation, and education) and industrial products (computer information systems, process machinery). In each case the focus groups led to improved insight into consumers' needs and desires.

For example, a focus group on high efficiency electric motors conducted for the Department of Energy (*Market Facts*, 1978) indicated that the common practice is to evaluate motors on the basis of initial cost rather than cost over the product's in-use life. The focus groups indicated that efficiency was not a purchase criteria. This strongly indicates a marketing problem that a new, higher-cost product will face. The group went on to suggest ways to educate the field through special programs, regulation, and incentives for manufacturers.

We recommend focus groups in all new product development processes. Even when a company feels they know their market, the development team will learn a great deal more at a low cost from observing focus group discussions.

Other individual exploratory consumer research is possible. In fact, the research conducted in the efforts to define the market (chapter 4) can be useful. For example, if the perceptual dimensions of the hand lotion market are effectiveness (healing red, rough hands) and application (not greasy, soaks in), positioning gaps may become clear when existing brands are placed on the maps. A *gap* in an area on the map where no products now exist and where consumer preference can be expected is a good opportunity (see chapters 8 to 10 for a full discussion of these methods and their use in positioning products to capture opportunities). The hierarchical definition of markets may suggest ideas. For example, a regular instant coffee was indicated as a high-potential area in the example in chapter 4. These general ideas could be expressed as concepts, and explored by personal interviews aimed at getting unstructured response to the ideas and insights that would be the basis of improvement.

Another kind of in-depth interview is oriented at finding problems consumers have and identifying opportunities for products to solve them. Other approaches concentrate on the benefits the consumer perceives the product as delivering and identifying situations where the customer wants to receive more benefit. Still others ask customers to describe product-use experiences and to express what needs the product fulfilled. Concentrating on likes and dislike of products can suggest ideas. Polaroid found that users were having problems storing pictures after they were developed instantly. Based on this insight Polaroid added a picture storage compartment to their new camera.

Although there is no general rule about which method of exploratory consumer study is best, it is clear that early consumer interaction should be achieved. (We present some data comparing focus groups and one-on-one interviews in chapter 9.) Whether one is interested in deodorants, machine tools, travel services, office systems, or banking, it is recommended that early contact be made with customers so that the problem of understanding needs and the usage process can begin. This understanding is vital for successful idea generation and later design of products.

Facilitating Lead User Analysis

As indicated earlier, users not only have needs but may possess solutions. Rather than wait for the users to bring solutions to us, we could expend effort to find and facilitate this problem-solving process.

Facilitating User Solutions.   As a first step in involving users in our idea generation efforts we survey users to find out what special problems they have solved and inspect their prototypes. We facilitate their solution process by supplying parts to innovative users at low cost. We could be more formal and develop a partnership with lead users as IBM has done in its key business application sectors. This kind of partnership may include technical support, reduced prices, or free equipment for the user in exchange for the manufacturer getting access to user needs and solutions.

Another approach is to set up a special program for custom one-of-a-kind work. This puts the company in a position close to the user need and solution process. A Boston electronics firm specializing in test equipment for integrated circuits decided to cut its one-of-a-kind production facility because it was not profitable. This decision was reversed when it was determined that most of the firms' products had developed from projects initiated as a one-of-a-kind machine. The user solution requirements had been generalizable to a wider market.

Innovation can also occur through product modification by users. Xerox's first machines were not used for copying as intended, but rather to make offset masters. This user adaption was important in carrying Xerox through its early period until the machine's speed and reliability could be improved to meet the market office-copying requirements. Flexibility of product design and tracking user adaptation is an important method for generating ideas for overall product improvement.

Users may have solved your development problem. It is useful to examine your organization's past history and see where successful ideas have come from. If users have been active contributors, you should devote effort to cultivating them and maximizing their input to the idea generation process.

Lead User Analysis.   Involving users is a positive activity, but identifying the true lead users is not always obvious and collecting their solution content may be done more formally than just asking them what they have done. First, let us define lead users more explicitly, and then define a set of steps to comprise a lead user analysis.

"Lead users" of a novel or enhanced product, process, or service are defined as those who display two characteristics with respect to it.

- Lead users face needs that will be general in a marketplace—but face them months or years before the bulk of that marketplace encounters them.
- Lead users are positioned to benefit significantly by obtaining a solution to those needs.

Thus, a manufacturing firm with a current strong need for a process innovation that many manufacturers will need in two years' time would fit the definition of lead user with respect to that process.

Each of the two lead user characteristics specified above provides an independent and valuable contribution to the type of new product need and solution data lead users are hypothesized to possess.

The first is valuable because, as studies in problem solving have shown (summarized in von Hippel 1988), users who have real-world experience with a need are in the best position to provide market researchers with accurate (need or solution) data regarding their experience. When new-product needs are evolving rapidly, as in many high-technology product categories, only users at the "front of the trend" will presently have the real-world experience that manufacturers must analyze if they are to understand accurately the needs that the bulk of the market will have tomorrow.

The utility of the second lead user characteristic is that users who expect high benefit from a solution to a need can provide the richest need and solution data to inquiring market researchers. This is because, as has been shown by studies of industrial product and process innovations (Mansfield 1968), the greater the benefit a given user expects to obtain from a needed novel product or process, the greater will be the investment in obtaining a solution.

In sum, lead users are users whose present strong needs will become general in a marketplace months or years in the future. Because lead users are familiar with conditions that lie in the future for most others, they can serve as a needs-forecasting laboratory for marketing research. Moreover, since lead users often attempt to fill the need they experience, they can provide valuable new product concept and design data to inquiring manufacturers in addition to need data.

Firms which undertake a formal lead user analysis:

1. *Specify Lead User Indicators.* A. *Find a market or technological trend and related measures:* Lead users are defined as being in advance of the market with

respect to a given important dimension that is changing over time. Therefore, before one can identify lead users in a given product category of interest, one must specify the underlying trend on which these users have a leading position and must specify reliable measures of that trend.

B. *Define measures of potential benefit:* High expected benefit from solving a need is the second indicator of a lead user, and measures or proxy measures of this variable must also be defined. In work to date, we have found three types of proxy measures to be useful. First, evidence of user product development or product modification can serve as a proxy for user benefit because, as we noted previously, user investment in innovation and user expectations of related benefit have been found to be correlated. Second, user dissatisfaction with existing products (services or processes) can serve as a proxy for expected benefit because it is logical that the degree of dissatisfaction with what exists will be correlated with the degree of expected benefit obtainable from improvements. Finally, speed of adoption of innovations may also serve as a surrogate for high expected benefit. Early adoption and innovativeness are often correlated with the adopter's perception of related benefit (Rogers and Shoemaker 1971).

2. *Identify lead user Groups.* Once trend and benefit indicators are specified, one may screen the potential market based on the measures specified via a questionnaire to identify a lead-user group. This is accomplished by a cluster analysis of the survey-based lead user indicators. The analysis identifies a subgroup which is at the leading edge of the trend being studied and displays correlates of high expected benefit from solutions to related needs.

3. *Generate concepts (products) with lead users.* The next step in the method involves deriving data from lead users related to their real-life experience with novel attributes and product concepts of commercial interest. This experience may include modifications to existing products or new products that they have created to meet their needs. Creative group sessions can be used to pool user solution content and develop a new product concept. In some cases the user solution may represent not only a concept but a fully implemented product.

4. *Test lead user concepts (products).* The needs of today's lead users are typically not precisely the same as the needs of the users who will make up a major share of tomorrow's predicted market. Indeed, the literature on diffusion suggests that, in general, the early adopters of a novel product or practice differ in significant ways from the bulk of the users who follow them (Rogers 1962). Therefore one assesses how lead user

data are evaluated by the more typical users in the target market. This is done by employing traditional concept (product) test procedures after segmenting lead and non–lead user responses.

These steps were applied in 1987–88 to the market of CAD/CAM systems for electronic systems (Urban and von Hippel 1988). Although the technology has continued to advance since then, the case illustrates lead user analysis and its enhancement with market research.

This case study focused on the submarket for CAD software employed in the design of printed circuit boards.[2] These PC-CAD systems play important roles in placing chips on the board, routing the solder wires called "vias," testing, and manufacturing. The objective of the study was to determine, first, whether lead users could be identified, and, then, whether their proposed "solutions" to a given problem could provide the basis for a product concept that would appeal to the remainder of the market. "Traditional wisdom," as expressed by a leading CAD supplier, held that it was unlikely that users would develop their own software, partly because the algorithms required were very sophisticated and the graphical interfaces very complex, and partly because such an effort required major resources.

The study attempted to identify lead users by specifying a series of indicators that reflected being at the leading edge of an important technological trend and the customers' propensity to create solutions to enable them to benefit from the trend. Consultation with experts in the field led to the identification of a significant trend toward greater density of integrated chips on a board (more chips per square inch). Higher density could be accomplished by using multiple layers in the board, making the vias narrower, or by using surface-mounted chips.[3] It was hypothesized that users who employed these technical methods, were innovative, felt dissatisfied with commercially available systems, and had adopted CAD early would be most likely to build their own PC-CAD systems.

It would be possible to use these indicators by informally calling on customers and potential customers, talking to sales and service personnel, interviewing industry experts, and contacting user groups. In this case, a more formal approach rooted in market research procedures was used. A questionnaire based on indicators was developed and administered to 136 electronic engineers and engineering managers. Contrary to industry expectations, CAD users were found to be very active in developing their own solutions: 25% had built their own PC-CAD systems, and 45% had modified commercial systems.

[2] Printed circuit boards hold integrated circuit chips and other electronic components and interconnect these into functioning circuits.

[3] In surface mounting, chips and other components are soldered to the board instead of being mounted on legs that fit into drilled holes.

A subset of lead users was identified through cluster analysis. Lead users in this cluster used more surface mounting (87% versus 56%), narrower vias (11 mills versus 15 mills), and more layers (7.1 versus 4.0). They were more likely to have built their own systems (87% versus only 1%), to be innovative (3.3 versus 2.4 on a 4-point innovativeness scale[4]), to be dissatisfied with existing commercial systems (4.1 versus 5.3 on a 7-point satisfaction scale), and to have adopted CAD earlier (1973 versus 1980).

Five of the lead users who had developed their own systems were invited to attend a group session where specifications would be established for a new PC-CAD system based on the solutions they had developed. Under the concept they came up with, the new CAD system would have direct links to numerically controlled machine tools, easier computer interfaces, central data storage, and functional simulation capabilities (electrical, mechanical, and thermal). It would be capable of designing boards of up to forty layers, routed with thinner vias, which used surface-mounted devices.

The customers identified in the screening phase of the study were then resurveyed to test the new concept versus each respondent's current system, and also what each respondent considered to be the best available commercial system. Each respondent's first-choice selection, preference (constant sum judgments), and probability of purchase, were assessed. It turned out that 78.6% of the respondents preferred the new concept, 25% more than for the best commercially available system. In fact, the concept developed by the five lead users in the group session was preferred to the best available commercial system *even at twice the price.*

Linking Marketing and Technology

Consumer input in terms of exploratory-user studies or lead user analysis is crucial to success in marketplace, but, as argued in chapter 2, new product strategies should be comprehensive strategies based on both consumer input *and* technology.

The success of a proactive new-product strategy is highly dependent on a firm's effectiveness in linking technology and customer needs. Because customers only buy products that they perceive as filling their needs, it is critical that customer input be brought to bear early in the new-product design process. "Marketing" in its broadest sense (the total fulfillment of customer needs) must be integrated closely with technology at every step in the design and engineering of new products if risks are to be reduced and innovation is to be successful. In today's rapidly moving and highly compet-

---

[4] This scale ranged from 1, "adopt a new technology only when it is established," to 4, "always on the leading edge of technology."

itive markets, most firms find it necessary to employ integrated strategies combining marketing and technology in the design of new products.

Three mechanisms have typically been used by firms to support strategies requiring the integration of marketing and technology: (1) formal organizational structures; (2) interpersonal relations; and (3) analytical support.

A variety of formal organizational structures can be utilized to facilitate the integration of marketing and technology. Table 5.3 enumerates a number of alternatives. These alternatives vary from formal organizational reporting relationships, matrix structures to entrepreneurial groups, venture teams, and "skunk works" (i.e., a team hidden in a "smelly basement" or remote isolated location with the task to get to market with a breakthrough new product fast—IBM did this with their PC). Empirical studies suggest that no one form is dominant and that most firms use multiple structures. A single organization might, for example, have a growth and development group with a charter to develop new business areas (reporting to a vice president); a new-products department charged with designing product-line extensions (located in the marketing department); a marketing research function to assess customer needs for new technologies (in the R&D group); and a separate entrepreneurial division intended to provide a home for innovators with new ideas (we will address these organizational alternatives further in chapter 20).

One reason why no one formal integrating mechanism is dominant is that the problem is fundamentally interpersonal. Marketing managers usually are not trained technically, tend to have short-run perspectives, prefer structured tasks, and often are outgoing. Engineers and scientists generally lack training in marketing and management, tend to focus on long-term results, are comfortable working on unstructured tasks, and are frequently reserved. Obviously, the potential for conflict is high. In some countries such as Japan this is not true because many engineers start working in sales and marketing before being transferred to engineering. In this situation the potential for cultural conflict is much less.

In his study of 289 new-product development projects across 56 firms, Souder (1987) classified firms as having "harmonious" or "disharmonious" relations between marketing and R&D. He found disharmony in 59.2% of the projects: "severe disharmony" (lack of appreciation and distrust) in 38.7% of cases, and "mild disharmony" (lack of interaction and communication, reluctance to criticize friends) in 20.5%. Harmonious relations were observed in only 40.8% of the projects. In 29.1% of these cases, either marketing or R&D was dominant, whereas in only 11.7% did the two functions appear to be engaged in equal partnerships. Perhaps the most important finding of this study, however, was the clear relationship Souder found between organizational harmony and success in new-product development. Of the projects characterized by severe disharmony, 68% failed, in contrast to a failure rate of

TABLE 5.3. Formal Organizational Structures to Integrate Marketing and R&D

1. R&D reports to V.P. marketing
2. Marketing reports to R&D
3. Growth and development department with assigned R&D and marketing staff
4. Matrix of R&D and marketing efforts assigned to new-product development projects
5. Venture teams including R&D and marketing/skunkworks
6. R&D representative assigned to each SBU
7. Dedicated marketing research group in R&D
8. Integrated design group consisting of marketing, R&D, engineering, and manufacturing
9. SBUs with budgets to buy internal (or external) R&D or marketing skills from corporate staff groups
10. Division to house entrepreneurs with access to corporate R&D and marketing resources

23% for those experiencing mild disharmony and only 13% for those enjoying harmonious relations between marketing and R&D.

Our opinion is that it is far too limiting to view the problem as merely one of integrating the marketing and R&D departments. For the two functions to work together rather than at cross-purposes, marketing and R&D personnel must be sensitized to the requirements and processes of each other's disciplines. In many leading companies, engineers attend formal marketing education programs, marketers study technology, and managers are transferred between engineering management and marketing management positions. Some companies have also found it effective to form "dyads" in which a marketer and engineer work together to accomplish a common set of tasks. In Japan it is common for an engineer to serve as a salesman before being placed in an R&D group. More and more business schools are teaching technology to their students, while engineering students frequently take at least some "marketing" electives. Clearly, the manager in the 21st-century will have to be well versed in both marketing and technology if he or she is to play a major role in strategic management.

The third component in a program to integrate technology and marketing is analytic support of the process. The lead user analysis cited earlier is one example. Quality functional deployment (QFD) is another example. It represents the formalization of good marketing, engineering, industrial relations, and manufacturing theory. First, customers define "quality" in *their* terms through techniques such as perceptual semantics and attribute/price/ value tradeoffs. These customer requirements are then transformed into detailed engineering specifications through an "integrated design" effort that evaluates alternative product designs and production processes simultaneously. The product is designed to meet both functional specifications and manufacturing constraints and efficiencies. If tradeoffs in design are made, they reflect all three aspects of customer preference: engineering requirement, production reliability, and cost. The product is manufactured with strict quality control and active worker participation. A strong customer service function is charged with ensuring that the customer ultimately receives the benefits originally identified as the "purpose" of the new product. This and similar processes are intended to *force* integration of customer needs, responsive product design, manufacturing quality control, and service (we discuss QFD and other methods to facilitate the design for quality in chapter 13).

A final example of analytic support to integrate marketing and technology is a matrix that helps align technology alternatives to target market segment. Here we focus the notion more specifically on one market and its possible subsegments and examine the engineering technologies that can be used to create concepts of products.

Figure 5.7 shows a hypothetical matrix of engineering technologies and markets for watches. The X's indicate when a given technology might be most relevant to a consumer segment.

The consideration of the rows suggest ideas for watches based on style, digital display, computer logic, and watches varying in weight, thickness, color, and shape. Most firms have looked at the market this way. This is not a very imaginative use of technology. Looking at markets (columns) rather than application of specific technologies may gives a different and creative perspective. For example, the business sector suggests watches with a beeper

Engineering Opportunities	Market Opportunities				
	Gift	Status	Jewelry	Woman	Men
Light-emitting diodes	X				X
Liquid-crystal diodes	X	X		X	
Thin case		X	X		
Three modules			X		
Five components				X	X
Self-charging battery					X
Instrument appearance	X	X	X		
Calculator plus watch	X				X

Figure 5.7 Engineering Terminologies and Market Segments for a Wrist Watch

feature such as those introduced by Motorola in the early 1990s. Extension of this notion might lead to a cellular phone on the wrist. Sports watches may include dive watches with computers to determine the allowable times and depths for safe diving as a function of actual dives completed. Sailing watches could include tides and weather alert alarms. A health sector might be developed based on watches that take pulse and blood pressure readings or allow biofeedback during business meetings to minimize stress. The matrix should be a stimulus for creative ideas; new segments, technologies, or concepts should be unearthed. For example, a watch with communication capabilities could be used to alert medical personnel when a chronically ill patient needs help. Such communication capability alternatively could be used to inform investors when their stocks moved out of prescribed ranges and allow sell orders to be transmitted after prices are displayed. This would create a new segment based on support of individual investors. Figure 5.8 shows a design

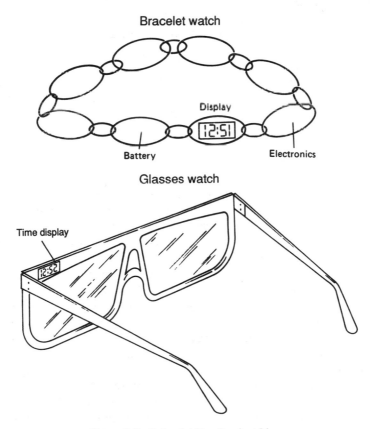

Figure 5.8 Potential New-Product Ideas

concept for a woman's watch to fill a status jewelry positioning. Here engineering is used in a unique way to tap the capability of the electronics to put components in separate units that are inlaid with black onyx and diamonds. Alternatively, a liquid-crystal display might change color to indicate the hour of the day. Another radical watch idea could use this electronic capability to have the display mounted above a pair of glasses and be activated by sensors which detect eye movement. Perhaps the time could be whispered in your ear. This could eliminate the embarrassment of "sneaking" a look at your watch when someone important is boring you. On the opposite tack, a wrist watch with a loud alarm and a big face could be used to remind those present that they are wasting your time and it is time to wrap up. The use of engineering to meet specific consumer needs in target segments can be the source of many new ideas.

Creative Methods

The matrix approach represents one method of encouraging creative thought. By viewing the matrix from a wide perspective, new ideas may be facilitated. In this section, we describe other individual and group methods to encourage the elusive notion of creativity. Most of the ideas that result from such efforts will not be feasible, but the few that are feasible represent successful outcomes of the idea generation process—a creative idea that can be produced to impact on the firm's chosen market segment(s) and profit.

Individual Creativity

The success of idea generation depends on using effective methods to search idea sources and on individual creativity. As shown in Figure 5.1, some ideas come directly from the idea sources while others require more structured search such as technological forecasting or exploratory consumer surveys. Turning the source information into an idea for a new product may be straightforward, or it may come from the spontaneous creativity of an individual within the organization.

The creative process is not well-understood and the specific determinants of creativity are not known. Bronowski, on reviewing the history of innovation in science and art, argues "Although science and art are social phenomena, an innovation in either field occurs only when a single mind perceives in disorder a deep new unity" (Bronowski 1987, p. 1). He finds the search for structure common across the disciplines. Innovation is an act of imagination; it is spawned by the discovery of an unexpected likeness.

New product development fits in somewhere between art and science so Bronowski's observations are relevant. Others have written about creativity more specifically directed at new product development. Prince (1970) describes (rather creatively) creativity as

> an arbitrary harmony, an expected astonishment, a habitual revelation, a familiar surprise, a generous selfishness, an unexpected certainty, a formidable stubbornness, a vital triviality, a disciplined freedom, an intoxicating steadiness, a repeated initiation, a difficult delight, a predictable gamble, an ephemeral solidity, a unifying difference, a demanding satisfier, a miraculous expectation, an accustomed amazement.

He believes each man and woman is born as a creative problem solver. Prince created Synectics to draw on this natural creative energy in a group process (see later). Roger von Oech believes that knowledge is the key input to creativity, but "creative thinking requires an attitude that allows one to search for ideas and manipulate your knowledge and experience. . . . You use crazy, foolish, and impractical ideas as stepping stones to practical new ideas. You break the rules occasionally, and explore for ideas in unusual outside places. In short, by adopting a creative outlook you open yourself up both to new possibilities and to change" (von Oech 1990, p.6). His book *Whack on the Side of the Head* describes how to free yourself from 10 mental locks that prevent individual creativity. These mental blocks include looking for the one right answer, excessive logical thinking, rigidly following the rules, being too practical, not being willing to have fun and play, overspecializing, avoiding ambiguity, fear of looking foolish, unwillingness to make an error, and believing you are not creative.

Edward de Bono proposes a creative approach based on "lateral thinking," which generates many new alternatives and new patterns rather than "vertical thinking" that restricts alternatives and concentrates on correct analysis and direct problem solution (de Bono, 1973). This process encourages new ways of looking at and structuring problems and solutions so that creative alternatives may be forthcoming.

Although many authors have written about creativity, there is no recipe for creative thinking. But breaking loose and having the confidence to let our ideas out in an open response to a problem can free an amazing amount of creativity if you do not evaluate prematurely the ideas for correctness and feasibility.

The organization can set up reward structures to encourage ideas. A willingness to accept "mistakes" in new products and a tolerance for the ambiguity of the invention process are positive cultural incentives for creativity in an organization. Another effective method is to designate idea generation as a responsibility for certain individuals and give clear organizational recognition to these people. A new product team or task force may be charged with coming up with new ideas to tap market opportunity.

Creative Group Methods

Because basic new ideas are so crucial to new product success, organizations may set up formal creative group methods to synthesize the information on new product potentials. Creative group methods are not magic, they cannot guarantee solutions to impossible problems, but they do encourage a fertile climate for creativity by removing inhibitions and unproductive structures. They force the organization to think beyond obvious solutions to those holding more potential. These techniques assume that each individual has a wealth of knowledge and is, by nature, capable of creativity. The task is to encourage individuals to draw upon their personal knowledge, no matter how irrelevant it may appear, and apply this knowledge to develop creative solutions, no matter how impossible to implement they may seem. For example, the next creative breakthrough might be triggered by something you know from a recent movie or book, or some common knowledge about the weather, or specific knowledge about opera librettos, football strategies, sailing, sewing, modern art, chemistry, mythology, auto races, physics, biology, or even management. Although at first this may seem absurd, experience has shown that "unrealistic" ideas can form the beginning of productive solutions.

In this section we discuss creative group methods of idea generation. We briefly outline several methods and then concentrate on some basic concepts that enhance the success of creative groups. Although formal methods may not be appropriate for every new product problem, we suggest that many of the ideas behind creative groups be carefully considered and incorporated in the new product development process.

One of the first group methods of creating ideas was "brainstorming" (Arnold 1962, pp. 251–268). In this approach a group tries to generate many diverse ideas. No criticism is allowed and group members are encouraged to improve on other people's ideas. It is hoped that through this method, a wide variance of ideas will result, and some will be really new. This basic meeting format has been modified by adding structure in "attribute listing" methods. Attributes are listed for the existing products and efforts are made to adapt, modify, magnify, substitute, rearrange, reverse, or combine them. For example, among the attributes of the Oreo cookie is the filling. This was magnified to produce the highly successful double-thick Oreo. Reversal produces a white cookie and black filling or an Oreo cookie with a chocolate covering. A new product may minimize an attribute and for example have less alcohol or fat. In "forced" relationship techniques (Osborn 1963), existing items are put together. For example, a new car might be both luxurious and economical or have performance and low maintenance.

A more highly structured creative method is represented by "morphological analysis" (Ayres 1969). There are five steps.

1. Explicitly formulate the problem.
2. Identify parameters.
3. List all possible combinations of parameters.
4. Examine feasibility of all alternatives.
5. Select the best alternatives.

For example, in the 1930s Zwicky (Arnold 1962, pp. 251–268) used this method on jet engines. He identified six parameters (e.g., type of ignition—self-ignition or externally ignited; state of propellant—gas, liquid, solid). Across the values, 576 combinations could be formed. His examination of these combinations are said to have led to several radical new inventions.

Many creative methods have been proposed. These range from unstructured methods such as meditation to structured approaches such as content analysis of advertising and functional analysis of products.

There are some common elements in the existing techniques that seem to work well.

1. Establish openness and participation.
2. Encourage many and diverse ideas.
3. Build on each other's ideas.
4. Orient toward problems.
5. Use a leader to guide discussion.

One method, using group sessions, has been developed by both Gordon (1961) and Prince (1972). These sessions arc based on four simple, but powerful concepts.

The first concept is to *listen.* Unstructured meetings can often become power plays, with each participant trying to express his pet solution. As a consequence, as someone starts to talk, many people will not listen with full attention but rather will begin formulating their response. A useful method to encourage listening is for a moderator to write down each person's statement on a flip chart. This reinforces the listening and assures that no ideas are lost. Because all ideas are written down, one participant does not need to interrupt another to be sure his idea is not lost. The moderator must control the discussion so that all members can express their views and so that the discussion considers an idea completely without unproductive shifting among ideas.

The second concept is that *most ideas have some good elements.* Because most ideas have some good points, the group must build on these good points while overcoming any bad points. This is done by first identifying the good points and then the concerns the idea generates. Then explicit effort is expended in overcoming concerns and making the idea acceptable. One sub-process called "itemized response" identifies the good elements, leads to positive thinking, and rewards the idea originator. For example, a self-thinking typewriter may have been infeasible in 1960, but it was a good idea which could prove useful once its technical problems were solved. Auto-correcting typewriters and typewriters with memory have been successful innovations in office equipment in the 1970s.

The third concept is *a common understanding of a specific problem*. Frequently a group will work simultaneously on what appears to be the same problem, but is in reality several different problems. For example, one person may interpret a goal of cleaner air as the problem of preventing pollution while another sees the problem as one of cleaning already polluted air, whereas still another views it as shifting pollution to another geographical area where it can be contained. Although each may satisfy the general goal and the final solution may combine all three, the group process will be difficult if each is simultaneously working on a separately defined problem. Some group meetings use a client to define the specific problem. For example, the client might be the vice-president of growth and development who has been told by the president of the company to establish a position in the teleconferencing market. The group then works with the leader and the client to achieve a working definition and common understanding that is used to address the problem of creating a new product idea.

The final concept is that of *a specific group leader*. In unstructured groups there is a tendency to jockey for leadership. The leader should be the facilitator and scribe. Because the leader does not have a personal interest in the problem, the leader can concentrate on encouraging effective group functioning.

These four concepts can be used to improve any group process. Prince's (1972) formal process makes good use of these concepts (Figure 5.9). After defining the problem and understanding its background, goals and wishes are generated. Usually the client will be asked to select one goal or problem to work on first. Then ideas are generated to meet the selected goal. For example, the goal might be to develop a remote conferencing system where users can have direct eye contact with a conference participant.

Simple techniques such as each participant listing one "real" and one "fantasy" idea can be used. More formal techniques based on the use of mental excursions, personal involvement, and metaphors can also be employed. Table 5.4 lists several specific idea-enhancing techniques. See Prince (1970) for more details. After a large number of ideas are generated, the client selects one for an itemized response. If the idea is made acceptable, it is called a "possible solution" and specific actions are outlined to implement it.

A usual session runs for three days, during which the basic flow is repeated many times. The group is usually comprised of personnel from the

FLOW   ACTIVITIES

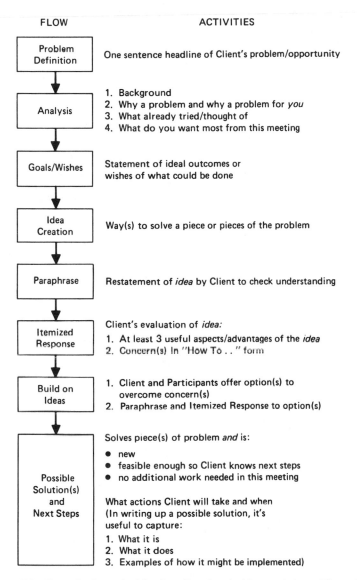

Problem Definition	One sentence headline of Client's problem/opportunity
Analysis	1. Background 2. Why a problem and why a problem for *you* 3. What already tried/thought of 4. What do you want most from this meeting
Goals/Wishes	Statement of ideal outcomes or wishes of what could be done
Idea Creation	Way(s) to solve a piece or pieces of the problem
Paraphrase	Restatement of *idea* by Client to check understanding
Itemized Response	Client's evaluation of *idea:* 1. At least 3 useful aspects/advantages of the *idea* 2. Concern(s) In "How To . . " form
Build on Ideas	1. Client and Participants offer option(s) to overcome concern(s) 2. Paraphrase and Itemized Response to option(s)
Possible Solution(s) and Next Steps	Solves piece(s) of problem *and* is: • new • feasible enough so Client knows next steps • no additional work needed in this meeting What actions Client will take and when (In writing up a possible solution, it's useful to capture: 1. What it is 2. What it does 3. Examples of how it might be implemented)

Figure 5.9   Flow of a Synectics Meeting (Reprinted with permission of Synectics, Inc., Cambridge, MA; Synectics is a registered trademark of Synectics, Inc.)

innovating organization, but consumer groups have also been used to create product ideas.

One remarkable feature of a creative group session is its ability to integrate marketing, R&D, engineering, and production viewpoints. We have

TABLE 5.4 Some Formal Techniques from Synectics

Technique	Description
Personal analogy	Participant puts himself or herself in the place of a physical object (e.g., a tuning fork) and gives a first person description of what it feels like to be that object.
Book title	Participant gives a two-word phrase that captures the essence and the paradox involved in a particular thing or set of feelings (e.g., familiar surprise).
Example excursion	Group discusses a topic seemingly unrelated to the basic problem to trigger thoughts or "take a vacation" from the problem.
Force fit—get fired	Participant thinks of an idea to force together two or more components of an idea. In the get-fired technique, the idea is to be so wild that his or her boss will fire him or her.

found it useful to frame a problem in some sessions based on market research studies. For example, considering the market definition findings, the organization may define an opportunity as a regular instant microwaveable coffee with improved mildness and aroma. The problem would then be to create such a product feasibly. In other sessions a technical issue may be the problem. For example, with digital watches the problem may be "how to use the electronic technology to create a watch that tells time and reads blood pressure." Combining a diverse group of people in a meeting and integrating basic technical and marketing research can facilitate creation of major new ideas for innovative products that meet market needs.

These concepts of a creative group may seem abstract and difficult to implement. Following is an edited transcript from an actual session that was used to develop a new service (Prince 1970, pp. 170–72). Examine this transcript for the four concepts outlined previously. You may wish to imagine yourself as either the client or a participant.

Problem as Given: How can we provide more diagnostic service with no more doctors?

Analysis: A large Boston hospital offers a 24-hour diagnostic service for emotionally disturbed people. This clinic examines patients and prescribes a course of therapy. Patient load is increasing 50 percent a year but the number of doctors remains the

same. How can this service be continued with no more doctors or money?

Problems as Understood: (1) How can one doctor be in three places at once? (2) How
can patients be spaced throughout 24 hours?

LEADER: Let's take number 1. In the world of nature, can you give me
an example of being in three places at once?

LIZ: Perfume.

LEADER: Yes?

LIZ: If a person wears a distinctive perfume and go from one room
to another that person remains present in each room.

LEADER: I think I see—you leave a trace or representation of yourself
in each room?

LIZ: Yes.

DICK: A fisherman's nets.

LEADER: Go ahead.

DICK: I was thinking of a Japanese fisherman for some reason. He
leaves one net in one place, another in another, and then
collects them with the fish.

LEADER: His nets act just as if he were there and catch the fish?

DICK: Yes.

LEADER: Let's examine this fisherman's nets.

DICK: Japanese fishermen have to be efficient because they depend
on a large catch to support their population. (Note: Dick is
more interested in the fish than the nets and his remarks lead
the team down an unexpected path. The leader, noting their
interest, happily goes with them.)

MORRIS: (Expertly) Some fish are considered great delicacies in Japan.

PETER: Yes, what is that poisonous fish that is so popular?

MORRIS: Poisonous?

DICK: I forget the name, but it has one poisonous part or a spot that
has to be removed.

LIZ: Who removes it? The person who eats it? I'd be nervous.

DICK: I am not sure, but it seems to me you remove it when you are
eating it. In the article I saw it said that it is not unusual for
people to get poisoned.

PETER: I would want to know all about that poison spot so I could
protect myself.

LIZ: You are right. I wouldn't trust the fisherman or the chef. I'd
want to remove it myself.

LEADER: OK, let's take these ideas about the fish. . . . How can we use
them to put one doctor in three places at once?
(Long silence.)

LIZ: There is something about do-it-yourself . . . get that poison
out yourself.

LEADER: Yes . . . this idea of protecting yourself? Can we help? . . .

Peter: I don't know if it makes sense, but could the doctor use a patient as an assistant?

MORRIS: (Expertly) We sure have plenty of patients and they have time to help—some have to wait for hours, which is another problem.

DICK: Could they help each other? Some kind of do-it-yourself group therapy while they are waiting to see the doctor?

DICK: Yes. (To Morris, the expert): Could you?

MORRIS: I like the part about the patients getting some benefit while they wait—even if some just listened it would probably be reassuring. But, I am a little concerned about their working without supervision.

LIZ: Could a nurse work with them, and perhaps get the history of the next one to see the doctor or something?

PETER: Or could the patient just finished take the history of the next one due to see the doctor?

MORRIS: If we push this thought to the end, we have a floating group-therapy session where everyone takes everyone else's history. We would want a doctor there.

This was the viewpoint. After experiments in the clinic the concept has evolved into a free-form meeting in the waiting room. The doctor presides. He and the group concentrate on helping one patient plan his own course of therapy. The doctor keeps an eye out for patients who are disturbed by the openness. Anyone who prefers can have a private interview. Most prefer the group treatment and find this waiting-room experience rewarding.

As the example indicates, an idea has its roots in many places—in this case in Dick's interest in the Japanese fishermen, in Peter's casual knowledge of Japanese delicacies, and in Liz's concern about trusting an important task to a chef or fisherman. Not all sessions will go this well and even this example is an edited transcript. But the openness, participation, teamwork, encouragement, and focus of creative group methods can lead to potential new product ideas that might not be recognized otherwise.

There have been some studies that indicate individual creative effort is superior to groups in terms of the quantity of ideas generated (see Lewis, Sadosky, and Connolly 1975; and Bouchard and Hare 1970). These studies are based on brainstorming and not the more advanced methods which stress the quality rather than the quantity of ideas. This area deserves more research, but one should not underrate individual effort as a component in the creative process.

In our experience, creative group methods have provided a useful tool for an organization to synthesize the diverse information obtained from direct search, exploratory consumer studies, technology forecasting, and lead user analysis and convert this information into potential new product ideas. Whether group methods or individual efforts are used, an organization should expend energy to tap its idea sources and generate a sizable number of exciting yet diverse ideas.

National Policy

While direct search, technological innovation, user research, integration of marketing and technology, and creative methods are very powerful methods of idea generation, other more macro methods of organizing innovation may produce meaningful new ideas. One macro method is based on government support. For example, in Japan, MITI has fostered major technological development in steel, textiles, and autos, as Japan rose to economic prominence in the 1960s to 1970s. Now MITI is funding fifth generation computers, superconductors, solar energy, advanced material machining, and unmanned space experiments among other growth areas. Participating and sharing the information from such a program can suggest many new product ideas and market growth opportunities for Japanese firms. In the United States, government consortia like MITI do not exist, but the Department of Defense and NASA R&D expenditures often create technological innovations that may be relevant for commercial products (e.g., aircraft engines, electronic instruments, materials, communication, and imaging). In Europe, government and industry are allocating $7.5 billion to consortia called EUREKA, which funds almost 300 projects in nine advanced technology areas (e.g., semiconductors and high-definition television). Other government and industry projects in Europe are ESPRIT ($6.7 billion and 400 programs to improve information technologies), RACE ($2.8 billion and 88 programs in fiber optics), and BRITE ($1 billion to fund advanced material and manufacturing technology). The scale of these programs is huge and the opportunity for the firm to leverage its technological competence is great. If such raw technological power can be integrated with market inputs, it becomes a major method of generation of high potential ideas.

Alliances, Acquisitions, and Licensing

Although governments are leading in some cooperative programs, in others individual private companies are forming consortia or alliances to generate new products. Sematech links 14 US computer companies (e.g., IBM, Motorola, and Intel) in an effort to create machines that will produce the 64- and 256-megabyte chips and advanced microprocessors. A consortium of U.S. auto companies is developing new battery technology that will enable improved electric vehicles. If these consortia are successful they represent new product opportunities for suppliers to these industries and manufacturers of the new products for the end users.

Increasingly, smaller-scale alliances are being formed between companies who have complementary skills in moving a strategic market and technology thrust forward. For example a small company may have the technology and a large company the marketing and production capacity. Microsoft and IBM had a very successful alliance in the 1980s based on software (DOS) by Microsoft and hardware by IBM. AT&T and Sun Micro Systems have an alliance for UNIX software, which, interestingly, led competitors to form the Open Software Foundation to counter this threat and establish its own standards and software. As well as providing complementary skills, alliances can also spread the risk and investment costs. GE and Boeing have worked together on major aircraft development with precommitments from airlines to minimize the multibillion dollar risks of aircraft programs.

A formal integration by acquisition can bring a new technology or product into a company. Current acquisition strategy has evolved from the 1980s when financial diversification and earnings per share dominated acquisition. Today acquisition strategies reflect priorities that reinforce the firm's core technology and target market presence. Few "bargains" are available in the acquisition market today and the key word for the 1990s is *focus*. Critical technologies in designated markets yield the synergy and lead to premium returns on investments in acquisitions. When the acquisition is focused, it can be managed effectively and integrated to produce an enhancement to the firm's competitive benefit proposition.

Often full acquisition is not feasible or not desirable. However, there is another alternative for the acquisition of technology. Licensing of technology is an option that gives rapid access to proven technologies. The cost may be high, but the risks are low and R&D funds do not need to be committed. In today's new product development arena a wide range of alliance and cooperative mechanisms are available to generate new ideas and products (see Roberts and Berry 1985 for more discussion).

IDEA MANAGEMENT

If an organization is successful in identifying sources of new ideas and using the methods outlined earlier to generate ideas, many exciting opportunities should be evident. Some may be the key ideas for a new product, but most of the remaining ideas will not have sufficient potential for further investigation. If each idea were advanced to the design phase costs would be prohibitive, thus we return to a managerial process to screen the ideas. Because the entire new product development process allows iteration, we select a small set of ideas based on the limited amount of information that is available for idea screening. This small set of ideas is advanced to the design phase to be analyzed in detail. Enough ideas are advanced so that it is likely that a sufficient number of ideas are developed into successful new products to meet the firm's growth goals. If not enough are successful in the design or testing phase of the process, the effort returns to idea generation and we iterate the process.

The two key managerial concepts in screening ideas are: (1) the selection process and (2) how many ideas to advance to the design phase.

Idea Selection

Idea selection comes early in the development process—before a final product is designed. Detailed information is not normally available and accurate estimation of financial outcomes is not always feasible. There are usually several human aspects reflected in the varying goals of R&D, marketing, production, distribution, and top management. For these reasons, most organizations should choose a relatively simple idea selection process tailored to their own unique needs. Although more complex processes may be appropriate after the design or testing phases, few organizations use such processes early in idea selection. Rather they choose a process that requires inputs that are feasible to obtain, is appropriate for early screening, and is flexible enough to allow the judgmental resolution of conflicting interests. We want to avoid two possible errors. First we do not want to waste development effort on ideas that are not good (will not be a success in the market), and second we do not want to eliminate ideas that are good (would be a success in the market). This second error is the most important to avoid in screening ideas. It is often advisable to carry forward an idea that may be a big winner because the cost of investigating in the design phase may be low.

One simple approach to finding the best ideas is to apply the same procedure to each idea that was proposed for screening markets. In chapter 4 we described "market profile analysis." The analogy for ideas is called "product profile analysis." When applied to product ideas the scales may be more refined and some new scales added. For example, specific scales on the probability of commercial success or the probability of successful technical development could be added. Individual cost scales such as development or production costs are useful. These scales and the ratings of the ideas by managers are a good way to be sure all aspects of each idea have been considered. This checklist function is important because although idea generation is a creative outburst, this outburst must be tempered by a disciplined look at the feasibility and reward potential of each idea.

Product profile analysis can be coupled with project selection indices. R&D management has specified and tested such procedures to select projects. Examining these methods and experience yields insights that are useful in not only R&D project selection, but in prioritizing ideas. The most basic procedure is to divide the expected return by the development cost:

$$I = \frac{T \times C \times P}{D} \qquad (5.1)$$

where I = index of attractiveness

T = probability of successful technical development

C = probability of commercial success given that it is technically successful

P = profit if successful

D = cost of development

If an idea is already feasible, the probability of technical success (T) will be high and the cost of development low (D). For the same profitability (P) and chance of commercial success (C), this project would be preferred to an idea that requires a technological breakthrough (low T and high D). This simple formula is one way of trading off the different risks, return, and levels of knowledge of various ideas. After the index I is calculated for each project, they are ranked and the projects with the highest I are considered for funding. (Final decisions include qualitative judgments that augment the index.)

As in market selection these formulas should be used more as a guide for discussion and judgment than as a final selection output. The model often oversimplifies the problem and biases towards small projects where uncertainty is low. Selection at this stage of development is more art than science. Many more complex models of project selection have been developed (E. B. Roberts 1974; Pessemier 1966; Baker 1974; Baker et al. 1976). Recently, financial option theory has been applied to R&D project selection (see Brealy and Meyers 1991 for a discussion of options). However, few of these advanced techniques are used by industry. Even the basic model in equation (5.1) is used with caution because of the difficulty in accurately estimating costs and probabilities. Meadows (1968) studied five firms (three chemical labs, one electronics lab, and one equipment manufacturer) and found that the correlation of actual to estimated cost was only 0.50. The ratio of actual to estimated cost varied from 4.25 to 0.96 over the labs. Marshall and Meckling (1962) found a ratio of 1.78 in ethical drugs and 2.11 in proprietary drugs, whereas Norris (1971) found the ratio varied from 1.5 to 0.97 for industrial products in England. It is apparently difficult to estimate accurately the cost of an R&D project. In addition to the uncertainty of estimation, Mansfield et al. (1971, p. 213) think that inaccuracies also stem from "deliberate under-estimations" used to marshal support for a project. In studying the discrep-ancies, Meadows found the ratio of actual to estimated costs to be greater for project failures than for successes. One explanation may be the tendency not to give up on a project and to continue to allocate funds to it even when success seems unlikely. Although costs are difficult to estimate, probabilities are even more difficult. Meadows found almost no correlation between the estimated probabilities of technical or commercial success and the observed fractions of success. Furthermore Rubenstein and Schroder (1977) found that personal, organizational, and situational variables have major impacts on estimated probabilities. For example, project originators and those with im-plementation responsibility tend to give more optimistic estimates than the average, whereas those with a "knowledge gap" about technical feasibility tend to give more pessimistic estimates.

These difficulties in cost and probability estimates suggest simplicity in the screening process because a more complex process tends to hide the inaccuracies in these estimates. Furthermore, these potential inaccuracies suggest that any estimates be treated with extreme caution and that steps be taken to minimize organizational bias on the costs and probabilities.

However, these cautions do not diminish the need for *some* process to screen ideas. Such a process should allow a critical look at the many aspects of the alternative ideas as they relate to new product development. Further-more, a process fosters dialogue among the disparate interest groups in-volved. It seems reasonable to consider costs and probabilities, but not to use a rigid formula to select ideas. We recommend the use of these factors as part of a product profile analysis. The profile analysis serves as a checklist and a guide to managerial discussion and decision making. The primary goal of such a formal screening process is to eliminate poor ideas and select those ideas which appear to be best.

Number of Ideas

How many ideas should be identified for design work? It is reasonable to assume that there are "good" ideas and "bad" ideas, with their distribution as shown in Figure 5.10.

If we consider generating an idea as making a random draw from the normal distribution of Figure 5.10 and we generate only one idea each time we develop a product, we will get an average expected reward. If we could generate two independent ideas and select the "best" one, the expected value would be substantially greater. As more ideas are generated for a development opportunity, the expected reward increases. The overall gain depends on how

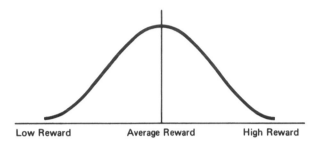

Low Reward   Average Reward   High Reward

Figure 5.10   Distribution of Potential Rewards for Ideas

many ideas are sampled, the variance in the distribution of ideas, the reliability and validity of our methods of finding the "best" idea, and the costs of generating ideas (see Marschak Glennan, and Summers 1967, pp. 13–48; and chapter 15 for more detail as we consider advertising copy generation).

In almost all cases, the rewards of generating several ideas are greater than the costs. We strongly suggest generating alternative ideas for each market opportunity or technological approach and not becoming committed to one idea alone. A common pitfall in new products is selecting the first idea and allocating large amounts of resources to it without considering alternatives that may be better.

The first idea may not reflect a major innovation in the market. It is important to allocate substantial creative attention to developing products that revolutionize markets. These may revise the structure of the markets by adding new dimensions to product performance through technology or by creating new market segments. To find these major innovations the market must be stimulated by major new idea concepts or prototypes. Consumer perceptions must be "stretched" to determine the potential of new dimensions and technologically challenged by ideas that may meet new major market needs. The examples of watches shown in Figure 5.8 stretch the market and technology. Watches that report pulse rate and blood pressure would represent new health dimensions for the product. We term these revolutionary ideas "stretchers." They represent new market and technical options. Many of the stretchers will not find market acceptance, but they may lead to understanding of major new opportunities in the market.

SUMMARY

The creation of major innovations and product ideas completes the opportunity identification phase of the new product development process. This opportunity identification begins with market definition. Many markets are identified with characteristics compatible with the organization. These are screened via market profile analysis to identify a high potential set for further analysis. More detailed information is gathered and the competitive structure of each market is modeled hierarchically. Target groups are specified through market segmentation. Finally these alternatives are examined carefully to select a portfolio of "markets" of attractive risk-return characteristics and to select the best initial, competitive definition for that market.

Given the market definition and target group, the organization then develops ideas for products to take advantage of the identified opportunities. A large number of ideas are generated through direct search, technological innovation, exploratory consumer studies, facilitating lead user solutions, integration of technology and marketing, creative group methods, national development programs, and alliances, acquisitions, and licensing. Emphasis is on breadth and creativity because alternatives enhance the chances for success and the greatest success often comes from the most innovative ideas. Finally, a relatively simple screening process is used to guide discussion and to select a few good ideas from those generated. These three or four innovative ideas represented by innovative concepts or product prototypes, as well as the market target group segmentation, are the initial inputs to the design phase. Because the market was chosen because of its strategic growth and profit potential and because the ideas were created to meet specific needs in this market through technological innovation, the opportunity defined by the set of ideas should be significant.

The next step in the new product development process is to design the product physically and psychologically to exploit the market opportunity by creating benefits for its customers. Use of measurement and models to understand consumer response and R&D, engineering, and production skills will lead to a final design. This design is then tested and, if successful, introduced.

REVIEW QUESTIONS

5.1. Why is idea generation important?

5.2. Investigate two recent and possibly significant technological advances. For each, generate three new product ideas for three different consumer needs.

5.3. Select three of the methods of generating new product ideas that were discussed in the chapter. For each method,
  a. Discuss the role of communication among individuals involved.
  b. Discuss the costs of employing the method.
  c. State which industries would find the method most valuable and why.
  d. Describe the generation of a hypothetical product when employing the method.

5.4. What are the advantages and disadvantages of creative groups?

5.5. The following table illustrates managerial judgments on the probability of successful technical development of an idea (*T*), the probability of commercial success given that it is technically successful (*C*), the profit if successful (*P*) and the estimated cost of development (*D*).

Idea	T	C	P	D
A	.7–.9	.2–.4	1.1–1.3	.1–.9
B	.1–.3	.7	2.2–2.5	1.2–1.9
C	.8	.4	1.3–1.4	.3–.4
D	.4–.5	.5–.9	.1–2.2	.1–.2
E	.2	.7	3.3–3.4	3.0
F	.6	.6	1.3–1.4	.9

    a. Compute the index of attractiveness for each idea.

    b. For each idea, discuss what information the index captures and what information the index ignores.

    c. What product ideas does the index dismiss as inferior? Would you dismiss those ideas?

    d. Where should managerial effort be directed when attempting idea selection?

    e. What are the limitations of this method of idea selection?

5.6. Suppose a single individual working alone would generate ideas of similar quality. Would it be more valuable for a single individual to generate 10 separate ideas or for 10 individuals to each generate one idea?

5.7. Suppose 10 individuals working alone would come up with 10 very different ideas. However, 10 individuals working together would generate 10 similar ideas but of better average quality. Should the individuals work apart or together?

5.8. How might a hospital supply firm encourage users to innovate? How might the hospital supply firm set up an information network to discover and use these innovations?

5.9. Develop two stretcher concepts for urban transportation service.

5.10. Develop two stretcher concepts for a warehouse heating system.

5.11. What are the advantages and disadvantages of focus groups? How do focus groups provide new product ideas?

5.12. Use a technology/market segment matrix to develop ideas for a new electric automobile.

5.13. Do a direct search of idea sources for a new environmentally sound packaging product for beverages.

5.14. What is the role of gatekeepers in idea generation? How can this role be encouraged? How does geographical layout affect the effectiveness of gatekeepers?

PART THREE

Design Process

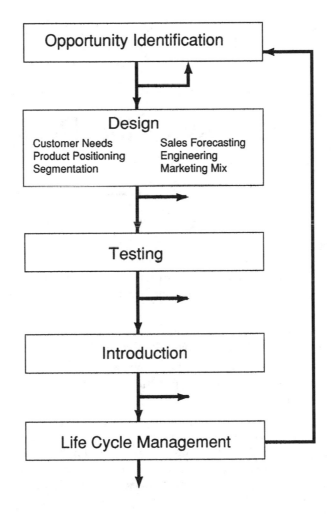

6

An Overview of the Design Process

DESIGN

We turn now to the goal of "designing" a profitable product and marketing strategy for the priority market that has been identified. We consider "design" to be the

1. Identification of the key benefits the product is to provide to customers
2. Positioning of these benefits versus competitive products
3. Development of a physical product, marketing strategy, and service policy to fulfill the key benefits

We summarize the key benefits in a statement called the *Core Benefit Proposition* (CBP). The CBP states the unique benefits that the product is to provide customers as well as those benefits required to meet and surpass competition. It must be clear and concise, striking immediately to the essential characteristics of the product's strategy in terms of the benefits it delivers to users. It forms the keystone upon which all elements of the marketing strategy are built and the vision that underlies the engineering design. For example,

- *American Express Traveler's Cheques.* Accepted everywhere; prompt replacement and complete protection if lost; prestige.
- *Hewlett-Packard Laserjet.* Quietly prints documents with excellent print quality on several media and in several types. Easy to use and maintain, reliable, and flexible.
- *Silkience Self-Adjusting Shampoo.* A shampoo that provides the appropriate amount of cleaning treatment (automatically) for different parts of your hair. Cleans the roots without drying the ends of your hair.
- *Personal-Care Hospital.* A full-service hospital committed to the personalization of health care. Provides high-quality primary care to the patient, increased accessibility of the staff, and a friendly, caring, "first-name" atmosphere.
- *Sear's Die-Hard Battery.* Longer-lasting battery with more power output.

Each CBP is short and to the point, stressing the key features of appeals that are special to the new product or market. In some cases, the target market is explicit in the CBP; in other cases it is implicit in the market definition. The CBP is stated from the customer's perspective indicating what is important to the customer and what will encourage the customer to purchase the product. It is not simply an advertising appeal, but rather a basic description of the overall strategy in terms of customer benefit. It is more than a technical description of the product because it specifies the benefits that the customer derives from the product.

Customers (consumers) buy products for the benefits that they perceive the product delivers. Consider, for example, General Motors and Toyota in the 1980s. Toyota built cars on the same production line in the "NUMI" joint venture. The Toyota Celica outsold the Chevrolet NOVA by a factor of 2, even though the only difference was the brand name. Customers perceived that the Toyota was a better product.

The CBP forces the design team of management, marketing, engineering, production, and other functions to reach a consensus on basic benefits and services. The engineering team makes tradeoffs in the physical product which reflect the CBP; the production process is implemented to assure that the benefits are delivered; the advertising agency develops advertising copy to communicate the CBP; the marketing strategists ensure that the price and distribution strategies are consistent with the CBP; and any quality control service activities are focused on characteristics of the product that are key to the CBP.

The CBP is simple to state—but not simple to attain. It is the end result of a careful new product design process that identifies the needs and priorities of the customer, develops a feasible design to deliver those benefits, and coordinates a marketing effort to communicate those benefits. For example, the Sear's Die-Hard Battery was a physically superior product and it was advertised as such. Conversely, General Motors discovered that quality must first be designed into a car before it can be advertised as such.

We now state a design process which develops a CBP. It is a conceptual representation of the key decisions that a design team must address to assure that the CBP does indeed reflect customer needs. The design process is based on an understanding of consumer behavior that recognizes that consumers (customers) make decisions about products based on their perceptions of those products and based on the priorities they implicitly assign to product benefits. Physical product characteristics affect these decisions but through the "lens" of product perceptions.[1] The design process recognizes and makes explicit the steps that the design team goes through to assure that the CBP is right for the market and that the product and marketing are right for the CBP.

THE DESIGN PROCESS

We represent the design process by a set of managerial responsibilities, the left side of Figure 6.1, and a set of customer analyses, the right side of Figure 6.1. The managerial subprocess represents the three phases of decisions the new product team must address—the market (opportunity definition), the product, technology, and marketing (refinement), and the business opportunity (evaluation). The managerial process draws information from and provides information to the customer analyses which represent key summaries of customer needs and desires. Customer measurement provides the raw data; the summary of the customer represents that data in a format that can be used by managers, and the "what-if" forecasts provide a means to evaluate the business opportunity.

Opportunity Definition

Market definition is a review and refinement of the markets and target customers that were the output of opportunity identification. A successful opportunity identification will have indicated a market that has the greatest potential to achieve managerial goals such as profit and growth. The design

[1] See E. Brunswick, *The Conceptual Framework of Psychology* (Chicago: University of Chicago Press, 1952). For a marketing example see A. M. Tybout, and J. R. Hauser, "A Marketing Audit Using a Conceptual Model of Consumer Behavior: Application and Evaluation," *Journal of Marketing*, 45, no. 3 (Summer 1981): 81-101.

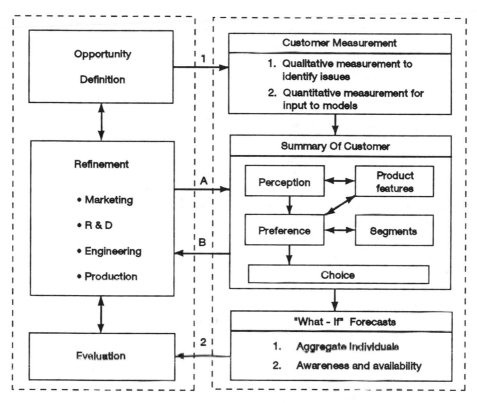

Figure 6.1 New-Product Design Process

process begins with this definition but uses the detailed information on customers and technology to refine the target so in the end the product, the marketing, and the strategy are coordinated. Similarly, as information is uncovered about the needs and desires of customers, management may decide to modify the definition of that target as well.

For example, consider the case of plentiful squid introduced in chapter 3. Seafood such as lobsters, cod, sole, and clams is becoming scarce and costly, whereas squid, a high-protein source, is plentiful off the coasts of the United States. There is little demand for squid in the American market, although many foreign markets such as Europe and Japan find squid a delicacy. In market definition the new product team must decide whether to promote squid to the gourmet delicacy market, the fresh produce market, the prepared frozen food market, the ethnic markets, or the canned food (chowder) market. Opportunity identification will have focused on one of these markets as high potential, but as information is gathered from potential customers the new product team may decide to refine the definition.

Within a market customers may vary in their tastes. Thus the new product team must decide further whether the target customers are affluent gourmets (squid as a delicacy), bargain hunters (squid is plentiful and easy to catch), or special nationalities (squid is considered a specialty by some). By gaining information of the size of the markets, the price range appropriate for the markets, the technical characteristics (does the average consumer want the squid precleaned and precooked?), and potential competition, the new product team hones the target market.

Customer Measurement

Successful new products deliver benefits that customers need. A cornerstone of the design process is to listen to the voice of the customer to understand customer needs.

The customer-response investigation begins with qualitative measurement that enables the design team to learn what motivates customers, how they see the current market, which products and combinations of products they now use, how they gain information about products, how they go about purchasing the products, and so on. For example, focus groups or one-on-one interviews might provide the new product team with initial insight and a list of customer needs which can be later quantified.

Qualitative measurement raises questions, suggests some answers, and directs investigation, but alone it is not sufficient. Quantitative measurement builds upon the qualitative insights to provide quantifiable measures of customer perceptions of existing products, of customer priorities with respect to alternative product benefits, and to provide input to the models underlying the "what-if" analyses. This measurement often takes the form of telephone, mail, or personal interview surveys. For example, after focus groups identify 20 to 30 key attributes of seafood, a 10-page questionnaire might be used to measure how customers evaluate lobsters, cod, sole, clams, and other seafood on these attributes. The same questionnaire might measure which attributes are most important to customers and provide some initial reaction to "stretching" concept statements for squid-based products.

Strategic Summary of the Customer's Input

Customer measurement provides information, but to be useful that information needs to be organized and summarized so that it can direct the strategic development of the new product. Figure 6.1 provides a structure with which to organize that information. This structure is organized around models of product features, perceptions, preferences, segmentation, and choice to help management diagnose the market. Together these models identify the product benefits that are key to a new product's success and they identify how to achieve those benefits in the design of the product. For example, airline customers prefer new aircraft designs to old ones, punctual arrivals to late arrivals, friendly and courteous stewardesses to aloof stewardesses, movies to magazines, no stops to one stop, no crowds to crowds, and more frequent service.[2] But if we are limited in the amount of money we can spend to improve service, if we are looking only for cost effective improvements, or we want a strategy consistent with a target market, which of these design features should we change? Or should we even limit ourselves to these improvements? Maybe the greatest impact comes from having news/shorts instead of movies, or free wine, or comfortable waiting areas, or bargain fares, or courtesy ground transportation, or more carry-on luggage compartments, or personal computer and facsimile service in the waiting area and on board? All are improvements—but which are the key improvements and how do you communicate these improvements to potential passengers?

To identify the key leverage points, we summarize the customer's input to highlight the information most relevant to the new product team. *Perception* models might tell the airline company that the key strategic benefit dimensions are quality service, a comfortable trip, convenient and on-time service, safety, low cost, and so on. *Preference* might tell the airline company that a comfortable trip is more important than low cost and *product features* might tell the airline company how to achieve comfortable trips with the design of the physical product (seats, aisles, waiting areas), with the management of the services (help from the stewardesses and gate attendants), and with ancillary features (food, magazines, etc.). Perception and preference helps the team select which benefits to include in the CBP and how much emphasis to put on each. Product features tells the team what can be done to realize the CBP. A key focus in these efforts is the quality of the resulting product or service.

Segmentation determines whether the best strategy is to have one product for all customers or whether to have a line of products, each directed at a specific group of customer benefits. For example, some airline companies have created an intermediate category of service between first class and economy class for the segment of business travelers who can pay the full coach fares. Although we may have segmented the market in the opportunity identification phase of development, we may want to make a more macro segmentation at this design phase based on benefit importances. Finally, *choice* determines what other events or phenomena affect the purchase decision in addition to the customers' perceptions and preferences. It tells the new product team what must be controlled, or at least considered, in the design and

---

[2] Paul Green, and Jerry Wind (1975), "New Way to Measure Consumer's Judgments," *Harvard Business Review* (July-August): 107–17.

marketing of the product. For example, an airline company must first make customers aware of a change in service and the service must be available to them (serve the routes they need). The product design team would also consider the influence of travel agents and company travel policies which affect the decisions of individual travelers. Taken together, the five component models summarize succinctly and effectively the information that the new product team needs to make the necessary strategic decisions in product design.

Preliminary "What-If" Forecasts

Before committing funds, often millions of dollars, to the launch of a new product, top management wants a forecast of customer response—sales. If the submodels of perception, preference, and choice are developed carefully, they can be used to forecast customer response. The idea is deceivingly simple. Customer measurement identifies how each customer (in a representative sample) perceives each existing product that they consider. The new product design includes a description of the product features that are linked through analysis and judgment to a prediction of how the new product will be perceived by each customer in the sample. The preference model predicts how each customer will compare the new product to the existing products in their consideration sets and the choice model forecasts the likelihood that the customer will actually purchase the new product. The forecast of sales is then an aggregation of the predictions of behavior for individual customers.

For example, suppose that an airline decides to offer a new service. Based on the features of the service and the marketing plan, the customer models will predict (1) how each potential customer (in the sample) will perceive the new service with respect to the quality of service, comfortableness of the trip, convenience and on-time service, safety, low cost, and other relevant dimensions; (2) how many customers will select the service as their first choice, their second choice, and so on; and (3) for potential passengers the probability that they would choose the service were they aware of it and were it available to them. If everyone were aware of the service and found it available, and if there were no influences because of travel agents and company travel policies, the expected demand for airline's service would simply be a sum of the individual predictions. Of course, the forecast would need to be adjusted for awareness, availability, and external influences in order to be accurate.

The output of "what-if" analyses is more than a single number representing a sales forecast. Rather it is a series of forecasts that depend on variables under the control of the new product team such as initial price and marketing strategy and, perhaps, product features. It will also depend on assumptions of competitive action and reaction.

Evaluation

The "what-if" forecasts form the basis for evaluation of the business opportunity. In evaluation the top management and the new product team weigh the forecasts, production costs, political constraints, technology considerations, material availability, labor issues, firm image, complementarity with product lines, and other aspects of new product introduction to arrive at a go/on/no go decision. Go means that the product concept has high promise and should go on to the next phase of development. No go means that the product is unlikely to return its investment even if it is vastly improved. On means that the evaluated product has potential but modification of the product or the marketing plan is necessary for it to be a success. An on decision means that the organization should continue with the design process looking for an improved CBP, product, and marketing plan.

Refinement

It is rare that a successful product is identified on the first iteration through the design process. Early in the design process, after an on evaluation, the new product team proceeds to refinement where the product and marketing are improved based on the diagnostic information summarized by the models of customers. For example, an airline might select as a target a superpremium coach service but find that while travelers prefer the service, it conflicts with the travel guidelines of many key corporate clients. The design team would then need to gather more information about these guidelines and reposition the service to meet these guidelines. Refinement would also include the modification of product features (in-flight amenities, waiting-area services, priority access to preferred seating, etc.) to assure that they fulfill the CBP in a cost effective manner and that it is feasible to deliver the service given the volume that is expected.

If the improvements are minor, the models which provide the strategic summary of the customer's input can be used to forecast the impact of the changes (see arrows A and B in Figure 6.1); however, if the improvements represent a major redesign, the new-product team may need to undertake new customer measurement and recalibrate the customer models (see arrows 1 and 2 in Figure 6.1).

As shown in Figure 6.1, refinement depends on the effective integration of marketing, R&D, engineering, production, and other functional areas of the organization. Successful new products deliver the CBP and to deliver the CBP each of these functions must be involved in the design. Marketing ensures that the customer's voice is represented and that the communication plan provides a positioning consistent with the CBP; R&D ensures that the best technology is used so that the product is "parity-plus" or "break-through"; engineering ensures that the physical product fulfills the CBP in a cost-effective manner; and production assures that the product can be built and the associated services delivered in a manner of consistent quality, low cost, and continuous improvement. The refinement activities are a part of a total quality commitment in effective organizations.

Summary

The output of this iterative process is the specification of the best CBP and a product that fulfills the promise through features and positioning. The final design is the specification of

- Target market and target group of customers
- CBP
- Positioning of the product versus competition
- Features of the product to fulfill the CBP
- Initial price, advertising, promotional, sales, and distribution strategies consistent with the CBP

After marketing, engineering, R&D, and production are satisfied with the product and its supporting advertising, and so on, we leave the design phase of new-product development and enter the testing phase.

KEY ASPECTS OF THE DESIGN PROCESS

The conceptual design process of Figure 6.1 is a logical way to proceed. In the chapters that follow we describe many details of the process, but before we turn to those details we would like to emphasize some key aspects of the design activity.

1. *A new product is both a physical entity and a psychological positioning.* A product must perform from an engineering viewpoint, but customers will not buy the product if they do not perceive that it delivers the benefits they need. For example, the right amount of fluoride is important in a toothpaste, but it is not enough. The toothpaste must be seen as decay preventing and must deliver on other attributes as well such as taste, cleaning, prevention of gum disease, and so on. This image depends on the advertising, the packaging, the color, the way the toothpaste is promoted, and of course the product's ingredients. Procter and

Gamble's Crest toothpaste positioned fluoride as a substantiation of decay prevention (reinforced with the American Dental Association approval), but within the image that using Crest was being a good parent. Their "Look Mom, No Cavities" advertising strategy showed peer group approval for the parents who had their children use Crest.

Similarly, new tartar control toothpastes and rinses must be perceived as effective before consumers will buy them. Even if they are effective clinically, consumers must believe they will deliver the benefits of tooth hygiene. Otherwise consumers will not adopt the new innovation.

Vitamins are perceived as a way of reducing stress in Japan, but do not have these perceived benefits in America or Europe where nutrition is the chief benefit. Perceptions and their link to engineering variables are critical to understand if good product design is to be achieved in meeting worldwide opportunities.

2. *The design process is iterative.* Design is not accomplished in one step. Evaluation, refinement, and learning occur sequentially. In the market-definition phase, the new product team is concerned with the potential of a category. Early in the process, the design team concentrates on developing a good basic appeal and image of the product. Later they concentrate on the specific physical and psychological features that achieve the chosen positioning. Finally, they select the full marketing strategy. As the product proceeds through this process from idea to concept to prototype to production, it is continually refined and improved. At all times the team must be willing to backtrack and reassess the market, position, product, and technology. But overall consistency is important in achieving the learning necessary to succeed.

3. *New product design is integrative. All* functions, marketing, engineering, R&D, and production, must cooperate if the new product is to be a success. R&D provides the technology, but technology is good only when it works. Engineering must assure that the CBP is delivered when the customer uses the product under field conditions. Marketing can identify customer wants and needs, but this information must be integrated with engineering to select the most profitable CBP. Products designed to be produced can deliver higher quality more consistently than products that work well as prototypes but are complex and expensive to produce. Production factors must be integrated early in the design process. Integration leads to better quality products, less expensive products, and products that are brought to market faster.

4. *Both prediction and understanding are necessary.* If prediction were the only goal of the marketing research in the design process, the strategic sum-

mary of the customer's input would be unnecessary. Because the design process is iterative and new product teams are fallible, the models of the customer provide valuable information with which to improve the product and marketing strategy and with which to refine the CBP. If an airline service is not "right" the first time, the models tell the new product team why and how to get it "right."

5. *The level of analysis should reflect tradeoffs between time-to-market and completeness.* It is always possible to spend more time and more funds on analysis, but this may delay the launch and cause the product to miss the "window" of opportunity. The required level of detail depends on the decision to be made. The "best" model is one that more efficiently supplies the required input at the specific point in the decision process. High accuracy may not be necessary early in the concept-development phase, but the need for accuracy increases when the product and its marketing strategy are evaluated for graduation to the testing phase. In the concept-development phase, money spent on predictive accuracy might better be invested in obtaining the understanding necessary to improve the product features and/or the positioning. All uncertainty cannot be removed so spending too much time on design could be a mistake, but not having sufficient customer response data could lead to an inferior design and poor fit of market needs and product features. These problems need to be balanced so that the time to market can be short and the quality of the product high.[3]

6. *The design process blends managerial judgment with qualitative and quantitative techniques.* Each aspect, managerial judgment, qualitative input, and quantitative analysis, is important. No one aspect can stand alone. Judgment is important but can be led astray. Quantitative techniques are "exact," but if they attack the wrong problem, they can be exactly wrong. Blending these aspects is an art, but once learned, it is a powerful art. The effective new product team combines quantitative and qualitative methods and creative thinking. New-product development is both an art and a science.

These six points help you keep the design process in perspective. By using a balanced mix of coordinated techniques and by integrating information obtained from the customer with cooperation between functions in the organization, you are in a better position to solve the basic problem: designing a successful new product.

---

[3] See Rosenbloom and Cusumano (1987) for a discussion of how six firms made these tradeoffs in the video cassette recorder (VCR) industry.

SUMMARY

The new product design process in Figure 6.1 is proactive. It stresses understanding the customer and the technical, production, and marketing capabilities of the organization to develop a new product based on customer needs.

The process of new product development entails (1) identifying an opportunity, (2) *designing* a product to exploit the opportunity, (3) testing the product and its marketing strategy, (4) launching and tracking the new product, and (5) managing the product life cycle. *Designing* a product is perhaps the most creative and challenging part of the new product development process. A product *design* involves

- Target group of customers
- The Core Benefit Proposition to be delivered (CBP)
- Positioning of the new product vis-à-vis the competition (if any)
- Product features and technology to deliver and substantiate the positioning and product quality
- Advertising, pricing, promotion, sales, service, distribution, and launch strategy to support the position

A new product design is complete when we know *who* will buy (target), *how* it will sell (benefits), *why* our offering is superior (positioning), *what* we will deliver to customers (features), and how to *communicate* and *distribute* the CBP (advertising, selling, channels, and technology).

REVIEW QUESTIONS

6.1. A key goal of the design process is the CBP. What is a CBP? Why is it important? What should a CBP contain?

6.2. Consider a new consumer packaged good, a new durable good, and, if you are familiar with the market, a new high-technology product. What are their core benefit propositions? Do you think that these CBP's are well developed for the markets? If so, why? If not, why not?

6.3. Discuss how the strategic summary of the customer's input facilitates the development of a core benefit proposition. What information is provided that helps the new product team refine the new product ideas?

6.4. When a go/on/no go decision is made, what costs and benefits must be considered? Be sure to consider opportunity costs.

6.5. Discuss the relationship between the physical features of the product, technology base of the product, positioning of the product, marketing mix, and the core benefit proposition.

7

Customer Measurement—
A Review

The success of a proactive design strategy depends on determining a product strategy that will be attractive to customers. Throughout this book several managerial and analytical techniques are introduced to design and position products in such a way as to attract and serve customers, but these techniques and the products they imply are only as good as the data on which they are based. The customer measurement that produces these data is critical to the success of new product strategy. Careful, exacting market research can lead to creative insights into customer wants and needs and result in superior products. Careless research will cause the new product team to miss opportunities and, in many cases, lead to errors in product design.

This chapter reviews some of the considerations in customer measurement that are particularly important in new product design. It is not a substitute for a course in market research; rather, it is meant to highlight briefly the relevant topics and provide specific examples relevant to new products. It serves as a review for those who have studied and practiced market research. For more detail on market research in general, readers are referred to Churchill (1991), Green, Tull and Albaum (1988), Lehmann (1988), and Payne (1951). A recent book by Barabba and Zaltman entitled *Hearing the*

Voice of the Market (1991) is a particularly valuable source book for market research in the 1990s.

LISTENING TO CUSTOMERS AND THE MARKET

Based on the arguments developed earlier we concluded that technology, marketing, and production must be integrated for effective product design. One would expect that the role of marketing research is firmly established in the process of development. Marketing research is well accepted but is not without controversy. Many writers still refer to the "marketing research failure" that was associated with the Edsel. Polaroid strategy is remembered as being based on technology and Mr. Land's knowledge of what people wanted and not market research. The New Coke reformulation disaster was undertaken after extensive market research. Akio Morita, the founder of the very successful SONY corporation said "Our plan is to lead the public to new products rather than ask them what they want. The public does not know what is possible, but we do" (Barabba and Zaltman 1991, p. 31).

It is worth looking at each of these situations and seeing what can be learned. First the Edsel was not completely researched—there was no styling research for example. The biggest research project was around the car name (two surveys of 800 people each probing names and feeling about cars) and largely it was ignored by the Ford executive committee (Barabba and Zaltman 1991, p. 27). One lesson here is to be sure to research all the critical aspects of product response and integrate the findings into the decision process.

Second consider the Polaroid experience. Although Polaroid was initially successful with Mr. Land's knowledge of the importance of the instant feature in photography, Polaroid is now using marketing research extensively to develop and forecast new products. A Market Research Director at Polaroid has said:

> Polaroid's driving force was its research and engineering; its new approach is market driven and has opened new doors for marketing and marketing research. Several primary studies were conducted to understand business and market shares. This new focus on the consumer revealed four segments—consumer pleasure, industrial, business amateur, and OEM—and helped the firm market effectively to these groups. Marketing information was instrumental in refining businesses into the right market sectors. (Krishnan, Marketing Science Institute, 1989, p. 10)

The lesson here is that technical breakthroughs can be the basis of successful products if the innovator's customer-need intuition is correct, but this technology driven process can be improved by supplementing technical creativity with market information.

New Coke's market response was unexpected, but the taste testing research did not include the Coke brand identification which was critical in the eventual market lack of acceptance. Changing the Coke formulation was in itself a major cue to response in the market. Again the lesson is that market research is valid only if it includes the key response variables. Coke executives did not include the coke identification in the tests because they did not want anyone to know they were considering changing the formulation. This is understandable, but it rendered the research invalid. Do the research "right" or do not do it at all.

Finally consider Mr. Morita's quote that indicates that market research is not needed and will be misleading. This reflects a technology-driven viewpoint and lack of knowledge of the state of the art of marketing research. It is true that you can not naively ask customers "What do you want?" Customers can not answer this question if they have not experienced the potential of a new technology. However, state-of-the-art market research represented by lead user analysis (see chapter 5) and new premarket forecasting techniques that accelerate the customer into the future technological environment and then ask for response to specific product designs (see chapters 12 and 16 for a discussion of "information acceleration" methods) can overcome the inability of customers to react to very new products. One can also now wonder if Sony could in fact have been more successful if it had integrated its technological creativity with some market tradeoff information. For example, Sony's commitment to BETAMAX rather than VHS could have been researched. This research would have been likely to show that standard availability rather than size of the tape is most important and helped to prevent SONY's commitments to the runner up technology. Market research is being adopted in Japan and many Japanese companies are joining American and European companies who view marketing as the critical competence for the 1990s and market research as its most important technology (see "Special Issue: Marketing Research in Japan" *Journal of Advertising Research* (1990) for a description of the level of practice in Japan).

We think that in the 1990s market research will be increasing in importance as this technology advances to include measurement of radical innovation and responses in the industrial and services as well as consumer product markets. As the capabilities of the methods improve it will become even more essential that the research be done well and properly integrated into the firm's decision support system (see Scott Morton [1991] for a review of the impact of information technologies on the firm). In this chapter we will review some of the elements essential for quality market research and some of the pitfalls to avoid when doing customer measurement.

Even with technological advancements in research methods, formal market research supplements managements' understanding of its markets; it does not substitute for it. Figure 7.1 shows that value increases even though the amount of information is reduced as the data is turned into information, intelligence, knowledge and wisdom. It is the wisdom of management that leads to the success of companies. In the future market research will be a valuable component in the system to create such wisdom.

CUSTOMER MEASUREMENT PROCESS

It is important to remember that in developing new products, market research is conducted to support decision making and to create knowledge, intelligence, and wisdom. Although many interesting behavioral issues might be addressed in a customer survey, the managerial usefulness is judged by the survey's ability to improve decisions and generate insight. In this book, market research provides the voice of the customer and supports models that lead managers to improved new product designs and to higher chances for new product success.

Figure 7.2 shows a measurement process that begins with decision requirements and proceeds to decision models. The decision requirements are key considerations in deciding the methodology for the study. Should a questionnaire be used? Will a different method yield the information more effectively? Should qualitative or quantitative measures be used? Is an experimental variation of decision variables necessary? These methodological issues must

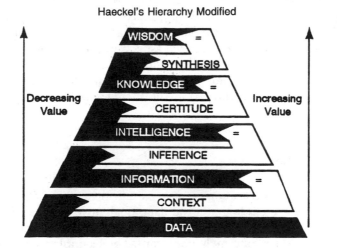

Figure 7.1   Haeckel's Hierarchy Modified (Barabba and Zaltman 1991, p. 45)

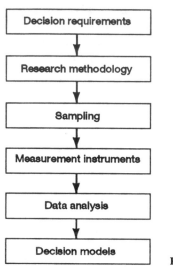

Figure 7.2   Customer Measurement Process

reflect the accuracy required, the costs, and the value in terms of improved decisions. One explicit cost tradeoff is in sampling. What sample size is required? Should the sample be random or is a purposive sample more appropriate? If the appropriate method is a survey, the questionnaire must next be formulated and tested. Many pitfalls await the untrained person in writing a questionnaire. Inaccuracies due to ambiguity or to unwillingness or inability to respond must be minimized. Once the measurement instrument (or qualitative protocol) is agreed upon, the data collection is undertaken and the data analyzed. If everything proceeds well, the process results in decision models that enable the new product team to design and market a profitable product.

In this chapter we review selected aspects in each phase of the measurement process. The issues presented are those most critical to successful design of new products. The remaining chapters present additional measurement issues and demonstrate the link of measurement to analysis and to managerial decision making.

RESEARCH METHODS

To be effective an organization must make effective use of all forms of customer information including archival data, qualitative studies, and quantitative research. Early in the new-product design process archival data and qualitative studies are extremely important. For example, focus groups are effective for idea generation because they do not constrain customer response to preconceived ideas. However, as the product development process proceeds, the quantitative measures become essential. But even then, quantitative measurements should not be used alone. Usually, the analysis process begins with qualitative techniques and an archival search to raise issues, to identify customer needs, to provide customer semantics, and to help direct the quantitative measurement to the areas that appear to be most productive.

Archival Search

A proactive strategy searches for new ideas, but this does not mean that existing data sources are to be ignored. Secondary data (i.e., data collected for reasons other than new product development) can provide useful information that may direct the search to more productive areas or save the expense of gathering data that is available from other sources. This data might come from internal sources, U.S. government statistics, special data services, or other external sources.

Internal Sources. Some internal sources may relate specifically to the product category under investigation. If the organization already has a product in the category or if we are considering a major change to an existing product, then sales records, advertising records, complaint/compliment files, or warranty records may provide useful clues to opportunities. For example, we have already illustrated how leading edge users develop their own new products. By sensitizing the sales force to these users, the new product team can gather useful input on user needs (and solutions). In another example, software firms might monitor help-lines to uncover features that cause users trouble—features that must be improved with new generations of the software. Occasionally market research will have been done to monitor a category or innovate in a related category, or product managers with experience in the category can provide insights worth further investigation.

Government Statistics. U.S. Census figures (population, retail trade, service industries, wholesale trade, manufacturers, mineral industries, transportation, agriculture, and government) or other government statistics (*Business Statistics, County Business Patterns, County and City Data Book, Economic Indicators, Economic Report of the President, Federal Reserve Bulletin, Federal Statistical Directory, Handbook of Cyclical Indicators, Monthly Labor Review, State and Metropolitan Area Data Book, Statistics of Income, Survey of Current Business*, etc.— see Churchill [1991] for a complete list) can be used to monitor demographic changes or for an estimate of category potential. For example, stackable washer/dryers are an innovation resulting from the recognition through governmental data of the number of apartment and condominium dwellers. Furthermore, the demographics can be used to check the representativeness of a customer survey. Another government source worth investigating is the *Statistical Abstract of the United States*—this secondary source can be used to search for primary sources of government data. Similar data can be obtained in Europe, Canada, the Far East, South America, Australia, and Africa but the quantity and quality of information varies by country.

    Special Data Services.   Some examples of special data services are (1) national retail scanning data (Information Resources Inc. [IRI]—Infoscan, Nielsen Retail Index, and GFK and AGB in Europe); (2) electronic Test Markets (e.g., Behavior Scan by IRI); (3) media ratings (e.g., Arbitron Ratings, Nielsen Television Index, the Starch Advertisement Readership Service, the Simmons Media/Marketing Services); and (4) consumer panel data (e.g., IRI, Nielsen, National Family Opinion [NFO] Panel). Although all of these are available at some cost to the user, they may be cost-effective for specific categories and for putting together components of the marketing strategy. Finally, there are published sources of archival data such as Moody's Manuals, the Rand McNally Commercial Atlas and Marketing Guide, and the World Almanac and Book of Facts. *Predicasts* compiles industry data from published sources and generates time series for forecasting many markets. For further information, see Churchill (1987), which contains detailed descriptions of the special data sources plus short descriptions of the published sources and a bibliography of additional published guides to archival data. The availability of syndicated primary data services is increasing worldwide and provides a high value source of data on markets.

    Archival data should be used with caution because it is collected for other purposes and may not fit exactly the category under investigation. But it is quickly obtained, may be less expensive, can lead to later efficiencies, and provides an external check to any qualitative or quantitative measurement. Although archival data may not meet all the managerial requirements, it is an important source to examine before primary measurement is undertaken.

Qualitative Measurement

    New-product development seeks to discover what the customer views as important in a product category. Qualitative measurement is based on in-depth probes into the customer's viewpoint. Its purpose is not to identify the best strategy, or to project demand, or even to select the most important product features. Instead, qualitative measurement raises issues by exploring the customers' basic needs and desires. The qualitative researcher enters the process with an open mind, seeking to learn by simply listening to the customer.

A popular method of qualitative research is focus group interviews. For example, in focus groups for "Shared Ride Auto Transit"—a form of organized hitchhiking—the U.S. Department of Transportation (1977) confirmed its intuition about the importance of safety, dependability, reliability, flexibility, and personal freedom in customers' reactions to various strategies. But they also uncovered some surprises. Major objections to "Shared Ride" were based on not wanting to be obligated or indebted to other people. Riders felt better if they paid the drivers, but drivers felt very uncomfortable in accepting payment. Several consumer misunderstandings were uncovered (e.g., most consumers felt they paid higher insurance for car-pooling when in fact they paid lower premiums). When Shared Ride was described as "community car-pooling," there was better initial reaction and greater willingness to experiment. When Shared Ride was called "organized hitchhiking"; however, consumers' attitudes immediately turned against the system.

Focus groups are employed in almost every industry: consumers talk about purchasing shaving creams, families meet to talk about vacation planning, CFOs discuss information software and communication systems, doctors meet over dinner to discuss ethical drugs and therapy innovations, and men or women share knowledge, attitudes, and experiences on the use of contraceptives. Typically several groups are run (minimum of three and typically five to seven) and the results are interpreted judgmentally by the observers and moderator. These groups should be conducted carefully to prevent bias and encourage open sharing of ideas (see chapter 5 and Calder, 1977). In some cases it is inconvenient for customers to meet as groups or it might be most effective if customers are interviewed one at a time. In these cases qualitative one-on-one interviews provide the qualitative input.

Often an important function of qualitative research in the design process is to generate a list of customer needs within the category to be used in the more formal research phase of the process. We describe in the next chapter how these customer needs relate to overall strategy, to the tactical design, and to detailed engineering decisions, and we describe in chapter 10 and 12 examples of how to use qualitative research to identify these needs. For now we provide an example of the tactical attributes which describe student needs with respect to management education. It is important that the list be as exhaustive as possible, covering a wide array of potential benefits, if they are at all relevant to the category. Ideas come from the transcripts of the focus groups, individual in-depth interviews, previous studies, and prior managerial beliefs. The emphasis is on breadth, even if redundancy is inherent, because later analysis will identify the underlying structure. Whenever possible, the qualitative research is used to select the wording of each of the statements.

Qualitative research does not provide final answers. It is a useful search

TABLE 7.1   Twenty Constructs that Describe Management Education

1. With a degree from this school, I'd be joining a worldwide fraternity, an effective alumni network.	11. Financial aid in the form of loans, grants, or assistantships is widely available.
2. The program emphasizes training in skills that can be used in advising decision makers on what course of action to take.	12. I would have a great deal of flexibility to structure a program to suit my own needs and interests.
3. The content of the program would be highly relevant to the decisions I expect to make in a management position in the next five years.	13. The majority of the faculty are academicians and have never been practicing managers.
4. I would be exposed to the newest, most advanced management techniques.	14. The students are very likely to be cooperative and friendly.
5. I'd be learning a commonsense approach to problem solving.	15. With a degree from this school, the most exciting job opportunities would be open to me on graduation.
6. The school provides excellent teaching.	16. I could not go wrong with a degree from this program.
7. The school is oriented toward those that want to take personal responsibility for making major decisions.	17. I would be able to command a very high starting salary with a degree from this school.
8. The program is very theoretical with limited real-world focus.	18. The program is very quantitative.
9. There would be a high level of contact with faculty members.	19. The school has an excellent location.
10. The school has a high-prestige reputation.	20. The school would emphasize how management is now conducted, not how it should be conducted.

technique that helps ensure that the quantitative measurements address the issues that are relevant to the design process.

Quantitative Measurement

Quantitative measurement (personal interviews, mail surveys, telephone surveys) provides the input to the analytical techniques used that identify the specific strategies that make the greatest impact on improving the success of a new product design. For example, analytic techniques summarize customer perceptions and preferences and provide preliminary estimates of purchase actions.

After archival and qualitative research are used to understand issues and semantics a quantitative approach is used to measure attitudes and customer response. As the product design proceeds through evaluation and refinement, estimates become more accurate, and the emphasis shifts to quantitative measurement.

The product concept or prototype can be an experimental treatment in the research; alternatives are presented and quantitative measures are taken. For example several "stretching" concepts may have been generated and will be evaluated. But in some cases an explicit experimental design is used to estimate response to product attributes or features.

Because quantitative measurement is often specific to the analyses used in the decision process, we defer some of the details to those sections that cover the specific analysis techniques. In this chapter we review sampling, questionnaire formulation, and attitude scaling.

To illustrate how qualitative and quantitative measurement is integrated, it is useful to consider the flow of marketing research at KAO corporation in Japan, a leading manufacturer of consumer packaged goods. See Figure 7.3 (Kuga 1990). First qualitative focus groups are conducted along with behavior and attitude studies. Then specific concept tests and component studies (brand name, package, and advertising) are undertaken. These are integrated with internal screening and product testing in a pretest market simulator. After test marketing, the product is launched and tracked by continuing survey, panel, and store data. Notice that the research steps roughly track the managerial phases of opportunity identification (focus groups, attitude studies), design (product tests, concept tests, naming and package tests), testing (sales forecasting, test market), introduction, and life-cycle management.

Computer-Aided Interviewing

A form of quantitative research that is growing in popularity is computer-aided interviewing (CAI). With CAI a customer is placed in front of a computer screen and asked to complete a series of questions by pressing one or more computer keys. In most cases a standard computer keyboard is used for input, but occasionally special keypads are used for input. Most telephone surveys now use computer input by the interviewer thus providing the advantages of branching, range checking, and rapid data summaries without the inherent disadvantages of a computer-customer interface. Recently mouse and touch screens have been employed. Voice input can be recorded in digital form for later analysis and new "surrogate travel" procedures allow customers to simulate walking through a store or showroom by pushing di-

Typical Flow of Marketing Research at Kao

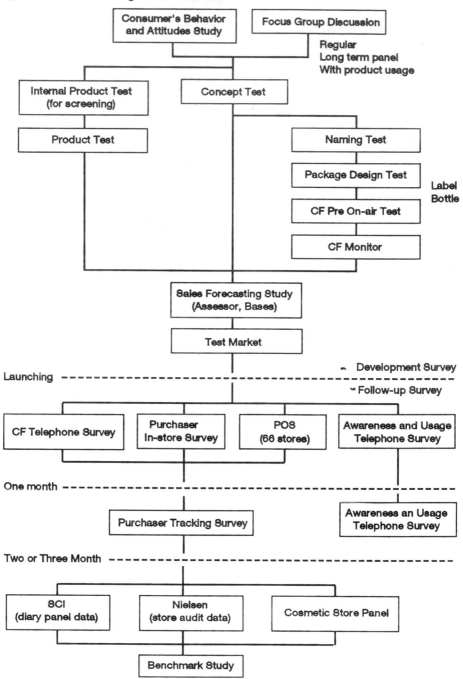

Figure 7.3 Typical Flow of Marketing Research at Kao (Kuga 1990, p. 24; reprinted with permission)

rection buttons (this is like seeing what a video camera on your shoulder would see as you move through an environment—see chapters 12 and 16 for more details on the use of multimedia measurement).

The advantages of CAI are many. First, because the computer reacts on-line to the customer responses, the questions can be tailored specifically to each customer via conditional branching and questions that depend upon the response to previous questions (see Singh, Howell, and Rhoads 1990, for an example). This results in a more efficient interview because only the questions that need be asked are asked. Second, because only certain responses are accepted, the data are "clean" in the sense that all answers are automatically within the allowed range. Third, because the data are stored electronically, they can be merged and analyzed almost immediately resulting in a more rapid turnaround of the analysis and more timely information to the new-product team. Fourth, the computer tracks the time and sequence of answering so that response time and protocol measures are generated automatically.

Conversely, although some customers can type well, most cannot—qualitative input is limited. Today's computers cannot yet react as a human interviewer to the complex potential of qualitative interviews. Thus, the new-product team should recognize the power and the limitations of CAI and use it for those studies that it can improve. In the future the capabilities of CAI will increase and many of these limitations will be overcome.

SAMPLING

After the research method is selected, sample sizes and sampling methods are determined. In the qualitative phase small samples are taken. Three or four groups of 8 to 10 people or 30 one-on-one interviews may be sufficient if issue identification and semantics are the primary concern. Later on, quantitative surveys require larger sample sizes. It is uncommon to collect fewer than one hundred respondents; in cases where segmentation is important there should be at least 100 respondents in each major segment. Samples to support design of new products are often more substantial, perhaps as large as 200 to 500. In fact, research by Srinivasan (1977) and Einhorn and Hogarth (1975) has shown that naive models which provide little diagnostic information may be indistinguishable from more sophisticated models when samples are too small.

Although there are theoretical methods of defining the best sample size (Schlaifer 1969; Green, Tull and Albaum 1988; Allaire 1975) based on the value of information, these are difficult to implement in a complex, sequential new-product development process. Classical methods of considering the standard deviation of the resulting estimate are useful, but vastly oversimplify the problem because information is collected on many variables and often analyzed by multivariate methods for which sampling properties are not easily determined. Judgment, norms, and experience are the best guides for sampling decisions.

In general, random samples are best if they can be obtained at a reasonable cost. They tend to be most representative and are less prone to sampling errors. But nonresponse can be a problem. If 30% to 40% of the random sample returns a mail questionnaire, the statistical analysis may be inappropriate unless it can be established that the nonrespondents are a random subgroup of the total sample. This requires that demographic and other characteristics be compared to external sources such as census figures, and corrections made if necessary. Response rates can be increased with prescreening (the respondent is called and asked to participate) or incentives (e.g., $5 is enclosed with each questionnaire or $10 to $50 is offered for a central location study), but such methods are costly and should be considered carefully before being used to assure that the incentive does not create its own response bias.

Alternatively, purposive samples can be used if they are done carefully and steps are taken to correct statistically any biases introduced by the sampling. For example, the use of a shopping mall as a site for market research is becoming common. A respondent is stopped while walking the mall and, by means of a few questions, qualified as having the desired target group characteristics. Quotas are established for age, sex, demographic, and product use groups. Although these samples are not random, response rates are high (more than 60%), and their representativeness can be established through statistical corrections. These mall interviews are attractive if personal interviews and product or advertising exposure is essential. Nonetheless, great care is required in the selection of criteria for screening the respondents and careful statistical analysis. They should be scrutinized for any potential biases. For example, people who have been in a study in the last three months should be removed to prevent the sample from being contaminated by "professional" respondents.

Purposive samples can be attractive due to their reduced cost, but lower cost should be weighed against potential biases. A good rule of thumb is that purposive samples are more appropriate early in the design process when the primary goal is exploratory analysis. Later in the design process when forecasting becomes important, the representativeness of the sample is crucial and randomness becomes more important.

Do not confuse purposive samples with convenience samples. In purposive samples, explicit selection and screening processes are established, potential biases identified, and steps taken to correct for those biases. In convenience samples such as man-in-the-street, church groups, office friends, and university students biases can be hidden. Interpretation of any analyses done on such groups can lead to incorrect strategies for new product development. Thus, in general, we recommend using a random sample with checks for nonresponse, but consideration should be given to the benefits and costs of purposive surveys with statistical corrections.

MEASUREMENT INSTRUMENTS

When questionnaires are used, a choice must be made between personal, mail, and telephone interviews. In some cases this is not difficult because personal interviews are the only feasible solution. For example, if a food product is to be tasted or an electronic component demonstrated, personal contact is required. In other cases, the format (mail, telephone, personal interview) depends on the information that is being collected. For example, for complex perception and preference questions personal interviews are best, but we have found the mail format represents an acceptable tradeoff when budgets are limited. The specifics of the questionnaire, the group to be interviewed, and the research budget must all be considered before a choice is made.

Questionnaire Design

A questionnaire must be constructed carefully to collect the appropriate information with a minimum of bias. Questionnaire design is an art. In this section we cover some representative considerations in questionnaire design and indicate some of the pitfalls to avoid.

Respondents must be motivated to participate. Convincing the respondents of the importance of the work is desirable. For example, a study of health services began with an explanation that the survey would measure health needs so that improved health services could be developed. Stressing the importance of each individual respondent's input is useful. In cases in which cooperation may be low, personal interviews with personable interviewers can be effective. Increasingly, respondents are given compensation for their cooperation. For example, in consumer products a coupon worth $25 may be given. Incentives to doctors or other professionals can be as high as $500 in cash or professional products. The use of an incentive helps to increase the response rate, thereby reducing the potential nonresponse bias, but nonfinancial motivations (a chance to have an impact, an enjoyable interview, etc.) should not be overlooked.

Proper motivation can be used to reduce nonresponse bias. But a good response rate does not necessarily mean good measurement. Improperly worded questions can be misleading to the respondent, to the analyst, and to the manager. For example,

"Do you like the taste of calamari?"

In this case the respondent may not know that calamari is the Italian word for squid. The question would underestimate consumer appreciation.

"Do you agree that the Massachusetts Health Foundation provides excellent care?"

This one-sided question, although good for public relations, tends to bias the response toward agree. A better question would give both sides of the argument, that is,

"In your experience, does the Massachusetts Health Foundation provide excellent care or does it provide poor care?"

Alternatively, one of the attitude scaling techniques, which are described subsequently, could be used. The pitfalls of question wording are numerous and can be avoided only through great care and careful testing of each question or set of questions. Both Payne (1951) and Oppenheim (1966) provide examples of many of these problems and how to overcome them. Payne provides an extensive list of problem words to avoid and a checklist of 100 points to consider before each questionnaire is taken to the field. Developing a good questionnaire can be costly and time consuming, but the rewards are great through more usable information and a better understanding of the customer.

A good questionnaire requires careful planning, which should begin long before questions are actually written. In preparing a questionnaire it is important to recall the managerial questions that need to be answered, the analytic techniques to answer those questions, and the specific information that the techniques need. First, the major sections of the questionnaire should be specified. This block layout allows the new product design team to (1) make rational tradeoffs about the length and the necessity of various sections, (2) ensure that all needed information is collected, (3) eliminate unnecessary redundancy, (4) construct a smooth flow of response throughout the questionnaire, and (5) check ordering requirements (e.g., preference valuation should come after attribute scales to avoid what are known as "halo effect"—Beckwith and Lehmann 1976). For example, Table 7.2 is the block design for a questionnaire used by the city of Evanston, Illinois, to identify

TABLE 7.2   Block Design for a Questionnaire to Investigate Consumer Views on Transportation Innovation

Block Description	Purpose	Analysis Technique
1. Cover letter	Generate interest, motivate respondents	Motivation
2. Warm-up questions	Gain rapport with consumer	Motivation
3. Recent-trip scenario sampling/transportation choice for scenario	Representative sample of scenarios/potential stratification by scenario	Benefit Segmentation
4. Instructions for rating transportation alternatives	Aid to response/consider recent trip/express *opinions*	Perceptual Mapping
5. Attribute scales for bus, walk, and car	Input to models of perception	Perceptual Mapping
6. Preference among available modes/frequency of use among all modes	Input to models of preference and choice behavior	Preference Analysis Demand Forecasting
7. Self-reported travel characteristics	Input to models of choice/link to consumer attitudes	Demand Forecasting
8. Stretching concepts for new modes of travel/attribute scales for stretching concepts	Enhance validity for changes in transportation system	Used with 4 and 5 above
9. Preference for available modes including stretching concepts	Estimate more complete models/internal validation of preference models	Preference Analysis
10. Conditional intent	Indicates behavior changes based upon changes in system characteristics	Intent Model
11. Importance ratings for attribute scales	Alternative measure of preference	Importance Model
12. Transportation facts such as the location of home, location of nearest bus stop, etc.	Enables measurement or estimation of benefits delivery	House of Quality
13. Demographics	Personal descriptions for use in segmentation	Benefit Segmentation
14. Open-ended comments	Qualitative input for completeness	Qualitative Input

new transportation services (see Hauser, Tybout, and Koppelman 1979). Note that each section has a specific purpose, and each section after the warm-up questions is specific to an analytic model. (The analytical methods are those described in subsequent chapters.)

After the block design is complete, focus groups and previous experience provide the input to word and reword the questions so that they accurately gather the information needed for the analysis. Small samples are used to pretest the questionnaire. Respondents are reinterviewed about their responses to be sure they were thinking of the same issues as the researcher when answering the questions. After the pretest, and possibly preanalysis, the questionnaire is revised and implemented with a representative sample of the target population.

Because questionnaire design is an art, each reader should try to develop this skill by designing a questionnaire and having a colleague critique it. Examine it in light of the pitfalls described subsequently. Everyone who uses market research should actually administer a questionnaire to some respondents at least once in order to understand the issues of nonresponse, ambiguity, and inaccuracy.

Some Pitfalls and How to Avoid Them

There is no simple formula for producing a good questionnaire. Instead we identify some of the common mistakes we have seen in questionnaires designed by our students and by professional market researchers. Recognition of these pitfalls should help you avoid many of them. In addition, we give guidelines that we try to follow in developing our own questionnaires. Some of these guidelines may seem costly, such as a major pretest and preanalysis, but considering the stakes in new product development, we feel this cost is justified. Among the major pitfalls we have seen are use of the wrong semantics, low motivation, poor initial questions, difficult questions to answer, products unfamiliar to the respondents, no pretest, no preanalysis, poor sampling, and underbudgeted marketing research.

Wrong Semantics.   Because you are trying to measure customers' responses, the questions must be phrased in the language which customers use. Rather than using the jargon of engineering, medicine, business, and so on, use the language of the customer. If a customer (consumer) talks about the time it takes to walk from the bus stop to the office, you do not ask, "What is the egress portion of your work trip via the bus mode?" If a consumer says a deodorant helps him stay "dry," you do not ask about "perspiration prevention." Rather than "minimization of propensity for cardiovascular infarction," you talk about "preventing heart attacks." A good way to discover the right semantics is through focus groups or other qualitative interviews. Careful pretesting is necessary to see that respondents understand all the words in the questionnaire. Remember that the words that are in common usage in the industry may be fine for the manufacturer or service provider, but not for the customer.

It is easy to write a biased question; difficult to write an unbiased one.

Although it is easy to ask, "Is the mayor doing a good job?," it is preferable to ask, "Is the mayor doing a good job or a poor job?" A useful exercise is to ask yourself the reporter's five questions: "Who? Why? When? Where? and How?" It should be clear to the customer which of these questions is being asked. If your question has more than one meaning, the customer may well choose the wrong meaning. Consider Payne's example of the five-word question, "Why did you say that?" This simple question can have five different meanings, depending upon which word the customer emphasizes in reading the question.

Why did you say that?

Why *did* you say that?

Why did *you* say that?

Why did you *say* that?

Why did you say *that?*

Without a pretest in which customers read aloud the question, the semantics problem might well go unnoticed.

Low Motivation.   It is important to the analysis that the customer is involved with the questions and gives them the proper thought. Because poor responses are often indistinguishable from thoughtful responses, poor motivation brings ambiguity and inaccuracy. Specific questions must seem real and relevant; the questionnaire must flow smoothly and be interesting.

The credibility of the research firm and the anonymity (if appropriate) of the survey must be established rapidly. It is useful to tell the respondent what the study is about, why inputs are crucial, how the respondent was selected, and how the results will be used.

Poor Initial Questions.   It is tempting to start immediately with the most important questions, but it is better to begin with some simple warm-up questions that give the respondent confidence, allow the respondent to voice personal opinions, and lead smoothly into the more difficult or substantive questions of the survey. The warm-up questions bring the respondents' frame of reference to the topic of the questionnaire.

Difficult Questions to Answer.   How many questionnaires have you completed that require a magnifying glass to read, or have so many circles and arrows that you never know which question to answer, or have computer precoding right in the margin so that you feel like a floppy disk? All these characteristics have some benefits, but they must be used carefully and with much forethought. Reducing the print and eliminating white space gets more questions on a page and thus reduces the number of pages, but it may also reduce the response rate. Branching in a questionnaire directs the right questions to the right people, but it can get out of hand. "Office use only" computerese in the margin saves coding time, but the small savings in coding may not be worth the loss in respondent rapport.

Products Unfamiliar to the Respondents.   There are almost thirty brands of deodorant on the market. Of these, how many could you seriously evaluate? In other words, how many: (1) have you used, (2) have on hand at home, (3) would you seriously consider using, or (4) would you definitely not use? Chances are that fewer than five brands of deodorant would pass any of the four criteria. In fact, in a study of more than 200 consumers, Silk and Urban (1978) found that the average consideration set size was about three deodorants when the consideration set was defined by the above criteria. (The consideration set is sometimes known as an evoked set or a relevant set; see Hauser and Wernerfelt 1990.)

If you ask customers to evaluate products on many attribute scales and you want these answers to be relevant, you must limit your questions to the respondents' consideration sets. Alternatively, you can expand the consideration sets by giving the customers a detailed description, say a concept statement, of the product that is being evaluated. Ignoring consideration set limitations can cause erroneous interpretations and lead to inappropriate strategies. Note that for new product research all four criteria (or reasonable modification) are important: "have used" to get experience, "have on hand at home" to get purchase and possibly consumption, "seriously consider" to get at dimensions the customer considers important in that category, and "definitely not use" to uncover the bad features of a product in the category. Reasonable modification includes changing "have on hand at home" to "have seen in use" for industrial products. Together these criteria ensure the consideration set gives the information that is necessary for proactive new product design.

No Pretest.   No matter how much experience you have or how carefully you examine and reexamine questions, you can still misword or misdirect a question or set of questions. Perhaps the most important element in questionnaire design is pretest. No matter how carefully you design a questionnaire, it is probable that you will make at least a few mistakes. Pretest is, in a sense, a carefully monitored ministudy where you give your questionnaire to customers in your target population and have them try to answer it.

A sample size of 10 is common. After a question is answered, you can ask respondents what they thought each question asked. You can try different forms of the questions. You can watch for careless response or no response. You can ask several similar questions and check the internal consistency, or you can check the responses against your prior beliefs (Campbell and Fiske 1959). You can do whatever is necessary to ensure that what you think is being asked is actually what is being answered. This step takes time and may delay a study, but without it you can never be confident that your measurement is reasonably unbiased.

No Preanalysis. Just as important as a pretest is a preanalysis where you try the analytical methods on the pretest data. Pre-analysis ensures that you have included the right questions to address the issues. For example, in one questionnaire we measured frequency of purchase with a category for "5 or 6" purchases, but discovered through pretest data analysis that it was important to distinguish between 5 times per month and 6 times per month. In another study we measured all the psychological characteristics of shopping centers, but had to construct an accessibility measure because it was not asked in the questionnaire. Preanalysis is not relevant to decision making because the sample is small, but it does help identify omitted data questions. If the results are interpretable within the small sample size limits, then you are ready for the full study; if not, then another iteration of the questionnaire may be necessary.

Poor Sampling. It is easy to hand out your questionnaire to anyone who will take it. You can increase your response rate if you have the respondent who does not want to answer your questionnaire pass it to someone who will. In transportation you have a captive audience if you do your survey on board a bus. An inexpensive way to reach consumers who buy color television is to have them fill out a questionnaire after they buy one of your television sets. You can poll your colleagues or your office staff, or you can intercept the man on the street. You can do all this, but don't treat the sample as random or representative of your target population. Although you can sometimes correct purposive sampling such as on-board surveys or point-of-purchase surveys, most of the models in this book are predicated on a random or stratified sample. Departure from randomness is sometimes done under extreme cost pressure, but methods of assuring representativeness must then be carefully considered.

Underbudgeted Market Research. Not allowing enough funds for survey research can result in insufficient sample sizes or can result in mail surveys when personal interviews are recommended. Costs of field work vary by such factors as the incidence of a target group in a population, complexity of questions, callbacks, and screening. For new product design market research can be expensive. Budgets for questionnaire formulation, analysis, report writing, and oral presentation can bring the total for an average study to five or even six-figure amounts. While this may seem high, it should be weighed against the benefits. For example, chapter 3 estimated the average benefits due to front-end design as equal to many times the cost of obtaining the information.

Conversely, not all organizations can afford survey research. Often "in-kind" support can be substituted for cash outlays. For example, many not-for-profit service organizations use trained volunteers for telephone interviewing, mailing, and questionnaire coding. This "in-kind" support makes efficient use of otherwise underused resources. But organizations should carefully consider all cost-saving strategies and use them only when sufficient accuracy can be assured. A poorly done survey can often be worse strategically than no survey at all. If funds are extremely limited, they are better directed at qualitative research rather than casual quantitative research.

Summary.   The pitfalls we have indicated should be avoided, but avoiding them does not guarantee a good questionnaire. Their avoidance is just a prerequisite for any questionnaire. Before preparing a questionnaire, study what others have done, gain some firsthand experience, or use consultants with proven skill in questionnaire construction.

ATTITUDE SCALING

Much of the information collected in quantitative measurement is based on attitude scales. Such scales are used primarily to measure the customer needs that are based on the constructs identified in the qualitative measurement, but they are also used to measure similarities between products, tradeoffs among customer needs, preference among products, intent to purchase, propensity to innovate, and demographics. We now summarize some of the techniques that are particularly useful in measuring attitudes toward new products. The scaling of these measures and their use is discussed more completely in subsequent chapters.

Likert Scale.   The most common form of scaling is to give the respondent a strongly worded statement about an attribute of a product and have the respondent react to that statement on a 5-point or 7-point agree/disagree scale. This is called a Likert-type scale (Figure 7.4a). The advantages of a Likert-type scale are that it measures intensity of feeling about the statement, it is easy to administer, and customers can respond to it easily. Its main

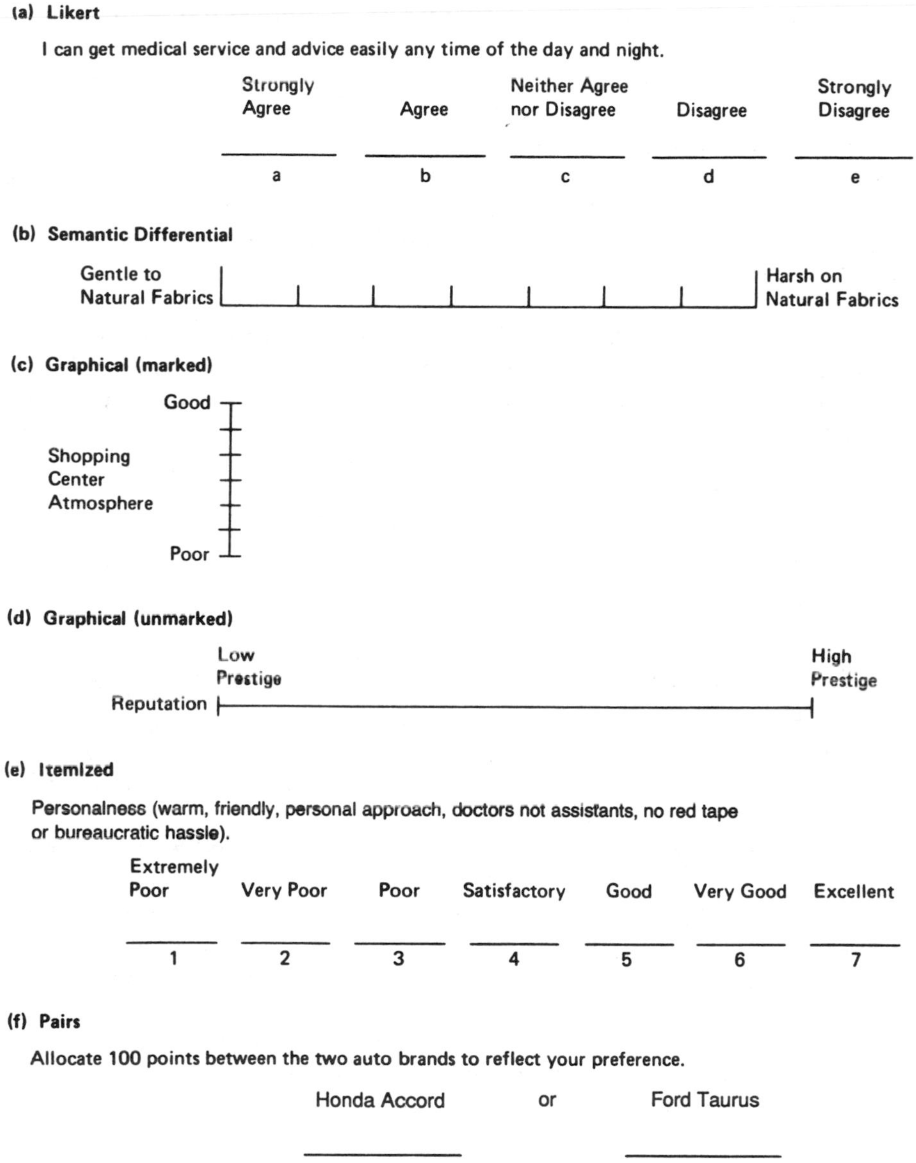

(a) Likert

I can get medical service and advice easily any time of the day and night.

Strongly Agree	Agree	Neither Agree nor Disagree	Disagree	Strongly Disagree
a	b	c	d	e

(b) Semantic Differential

Gentle to Natural Fabrics |___|___|___|___|___|___|___| Harsh on Natural Fabrics

(c) Graphical (marked)

Shopping Center Atmosphere

Good — ... — Poor

(d) Graphical (unmarked)

Reputation

Low Prestige ⊢————————————————⊣ High Prestige

(e) Itemized

Personalness (warm, friendly, personal approach, doctors not assistants, no red tape or bureaucratic hassle).

Extremely Poor	Very Poor	Poor	Satisfactory	Good	Very Good	Excellent
1	2	3	4	5	6	7

(f) Pairs

Allocate 100 points between the two auto brands to reflect your preference.

Honda Accord   or   Ford Taurus

Figure 7.4 Different Types of Attribute Scales

disadvantage is that it measures attributes on an ordinal rather than on an internal scale. For example, in the scales in Figure 7.4a going from "neither agree nor disagree" to "agree" means the health service has higher quality, but we cannot infer that going from "neither agree nor disagree" to "strongly agree" means twice the improvement in quality. Nonetheless, in empirical experience the scales have proven rather robust with respect to the interval assumption; some manipulations (such as factor analysis and regression) can be performed if the analyst proceeds with caution (see Singh, Howell, and Rhoads 1990, for recent developments).

Semantic Differential.   In marketing, the most common form of a semantic differential scale is to give the respondent bipolar adjectives or phrases and have the respondent express feelings about the product by checking a category to indicate how close the respondent's feelings are to one or the other of the phrases (Figure 7.4b). Like the Likert scales, semantic differential scales measure intensity of feeling and are easy to administer or respond to. They can often be used interchangeably with Likert scales, but in some cases it is difficult, if not impossible, to generate the necessary bipolar adjectives or phrases.

Graphical.   Rather than using categories, you can have the respondent react to a statement or to bipolar adjectives by indicating his strength of feeling as a position on a line. The line can be marked as in Figure 7.4c, or unmarked as in Figure 7.4d. If marked, the divisions can be few, as shown, or many as in a "thermometer scale." Most applications require that words be associated with at least the endpoints of the scale, although some applications, particularly those with only a few divisions, have been used with no anchor points. As with the Likert and semantic differential, these scales measure intensity of feeling and are easy to administer. Often the respondent finds them more difficult to answer and unmarked or finely marked scales are difficult to encode for analysis. The interval properties of some of these scales may be slightly stronger than Likert or semantic differential, but not nearly as strong as might be inferred from the seemingly close relationship to the interval properties of a line. We cannot be assured that customers react to graphical scales in a linear fashion.

Itemized.   The itemized scale presents the respondent with an attribute description from which to select a category indicating the respondent's belief about how the product rates on the attribute (see Figure 7.4c). These scales also measure intensity of feeling and are easy to administer and answer. They do not allow the fine distinctions of graphic scales but are generally more reliable. They have only ordinal properties, but careful selection and testing of categories can get them closer to interval-like scales than either Likert, semantic differential, or graphical measures. Unfortunately, preparing the questions is difficult and tedious, and they require more space on the questionnaire than other scales.

Pairs.   Paired comparisons yield data that can be scaled to produce interval or ratio measures. The example in Figure 7.4f is called a constant-sum paired comparison. Customers are asked to allocate a fixed number of points between the two products to indicate their relative intensity of preference. If sufficient pairs are evaluated, a least-squares procedure (Torgerson, 1958) or a linear programming procedure (Srinivasan and Shocker, 1973) can be used to develop an overall preference scale. For more details, see Hauser and Shugan (1980) or Huber and Sheluga (1977).

Other Scales.   These are other scales used in attitude scaling that have strong underlying theory, provide good tests of reliability and validity, and are similar in appearance to those we have discussed. Despite these properties, these scales are rarely used in studies that require customers to rate many products on many scales. They are not used because to achieve these properties each scale requires a major empirical effort. For example, the classical Thurstone scales require roughly 100 individuals to sort 100 to 200 items into 10 piles. Use of Thurstone scales results in an exorbitant amount of money and effort spent on scaling rather than analysis or strategy.

SUMMARY

Customer measurement provides key input to the design of new products. Careful customer measurement enhances creativity, uncovers greater opportunities, leads to more accurate forecasts, supports improved new-product decision making, and generates insight and knowledge. The guidelines presented in this chapter should be carefully adapted to the special needs of each particular study. Probably the best advice in customer measurement is to proceed carefully and cautiously, continually critique the questionnaire or group procedure, and pretest it on customers. Seek advice when necessary and avoid making assumptions about how a customer will respond.

Good customer measurement is difficult, but when done properly it is an extremely powerful tool for the design of new products. We provide more examples of measurement and scaling as we consider models of customer perception, preference, and choice. Good measurement means good analysis and good decisions in the managerial evaluation and refinement process of new product design.

REVIEW QUESTIONS

7.1. What is the ultimate objective of customer measurement?

7.2. How can customer measures be made synergistic with technological creativity?

7.3. Discuss the relationship between qualitative and quantitative measurement.

7.4. Generate a list of attributes for electric cars. For financial services. For office furniture systems. How would you scale these attributes?

7.5. What factors must be considered when selecting the sample size for a customer study?

7.6. In customer sampling, how is nonresponse a problem? How can nonresponse be minimized?

7.7. How can the manager measure and control the quality of information provided by a customer with a questionnaire?

7.8. Why is preanalysis important when doing a customer questionnaire study?

7.9. A company considering the marketing of a new financial service uses a *Fortune* magazine mailing list for sampling perspective buyers. Could this procedure distort the conclusions which will be reached by the study? If so, how?

7.10. Suppose you were attempting to position a new type of resume service for your fellow students. Construct a questionnaire which attempts to measure the needed information.

7.11. You are introducing a new line of premium wines and want to measure how many customers will try your product. Write a biased question that will overestimate demand. Write a biased question that will underestimate demand. Write a confusing question. Write a question that will accurately estimate demand.

8

Perceptual Mapping: Identification of Strategic Benefits

PERCEPTION AND THE CORE BENEFIT PROPOSITION

Now that we have a basic understanding of the measurement issues surrounding customer inputs, we are ready to study each component in the design process (see Figure 6.1). The unifying concept is the CBP and our efforts to build quality products that create value for customers better than competitive alternatives. In this chapter we present perceptual maps as a tool to understanding the relationship of the CBP and customers' choice process while Chapter 9 outlines the technical methods of mapping. We then add customer preference to the maps (Chapter 10) and study benefit segmentation and its representation through perceptual maps (Chapter 11). Chapter 12 discusses in depth the links of perception to features and engineering design elements and we close this section with a look at "what-if" forecasting methods to gage the sales potential of the design.

CUSTOMERS BUY BASED ON PERCEPTIONS

On any day when you turn on the television, read the newspaper, or pick up a magazine you find many claims. You might turn on the television and notice a commercial image of a beautiful young woman in a flowing dress crossing a bridge over the Seine River. In the background is the haunting melody of the Puccini aria, *O mio babbino caro*. Your mood is that of an elegant, romantic trip to Paris, a mood the sponsor wants you to attribute to Tott's champagne—a mood you may not have otherwise attributed to a Gallo product. Flipping channels to another program you notice that Ivory soap gives you that "clean fresh feeling of clean," and that Glad bags are "strong and thick, with lots of room."

Turning off the television, you decide to catch up on your *PC Magazine* and find that the latest version of Borland's Paradox database software gives you "power without pain," that a brand of personal computer gives you "dazzling performance," or that a video card enables you to "see the full spectrum." In *Business Week* you notice a full page of amenities such as a shaver, a toothbrush, a shoehorn, and a comb and discover that British Airways "provides the tools for a successful presentation." Of course you might be successful enough in your career to deserve your own private corporate jet, in which case you might choose a Gulfstream IV for the "pursuit of perfection." More down to earth, Toshiba copiers would like you to "think dependable," and the Bank of Boston promises that they will "put our strength to work for you."

In the *Wall Street Journal* United Airlines promises to bring you "the character of Japan," and Bertram-Trojan, Inc. advertises their yachts with the challenge, "never send a boy to do a man's work." In the *New York Times* a retail outlet, U.S. Athletics, offers to sell "limousines for your feet," and Metro-One, a Cellular telephone company, points out that their product makes the difference between "keeping your client waiting and keeping your client."

These advertising claims reflect the careful efforts of these organizations to portray the benefits they offer customers and to differentiate themselves from competition. Borland's advertising claim (supported in the advertisement by features and examples) is an attempt to state that they can do what competitive database programs do, but that their software is easier to learn and easier to use. They do not name the competition but there is an implicit reference to the perceived difficulty of the Ashton Tate's dBase language. The detailed advertising copy contains technical features such as "Query-by-Example," "Auto-refresh," and graphs with one key stroke, but these features support the perceptual positioning of powerful and easy to use; the features are not themselves the CBP.

Positioning is critical for a new product. Not only must a new product deliver the benefits the customer needs, but it must do so better than competition. When it was initially introduced, Sure deodorant positioned itself as drier than other deodorants with a commercial message that encouraged consumers to try Sure under one arm and their current favorite deodorant under the other arm—they were "sure" that consumers would notice the difference. The introduction succeeded because the product delivered superior dryness and because a sampling campaign placed free samples of the product to a large percentage of households. It would have been difficult for Sure to have succeeded with a parity position in the crowded deodorant market—it was much better to surpass existing products in both the CBP and the fulfillment of the CBP.

Subjective Benefits and Objective Features

All of the examples stated thus far have been stated in terms of subjective benefits such as "power without pain," "dazzling performance," and "drier than other deodorants." Features such as one-stroke graphing (Paradox), number of pixels (video card/monitor), or chemical ingredients (deodorant) are important, but they are important because they deliver the subjective benefits. This philosophy is based on a model of customer behavior in Figure 8.1 known as Brunswick's Lens model.

The Lens model states that customers form their preferences for products based on subjective perceptions. They use these perceptions as a "lens" to filter the complex set of cues they receive about the product based on its features and based on communications (advertising, salesforce, word of mouth, PR, channel of distribution, etc.) they receive about the product. Thus, to affect preference we must select the CBP based on the perceptions and fulfill it with features and communications.

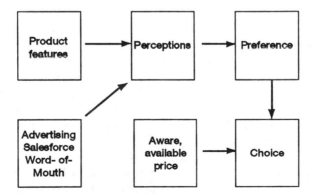

Figure 8.1 "Lens" Model Illustrates Key Concepts of Customer Response to a New Product and Its Marketing Mix

Of course, customers may not buy their most preferred product. It might be too expensive or unavailable. Thus, the Lens model recognizes explicitly that preference is moderated by price/value considerations and constraints such as awareness and availability. To achieve the goal of sales (i.e., the customer's choice of our product), the product, its service, its distribution, and its communication must be consistent and deliver the CBP.

Benefits and Value

Customers buy based on perceived benefits as shown in the Lens model. But benefits are often expensive—expensive to deliver and, because of the resulting price, expensive for the customer to purchase. The concept of value is one of benefits versus the price paid. In this chapter we discuss two tools for benefit positioning—perceptual maps and value maps.

Perceptual maps visually summarize the dimensions that customers use to perceive and judge products and identify how competitive products are placed on those dimensions. We must know the number of dimensions, the names of those dimensions, what more detailed customer needs make up the dimensions, where competition is positioned, and where there are gaps for a new product to fill. By focusing on key benefits and forcing an explicit comparison to competition, perceptual maps assure that the CBP provides a differential advantage.

Value maps augment the information in perceptual maps. For example, IBM Personal Computers might have a position as extremely reliable, running all software, and easy to get repaired, but IBM clones sell well because, in some cases, customers perceive them as providing better value. Similarly, private label aspirin might be perceived as a better value than a branded aspirin such as Bayer.

Value maps portray the benefit versus price tradeoff by displaying products on a "benefit per dollar" basis. For example, if product A delivers 4 units of "effectiveness" for a price of $2, then it delivers 2 units of "effectiveness per dollar." Another product might deliver 3 units of "effectiveness" for $1 and be perceived as a value leader because it delivers 3 units of "effectiveness per dollar." Given a definition of the market segment, value maps provide a discipline to help recognize the interrelationship between benefits and price. When used in conjunction with perceptual maps, value maps provide important strategic information.

We first turn to perceptual maps and examine their role in providing the key managerial concepts and then discuss their evolution into value maps. In the next chapter we present the analytic methods needed to identify customer needs, sort those needs into hierarchies, and to develop the perceptual and value maps.

PERCEPTUAL MAPS

Some Examples

Perceptual maps represent the positions of products on a set of primary customer needs. Figure 8.2 is a perceptual map which displays brands of pain relievers on the dimensions (needs) of "effectiveness" and "gentleness." "Effectiveness" reflects more detailed needs of strong, fast, long-lasting relief and the ability to make headache pain go away fast. "Gentleness" represents perceptions that the product would not upset one's stomach, cause heartburn, or result in a nervous jittery feeling. Tylenol is the most gentle relative to other brands. There appears to be a positioning opportunity for a CBP of gentle *and* effective; if a product and marketing campaign were developed to make and fulfill credible claims on both gentleness and effectiveness a unique position could be achieved. Indeed, Extra Strength Tylenol is a product that was introduced in an attempt to fill this gap.

Perceptual mapping is not restricted to frequently purchased consumer goods. Services and industrial products can be represented by perceptual maps. Figure 8.3 shows consumer perceptions of transportation services along three primary needs.

Figure 8.2   Perceptual Map of Pain Relievers

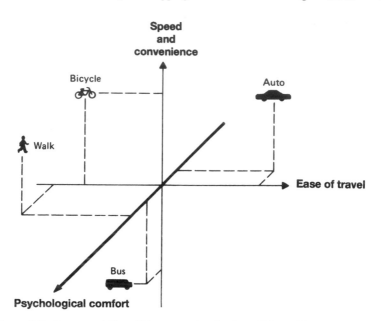

Figure 8.3   Perceptual Map of Transportation Services (Adapted from Hauser and Wisniewski 1979)

1. *Quickness and convenience* reflects the ability of a mode of travel to provide on-time service that gets consumers quickly to their destinations with no long wait, is available when needed, and allows consumers to come and go as they wish.

2. *Ease of travel* includes correct temperature, no problems in bad weather, little effort needed, not tiring, and easy to carry packages or travel with children.

3. *Psychological comfort* includes attributes such as relaxing, not worry about assault or injury, and not made uncomfortable or annoyed by others.

   If you were a transit manager or community planner trying to increase utilization of public transportation, Figure 8.3 suggests that you would need to improve drastically consumers' perceptions of public transportation with respect to both ease of use and quickness and convenience. You might try to modify the existing bus system or introduce a new type of service that is quicker, more convenient, and easier to use.

   Product positioning for industrial products is illustrated for solar-powered air conditioners in Table 8.1, which lists the needs of corporate engineers associated with each of two benefit dimensions, "risk" and "benefits." In industrial buying, there is often a further managerial consideration

TABLE 8.1 Primary Customer Needs for Air-Conditioning Systems as
Perceived by Corporate Engineers

	Risk	Benefits
Corporate Engineers	Reliability	Reduced pollution
	Field tested	Energy savings
	First cost	Protection
	Noise level	Modernness

(Adapted from Choffray and Lilien 1978, p. 220)

that more than one person may be involved in the buying process. Table 8.2 lists the perceptual structure for four groups of customers: plant managers, production engineers, top managers, and heating-ventilation-air-conditioning (HVAC) consultants. Generally, all perceive "benefits" and "risk" as primary needs, but "noise" and "cost" perceptions differ and the composition of these factors vary. In this case a good product positioning must balance the needs of the four interest groups. If one were considering a new solar-powered air conditioner, these perceptions would be important in the design and communication positioning decisions.

How Many Dimensions

Figure 8.2 uses two primary dimensions; Figure 8.3 uses three; and Table 8.1 groups eight customer needs into two or more primary needs. Clearly both levels of information in Table 8.1 are important, but for whom and at which stage of the design process? To illustrate the impact of the number of customer needs being considered, examine Figure 8.4, which shows average customer ratings on 25 customer needs for communication systems. The data displayed in this figure are obtained by asking potential customers to rate existing products and new product concepts on 5-point scales that measure their perceptions of the products (new and old) on the detailed customer needs. Figure 8.4 plots the average ratings.

This "snake plot," so-called because a line connecting the ratings "snakes" down the page, allows you to interpret visually the perceived positions of all existing products. This map indicates how scientists and managers at the Los Alamos Scientific Laboratory in New Mexico viewed telephone and personal visit relative to dedicated closed-circuit television, teletype terminals, and a potential new product, Narrow-Band Video Television (NBVT). NBVT transmits still pictures of normal TV resolution over standard telephone lines at the rate of two to three per minute. The map represents the communications market prior to the introduction of low-cost FAX devices.

Careful examination of Figure 8.4 indicates the detailed strengths and

TABLE 8.2   Primary Customer Needs for Air-Conditioning System Vary by
Participants in the Buying Process

	Customer Need "A"	Customer Need "B"	Customer Need "C"
Plant managers	*Benefits* Energy savings Protection Modernness Low-operating cost	*Risk* Reliability Field tested Modularity Noise level	
Production engineers	*Benefits* Energy savings Protection Low operating cost Modernness Less pollution	*Noise* Noise level Modularity	*Risk* Complexity Field tested Reliability
Top managers	*Benefits* Energy savings Protection Low operating cost Modernness Protection against power failure	*Risk* Reliability Field tested Initial cost Complexity	*Noise* Noise level
HVAC Consultants	*Benefits* Energy savings Protection Modernness Less pollution	*Risk* Reliability Field tested	*Cost* Initial cost Noise level

(Adapted from Choffray and Lilien 1978, pp. 220–221)

weaknesses of each technology as compared with the more generic alternatives of telephone and personal visit. However, it is difficult to identify with Figure 8.4 a simple, strategic positioning strategy for the new product, NBVT. Although the detailed list of customer needs will certainly influence the adoption of the new technology, Figure 8.4 does not capture the essence of the adoption process.

An analysis of the data which produced Figure 8.4 provides a simpler, more strategic picture of the communications needs of the scientists and managers at Los Alamos by reducing the 25 detailed needs to two primary needs (see Chapter 9 for analytic methods). The correlations between the

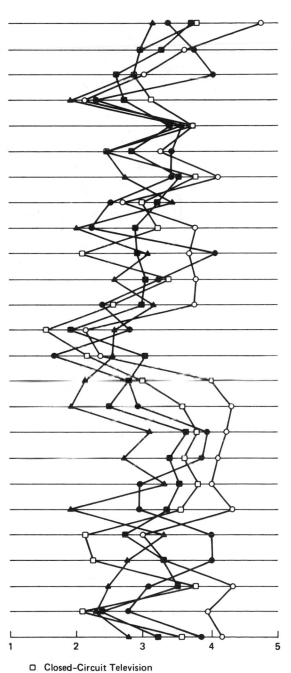

1. Effective information exchange
2. Find and reach the right person
3. Save time
4. Not need visual aids
5. Not get trapped
6. Eliminate paper work
7. Persuade
8. Focus on issues
9. All forms of information
10. No hassle
11. Control impression
12. Good for security/privacy
13. Must plan in advance
14. Eliminate red tape
15. Monitor people and operations
16. High level of interaction
17. Solve problems
18. Express feelings
19. Not misinterpret
20. Good for group discussion
21. Inexpensive
22. Quick response
23. Enhance idea development
24. Works well for commitment
25. Can maintain contact

● Telephone
○ Personal Visit
■ Narrow Band Video Telephone
□ Closed–Circuit Television
▲ Teletype

Figure 8.4 ''Snake Plot'' of Scientists' and Managers' Perceptions of New Communication Options

twenty-five detailed needs and the two primary needs are shown in Figure 8.5. If you read the detailed needs that correlate with the first primary need, you might name that primary need "effectiveness." You might name the second primary need "ease of use." Figure 8.6 plots the alternative technologies in this reduced space of "effectiveness" and "ease of use."

Compare Figures 8.4 and 8.6. The snake plot presents more detail but tends to obscure the basic structure; the two-dimensional plot defines the market more clearly. There is definitely a gap for a technology that is easier to use than personal visit and more effective than telephone, but neither NBVT, closed-circuit television, or teletype fill that gap. If a new product team develops a product in the starred (*) position, it would capture a significant share of the communications market if the price were right. However, the star is the strategic goal; we need the detailed plot to develop tactics to reach that goal. (We might need even more detailed measures of customer needs to engineer the product in order to operationalize the tactics.)

Figures 8.4 and 8.6 illustrate how perceptual maps clarify strategic issues. To develop creative strategies and the CBP, the new product team uses the perceptual map to internalize and visualize the market along its primary dimensions. Fortunately there is evidence that customers tend to simplify judgments by reducing dimensionality to prevent cognitive strain and information overload. In addition, in Chapter 10 we will see that preference analysis based on statistical methods works well with the reduced dimensionality of the perceptual map but runs into technical difficulty (multicollinearity) with the many detailed customer-need attributes.

Relationship to the Design Engineering

The perceptual maps in Figures 8.2, 8.3, and 8.6 correspond to the primary needs in the market. They are strategic summaries of the benefits that the product delivers. Their most important use is in the development of the CBP for strategic product positioning versus competition. The more detailed customer needs in Figures 8.4 and 8.5 can be called secondary needs. They are necessary for tactical decisions on the product and the marketing program. For example, if we decide to reposition NBVT along "effectiveness," we must improve it for the more tactical needs of "effective information exchange," the ability to "persuade" people, the ability to communicate "all forms of information," "control impressions," "monitor people, operations, and experiments," "solve problems," encourage group discussions," and "enhance idea development." (These are the large correlations in Figure 8.5.)

To engineer the product the secondary needs of Figures 8.4 and 8.5 are not sufficient. Engineers need to know more than "enhance idea development." Thus, for product engineering we deal with still more detailed

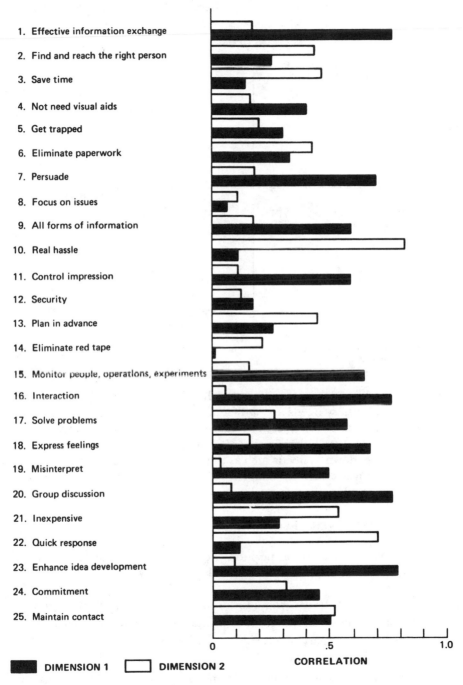

1. Effective information exchange
2. Find and reach the right person
3. Save time
4. Not need visual aids
5. Get trapped
6. Eliminate paperwork
7. Persuade
8. Focus on issues
9. All forms of information
10. Real hassle
11. Control impression
12. Security
13. Plan in advance
14. Eliminate red tape
15. Monitor people, operations, experiments
16. Interaction
17. Solve problems
18. Express feelings
19. Misinterpret
20. Group discussion
21. Inexpensive
22. Quick response
23. Enhance idea development
24. Commitment
25. Maintain contact

0   .5   1.0

■ DIMENSION 1   □ DIMENSION 2   CORRELATION

Figure 8.5 Correlations between the Detailed Customer Needs and the Primary Strategic Needs

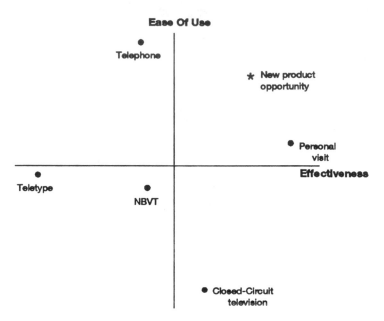

Figure 8.6 Perceptual Map for Communications Technologies (Hauser and Shugan 1980)

tertiary needs which elaborate concepts such as "enhance idea development." Sometimes the tertiary needs are sufficient to link to engineering characteristics; sometimes the product team decides to go deeper still. For example, in a study by Toyota Autobody of rust protection, the new product team went eight levels deep, down to needs such as the ability to withstand rotting apples in the trunk or truck bed. In Chapter 13 we address the detailed issues in using detailed needs to design quality products.

Summary: Managerial Requirements

To develop a CBP and to position the new product relative to competitive products, the new product team needs to identify

- Customer needs underlying a reduced summary of primary needs
- Grouping of customer needs into primary needs and, in particular
  - Number of primary needs
  - Names of those needs
- Positioning of existing products along the perceptual dimensions corresponding to primary needs

- Preference of groups of customers regarding placement of products relative to the primary needs

To engineer the product, the team will need

- Tertiary customer needs and how they relate to the secondary (tactical) needs and the primary (strategic) needs
- Engineering characteristics, product features, and part characteristics that relate to the customer needs

In Chapter 9 we present analytic methods to help identify customer needs, group them, map the primary needs, and position products relative to those needs. Chapter 10 covers the prioritization of customer needs as they relate to customers' preferences. It also provides analytic methods to map the relationship of product features to customer needs. However, before we turn to the analysis procedures we discuss the relationship of price to the product's core benefit proposition.

VALUE MAPS AND CUSTOMER PRIORITIES

Many new products exploit improved technology or features that deliver customer benefits better than competitive products. Other new products exploit process improvements that deliver the same benefits at a lower cost. To evaluate fully such new product opportunities we consider price as well as the core benefits. Value maps provide a means to incorporate price in a new product's perceptual position. We begin with the concept of customer value.

Value Priorities

How many times have you heard phrases such as "you get what you pay for," "I want my money's worth," "good value for the money spent," "I want the most for my money," "when you buy a . . . you shop value," and so on. Such phrases reflect a customer's concern for value, that is the tradeoff between the benefits of a product and the price paid for the product.

The concept of value, or net value, comes from considering a budgeting problem in which a consumer is trying to allocate money across a number of products. For example, a typical consumer may wish to budget money for a car, appliances, home improvements, video equipment, food, clothing, and so on. The customer wants to do this in a manner that provides the most "utility." It is not hard to show mathematically (Hauser and Urban 1986) that a good budgeting rule is to choose first the product with the most utility per dollar, then the product with the next most utility per dollar, and so on until the budget is exhausted.

Furthermore, this budgeting rule has some empirical validity. For example, in a sample of 522 budgets we asked consumers to allocate their budgets among the products that they planned to buy over the next three years (Hauser and Urban 1986). In the same study we obtained four independent measures of the utility of each of these products, combined the measures to get a convergent measure of utility, and divided that utility by the price they planned to pay. The rank order correlations between budget plans predicted by the value priority rule and the actual budget plans were good (35% were perfectly correlated and an additional 25% had a correlation of .75). Although such predictions are not perfect, they are sufficient to motivate the concept of value as affecting consumer purchases. Although we have no data for business purchases, we expect that the more rational business decisions would be explained even better by a value-priority rule.

Based on both the theoretical arguments and on the empirical evidence we feel that it is useful to consider value in a product's position. One way to do this is with a value map.

Value Maps

Review Figure 8.2, a perceptual map of pain relievers. In that map Tylenol provides the most gentleness and Advil and Nuprin the most effectiveness. Bufferin is a nice compromise, but Bayer and Anacin appear to be dominated by Tylenol and Bufferin—they each provide more gentleness *and* more effectiveness. Private label Aspirin provides the least of both perceived dimensions and appears to be dominated by almost every brand on the map. If all eight of these brands were priced identically, then few consumers would be rational if they bought Bayer, Anacin, or, especially, private label brands. But consumers do buy these brands! They are not irrational; they consider price in addition to effectiveness and gentleness.

Perceptual Dimensions and Price.   Suppose that we obtain the prices (per unit dose), rescale the perceptual map such that the lowest brand on each dimension defines the origin of the map, and divide each brand's position by its price. If we do this for the market prices which were prevailing at the time that Figure 8.2 represents, then we get the value map in Figure 8.7. Notice that no brand is now dominated by another brand on both dimensions. A rational consumer could find a reason to choose each brand, de-

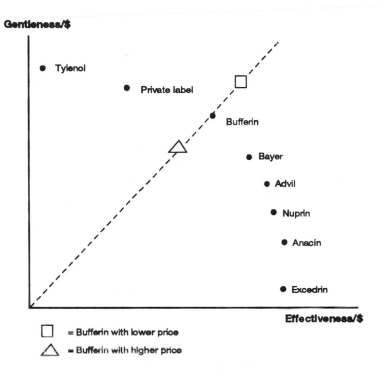

Figure 8.7   Value Map for Pain Relievers

pending on the tradeoffs that they wish to make between gentleness per dollar and effectiveness per dollar.

To understand better the relationship between benefits and price in a value map, consider a change in the price of Bufferin. If we lower its price, then consumers obtain more value—more effectiveness and gentleness per dollar. This is shown in Figure 8.7 by a movement *out* to the position shown by a square. If we raise Bufferin's price consumers get less value moving the brand *in* to the position shown by a triangle in Figure 8.7. Thus, managers can modify the price (and perhaps benefits) of Bufferin to obtain a value positioning that is likely to attract consumers.

Use of Value Maps.   Value maps provide the new-product team with a means to set an initial price for their product. To succeed the new product should provide superior value to the customer. This means that the benefit-price ratio should be high and the product should be positioned such that it is not dominated by another product on the value map.

The exact price depends on several conditions. If the price is set too low the customers will get a very high value, but the firm may not earn sufficient margins to market the product profitably. (Early in the life of a new product good margins may be important to fund product refinement.) However, if there are manufacturing efficiencies for high volume or if the firm expects to exploit an experience curve to lower manufacturing cost, a low price may be justified to penetrate the market. Another concern is competitive response. Low prices often evoke competitive retaliation leading to unprofitable price wars. This would be true if competitors have high fixed costs such that they must defend their volume in order to function profitably. All said, the price decision is extremely complex; the value map is an important input to that decision.

Value maps should be used synergistically with perceptual maps because value maps make strong assumptions. When a value map is drawn it assumes implicitly that the perceptual dimensions are linear such that 4 units of effectiveness at $2 is the same as 2 units of effectiveness at $1. This may not always be true, so the team should use inputs from both perceptual and value maps to set the product's core benefit proposition. There are other technical concerns such as the choice of a "zero-point" and the choice of which price to use. In Figure 8.7 we chose the origin of the map to be just below the lower left point of the perceptual map. This choice seems to work empirically (Hauser and Gaskin 1989), but value map positions can be sensitive to the choice of the zero point.[1] We recommend this rule of thumb but suggest that the new product team be aware of the sensitivity of the map. The other concern is that there is not always a single price. Package sizes can vary between brands or even within a product line; some package goods or pharmaceuticals are concentrated, others are not; price can vary by region, and so on. In practice the best choice seems to be the average price per use. For example, in Figure 8.7 we used the average price per dose based on 100-tablet packages (the most commonly sold package size). In cases where the per-dollar dimensions are troublesome, a default approach is to add a price dimension to the perceptual map. This makes the perceptual map more complex, but does capture the price tradeoffs critical in many markets.

---

[1] A recent development provides the capability of drawing a value map directly from sales and price data such as that obtained from automated supermarket checkout systems. For such a map the zero-point estimation is implicit in the algorithm that produces the map. However, because such maps are obtained directly from sales data rather than directly from a perceptual map, the new product team must be cautious in comparing the value maps so obtained to the corresponding perceptual maps. Nonetheless, such implicit maps have tremendous potential because they can be developed easily and inexpensively. For more details see Shugan (1985).

DESIGN AND THE USE OF MAPS

Benefit Opportunities

Perceptual maps help managers understand a product category and recognize opportunities by providing a succinct representation of how customers view and evaluate products in a category. Value maps complete the Core Benefit Proposition by enabling managers to set a target price for the new product such that customers perceive it to be of high value. These inputs enhance the creativity of the new product team and encourage marketing, engineering, and R&D to work together to focus their creativity on achieving a successful position in the market.

The emphasis in perceptual mapping is on benefits and needs rather than the physical characteristics of the product. Customers make judgments based on perceived reality. Early in the new-product design process it is extremely important to identify opportunities, select a target position, and direct the product development process, that is, establish the Core Benefit Proposition. This does not mean that physical characteristics are not important. On the contrary, physical characteristics and psychological cues such as advertising and salesforce messages communicate and fulfill the CBP. By identifying the structure of perceptions and by linking it to customer needs and benefits the new product team identifies better the physical and psychological aspects of the new product.

Concept Positioning

The use of concepts in perceptual mapping is important because they test the CBP and the product's ability to fill a positioning opportunity. Even if there are no products now in the category, perceptual mapping based on product concepts reveals the structure of perceptions and targets the key benefit dimensions. For example, Figure 8.3 mapped consumer perceptions of existing transportation alternatives. Close examination of the map suggests a need for a new service that provides for ease of travel and psychological comfort. To test this area of the map potential transportation consumers can be asked to evaluate new concepts such as a Budget Taxi Plan (BTP) in which a privately operated system provides service similar to that provided by taxis, but at a lower price. The only change is that if you request the budget plan, the driver may pick up or drop off other passengers on the way to your destination. Another concept, Personalized Premium Service (PPS) claims to be a publicly operated version of BTP except that the service is provided by minibuses rather than taxicabs. Consumer perceptions of these concepts are displayed on the perceptual map in Figure 8.8. Notice that the new systems are perceived as significantly better than the existing bus service on speed and convenience, and ease of travel, but that they do not achieve the goal of improved psychological comfort. To achieve this goal they will need to be improved to fulfill the more detailed consumer needs that make up psychological comfort.

Identifying a New Dimension

Because most products are evaluated within the perceptual structure of the segment, the most common positioning question is where to place our product in that space. Sometimes, however, a more revolutionary approach based on identifying a new dimension may be our best choice. If we identify a new dimension that is important to consumers and position uniquely upon it, we will enjoy high market share and profits.

Identifying a new dimension is difficult. New dimensions are based on latent, exciting needs, that is, needs which customers would view as important if they could be fulfilled. In many cases a new technology fulfills such exciting needs and makes them more salient to customers. In essence, the new technology "creates" the need. For example, the use of micrologic chips in pacemakers created the dimension of functional sophistication. In soft drinks, the

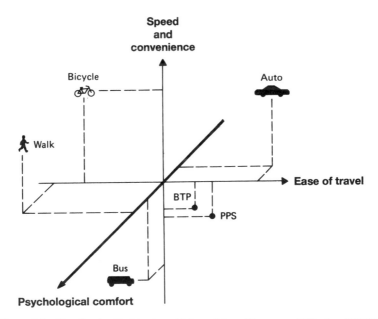

Figure 8.8   New Service Positionings (Adapted from Hauser and Wisniewski 1979)

use of saccharin and aspertame created the low-calorie dimension. Most new dimensions result from major product innovations. Minor product changes, though they may be intended to create a new dimension, are often reflected instead in the existing perceptual structure. For example, introducing a retractable hardtop on a car may not create a new dimension, but rather lead to a change of position on the sportiness dimension. Likewise, a new remote radio reprogrammable heart pacemaker may not create a new dimension, but lead to a change in position on the reliability dimension through its subattributes of lack of side effects and long life.

The English retail chain called "The Body Shop" created a dimension of ecological responsibility in health and beauty aid retailing. No products are sold that were tested on animals, all employees work for public service organizations one-half day per week (the company pays them), all products are biodegradable and environmentally safe, and packages can be refilled at the store. This strategy positions the Body Shop well on the "healthy" dimension and differentiates them on the new ecology dimension.

Sometimes an innovation is so major that it creates both a new dimensional structure and an entire new segment. In pacemakers, the use of micrologic components segmented the market into simple and sophisticated pacers, besides creating the dimension of functional capability in the sophisticated segment. Conversely, the use of microcomputers in autos did not create a new segment or dimension, but rather enhanced perceptions of reliability.

The final result of innovation may be either a new positioning within the current structure or the identification of a new dimension or an additional segment. When a firm sees no opportunities for improvement in the existing positioning structure, it should strive to add a dimension by identifying previously unmet exciting needs. One caution here is that managers often think they are revolutionizing a category when consumers feel nothing but a mild perceptual perturbation. Customer reaction must be measured to determine what is really occurring. This can be done informally by contact with key customers or by more advanced analytical methods such as those discussed in Chapter 9.

After-Use Positioning

Maps are also useful to compare perceptions of a product concept to those of the actual product that is developed based on the concept. By collecting evaluations after the customer is exposed to the actual product (or prototype), the new product team assesses if the product fulfills the core benefit proposition. For example, Figure 8.9 shows the position of a new pain-relief product after four weeks of use. Note the good, but not perfect,

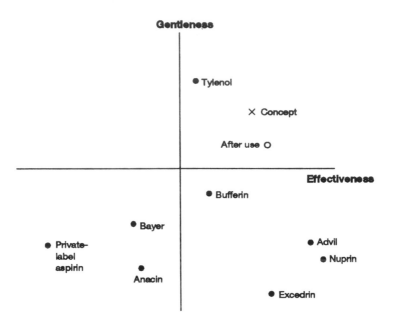

Figure 8.9   Perceptual Map of a New Pain Reliever after Home Use

match between consumer perceptions of the concept and the actual product. When perceptions of the product do not match the concept positioning, the team should modify the physical product or rethink its initial positioning claims.

Summary

This chapter has discussed methods of mapping and how they are used to identify gaps in markets, check positioning of the concepts, and determine if the products fulfill the Core Benefit Proposition. The next chapter reviews the analytic methods used to identify customer needs and produce perceptual maps. However, we have not yet answered a key design question: Which gap should we fill? Chapters 10 and 11 show how preference analysis is used to designate the best gap to fill.

REVIEW QUESTIONS

8.1. The "lens" model postulates that product features impact preference through the lens of perceptions. What are the advantages and disadvantages of this interpretation? How does the lens model impact new-product strategy?

8.2. Discuss the difference between a perceptual map and a value map. Why might a new-product team find both useful?

8.3. In some situations, particularly large industrial products, different members of the buying center might perceive the product differently. Why might perceptions differ? How does this affect new-product design?

8.4. What is the relationship between market definition and perceptual mapping? And value mapping?

8.5. Figure 8.6 is a perceptual map for communications technologies. One opportunity for a new product is indicated by a gap—there is no product that is dominant on both dimensions. If such a product were developed could you guarantee that it would be profitable? If so, how? If not, why not?

8.6. How might you represent customer preferences on a perceptual map? On a value map?

8.7. Does the cost of making a product affect its position on a perceptual map or a value map? If so, how? If not, how might you represent cost in the deciding how to position a product on a map?

9

Customer Needs and Perceptual Mapping: Methods and Procedures

IDENTIFYING CUSTOMER NEEDS

A perceptual map, a value map, or a CBP is only as good as the data upon which it is based. Thus we begin the analysis of customer perceptions by an in-depth search for customer needs—statements in the words of the customers that describe the benefits they need, want, or expect to get from a product. These needs often include the entire process by which customers use the product and they often include the needs of customers other than just the end users.

Consider a new-product team designing a laundry product. They might collect customer needs with respect to brands of laundry detergents, but opportunities might also be developed by understanding customer needs with respect to buying the detergent, bringing it home from the store, storing it in the laundry room, or, perhaps, laundry functions of sorting, carrying down (up) to the laundry room, folding after washing, and hanging in closets. Indeed, Kao Soap, Inc., a major Japanese packaged goods company developed a very successful brand called "Attack" by understanding how Japanese consumers buy, use and store detergents. In Japan, there is little storage space and consumers make almost daily trips to the store bringing home groceries and packaged goods by foot or bicycle. Attack fulfilled an unmet need by concentrating the detergent and putting it in a compact package. In addition, Attack is easy to stack at the store, thus fulfilling a need of another "customer," the small retailer that characterizes the Japanese distribution system. A few years later both American and Japanese companies introduced "Ultra" brands in imitation of Attack.

What is a Need?

In Chapter 8 we argued that customers buy based on perceptions. In searching for customer needs we keep this in mind—we want to understand the needs not the solutions. For example, in describing a computer monitor a customer might say that they need a noninterlaced megapixel monitor. However, "noninterlaced" and "megapixel" are solutions, not needs. Noninterlaced means that every line is scanned sequentially rather than the usual procedure where every even-numbered line is scanned, then every odd-numbered line is scanned.[1] If the lines are scanned frequently, then a noninterlaced monitor has less flicker, particularly when graphical images are shown as they are in CAD applications, business graphics applications, and graphical user interfaces. The *need* is "less flicker" or "easy to read" or "easy on my eyes." By understanding the need rather than the current solution we do not limit the creativity of the new-product team and we encourage them to seek new solutions that might address the needs better and at lower cost. For example, in Chapter 14 we illustrate how a medical instrument solved the need for improved hard-copy output by using computer printers that are in every doctor's office. Not only did this solve the need better, but it saved cost because the printer did not need to be built into the printer.

We must also keep in mind that some needs are easier to articulate than others. For example, industry often uses a "Kano-chart" characterization (King 1987), which characterizes needs by

- *Basic needs.* Those needs that the customer will just assume that the product satisfies. For example, a consumer assumes that a shampoo cleans hair.
- *Articulated needs.* Those needs which the customer can articulate readily. They usually are met by at least one current solution or are easily imagined as being met. For example, a customer can imagine a monitor that has no flicker.

---

[1] Megapixel means that there are 1 million pixels (dots) that make up the image. They are arrayed in a 1024×1024 matrix.

- *Exciting needs*. Needs such that the customer will be delighted and surprised if they are fulfilled. They are usually not met by current solutions and, in many cases, the customers find them hard to articulate. For example, some computer users would be excited if they never again had to spend time loading software updates. (Exciting needs are also known as unarticulated needs.)

In searching for these needs we must keep in mind that some needs change categories over time. For example, once exciting needs are met, they become articulated needs. Once every solution satisfies an articulated need all the time, the articulated need becomes a basic need. All three classes of needs must be identified. A product will not succeed if it does not satisfy basic needs, articulated needs usually define the basis of competition, and exciting needs represent opportunities upon which to excel and attract new customers.

To cast a wide net for customer needs, we begin with open-ended, qualitative methods.

Qualitative Methods

One-on-One Interviews.   Perhaps the most widely used and most effective technique for eliciting customer attributes directly from customers is experiential open-ended interviews. Individual customers are asked to describe existing products and how they use them and to speculate about needs they have that are unmet. The interviewer probes deeply on any stated need hoping to get clarification of that need and, sometimes, an unstated need. For example, if an automobile customer states that they are uncomfortable on a long trip, the interviewer would probe: "What do you mean by uncomfortable?—Describe the feeling and describe what aspects of the car make you uncomfortable." Some may discuss stiffness and back pain, whereas others mention motion sensitivity or the lack of fresh clean air. The interviewer also might probe on what is meant by a long trip or whether there is some uncomfortableness on short trips.

The interviews provide the raw material. Team members might listen to the interviews (or interview tapes) and/or read transcripts of the interviews. Team members should note any and all needs; reduction of the needs comes later in the process. In general, 20 to 30 qualitative interviews are sufficient per customer segment. For example, Figure 9.1 plots the expected percentage of total (detailed) needs identified as a function of the number of customers interviewed. The product category was a moderately complex durable good. Customers had heterogeneous needs. The plot for "important" needs is almost identical to Figure 9.1 indicating that 20 to 30 interviews are necessary

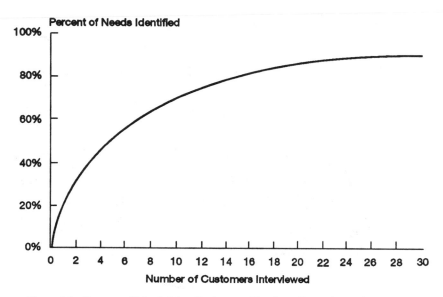

Figure 9.1   Percent of Needs Identified versus Number of Interviews (Griffin and Hauser 1993)

whether we cast our net for all needs or just the "important" needs.

With experience, interviews can be made more efficient. Figure 9.1 reports the needs obtained from independent interviews. However, recent improvements in interviewing techniques have led to a sequential procedure in which 5 to 10 interviews are conducted and reviewed, then subsequent interviews focus on the differences—new needs. With such techniques, 10 to 20 interviews might suffice.

Another important consideration in the analysis of qualitative data is that each member of the new-product team brings different perspectives to the analysis. Some team members will identify customer needs that other team members might miss. For example, Figure 9.2 plots the percent of needs identified as a function of the number of analysts that examined the transcripts. Experience matters—more experienced analysts do better than naive analysts, but only slightly better. To be safe, two or more team members should examine the transcripts.

Focus Groups.   An alternative qualitative technique is focus groups where groups of six to eight customers are asked to talk about their needs. Focus groups have some advantages; statements by one customer in the group can trigger comments by others and focus groups are excellent for uncovering shared perceptions. Conversely, in a typical 2-hour focus group the aver-

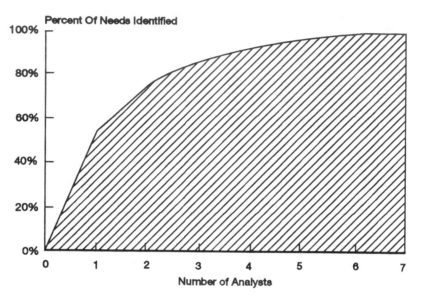

Figure 9.2   Percent of Needs Identified versus the Number of Analysts Examining the Data (Griffen and Hauser 1993)

age customer talks for 15 to 20 minutes versus the one hour that is typical for one-on-one interviews. It is common in focus groups that managers actually watch the groups from behind a one-way mirror or by remote video. For more details on focus groups review Chapter 5 on idea generation or see Calder (1977).

Recently Silver and Thompson (1991) compared the relative efficiency of focus groups and one-on-one interviews. (The interviews were the sequential interviews described earlier.) The product category was a complex office product. For that product two one-on-one interviews were about as effective as one 2-hour focus group. In other words, an hour of qualitative interviewing appears to be an hour of qualitative interviewing independent of whether one uses focus groups versus one-on-one interviews.[2]

Structured Methods.   Some firms prefer structured qualitative techniques. For example, the Repertory Grid Technique (Kelly 1955) asks customers to consider existing products three at a time. They are asked to select the two which are the most similar and to state why they are similar. They then select the two products which are the most dissimilar and state why they are

---

[2] For detailed analysis see Griffin and Hauser (1993a). This result is also supported by Fern (1982).

different. This continues for all triplets of products with probes for elaborations of the similarities and differences. In the Echo technique (Barthol and Bridge 1968) the interviewer probes on "good things," "bad things," "useful things," "useless things," and so on about the product. The probing continues until the customer can provide no further answers. In laddering or means-ends analysis, customers are asked for more basic or fundamental antecedents of their needs (Gutman 1982 and Reynolds & Gutman 1988).

Another technique is the use of verbal protocols to find needs (Bettman 1970, 1971; Bouwman, Frishkoff, and Frishkoff 1987; Ruiz and Jain 1991). In the method consumers talk aloud as they buy, use, describe, evaluate, or carry out a task. For example, a manager may talk out loud as she or he uses a decision support system. The verbal record is divided into individual clauses, goal and method statements, and problems and then needs are identified for input to the design process.

The structured methods are helpful, but in our experience less structured, more open-ended input procedures can do as well in generating a complete set of customer needs.

Other Sources of Customer Needs

Some firms may not have the resources or the time for qualitative market research or prefer alternative methods to obtain customer needs. One Japanese technique, called the "murmur of the customer," places products in public places such as shopping malls and allows customers to examine and or try the products. Developers stand in close proximity to the displays and record the comments that the customers make about the products. In other situations, firms talk to user groups or examine complaint/compliment files, previous market research, and warranty information. It is common in some industrial firms for new-product teams to use the team's experience to generate an initial list of the customer needs. With discipline and practice such managerial judgment is a valuable beginning, but there is no real substitute for talking directly to customers.

SORTING CUSTOMER NEEDS INTO HIERARCHIES

In Chapter 8 we illustrated how perceptual mapping identifies structure within a set of needs to highlight the two or three strategic dimensions upon which products are differentiated. This structure was important because it allowed managers to understand the fundamental directions that a new-product project must take if it is to succeed in the market place. However, the greater detail in the "snake plots" was also important because it specified the tactics with which to meet that challenge. When it comes to actually engineering the product, we will need even more detail—operational needs which elaborate the tactical needs. (In the language of product development, strategic needs are known as primary needs, tactical needs are known as secondary needs, and operational needs are known as tertiary needs.)

The method used to identify structure within a set of customer needs depends upon the detail with which the needs are elicited. When the goal is strictly one of positioning, marketing, or early ideas for the new product it may be sufficient to generate 20 to 30 customer needs such as those in the telecommunications example of figures 8.4 to 8.6. In other situations when the goal is engineering design it is necessary to identify customer needs that can be linked directly to engineering characteristics. In this case, the design team may identify 200 to 300 operational customer needs to design a quality product (see Chapter 13).

There are at least two analytical techniques that are used widely for the reduction of 20 to 30 tactical customer needs: factor analysis and similarity scaling. We cover these analytical techniques in the next section of this chapter. In this section we cover two methods to sort a larger number of needs (100-300 operational tertiary customer needs) into hierarchies: (1) managerial affinity diagrams and (2) cluster analysis of customer sorts. These techniques are growing in popularity as managers are more concerned with integrating the marketing and the engineering functions.

Managerial Judgment (Affinity Diagrams)

In the affinity diagram technique, the new product team sorts the customer needs themselves. While there are many variations in the methods by which a team of people can sort customer needs, a typical session might go something like the following.

Suppose that we begin with 240 customer needs and eight team members. Each customer need is written on either a $3'' \times 5''$ index card or a $3'' \times 5''$ Post-it note and each team member randomly selects 30 customer needs to sort. One team member begins by selecting a card from his or her pile, reading it aloud, and placing it on the table (or the wall if Post-it notes are used). The remaining team members select cards from their piles which they feel express a similar customer need, read them aloud, and place them next to the seed card. If the team agrees that the new need is similar to the needs in the pile, the card stays there; if not, a discussion ensues resulting in either a new pile or an agreement that the card is indeed similar. Piles continue to be generated through team discussion and, if necessary, new "seeds" are selected until all of the customer needs are sorted. The team then discusses the piles and imposes a hierarchy reflecting their judgment on how the detailed (tertiary) needs cluster to tactical (secondary) and strategic (primary) needs. Titles are added to the groupings for clarification. If possible, a card is chosen from the pile as a title; otherwise, the team chooses a title. Finally, the team reviews the structure, rearranging and retitling as appropriate.

The advantages of a managerial sort are that it is quick, inexpensive, and feasible for all organizations and that it helps team members reach a consensus on the structure of customer needs. Its disadvantage is that the structure may represent management's viewpoint, not that of the customer.

Customer Sort and Cluster Analysis

Customers can provide the data on structure. The input is simple; each customer is given a pile of cards representing customer needs and asked to sort them into piles putting together those that represent similar ideas. Each customer is allowed to use the definition of similarity that he or she feels is appropriate. After the cards are sorted the customer is asked to review each pile and select one card in each pile (an exemplar) that represents the pile. In a typical study, about thirty customers per unique segment provide the data. Although the piles differ slightly, it is hoped that such a summary represents a common underlying structure.

The data are summarized with a "co-occurrence matrix." The entry in the ith row and the jth column represents the number of times the ith customer need appeared in the same pile as the jth customer need. (If the number of piles differ, one can weight each customer's input to reflect more discrimination among needs.) For example, Table 9.1 gives a hypothetical example of entries from a co-occurrence matrix for the 25 tactical customer needs that were identified for telecommunications technologies. Table 9.1 suggests that customers sort "persuade" and "enhance ideas" in the same

TABLE 9.1 Co-Occurrence Values for Four (of Twenty-Five) Customer Needs for Telecommunications Technologies

	Persuade	Enhance Ideas	. . .	Quick Response	No real Hassle	. . .
Persuade	—	27		4	3	
Enhance ideas	27	—	. . .	2	3	. . .
. . .		. . .			. . .	
Quick response	4	2	. . .	—	25	. . .
No real hassle	3	3	. . .	25	—	. . .

piles and that they sort "quick response" and "no real hassle" in the same piles and that there was little overlap among the piles. If this data were representative of the full set of 25 customer needs, it might identify the same "effectiveness" and "ease-of-use" hierarchy as plotted in Figure 8.6.

In Table 9.1 it is easy to look at the co-occurrence matrix and decide that "persuade" and "enhance ideas" and that "quick response" and "no real hassle" group together. An experienced analyst might be able to see structure within such a table for 25 customer needs, but for 100-300 customer needs it would be extremely difficult to see structure by inspection. Thus, we turn to an analytical technique called hierarchical cluster analysis.

In a hierarchical cluster analysis we treat the co-occurrence values as aggregate similarity measures and seek a grouping of customer needs such that any two needs within a group are similar (have high co-occurrence values) and such that any two needs in different groups are dissimilar (have low co-occurrence values). A hierarchical cluster procedure begins with each customer need as a separate cluster and then joins the two most similar. It continues joining needs to clusters or clusters to one another to form a tree (or hierarchy) known as a dendogram. By visually examining this tree, the new product team identifies the structure. For example, Figure 9.3 gives a hypothetical hierarchical structure based on the co-occurrence matrix in Table 9.1. We have added two needs, "solve problems" and "inexpensive," to illustrate better the dendogram. Notice that at the first four stages the dendogram joins customer needs to clusters. It is only at the final stage that two clusters are joined. A new product team examining Figure 9.3 might readily decide that there are two primary clusters, "persuade-enhance-solve" and quick-no-hassle-inexpensive."

The final step is to name the clusters. To do this the team labels each of the customer needs in the dendogram with the number of times that needs were identified by customers as an exemplar. For example, had "effectiveness" and "ease-of-use" been in the dendogram in Figure 9.3 we would have

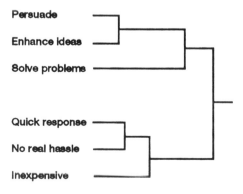

Persuade

Enhance ideas

Solve problems

Quick response

No real hassle

Inexpensive

Figure 9.3 Hypothetical Hierarchical Clustering of Telecommunications Customer Needs (Dendogram)

TABLE 9.2 Comparison of Two Methods to Identify the Structure of
Customer Needs for Coolers and Picnic Baskets

Affinity Diagram	
Strategic Needs	Tactical needs
Container utility	Container serves multiple purposes
	Suitable for year-round use
Convenient	Access to container
	Container is organized, neat
	Easily movable
	Easy to keep between uses
	Everything fits in one container
	External container dimensions
	Lets me carry liquids
	Lets me carry nonfood items
Physical characteristics	Attractive, good looking
	Container does not leak
	Container is durable
	Container is rugged
	Container movement
	Easy to drain excess water
	Flexible construction, moldable
	Made of nontoxic materials
	Protects things
	Waterproof
Container price	Cooling material is cheap
	Good price for the performance
	Inexpensive over the long run
	Reasonably priced
Thermal characteristics	Contains a cooling mechanism
	Maintains desired temperature
	Maintains multiple temperatures
	Temperature is regulated

expected them to cluster with the first and second clusters respectively and to have been chosen more often than other customer needs as exemplars. We would name the primary clusters accordingly.

Clustering algorithms are widely available as part of most standard statistical packages. While a debate on the relative merits of alternative methods for clustering is beyond the scope of this chapter, we have found that squared distance algorithms (e.g., Ward's[3] method) produce very interpretable re-

[3] In Ward's method, at any step in the hierarchy, the squared distance (similarity) from each customer need to the cluster centroid is calculated. Two clusters are merged in the next step to give the largest increase in the overall sum of squared within-cluster distances (see Norušis [1988, p. B-83]).

TABLE 9.2 (Continued)   Comparison of Two Methods to Identify the
Structure of Customer Needs for Coolers and Picnic Baskets

Customer-Sort Diagram	
Strategic Needs	Tactical needs
Attractive, good looking	Container edges, etc. do not cause problems
	Container is durable
	Elegant design
	Reasonably priced
Convenient	Easy to use
	Lid works well
	Easy to drain excess water
	Container is organized, neat
Works well	Does not leak
	Separates things
	Protects things
	Everything fits into one container
	Serves multiple purposes
Right size	Efficient use of space
	Suitable for year-round use
	Useful for traveling
Maintains food temperatures	Uses a convenient cooling mechanism
	Temperature is controllable
Carries many kinds of things	Lets me carry nonfood items
	Lets me carry food items
Easily movable	Easy to transport
	Convenient to carry

Adapted from Griffen (1989, Appendix 6).

sults. Most available packages allow a number of clustering algorithms to be applied and sensitivity can be examined easily.

The advantage of a customer-sort/hierarchical-cluster method of identifying the structure is that the structure is based on the voice of the customer not the voice of the team. The disadvantage is the cost and time involved in the collection and the analysis of the data.

For example, Table 9.2 compares the affinity and customer-sort methods in their ability to identify primary and secondary levels of the customer needs for portable food carrying devices (e.g., picnic baskets and coolers) from a list of 220 detailed customer needs. After seeing the customer-sort hierarchy, the team felt that it provides a richer and more category-specific structure than that identified with affinity diagrams. In another situation in a consumer packaged-good firm there was more agreement between the hierarchies identified by judgment and the analysis of consumer data for a major product category. However, the customer-sort data provided a structure that appeared to represent customers better. The team accepted the customer-sort structure once they saw it. In general, when managerial-judgment and customer-sort hierarchies are compared, the product-development teams tend to sort needs according to how the product was built while customers tend to sort needs according to how they use the product. In every application that we have seen where both techniques have been tried, the customer-sort hierarchy was accepted as the better representation.

ANALYTICAL METHODS FOR PRODUCING PERCEPTUAL MAPS

Now we turn from detailed consumer need structures that build up strategic needs to methods of directly assessing strategic benefit dimensions. We examine two methods to produce perceptual maps that support a strategic positioning for the new product. The first is factor analysis. It begins with a set of 20 to 30 tactical customer needs and identifies a structure within those needs based upon the way customers evaluate products. The second is similarity scaling, also known as multidimensional scaling. It infers the strategic dimensions based upon customers' perceptions of similarity among products. After presenting the techniques, we compare their advantages and disadvantages and present a case which illustrates the managerial use of perceptual maps.

Factor Analysis of Customer Needs

Factor analysis attempts to find a reduced set of strategic dimensions that represents the information contained in a larger set of customer needs. In factor analysis we view the tactical needs as imperfect indicators of the primary needs. We hypothesize that customers reveal their primary needs by the way they evaluate existing products and concepts or the attributes that characterize them. This differs from our use of cluster analysis, where we view the primary needs as a summary of the secondary tactical needs.

A perceptual mapping study based on factor analysis begins by asking 100 to 300 customers to rate the products with which they are familiar on a set of measurement scales such as shown in Table 9.3. The averages of these ratings provide the snake plots such as that shown in Figure 8.4 for telecommunications technologies. But as we have seen, snake plots are too detailed for strategic positioning. A better summary of customer perceptions may be provided through some aggregation.

Underlying Model of Customer Ratings.   Although customers may evaluate products on many needs, we expect that these evaluations can be sum-

TABLE 9.3 Measures of Customer Evaluations of Products with Respect
to the Customer Needs

	Strongly Disagree	Disagree	Neither Agree nor Disagree	Agree	Strongly Agree
I can convey all forms of technical information by NBVT.	[ ]	[ ]	[ ]	[ ]	[ ]
I can find and and reach the right person with NBVT. . . .	[ ]	[ ]	[ ] . . .	[ ]	[ ]

marized strategically by a smaller number of dimensions. Even for complex products such as automobiles, we expect that customers remember the basic benefits of different brands and summarize those brands (in memory) by those basic benefits. For example, for a laundry detergent there might be 5 to 10 strategic needs that are summarized by two basic benefits such as "efficacy" and "gentleness." It is likely to be more for an automobile, but still far fewer than twenty to thirty. When selecting a strategic positioning vis-à-vis competition, we want to be sure that the core benefit proposition provides the strategic positioning and reflects the basic benefits that customers use to summarize their perception of products. Factor analysis seeks to identify these basic benefits.

For example, Figure 8.6 suggests that customers summarize telecommunications technologies by the basic benefit dimensions of "effectiveness" and "ease of use." Suppose, as in Figure 8.5, we ask a customer to rate a technology on a tactical customer need such as "convey all forms of technical information." Then, if our model of customer memory is correct, we expect that the customer's summarization—effectiveness and ease of use—will influence the way she/he rates a technology on "conveys all forms of technical information." As shown in Figure 9.4 we expect that there will be some component of this rating that is due to the basic "common" structure, in this case the customer's perception of the technology's effectiveness, some component

Figure 9.4 Components of a Customer's Response to a Measurement Scale

that is unique to the attribute we are measuring, and, of course, some component that is due to the inexact measurement—the error.

For example, the average rating of convey "all forms of information," scale 9 in Figure 8.4, is 3.7. This scale is related to effectiveness, so suppose that of this 3.7 rating, 3.0 is due to the customer's perception of the effectiveness of personal visit, 0.5 is unique to the customer's perception of personal visit on the "convey all forms of information," and 0.2 is error. Then we would decompose the customer's rating as follows:

$$4.7 \qquad = \qquad 3.0 \qquad + \qquad 0.5 \qquad + \qquad 0.2 \qquad (9.1)$$

(Rating of "conveys	(Contribution	(Unique contri-	(Error)
all forms of	of "effective-	bution of scale)	
information")	ness" factor)		

If equation 9.1 does represent how customers react to the scales they use to rate products, then we would hope to uncover the underlying structure by observing how they rate products. For example, we would expect that a customer's rating of "conveys all forms of information" would be correlated with their perceptions of "effectiveness." Because two "effectiveness"—scales are correlated with "effectiveness" we expect that those two scales would themselves be correlated. This means that the correlations among attribute scales should contain the raw material we need to infer structure.

Identifying the Factor Dimensions.   If we already knew the factor dimensions, "effectiveness" and "ease of use," we would just look at the correlations among the attribute scales, e.g., "conveys all forms of information," and the factor dimensions in order to decide which attribute scales measure which factor dimensions. But we cannot observe the factor dimensions directly. Instead, the computer algorithm that is factor analysis searches for a set of common factors that can explain as much as possible of the variation in the customers' ratings of the attribute scales. For a given number of factors, the computer algorithm outputs a set of correlations, called *factor loadings*, that represent the correlations between the attribute scales and the factors that the algorithm identified. For example, the plot of relationships in Figure 8.5 is based on the factor loadings for the telecommunications attribute-scales in Table 9.4. It is by examining the scales with which dimension 1 correlates, that we name dimension 1 "effectiveness."

Notice that "effectiveness" is the name that the new product team uses to summarize the scales; the word "effectiveness" is not determined directly from the customer. Nonetheless, if the attribute scales were a good summary of the customer's tactical needs, the name given via factor analysis is a good strategic summary of the customers' basic benefit dimensions.

TABLE 9.4 Factors Loadings are Used to Name the Dimensions of the Perceptual Map

Attributes	Effectiveness	Ease of Use
1. Effective information exchange (−)	−0.77	−0.17
2. Find and reach the right person	0.25	0.43
3. Save time	0.17	0.47
4. Not need visual aids	0.39	−0.16
5. Get trapped (−)	−0.33	−0.20
6. Eliminate paperwork	0.31	0.43
7. Persuade (−)	−0.70	−0.20
8. Focus on issues	−0.04	−0.07
9. All forms of information	0.65	−0.18
10. Real hassle (−)	−0.11	−0.83
11. Control impression	0.56	0.07
12. Security	0.18	0.11
13. Plan in advance (−)	0.23	−0.44
14. Eliminate red tape	−0.00	−0.21
15. Monitor people, operations, experiments	0.65	0.15
16. Interaction	0.78	0.05
17. Solve problems (−)	−0.55	−0.27
18. Express feelings	0.66	0.17
19. Misinterpret (−)	−0.49	0.00
20. Group discussion	0.75	0.05
21. Inexpensive	−0.27	0.52
22. Quick response	0.07	0.71
23. Enhance idea development	0.77	0.09
24. Commitment	0.44	0.32
25. Maintain contact	0.50	0.52

(−) Indicates the question was worded so that a high attribute rating would mean a poor evaluation.

For more details on the mathematics of factor analysis see Rummel (1970), Cooley and Lohnes (1971), or Harman (1976). There are many variations on factor analysis including common (with a uniqueness component), principle components (without a uniqueness common), and confirmatory (testing rather than searching for structure). There are issues around "rotation" which represents the orientation of the perceptual map and issues around the algorithm used to obtain the factor loadings. From the managerial perspective, it is important that a statistically valid factor analysis procedure be used and, if necessary, that advice be obtained from a statistician or market researcher. One of several PC-based or mainframe-based statistical packages (SPSS, SAS, Systat, Statgraphics, etc.) can be used to run the analyses.

Determining the Number of Factor Dimensions.   The perceptual map for telecommunications technologies in Figure 8.6 uses two factor dimensions. Although two dimensions clearly simplify the message conveyed by the twenty-five more-detailed attribute scales, we might wonder why two rather than three or four factors were chosen. There are two classical rules for determining the number of factors: the "scree" rule and the "eigenvalue-greater-than-one" (EGO) rule.

The factor analysis computer program identifies factors by examining the matrix of correlations among the detailed attributes. It extracts factors one-by-one in order of variance explained. Thus each successive factor explains less variance. In fact, if there are 25 attributes it is possible to have 25 factors that, taken together, explain the same amount of variance as the attributes. The judgment that the analyst must make is how many factors are needed to explain enough variance that the basic information is still retained but in a simpler form.

Figure 9.5, an illustration of the *scree rule,* plots the incremental variance explained by each factor. The interpretation of Figure 9.5 is that after so many factors the amount of variance that additional factors explain will level off such that the explained variance is just barely above the noise level. This leveling off is shown in Figure 9.5 after the second factor. (The scree rule takes its name from geology where the "scree" is the pile of rock that accumulates at the bottom of a rock slide.)

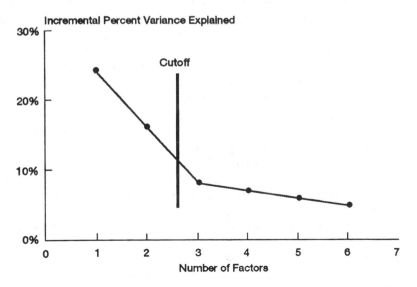

Figure 9.5 Example of the "Scree" Rule for Determining the Number of Factors to Use

The EGO is similar in concept. Because the attributes are standardized to have variance 1.0 a factor is no better than a single attribute if it cannot explain more variance than 1.0. Statistically, the variance explained by each factor is equal in numerical value to a mathematical construct called an eigenvalue (of the correlation matrix). Thus, if the eigenvalue drops below 1.0, the EGO rule suggests that it not be retained.

In practice, either the scree rule or the EGO rule can be used to select the appropriate number of factors, but only if tempered by managerial judgment. It is good practice to consider retaining the number of factors indicated by a combination of the rules and to consider retaining slightly more or slightly fewer factors. The final selection should balance the variance explained with the ease of interpreting the factors and their usefulness to the new product team.

Producing the Perceptual Map.   Once you have decided on the number of factor dimensions and have named them using the factor loadings, it is time to produce the perceptual map. We used the correlations among the attribute scales to identify the factor loadings. To identify the map positions we use the attribute scales themselves.

Table 9.5 is an example of the data. Each customer rates each product (telecommunications device) on each attribute scale. We cannot observe directly the customer's rating of the products on the factor dimensions (effectiveness and ease-of-use), but we can estimate from the data how they would have rated the products on the factor dimensions. These estimates are called *factor scores*. In a regression-like procedure the factor-analysis computer algorithm uses the correlations among the attribute scales and the correlations among the attribute scales and the factors (i.e., the factor loadings) to compute a set of "regression" weights, called *factor-score coefficients*. The factor scores are then estimated by multiplying the factor-score coefficients times the attribute weightings and summing over attributes.

Fortunately for most applications the factor scores themselves are output directly from the computer programs. For example, in Table 9.5 the factor score of -0.3 represents customer 1's evaluation of telephone on the factor dimension of effectiveness. This value is based on a weighted sum of customer 1's rating of telephone on the 25 more-detailed attributes (the first row of data in Table 9.5). The map position of telephone (in Figure 8.6) is then the average over all customers of the factor scores for telephone.

Estimating the Position of a New Product.   If the customers were given a "stretching" concept (i.e., one that is a breakthrough on some benefit dimension) for a new product and asked to rate it, then you have measures of their evaluations of the new product on the more detailed attributes. In this

TABLE 9.5 Example of Attribute-Ratings Data Matrix with Factor Scores

	Attribute Scales				Factor Scores	
	Effec. Info. Exch.	Find and Reach	Save Time ...	Main- tain Contact	Effec- tiveness	Ease of Use
Customer 1						
Telephone	4	2	4	1	−0.3	0.9
Personal Visit	1	3	2	3	1.0	0.2
NBVT	2	2	2	2	0.0	−0.2
TTY	3	2	2	1	−0.1	−0.1
CCTV	3	1	1	1	0.2	−0.9
Customer 2						
Telephone	3	1	5	1	−0.4	0.8
Personal Visit	2	2	3	2	1.1	0.1
NBVT	3	1	3	1	0.1	−0.3
TTY	4	1	3	1	−0.9	−0.2
CCTV	2	1	2	1	0.3	−1.0
Customer N						
Telephone	5	3	3	2	−0.2	1.0
Personal Visit	2	4	1	4	0.9	0.3
NBVT	5	3	1	3	−0.1	−0.1
TTY	5	3	1	2	−1.1	0.0
CCTV	4	2	1	2	0.1	−0.8

NBVT=narrow band video telephone; TTY=teletype terminal; CCTV=closed-circuit television.

case the map position of the new product is determined from those ratings by the procedure described above. In Figure 8.6 the map positions of NBVT and closed-circuit television were obtained in this way.

However, in some cases you may want to estimate where a concept might be positioned if it were improved along some attribute. In this case you must first estimate quantitatively how much that improvement would be. For example, you might estimate that the average rating of NBVT on "effective information exchange" would improve by 10%. The movement of NBVT on effectiveness and ease-of-use would then be obtained by weighting the new simulated ratings of NBVT by the factor-score coefficients and summing. The new map position is then an estimate of the position that would have been obtained had customers been asked to rate directly the new NBVT concept.

Some Hints.   Factor analysis is a powerful technique, but it has its dangers. Perhaps the most common danger is "concept hype." When customers are asked to rate a new product they may provide artificially inflated ratings of the product because the concept statement calls their attention to the product, the concept statement makes the benefits extremely salient, or respondents just want to please the interviewer. To test for (and correct) concept hype we recommend that a sample of customers be asked to rate an existing product as if it were a concept. By comparing customer ratings of the concept to ratings of the actual product, you can measure the magnitude of concept hype.

Another danger is that different customers use different parts of the rating scale. Some may give uniformly high ratings and some may give uniformly low ratings. Some may use the whole scale and some may use just the upper part of the scale. To correct for this potential bias we recommend that you standardize the ratings by respondent. That is compute the mean and standard deviation of the customer's responses to all of the rating scales then subtract that mean and divide by that standard deviation. An alternative is to normalize the individual's ratings so they sum to one.

Sometimes an attribute scale is unique. It may load on no factor but still be important or it may not differentiate between currently existing products. Thus it is useful to examine carefully any attribute that does not load on any factor. It should not be neglected without further investigation. Indeed, these unique attributes sometimes represent opportunities for identifying new customer needs.

Finally, remember to ask customers about brands they know. We suggest a "consideration set" of brands they would consider and others they would reject plus concepts you present in a complete enough form so they can be evaluated.

Discussion and Summary.   Factor analysis has been used successfully in thousands of product categories. It is an effective technique to identify structure within a complex set of detailed attributes. To use factor analysis simply:

- Obtain the structure of perceptions by factor analyzing customers' ratings of product attributes across considered products and individual customers. Interpret and name the factor dimensions by examining the factor loadings.
- Select the appropriate number of dimensions by combining judgment and the analytical rules (e.g., scree and EGO).
- Estimate the positions of the existing products, the test products, and the concepts by using the factor scores or the factor-score coefficients.
- Examine the gaps in the map to determine the potential opportunities and examine the weaknesses and the strengths of the concepts to identify potential improvements.

Factor analysis is easy to use and has a proven track record. The behavioral assumption of how customers react to rating scales is intuitively appealing and, empirically, factor analysis usually leads to results with strong face validity. It is a natural statistical complement to direct cluster analysis of the rating scales. The major disadvantage of factor analysis is that it depends on a well-specified set of customer needs (attributes); it can only identify structure *within* a set of needs, not beyond them.

In the next section we review a technique, similarity scaling, which identifies a reduced set of dimensions directly from customers' ratings of interproduct similarity.

Scaling of Similarity Judgments

In some cases new product managers want to enhance creativity by looking beyond the attribute structure and identifying a perceptual map that is not based directly on a grouping of attribute ratings. One such technique is based on customer's direct ratings of how similar/dissimilar products (and concepts) are to/from one another.

We illustrate this technique with an example based on business schools. Consider three business schools, Harvard, Stanford, and the University of Chicago. Most students would judge Harvard and Stanford to be the two most similar schools of this set. The University of Chicago is likely to be perceived as quite dissimilar from Stanford and even more dissimilar from Harvard. Now consider what these similarity judgments would imply on a perceptual map. If we were to place Harvard on the far right of a perceptual map, we might place the University of Chicago on the opposite end of the map, the far left of the map. This large distance would reflect the dissimilarity among the schools. Stanford would be placed close to Harvard and far from Chicago, but, perhaps, between Harvard and Chicago to reflect the fact that it is not as dissimilar from Chicago as is Harvard.

If instead of asking you just about Harvard, Stanford, and Chicago, we asked you to also consider Northwestern, Wharton, Michigan, Cornell, and Columbia, you would need to provide more similarity judgments resulting in a more complex map. In fact, if you were really discriminating in your judgments we might need many dimensions to represent your similarity judgments. Fortunately, customer perceptions underlying similarity judgments often can be mapped in a relatively few dimensions. For example, Figure 9.6 shows a similarity map derived from the judgments of 100 entering students at Northwestern University. Notice that Harvard and Stanford are indeed close together and that Chicago is on the far left.

In Figure 9.6 the axes are labeled "realism" and "outcomes." These labels are not endogenous to the analysis, but rather chosen in an attempt to

Figure 9.6   Similarity Map of Business Schools (Adapted from Simmie 1978)

explain the positions of the points on the map. In this case the analyst was familiar with the programs at all of the eight schools and was able to identify labels. We discuss below how one might use other means to name the dimensions.

The Data.   Customers are first asked to evaluate existing products and product concepts with respect to similarity. For example, Table 9.6 provides one example of similarity ratings for telecommunications technologies. The data collection in Table 9.6 asks customers to provide a metric measure of similarity. Alternatively, customers can be asked to rank each product in relationship to each other product or to rank all pairs of products in terms of similarity. The advantage of the rank-order (nonmetric) measures is that they are easier judgments to make. The advantage of the metric measures is that they provide more data per judgment and, if the data is accurate, can produce maps with fewer data points.

These measures are tabulated for each customer or averaged across customer groups to produce a proximity matrix whose entries represent the similarities or dissimilarities among the products. For example, Table 9.7 represents the average similarities among telecommunications technologies. Of all the pairs of technologies, NBVT and CCTV are the most similar and

TABLE 9.6 Measures of Customer Evaluations of Products with Respect to Similarity

	Very Similar				Very Different
	1	2	3	4	5
Telephone and narrow band video telephone	[ ]	[ ]	[ ]	[ ]	[ ]
Personal visit and narrow band video telephone with NBVT	[ ]	[ ]	[ ]	[ ]	[ ]

telephone and CCTV are the most dissimilar. If you compare these measures to the interpoint distances in Figure 8.6 you will note that the interpoint distances are proportional to the dissimilarity measures in Table 9.7.

Producing the Perceptual Map.   Based on the relative similarities of Harvard, Stanford, and Chicago we were able to guess the map positions by placing the points in such a manner as to reproduce the judged similarities among the schools. If we were able to visualize maps easily we might take the data, place the points on a map, and adjust them so that the interpoint distances reproduce the perceived dissimilarities. Conceptually this is what the computer algorithms do in similarity scaling. Given an initial choice of positions, the distance between the points is calculated and a statistical measure, called "stress," is calculated to summarize how well the map fits the data. A large value of stress means a poor fit; a small value a good fit. The computer algorithm adjusts the points to reduce stress and continues doing so until stress is minimized. The resulting map is the best representation of the data using the map's dimensions.

The number of dimensions is determined in a manner that is similar conceptually to that used for factor analysis with stress playing the role of variance explained. As we increase the number of dimensions we represent the data better and the value of stress is reduced. By plotting the stress values

TABLE 9.7 Perceptual Distance Measured in Dissimilarity

	Personal visit	Telephone	NBVT	CCTV	TTY
Personal visit	—				
Telephone	10.5	—			
NBVT	7.3	8.2	—		
CCTV	8.5	13.8	5.8	—	
TTY	13.4	8.4	6.7	11.1	—

versus the number of dimensions we look for the "elbow" or "scree" where the incremental improvements in stress taper off. The final choice of the number of dimensions is a balance between the stress values and the ability to interpret and use the map.

Naming the Axes.   One method to name the axes was illustrated in Figure 9.6. Using knowledge of the category the analyst names the dimensions to explain best the products' positions. While this may seem arbitrary, it is just this creativity that similarity maps seek to elicit. Sometimes the new product team becomes tied to the attributes that are generated; the similarity map suggests new directions that the customers may not have articulated or that the new product team may not have understood.

Another method to name the dimensions is to regress the attribute measures on the coordinates of the map. The resulting regression coefficients are called *directional cosines* and represent the relationship between the measured attributes and the axes derived from the similarity measures. The manager can then name the dimensions based on the attributes. For example, Figure 9.7 lists 16 attributes of shopping centers in the Chicago area and plots the perceptual map based on similarity judgments among seven of those shopping centers. The directional cosines shown on the left of Figure 9.7 enable us to label the axes as "variety" (variety of merchandise, availability of credit, "specials," store availability, and variety of the stores) and "quality/ price" (prestige of the stores, quality of merchandise, reasonable price, specials, and free parking).

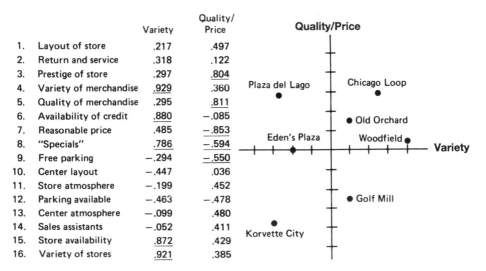

		Variety	Quality/ Price
1.	Layout of store	.217	.497
2.	Return and service	.318	.122
3.	Prestige of store	.297	.804
4.	Variety of merchandise	.929	.360
5.	Quality of merchandise	.295	.811
6.	Availability of credit	.880	−.085
7.	Reasonable price	.485	−.853
8.	"Specials"	.786	−.594
9.	Free parking	−.294	−.550
10.	Center layout	−.447	.036
11.	Store atmosphere	−.199	.452
12.	Parking available	−.463	−.478
13.	Center atmosphere	−.099	.480
14.	Sales assistants	−.052	.411
15.	Store availability	.872	.429
16.	Variety of stores	.921	.385

Figure 9.7   Perceptual Map of Shopping Locations (Koppelman and Hauser 1979)

Position of the New Products.   New products are positioned in a similarity map by

- Measuring new similarities for the new product
- Judgmentally shifting the product directly on the perceptual map

The pros and cons of each technique depend on the product category, the creativity of the new product team, and the stage of the new product development process.

Some Hints.   Similarity scaling is a powerful technique, but it must be used with caution. Practice has shown that seven or eight stimuli are necessary for a good two-dimensional map. For more than two dimensions it is a good rule of thumb that there be at least three times as many stimuli as there are dimensions. Another concern is that similarity may or may not be representable by a structure based on interpoint distances. For example, a friend may comment that your appearance is similar to that of your parents, but that same friend would be unlikely to comment that your parents' appearance was similar to yours. In such cases a treelike structure might prove a better representation of a similarity structure.

Naturally, one should limit data collection to those products with which the respondents are familiar. Such caution leads to more accurate maps that better represent customer perceptions. Recent algorithms (Katahira 1989) facilitate such limitations in data collection by allowing customers to rank only those products or concepts that they would consider seriously.

Discussion and Summary.   Similarity scaling has been applied in a variety of product categories providing creative insight that might not have been otherwise available. To use similarity scaling:

- Have customers evaluate existing products or product concepts according to their relative similarity and form an average proximity matrix for each group of customers you wish to analyze.[4]
- Use a computer algorithm to produce a map in 2, 3, . . . dimensions.
- Based on managerial judgment, limitations owing to the number of stimuli, and a plot of "stress" select the appropriate number of dimensions.
- Name the dimensions based on the relative position of the stimuli or a regression of the map coordinates on attribute ratings.

[4] In some cases one may wish to analyze each customer separately or to use an algorithm that produces a common perceptual map in which the dimensions are scaled differently for each customer.

- Identify gaps and opportunities by examining the positions of the existing products and, perhaps, the new product concepts.

A Comparison of the Quantitative Analytical Techniques

Factor Analysis and Similarity Scaling.   There are advantages and disadvantages to both factor analysis and similarity scaling. In factor analysis, ratings directly measure customers' evaluations of products. These evaluations are easy to interpret and can be linked to potential product improvements. However, factor analysis cannot identify any perceptual dimensions that are not represented by the attribute measures and, hence, is dependent on the ability of new product managers to accurately and completely identify customer benefits.

Similarity scaling gathers its input independently of stated customer benefits. Customer statements about which products are similar and dissimilar indicate which products are likely to be considered as substitutes and, thus, competitive. Similarity scaling is particularly useful if some attributes of a product are difficult to scale—the allure of a perfume—or are latent and difficult for the customer to articulate. However, because attributes are not used to generate structure it may be difficult to name and interpret the similarity-based dimensions. The new product designers must depend to some extent upon their personal knowledge of the market.

Both techniques are useful in product design. No one technique is suited to every situation. Rather it is important to understand the strengths and weaknesses of both techniques and match their use to the needs of the creative team. Factor analysis is best if customer needs and benefits can be described and measured accurately. Similarity scaling is best if customer needs are difficult for customers to verbalize or if the team is looking for additional creative input.

Other Analytical Methods.   Many specialized techniques have been developed to generate maps. For example in consumer packaged goods, brand switching data can be used to generate maps based on similarity measures (Lehmann 1988; Fraser and Bradford 1983, 1984) or more elaborate choice models based on UPC and panel data (e.g., Shugan 1986; and Elrod 1988). These methods use the availability of purchase rather than survey data to estimate maps. In package goods this kind of approach can reduce the cost and time of generating maps, but may not provide the attribute richness of say factor analysis. Other examples are algorithmic procedures based on probabilistic models (Mackay and Zinnes 1986; and Katahira 1989), which represent the most recent mapping extensions.

As you begin perceptual mapping consider alternative data sources for your industry and the various statistical procedures. You should get advice from a statistician or modeler to help you evaluate the best measurement and estimation method for your product class.

We now close this chapter with a managerial example of the use of perceptual maps. In this case, factor analysis was used to identify the positioning of a new health service.

EXAMPLE APPLICATION: HEALTH MAINTENANCE ORGANIZATION

The MIT Health Department was considering conversion to an HMO that would provide most medical care for a fixed annual fee. They wanted to design the HMO so that it would attract enough consumers to support both the fixed costs and the operating costs. They commissioned a perceptual map to compare a new product concept to existing care, to a pilot HMO that had been operating for one year, and to the major competition—Harvard Community Health Plan.

Questionnaires were sent to 1,000 members of the community. Of the 447 that were returned, 367 were prospective members of the new HMO and 80 were members of the pilot HMO. Figure 9.8 is the snake plot for sixteen detailed attributes, the factor loadings, and the resulting perceptual map.

By examining the high loadings on each dimension, the factors were labeled (1) quality, (2) personalness, (3) value, and (4) convenience. Quality correlated with trust, preventative care, availability of good doctors, and hospitals. Personalness reflected a friendly atmosphere with privacy and no bureaucratic hassle. Value was not just price, but rather paying the right amount for services. Convenience reflected location, waiting time, and hours of operation.

Based on the perceptual map it became clear that the average perceptions of existing care were superior to the new HMO on all dimensions except convenience. It was unlikely that the concept, as stated, could draw a large number of consumers from existing care providers. Now compare the concept's ratings to those for the pilot program. The pilot plan exceeds the concept in all dimensions, even though the concept and the pilot are essentially the same service. Although this could be self-selection or post-purchase rationalization, it was more likely to be a case of a good product where few people perceived it as such until they had experience with it. To be successful the HMO would have to develop an aggressive campaign to communicate performance to perspective members. Testimonials and "live" media such as

1. I would be able to get medical service and advice easily any time of the day and night.
2. I would have to wait a long time to get service.
3. I could trust that I am getting really good medical care.
4. The health services would be inconveniently located and would be difficult to get to.
5. I would be paying too much for my required medical services.
6. I would get a friendly, warm and personal approach to my medical problem.
7. The plan would help me prevent medical problems before they occurred.
8. I could easily find a good doctor.
9. The service would use modern, up-to-date treatment methods.
10. No one has access to my medical record except medical personnel.
11. There would not be a high continuing interest in my health care.
12. The services would use the best possible hospitals.
13. Too much work would be done by nurses and assistants rather than doctors.
14. It would be an organized and complete medical service for me and my family.
15. There would not be much red tape and bureaucratic hassle.
16. Highly competent doctors and specialists would be available to serve me.

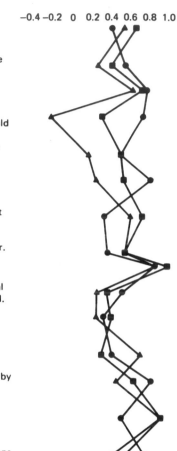

● Existing   ▲ HCHP   ■ MIT

(a) Average Ratings

Figure 9.8 Perceptual Analysis of Health Care Delivery (Hauser and Urban 1977)

slide shows would communicate a core benefit proposition based on proven quality, personalness, value, and convenience.

But communication was not the only answer. Note that relative to the major competition, Harvard Community Health Plan, the MIT concept (or pilot) is perceived to be better on all factor dimensions except quality. At this

ATTRIBUTE SCALE	QUALITY	PERSONAL	VALUE	CONVENIENCE
1. Day & Night Care	0.37244	0.07363	−0.31379	0.63939
2. Waiting Time	−0.22082	0.26204	0.15514	−0.64370
3. Trust-Good Care	0.72125	−0.21826	−0.09556	0.24703
4. Location	0.01144	0.24706	−0.12544	−0.72454
5. Price/Value	0.03066	0.12810	0.72884	−0.08461
6. Friendly/Personal	0.40986	−0.51317	−0.12265	0.16768
7. Preventive Care	0.55403	−0.14187	−0.44353	−0.01653
8. Easily Find Good M.D.	0.64412	−0.15036	−0.21491	0.27113
9. Modern Treatment	0.72288	−0.13441	−0.15906	0.08018
10. Access to Records	0.43412	−0.49053	0.18749	−0.06982
11. Continuity of Care	0.20491	0.47900	0.47727	0.04725
12. Associated Hospitals	0.68006	−0.08256	0.10854	0.00555
13. Use of Paramedics	−0.05303	0.67083	0.12299	0.16722
14. Organized/Complete	0.47725	0.01627	−0.52893	0.14316
15. Hassle/Red Tape	−0.13031	0.69824	0.11830	−0.27903
16. Competent M.D.s	0.73953	−0.19335	−0.13971	0.18691
Eigenvalues	5.34	1.4	1.1	1.02
Cumulative Variance	0.33	0.42	0.49	0.55

(b) Factor Loadings

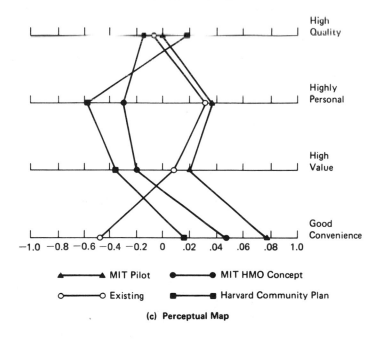

(c) Perceptual Map

Figure 9.8 (*Continued*)

point in our analysis we have no indication of the relative importance of quality to consumers and we do not know whether a change in quality would have a major impact on consumer response. These questions will be addressed in the next chapter. However, for now we state that not only was quality an important factor, it was the most important factor—the quality gap should be closed if possible. By examining the factor loadings we see that attributes 3, 7, 8, 9, 12, 14, and 16 load on quality. By examining the snake plot, we see that the lower rating for MIT on quality is based almost entirely on a low score for MIT on hospital quality. However, most people had not actually been sick so the ratings were largely perceptions. Thus, if the MIT HMO were to be successful, the HMO managers must identify some method to improve the perceptions of hospital quality. For the MIT HMO it was possible to accomplish this by switching some affiliations and by emphasizing the best hospital of those affiliated.

In summary, the perceptual map indicated two key strategies: (1) a more aggressive communications based on quality, personalness, convenience, and value and (2) a shift in hospital affiliation. The improvements were expected to move the perceptual position of the MIT concept one-half of the distance from the concept to the pilot on personalness, value, and convenience, and one-half the distance to the Harvard plan on quality. Based on the preference analyses of Chapters 10 and 11 and the forecasting procedures of Chapter 12, these changes increased the expected enrollment from 3,622 families to 5,405 families—an increase of almost 50%. Actual experience confirmed that the projections were reasonably accurate.

This example illustrates the synergy between the analytical technique and managerial judgment. Major improvements were identified because the design team was able to interpret the analysis and identify creative means to improve the concept. Without managerial interpretation, the analysis would have been just an accurate report of the situation. Without the analysis, the managers may not have identified the key leverage points.

Notice the key input that quality was an important dimension. In the next chapter we discuss how to obtain and use such information on customer preferences in determining the importance of dimensions.

SUMMARY

In this chapter we have described several approaches to the development of perceptual maps. Qualitative methods are important in gaining an initial understanding of needs, but in the area of perceptual mapping we have available a number of analytical techniques that are very powerful and should be used to supplement judgment. Four available analytic techniques are proved: (1) judgment-based affinity diagrams, (2) customer sorts with cluster analysis, (3) factor analysis, and (4) similarity scaling. The first two describe the structure of needs by building up from the detailed tertiary customer needs. The third and fourth techniques develop perceptual maps that define macro dimensions and position of brands on these perceptual dimensions.

The approaches can be used synergistically by using affinity diagrams and customer sorts to define the need attributes to be used in factor analysis to develop maps or in similarity mapping to name dimensions. For example the affinity and sort tasks can be used to reduce 200 to 300 needs into 15 attribute scales. Customers would be asked to use these scales to evaluate their considered products as input for factor analysis. The three or four factor dimensions can be compared to the highest levels in the need hierarchies which are obtained from the customer sorts. Finally managers have customers could rate the competitive brands on the highest dimensions in the need diagrams as well as fill out the questionnaire items for the factor analysis ratings to see if their inputs to the two approaches lead to the same diagnosis of the core benefit positioning of the various products.

REVIEW QUESTIONS

9.1. What are the relative advantages of using affinity diagrams and hierarchical clustering of customer-sort data? Would there ever be organizational advantages of using both?

9.2. Discuss the relative advantages and disadvantages of factor analysis and similarity scaling as analytical means by which to produce perceptual maps.

9.3. What is the role of product concepts in perceptual mapping? Do you expect that product concepts provide accurate positions for products?

9.4. Both hierarchical clustering of customer-sort data and factor analysis of customer-ratings data provide a structural grouping of customer needs. How do these methods differ? How can they be used to complement one another?

9.5. When confronted with the details of factor analysis, Mr. Rolandas, a vice-president of new product development, stated, "Sure analytical methods are used to generate perceptual maps and these maps are very useful. But my job is to make decisions. I must apply the perceptual maps to come up with real actions. It's not important for me to know a lot of the theoretical details. Academics worry about how the computer makes the map. I only worry about how to apply it."

Discuss Mr. Rolandas' statement and its implications for the new product team and the new product design process. Do you agree with Mr. Rolandas?

9.6. Draw a judgmental perceptual map for the toothpaste market. For the personal computer market. For financial services. For heavy-duty industrial compressors.

9.7. You are about to graduate and venture into the ominous job market. Being an aggressive, hard-working and enterprising person, you decide that your excellent grades and outstanding personality are not enough. A proper perceptual positioning is required at your interview. From the placement office and from talking to recent graduates you discover the following key dimensions by which employers evaluate potential hires.

A = Preparedness	(0–10, 10 best)
B = Group skills	(0–10, 10 best)
C = Technical skills	(0–10, 10 best)
D = Ability to handle pressure	(0–10, 10 best)

You know your competition because you have seen them in class and have observed them in social settings. The following ratings represent your judgment of how you will be perceived relative to your peers.

	A	B	C	D
John Smith	7	3	2	3
Jane Doe	7	5	9	4
Marius Aleksas	2	5	8	9
You	6	2	8	6

    a. If only you and John Smith compete for the job, how should you handle the interview?

    b. If only you and Jane Doe compete for the job, how should you handle the interview?

    c. How would your strategy for the interview depend on the relative importances that the interviewer places on preparedness, group skills, technical skills, and the ability to handle pressure?

10

Strategic Product Positioning and Customer Preferences

Perceptual maps and value maps identify the benefit dimensions that customers consider, indicate competitive positioning, and suggest opportunities for competitive advantage. Operational customer needs from affinity diagrams or customer sorts and their links to perceptual dimensions help engineers design the product to hit a target position. But the maps do not tell us which position is best nor do they tell us which customer needs should be given the highest priority. To select the best core benefit proposition we need information on customer preferences.

CUSTOMER PREFERENCES AND PRODUCT POSITIONING

The perceptual maps and value maps in chapter 8 identified new product opportunities for pain relievers as gaps in the effectiveness and gentleness dimensions. There might be an opportunity for a highly effective pain reliever or for an extremely gentle pain reliever, both, or neither—it depends on the tradeoffs consumers make between effectiveness and gentleness. The right choice could lead to a highly successful new product while the wrong choice could lead to financial disaster. Analysis of consumer preferences gives the manager the information necessary to make this choice. For example, suppose that all consumers believe that effectiveness is extremely important and that gentleness is of little importance. A positioning strategy based on effectiveness is much more likely to lead to high sales volume than a positioning strategy based on gentleness. But if the analysis indicated that different groups valued the dimensions differently, the choice of a position would depend upon the size of the groups and how strongly each group valued each dimension. If there is more than one large group the best strategy might be a product line with two or more offerings.

Segmentation of target groups by their preferences is called "benefit segmentation" (Haley 1968). This segmentation is related to market structure segmentation (chapter 4), which was used to decide which products were most competitive. Benefit segmentation cuts to the heart of the strategic decision of designing products to meet customer needs. If it can be related to demographic, psychographic, or usage variables, so much the better for targeting of communications and distribution strategies. But even if there is no direct link, benefit segmentation identifies the best positionings for a product or a product line.

To make the role of preferences clear, consider the following examples.

1. The perceptual map in chapter 8 suggests that there is an opportunity for a telecommunications technology that is more effective than telephone, but easier to use than personal visit, but should R&D focus on effectiveness or on ease-of-use?

2. The similarity map in chapter 9 indicates that the variety of stores and the availability of parking are important to consumers in the choice of which shopping center to patronize. But in a given land area, more parking space means fewer stores. How should the developer or shopping center manager allocate parking and retail space?

3. Automobile consumers want controls that are easy to reach and use. One design option is to place controls for cruise control, the horn, the radio, the heating/air-conditioning system, and so forth on the steering wheel. But if too many controls are on the steering wheel, they will be crowded and difficult to use. Which controls should be given the highest priority?

This chapter and the next chapter provide the tools with which to address these issues. Preference measures, both direct and revealed, indicate which perceptual dimensions are most important to customers and help the new product team establish a target position. Feature-based measures, direct measures, and conjoint analysis, enable the engineering design to focus on the most efficient means to attain a target position. Benefit segmentation identifies whether or not to focus on a niche of the market or the overall market. We begin this chapter with a discussion of the strategic role of product positioning, then present both direct and revealed methods to identify customer preferences. The next chapter will discuss benefit segmentation strategies based on customer preferences.

STRATEGIC ROLE OF PRODUCT POSITIONING

Managerial Needs

Suppose we were developing a new pain reliever. From Figure 8.2 we know that effectiveness and gentleness are key, but we don't know which dimension to stress. One means to identify a priority is to develop several different products, say 10, each with a different position. We could measure consumer reaction and choose the best received. However, such a trial-and-error method is expensive and time consuming and, even when we know the best concept of the group, we don't know why that concept was chosen, how to improve it, or whether an 11th concept might do even better.

An alternative to trial and error is demonstrated in Figure 10.1. The

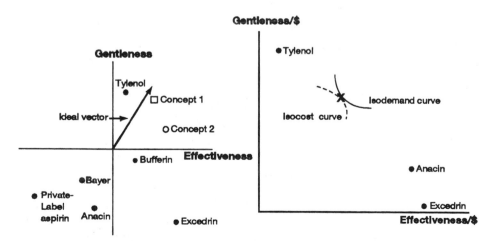

Figure 10.1 Illustration of the Managerial Use of Perceptual Maps and Value Maps

arrow in Figure 10.1a, called an "ideal vector," indicates the relative tradeoffs that represent how the market reacts to effectiveness and gentleness. Because the ideal vector is angled toward gentleness rather than toward effectiveness it says that on average the market would react more favorably to a product positioned toward gentleness than toward effectiveness—assuming they were priced equally. Concept 1 is more likely to achieve a sales goal than is concept 2. Furthermore, if we could improve concept 1 in a direction parallel to the ideal vector it would be likely to achieve even more sales.

But suppose that we could produce concept 2 much more cheaply than concept 1. Might not concept 2 be more profitable? Figure 10.1b illustrates some cost/position tradeoffs from the viewpoint of the product developer. Note that Figure 10.1b is a value map. We use the value map to take price into consideration. Taking price into consideration enables us to calculate sales from a position on the map. (Alternatively we could plot three dimensions, effectiveness, gentleness, and price.) First we label each potential product position with its forecast sales and connect those positions which have the same sales. The points of equal sales potential generate an "isodemand" curve such as the solid line in Figure 10.1b. Because each point on that curve gives the same revenue, the most profitable point will be the product that costs the least to produce. Similarly we can calculate the projected production (and design) costs of each position, label the points with that cost, and connect those points that have the same costs. Such a curve, shown as a dotted line in Figure 10.1b, is called an "isocost curve." Because each point on the isocost curve has the same costs, the point that generates the most revenue will be the most profitable.

Putting this information together, if the isocost and isodemand curves are of a shape similar to those drawn in Figure 10.1b, the most profitable position will be at the intersection of the curves (shown with an X in Figure 10.1b). In theory one could draw a collection of such curves for various consumer segments, plot their intersections to obtain a set of potential profitable positions, and choose the most profitable position. This is, of course, rarely feasible. More likely the new product team uses the ideal vector or isodemand curves to find areas of high demand and they use cost estimates to find areas of low cost. They temper their judgment with concerns about feasibility, future technology, changing markets, and competitive response. Alternatively, the team can test a number of stretching concepts labeling each with sales and cost and begin to focus on highly profitable areas of the map.

A final managerial input from the perceptual and value maps is a forecast of the nature of competitive response. If the new product position is close to a major competitor, say Tylenol in Figure 10.1, we expect a strong defensive reaction by the incumbent brand. This could lead to price wars, positioning wars (e.g., new stronger Tylenol), or strong reactions on other marketing variables. The team may decide to proceed anyway, especially if they have a superior product, but the initial understanding of which brands will have incentives to respond provides further input in the choice of a position for the new product. (We return to competitive response considerations in chapter 11.)

Engineering Needs

The engineering use of customer preference information is synergistic with the managerial use. Once management decides on a target position or perhaps as input to that decision, the new product team selects the engineering characteristics of the product to meet a target position. (Also see chapter 13, Designing for Quality, for an in-depth discussion of these issues.) Naturally many, but not all, engineering decisions will involve tradeoffs. To make these tradeoffs the engineering team needs to know how operational engineering decisions relate to the target position.

The engineering priority information comes in a number of forms. The structure of perceptions from either an affinity diagram, a customer-sort hierarchy, factor analysis, or similarity scaling tells the team which tactical customer needs make up the more-primary perceptual dimensions. For example, if the managerial positioning goal is a telecommunications technology that is easy to use the engineering team can concentrate on the tactical needs (figure 8.5) that correlate with ease-of-use.

In addition to importance weights on the strategic dimensions, the engineering team often wants a prioritization of the tactical and operational needs. This is a nontrivial task because the operational needs often number in the hundreds, but the detail is needed. In the instrumentation example (#3) that began this chapter the tradeoffs were at the level of a cruise-control button versus a sound-system knob. Even in products such as pain-relievers, chemists may want to distinguish effectiveness for stress headaches from effectiveness for arthritis.

The last engineering task is that of selecting a product's major features. Should an automobile have a five-speed manual transmission or a four-speed automatic transmission as standard equipment? Or, should rear windows go all the way down even if it means that there is less interior room in the back seat? In this case the new product team needs measures, called "part-worths," that quantify the tradeoffs customers are willing to make. In some cases the data indicate how features affect overall preference and in some cases how the features affect each of the perceptual dimensions. While the latter is consistent with the concept of a "lens" model (chapter 8), both forms of feature priorities are valuable to the team.

THE CONCEPT OF IMPORTANCE WEIGHTS

We begin by defining what is meant by customer "importance." Suppose that we seek to introduce a new pain reliever, called HALT, to the market described by the perceptual and value maps of Figure 10.1. We assume that gentleness and effectiveness are the only relevant perceptual dimensions. The ideal vector in Figure 10.1 favors gentleness over effectiveness causing us to make a statement that "gentleness is *more important* to the market than effectiveness." But what does this mean?

Quantitatively the ideal vector represents a set of numbers called importance weights, or "importances" for short. Suppose that these numbers are w_g and w_e for gentleness and effectiveness, respectively. Suppose further that a consumer, Sharon, evaluates Tylenol, Anacin, Excedrin, and Halt as displayed in Table 10.1.

In Table 10.1 we compute Sharon's preferences by weighting gentleness and effectiveness by the importance weights and summing. That is,

$$\text{Preference of Tylenol} = (2) \times (5) + (1) \times (1) = 11 \qquad (10.1)$$

Or, more generally, if G_j is Sharon's evaluation of gentleness for brand j and E_j is her evaluation of effectiveness, then her preference value for that brand is:

$$\text{Preference of brand } j = w_g\, G_j + w_e\, E_j \qquad (10.2)$$

Thus, according to Table 10.1 Sharon would prefer the new product, Halt, to her currently most preferred brand, Tylenol. (Halt would be positioned like concept 1 in Figure 10.1. Notice that she would not prefer concept 2, which would obtain a preference rating of 8, based on a gentleness of 2, and effectiveness of 4.)

Clearly we can generalize equation 10.2 to more than two perceptual dimensions and to different perceptual dimensions. Indeed, for operational measures we might have as many as 100 to 300 different importance values corresponding to the 100 to 300 operational tertiary customer needs.

TABLE 10.1 Perceptual Ratings of Pain Relievers and Implied Preferences

Brand	Gentleness (w_g=2)	Effectiveness (w_e=1)	Preference
Tylenol	5	1	11
Anacin	−4	−2	−10
Excedrin	−5	5	−5
Halt	4	4	12
Concept 2	2	4	8

When we have a relatively few dimensions as in a perceptual map, we graph the importance values with an ideal vector whose slope corresponds to the ratio of the importance values. For example, in Figure 10.1 the ideal vector has a vertical slope of 2:1 corresponding to the 2:1 ratio of w_g/w_e. Geometrically this means that the customer will prefer the product that is farthest out in the direction parallel to the ideal vector. (Alternatively one can draw a perpendicular from each point to the vector; the perpendicular farthest out the vector reflects the most preferred brand.)

We now describe the means by which preference information is obtained. We begin with direct measures of customer importances.

DIRECT MEASURES OF CUSTOMER IMPORTANCES

Suppose that you are the city manager of a suburban community. You have a fixed transportation budget and want to consider improvements in your community's transportation service. Because your budget is fixed, you are limited in what you can do, so you want to know what aspects of transportation services are most important to residents of your city. One method is to measure directly the importances of a list of identified consumer needs. One such measurement is shown in Figure 10.2. The consumer needs are the first 5 needs, out of a total of 25, that were measured by the city manager of Evanston, Illinois. Note that each consumer need has an indicated directionality ("will get me places on time" rather than "on time performance") and that the 5-point scale begins with "of no importance" rather than "unimportant."

Managerial Diagnostics

The results of this measurement are plotted in Figure 10.3 where a snake plot, giving consumer evaluations of bus, walk, car and two concepts,[1] is labeled with the average importances obtained with the scales in Figure 10.2. Notice that "on time," "come and go as I wish," "available when needed," and "no long waits" are among the most important consumer needs and that car does well on all but one of these. Notice further that the two concepts do better than bus on each of these needs. Thus, on the important travel-convenience consumer needs, the new product concepts do better than the city's existing bus service, but work needs to be done if the concepts are to exceed the ability of car to fulfill these needs.

[1] Recall that the two concepts are PPS—a publicly operated shared-ride, minibus system and BTP—a privately operated shared-ride taxi system for a reduced fare.

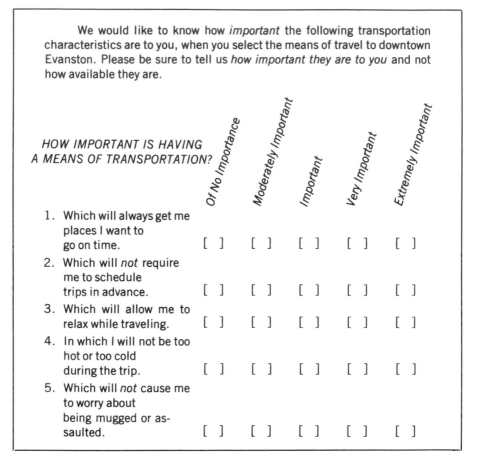

Figure 10.2 Examples of Direct Measures of Importances (Self-Rated Importances) This figure represents the first 5 out of 25 scales.

Forecasts of Customer Response

Direct measures of customer importances are collected from every customer that is surveyed. To forecast customer response, these importances can be used at the level of the individual customer or they can be averaged, by customer segment if necessary. To illustrate how the importances might be used at the level of the individual customer suppose that the Evanston city manager wants to increase the frequency of bus service. As a rough estimate, he/she might postulate that this would increase each consumer's average rating on "come and go as I wish," "no long waits," and "available when

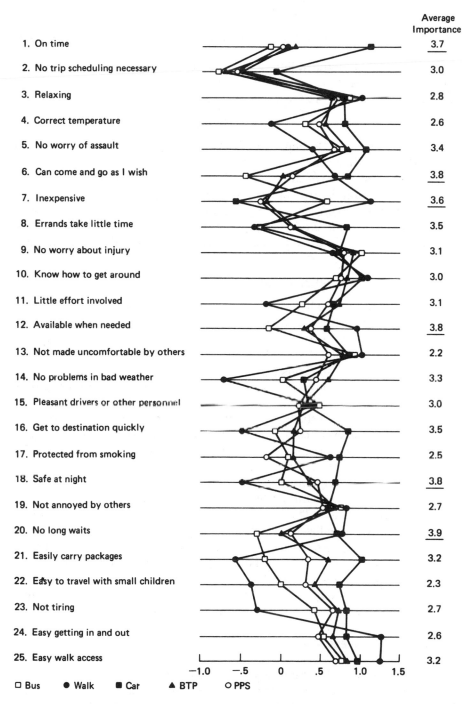

Figure 10.3 Average Ratings of Transportation Service Ratings and Average Importances (Adapted from Hauser, Tybout, and Koppelman 1979)

needed" by 50% of the difference between bus and PPS. Thus, if y_{ibl} is consumer i's rating of *bus* on scale l before the change, and y_{ipl} is consumer i's rating of PPS, then the forecast rating, y'_{ibl} after the change is just l

$$y'_{ibl} = y_{ibl} + 0.50 \ (y_{ipl} - y_{ibl})$$

for the consumer needs improved by the strategy. The forecast rating is unchanged for other consumer needs.

We then estimate consumer i's preference with a generalization of equation 10.1. For example, if consumer i's rating of bus after the change were -0.2 for "on time," -0.7 for "no trip scheduling necessary," ..., and 1.3 for "easy walk access," and if consumer i's importances were 3.7, 3.0, ..., 3.2 for those consumer needs, then we would compute consumer i's new preference value for bus by

$$(3.7)(-0.2) + (3.0)(-0.7) + \ldots + (3.2)(1.3)$$

Because car and walk remain unchanged, the preference values for car and walk would remain unchanged. (Their preference values would equal the sum of the importances times the unchanged evaluations.) We then predict that consumer i would choose the service with the highest forecast preference. If that service were bus, we would predict that the consumer would choose bus. If it were another service we would predict that he would choose that.

To forecast market share, we compute preferences and predict behavior (via computer) for every consumer in the sample and count the number of people who would ride the bus after the improvement. We then compare the number (or share) of consumers choosing bus to a forecast based on the preimprovement evaluations. For example, when this strategy was simulated for the city of Evanston, the preference model predicted a net increase of 28.3% in performance. The base case prediction was 16.5% bus riders, whereas the model predicted a 21.2% ridership under the improved strategy.

In some cases the manager will want to use average importances rather than individual-level importances. This might be the case if importances were collected from one sample of customers and evaluations were collected from another set of customers. In this case the procedure is the same except that average importances are used for each and every customer in the segment.

Alternative Measures

There are several possible ways to measure importances. In this section we review the methods and several technical issues related to their use. Although managers need not deal with the technical issues they should be sure their market research staff does consider them.

Self-Rated.   Figure 10.2 illustrates self-rated importances. With such scales each customer is asked to provide an estimate of importance directly on a 5-, 7-, or 9-point scale. The scales are worded carefully to reflect the customer need or perceptual dimension providing a directionality and, if possible, an anchor. Although there is no guarantee that the scaling implicit in the direct self-rated importance measurements is the scaling appropriate for the model of preference used in equation 10.1, experience suggests that if care is taken self-rated scales do surprisingly well.[2] For example, the scales in Figure 10.2 were able to forecast the preferences of 72% of the respondents correctly. The empirical accuracy of self-rated scales is true in part because equation 10.1 requires only that *relative* importances be measured; thus the fact that a scale is a 9-point rather than a 5-point scale should have no impact other than providing more categories to which the customer can respond.

Anchored Measures.   In an anchored measure the respondent is asked to state importances on a 10-point scale such that the most important need or dimension is given 10 points and every other need or dimension is given some number of points between 0 and 10. One such scale is illustrated in Figure 10.4 for effectiveness and ease of use, the two dimensions that we have been using for telecommunications technologies. Naturally, many of the same concerns and caveats that were true for self-rated scales are also true for anchored measures.

The advantage of anchored measures is that they work naturally with hierarchies of customer needs. For example, suppose that "effective information exchange," "eliminate paperwork," "focus on issues," and "enhance interaction" are four tactical customer needs that make up the effectiveness dimension. (In earlier examples effectiveness was made up from eleven detailed needs. Here we have simplified the example.) As illustrated in Figure 10.4 the anchored importances are now used with the tactical needs in a manner that makes clear the hierarchical relationship to effectiveness.

The importance of a tactical need, say "effective information exchange," is then the product of the importance of the more aggregate dimension, effectiveness, and the importance of "effective information exchange" relative to effectiveness. For example, if effectiveness is given 8 points in Figure 10.4a and "effective information exchange" is given 7 points in Figure 10.4b, then the imputed importance of "effective information exchange" is 8 times 7 divided by 10 ($8 \times 7 \div 10$). (For convergence of interpre-

---

[2] Technically, we can adjust the scaling by computing an "equal-weights" index, which simply sums the evaluations. We then regress the preference index (equation 10.1) and this equal-weights index on measured preference. The value of the regressions weights gives us the scaling constant.

(a) Tell us how important each statement is by

- First read all the statements in the group.
- Find the statement that is the most important to you in the group and place a "10" in the space to the left.
- Rate all the other statements in that group with numbers from "0" to "10" indicating their relative importance. ("0" means no importance.)
- You may use any number more than once. The only requirement is that every group should have at least one statement rated "10."

(b) When considering telecommunications technologies, how important is it that:

_____ The technology is effective.
_____ The technology is easy to use.

When considering about the effectiveness of telecommunications technologies, how important is it that:

_____ You can achieve effective information exchange.
_____ You can eliminate paperwork.
_____ You can focus on issues.
_____ You can enhance interactions.

Figure 10.4. Simplified Examples of Anchored Measures of Importance for Primary and Secondary Customer Needs

tation we divide by 10 to maintain a 0–10 scale.) If there are tertiary customer needs related to the secondary, customer needs such as "effective information exchange," then we continue to *cascade* the importances from the more aggregate to the more-detailed customer needs.[3]

Constant-Sum Measures. In constant-sum measures the customer is given a fixed number of points (chips) to divide among the dimensions or customer needs. One such scale is illustrated in Figure 10.5. Like anchored scales, these directly assessed constant-sum scales can be cascaded from more aggregate to more detailed levels. Similar scaling concerns apply as to the previous scales. Constant sum scales can also be collected by allocating 100 chips between each pair of scales and statistically estimating the importance values (Torgerson 1958).

---

[3] In some applications firms multiply by the mean importance rather than 10 to maintain consistency of scale with the primary importances.

Tell us how important each statement is by dividing 100 points among the statements in a group.

- First read all the statements in a group.
- Give the most important statement the largest number of points.
- Give the least important statement the fewest points.
- Give other statements the remaining points in relation to their relative importance to you.
- The only requirement is that the points assigned to a group must add up to 100.

When considering telecommunications technologies, how important is that:

_____ The technology is effective.
_____ The technology is easy to use.

Figure 10.5.   Example of Constant-Sum Measures of Importance for Primary Customer Needs

The advantage of directly assessed constant-sum scales is that customers are forced to make difficult tradeoffs among needs or dimensions. If one need is given 60 points, there are only 40 points to divide among the other needs within that group. However, this advantage can produce a problem when a hierarchy of needs are assessed. This is illustrated in Table 10.2. Suppose that one primary customer need has four secondary needs associated with it and that a second primary need has two secondary needs associated with it. If we simply multiply through to cascade the importances, we can

TABLE 10.2 Illustration of the Necessity of Rescaling Constant-Sum Measures to Address Independence of Irrelevant Needs

Primary constant-sum rating	Secondary constant-sum rating	Cascaded	Cascaded and rescaled
60	Primary need 1		
	30 Secondary need 1	18	36
	30 Secondary need 2	18	36
	20 Secondary need 3	12	24
	20 Secondary need 4	12	24
40	Primary need 2		
	52.5 Secondary need 5	21	21
	47.5 Secondary need 6	19	19

generate a case where the least important secondary need within the least important primary need generates an importance value that is larger than the most important secondary need within the most important primary need (19 points versus 18 points in Table 10.2). This problem is called independence from irrelevant needs (IIN). Why does this happen? It happens because the nature of a constant-sum scale is to divide up points; hence if there are a larger number of needs in a grouping this forces a finer division of points. To correct for the IIN problem we rescale the points such that twice as many points are divided among the four customer needs in primary 1 as are divided among the two customer needs in primary 2. These rescaled importances are shown in the last column of Table 10.2. We have not done so, but we could have rescaled them such that the sum of all secondary importances equals 100 points. Such rescaling would not affect the computations in equation 10.1.

Comparison of Measures.   The advantage of the self-rated measures is that they are easy to develop and easy to administer. The customer provides direct ratings on all levels of customer needs. The disadvantage is that they do not force tradeoffs among the customer needs, it is easy to say all needs are extremely important, and they do not make any hierarchical structure explicit. The advantage of the anchored scales is that they make the hierarchical structure explicit without raising the issue of IIN. They are more difficult to administer than the self-rated measures but easier for the respondent to answer than the constant-sum measures. Finally, the constant-sum measures make the hierarchical structure explicit *and* force clear tradeoffs among the needs within a grouping. However, they also raise the issue of IIN. The disadvantage of constant-sum measures is that they are the most difficult for the respondent to answer and, potentially, can lead to confusion among respondents.

All three measures predict reasonably well if the questions are phrased carefully and if the customer is given a reasonable description of the context in which the choice is being made. For example, Griffin and Hauser (1993) present data in which a consumer-packaged-goods company developed seven product concepts such that each product concept stretched one of the seven primary consumer needs but left the other primary consumer needs unchanged. Consumers were then asked to express their preferences among the seven (equally priced) concepts and these preferences were compared to self-rated measures, anchored measures, and constant-sum measures. In all cases the preferences among the concepts were highly correlated (Spearman correlations of .96) with the directly measured importances.

Frequency of Mention.   It is a reasonable hypothesis that, in qualitative research, customers will mention most frequently those customer needs that are most important. If this were true, then we could obtain a rough measure of importance from the qualitative interviews. Indeed, some consulting firms have used such measures for their clients. Regrettably, customers do not seem to mention important needs any more frequently than other needs. Frequency of mention is a poor measure of importance. See Griffin and Hauser (1993) for empirical evidence.

One reason that frequency of mention is a poor surrogate for importance is that needs that could excite customers are often mentioned infrequently, but once identified these exciting needs can be extremely important to customers and can form the basis of a competitive advantage for the innovating firm. Another reason that frequency of mention is a poor surrogate is that today's efficient interviewing techniques probe new respondents for new needs rather than treating every respondent as an independent observation.

REVEALED PREFERENCE METHODS

While direct measures of importances often work well, there is no guarantee that the measures which customers provide match the scaling requirements of the preference model (equation 10.1) with which we interpret the measures. Also, in some cases customers may be unable or unwilling to express their preferences. For example, consumers will say that they prefer ready-to-eat cereals that have less sugar, but many prefer the taste of sweet cereals and continue to buy them. Similarly, automobile consumers will say that safety is extremely important, but they may be willing to buy a car that is less safe if it delivers other important benefits.

The concept behind revealed preference is that if we just ask customers to express preferences for products (cereals, automobiles, etc.) we might be able to use statistical analyses to infer the importance weights that led to those preferences. To illustrate the concept of revealed preference, reconsider Figure 10.1a. If we knew that a consumer preferred Tylenol to Bufferin to Bayer and that the consumer preferred concept 1 over concept 2 and over Tylenol, we could try to place an ideal vector on the map to recover these observed preferences. Although we might not get exactly the ideal vector in Figure 10.1a, we would get close. If we observed the preferences of not just one consumer but hundreds, we could estimate an ideal vector that best described their aggregate preferences.

In the preceding example we used preferences with respect to products and concept statements to draw an ideal vector, when this is done formally it is called *preference regression*. We might also have created product concepts by describing product features. For example, we might describe a number of alternative telecommunications technologies by listing features such as the speed of transmission, the ability to produce hard copy, and the availability. If customers state their preferences with respect to these lists of features then we can use statistics to impute the importances they place on each feature. Revealed preference techniques based on feature combinations are called *conjoint analysis*. We begin with preference regression.

Preference Regression

Preference regression "reveals" the relative importance weights (the w's in equation 10.1) by relating preference on products to perceptions of those products. Figure 10.6 provides one example measurement of rank-order preference. One can also use intensity measures (see Hauser and Shugan 1980) where customers are asked to (1) allocate 100 points to their most preferred product and less to other products (similar to anchored importance measures); (2) allocate 100 points among products (similar to constant-sum importance measures); or (3) make paired comparison judgments across the set of evoked brands which are statistically scaled (see Hauser and Urban 1977). Naturally, if we collect data such as that in Figure 10.6 we would rescale the data such that the most preferred product received the highest preference measure and the least preferred product received the lowest preference measure.

We are interested in your preferences for alternative pain relievers. Below are listed a number of products. Place a "1" next to the product you prefer. Place a "2" next to your next most preferred product. Place a "3" next to your third preference, a "4" next to your fourth preference, and a "5" next to the product you least prefer. Be sure to rate all the listed products.

Anacin   5

Bayer   4

Bufferin   2

Excedrin   3

Tylenol   1

Figure 10.6. Simplified Example of Rank-Order Preference Measurement for Preference Regression

Methodology.   If we collect perceptions of the products, effectiveness and gentleness for pain relievers, in the same survey, then we can set up the following linear regression equation:

$$\text{Observed preference} = \beta_o + \beta_e * \text{effectiveness} + \beta_g * \text{gentleness} + \text{error}$$
$$(10.2)$$

The data used to estimate the revealed importance weights (β_e and β_g) and the constant (β_o) are the overall preference as the dependent variable and the perceptual dimensions (factor scores or direct measures) as the explanatory variables. The data include each customer's preference and perceptions for each product that is evaluated. For example, if 300 customers are asked to evaluate (on average) three products, then there are 900 observations (300 × 3) in the regression. Example input and output is illustrated in Table 10.3.

The linear or monotonic regression coefficients in equation 10.2 become the importance weights in equation 10.1. The constant term, β_o, just establishes the scale and can be ignored for relative comparisons. The ratio of the importance weights, β_g/β_e, gives the slope of the ideal vector in Figure 10.1a.

TABLE 10.3   Input and Output of Preference Regression

		Preference	Effect-iveness*	Gentle-ness*	
Customer 1	Anacin	2	−0.31	−0.50	
	Bayer	1	−0.40	−0.51	
	Bufferin	3	0.09	−0.09	
	Excedrin	4	0.39	−0.11	
	Tylenol	5	−0.99	0.10	Input
Customer 2	Anacin	3	−0.41	−0.40	
	Bufferin	4	0.19	0.12	
	Excedrin	2	0.21	−0.93	
	.	.	.	.	
	.	.	.	.	
	.	.	.	.	
Customer 3	Bayer	1	−1.10	−0.20	
	Bufferin	3	0.11	0.90	
	Excedrin	2	0.10	−0.30	
	Tylenol	4	0.11	1.30	
Estimated Importance Weights			(0.35)	(0.65)	Output

* The measures of effectiveness and gentleness are obtained as factor scores computed from consumer ratings of tactical (secondary) needs.

Managerial Diagnostics. The ideal vector in Figure 10.1a indicates that gentleness is more important than effectiveness (a ratio of almost 2:1), but that effectiveness cannot be neglected. This means that, all else equal, the new product design team should concentrate on designing and positioning a product that delivers both gentleness and effectiveness but, if they must make a tradeoff, that tradeoff should favor gentleness. Naturally, cost and price influence the decision as well as illustrated in Figure 10.1b.

Prediction of Response to Product Revision. Once one estimates the regression coefficients, preference regression is used to forecast customer response to changes in a new product concept. The technique is similar to that used for direct measures except that the regression coefficients rather than the direct measures are used to forecast changes in preference. For example, in the HMO case of chapter 9, we identified improvements in quality, convenience, personalness, and value. To forecast the impact of these changes we modify for every consumer in the sample that consumer's perception values on the four factor dimensions. Equation 10.1 predicts their new preference values, we assign each consumer to their most preferred health care plan, count the number of consumers preferring each health care plan, and compute market share. In this way we can simulate the sales for any planned improvement in the positioning of the HMO.

The Bane of Colinearity among Customer Needs. It was no accident that we chose to illustrate preference regression with factor dimensions as the explanatory variables. Factor scores are by construction uncorrelated (Rummel 1970, Harman 1976) hence colinearity will be no problem when factor scores measure perceptions. On the other hand, more detailed tactical and operational customer needs are likely to be correlated. In fact, it was their very correlation that allowed us to use factor analysis to group them. Even if factor analysis is not used they are likely to be redundant measures such as (for the car door example) "easy to close from the outside," "easy to close from the inside," and "stays open on a hill." If we were to attempt preference regression for the more detailed customer needs, the colinearity would make it extremely difficult to obtain clean and clear estimates of relative importance weights. Thus, preference regression works best for more aggregate customer needs such as the primary customer needs. For more detailed customer needs colinearity is likely to force us to rely on direct measures.

Leading-Edge User Maps and an Example of Preference Regression Estimation of Importances. In chapter 5 (Idea Generation) we described the case of lead user analysis for CAD/CAM systems for printed circuit board design. Recall that the lead users were identified and brought together in a focus group to design a new concept based on their own innovations. Furthermore this concept, when tested with other customers, was preferred more than 75% of the time to existing products. As well as overall concept preference measures, perceptions and preferences were collected for existing software systems and preference regression was used to estimate the importance of the underlying factor dimensions.

Urban and von Hippel (1988) factor analyzed the perceptual ratings and selected five dimensions. The principal components five-factor solution explained 66% of the variation; the eigenvalue of the last factor was 1.0. The six-factor solution explained only 5% more variation, the sixth eigenvalue dropped to .81, and the final factor was not clearly interpretable. The five-factor interpretation was supported by a common factor analysis. The same loading structure was observed and the same number of dimensions indicated. These dimensions were (1) "power/value" (loadings of more than .6 were found on attributes of placement/routing power, value for the dollar, powerful, and high density); (2) "ease of use" (high loading on easy to learn and easy to use); (3) "manufacturable" (high loadings were found on manufacturable and enough layers for my needs); (4) "integratibility" (high loadings on easy to customize, integrate with manufacturing and other CAD systems); and (5) "maintenance/upgrading" (high loadings on easy to maintain, upgrade, and reliable).

The importance of the five dimensions to users were estimated by a linear regression. Constant sum preference values were the dependent variables; the factor scores and a dummy variable for each concept were the explanatory variables. The most important needs were power/value (coefficient of .54) and integratibility (.38). Manufacturable (.21), ease of use (0.16), and maintain/upgrade (.13) were less important. The regression was significant at the 1% level ($F(9, 230) = 14.4$) and the R^2 value was 0.36. All t statistics were significant at the 10% level except maintain/upgrade, which was significant at the 15% level.

The perceptual maps showed the leading-edge-user-developed concept to be rated higher than other concepts on the power/value and integration needs, but lower on manufacturable (board design can be easily and reliably manufactured in the plant) and maintenance/upgrade dimension and the same on an ease of use dimension. The existing system excelled on manufacturable but was lower on other dimensions. On the basis of this analysis, it appears that the appeal of the leading-edge-user concept could be improved still further if users in general were convinced that the system would be easy to maintain and upgrade, and the system would specify board designs which are simple to produce.

Discussion.   Preference regression has been used successfully for frequently purchased products such as pain relievers, services such as HMOs, durable goods such as automobiles, and high tech products such as computers. To use it for a product category simply obtain preference rank orders or, better yet, intensity measures (e.g., constant sums or pairs), compute the product positions, and form a data matrix similar to Table 10.3. The regression is run and the model tested by its ability to predict observed preference. You then use the model to explore the potential product positions and product strategies. Remember that the changes in positions are based on judgment. Preference regression gives reasonable guidelines but not exact predictions.

One advantage of preference regression is that it is relatively easy to use. Regression software is available for both mainframes and PCs. A disadvantage is that the estimated regression weights are "average" weights. Although these average weights are useful early in the design process to establish priorities they must be modified later to reflect variation among customers. We address this variation in the next chapter when we introduce a "search and test" procedure for identifying benefit segments with preference regression and when we introduce a revealed preference method that provides a distribution of importance weights rather than just average weights.

Conjoint Analysis

Preference regression is suited well to the identification of a perceptual position. But once that position is identified, the new product team must select the engineering characteristics and/or the features of the product. One can do this with a judgmental relationship between customer needs and engineering characteristics as indicated in chapter 13. Conjoint analysis provides an alternative methodology that links features directly to preference, links features to perceptual dimensions, or links features to customer needs.

For example, a target position of a new deodorant might be that it "goes on dry, keeps you dry." To achieve this position the new product team must determine the features (chemical ingredients, scent, form (powder, stick, spray, roll-on), package size, package color, etc.) that best achieve the target position. One method to identify the best features might be to try every combination of features, determine which is the best, and select that combination. That is basically what conjoint analysis does except that only a fraction of all combinations need be tried and a formal model is used to help the team measure and quantify the effect of each feature.

In chapter 8 (see Figure 8.1), we introduced the Lens model which made explicit the fact that customers use perceptions as a "lens" to filter

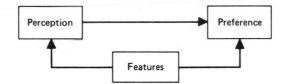

Figure 10.7 Conjoint Analysis Can Link Features to Perceptions and Preference

product features and other cues. Our focus on developing a core benefit proposition is based on this recognition. Preference regression and direct measurement provide an explicit link from perception to preference. Conjoint analysis provides the link from features to perception. However, management sometimes likes to see the direct link from features to preference. As shown in Figure 10.7 conjoint analysis can provide this link as well.

Method.   Consider the telecommunications example and suppose that preference regression indicates that the relative importance weights are 57% for effectiveness and 43% for ease of use. From previous maps we know that NBVT is dominated by telephone and personal visit. If NBVT is to be a viable technology, it must be improved so that it moves out along the ideal vector to fill the gap between telephone and personal visit (see Figure 10.8).

The problem is to adjust the features of NBVT to achieve this needed improvement. For example, we might increase the resolution of the video picture, decrease the transmission time, increase its accessibility to users, or make hard copy available. Table 10.4 lists these features. Note that there are $2 \times 2 \times 2 \times 3 = 24$ possible products, each of which can be described by a particular combination of features, such as illustrated in Figure 10.9. In this conjoint analysis we give each customer 24 3" × 5" cards, each of which describes a possible communication product. We ask each customer to rank these cards in order of preference from 1 to 24.

Conjoint analysis is a mathematical technique to summarize the ranking information in a form that is useful to the new product team. In particular, we assume that the preference for NBVT is composed of some preference for the base-level NBVT plus some "part-worth" or utility for each of the features. That is, if m indexes the product profile ($m = 1$ to 24) then, for each customer in the sample, we say that the preference, P_m, for the mth profile is given by

$$
\begin{aligned}
P_m = \; & u_r(\text{resolution of } m) + u_a(\text{accessibility of } m) \\
& + u_h(\text{hard copy of } m) \\
& + u_t(\text{transmission time of } m) \\
& + \text{base level preference for NBVT} \qquad (10.3)
\end{aligned}
$$

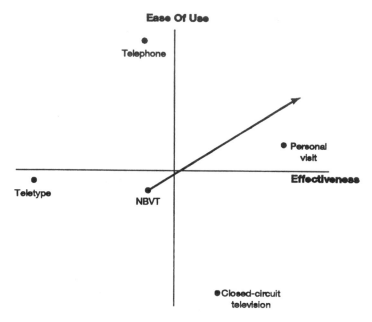

Figure 10.8   Needed Perceptual Improvement

where the $u_j(\bullet\ )$'s are the utilities of the various features. For example, u_r (resolution = four times home TV) represents the contribution to the customer's preference of having the resolution of NBVT boosted to four times that of home television.

Figure 10.10 gives the part-worths for the features of NBVT. The most important features are accessibility and a 30-second transmission time—they have the largest part-worths. Improving the transmission time has a much larger impact (0.42 versus 0.09) than improving resolution, but only if that transmission time is reduced all the way to 10 seconds. A reduction to 20 seconds is just not sufficient.

TABLE 10.4   Product Feature Combinations for Narrow Band Video
Telephone

	Resolution	Accessibility	Hard Copy	Transmission Time
Level 1	Equal to home television	30-minutes notice	None available	30 seconds
Level 2	Four times home television	Every office has one	Hard copy available	20 seconds
Level 3	—	—	—	10 seconds

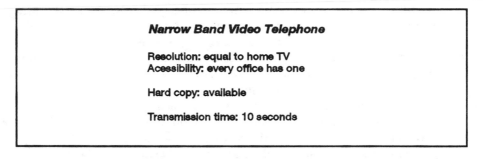

Narrow Band Video Telephone

Resolution: equal to home TV
Acessibility: every office has one

Hard copy: available

Transmission time: 10 seconds

Figure 10.9 An Example of One of Twenty-Four Possible Types of Video Telephones

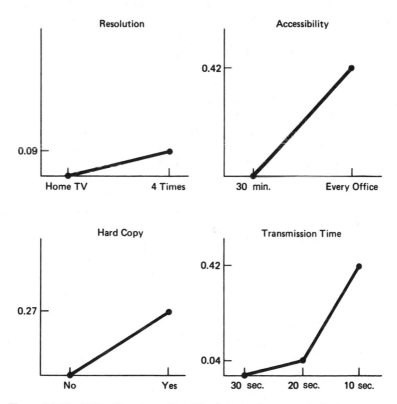

Figure 10.10 Utility Functions (Part-Worths) for Features of NBVT (Adapted from Hauser and Simmie 1981)

Because we only specify the features at discrete levels, we use dummy-variable regression (or, equivalently, analysis of variance) to estimate the part-worths for each level of each of the features. (Because the base level does not vary across the profiles we use the rank orders as the dependent variable and the levels of the features as the explanatory variable. Due to degrees-of-freedom considerations we arbitrarily set the lowest feature to have a part-worth of zero causing all improvements to be measured relative to a base level.) In many cases the researcher will use monotonic regression (Kruskal 1965) or linear programming (Srinivasan and Shocker 1973) to recognize that the rank orders are monotonic rather than interval-scaled data. Alternatively, one can collect intensity measures for the preferences such as asking customers to provide preferences on a 100-point scale.

Conjoint analysis has many advanced features which enable the analyst to customize the studies to the special needs of the new product team. Fractional factorials (Cochran and Cox 1957, Addleman 1962) enable the researcher to use only a small fraction of the profiles to estimate the part-worths. Alternatively, if enough profiles are used, the researcher can estimate interactions. For example, the part-worth of transmission time may depend upon whether or not hard copy is available. Aggregate importances can be estimated by simplified measures and new discrete choice models (Louviere and Woodworth 1983; Wiley and Low 1983; Ogawa 1987). These advanced models collect measures by asking for overall preference among the profiles and then generating importances and interactions. Individual importances are not derived, but good aggregate values can be obtained.

Interactive computer interviewing systems are widely available decreasing the difficulty of the task for the respondent and providing overnight analyses of the data so that the new product team can act as soon as the data collection is completed. Furthermore, it is possible to use many different stimuli besides $3'' \times 5''$ cards. In some cases the team can use concept statements or even build prototype products. Conjoint analysis is an extremely flexible technique that can be modified to the needs of the task at hand.

Hybrid Conjoint Analysis.   Hybrid conjoint analysis is one technique to obtain part-worths for a large number of features. In hybrid conjoint analysis respondents are asked to provide direct measures of importances for the features and, in addition, to provide preferences for a limited number of profiles such as Figure 10.9 where the profiles are drawn from a much larger set—a master design. The data are merged across respondents, overall part-worths are obtained, and adjusted (via regression) by the directly-measured importances. (For more details see Green and Srinivasan [1990] and Green [1984].)

Managerial Diagnostics.   Conjoint analysis is best used to select features. The "utility" functions indicate how sensitive customer perceptions and preferences are to changes in product features. By examining graphs such as Figure 10.10 the new product team gains insight into which features to select for a new product. In general, the best features are those that give the greatest gains in preference at the lowest costs.

Figure 10.10 gives the relationship of features to preference. But conjoint analysis can also be used with perceptual dimensions as the dependent variables. For example, Table 10.5 gives the part-worths of the features as they relate to effectiveness and ease of use. Based on Table 10.5 we see that if we want to position the telecommunications technology on effectiveness we must improve the hard-copy availability (such as today's FAX products). If we seek an ease-of-use positioning the key feature is accessibility. While these insights may seem obvious after the fact, Table 10.5 provides a quantification of the feature impacts. By using the part-worths in Table 10.5 scaled with the base-level NBVT perceptions, we plot each of the concepts on a perceptual map or a value map. If we also plot production costs we can begin to identify a most profitable position as is indicated in Figure 10.1b.

Market Simulation.   Conjoint analysis can be used to simulate the sales or market share of a product profile. In a technique conceptually similar to

TABLE 10.5   Part-Worths Relating Features to Perceptions
(Adapted from Hauser and Simmie 1981)

	Effectiveness	Ease of Use
Resolution		
Equal to home television	—	—
Four-time home television	*	*
Accessibility		
30 minutes notice	—	—
Every office has one	0.13	0.36
Hard copy		
None available	—	—
Hard copy available	0.45	0.27
Transmission time		
30 seconds	—	—
20 seconds	0.11	0.09
10 seconds	0.38	0.31

(* Indicates the coefficient was not satistically significant.)

that used for direct measurement and preference regression, equation 10.3 is used to assign preference values to a product concept. If the preferences for the existing products are measured on the same scale, we assign each customer in the sample to their most preferred product, count up the number who are forecast to choose the new product, and compute market share. We illustrate market simulation with conjoint analysis in the next chapter on segmentation with a case based on fork-lift trucks.

Discussion.   Each year there are hundreds of applications of conjoint analysis (see Cattin and Wittink 1982; Green and Srinivasan 1978; Reibstein, Bateson, and Boulding 1988). Conjoint analysis is appropriate when the features of the new product need to be set. Judgment or simulation can be used to assess new combinations of features. Recently optimal product design models have been extended to use perceptual or conjoint data to develop a recommended product design (Albers 1982; DeSarbo and Rao 1986; Dobson and Kalish 1988; Green and Krieger 1987; Green, Krieger, and Carroll 1987; Green and Krieger 1989; Kohli and Krishnamurthy 1987; McBride and Zufryden 1988; Sudharshan, May, and Shocker 1987; and Sudharshan, May, and Gruca 1988). These models represent the advancing state-of-the-art of conjoint analysis and new product development. We can expect further elaborations in the future.

Basic conjoint analysis is not difficult. To use conjoint analysis in a product category, select the features that need to be tested. These features are the result of strategic positioning decisions and available technology. Then prototypes are made, pictures drawn, concepts written, or cards made to depict the feasible combinations of product features. Customers are asked to rank these "products" or indicate their preferences in other ways. A conjoint analysis or regression computer program is used to estimate the part-worths (programs are now available for personal computers). The results are used to select features and to predict market response (Green and Krieger 1991, 1992).

The advantage of conjoint analysis is that it can deal with physical product features. One disadvantage is that as the number of features escalates, the number of potential "products" escalates even faster, thus the new product team must be frugal in their choice of features to test. For example, Wind and Mahajan (1981) use hybrid conjoint analysis to evaluate 50 features for a new hotel chain (Mariott's Courtyard). They state that 50 features are about the limit of the technique. If there are indeed a large number of features, then a direct measurement or judgmental technique may be better suited to the task. Another disadvantage is that the product profiles used in the measurement may not be perceived as realistic to the customer. The team should use caution when interpreting any conjoint analysis that is based on profiles that include abstract representations of products.

SUMMARY

Preference analysis plays an important role in new product design. If there are many customer needs or the engineering team needs detailed specifications, direct measures are best. Preference regression excels in analyzing the importance of the dimensions used in perceptual maps. It identifies an "ideal vector" along which a product should be moved to maximize customer preference. Conjoint analysis is best when there are a modest number of specific features being considered in product design.

The three techniques are a powerful set of methods for analyzing customer preferences. A successful product team should know how and when to use each of these methods.

These tools of preference analysis are important strategically for identifying the best position with which to enter the market. By understanding the tradeoffs that the customers make in terms of their desires for product benefits and by designing the product based on those tradeoffs, the new product team is more likely to design a product that customers will accept. Furthermore, by carefully balancing the product's position with the strengths of competitive products and with the cost of achieving that position, the new product team identifies a strategic opportunity that is likely to be profitable for the firm and to lead to competitive advantages.

In the techniques reviewed in this chapter we either analyzed preferences at the level of the individual customer or at the market level. Even when we analyzed the data at the level of the individual customer we presented overall averages as managerial diagnostics. In practice, markets are rarely homogeneous. Some customers may have one set of tradeoffs while other customers have a completely different set of tradeoffs. When this happens using average response can lead to average products that satisfy no one. The next chapter considers this heterogeneity and introduces means by which to deal with the heterogeneity through benefit segmentation.

REVIEW QUESTIONS

10.1. There are several approaches to selecting the best positioning for a new product. One approach might be to construct a concept description for each possible new product position and have customers evaluate the various descriptions. A second approach would be to use preference analysis to understand customer tradeoffs and select a target position. Discuss the advantages and disadvantages of each approach.

10.2. Summarize the various preference analysis methods, direct measurement, preference regression, and conjoint analysis. What are the advantages and disadvantages of each? When should each be used?

10.3. What are the managerial implications of the relationship among product features, perceptions, and preferences? How is conjoint analysis used to provide the manager with the information necessary to select the product features?

10.4. The best position in terms of customer preference may be the most costly for the firm to achieve. How can the team select among potential positions that vary in terms of position and cost? How can value maps be used to summarize this information and to consider alternative pricing strategies?

10.5. In all of the analyses in this chapter we have treated competitive products as fixed positions on the maps. In fact, competitors are likely to respond to any new product we develop—especially if that new product has the potential to impact their sales. How can value maps and preference analyses be used to understand potential competitor response and to develop defensible strategies?

11

Benefit Segmentation and Product Positioning

SEGMENTATION AND NEW PRODUCT DESIGN

The PC industry is a diverse industry offering a wide variety of products for the lab, office, and home. At the low end there are machines based on the simple chips. These machines will do basic computing including word processing and spreadsheets. At the high end are powerful workstations based on very fast chips. These work-stations are used by "power users" who need the computing power these machines offer in order to be competitive in their jobs. These advanced chips are now being used for ultra-light-weight portable computers that will fit in a briefcase and can be used by executives while traveling. The new next generation chips are trying to put supercomputer capability on the desk of engineers and scientists. But even beyond the basic technology manufacturers stress different service and price images. Some position themselves as the standard (e.g., IBM, Compaq), or reliable (e.g., Hewlett-Packard), easy to use (e.g., Apple), outstanding service, or the lowest price. Some target the business environment, others the engineering environment, others the "hacker," and still others the home user. Today's personal computer market has evolved well beyond the early days when there were one or two major choices and a wide variety of commodity-like clones.

One of the messages that we have stressed in new product design is that successful new products meet the needs of their customers. But not all customers have the same needs! Clearly, in the personal computer market there are a variety of users, each using the computers in different ways and hence needing different benefits. Indeed, most manufacturers, whatever their basic product-line positioning, offer a variety of products to meet these needs. IBM, Apple, Compaq, Hewlett-Packard, NEC, Zenith, AST, Digital, Dell, Zeos, Gateway, and so on all offer a wide product line.

The message of benefit segmentation is that to meet customer needs a line of products may be better than a single product. This concept is illustrated in Figure 11.1. Suppose that there are some consumers who feel that gentleness is much more important than effectiveness. These may be heavy users that are concerned with side effects. There might be another set of users who feel that effectiveness is much more important than gentleness. These users may have severe headaches that must be relieved even if the product upsets their stomachs. If we pool these consumers and estimate the average ideal vector (see Figure 11.1) we will be led to infer that a product that balances gentleness and effectiveness is best. Alternatively, if we could identify the benefit segments, we would estimate two segmented ideal vectors as shown in Fgure 11.1. In this case the best new product strategy might be a two-product strategy with product 1 aimed at segment one and product 2 aimed at segment two (see the starred products in Fgure 11.1).

The final decision on which product to offer or whether to offer both products will depend upon the manufacturing costs, efficiencies or inefficien-

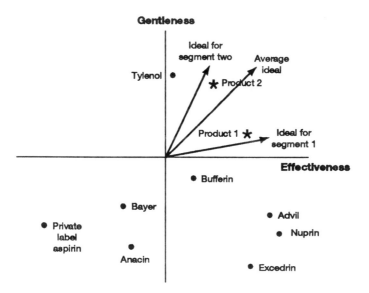

Figure 11.1   Benefit Segmentation for Selected Pain Relievers

cies due to assortments, the size of the segments, and competition. Figure 11.1 illustrates that the new product team can make informed decisions if they consider heterogeneity of benefit needs.

There are competitive considerations in benefit segmentation as well. If everyone enters the market with a product designed for the average customer, then the market begins to look like a commodity market and competition for customers drives down prices (and margins). Alternatively, if each manufacturer chooses a well-targeted niche of the market, each manufacturer can enjoy a "local monopoly" and maintain profitable margins. Thus, benefit segmentation can have strategic implications above and beyond the desire to serve customers better.

In this chapter we look at segmentation from the viewpoints of matching customer benefits and maintaining margins. We consider methods that identify discrete segments as well as methods that assume a more continuous variation in customer-benefit needs. We begin with benefit segmentation as it relates to discrete segments.

BENEFIT SEGMENTATION WITH DISCRETE SEGMENTS

The basic idea behind discrete segments is that customers vary in the importance weights that they assign to different benefit dimensions and that there are two or more types of customers that can be distinguished by the importances that they assign to the benefit dimensions. This concept is illustrated in Figure 11.2.

Suppose that we have measured the importance weights that each consumer (in a sample of consumers) assigns to the effectiveness and the gentleness of pain relievers. We plot each customer as a point in a two-dimensional space where the axes are the *importance* weights (not brand perceptions). If the data is as indicated in Figure 11.2, then we can identify visually that there are two sets of consumers—cluster 1 feels that gentleness is extremely important and cluster 2 feels that effectiveness is extremely important. These clusters are indicated by the dense cloud of points in the upper-left and lower-right corners of the space. The sparsity of points elsewhere suggests that these two segments encompass most consumers. Product developers might consider two products, one for each segment.

Clustering of Direct Measures

Once you understand Figure 11.2, you understand the basics of the analytic method to identify benefit segments when importance weights are

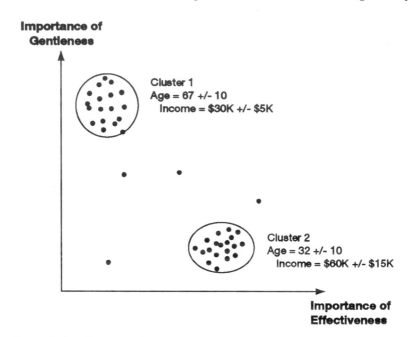

Figure 11.2   Cluster Analysis of Customer Importance Weights to Reveal Two
Benefit Segments for Pain Relievers

measured directly. If there are but two dimensions you can plot the customer importances. If there are many dimensions, such as when detailed
customer needs are measured, it is better to use a formal cluster analysis
program. The computer program will group customers such that the variation in importance weights within segment is small and the variation between segments is large. As was the case in the clustering of detailed
customer needs into groups of needs, the computer program will identify
one-cluster, two-cluster, three-cluster, and so on, solutions. You will have to
use judgment tempered with a plot of variation versus number of clusters to
decide on the appropriate number of potential benefit segments. Several
advanced methods of benefit clustering (Kamakura 1988; Hagerty 1985,
1986) are emerging and models based on the optimal design structures
identified in the last chapter are being developed to help managers in dealing with the complexity of benefit segmentation (Ogawa 1987; Green and
Krieger 1989).

   In some cases the new product team will want to identify the demographic, psychographic, sociographic, or use-characteristic makeup of the
segments. One method to do this is to compute the means and standard

deviations of each relevant variable and identify the differences.[1] For example, in the hypothetical case of Figure 11.2, the segments differ on age and income. In more complex situations multiple discriminant analysis can be used to find the best set of variables to distinguish among the clusters.

Of course not all clusters will be distinguished by demographic, etc. variables. In such cases it is more difficult to target advertising or sales messages to the segments, but the existence of benefit segments is still important because it allows the new product team to design products that best meet customer needs.

The example in Figure 11.2 is for the importances of benefit dimensions, but the basic idea applies as well to the importances of the secondary and tertiary customer needs or the part-worths identified by conjoint analysis. The interpretation and use is the same—design one or more products to meet the diverse needs.

Search and Test with Revealed Measures

Revealed preference techniques present an inherent paradox for benefit segmentation. If an analyst knew which individual customers belonged to a segment, the analyst would run a preference regression for those customers only and report a set of importance weights for that segment. However, to assign customers to segments the analyst must know their importance weights. To finesse this paradox, we use a two-step technique known as search and test.

First candidate segments are generated by prior beliefs ("sports car drivers want high-performance tires") or by heuristic search of preference indicators (demographics, psychographics, usage, or attitude measures). Next, for each candidate segmentation scheme preference regressions or other revealed techniques are run within each segment in the scheme. Finally, the explanatory power of the segmentation scheme is tested against an unsegmented preference regression to determine whether or not the segmentation scheme provides improved insight and whether or not it can predict preferences better.

The technique is best illustrated with an example. Recall from the HMO case of chapter 9 that there were four perceptual dimensions—quality, personalness, convenience, and value. The first step, identifying candidate segments, was done with Automatic Interaction Detection program (Sonquist, Baker, and Morgan 1973) on intent to purchase. This program searches over a candidate set of variables selecting a variable, say age, and a set of groupings,

---

[1] Naturally, one would test for the significance of these differences based on the means and standard deviations. See Mood and Graybill (1963).

say under 30 years old and over 30 years old, such that there is low variance within groups and high variance between groups. Throughout the analysis there was a common but weak indication that the pattern of existing care—MIT versus private—was a possible variable for segmentation. Table 11.1 reports the results of the second step—preference regression for each of three segments within this segmentation scheme and for the overall population.

Finally, we test to see whether the segmented regressions are better statistically than the overall regression. The formal statistical test is an F-test (Fisher 1970; Johnston 1972; Chow 1960). The basic idea is simple. The group of unsegmented regressions can be thought of as a single regression with added parameter weights applied depending upon the segment to which the observation belongs. The F-test is a standard regression test used to determine whether the added parameters are significant.

Based on Table 11.1 we can compute $F = 0.50$ with $(10,195)$ degrees of freedom. This F-statistic is not significant indicating that a segmentation by pattern of care does not distinguish consumers via preferences—it is not a benefit segmentation. In this case no benefit segmentation scheme was found, not even the scheme of faculty versus students versus staff that was favored by the management team. We chose it to demonstrate the technique and to caution the new product team that not all markets can be segmented.

In other cases search and test has proven quite successful. For example, in the telecommunications case there were clear benefit segments identified based on (1) the need to use visuals, (2) the amount of people involved in the interaction, and (3) the length of time of the interaction (Hauser 1984).

Managerial Use of Benefit Segmentation

Benefit segmentation makes sense when customers vary in the benefits that they demand of products. Because a key success criterion for new product development is satisfying customer needs, benefit segmentation provides the new product team with a chance to tailor the product directly to the diverse

TABLE 11.1   Preference Regressions within Each Segment

	Quality	Personalness	Value	Convenience	R^2
Overall ($n = 210$)	6.2	3.9	5.7	3.3	.27
Segmentation:					
Private ($n = 88$)	6.1	4.6	4.9	4.5	.28
MIT ($n = 109$)	6.9	3.6	6.5	2.8	.29
Mixed ($n = 12$)	2.6*	5.5*	4.2*	-1.0*	.26

All regressions are significant at the .01 level. All coefficients but those starred (*) are significant at the .05 level.

needs. By providing two or more products, each designed with a specific benefit segment in mind, the team assures that customer needs are met.

Of course multiple product strategies may not be appropriate for all markets. Certainly when importance weights do not vary, as in the HMO case, a segmentation strategy will not be cost-effective. But even if importance weights vary, the new product team must weigh the added costs of designing, manufacturing, and administering multiple products against the improved ability to meet customer needs. For example, if a product line gets too broad then manufacturing may not be able to exploit economies of scale or may not be able to switch among output quickly enough—costs will escalate, the resulting price to the customer will increase, and the perceived value of the product will decrease. Alternatively, a less standardized production strategy may mean batch processing resulting in a reduced ability to provide on-time delivery. Finally, sales and service may suffer because of the inability of the salesforce or the service department to deal with the complexities of the product line. In the end, it is a difficult decision, but benefit segmentation provides the insight into customer needs that is so critical to a decision on the breadth of a product line.

We close with a final example on fork-lift trucks for the Brazilian market.[2] At the time of this example, Brazil had recently passed a law requiring that Brazilian parts be used in the manufacturing of trucks sold in Brazil. In response Clark Equipment Corporation had used a Brazilian-produced transmission in its trucks. Unfortunately this transmission often broke down and became a major headache for Clark and its distributors. Meanwhile, a competitor, Hyster, used a transmission made from Brazilian parts that provided superior performance and which allowed Hyster to gain market share at Clark's expense.

In seeking to regain its share and position for the future, Clark commissioned a conjoint analysis study to determine which new products, if any, should be introduced. One option being considered was a new offering based on a powershift automatic transmission, thus "transmission" was a key factor in the conjoint design. Other factors included performance, reliability, durability, parts availability, brand name, and price. We focus on brand name and transmission for the remainder of this example.

Figure 11.3a is a plot of the part-worth importance weights for brand name and transmission. Based on Figure 11.3 (top) it appears that the automatic transmission does not serve customer needs as well as the standard transmission and that Clark is an okay brand name, much better than the

---

[2] This example is taken from a case on "Clark Equipment" in Chapter 4 of Darral G. Clarke, *Marketing Analysis and Decision Making: Text and Cases with Lotus 123*, (Redwood City, CA: The Scientific Press, 1987), pp. 180–211.

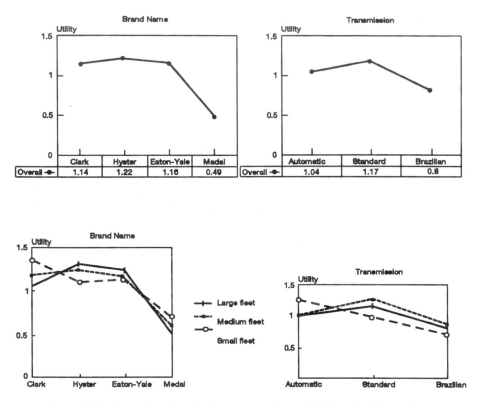

Figure 11.3   Example of Benefit Segmentation for Fork-lift Trucks (Adapted from Clarke 1987)

Brazilian brand of Madal but slightly worse than the international brands of Hyster and Eaton-Yale. However, a different picture emerges when the part-worths are segmented by the size of the fleet owned by the customer (see Figure 11.3). It becomes clear quickly that the automatic transmission is favored by small-fleet owners and furthermore that, for those owners, the Clark brand name is most preferred. The automatic transmission will serve these core customers, but if Clark is to expand its share, it must develop a product to meet the need of medium- and large-fleet owners, which account for 90% of the fork-lift trucks sold in Brazil.

Naturally the case is more complex than that illustrated in Figure 11.3. Clark must face organization and distribution issues in developing the new products and Clark must position itself to anticipate new competitive offerings, but Figure 11.3 illustrates how benefit segmentation is often key to understanding the needs of customers and to designing the right product(s) to meet those needs.

TASTE DIAGRAMS

Figure 11.1 illustrates how tastes might vary among segments of customers—segment one cares more about effectiveness than gentleness while segment two cares more about gentleness than effectiveness. But perhaps the variation in customer tastes is not so abrupt. Perhaps tastes vary in a more continuous manner. Taste diagrams are one means to represent such variation.

Illustrative Taste Diagram

Figure 11.4a reproduces the value map for the analgesics market, but we have taken the liberty of simplifying the map by limiting the number of brands to three. This will allow us to explain the technique; naturally it is readily applicable to the full market. To represent the variation in tastes we replace the segmented ideal vectors of Figure 11.1 with the taste diagram in Figure 11.4b.

The interpretation of Figure 11.4b is simple. Consumers are represented by the tradeoffs they make between effectiveness and gentleness—consumers who place a high weight on effectiveness are represented by the right-hand side of the x axis while consumers who place a high weight on gentleness are represented by the left-hand side of the axis. Consumers who feel that effectiveness and gentleness are equally important are represented by the middle of the axis. A solid line is then drawn to represent the number of consumers with various tastes. For example, in Figure 11.4b there are more "effectiveness" consumers than there are "gentleness" consumers.

Taste diagrams also indicate the type of consumers that buy each of

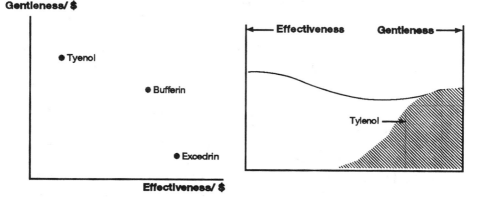

Figure 11.4   Illustrative Taste Diagram Portrays the Heterogeneity of Customer Tradeoffs

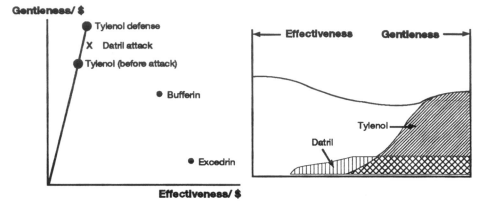

Figure 11.5   Interpretation of the Tylenol versus Datril Case

the brands. For example, in Figure 11.4b the shaded region indicates that Tylenol attracts consumers who care more about gentleness than about effectiveness.

Tylenol vs. Datril

In the early 1970s Tylenol was an effective and profitable analgesic, but it was not heavily advertised. (Its awareness came from doctors' recommendations, which in turn were strongly influenced by McNeil Laboratories', a division of Johnson & Johnson, "detail" force.) Bristol-Myers recognized an opportunity and introduced a competitive brand called Datril with the selling proposition that Datril was just like Tylenol, but that it cost much less. This positioning is shown on the value map in Figure 11.5a; Datril (X) is shown as dominating Tylenol because it delivers the same benefits, but for a lower price.

Datril now had the potential to have a dramatic impact on Tylenol's share. Even if national advertising would not reach all of Tylenol's consumers, it would reach some Bufferin and Excedrin consumers.[3] Furthermore, Datril was now positioned better than Tylenol to compete with the other brands. Had Tylenol done nothing, Datril might have captured the area shown in the taste diagram in Figure 11.5b.

In top-level strategy meetings, Johnson & Johnson decided to fight back strongly. Literally over a weekend, they mobilized the Johnson & Johnson salesforce (not just the salesforce of the McNeil division), matched Datril's price, persuaded television networks that Datril's price advantage was now

---

[3] As well as the other brands not shown on this simple map.

false advertising, and began other defensive measures. The result was that Tylenol, with its strong image from years of detailing, leap-frogged Datril and successfully trumped Bristol-Myers' challenge. This strategy is shown on the value map by Tylenol's defensive position. With this new position Datril could capture but a small fraction of Tylenol's consumers; this would be shown in Figure 11.5b as a much-shrunken area for Datril.

Awakened to the potential of the Tylenol brand, McNeil Laboratories became a national advertiser, added the Extra-strength Tylenol brand to capture the effectiveness consumers on the left-hand side of the taste diagram, and undertook a number of effective marketing strategies. Until the ibuprofen challenge in the mid 1980's and early 1990's by Nupril, Advil, Motrin, and others, McNeil's marketing had been so strong that identical physical products, Datril, Panadol, and generic acetaminophen, had not been able to draw substantial share from Tylenol. Tylenol was even able to weather tragic poisonings in 1982 and 1986.

Managerial Diagnostics

The Tylenol-Datril case illustrates the power of taste diagrams. Because they represent a more continuous set of tradeoffs the taste diagrams indicate which customers are affected by new products, competitive new products, and competitive actions. This "what-if" simulation capability is a powerful tool with which to fine-tune a launch or, as in the Tylenol-Datril case, a defense.

The diagram in Figure 11.4 is quite smooth; there are no clear segments. But such is not always the case. Figure 11.6 illustrates how sharp segments appear in taste diagrams. The market in this case is actually a $100 million plus market, but for confidentiality we disguise the category with the fictitious name "gypsy moth tape." Figure 11.6 shows that there are four major national brands plus the regional store brands competing in a market defined by the benefit dimensions of "professional quality," "effective control," and "ease of use."

The taste diagram, Figure 11.6b, is more complicated than that in Figures 11.4 and 11.5 because instead of two dimensions there are three. Thus one axis of the taste diagram represents tradeoffs between effective control and ease of use, whereas the other axis represents tradeoffs between effective control and professional quality. The taste diagram is now a surface rather than a line representing the number of consumers with each combination of tradeoffs. In Figure 11.6b it is clear that there is a distinct segment of consumers who care about professional quality almost to the exclusion of all else. Clearly there is an opportunity here for a professional-quality product if one can be developed to dominate "Pro-strip." Conversely, any product that is weak on professional quality would miss this opportunity.

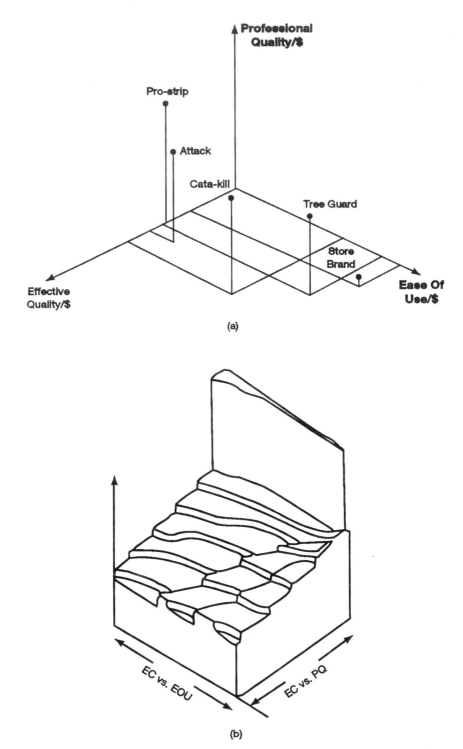

Figure 11.6. Example Value Map and Taste Diagram for "Gypsy-Moth Tape." Note the "professional-quality" segment in the Taste Distribution. (Value map and taste distribution from Hauser and Gaskin 1984)

Methodology

Generating taste diagrams is simple in concept as illustrated in Figure 11.7. By "tastes" we refer to the relative importance weights that a customer places on the two (or more) dimensions. In chapter 10 we plotted these weights as an ideal vector indicating the direction along which preference increases most rapidly. We can also represent the relative importance weights by an "indifference curve," a line or curve which connects those positions on the perceptual map that are equally preferred. (Geometrically, an indifference curve is perpendicular to the ideal vector.) Figure 11.7a illustrates indifference curves for those consumers who place heavy weight on gentleness, equal weight on both dimensions, and heavy weight on effectiveness.

Now let us consider those consumers who choose Tylenol. Consumers who place all their weight on gentleness will choose Tylenol (the horizontal indifference curves in Figure 11.7a). But consumers who place most of their weight on gentleness will also choose Tylenol. In fact, as long as the indifference curve touches Tylenol before it touches Bufferin (moving in from the top and/or right of the diagram), consumers represented by the indifference curve will choose Tylenol. As we rotate the indifference curves by changing the relative weights we will reach a point where the curves now touch Bufferin first. Those consumers will choose Bufferin. This boundary is shown in Figure 11.7b. We also compute a boundary between Bufferin and Excedrin.

We now set the height of the taste diagram within each region. To do this we recognize that the area under the taste diagram will be proportional to the number of consumers who choose the brand that corresponds to a region of the x axis. Thus, if Tylenol has a bigger share of the market, the area under its portion of the diagram will be larger. If the relative market shares of

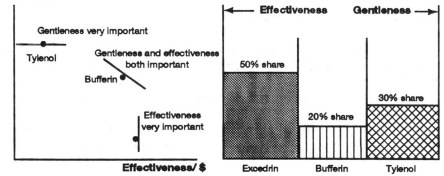

Figure 11.7. Illustration of Revealed-Preference Method to Estimate Taste Distributions (a. value map, b. taste diagram)

Excedrin, Bufferin, and Tylenol were 50%, 20%, and 30%, respectively, and if the portions of the x axis corresponding to each brand were equal, then we would get a diagram such as that in Figure 11.7b.

Finally, to get a smooth diagram such as in Figures 11.4 and 11.5 we recognize that consumers vary in the brands that they consider. For each set of considered brands we compute a diagram such as that in Figure 11.7 and combine them to get the smoother overall diagram. We also adjust the boundaries to recognize that they are fuzzy because of the fact that consumers vary in their perceptions as well as their preferences.[4]

Discussion

Taste diagrams provide an alternative means to model preferences. They are most effective when one suspects that consumers vary in their tastes but that the variation is smooth rather than abrupt. Taste diagrams can uncover segments as in the case of "Gypsy Moth Tape" or indicate that the market is heterogeneous as in the case of Tylenol versus Datril. In either case the improved understanding of the variation in customer tastes leads to targeted products that serve customers, perhaps better than a single product.

Taste diagrams do have their limitations. The revealed-preference methodology used to generate taste diagrams is sensitive to the number of dimensions and the number of brands. Because of computational and measurement issues it works best if the number of dimensions is limited to three or four and the number of major brands in the category is well under 10 brands. When these limits are exceeded, the new product team is best advised to use one of the preference/segmentation techniques described in the section on benefit segmentation.

STRATEGIC VALUE POSITIONING

Our final topic on segmentation deals with the competitive implications of segmentation strategy. Consider again the Tylenol versus Datril case. In that case Tylenol had basic advantages due to years of detailing effort and due to the "deep pockets" of Johnson & Johnson. But suppose that both were relatively new brands and that both Johnson & Johnson and Bristol-Myers were willing to invest heavily in their brands. If this were the case, Tylenol and Datril might have kept lowering their prices to move further and further out

[4] The resulting correction is a matrix-valued logit model. For detailed equations see Hauser (1986b). For derivation of the basic technique see Hauser and Shugan (1983) and for implementable equations see Hauser and Gaskin (1984).

on the map. The resulting price/positioning war would have made the market unprofitable for both players.

Conversely, suppose that Excedrin lowers its price. Tylenol would lose share but not at the same rate that it would lose share to a Datril price reduction. It is conceivable that after one or more rounds of price cutting, the market might stabilize at a price that would allow both brands to remain profitable. Thus, one reason a brand might want to consider selecting a niche—a segment—would be to avoid destructive price competition.

Competitive Price and Positioning Interactions

We illustrate these competitive effects with an idealized market. Suppose that there are three equal-priced brands in a market all positioned at the same distance from the origin on a value map. Suppose further that customers vary in their tastes such that there are equal numbers favoring each dimension and, in fact, every intermediate tradeoff in a taste diagram. One such market is illustrated in Figure 11.8 where we have placed three hypothetical brands, Robologic, Rocon, and I.Robot, on a value map defined by power/$ and ease of use/$.

Consider now a competitive environment where by fiat the brands cannot compete on price; they can only compete on position. Then it is not hard to show by mathematics or simulation (see Hauser 1988) that the brands will have unilateral incentives to reposition toward the "center" of the market. Why? Because as the exterior brands (Robologic, I.Robot) move toward the center they keep the customers with extreme tastes (all power or all ease of use) and gain customers with more moderate tastes. This repositioning will continue until all brands are offering similar benefits—the market will look like a commodity market.

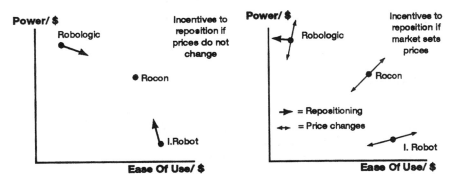

Figure 11.8. Competitive Price and Positioning Strategies (adapted from Hauser 1988).

But Figure 11.8a is not realistic. Brands will compete on price. In a value-map price competition is represented by movements in and out, toward or away from the origin, as brands change price but keep their benefits the same. It is also easy to show by mathematics or simulation that unless the brands are right on top of one another, as long as they hold their benefits constant, the price changes will ultimately stabilize and the market will reach an equilibrium. Of course the equilibrium that the brands reach will depend on their relative positions. The closer they are to one another, the lower the equilibrium price will be. In other words, if the brands are too close to one another, the market will look like a commodity market and competition will drive down the price. If the brands are sufficiently distinct then each brand will, in a sense, have a local monopoly and will be able to maintain higher prices.

Consider now a two-stage strategy where brands decide first on a position and then compete on price. In such a situation there will be incentives to move toward the center as in Figure 11.8, but there will also be incentives to move away from one another to maintain higher prices. In complex markets with many products and many segments it is hard to predict the net outcome of these conflicting incentives, but in our simple three-brand market it is possible to show that the net (unilateral) incentive is to reposition away from one another as shown in Figure 11.8b. In fact, the unilateral incentives make the market more profitable for everyone.

Real markets are very complex. Tastes vary, costs vary, different firms have competitive advantages. But Figure 11.8 does illustrate that the new product team should think carefully about the implications of competitive positioning. A core benefit proposition that delivers benefits to the most customers may, at first, seem quite attractive, but if such positioning toward the "center of the market" invokes competitive retaliation, such retaliation should be considered carefully. The new product team may wish to identify a segment where they can serve a "local monopoly" or, alternatively, delay for further improvements and cost reductions so that they can withstand the competitive pressure.

How Markets Evolve

Figure 11.8 suggests how markets might evolve. Suppose that a market is new; no one has yet entered. The first brand in is likely to attempt to identify customer preferences and position such that the most customers are satisfied—the "center" of the market. As further brands enter, they will attack the center of the market. These brands will survive as long as the market is growing, but as the market matures, price competition will drive down profits, a shakeout will result, and only the most efficient brands will survive. At this time they will begin to recognize segmentation opportunities and reposition to avoid destructive price competition. Over time the market will evolve to a differentiated oligopoly.

Naturally all markets will not evolve in this way, but there is some evidence that markets have evolved in this way (Fulga 1986, Goldberger 1985, Gupta 1986, Isaacs 1986, Shield 1986, Werner 1986). Whether or not a given market is evolving in this way, the new product team does well to consider whether such trends are occurring and, if they are occurring, how to anticipate the trends. For example, if the market is becoming a commodity-like market, the designer should be looking for profitable niches. If the market is still "young and growing" the team might want to meet competition head-on in the center of the market.

SUMMARY

Customers vary in their preferences. To design the most profitable new product or products the new product team must understand this variation. Benefit segmentation is one means by which this variation is understood. By clustering customers based on their importance weights or by estimating different preference models within segments, managers identify whether a multiple-product strategy is necessary. Alternatively, if the number of dimensions and the number of brands is small, the team can represent this heterogeneity as a more continuous taste distribution. Both benefit segmentation and taste distributions help in the design of products that meet customer needs. Positioning and benefit segments also are used to examine the implications of competitive price and positioning actions. Entering a market may cause existing brands to take actions to protect their market share so these defensive strategies should be considered when developing a new product.

Given a clear understanding of how customers perceive products, trade-off dimensions, and are segmented by their importances, we next need to translate our understanding into a sales forecast. This is a "what-if" exercise that explores competition and product designs. In the next chapter we present methods of forecasting sales potential at the design stage of development.

REVIEW QUESTIONS

11.1. What is the managerial goal in benefit segmentation?

11.2. Why can average preferences be misleading?

11.3. Suppose that the new-product team clusters direct measures of customer preferences and finds benefit segments, but suppose that no demographic, psychographic, or sociographic variables can be found to distinguish among the segments. Is the segmentation still useful? If so, why? If not, why not?

11.4. Describe a taste diagram and indicate how it might be used in new-product design.

11.5. Develop another geometric representation of heterogeneous customer tastes besides taste diagrams. (Hint: Draw many ideal vectors.)

11.6. Explain the intuition behind the seeming paradox that brands have the incentive to "position toward the center" if they do not consider price, yet have the incentive to differentiate if they do consider price.

12

Estimating Sales Potential: "What-if" Analyses

The preceding chapters have discussed the concepts and techniques that are used to identify and prioritize customer needs and have indicated how customer perceptions and preferences affect the development of a core benefit proposition. The chapters focused on diagnostic information that identifies the "best" product design. But is the "best" product good enough to warrant the cost and time involved in final development and testing? To answer this question we evaluate the sales potential of the new product.

ROLE OF SALES POTENTIAL IN THE DESIGN PROCESS

Consider a new-product team designing the next generation of a popular software product. Decisions are being made as to which features need to be updated in the next generation and which features can wait for succeeding generations. The team must decide now how much effort to allocate, how long the generational update can be delayed, and, roughly, what price the update should sell for. Early in the design the team need not forecast weekly sales for the next five years. To make these decisions, the team needs forecasts of *potential* sales—forecasts that vary depending upon the decisions being made.

Accuracy Depends on Decision Needs

The accuracy of the forecasts must be tailored to the decisions being made. Early in the design process the product is just an idea, a positioning, or at most a concept description. The investment has been relatively small and there are still many competing potential ideas. The team needs a rough estimate—an indication of whether the product will be a "bomb," a moderate success, or a spectacular "winner". Furthermore, because much can change as the idea is refined and the product designed, estimates can be "ballpark" estimates. Thus, the first forecasts that are likely to be made will combine the results of the perception and preference analysis with rules-of-thumb and managerial intuition.

As a product progresses through the design process, it becomes more refined and more like the final product. As a result, the evaluation of sales potential becomes more refined and the estimates become more exact. The investment in the product has grown and there are relatively fewer ideas or concepts that have passed the early screens. Thus, not only are more sophisticated techniques possible, but they are required to fine-tune the marketing strategy and to make the difficult, but crucial go/no go decision. An investment in the development of sophisticated customer purchase models is justified by the importance of the go/no go decision.

In this chapter we present both the simple rule-of-thumb methods of translating preference into purchase estimates and a more formal model of the customers' probability of purchase. This model, called the "logit model," is valuable in the final design and evaluation. We close the chapter with a description of a new measurement technology called "Information Acceleration," which holds promise for better estimates of potential and faster time to market.

Long-Run Potential versus Short-Run Sales

Consider a new antacid. Once launched OTC, sales of the new antacid depend on how well the product satisfies consumer needs. But the sales also depend on the marketing effort allocated to advertise the brand, promote the brand, distribute the brand, and so on. A product with great *potential* may fail because of a poor marketing effort. Thus, any forecast must include a "free-expression" forecast—a forecast of the potential sales that assumes a first-rate marketing effort. In this chapter we discuss techniques that forecast customer reaction based on an assumption that every customer is aware of the product and finds it available. The team then adjusts the forecasts to reflect projected awareness and availability.

Even if the long-run sales are 100 million units, these sales will not materialize over night. Sales may start at a low level and grow as more customers try the product, as more stores stock the product, as more uses are found for the product, or, in some cases, as existing products wear out. Thus, the product-development team must recognize the difference between forecasts of long-run sales—the sales once the transient phenomena stabilize—and the short-run sales that include the transient phenomena. This is particularly important when decisions to continue marketing a product are made on early sales data.

"What-If" Capability

Consider the software update. A major improvement such as going from two graphic dimensions to three graphic dimensions might result in one forecast while a minor update making the product easier to use and easier to network might result in another sales forecast. Similarly for the antacid, a positioning of "fast-relief" might result in a different sales potential for the same physical product than a positioning of "gentle." If the new product team is faced with these decisions it needs more than a generic forecast for the new product. It needs forecasts that depend upon the decisions being made (update to three dimensions versus minor update; fast-relief versus gentle).

In this chapter we discuss two methods for "what-if" capability in the forecasts. The first is measurement-based; an actual measurement of customer intentions is made for the "what-if" conditions. The second is model based; one set of measurements are made and analyzed to develop a mathematical model that can be used to simulate alternative designs and strategies.

Sensitivity to Competitive Actions

Customer reaction to a three-dimensional software package depends on whether that package is the first three-dimensional software package on the market or whether it is the tenth. Consumer response to a new antacid depends on whether or not competitive antacids double their advertising and send out 50 million free samples. Thus, an important characteristic of new product forecasts is that they depend upon competitive products and competitive marketing in an explicit manner. The go/no go decision, the positioning of the product, its features, and its introductory marketing mix all depend on planned (or threatened) competitive reaction. Forecasts must recognize this decision need.

The Goals of the Organization

In private organizations the goal is profit. However, profit is a complex construct. An organization might develop a new product for its own profitability, as a flagship to attract customers to other products in the line, as a move to preempt competition, or as a means to develop expertise in a market that holds promise for the future. Thus, while sales potential is an input to profit potential, this translation should be made carefully with the goals of the organization in mind.

In public services, goals may be different. A regional transportation agency may be concerned with increased energy efficiency and less pollution, and may measure success through a reduction in vehicle miles traveled (VMT). But VMT is a result of the trips people make and what mode of travel they use to make those trips. In this case sales potential is interpreted more broadly. For example, in health care delivery it is enrollment, in hospitals it is admissions by illness, in universities it is applications and placement, and in energy policy it is efficiency of energy use.

We now turn to models and measurements which enable the new-product team to forecast sales potential with an accuracy that is appropriate to decision needs.

MODELS OF SALES POTENTIAL

Several indicators of sales potential can be obtained from the customer. The simplest is a direct question which asks the customer either his or her intent to purchase or her or his probability of purchase. These measures must be treated with caution but can be translated to a rough measure of sales potential. An alternative procedure is to use historical relationships among preference and choice to transform the preference measures developed in chapter 10 into rough predictions of purchase probabilities. These methods are used early in the design process. Later in the design process, actual purchase is observed for some forms of the new product. When this is possible, the more complex logit model is used to translate preference measures into purchase predictions. We discuss each of these models and indicate how to use them in the design process.

Intent Translation

Intent Scales.   Figure 12.1 is an intent scale administered for the communications case described in previous chapters. Customers are simply asked to make a subjective estimate of their likelihood of using the new com-

If you selected the Narrow Band Video Telephone, which of the following statements reflects how you feel about your choice? Check one.

_____ I definitely would use the Narrow Band Video Telephone.

_____ I probably would use the Narrow Band Video Telephone.

_____ I might use the Narrow Band Video Telephone.

_____ I probably would not use the Narrow Band Video Telephone.

_____ I definitely would not use the Narrow Band Video Telephone.

Figure 12.1   Intent-Scale Communications Example

munications device. From past experiments and from experience in the product category, a manager can often translate customer response to these scales into estimates of probability. For example, Figure 12.2 illustrates the average relationship between stated intentions and actual purchase probabilities over the first six months of market experience. However, the percentages in Figure 12.2 should not be used blindly because there is a large variation across product categories and six months does not capture the full trial po-

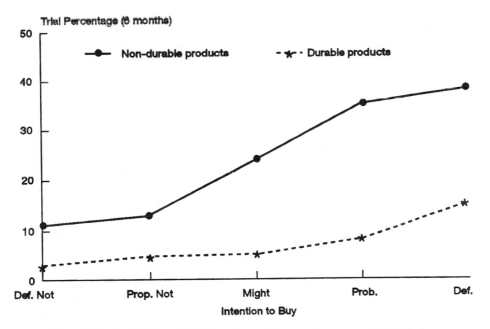

Figure 12.2   Probability of Trial Based on Customer Response to Intent Scales (Adapted from Jamieson and Bass 1989)

tential. In package goods 6 months may represent less than two-thirds of eventual trial and for consumer durables even less. In the study by Jamieson and Bass (1989) that led to Figure 12.2, the percentages varied from lows for cordless irons and stay-fresh milk to highs for home computers and pump toothpastes (see Silk and Kalwani 1982; and Morrison 1979a for other studies). In a study of new services, it was found that the probability of actual purchase varied from a value of .45 for "definitely would buy" to .05 for "definitely would not buy" (there were 10 points on the scale) when the service was offered with promotion (Infosino 1986). The translation values were much lower when the product was not under promotional incentives (e.g., .24 for "definitely would buy"). It is clear the "norms" for translating intent into purchase must be developed carefully within the specific market and launch practices.

Similarly, although Tauber (1975) reports a high correlation between intent scales and repeat buying (on average, 57% of the definites, 28% of the mights, and 13% of the mights purchased consumer package goods), he cautions that the variation between categories is sufficiently large that additional measures are necessary. In keeping with our emphasis on satisfying customer needs (chapter 8), Tauber suggests that one also measure satisfaction with the product and whether the product fulfills the customer's needs. In his data if customers said they were satisfied, they were 14 times more likely to be repeat purchasers than if they said they were not satisfied. If they felt the product fulfilled their needs, they were three times as likely to be repeat purchasers.

To illustrate the technique, assume that 90% of the "definites," 40% of the "probables," and 10% of the "mights" will actually purchase the product once it is available. (Assuming that the customers are aware of the product and it is available to them.) Applying these numbers to the communications case yields an overall estimate that 13.1% of the sample population would use NBVT if they were aware of it and the equipment were available, that is, the market research indicated no one would definitely use NBVT, but 23.7% would probably use NBVT and 36.1% might use NBVT. Thus $0.131 = (0.90)(0.00) + (0.40)(0.237) + (0.10)(0.361)$. Finally, to get an actual purchase prediction we would multiply the 13.1% by the expected awareness-availability percentage, say 50%, to get an unconditioned estimate of 6.7%. (That is, we assume 50% of the population will be aware of NBVT *and* find it available. Both awareness and availability are necessary for purchase.)

Notice that the predictions are conditioned on awareness and availability. The percentages in Figure 12.2 are unconditioned, customers may or may not consider the relevant product, thus these percentages indicate the linkage of intentions to sales rather than to conditioned sales potential. In cases where the research design makes the customer aware of the product and implies it is available, the intent scales estimate sales potential. To forecast sales we modify this estimate of sales potential by independent estimates of awareness and availability. The translation percentages for *sales potential* are likely to be higher than those in Figure 12.2. For example, for the telecommunications product above the 50% awareness-availability percentage imply that the 90/40/10 percentages for sales potential are halfed to become 45/20/5 for sales (see section below or models of sales formation for more detail).

While one cannot say for certain how intent-to-purchase scales will translate to actual purchase for a new product category, the above examples provide some initial estimates. In each industry studies of past products or managerial judgment must be used to derive the coefficients to be used to translate the levels of intent into purchase. When possible a new product team should also collect measures of satisfaction and need fulfillment to provide additional support to the decision on whether the product is likely to be a winner or a loser.

In some industries, such as packaged goods, market research suppliers have calculated norms for translating these measures across a wide range of products and sample screening procedures.

Modified Intentions.   If we wanted to find the effect of design changes, the intent question would have to be asked for each design. Figure 12.3 provides an example from the telecommunication study. Only a few design alternatives can be tested in this way before the data collection burden soon becomes overwhelming.

Probability Scales.   Some market researchers prefer probability statements to intent statements because probability statements provide the respondent with more categories and because the categories are more exactly defined. For example, Juster (1966) recommends a scale similar to that in Figure 12.4.

The probability scale is used in the same way the intent scale is used. Each category is an estimate of some probability of purchase. Juster compared actual purchases projected from 6 months data to intentions to purchase over "the next 12 months." As Table 12.1 indicates, the stated probabilities are monotonically related to the actual purchase probabilities, but the stated probabilities are not equal to the actual probabilities. Morrison (1979) suggests an underlying behavioral process model based on true intentions and extraneous events. Simply stated, Morrison's model suggests that the stated intentions, as measured by Figure 12.4, are linearly related to the observed probability of purchase. For example, Figure 12.5, which is based on the data for automobiles in Table 12.1, suggests such a linear approximation.

To use the probability scale, first establish the translation for the scale

How likely would you be to choose Narrow Band Video Telephone?

	Definitely not Choose	Probably not Choose	Might Choose	Probably Would Choose	Definitely Would Choose
If it were exactly as described:	[ ]	[ ]	[ ]	[ ]	[ ]
If every office had one:	[ ]	[ ]	[ ]	[ ]	[ ]
If hard-copy were available:	[ ]	[ ]	[ ]	[ ]	[ ]
If transmission time were improved from 30 seconds to 10 seconds:	[ ]	[ ]	[ ]	[ ]	[ ]
If resolution were improved to 4 times that of a home TV:	[ ]	[ ]	[ ]	[ ]	[ ]

Figure 12.3   Conditional Intent Scales Communications Example

values to purchase probabilities based on past data or judgment. This can be done with a table such as Table 12.1 or a graph such as Figure 12.5. Then use your model to translate stated customer intentions to estimated probabilities for each customer or group of customers. Use the average estimated probability as an estimate of market potential. In some cases the new product team may wish to use both a 5-point intent scale and an 11-point probability scale. Fortunately, the two scales provide predictions that are correlated. Gruber (1970) found that the stated probabilities on the 11-point scale, when reduced to a 5 point scale, were 99% for the definites, 76% for the probables, 40% for the mights, 12% for the probably nots, and 1% for the definitely nots. The correlation is not perfect, so again, product specific research may be needed to get an accurate translation.

Preference Rank-Order Transformation

Direct measures of intent are useful in evaluating concept statements, however we also want to uncover strategic refinements in positioning. Recall that in previous chapters analyses of customer perceptions and preferences were used to identify potential product improvements and to predict preferences for the refined product. If predictions are to be made at the purchase

Taking everything into account, what are the prospects that you will adopt Narrow Band Video Telephone for your daily communications?

Certain, practically certain (99 in 100).   ____

Almost sure (9 in 10).   ____

Very probable (8 in 10).   ____

Probable (7 in 10).   ____

Good possibility (6 in 10).   ____

Fairly good possibility (5 in 10).   ____

Fair possibility (4 in 10).   ____

Some possibility (3 in 10).   ____

Slight possibility (2 in 10).   ____

Very slight possibility (1 in 10).   ____

No chance, almost no chance (1 in 100).   ____

Figure 12.4   Probability-Scale Communications Example

level for each of the many design combinations, a final link between preference and choice is needed. One simple approach is to assume that everyone would choose their first preference. Alternatively, we can acknowledge that the preference measures are good approximations, but not perfect. Thus, we can expect that only some percentage of the customers will select their first preference. But if everyone does not select their first preference, some will select their second or even third preference product. The *preference rank- order transformation* simply assigns probabilities according to whether the new product is ranked first, second, third, etc. The values reflect the probability of an

TABLE 12.1   Relationship between Scales Probabilities and Observed Purchase Behavior (Adapted from Juster 1966)

Probability-Scale Value	Automobiles	Appliances
1 in 100	.07	.017
1, 2, or 3 in 10	.19	.053
4, 5, or 6 in 10	.41	.111
7, 8, or 9 in 10	.48	.184
99 in 100	.55	.105

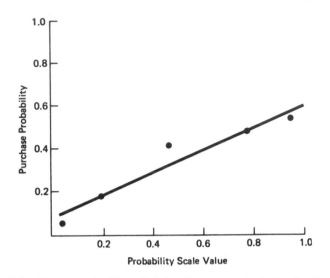

Figure 12.5   Representative Linear Relationship between Scaled Probabilities and Observed Purchase Probabilities (Morrison 1979)

individual buying his first choice product, second choice, third choice, etc. Since these probabilities vary somewhat by product category, you should base estimates on past experience, reported results, and personal judgment about the product category.

For example, Silk and Urban (1978) found that for deodorants, 83% of the first preferences, 15% of the second preferences, and 2% of the third preferences purchased the product. For transportation Hauser, Tybout, and Koppelman (1979) found these percentages to be 76%, 16%, and 8%.

Suppose that these numbers are reasonable for the communications case. In fact, for simplicity, take 80% of the first preferences and 20% of the second preferences. Based on these proportions, we estimate 11.8 percent of the target population would adopt if they were aware of Narrow Band Video Telephone (NBVT) and it were available to them; 9.2% ranked NBVT first and 22.4% ranked NBVT second. Thus $0.118 = (0.80)(0.092) + (0.20)(0.224)$. Comparing this to the 13.1% estimated through the intent measures, we see that although the techniques are not exact, they can give reasonably consistent estimates.

An advantage of the rank-order transformation is that it can be used to estimate purchase for refinements in positioning without remeasuring intent to purchase for concept descriptions. Simply use the techniques of the previous chapters to obtain estimates of the preferences and convert these to purchase via the ranked probabilities.

Both the intent translation and the rank order transformation are most useful early in product design when the new product is still a concept state-ment or a mathematical position on a perceptual map. Both models are approximations and both rest to some extent upon managerial judgment. But they do give reasonably consistent "ballpark" estimates of purchase and are used to make early evaluations which isolate the concepts or positionings with the greatest potential.

To use these models in a product category, measure intent or use the ranked probabilities to transform preference to choice. In fact, some manag-ers use both models in parallel to get alternative estimates of potential. If the estimates are similar, the managers have more faith in the numbers; if they diverge, then it is useful to reexamine both models and compare assumptions and measures until you understand the discrepancies and know what must be done if they are to converge.

The ranked probability model uses only the ordinal properties of the preference measures. We turn now to a more sophisticated model that bases predictions on the magnitude of the preference measures as well as their rank orders.

Logit Analysis: An Analytical Technique to Estimate Purchase Probabilities

As the design phase progresses, the measures of preference become more refined because the risks are higher. There is a need for more accurate estimates of purchase.

For example, suppose we used preference regression to develop a pref-erence model for the analgesics example. The first column of Table 12.2 shows the preferences from the model for four typical consumers. The second column shows the preference rank order transformation. Compare consumer 1 to consumer 2. From the preference values, intuitively, we would expect that consumer 1 would be almost as likely to purchase Tylenol as the new product, whereas consumer 2 would be much more likely to purchase the new product. (Compare relative preference values). The rank-order transformation ignores the intensity information contained in the preference values and uses only the fact that one is larger than the other. The rank-order transformation just does not distinguish between consumers 1 to 4.

Logit analysis is an analytic technique that uses intensity information contained in preference values to produce potentially more accurate esti-mates of purchase probabilities. For example, a logit model produced the estimates in the third column of Table 12.2.

Logit Model Structure.   The basic idea behind logit analysis is a math-ematical function that translates the preference values into purchase proba-

TABLE 12.2   Comparison of Rank-Order Transformation to Logit
Predictions for Four Typical Analgesics Customers

	Preference Value	Rank-Order Transform	Logit
Customer 1			
Bufferin	1.3	—	.08
Advil	2.1	—	.09
Tylenol	9.8	.20	.41
New product	9.9	.80	.42
Customer 2			
Anacin	1.4	—	.11
Private label	2.0	—	.13
Tylenol	2.3	.20	.14
New product	9.9	.80	.62
Customer 3			
Bayer	1.2	—	.10
Nuprin	2.2	—	.12
Tylenol	5.0	.20	.21
New product	9.9	.80	.57
Customer 4			
Anacin	5.9	—	.33
Tylenol	6.0	.20	.33
New product	6.1	.80	.34
Share of new product		.80	.49

bilities based on a theory of customer behavior developed by McFadden (1970). To present the logit model, we introduce the concepts of "true" preference, measured preference, and error. Suppose that there is some "true" preference and that this "true" preference is such a good measure that the customer always purchases the product with the largest value of "true" preference. Naturally, it is extremely difficult to measure "true" preference, but we try. Any measure we actually use will contain measurement error; the "true" preference will differ from this measured preference by this error. That is,

$$\text{true preference} = \text{measured preference} + \text{error} \qquad (12.1)$$

If we measure preferences (imperfectly) and we know something about the probability distribution of the error then we can begin to predict the probability that the "true" preference for the new product is larger than the "true" preferences for the other products. This prediction will be some mathematical function based on the measured preferences. In particular, if the probability distribution is a "double exponential extreme value distribution" then McFadden (1970) shows that the following equation predicts actual probabilities as a function of observed preferences.

Let L_{cj} be the likelihood that customer c purchases product j and let p_{cj} be the measured preference for product j. Let 1 index the new product and let β be a parameter that is used to fit the model to the data. Then the logit model is given by equation 12.2.

$$L_{c1} = \frac{\exp\ (\beta p_{c1})}{\Sigma_{j=1}^{J}\exp(\beta p_{cj})} \qquad\qquad (12.2)$$

where $\exp(\beta p_{cj})$ is the number e (recall $e = 2.71828...$) raised to the βp_{cj}th power.

We illustrate equation 12.2 with an example from Table 12.2. Suppose that $\beta = .2$, the probability that consumer 1 in Table 12.2 choose the new product is given by

$$L_{11} = \frac{\exp\ [(.2)(9.9)]}{\{\exp[(.2)(1.3)] + \exp\ [(.2)(2.1)] + \exp\ [(.2)(9.8)] + \exp\ [(.2)(9.9)]\}}$$
$$L_{11} = 0.42$$

Thus, once we know the value of β for a product category and a particular preference measure, we can estimate more accurately purchase probabilities. To estimate β we use statistical analysis.

Estimation of Parameters.   To estimate β, we need a data sample. In that sample we must measure preferences (p_{ij}'s) by one of the techniques of Chapter 11 and observe or measure customer choice behavior. Among the measures of the latter are: (1) brand chosen in a simulated purchase environment, (2) reported last brand chosen, or (3) reported frequency of purchase of all brands. The first measure is appropriate when an actual product is ready for testing and stated choice correlates well to actual market choice. The other measures are used in early design or in product categories such as services, industrial products, or consumer durables where the interpurchase interval makes simulated purchase infeasible. Of course other choice measures can be used if they are available.

Based on observed choice or frequency and based on the measured explanatory variables, we use a statistical technique known as maximum likelihood technique to estimate β. The resulting estimate has good statistical properties. It approaches the true value as the sample sizes increase and has lower variance than values from other estimators. The estimates are normally distributed and empirical experience indicates that the estimate is quite good even in relatively small samples ($n \geq 100$). Fortunately, a number of computer programs are available to perform logit analyses including most popular statistical packages (Ben-Akiva and Lerman, 1985).

To illustrate the logit model in application we return to an example we discussed in chapter 10 when we used preference models to project the impact on preference of a change in transportation service in Evanston, Illinois. Further analysis with a logit model based on the last mode of transportation chosen produced an estimate of $\beta = 3.35$ when preferences were measured by a form of preference regression. This model was then used to predict the number of consumers who would ride the improved bus service for alternative strategies as shown in Table 12.3. This table was produced by judgmentally predicting the impact of the strategies on perceptions (factor scores), then using the preference regression model to predict preference values for each consumer in the sample. The logit model translates preferences into purchase likelihoods and the likelihoods are aggregated (added up) to predict the market share of bus. The numbers in Table 12.3 are ranges which depend upon alternative assumptions of how the improvements affect consumer perceptions.

Managerial Use of the Model. Intent translation and ranked probability models give estimates of demand that are used early in the design process. Logit analysis is used to refine these estimates as the product progresses through the design process. Because the logit model is based on the magnitudes or intensities of preference via a model of customer choice behavior, it has the potential to provide more accurate estimates of demand. This accu-

TABLE 12.3　Forecasts of Strategy Impact on Bus Usage

Modification	Forecast Increase (%)	Modification	Forecast Increase (%)
Information campaign to increase knowledge of bus system	.3–7.6	Constrain auto availability	3.8–20.8
Add bus stop signs with information	.2–5.8	Reduce perceived auto availability	1.4–3.6
Increase bus frequency by one bus per hour	2.8–19.3	Increase perceived bus availability	.9–6.1
Add bus shelters	2.1–4.1	Increase perceived bus reliability	2.5–5.7
Improve bus safety	1.1–2.2		
Make the bus more relaxing	.7–2.2	Make bus environment more pleasant	0–1.5

racy is important in making a commitment to complete the new product design and to initiate the testing phase of new product development.

To use logit analysis (equation 12.2) in another product category, the analyst must first determine the parameter β. This is done by collecting preference and choice information for a sample of customers and using standard computer packages to estimate β. To use the model to predict demand for a new idea, concept, or product the analyst must then:

1. Use the preference model (direct measures, preference regression, conjoint analysis) to determine how preferences change as the result of design changes in the new product.
2. Use the logit model (equation 12.2) to estimate the probabilities that each customer will actually try (or use) the new product if it is available and the consumer is aware of it.

These estimates of demand for the new product then serve as input to the full evaluation process to select the product and the marketing strategy that are best for further analysis or for advancement to test market.

The advantages of logit analysis are that it is based on a realistic model of customer behavior that acknowledges and measures error and tries to explain as much of behavior as is feasible. It is relatively easy to use, provides reasonably good estimates of demand, and provides explicit statistical measures that can be used to judge the usefulness, accuracy, and significance of the model (see Hauser 1978). A disadvantage is that the logit model assumes the same preference-to-choice process for all customers and that it does not take into account complementarities or similarities among products.[1] Another disadvantage of logit analysis occurs if the new product does not fit in an existing category. The observed choice for existing products is not available and the logit coefficients cannot be estimated based on actual purchase data. Choice among concepts can be used, but one must realize in this situation that the critical link of choice to actual purchase is missing.

When past sales data are available for a market a new product is entering, logit analysis is the best practical means to link preference to sales

---

[1] Logit analysis is of a class of models that are subject to independence of irrelevant alternatives (IIA). Basically, IIA states that the model does not account for similarities among products that may cause the new product to attract more customers from products to which it is similar than from products to which it is dissimilar. While the logit model is subject to IIA at the level of the individual customer, it is less sensitive when shares are aggregated to the market as a whole. In part, the heterogeneity in perceptions, preferences, and consideration sets mitigate the potential IIA problems.

potential and is sufficiently accurate for the managerial go/no go decisions in the design phase. Logit analysis can also be used for the analysis of preference and for benefit segmentation. The only modification is that the factor scores (or other measures of customer benefits) are used as explanatory variables in the estimation. Instead of one parameter, β, one obtains a parameter for each customer benefit and interprets these parameters as relative importance weights for the customer benefits. Benefit segmentation is based on variation in these importance weights. Finally, logit models can be used along with conjoint measurement to predict probability of purchase as a function of product features (review chapter 10, and see Green and Krieger 1989) and to model share as well as total category expansion (Mason 1990).

Summary of Purchase Potential Models

This completes the basic discussion of purchase potential models. Together, the intent translation, preference rank order transformation, and the logit model give the new product manager a set of techniques to estimate the purchase potential of new product ideas.

The intent or probability scales give a direct measure of the customer's beliefs about whether the customer will actually choose the new product. While not exact, the scales provide a good indication of behavior that is sensitive to effects that may not otherwise be captured in our models. The disadvantage of direct scales is that they are limited to testing specific concepts or a relatively few changes to those concepts.

The preference rank order transformation is more useful for a wide range of strategies because it can be based on the multi-attributed preference models of chapter 10. Its disadvantage is that it may miss extraneous events, not modeled in the preferences. Thus, we advocate the combined use of both the direct measures—intent scales—and the indirect measures—preference—as well as diagnostic information on customer satisfaction and the fulfillment of customer needs.

The logit model provides a more sophisticated and potentially more accurate model that is sensitive to the intensity of the measured preferences. It is used later in the design process than the rank order transformation and can update or confirm predictions made by earlier analysis.

We feel that it is sound practice to use multiple techniques to get the best estimates of purchase potential. When used appropriately, these combined models provide accurate estimates that are relevant to managerial design decisions. We now turn to a set of analyses that modify purchase potential to provide estimates of sales formation.

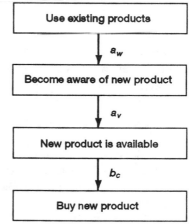

Figure 12.6 Simplified Model for the Evaluation of
Sales Formation

MODELS OF SALES FORMATION

The models of sales potential predict the sales that would occur if customers were aware of the new product and it were available to them. In most cases the preference and intent measures are collected from respondents after exposure to a new product or a new product concept. In an actual new-product introduction, not all customers will be aware of the product nor can an organization always achieve 100% availability of a new product. Awareness and availability are often managerial control options that depend upon advertising and distribution strategy. In order to forecast accurately sales as opposed to potential, we modify the probability of purchase estimates by the probabilities that the customers are aware of the product and it is available to them. Figure 12.6 presents a simplified model of sales formation.

The model says that before a customer can buy a product, the customer must become *aware* of it (a_w) and it must be *available* (a_v). For example, suppose that there is a .8 chance that customer c will become aware of a new analgesic and a .9 chance that the customer's regular store will carry it. If the sales potential model predicts that there is a .5 chance the customer will buy and continue to buy it if the customer is aware of it and it is available, then the expected probability of actual buying will be $(.8)(.9)(.5) = .36$ for that customer. If there are 100,000 customers just like customer c, then the expected purchase potential is 36,000 unit sales per period. If customers are not identical, but vary in terms of sales potential, then we must sum purchase probabilities over all customers. That is, the estimated number of purchases (durable goods) or purchase rate (frequently purchased goods), P, is given by

$$P = \sum_{c=1}^{N} a_w a_v b_c \qquad (12.3)$$

Purchase rates (b_c) can vary by individual, but unless the analysis is done by segment, all models in this chapter compute average awareness (a_w) and availability (a_v). N is the number of customers.

Awareness and Distribution Adjustments

Take out a piece of paper and try to write down all the deodorants you can think of—this is unaided recall. Now suppose you were asked if you have heard of Right Guard, Sure, Ban, Secret, Old Spice, Mennon, Arrid, Arm & Hammer, Soft & Dri, Brut, Mitchum, Safe Day, Tickle, Dial, Dry Idea, and Calm. If you have, that is aided recall. But how many of those deodorants do you know sufficiently well that you can describe them with respect to the many detailed attribute scales that are applicable to deodorants? For new-product awareness, we want to know how many customers will become aware of the product at a level that is sufficient so that they have the information to consider the new product seriously. The concept we are concerned with is known as the consideration set. (This concept is sometimes referred to as the evoked set or the relevant set.) For example, one common way to measure a consideration set is those products that the customer has used, has on hand or would seriously consider (or definitely not consider). Thus, a_w is defined formally as the percentage of customers who will consider the new product.

There are two ways to estimate this percentage. The first is to estimate judgmentally the consideration percentage. This was done for the HMO case that was introduced in an earlier chapter. For the HMO case, we estimated that 70% of the target group would be made aware of the HMO by the planned marketing effort. (That is, they would be exposed to the brochure which they would have read carefully.) The intent model forecast that 23.3% of the target group would enroll if they were made aware of the HMO plan at a level equivalent to the survey. Because of its location and the planned benefits program at MIT, the HMO would be available to all members of the community. Together these numbers imply that the new enrollment forecast (P) was the purchase probability (.23) times at the awareness (.70) times the availability (1.0) times the size of the target group (17,200). The enrollment forecast was 2,800 patients.

It is often difficult to estimate the awareness percentage directly. An alternative method is to estimate judgmentally unaided-recall awareness and use it to estimate awareness (consideration). Unaided recall is often easier for advertising managers to estimate than consideration and it can be linked to an advertising budget. Fortunately, unaided recall and consideration are highly related. For example, Silk and Urban (1978) estimated the relationship with a least squares regression equation. If historic data is available, such linkages can be estimated for a product category. Then the level of unaided brand awareness that the introductory marketing campaign is expected to obtain would be substituted in the equation to estimate the consideration proportion. If necessary, a number of estimates are made at varying levels of marketing expenditure. Advertising agencies often develop models linking advertising expenditure (dollars, gross rating points, reach, and frequency) to the aided or unaided awareness resulting from an advertising campaign. These are useful if the new product is in the same product class as the data collected to develop the relationship.

The measure of availability is based judgmentally on the percentage of retail outlets, distributors, and so on (adjusted for volume) that will carry the product in the target area. For some industrial products, it is the percentage of buyers that are within a feasible delivery area. In health care it might be the fraction of eligible customers in a service area. In transportation it may be more complex (e.g., what percentage of consumers are within one-quarter mile of the bus line or how many can afford an automobile). For most categories, past experience or managerial judgment is sufficient for design-phase estimates.

Dynamics

Sales potential of a new product will not occur immediately. For products that depend on repeated purchases, we consider the trial and repeat processes that lead to the dynamic growth of sales. For a major new product such as a home appliance, we consider the phenomenon known as the "diffusion of an innovation."

Trial and Repeat.   The sales of new products that rely on repeated purchases are modeled by two components. Examples of such products are consumer packaged goods, service plans (e.g. for cellular phones), or industrial supplies (e.g., buy-rebuy decisions). The first component is trial and can be represented by the simplified model that was shown in Figure 12.6. The second component is repeat purchasing which applies only to those customers who have tried the new product.

For example, in the HMO case, sales came from new enrollment plus reenrollment from the 1,000 patients who were in the pilot HMO program for a year. Table 12.4 shows the calculation of total enrollment for the first year of full operation. The reenrollment rate was high (.95) because respondents evaluated the plan as excellent and had strong preferences for it over other existing health services. The actual reenrollment prediction was lowered

TABLE 12.4 Calculation of Purchase Potential of New HMO

	Number Not Now in Pilot Program	Enrollment, If Aware	Estimated Awareness	Estimated New Enrollment
New enrollment	17,200	× 0.233	× 0.70	= 2,800

	Existing Subscribers	Estimated Repeat Rate	Estimated to Remain at MIT	Estimated Repeat Enrollment
Reenrollment	1,067	× 0.95	× 0.863	= 874

Total enrollment = 2,800 + 874 = 3,674

somewhat because some percentage of the target group of students, faculty, and staff (13.7%) would graduate or leave the area for other reasons.

For frequently purchased products the projection of sales is more difficult because of the issue of continued repeat buying. Management is interested in the long-run market share. For frequently purchased products a forecast of sales must consider the issues of both trial and repeat. Thus, when we forecast sales, P, we include terms for trial and for repeat. That is,

$$P = \sum_{c=1}^{N} a_w a_v t_c r_c \qquad (12.4)$$

where t_c = trial probability for customer, c, given awareness and availability
   r_c = long-run share of purchases per period for new brand by
       customer c, given that customer c tried the product.
   a_w = awareness of new brand
   a_v = availability of new brand

Trial probabilities are obtained from models based on customer response after being exposed to concepts, while repeat shares are based on measures taken after home use of the new product. Note that this model is most relevant late in the design process when an actual product is available to give to customer for in-home use. Earlier in the design process we replace customer-level estimates of trial and repeat with more aggregate measures. For example, early in the design process we might estimate a target repeat rate of 50% to serve as a goal, recognizing that we will modify those estimates when the product design is more complete.

Once one or more candidate products are selected for design evaluation, the value of P can be calculated from the aggregate equation. Here we make population estimates of trial and repeat rather than summing individual estimates:

$$P = N_p \, a_w \, a_v \, T \, R \qquad (12.5)$$

where T = ultimate proportion of the target group who would try the product conditioned on awareness and availability

R = long-run share of purchases of the new product among those customers who try the product

N_p = number of customer purchases in category per period

The long-run share of purchases among triers, R, is estimated by analogy to products where repeat purchase data is available. In package goods or doctor prescriptions, panel data is analyzed to calculate a share of purchases given trial. If the new product has similar properties, these estimates are used for initial forecasting. Models that relate the repeat purchase rates after each repeat purchase provide the foundation to estimate R (see Silk and Kalwani, 1982). In some cases R is approximated by the simple switching process shown in Figure 12.7. Customers either repeat-purchase the product immediately or switch back to their existing product(s) and repeat-purchase at a later date. The process will stabilize to a point where the number of customers switching in equals the number of customers switching out. Once the process stabilizes the repeat rate, R, is calculated by $R = R_{E1}/(1 + R_{E1} - R_{11})$ where R_{E1} is the proportion of customers who switch to the new product and R_{11} is the proportion of customers who repeat-purchase the new product (Urban 1975a). For example, if 40% of the customers are observed to switch from existing products to the new product (R_{E1}), and if 50% of the customers are observed to repeat-purchase the new product after trying it (R_{11}), then the long-run share among triers (R) is given by $R = (.40)/(1 + .40 - .50) = .444$. Note that the long-run share (R) is not necessarily equal to the transient observed repeat rate of those who have tried the new product (R_{11}). The correction

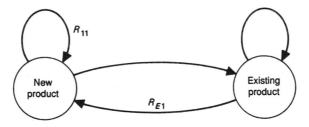

Figure 12.7   Two-State Switching Model to Derive "Repeat" Proportion (R = Representation of Consumer Switching among Products)

takes account of those customers who are not 100% loyal to the new product.

To illustrate equation (12.5) suppose we achieved 40% trial (T), 80% awareness (a_w), 90% availability (a_v), and that there are 1 million consumers in the target group (N_p). Equation 12.5 predicts that the long-run sales rate (P) of the new product would be

$$P = (1,000,000) \cdot (.80) \cdot (.90) \cdot (.40) \cdot (.44) =$$
$$126,720 \text{ purchases} \qquad (12.5)$$

Normally, these proportions are measured by giving consumers, first, an opportunity to purchase the new product and then, second, an opportunity, after in-house use, to repeat the purchase of the product. This model is an approximation to equation 12.5 because it confounds transient behavior (the market has not yet reached steady state) and aggregation error (the product of the averages of two numbers is not equal to the average of the product of two numbers). Despite the potential errors, we have found that these theoretical effects do not cause major empirical bias. Experience suggests the model is reasonably accurate when used to forecast long-run share.

Diffusion of Innovation.   Diffusion of innovation occurs when "innovators" (customers with a high propensity or high need to try in the product category) buy first and then, through an influence process, encourage others to adopt. This phenomenon is difficult to handle in new-product sales forecasting because, in the short run, only the responses from innovators are measured. Models based only on short-run measurements which do not consider the influence process could seriously underestimate the long-run adoption level. This is particularly true in consumer durables or industrial products.

The approach to modifying short-run estimates relies on analogies to previous products or specific laboratory measures. (We return to this issue in chapter 16 when we discuss laboratory measures for prelaunch forecasting.) For example, suppose we are forecasting sales for a new office automation product. Figure 12.8 (dotted line) describes an observed adoption rate for an existing office-automation product. If the existing product serves a similar population, has a similar price, and fulfills analogous customer benefit as the new product, then it can serve as an analogy to the new product. Through judgment or measurement, the new product team compares the analogous product to the new product to estimate long run potential. In this example, suppose that preference measures and intent scales suggest that the new product will do better than the analogous product. This increased forecast is shown as the solid line in Figure 12.8. Once the long run potential is estimated, the year-by-year forecast then uses the analogy as a template with which to predict the growth in sales. In some cases this judgmental process is formalized by the use of a diffusion model such as the one developed by Bass

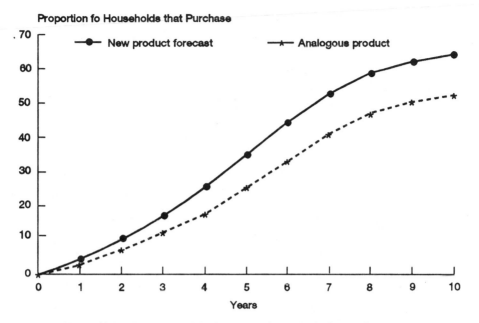

Figure 12.8   Illustration of the Use of Analogies for Diffusion Forecasting

(discussed in Chapter 4.) Alternatively, prior descriptions of the diffusion curves can be updated with a formal Bayesian approach (Lenk and Rao 1990).

Figure 12.9 gives the sales history for seven products. The thick line is the Bayes expected sales rate after observing the seven products. The dashed lines are plus and minus one standard deviation of the expected sales rates (Lenk and Rao 1990). This prior description could be modified by judgment, comparative concept scores for the old and new products, or eventually by early sales results when the product is test marketed or launched.

Multiperson Decision Making—The Buying Center

Not all purchase decisions are made by independent customers. Often more than one person is involved in the purchase decision. For example, the choice of a family car or a home may be the result of some deliberation or bargaining process among the various members of the family. Multiperson decision making occurs most often in the purchase of industrial products where a buying center consists of many buyers with diverse needs. For example, engineering, purchasing, consultant, and top management all may be involved in large procurements for items such as office furniture, production machines, and buildings.

New Product Diffusion (Adoption) Rate

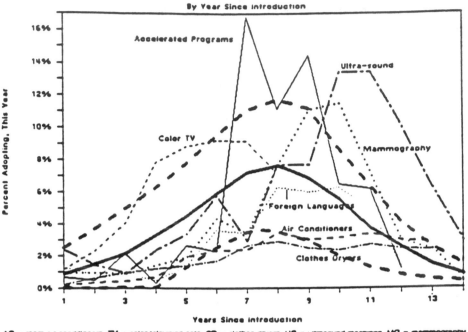

By Year Since Introduction

AC = room air conditioners. TV = color television sets. CD = clothes dryers. US = ultrasound machines. MG = mammography machines. FL = foreign language programs. AP = advanced programs.

Figure 12.9 Observed Sales Rates for the Seven Products (Lenk and Rao 1990)

In those cases the role of each participant must be understood. One approach to understanding roles is through a "decision matrix" which describes the role of each decision participant in each phase of the decision process. Figure 12.10 shows the decision matrix used by Choffray and Lilien (1980) in their study of solar air conditioning. The participants are divided into internal and external influences and the decision process is represented by five steps: (1) evaluation of needs, (2) budget approval, (3) search for alternatives, (4) equipment evaluation, and (5) final selection. After each participant's role is understood, his perceptions and preferences are integrated to predict passage of the new product through each phase. Information to complete a decision matrix and to translate the multiple participants' preferences into purchase are based on judgment or qualitative interviews with participants in the target firms. In Chapter 8 we described the needs of each participant. These needs will determine the participant's decision in each phase of the process where they are active.

In some public systems, multiple groups are important to the success of

Decision phases / Decision Participants	Evaluation of a/c needs, specification of system requirements	Preliminary a/c budget approval	Search for alternatives, preparation of a bid list	Equipment and manufacturer evaluation*	Equipment and manufacturer selection
COMPANY PERSONNEL					
Product and Maintenance Engineers	%	%	%	%	%
Plant or Factory Manager	%	%	%	%	%
Financial controller or accountant	%	%	%	%	%
Procurement or purchasing department	%	%	%	%	%
Top Management	%	%	%	%	%
HVAC/Engineering firm	%	%	%	%	%
EXTERNAL PERSONNEL					
Architects and building contractor	%	%	%	%	%
A/C equipment manufacturers	%	%	%	%	%
COLUMN TOTAL	100%	100%	100%	100%	100%

Figure 12.10 Sample Decision Matrix: Industrial Cooling Study (Adapted from Choffray and Lilien 1980)

a new program. While they may not interact as a formal decision-making body, their responses are important. For example, in designing a new management program leading to a master's degree, reactions of prospective students are important, but so are responses from recruiters who hire the graduates of such a program. Remember that the important dimension for the student target group in the management education case was "outcomes." A good positioning of the new programs for the recruiters leads to long-run substantiation of the "outcomes" dimension for students. In MIT's efforts to redesign its master's program, recruiters were interviewed and their perceptions and preferences modeled. Based on responses from twenty-five recruiters, a perceptual map was drawn. Four dimensions were identified by factor analysis of the recruiters' ratings of MIT, Harvard, and the new concepts (Young Executive Program [YEP] and the Intensive Program in Management [IPM]). The first dimension was correlated to scales that reflected graduates having real-world knowledge, action orientation, practicality, relevant skills, the ability to choose a career, and contact with business people. It was named "job preparedness." The second reflected "group skills" and was correlated with the graduates' sensitivity to people, leadership abilities, generalist aptitude, and interpersonal skills. The scales loading heavily on the third dimension involved graduates having sophisticated skills, familiarity with analytical techniques, research orientation, contact with faculty, and creativity in attacking problems. We called this the "technical skills" dimension. The final dimension represented the degree of competitive "pressure" the program placed upon the student.

The average standardized factor scores are shown in Figure 12.11. The existing program at Sloan was rated lower than Harvard on job preparedness and group skills, but higher on technical skills. Recruiters saw Harvard as a high pressure environment, while MIT was low. The recruiters rated the new programs favorably. Both the YEP and IPM programs exceeded Harvard on job preparedness. Measuring recruiter preferences for schools was difficult because preferences depend on the particular job to be filled and the individual student being considered. Therefore, in order to get an overall evaluation measure, ratings of programs and schools were weighted by direct measures of the recruiter's self-designed importance for each scale. Based on the weighted ratings, 63% of the recruiters rated one or both of the new concepts superior to Harvard and the existing Sloan programs. A weighted average of the importances indicated each of the four overall dimensions to be approximately equally valued.

In examining student and recruiter responses, there was agreement in a positive response to the new programs. Comparing the students' perceptual maps to those of recruiters revealed some common interests. The students and recruiters were both interested in career success. The student percep-

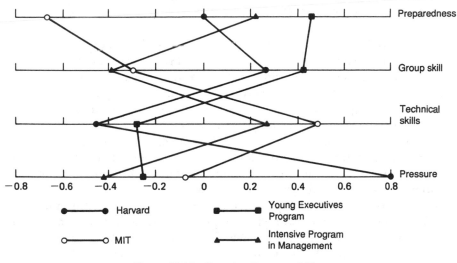

Figure 12.11   Recruiter Perceptual Map

tions of realism and relevancy were also a component of the preparedness dimension of recruiters. Recruiters seemed particularly concerned with group skills as a positive attribute of graduates. Although both recruiters and potential students perceived Harvard high and MIT low on pressure, recruiters had a preference for more pressure, whereas students preferred a friendly and cooperative atmosphere.

Summary of Sales Formation Models

This completes the basic discussion of sales formation models. The basic concept is that estimates of sales potential are modified because of complexities that occur in new product introduction. The first modification is for awareness and availability. Purchase usually does not occur unless customers know about the new product and can obtain it if they want. Thus, we forecast sales by first conditioning sales potential on estimates of awareness and availability and then correcting for forecast awareness and availability. The second modification is for dynamic effects. Long-run sales are not obtained immediately; we modify forecasts to account for trial/repeat phenomena and for influence processes that lead to diffusion in the innovation process. Finally, in some industrial products, some customer durables, and some public services, we explicitly consider multi-person decision making. New models are being developed for *specific* situations and a new product forecaster should review the range of possible techniques and find the one that best fits the particular product situation (see Mahajan and Wind 1988, for a review).

INFORMATION ACCELERATION

The models of sales potential and sales formation are based on data collected from customers who react to a representation of the new product. Early in the design process this representation might be a short one-sentence concept. As that concept is developed, the new-product team might expose customers to a longer one-page concept, sometimes with pictures and other supporting documentation. Still later, prototypes and one-of-a-kind production models might be available, etc. In each case as the concept or prototype becomes a better representation of the product as it will appear once launched, the information from the customer is better. When the information from the customer is better, the forecasts are more accurate.

Recently, a number of researchers have been experimenting with multimedia computer systems in an effort to provide realistic stimuli to customers (Johnson, Payne, and Bettman 1988; Johnson et. al. 1986; Johnson and Schkade 1989; Payne, Bettman, and Johnson 1988; Brucks 1988; Burke et. al. 1991; Meyer and Sathi 1985; Painton and Gentry 1985; Urbany 1986; Hauser, Urban, and Weinberg 1992). A multimedia computer system combines images from a videodisc (or other media) to provide full-motion, realistic visual images on a computer screen. The computer interface allows the customer to interact with the images to produce a more realistic purchase environment. This means that not just the product can be simulated, but the full marketing environment including brochures, print advertisements, television advertising, word-of-mouth, shopping visits, and even personal selling. While no system will ever be a perfect substitute for the final environment that the customer sees when making a purchase and no system will be fully able to model the "in-use" system or the full effects of customer satisfaction feedback, these multimedia systems are providing new opportunities for greater realism at earlier stages of the new-product design process. Because the customer gets information in these systems at a more rapid pace than in an actual purchase environment, we call these systems information acceleration systems.

Consider the purchase of a new car. At the design stage, the production version of the car is not available, but the design and styling is. Advertising, print media, hypothetical consumer journal reviews, and word-of-mouth communication can be developed. For example, Hauser, Urban, and Weinberg (1992) describe a system in which the following media are available:

- *Print advertisements.* Hypothetical magazine and newspaper advertisements are created, stored on a videodisc, and retrieved to the computer screen.
- *Television advertisements.* Actual 30-second television spots are produced

and stored on the videodisc. When the customer asks to see them, the computer monitor acts like a television screen to show the advertisements.

- *Articles.* Because magazines such as *Consumer Reports,* and *Road & Track* are influential in the automobile purchase process, we develop potential magazine articles. Actual reproductions with full-color pictures appear on the screen and the customer can read them at his (her) own pace.
- *Interviews.* To simulate word-of-mouth we produce video tapes of unrehearsed interviews with actual customers (or actors). To make the situation more realistic, four to six "word-of-mouth" customers are available. For example, Figure 12.12a shows a screen with five potential word-of-mouth customers, each with a picture and a phrase so that the customer viewing the material can get cues about the overall opinions and biases of the source. When the customer viewing the word-of-mouth selects a source, he or she sees another computer screen and can select topics on which to query the source. In this way the interviews become interactive and more realistic.
- *Showroom.* The showroom or shopping environment is simulated with tapes of the actual (prototype) car. The customer can "walk around" the car by clicking on the arrows in Figure 12.12b. The car rotates as if the customer were actually walking around the car. If the customer "opens the door," he (she) sees interior shots which change as he (she) moves around the interior. Similarly the customer can open the trunk and look under the hood.

We have not yet developed an actual drive simulator on the computer, but prototype cars can be used to augment the multimedia computer. For example a 1992 Geo Storm may be retrofitted with solar power and electric motors in 1992 to simulate a new 1996 "Supernova" drive experience. Eventually drive simulators (analogous to flight simulators) may eliminate the need for prototypes.

If we integrate the notions of leading-edge users into the multimedia "information accelerator," we have all the ingredients for forecasting more radical innovations. The leading-edge users give responses based on their advanced use experience and knowledge and we capture this information to accelerate the other potential customers to the point in time where the middle majority of the market are ready to consider purchases. With a model of diffusion from leading-edge to majority users, a time path forecast can be generated.

With a multimedia computer system measures of attitude, intent, and

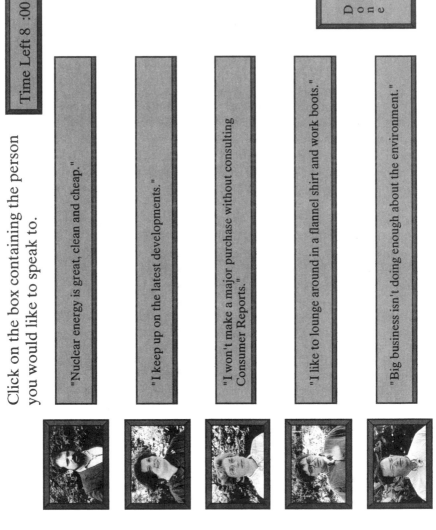

Click on the box containing the person you would like to speak to.

Time Left 8 :00

"Nuclear energy is great, clean and cheap."

"I keep up on the latest developments."

"I won't make a major purchase without consulting Consumer Reports."

"I like to lounge around in a flannel shirt and work boots."

"Big business isn't doing enough about the environment."

Done

Figure 12.12a Multimedia Word of Mouth

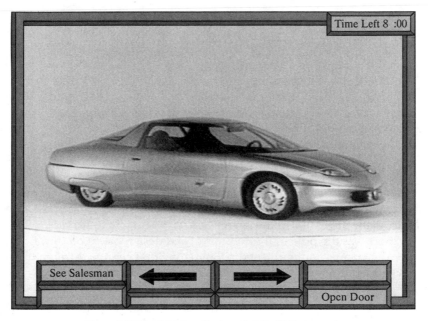

Figure 12.12b   Multimedia Automobile Walk-Around

purchase probability information are based on more realistic stimuli. After the design is complete and the product proceeds to the production stage this same methodology can be used to obtain more accurate forecasts based on final advertising, pricing, promotion, product, and distribution strategies.

The use of the most realistic stimuli at the design stage serves to integrate the efforts of engineering, marketing, and production who participate in the development of the initial concepts, prototypes, advertising, and word-of-mouth simulations. This means the product gets to market faster because it is designed right in the beginning. Rapid testing of prototypes enables changes to be made without delay. Risks are minimized and the final testing is completed to hit the launch window of opportunity.

MANAGERIAL USE OF SALES MODELS FOR "WHAT-IF" FORECASTING

The models of sales potential and sales formation described in this chapter serve two purposes: (1) they determine if the new product has sufficient sales potential to proceed with the full design and testing effort, and (2) they aid in improving the product design.

The sales models give approximate results which enable the new product team to make go/no go decisions in the advancement of ideas, concepts, or products through the design process. Diagnostics are used to refine the forecast after the core benefit proposition has been identified and the physical product has been formulated to substantiate the positioning. All of the models require some judgmental estimates and some averaging of individual effects, but they have proven adequate for screening new product designs and setting resource and timing priorities.

The second purpose of sales forecasting models is to aid in improving the new product design by simulating the effect on sales of improving features or perceptions of the product. For example, the HMO forecast used preferences that were measured for the new HMO concept to give a rough, early design estimate of demand. The result was 2,800 consumers (see Table 12.4). But we know from the discussion of the perceptual positioning of the HMO in Chapter 9 that there was the potential for an improved design based on new hospitals and more personal communication. Simulating that change through the preference model and rank order transformation gives a trial probability of 31%, which produces a demand estimate of 3,700 consumers (100% available, 70% aware, 17,200 in the total market). But part of the improved strategy was an aggressive marketing campaign to make consumers aware of the personalness of the HMO through strong testimonials. It was quite likely that this campaign would increase awareness as well as trial. Suppose it increases awareness to 85%. Then the demand estimate would be 4,530 consumers who would sign up in the first year. This new enrollment, plus the returning enrollment of 875, brings the total enrollment to 5,405. These enrollment increases justify revising the HMO design. Subsequent to the analyses described here, the new plan was implemented successfully based on the new design.

Another example is a new aerosol hand lotion. Based on concept statements, the hand lotion was perceived as good on performance and application dimensions, but after use, it was perceived as only average on performance. In fact, after use, the product with the concept description was significantly less preferred than the product with no concept claims (i.e., "blind test"). The advertising claims of performance were not fulfilled by the product; this appeared to produce an adverse effect. The initial strategy generated trial and repeat predictions that implied a 5% share. Two alternate positions were simulated. The first represented a strategy of aligning the product claims and performance, which resulted in a 6% market share. The second strategy was (1) to improve the product physically so that it would perform better and (2) to align the advertising to this improved performance. This strategy implied an 8% market share. These simulations led to design changes in the product advertising and additional R&D. Ultimately, however, even these improvements were not sufficient. The product was unable to substantiate performance superiority, the project was dropped, and resources were allocated to other new product development efforts.

In general, we have found that the focus on understanding and improving customer benefits through the analysis of customer perception, preference, and choice leads to new products that are more profitable. These analyses provide their most substantial rewards by generating creative insights through enhanced understanding of customer response and the ability to generate "what-if" forecasts. The enhanced understanding and the "what-if" forecasts enable the new product team to weigh the costs and benefits of changes in the product or its marketing strategy and get to market fast with a superior product.

SUMMARY

Success in new products is linked to the ability of a new product to attract and retain customers. Whether the goals are profit, market share, or increased use, the key marketing input is an estimate of how many customers will purchase or use the new product. Previous chapters presented techniques to design a product that would be preferred by customers. This chapter presents techniques to select the best strategy and to ensure that the chosen design strategy will provide a sufficient return on investment.

The primary input to demand estimation is the preference measures developed in Chapter 10. These measures are used in the purchase potential and sales formation models to get estimates of how many customers actually buy or use the product. On this estimate rests the potential success or failure of a product positioning. Information acceleration has the potential of portraying the future in a natural and realistic fashion so that good preference measures can be obtained.

We discussed how to modify sales-potential estimates for advertising (awareness) and distribution (availability), but a complete design needs detailed marketing inputs such as advertising copy, pricing schedules, sales manuals, and final engineering specifications if a quality product or service is to be produced. In the next chapter we incorporate this information to detail the complete product strategy and assemble the marketing mix and physical product to support that strategy in an activity stage we call "designing for quality."

REVIEW QUESTIONS

12.1. Why is sales forecasting important to the design of new products?

12.2. What is preference rank-order transformation? What are its uses and its accuracy?

12.3. Intent-to-purchase measures seem to provide the manager with all the necessary information required to make new product decisions. If the product is described in full detail including price, physical features, customer benefits, packaging, and so on, and the customer states intentions to buy, why should the manager then augment intent measures with forecasts based on a transformation of rank-order preference to choice probabilities?

12.4. What are the advantages of the logit model? If the logit model provides the most accurate demand estimates when compared to other preference models and measures why employ any other technique?

12.5. What diagnostic information is produced by each of the models of sales formation? How is this information used to improve the new product?

12.6. What are the advantages of making probabilistic forecasts? Why not simply assume customers will choose the product that preference regression or conjoint analysis says they should prefer?

12.7. Give an example of multiperson decision making in the industrial sector. How would you use the inputs from the multiple decision participants to arrive at a sales forecast?

12.8. How can Bass's model (introduced in chapter 4) be used to forecast the dynamics of the diffusion process?

12.9. Why is it important to consider awareness and availability when forecasting sales? How do you estimate awareness and availability? What is the difference between sales potential and sales?

12.10. Voras Chemical Supply Company is launching a new brand of exotic dinners designed for picnics where insect pests pose a potential problem. They estimate product awareness to be approximately 99% because the product has received an unexpectedly high press coverage. One supermarket chain that sells 37% of picnic dinners in the target market will carry the product. The probabilities of purchase given awareness and availability are

Percent of Population	Purchase Probability
50%	.00—will not even buy adjacent products on shelf
40	.20—good souvenir
10	.90—definite collector's item

If the target market consists of one-half-million families each buying one dinner per purchase occasion, what will be the expected number of consumers buying the product? Do you expect that this product will be successful in the long run? Why or why not?

12.11. What are the limitations of a multimedia computer system for presenting customers with information on new products? Could information acceleration be used to assess new services like computer homeshopping? Could it be used for industrial low-frictional high-efficiency motors? Ethical pharmaceutical products prescribed by doctors?

13

Designing for Quality

COMPLETING THE DESIGN

Design and Quality

We now have a carefully crafted CBP, a set of features that substantiate that consumer value generating promise, and an indication of the potential to generate profits. Next we need to translate the proposition and features into detailed engineering and production designs. In this chapter we discuss the translation of the overall product position into the actual product or service and its associated marketing strategy. Throughout this process *quality* is the dominant factor. We must have products that consistently are manufactured to meet their design targets. The design targets provide customers with products that meet their needs and generate a high level of value. Originally quality was thought of as only quality control—manufacturing within narrow specifications for error, consistently aiming for zero defects, and narrow variances on product design characteristics. Today quality means building products that customers want and doing it in a way that delivers high value and meets customers expectations. Naturally a $50,000 Mercedes will have higher absolute performance than a $9,500 Saturn, but both will be high quality if they deliver consistently high utility to their customers per unit of price expenditure throughout the life of the product. Quality means each design and manufacturing element is aimed to satisfy customers. A carefully designed car door will be viewed as high quality if it functions well on all dimensions (e.g., easy to open, seals quietly, feels solid) and its costs lead to price tradeoffs that reflect customer preferences. Good design in this sense may reduce costs and increase satisfaction by removing components and cost that do not deliver benefit to customers and by providing a holistic design in which all components work together to generate customer satisfaction. However, quality might also mean higher cost components that provide the right value.

In the following sections we discuss the customers' role in driving detail tradeoffs and the need for designs that reflect manufacturing cost. The physical product specification and the marketing mix are specified carefully in total-quality terms. Cost-effective and creative strategies for advertising, sales effort, distribution, promotion, and service are developed. We close this chapter by emphasizing that engineering design must be integrated with marketing and manufacturing to produce a *total quality* effort that permeates all aspects of the organization.

Primary, Secondary, and Tertiary Customer Needs

In chapter 8 we introduced the notion of primary, secondary, and tertiary customer needs. At the *primary* level are the strategic benefits that characterize the Core Benefit Proposition; at the *secondary* level are the tactical features that are associated with the perceptual dimensions of the core benefit proposition; and at the *tertiary* level are the operational needs that correspond to detailed engineering attributes of the product or service and that establish the design features. Table 13.1 provides an example of a simplified hierarchy of needs for a car door. Here we have specified one primary (strategic) need, "good operation and use," three secondary needs, and fifteen tertiary needs. Notice how the complexity increases as one gets to the final design level where products are specified with enough operational detail to be manufactured.

Top management strategists are concerned most with the primary needs as they relate to the core benefit proposition and the overall image of the product. To implement and communicate the CBP, the design team must assure that the secondary needs fulfill the primary promises. At the most detailed level, the team "gets all the little things right" to deliver the core benefits in the most effective and cost-efficient manner. The use of the hierarchy assures that the detailed design decisions are "on strategy" with respect to the customer benefits to be delivered when those potential customers vote with their money and choose products and services that maximize value.

In typical applications, the lowest level of the hierarchy, tertiary needs, is a list of the 100 to 300 need statements used in detailed product design. Typically, these are grouped into 10 to 30 secondary needs and the secondary needs themselves are grouped into a relatively few (2–8) primary needs. By

TABLE 13.1 Customer Needs Arrayed in a Hierarchy

Primary Needs	Secondary Needs	Tertiary Needs
Good operation and use	Easy to open and close door	Easy to close from outside
		Stays open on a hill
		Easy to open from the outside
		Doesn't kick back
		Easy to close from inside
		Easy to close from inside
	Isolation	Doesn't leak in rain
		No road noise
		Doesn't leak in car wash
		No wind noise
		Doesn't drop water when open
		Snow doesn't fall in car
		Doesn't rattle
	Arm rest	Soft, comfortable
		In right position
Good appearance	Interior trim	Material won't fade
		Attractive look
	Clean	Easy to clean
		No grease from door
		Stay clean
	Fit	Uniform gaps between panels

From Hauser and Clausing (1988, p. 65); reprinted with permission.

focusing on one or more critical primary needs and by assuring that all primary needs are considered, the new-product team develops a consistent CBP that is implemented through the secondary and tertiary needs.

Chapter 8 describes approaches to understanding the primary needs. Chapter 10 describes conjoint techniques that can be used to study secondary level needs and their tradeoffs. Chapter 9 provides several techniques for the measurement of tertiary needs and their grouping into higher order needs. In this chapter we discuss the integration of tertiary level needs into the features and benefits by customer driven engineering and design for manufacturing efforts.

CUSTOMER-DRIVEN DESIGN

Voice of the Customer

Quality design begins with the needs of the customer. These customer needs are statements or phrases, stated in the customer's own words, that enable the design team to focus on delivering the benefits the customer wants. A list of customer needs, a hierarchical structure for those needs, a set of importances to prioritize those needs, and evaluations of competitors on those needs are known as the "voice of the customer." The "voice of the customer" must be heard accurately and interpreted accurately if high quality products are to be designed and marketed successfully. These statements are best obtained with focus groups, one-on-one qualitative interviews, customer sorts, and affinity diagrams (review chapter 9), but some companies use other, less formal techniques. Some Japanese firms simply place their products in public areas and encourage potential customers to examine them, and design team members listen and note what people say. Other firms examine complaint files or talk to user groups or poll representatives and distributors. The most important lesson is to listen to your customers for input to the design process.

The voice of the customer must be understood by the entire new-product team so that engineering, manufacturing, and marketing can participate in the final product design. Consensus at this level leads to enhanced team building. At the most detailed level, a team might identify 100 to 300 phrases that describe customer needs. Some will be redundant, but many will relate to distinct, but subtle, differences in the potential product. For example, Table 13.1 lists 21 of the 100+ customer needs for a car door—a good car door is "easy to close from the outside," "stays open on a hill," is "easy to open from the outside," "doesn't kick back," and so on.

Two customer needs for a car door are that it is easy to close and that its power windows operate quickly and easily. But rapid operation might call for a larger motor which makes the door heavier and, perhaps, more difficult to close. Ideally, the engineering team will find a creative solution to satisfy both needs, but if they can not, they will need to trade off one benefit versus the other.

To bring the customer's voice to such deliberations among the design team, the relative importance to the customer of the customer needs is determined. Larger relative importance numbers indicate that the customer makes tradeoffs in favor of those customer needs. For example, "easy to close from the outside" might have a relative importance of "7" while "no road noise" might have a relative importance of a 2. If the customer were faced with two cars and all else was equal, the customer would choose the car with the easy-to-close door over the car with less road noise. Clearly these tradeoffs are essential in designing the best product for customers.

To design a successful product we want to meet or exceed competition on important customer needs (benefits). But to do so we must know how customers perceive competitive products. Thus, quality design requires customer evaluations of competitive products (and evaluation of our existing products if relevant) with respect to the customer needs at all three levels. Figure 13.1 gives an example of such competitive measurement at the tertiary level of need. For example, competitive cars have doors that are easier to close than our existing car. One design opportunity might be for a car with a door that is much easier to close. Furthermore no car door, neither ours nor competitors', satisfies customers on the relatively important benefit of staying open on a hill. A new car door that fulfills this need will provide a competitive advantage.

Engineering Characteristics

Parallel to the customer needs are the physical means to deliver the benefits that meet the customer needs. For example, most car doors have a "check-position," a position of the car door where it "checks" into position such that it will stay open on a hill. One measurement of this engineering characteristic is the "check force on a 10% slope" (in pounds). B's car door might have a level-ground check force of 11 pounds while A's car and our existing car might have car-door level-ground check forces of 12 pounds. The customer wants the door to be easy to close but stay open on a hill; the engineer fulfills those needs via engineering characteristics such as the check force.

In specifying engineering characteristics we avoid stating solutions too quickly. Such quick solutions constrain creativity by implicitly ruling out all

Secondary Needs	Tertiary Needs	Importances
Easy to open and close door	Easy to close from outside	7
	Stays open on a hill	5
Isolation	Doesn't leak in rain	3
	No road noise	2

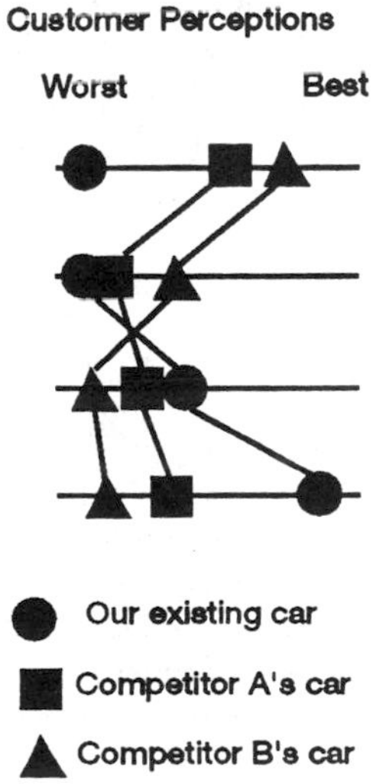

Figure 13.1 Customers' Evaluations of Competitive Products

but the standard solutions. Notice that we did not specify the solution "stays open in check position" but rather the force holding the door open. This does not constrain the engineer to design in a check position. Alternative solutions such as a more continuous resistance system could also be considered. The customer wants the door to stay open on a hill; the customer would prefer a solution that did not require a check position if that solution fulfilled needs better.

Table 13.2 lists a partial hierarchy of some of the many other possible engineering characteristics for a car door. Note that engineering characteristics are not product features (gull-wing doors, manual or power windows) nor are they parts characteristics (steel or aluminum, an XYZ hinge). The product features and parts characteristics are important to the new product design and need ultimately to be linked to the engineering characteristics in a hierarchy analogous to the customer needs hierarchy (see following section for a discussion of this issue).

Customer–Engineering Relationship

We clearly need a way to communicate customer needs to engineers so they can use the engineering characteristics at their disposal to design products that meet customers' tertiary, secondary, and primary needs. To enhance communication we need to describe the customer needs in the language of the engineer. Thus, we must identify descriptions of the physical product that are measurable and quantifiable and that relate to the customer needs.

Before the industrial revolution, producers were close to their customers. Marketing, R&D, engineering, and production were integrated—in the same person. If a knight wanted armor, he talked directly to the armorer, who translated the knight's desires into a product. The two might discuss the material—plate rather than chain armor—and details like fluted surfaces for

TABLE 13.2   List of Engineering Characteristics for a Car Door

Energy to close door	
Check force on level ground	
Check force on 10-degree slope	Open-Close Effort
Energy to open door	
Peak closing force	
Door seal resistance	
Acoustic transmission, window	Sealing Insulation
Road noise reduction	
Water resistance	

Adapted from Hauser and Clausing (1988, p. 72).

greater bending strength. Then the armorer would design the production process. For strength he cooled the steel plates in the urine of a black goat (perhaps because of its acid content). For a production plan, he arose with the cock's crow to light the forge fire so that it would reach its critical temperature at midday.

Today, we face the challenge of assuring that all parts of an organization work together on new product design. For example, Figure 13.2 illustrates the amount of communication among members of two new-product teams. Communication is measured on a three-point scale where a "three" denotes a large amount of communication and a "zero" denotes little or no communication. Both products were developed by the same organization, but the film cover was a success and the battery product was a failure. The difference seems to be communication—team members exchanged information on *all* aspects of design for the film cover but not for the battery. Indeed, Figure 13.2 is representative of new product success and failure at several organizations—it is a typical result from a retrospective study of sixteen new product projects.

This need for communication was also documented in a study of 167 firms (109 marketing managers and 107 R&D managers) by Gupta, Raj, and Wilemon (1985). They found that the primary barrier to integration across functions was lack of communication. The second most prevalent reason was insensitivity to the viewpoints of others. They also found that there was a significant discrepancy between the perceptions of marketing managers and the perceptions of R&D managers, especially on the topic of whether or not marketing provided an adequate representation of customer requirements, appropriate feedback on product performance, and information on competitive activities—R&D managers did not find marketing's input to be of the same level that marketing perceived that same input. However, marketing and R&D managers did agree that the five most important areas where integration is needed are

- Customer requirements
- Feedback on product performance
- Information on competitors
- Development of products according to market needs
- Setting of new-product goals and priorities

Quality Function Deployment (QFD)

The challenge to an organization is to encourage the communication necessary for success while retaining the creativity so essential to new product design. In this section we present one technique for integration called QFD.

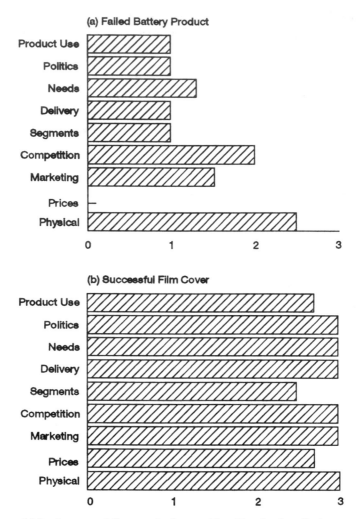

Figure 13.2 Amount of Communication on Two New Product Projects at the Same Firm (From Dougherty 1987, pp. 68 and 70; reprinted with permission)

Other techniques are likely to be forthcoming, but this demonstrates the key concepts of integrating customer needs with engineering product characteristics in the design and manufacturing of quality products.

QFD originated in 1972 at Mitsubishi's Kobe shipyard and is used widely in both Japan and the United States. By various claims QFD has reduced design time by 40% and design costs by 60% while maintaining or enhancing the quality of the design (Hauser and Clausing 1988).

QFD achieves these goals by encouraging communication among functional groups early in the design effort and by assuring that the design is focused on the voice of the customer. This impact is illustrated in Figure 13.3. Figure 13.3a shows the startup and preproduction costs at Toyota Auto Body before and after the introduction of the QFD. Notice that the 60% cost reduction comes because *more* effort is allocated in early design—startup costs are avoided because manufacturing and production need not modify the design. Figure 13.3b illustrates the same message by comparing a Japanese car company using QFD to an American car company not using QFD. More activity early in the design process means that fewer engineering changes need to be made as the car nears production and this means time to market is shorter. Notice also that for the American car company a large number of changes are made after the car is in the market, presumably in response to the customer's experience with the new car.

We present the QFD technique to illustrate the issues that an organization must address to assure communication. The success of any specific management technique depends upon organizational issues such as commitment and management style, but the need to communicate and the topics of communication cut across organizations. Readers should customize the concepts illustrated to their organization's culture.

Linking Customer Needs and Engineering Characteristics—House of Quality Approach.

One convenient diagram to help in linking engineering variables to the detailed customer needs is shown in Figure 13.4. Because of the distinctive shape it is called the "House of Quality." The interfunctional team—marketing, engineering, R&D, production, and so on—build the house together. Naturally, for an actual car door there would be many more customer needs and many more engineering characteristics than the few shown in Figure 13.4.

In the center of the house, a "relationship matrix" indicates how each engineering characteristic affects each customer need. For example, decreasing the energy to close the door has a strong positive relationship on the customer's perception that the car is easy to close from the outside. On the other hand, increasing the door's seal resistance might make the door more difficult to close leading to the judgment in Figure 13.4 that door seal resistance has a medium negative impact on the customer's perception that the car is easy to close from the outside.

The values in the relationship matrix are obtained by consensus of the interfunctional new-product team. In many cases this judgment is influenced by market research studies measuring the impact of product features on perceptions (chapter 10, Conjoint Analysis) or by experiments with alternative features or part characteristics.

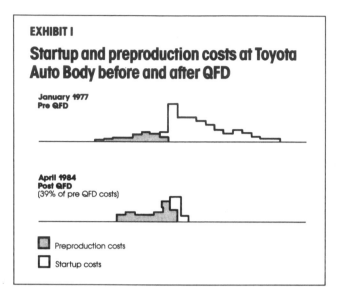

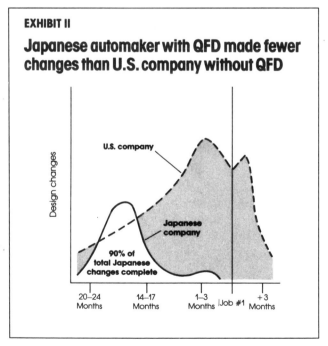

Figure 13.3 Communication Reduces Design Costs and Design Changes (Hauser and Clausing, 1988, pp. 63–73; reprinted with permission)

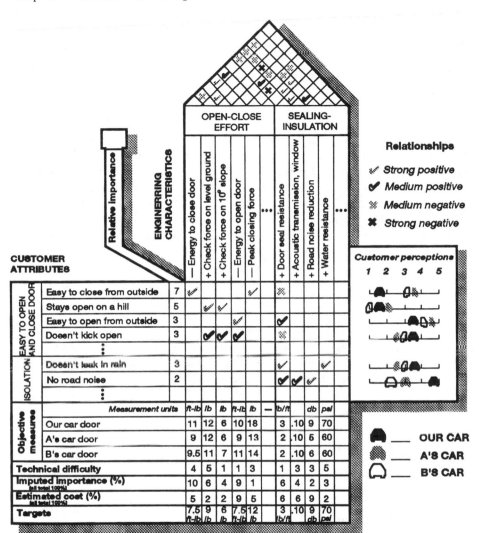

Figure 13.4 The House of Quality (Hauser and Clausing 1988, p. 72; reprinted with permission from Harvard Business Review)

Once the relationship matrix is complete, the new-product team compares the customer perceptions to objective measures. For example, if the car door with the least energy to open is perceived by customers as the most difficult to open, then either the measures are faulty or the car suffers from an image problem that might be addressed with an improved marketing program.

A change in the gear ratio on a car window may make the window motor smaller, but cause the window to go up more slowly. If the design team decides to enlarge or strengthen the motor, the door might be heavier causing it to be more difficult to open, especially on a slope. The House of Quality represents these engineering tradeoffs with a "roof" matrix (see Figure 13.4) that links each engineering characteristic with every other engineering characteristic.

The roof matrix helps the team balance engineering changes to ensure that important customer benefits are not inadvertently adversely affected. Together the relationship matrix and the roof matrix indicate the complex interrelationships among various product changes. A careful consideration of this information leads to an effective design with few unpleasant surprises.

The House of Quality is a living process—it is more than a chart on the wall. Many organizations customize it to their organizational culture. Some engineering-oriented organizations add imputed importances of the engineering characteristics. (Imputed importances are obtained by multiplying the importances of the customer needs by numbers assigned to the entries in the relationship matrix.) Some organizations add information from complaint and compliment files and some organizations add marketing information such as the influence of advertising copy. Most organizations add technical difficulty, and estimated cost for engineering characteristics as indicated in Figure 13.4. Any customization is good if it helps to integrate the information that is used by that organization in new product design.

Use of the House of Quality. The House of Quality is most useful after determining the primary customer needs, customer perceptions of competitive products with respect to those needs, and the CBP. QFD delivers value as the design proceeds, R&D provides creative solutions to improve the engineering characteristics that relate to the tertiary customer needs which fulfill the primary and secondary needs of the CBP and engineering produces the final product design that is consistent with the CBP. Marketing uses the secondary customer needs to develop the marketing program and looks to the relationship matrix to select demonstrations that establish the credibility of the CBP. More importantly, the House of Quality approach encourages all of these functions to work as a team to produce a coordinated CBP, physical product, and marketing plan.

Let's run through a hypothetical situation to illustrate how the House directs the engineering design. Look at figure 13.4. Notice that our existing doors are much more difficult to close from the outside than those on the competitor's cars. We decide to look further because our marketing data say this customer need is important. From the relationship matrix we identify the engineering characteristics that affect this customer need: energy to close the door, peak closing force, and door seal resistance. Our engineers judge the energy to close the door and the peak closing force as good candidates for improvement together because they are strongly, positively related to the customer's desire to close the door easily.

In the roof of the house, we identify which other engineering characteristics might be affected by changing the door closing energy. Door opening energy and peak closing force are positively related, but other characteristics (check force on level ground, door seals, window acoustic transmission, road noise reduction) are bound to be changed in the process and are negatively related. It is not an easy decision. But with objective measures of competitors' doors, customer perceptions, and considering information on cost and technical difficulty, the design team decides that the benefits outweigh the costs. A new design target is set for the door of the new car—7.5 foot-pounds of energy. This target, noted on the bottom of the house, establishes the goal that leads to a door which the customer perceives to be superior on an important customer benefit.

Look now at the customer need, "no road noise" and its relationship to acoustic transmission of the window. "Road noise" is only mildly important to customers and its relationship to the characteristics of the window is not strong. Window design will help only so much to keep things quiet. Decreasing the acoustic transmission usually makes the window heavier. Examining the roof of the house, we see that more weight would have a negative impact on characteristics (open-close energy, check forces, etc.) that, in turn, are strongly related to customer needs that are more important to the customer than quiet ("easy to close," "stays open on a hill"). Finally, the perceptual map shows that we already do well on road noise; customers perceive our car as better than competitor's.

In this case, the team decides not to tamper with the window's transmission of sound. The target shown at the bottom of the house stays equal to the acoustic values of the door on our existing car.

We stated early in this chapter that successful new products require communication on all issues of new product design. Does the House of Quality lead to such communication?

In a study of two product design processes within the same organization, Griffin and Hauser (1992a) found that the House of Quality led to more efficient communication. The team which used the more traditional process spent more time communicating with other members of the organization than the House of Quality team, but much of that communication was "up-over-down," from team members up to management and from management back down to team members with other functional responsibilities. Similarly communication between the manufacturer and parts supplier for the more traditional team was more often through management. On the House-of-

Quality team, team members exchanged information among themselves, leading to enhanced mutual understanding and freeing management for more strategic thinking.

In a study of 35 projects Griffin (1992) identified that the House of Quality requires strong top management support and buy-in from the team members. The House of Quality is an up-front investment that leads to more efficient and effective design efforts, but without the willingness to see the process through, it can look like a major investment without immediate payback. However, when the team buys into the process and receives the resources (time and expense) necessary to build the house, products are designed more effectively.

Beyond House-of-Quality Integration. The House of Quality is one approach of linking customer tertiary needs to engineering characteristics. Such approaches are essential to defining quality in terms of customer needs, but doing so in a way that makes sense to actually designing the product.

However we must address more than the customer need-engineering integration if we are to have a design that is ready for production. For example, suppose that the new-product team decides that doors closing easily is a critical design need and that a relevant engineering characteristic is closing energy. Setting a target value for closing energy gives the team a goal, but it does not give the team a door. To design the door, the team must specify the right parts (frame, sheet metal, weather stripping, hinges, windows, etc.), the right process to manufacture (or buy) these parts, the right process to assemble the door, and the right production plan to get it built and installed in a car.

The House of Quality links the "whats," the customer needs, to the "hows," the engineering characteristics. The next task is to take the engineering characteristics as the "whats" and link them to another set of "hows"—parts characteristics or product features. One approach to this task is to use the house diagram again, but in a revised manner. Engineering characteristics such as foot-pounds of closing energy become the rows of the next house, while parts characteristics such as hinge properties or the thickness of the weather stripping, become the columns.

In some organizations the process continues as shown in Figure 13.5 as the "hows" of one stage become the "whats" of the next. Weather stripping, a "how" in the parts deployment house, becomes a "what" in the process planning house. Process operations such as "rpm of the extruder producing the weather stripping" become the "hows." Finally, the organization might link process operations such as "rpm of the extruder" to production requirements such as knob controls, operator training, and maintenance.

The use of a QFD approach links customer needs to engineering and manufacturing decisions so that products can be manufactured efficiently

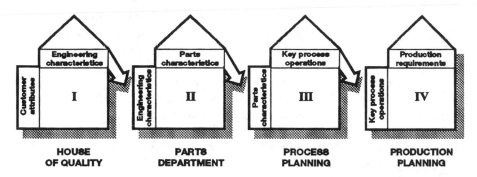

Figure 13.5 "Houses" of Parts Deployment, Process Planning, and Production Requirements (Hauser and Clausing 1988, p. 73; reprinted with permission)

and exactly. By linking the houses, the new-product team assures that the voice of the customer is deployed through to manufacturing. A knob control setting of 3.6 gives an extruder speed of 100 rpm, this helps give a reproducible diameter for weather-stripping bulbs, which gives good sealing without excessive door-closing force. This, in turn, satisfies the customer's need for a dry, quiet car with an easy-to-close door.

The design of successful new products requires effective communication among a variety of functions and people within an organization. This section has introduced QFD and the House of Quality. The House of Quality begins with the voice of the customer as summarized in a set of statements known as customer needs. These customer needs are drawn from qualitative market research and grouped to provide strategic (primary needs), tactical (secondary needs), and operational (tertiary needs) insights. Importance weights provide priorities and competitive evaluations identify opportunities.

The customer needs are linked to engineering characteristics, technical descriptions of the product providing insight to engineering and R&D team members without stifling creativity. In turn the engineering characteristics are linked to parts characteristics, product features, process operations and production requirements.

The advantage of the House of Quality is that it displays the key information that the new-product team needs for a successful design. By making this information explicit it removes hidden agendas and helps the team avoid unnecessary mistakes. Effective communication means more productive opportunities.

QFD is not the only way to assure that customer input is reflected in designs that can be implemented effectively in production operations. Some organizations find QFD overall formal and burdensome. This may be true because construction of a set of houses for QFD can take a tremendous amount of time. However, when this is the case the steps should be reduced in scope and detail only if other methods are found to address the same issues of communication and integration of marketing, engineering, and manufacturing. Without this integration quality products will not be forthcoming. If organizations find that other integration mechanisms match their organizational culture better than QFD and the House of Quality, then by all means they should be used. However, the concepts—customer voice, levels of needs, importances, competitive evaluations, link to engineering characteristics, deployment through to features, process, and manufacturing, and communication—should be part of the mechanism. These concepts are key to a successful design effort. To illustrate how QFD can be modified and applied we present nine applications vignettes.

Applications Vignettes.[1]   A *manufacturer of medical diagnostic equipment* was faced with a well-financed competitor whose new product was being sold at half the price. However, the competitive product did not have a feature that the manufacturer considered important. The voice of the customer suggested that the product could be redesigned totally to satisfy important customer needs. A modular design would enable customers in different segments to pick and choose those features that best satisfied their needs. Within a year, a new product was developed based on the voice of the customer. The basic module is priced below competition, but a fully featured product commands a high price. The sales are five times higher than the previous year.

A *consumer stationary-products manufacturer* observed a year-by-year decline in the sales of a key replacement component in their line. They did not know whether the decline was due to the perceived quality of the component or the appeal of the product itself. QFD identified the important customer needs which, in turn, identified key design attributes. Laboratory measures of the design attributes indicated that a modest improvement in the component's quality would reverse the decline in sales.

A *manufacturer of tools for the construction industry* was considering a new technology that promised to save significant manpower at construction sites. These tools would have applications in a variety of industries and market segments. Although the basic technology existed, the firm would need to invest in significant design efforts to create an actual product. The voice of the customer identified key customer needs that were important to a target segment and which would distinguish the new product if it were developed based on the technology. The manufacturer focused the product-development program to this segment and these needs.

A *financial institution* used the voice of the customer to evaluate their

---

[1] These applications were described to us by Robert Klein of Applied Marketing Science, Inc. These vignettes are modified from descriptions in Hauser (1993).

formal customer communications program. They identified eight important customer needs that were not being addressed effectively by current communications. They revised the communications programs and achieved increased sales.

The information-systems group in an *insurance company* had a substantial backlog of information-systems requests from other functions, each of which was labeled as high priority. By linking the benefits provided by the projects to important customer needs, the company was able to eliminate some projects, identify new projects which where important to the customer, and establish priorities for the remaining projects.

A *manufacturer of a lightweight chemical mixing device* had positioned its product on "greater portability." However, the voice of the customer suggested that "ease of use" and "accuracy" were of much greater importance. Through QFD they modified the design attributes of training requirements and the predictability of the mixing result. They improved these attributes via a modification in the design of the mixing device and through a new sales package. Sales increased.

An *entertainment provider* with 350 separate locations discovered that customers viewed one specific area of its operation as very important. However, customers did not perceive that the entertainment provider satisfied their needs in that area. A crash program was undertaken to identify and implement programs that would impact that area and beat out competition.

A startup *manufacturer of a new surgical instrument* had contracted with a design firm to develop prototypes for a new scalpel. The choice of the final design would depend upon accommodating the constraints of the technology in a package that fit the way surgeons operated. The voice of the customer reoriented the development and design effort, and significantly improved product acceptability.

A *manufacturer of office equipment* was designing the next generation of a product that held a dominant market position. A competitor, using digital technology, was making rapid inroads in a related market segment. The voice of the customer suggested that the benefits of the digital technology were important for the related market segment. However, they were of only minor importance for the manufacturer's market segment. As a result the manufacturer refocused its development effort to more important customer needs and avoided the expense and delay of moving to the digital technology.

DESIGN FOR MANUFACTURING

QFD integrates manufacturing and engineering into the design and marketing process. In this section we elaborate on this issue by considering computer integrated manufacturing (CIM), robust design, experimentation, and continuous improvement.

Computer-Integrated Manufacturing (CIM)

The link of design to manufacturing is facilitated by computer systems to speed up and improve design efforts (CAD) and the links to manufacturing (CAM). These CAD/CAM systems are well established procedures that generate improved designs at lower cost and do it faster (Adler and Helleloid 1987; Gagnon and Mantel 1987; and Hayes and Jaikumar 1988). CAD/CAM systems that include data storage, sharing, and access along with artificial intelligence models become CIM systems.

Recently the concept of CIM has been widened further to include many of the design functions and their integration with marketing and engineering. For example cost tradeoffs in design are now included in some CAD/CAM systems. In this case not only are alternative engineering characteristics considered in the design, but also the costs of each of the manufacturing elements. With this capability it is only one more step to tradeoff the cost and, therefore price, changes through the House-of-Quality matrix to design the simultaneous effects of cost changes and price changes that compel consumer response. This domain has also been called "simultaneous engineering" or "concurrent engineering" (see Barkan [1991] for a review). The name seems to depend upon the initial background of the writer: if manufacturing—CIM, if engineering—simultaneous engineering, and if marketing or management—total quality. By whatever name the key concept is the integration of functions of product engineering, design, R&D, manufacturing, marketing, service, distribution, and management. The desired output is more and better innovation and faster times to market.

Robust Design

Consider the engineering of the mixture of ingredients for a chocolate cake. Working with engineering characteristics of moistness, springiness of the cake when depressed with a fork, the ability to take icing, the flavor "notes" for chocolate, sweetness, vanilla, and so on, and perhaps some targets on the difficulty of preparing and baking the cake, the engineering team might determine an "optimal" product that includes an ingredients mix, a method of preparation, an oven-baking temperature, and a baking time. Indeed, if the consumer follows all of the instructions exactly, the consumer bakes a perfect chocolate cake.

But will the consumer follow the directions exactly? Ovens vary; oven temperatures are not exact; altitude can affect baking characteristics (Denver versus Paris); the phone may ring and the cake will be overbaked; much can happen in the baking of a cake that is not under the control of the manufacturer. The concept of robust design states that instead of designing a cake mix for ideal conditions, we are better to consider the range of conditions under which the product will be used. It might be that the ingredients mix that is best under ideal conditions degrades rapidly as oven temperature and baking time vary. An alternative ingredients mix or an alternative baking procedure might be very close to the best under a wide variety of conditions. The latter procedure makes it more likely that the consumer gets the best cake possible.

Naturally, robust design concepts apply to a variety of products and services. A naval helicopter may work well over water, but be a poor choice for pursuing the enemy inland over desert terrain. A robust design would consider such potential uses. In other examples, a laser printer should work in many office environments including those that are well heated, ventilated, or air conditioned, and those that are not. A snow-blower must be tolerant of misuse by customers. A packing material must cushion goods against a variety of shocks. A laundry detergent must work over a range of water temperatures.

Of course in many cases a product cannot be designed for all conditions. For example, the best ingredients mix and even the best form (liquid versus powder) for a laundry detergent vary depending upon the conditions of the water (hard water versus soft water areas) and the local regulatory environment (amount of phosphates allowed). One option is to choose a single product that works well under all conditions; another option is to design a variety of products and allow the customers to select the product that is best for their environment. The choice of the exact product line mix depends on customer needs and production costs. The techniques of the previous chapters provide valuable input to this decision.

Experimental Design and Continuous Improvement

An initial pass through the design process should produce a product that fulfills most of the CBP. But there is often room for improvement. In some cases the new-product team may wish to experiment with alternative designs. If the design alternatives are relatively controlled—ingredient changes in a laundry product, keyboard differences in personal computers, a change in a car-door hinge, or a service procedure—experimental design is a useful tool.

The procedures of engineering experimental design are similar to the concepts of experimental design in conjoint analysis. Potential design changes are varied systematically and customer benefits (or cost, or robustness, etc.) are measured to determine the best design. If the number of features is large such that a full factorial design is not feasible, fractional factorial designs (Addelman 1962; Box, Hunter, and Hunter 1978) provide an efficient alternative.[2]

Recently many firms have adopted an experimental design technique known as Taguchi methods (1983, 1988) in which orthogonal arrays (similar in concept to fractional factorial designs) are used to develop a robust design that maximizes the "signal-to-noise" ratio—a sum-of-squares measure comparing the variation in measurement to the errors of measurement.[3] For further discussion see Box et al. (1988), Taguchi (1983, 1988), Ross (1988), Schmidt and Meile (1989), or Taguchi and Clausing (1991).

A concept that is important to both traditional experimental designs and to Taguchi designs is the concept of inner and outer designs. Consider the design of a cake mix given above. Some factors (ingredients, recommended baking procedure, etc.) are under the control of the manufacturer—"call these inner factors." Other factors (actual baking time, oven temperature, altitude, etc.) are either under the control of the customer or determined by environment—call these factors "outer factors." To determine a robust design the experiment should systematically vary both the inner and the outer factors computing an overall measure of how much the actual benefits delivered vary from the target benefits. The exact means of calculation can follow traditional sum-of-squares methods, Taguchi loss-function measures, or other criteria set by the new-product team. The important consideration is that the new-product team consider a variety of conditions and take steps to ensure that the product-in-use delivers the benefits that the customer demands.

Engineering Design Dynamics and Creativity

Even with the aid of the QFD, CIM, and robust experimental design methods, engineering is still a task that requires creative solutions from human beings. Research on parallel projects indicates that better-rated engineering solutions are produced by groups that generate relatively few approaches at any one time and, during the course of a project, use a strategy of trading off approaches two at a time rather than generating many alternatives and considering them simultaneously. See Allen et al. (1978). By studying how R&D laboratories actually work Allen suggests a description of the R&D problem-

[2] For example, if there are 10 alternative features or procedures and for each feature there are two choices, this means that there are 2^{10} (1024) potential alternative designs. A fractional factorial design can reduce this number of alternatives to as few as 16, although a design of 32 alternatives may be less sensitive to measurement error.

[3] There are actually several signal-to-noise ratios depending on the conditions of the experiment and the loss functions that are used. For greater detail see the references given.

solving process. See Figure 13.6. In this process the new-product design task is first factored into subproblems then alternative approaches are generated and evaluated on critical dimensions. Alternative approaches are generated only if the design can not pass or exceed the critical dimensions.

To proceed successfully through a process such as that in Figure 13.6, the new-product team members tap all sources of information to generate creative solutions. Table 13.3 shows the relative information usage from two pairs of projects at the development phase of R&D work. In the early functions, information is greatest from outside sources (customers, 36%; vendors, 12%) and in later functions, internal analysis is relied upon more heavily (you may want to review the discussion of gate keepers in chapter 5 for more discussion of information flows in the lab).

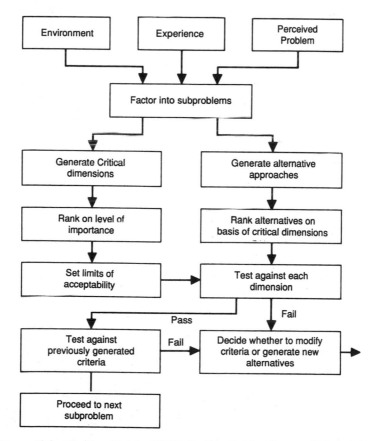

Figure 13.6 Working Model of R&D Problem-Solving Process (Adapted from Allen 1966)

TABLE 13.3 Information Sources Used Related to Function Served in Engineering Design

Function	Literature	Technical Staff	Sources Outside Laboratory	Vendor	Customer	Memory	Analysis and Experimentation	Number of Messages
1. Generate Alternative Approach	2%	10%	2%	12%	36%	12%	26%	106
2. Reject Alternative Approach	0	12	2	13	2	10	62	68
3. Generate Critical Dimensions	3	17	4	10	9	4	54	71
4. Set Limits of Acceptability	4	15	5	19	4	5	49	75
5. Change Limits of Acceptability	0	25	17	3	25	0	25	12
6. Decide Whether to Modify Criteria or Generate New Alternatives	0	0	9	0	9	9	73	11
7. Test Alternative	9	7	4	10	3	2	65	106
8. Expand Alternative	8	0	0	33	17	17	25	12
Total	4%	11%	4%	13%	12%	7%	30%	461

In the new-product development process described in this book, the customer research on the concept and product help specify the critical dimensions (engineering characteristics based on customer needs) and limits of acceptability (target values for those characteristics). The function of expanding alternatives is supported by creative idea inputs and evaluation of "stretchers." Coordination between R&D and marketing via QFD encourages an iterative design in which the dimensions and limits are modified based on customer input and engineering difficulties. Customer reactions establish and prioritize new criteria.

Proximity and Coordination

A final consideration in integrated design is the physical interactions among new-product team members. We have already seem that coordination is desired, but to coordinate a team must talk. Figure 13.7 plots the probability that two people (within an R&D lab) communicate as a function of the physical distance separating them. Figure 13.7 suggests that communication can degrade quickly as a function of distance —dropping off dramatically over as little as 10 meters. Recall that in chapter 5 on idea generation we also discussed the effects of physical location on creativity. The same concepts deserve to be re-emphasized here. Proximity is important because in creative processes such as new-product development informal interaction may be more

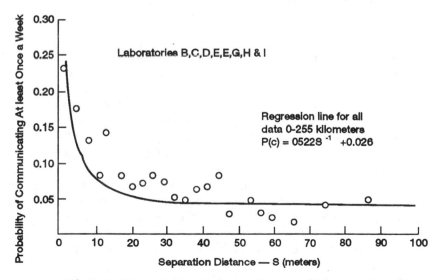

Figure 13.7 Probability of Communication as a Function of Distance (Allen 1977, p. 239; reprinted with permission)

effective than formal meetings. Chance meetings in the halls, at the coffee machine, in the lunch room, or in a group lounge may result in the exchange of ideas. These informal and formal exchanges are necessary if marketing, engineering, and production are to be coordinated.

The proximity arguments suggest that the new-product team should be physically together in a carefully designed space. Some companies recognize these formal and informal contacts are productive exchanges and plan their facilities to encourage them. For example, the Steelcase design facility in Grand Rapids, Michigan, was built from the ground up to encourage interaction. The building is in a pyramidal shape such that people on each floor can see the people on other floors; escalators rather than elevators are encouraged; balconies are furnished to encourage use; blackboards are placed near coffee areas; and open architecture is used throughout.

Engineering Services

Engineering and production functions must be carried out for new services as well as manufactured products. For example, in defining a new MIT MBA program the following service-delivery features had to be developed:

1. Trip to visit businessmen
2. Summer job internship
3. Close faculty-student interaction on company-sponsored projects

The design process was similar to Figure 13.6. Alternative specifications were examined and evaluated. The trip could be to Europe or to New York. It could be in-depth visits to a few companies or an overall view of many companies. The design selected was a three-day, in-depth visit to a company. The first experimental trip was to Xerox, and post-trip evaluation indicated it met the program criteria. Similarly, an experimental program was established in the management science area to examine the issues of faculty/student interaction and summer job placement. A special seminar and pairing of faculty and students for joint research was implemented. These were successful and naturally led to successful summer placement through personal contacts of the faculty and the placement office. Although these are not the usual features developed by an R&D laboratory, the engineering design of service plans is just as critical as in products. The service plan must deliver the benefits of the CBP or it will fail.

Of course most physical products have service components. In the mid-1980s the Japanese automobiles gained a reputation for reliability because they required less service. Indeed, the amount and quality of the service provided by a dealer is an important component in many consumers' choices of which car to buy. To fulfill the CBP the new-product team should pay close attention to engineering services as well as the physical product.

MARKETING MIX

Careful analysis and a focus on quality is also relevant to the marketing effort which fulfills the CBP. The final set of decisions that are made before a product is ready to be tested is the specification of the advertising copy and budget, personal selling approaches, distribution variables, prices, promotion, packaging, branding, and service. Although our goal is to set these variables at the "best" levels, it is difficult to know exactly what "best" means because at the design stage there is still too much uncertainty with respect to customer response and competitive response. Thus, we set an initial marketing mix that is consistent with the CBP, our initial sales forecasts, our best estimates of customer response to marketing efforts, and our best estimates of competitive reaction. As more information becomes available during the testing phase of new product development this initial marketing mix is refined for greater strategic advantage and profitability.

Coordination in the Marketing Elements

It may not make sense to introduce a high-quality product and price it at a low level relative to competition. Premium products justify premium margins—quality justifies increased long run profits. A high level of advertising requires either a high volume of sales, a premium margin, or both—otherwise there is insufficient revenue to justify the advertising budget. Of course it is also true that advertising may be needed to justify a premium price. Such advertising might be necessary to make customers aware of the product and communicate its benefits or it might be necessary to signal retailers and distributors that the manufacturer will stand behind the product and that the manufacturer expects sales to be high enough to justify the advertising expenditure.

Beyond price and advertising there are many interactions among the elements of a marketing strategy. A good advertising message could encourage customers to use a free sample, to react to an end-aisle display, or open the door for a salesperson. The message in an advertising campaign should match the message of a sales campaign. On the other hand, too much promotion or too many rebates or distribution through the wrong outlets can undermine an image of "high quality." In short, the marketing strategy must be coordinated. Each element should consider the impact of the other and work together to fulfill the CBP.

We now turn to specific elements of the marketing mix—advertising, selling, distribution, pricing, and promotion—to review some conventional wisdom with respect to developing creative executions and setting budgets for these tactics. However, we caution the reader that the one-variable-at-a-time approaches provide input to an integrated profit maximization approach that recognizes the interactions among the mix elements.

Developing Advertising and Sales Copy

Advertising and selling efforts complement the engineering design by communicating the CBP. For consumer products advertising copy for television, radio and print media must be created. For industrial products, the salesperson presentation and sales aids must be designed. In this section we briefly address the issues of creating advertising copy and sales promotion materials. Readers are referred to Aaker and Meyers (1987) for a more complete discussion of advertising management.

Advertising Copy.   Figure 13.8 shows a concept board for a new aspirin. It describes the CBP and provides cues to substantiate the CBP. Based on consumer reaction it is refined for more effective communication of the CBP. Figure 13.9 shows a story-board that would be the basis of a television commercial. Here the CBP is refined and shown as a puzzle. The ad attempts to establish that strength, speed, and gentleness have been combined in this new product.

Figure 13.10 shows a print advertisement for Pacific Data's ProTracer. The core benefit proposition, "All the benefits of a laser printer on a much larger scale," is featured prominently and supported with graphics showing the larger scale. Substantiation of the CBP, "desktop convenience, reliability, low cost, sharp high-quality output, fast printing speed, and plain paper," all accepted benefits of laser printing, are shown in the upper right corner. Finally, technical substantiation (the top of the House of Quality) are given in the text. This advertisement appeared in *PC Magazine*, a medium that was likely to reach the target audience.

An advertisement may be more effective if it concentrates on one unique aspect of the CBP rather than briefly describing all the attributes. Figure 13.11 provides another example of a print advertisement. This is one of the advertisements that NEC used when introducing their FG-series of computer monitors. Here, despite the fact that the monitor has a number of other features, the advertisement stresses its ergometric design, "NEC makes a hard day's work a little easier." Substantiation is given with technical features and a

ATTACK—A New Kind of Pain Reliever

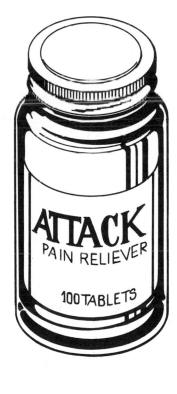

Pain relievers are one of the most widely used home medications and the main ingredient of those products is aspirin. That's because aspirin works so effectively to relieve headaches, muscular pain, fever due to cold, and "flu."

But clinical studies have recently discovered that aspirin and the extra-strength pain relievers also have side effects—and not just among people with sensitive stomachs. As many as 70% of the people who frequently take pain relievers can suffer from upset stomach, heartburn, gastric irritation, thinning of the blood, hidden stomach bleeding, and even certain allergic reactions.

Now a new pain reliever called ATTACK is available in two strengths, regular and extra-strength, whichever is appropriate.

ATTACK has all the effectiveness but it has none of the side effects. ATTACK gives you fast, effective, extra-strength relief, but it won't irritate or upset your stomach. That's because the pain reliever in ATTACK is acetaminophen—a pain reliever which has long been known for its effectiveness and absence of side effects.

Next time you need fast, effective pain relief, without side effects, try ATTACK.

Figure 13.8 Concept Board for "Attack"

1. (Anncr VO) You wouldn't bring out a new pain relief tablet ... against all this competition if you really didn't have something.

2. Introducing ATTACK ... ATTACK has Acetaminophin.

3. ATTACK is ...

4. ... strong ...

5. ... FAST and an important advantage ...

6. Gentle -- ATTACK does not cause stomach upset -- no heartburn -- no indigestion.

7. Fast and strong for effective pain relief without stomach upset.

8. Get ATTACK.

9. We think we really have something better.

Figure 13.9 "Attack" Story Board

Figure 13.10 ProTracer Advertisement Features the CBP (*PC Magazine*, May 12, 1992, p. 36; reprinted with permission)

9:27 PM

NEC makes a hard day's work a little easier.

Often, a day at the office runs well into the night. That's one of the reasons NEC places a high priority on user comfort and safety in the development of new products.

We call this people-minded thinking our ErgoDesign™ philosophy, and our new line of MultiSync® Monitors is a prime example.

Their reduced ELF/VLF emissions meet the strictest safety guidelines in the world. They're flicker-free, with anti-glare protection for less eyestrain. A tilt-swivel base for less neckstrain. An anti-static screen coating that eliminates dust and static shock. And up-front controls that are easy to reach and use.

It's no wonder you'll see NEC products in corporations large and small. In public and private institutions. In homes across the country. At NEC, we don't consider our work done until we've made it easier to do yours.

For more information, call us at 1-800-338-9549.

Caring through technology.

Communications • Computers • Electron Devices • Home Entertainment.

Figure 13.11 NEC Advertisement features a Unique Benefit (reprinted with permission)

quality image is maintained by refering to the previous, well-received line of NEC monitors. Which of the two approaches is best? It depends on the specific product and target market and whether or not a single advertisement is run or the advertisement is part of a campaign. At this phase it is important that the advertisement communicate the product benefits in a manner that is consistent with the CBP. We return to the selection of advertising in the testing phase of development. Here we consider how such advertisements are created.

In creating ads, advertising strategists concern themselves with product advantages, differentiating characteristics, and the customers' buying motives to generate a message that will "sell" the product. They use this information to generate a unique selling proposition (USP) to make a consumer Aware, generate Interest in the new product, motivate a Desire to purchase, and hopefully cause the consumer to Act. This is called the AIDA model (Strong 1925). Others like it, such as hierarchy of effects (Lavidge and Steiner 1961), which identifies a hierarchy of steps (unaware, aware, knowledge, liking, preference, conviction, and purchase), are used to identify and address the multiple strategies of advertising necessary to affect purchase. Good advertising addresses each phase in the model to achieve the final outcome, purchase.

Generation of the message is a creative process, but this creativity is enhanced and focused with information from the design process. Focus groups and design analyses provide information about the buying motives for the product category and the customer semantics for the advertising copy. The product positioning strategy directs the advertising positioning and helps define the unique aspects of the core selling proposition. The perceptual mapping tells the advertiser which dimensions to stress and which product characteristics and psychological appeals make up these dimensions (see Aaker and Stayman [1990] for ad impact correlates). In some cases these approaches are automated with rule-based systems (artificial intelligence) that are applied in advertising design (Burke, Rangaswamy, Wind, and Eliashberg 1990).

Interest can be generated because the product fills previously unfulfilled needs. But this must be augmented with the advertiser's skill in creating interest in the advertisement per se. If the CBP is good, then the advertiser must generate sufficient belief in the appeals to cause trial, but one must be careful not to overstate product features. Otherwise, the customer might be disappointed because the product did not live up to the advertising's claims. For example, Urban (1975a) shows that a positioning that was too strong relative to blind test caused enough advance reaction in consumers that, after using the product, they perceived the product as much worse than it actually was. In his example, Urban found that the lower level of repeat purchase more than offset any gains in trial. Thus, while an advertiser might enhance a positioning with a good message, it must be done cautiously because stronger appeals are not necessarily better. The perceptual position that describes accurately the physical product is a good starting point.

The advertising copy (words, pictures, headlines, border, trademarks, slogans, etc., in print media; words, music, sound effects illustrative material, action, camera cues, etc., in radio and TV) must be set to attain this message. The important consideration in the message is that it is not independent of the product strategy, but rather enhances that strategy by using the CBP and the knowledge gained in the design process.

Who actually creates ads? In most cases, advertising agencies carry out this function; the new product developer delegates much of the creative responsibility. The new-product team selects the agency and approves the final copy. Some firms take a much more active role by participating in copy development, whereas others expect the agency to deliver an effective advertising campaign and give the agency much freedom to develop it.

Selecting an advertising agency is not an easy task. The sales presentations that agencies give are almost all uniformly good and usually overwhelming. Although the agency's "track record" is important, we suggest the following additional considerations in choosing an agency to participate in the new product process.

We recommend an agency that accepts the notion that they are part of the development team. In many cases, this involvement can begin very early, in opportunity identification or soon after initial ideas are developed. The new-product team identifies a market opportunity and develops a CBP to exploit that market. The most successful advertising strategy uses this information; its advertising is integrated with the total new product strategy. While most agencies use this information to enhance their creative output, some agencies hold the attitude that: "If you want a winner, turn the project over to us and we'll give you the best ad this market has even seen." We feel there is a real danger that the underlying R&D and marketing development strategy may be lost if the agency has this attitude. With participation by the agency and the sponsoring organization, the CBP strategy is more likely to be implemented effectively in the advertising campaign.

The specific people to be assigned to the project should have a record of successful creative output, but they also should understand marketing strategy and acknowledge that their copy will be tested. Some creative copy writers believe that testing should not be done. Although copy testing is subject to limitations, we argue in the next chapter that it is a critical part of new product testing.

A final desirable attitude in an agency is the willingness to create very different alternatives. Some agencies develop one campaign and give the client an accept or reject alternative. It is better to be given a set of good alternatives that reflect different creative executions and use testing and judgment to select the best one (Gross 1972). The more creative alternatives available, the more likely it is that an outstanding campaign will be found.

Sales Presentations.   It is natural to think of copy development as applying to advertising, but it also is important in managing a sales force. In some industrial products advertising budgets are small (Lilien and Little 1976) and the salesperson is relied upon to deliver the CBP message. The salesperson identifies prospects, obtains appointments, presents the message (Core Benefit Propositions), overcomes objections, and attempts to close the sale (Figure 13.12). An important design activity is to lay out the selling presentation. This usually is a 10- to 15-minute sales message that presents the CBP. Most companies do not spend enough time designing this message and training the salesperson to deliver it at a professional level. As much care should be taken in designing the salesperson's selling proposition as in designing advertising copy.

As well as preparing the layout and content of the CBP message, sales aids and brochures must be designed. These sales-support devices, brochures, and the message should be coordinated with advertising to present the buyer with a unified CBP positioning. Increasingly today telemarketing, tradeshows, direct mailings, and video aids are being used in the selling process. These should also be designed carefully to support the communication of the CBP and to be consistent with the personal selling tactics.

Advertising Budgeting

We must recognize that advertising has at least two roles —it encourages customers to consider the new product and, among those customers, it encourages trial (or purchase) by communicating the CBP. We have already

Prospecting

↓

Approach and qualify
Potential buyers

↓

Presentation

↓

Overcome objections

↓

Close sale   Figure 13.12 The Personal Selling Process

discussed the qualitative aspects of advertising copy—what it says—we turn now to the more quantitative aspects—how often should we say it. That is, we will assume that we have the best copy and attempt to select a level that is most profitable.

For the sake of exposition assume that competitive advertising levels are fixed and that the only action we are taking is to change the magnitude of our advertising. Then following the ideas of the previous chapter we forecast the actual purchase rate, P, as the purchase potential, B, modified by awareness, a_w, and availability, a_v. (For frequently purchased products purchase potential is the trial times repeat. Here B is the market response, the sum over the individual customers in equation 12.3). That is,

$$P = a_w \, a_v \, B \tag{13.1}$$

The advertising budget affects both the awareness level and the purchase potential. Consider now its effect on the awareness level—the likelihood that a customer considers our product. This awareness level is created by purchasing advertising media insertions and by the advertising being seen and comprehended by customers to produce attitude changes and purchases.

The budget can be set by estimating the relationship of the budget to the awareness level. One approach is to set an awareness goal and determine how much money should be budgeted to meet it. For example, if 70% of the target group should see at least one ad (i.e., "reach"), and on average two ads should be seen by each person across the target group (i.e., "frequency"), media schedulers can estimate the cost and schedule to meet these goals.

But this approach leaves open the question: Why not 90% reach and frequency of three rather than 70% reach and frequency of two? To answer this question, expenditure must be linked to awareness. For example, Figure 13.13 shows a hypothetical graph of awareness as a function of dollar expenditure. Initially, big gains occur, but then diminishing returns set in.

We use the advertising function to calculate awareness (or consideration) as a function of dollars spent. Equation 13.1 then provides an estimate of sales at this advertising level. For example, suppose that our best estimate of purchase potential, B, is 20 million units. Suppose further that from Figure 13.13 an advertising rate of $7.5 million per year gives us a 50% awareness level ($a_w = 0.50$) and that we have spent $1 million to assure 100% distribution in all outlets ($a_v = 1.0$), then equation 13.1 estimates that our sales will be (0.50) (1.0) (20 million units) which equals 10 million units. Of course if we had spent more, say $10 million, we would have achieved more awareness (55%) and more sales (11 million units).

To determine whether the increased spending is justified we turn sales into profitability. In general this accounting function is complex, but we get an initial estimate by considering the case of constant returns to scale. For

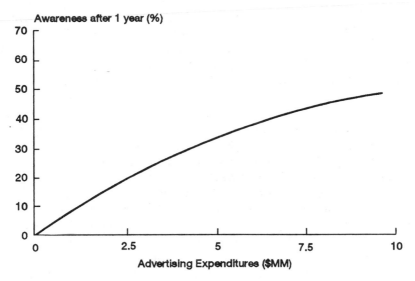

Figure 13.13 Typical Advertising Response Function

example, suppose that our sales potential estimates are based on a price of $2 per unit and that the marginal cost of production is $1 per unit—this gives margin (not including fixed costs) of $1 per unit. To get profit we multiply sales times the margin and subtract the advertising and distribution costs. For example, for an advertising rate of $7.5 million our projected profit is

$1.5 million = ($1 per unit margin) (10 million units)

− ($7.5 million for advertising) − ($1 million for distribution)

Table 13.4 shows similar profit calculations for various levels of advertising expenditures. While the advertising level of $7.5 million looks best, we

TABLE 13.4 Sample Calculations to Establish Initial Advertising Rate

Advertising Rate, A ($MM/yr)	Awareness, a_w (%)	Sales Rate (MM units/yr)	Profit Rate, π ($MM/yr)
1.0	10	2.0	0.0
2.5	20	4.0	0.5
5.0	35	7.0	1.0
7.5	50	10.0	1.5
10.0	55	11.0	0.0

note that it is only an approximation. Figure 13.13 is based on judgment and discussions with the advertising agency. Furthermore, several factors such as the lagged effects of advertising, diffusion, and the interaction with other marketing mix variables are not reflected in Table 13.4. Nonetheless, calculations of the type in Table 13.4 give the new-product team valuable perspective on setting the initial advertising budget (see Hanssens, Parsons, and Schultz [1990] for an econometric approach to estimating market responses).

Another concern is the response of competition. If we enter the market with a new product and invest heavily in advertising, we do not expect the existing brands to ignore us. Rather, it is likely that they will adjust their advertising to a new level. In most cases their initial response will be to defend their market share by increasing advertising, but such initial response may not be profitable in the long run. Once we enter, the market is less profitable for them and they may find it in their interest to cut back advertising if we gain a foothold in the market. In some cases if enough is known about the competitors' cost structures, the new-product team can simulate (or calculate) competitors' incentives and hence competitor's reactions (see Hauser and Wernerfelt 1990a[4]). In other cases the new-product team will have to estimate competitive response and run a number of "what-if" analyses. In either case, the new-product team must consider competitive response if they are to select the best initial advertising level.

In addition to setting the advertising budget, the media mix is necessary for the initial design strategy. The message copy determines what to say and the media plan determines how to channel it most effectively to the target group. The media plan is set to maximize results considering advertising-budget constraints. For example, a stock-brokerage service might emphasize the *Wall Street Journal* and *Forbes*, while a cosmetic product might emphasize the *Ladies' Home Journal* and daytime television. The advertiser chooses the media to achieve the best exposure, reach, and frequency levels within the target market.

Selling Effort

Although advertising plays a role in industrial products, sales representatives carry more of the communication responsibility. The budget for selling is expressed in the allocation of sales time to the new product.

Each sales call exposes the potential customer to the core benefit prop-

---

[4] Hauser and Wernerfelt (1990a) demonstrate that, in equilibrium where every firm is using its most profitable strategy in response to other firms' advertising levels, the equilibrium advertising level is higher than would be calculated assuming that competition does not respond. They demonstrate one case where it is almost nine times as large as well as other cases where it is only slightly larger.

osition and is analogous to creating awareness levels by advertising. The number of customers and the rate at which the calls are made must be determined. Figure 13.14 shows two rates of sales coverage. One curve shows rapid and almost complete coverage, while the other shows a gradual growth in coverage.

The results of sales calls are estimated by an equation similar to that for advertising. Sales calls make the customer aware of the new product and in many cases make it available to the customer.

In some cases there is a cumulative effect of sales calls and the probability that the customer purchases the new product grows as more sales calls are made to that customer. For example, Figure 13.15 shows one possible relationship between the probability of ordering the new product and the number of calls made on the customer. If customers vary in their susceptibility to sales calls, then separate calculations are made for each type of customer.

The *net* effect of the sales effort is more difficult to measure because the existing products may be affected. Usually total sales time is fixed and allocations of selling time to a new product reduce the time available to other products. If the effects of reduced effort on other products can be estimated, the net sales and profit effects of sales allocations are calculated.

Distribution

Availability is affected primarily by the distribution system (e.g., distributors, wholesaler, jobbers, and retailers). Like the other elements of mix,

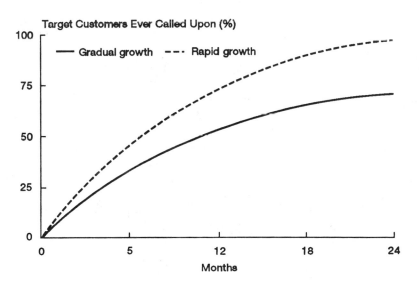

Figure 13.14   Rates of Sales Call Coverage

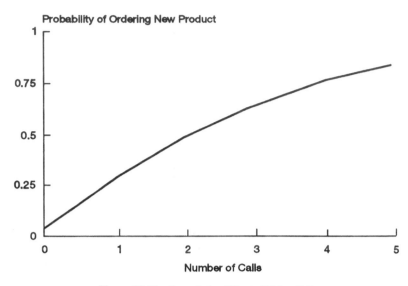

Figure 13.15 Cumulative Effect of Sales Calls

good distribution does not ensure success, but it is necessary for success. For example, even with a good positioning, a manufacturer of a new antacid found sales down due to poor distribution. A major portion of the market buys antacids at the special displays near supermarket checkout areas. Without good coverage of these displays, the firm could not be successful.

But availability is not the only function of a distribution channel; information is also provided. By providing information, channels also play a role in communicating the CBP. For example, many audio component (Hi-Fi) stores have listening rooms where consumers listen to components within a full audio system. Other stores supply "loaners" that enable consumers to try components in their home system.

In industrial products, often selling is done by the firm's sales force. But if the firm does not have its own sales force for a new market, it may use middlemen to carry out this function. Distribution channels perform needed service by fulfilling warranties and providing diagnostic and corrective maintenance when needed. A good distribution system might be critical to fulfilling the CBP. For example, the servicing function may be a crucial part of the CBP if reliability is emphasized or if the delivery of product benefits is significantly better when the product is used properly.

Channels of distribution vary widely and are usually institutionalized. Consumer goods usually have a long chain of distribution from manufacturer to distributor to wholesaler to retailer. Industrial products may use middlemen or direct distribution. In new-product development, there may not be a large number of alternative channels due to inertia in the distribution institutions and practices. However, in many cases, new products need more support from the channel than an average mature product. If the new-product team wants the channel members to provide extra availability; information exchange, demand creation, and service they must pay for it or provide incentives to encourage it.

Among the incentives offered to retailers are cooperative advertising or "slotting" allowances (direct payment to retailers to give a manufacturer a "slot" in the inventory and shelf space systems). Some manufacturers give selling assistance, supply promotion material, or supply direct advertising materials. Some manufacturers supply store traffic stimulators such as free offers and product demonstrations, or the manufacturer may sponsor clinics and special events. Point-of-purchase promotions such as signs, window displays, wall displays (clocks, thermometers), display cards, and merchandise racks (e.g., razor blades) reward the retailer and serve to aid awareness and induce trial. The product itself is an incentive to the channel member. Proactively designed products are products that consumers will buy. As a result, some manufacturers emphasize a "pull" strategy in which the consumers demand the product and pull it through the channel.

It is possible to support the channel's selling function by the use of missionary salespeople. These salespeople represent the company, but orders are placed with middlemen. For example, L'eggs representatives set up displays and stock them directly, but sales are by the local grocer. Pharmaceutical companies "detail" products with their representatives, but prescriptions are filled by local druggists. Another way to add more selling emphasis in the channel is by increasing the margins to the trade. It is common in consumer products to give middlemen (retail food stores, auto dealers) higher margins in exchange for special displays or to encourage extra selling push.

For new products, manufacturers must make both macro and micro distribution decisions. Macro decisions involve a selection of the channel itself. For example, should a manufacturer of a swimming pool chemical reach consumers through

1. Conventional retail outlets such as hardware stores and drug stores
2. Specialized swimming pool supply and equipment retailers
3. Swimming pool service companies
4. Mass retailers such as supermarkets, department stores, and discount houses

5. Direct-mail supply companies

6. A combination of these alternatives

Micro decisions involve the allocation within the channel to elements such as advertising assistance, point-of-purchase displays, and economic incentives. A key determinant in the macro decision is the CBP which identifies the consumers who are the target market. For example, a low-priced camera would be better sold in department stores or discount houses rather than in professional photography shops; whereas, a luxury telephone attachment may be priced out of a discount store distribution strategy. Avon products are better sold by neighborhood representatives who give personal service and advice. Tupperware is sold at "parties" where their superior seal is demonstrated. Finally, part of the macro decision is based on economic considerations balancing the gains in availability (a_v), awareness (a_w), and purchase (B) against the cost incurred by using the channel.

The microdecisions are the result of detailed negotiations, which are highly dependent on the relative power, conflict, and regulation involved for each potential channel. It is important for the new-product team to set margin and special incentives to obtain the desired availability, information, demand creation, and service effort (see Stern and Ansary [1988] for a complete discussion).

Pricing

There are several methods of selecting a price for a new product. A common approach is to mark up costs by some amount. Another is to calculate a price which will result in a break-even of profits for a conservative sales estimate. A third is to set prices at a level slightly below competitive products.

These are simple methods to implement, but may underprice or overprice a product. The best approach would be to understand the sales effect of changing price. In theory, the price of the new product is set by considerations of profitability. A higher price means more profit per product sold while a lower price means more volume but lower profit per unit.

In the design process, some measures of price response are obtained. For example, price is often a variable in preference regression or conjoint analysis. Alternatively, value maps provide a tradeoff between benefits and price. (A greater price means fewer benefits per dollar in a value map.) If the new-product team has used a value map to select a target position, they can use this value map to simulate the effect on sales of alternative prices. As illustrated in chapter 10 (see Figure 10.2), the team can use isocost and isodemand curves to select the most profitable position for a variety of prices and then select the most profitable price (and position). However, as in advertising, this "most profitable" price assumes competitors do not change their prices. More realistically, the new-product team should identify a price that is profitable under a variety of competitive scenarios.

Of course setting the right price involves more than just selecting the price that is best for short-run profits. For example, one might consider a pricing strategy to build a market, that is, price low initially to build sales volume and customer loyalty (see Narasimhan [1989] for an analytical approach to pricing and the diffusion of innovation). Such penetration pricing scenarios make the most sense if the firm uses the production experience to lower costs and improve the engineering design. Such experience solidifies the firm's competitive capabilities and leads to long-run profitability. Another reason for penetration pricing is to stimulate word-of-mouth recommendations or acceptance by the channel of distribution. A disadvantage of penetration pricing is that profits are low; if the market does not grow at the expected rate, the product may never be profitable.

Another consideration is that of quantity discounts. Such discounts encourage larger orders. As Jeuland and Shugan (1988) demonstrate, quantity discounts are a profit sharing mechanism—if the channel sells more its costs per unit are less and its profitability per unit can be more. Such quantity discounts to channels encourage greater service by the channel and greater sales pressure.

The final consideration is to establish a price that is consistent with the CBP. A premium product should command premium margins. This is particularly important as an incentive to the channel to push the new product at the expense of existing competitive products.

Naturally, the team will want to leave open the option to respond to competitors. Thus, we encourage the price to be set on the basis of a full set of "what-if" competitive price scenarios. Look for a robust price that leads to a profitable new-product introduction under most reasonable competitive and environmental scenarios. However, remember that the price is likely to be modified as more information becomes available in pretest, prelaunch, or test-market analyses.

Promotion

In many new products, special promotions are used to encourage initial acceptance. For example, in industrial products, these promotions may be special introductory prices or they may be special deals in which the purchase of the new product results in lower prices for existing products or includes free service for a specified period of time.

Early in the introduction of a new consumer product, there is a desire to induce trial to obtain more rapid market penetration. Various strategies are used to entice the consumer to try the new product in a way that does not lower the overall probability of repeat purchases. Although there are several strategies including premiums (such as towels in laundry detergents), contests (such as drawings and puzzles), and combination offers (such as Bic pens and lighters), by far the most widely used strategies are the economic incentives that effectively lower the initial purchase price of a new product. These strategies (sampling, couponing, and price-off) can be used alone or in combination. Recently several books have been written about promotion (Quelch 1989; Lodish 1986; and Blattberg and Neslin 1990). These books reflect the increasing use of promotions as a competitive tool. You are referred to these books for more information.

Sampling.   When Sure deodorant was introduced, Procter & Gamble gave out approximately 30 million free 2-ounce samples. Polaroid made available the sonar range detector from its camera at minimal cost to original-equipment manufacturers so that they could evaluate it as a component in their products. The goal of these strategies is to encourage trial in the hope that if customers try the product, they will buy more. In this way sampling substitutes for awareness and first trial.

Suppose that a percentage of the target consumers are sampled. From this group initial awareness and initial availability is assured. However, repeat purchases will be affected by market availability and there is the danger that the repeat rate might be lowered. Some customers may try the sample even though they would never use the product at full price. Others try the product because it is "free," but the "free" image will lower their expectations and they will not seriously consider its features (Scott 1976). The new-product team considers this potential lowering of repeat rate when suggesting a promotion strategy.

The economic effect of sampling can be modeled by considering separately consumers who are sampled and those who are not. For example, suppose that s percent of the target group is sampled. Then, by logic, $(1 - s)$ percent are not sampled. The normal trial-repeat forecasting equation (equation 12.5) applies to them. The sampling program makes the s percent aware of the new product. We must still consider availability. We must also consider the fact that not everyone will try the sample and that the sample may alter the repeat rate. Defining terms and putting these ideas together gives equation 13.2.

$$P = (1-s)\ N_p a_w a_v TR + s\ N_p a_v U_s R_s \tag{13.2}$$

where s = percent of target group sampled

    N_p = number of consumer purchases in the
           product category per period

    a_w = awareness

    a_v = availability

    T = ultimate proportion of target group who try the new product

    R = long-run share of purchases for new product among those who
          have even made a trial purchase

    R_s = long-run share of purchases for new product among those who
          received and used a sample

    U_s = proportion of samples sent that are used by member of target
          group

A numerical example of this equation is given in the case in the next chapter. Naturally, this equation can be modified to include more phenomena should the new-product team need to do so.

Couponing. When Spiffits (moist towels with a soft-scouring cleanser [red] or a furniture polish/cleanser [brown]) was introduced, many consumers received coupons worth 75¢ off the purchase price of a package of Spiffits. Jiffy-lube, a car maintenance service encouraged customers with a coupon worth $5 off their automatic-transmission service. Teddy Grahams, a very successful new snack product used coupons worth 30¢ off. These strategies, like sampling strategies, try to produce awareness, induce trial, and, it is hoped, not undermine repeat sales. At this stage of strategy development, couponing is handled in a similar manner to sampling. Volume is computed by separating those who receive a coupon from others and calculating their sales based on a higher trial and potentially altered repeat rate (see Neslin [1990] for a coupon model).

Price-Off. A third incentive is to lower the price that consumers pay. In some cases this strategy will be less effective than couponing because it requires that consumers notice the price differential in the store. In other cases, it may reach consumers who could not be reached by couponing. The effects are similar to that for sampling and couponing. For those who are presented with the price off, trial rates would be higher but repeat rates potentially lower.

Some new-product teams may wish to combine sampling, couponing, and price-off strategies. In calculating the net effect, care must be exercised to avoid double counting in the volume equation. This can be done by dividing the target group into parts who receive one, two, or more specific promotions and estimate a trial (T) and repeat share (R) for each relevant combination.

Packaging, Product Name, and Point-of-Purchase Display

In consumer products, packaging and the display at the point of purchase are critical. In the 1970s L'eggs pantyhose used innovative "plastic egg" packaging and point-of-purchase displays to create a major business in low-priced pantyhose distributed through mass merchandisers. This was very successful in building the brand franchise. However, in 1991 L'eggs reduced the cost of the package and used a box with an oval top in an effort to earn more profit as the product reached the mature phase of its life cycle and price competition emerged.

As with other communication, the package and display should support the CBP. If a new hair conditioner was positioned as "bright" and "uniquely you," it might be packaged in a bright yellow box with a mirrored surface on top. The package is important in enabling ease of use. Although Contact's claim is based on "time release capsules," it is packaged to allow easy dispensation of the tablets and in a package with a facing that is large enough to allow restatement of the CBP message.

A final component of the product is its name. As with advertising copy this is a creative input that communicates the CBP. For example, a product with sophistication as part of the CBP should have a sophisticated name; a product with strength as part of the CBP should have a name that connotes strength. The product name is important. Several alternatives should be generated and tested for effectiveness and consistency with the CBP. If the new product is a potential product-line extension, then its CBP should be consistent with the CBP of the product line. In some cases the product line already has a well-established CBP that can be used to communicate the CBP of the new product.

In each specific product there are variables that can be designed to communicate the CBP. Advertising copy, product name, selling messages, package, and point-of-purchase displays are the most common. A good marketer is careful to consider each aspect and coordinate it with the underlying new product positioning strategy.

Service

Service is a most important function in assuring quality delivery of the benefits promised consumers. Careful plans should be laid to be sure sufficient resources are allocated to postpurchase service. How will product repairs be handled? Manufacturer service facilities are one approach but sometimes they are expensive. In this case the channel of distribution may be able to provide support effectively. Increasingly, manufacturers maintain 800-number telephone lines to handle questions and facilitate service to maximize customer satisfaction.

Guarantees are one method of assuring customers that they will get the benefits of the product in use. Sometimes these are included as a feature of the CBP and in other cases they are sold as separate service contracts. For example in the computer industry, the service division is a major contributor to the profit of the firm. Sometimes the initial price competition is so severe the profits on the initial sales are almost zero and profit is earned by service revenue generated with high margins. For example in the jet engine business as much as 90% of the profits are earned on service and parts revenue. The pricing of service and the possible inclusion of guarantees depends upon the customer's initial price elasticity and the costs of the service provided. Careful modeling is necessary to integrate customer tradeoffs (conjoint analysis or the House of Quality is useful here) with costs to maximize profit and assure long run perceptions of quality product, service, and customer satisfaction.

Summary of Marketing Mix Determination

The discussion above provides the new-product team with usable techniques to set each of the marketing mix variables. Each technique requires direct market measurement or managerial judgment. Furthermore, initial estimates can be updated as more information becomes available. The important point is to use simple models to summarize the essential elements of the managerial decisions and evaluate initial strategies. Naturally, the new-product team recognizes that the initial strategies will be refined in market testing.

In using these models, the new-product team should recognize that the elements of the marketing mix are interrelated. Price cannot be set independently of service and advertising, nor advertising set independently of promotion strategy. We return to the integration and coordination of the marketing mix in chapter 19, Managing through the Life Cycle.

For example, one strategy is an aggressive introduction through high advertising and selling effort along with a "low" price. This implies a large investment in the marketing strategy with a goal of long-run payback. An alternative strategy is a low-keyed introduction with moderate advertising, moderate sales effort, and "higher" prices. This strategy tends to pay for itself as it goes but holds sales volume at a low rate and, if the market is large enough, makes competitive entry attractive.

The choice of these or other strategies depends upon the strengths and goals of the firm. For example, large firms such as Procter and Gamble, General Electric, or General Motors, which have investment capital and marketing expertise, may opt for an aggressive strategy; whereas, a smaller firm may, by necessity, be limited to a less aggressive strategy.

In practice, aggressive strategies are becoming more common. Such strategies are especially important if the proactive development strategy has resulted in a differential advantage based on the recognition of customer needs. In this case, the organization exploits the advantage by rapidly developing the market and establishing a strong market position before competitors can imitate the innovation.

TOTAL QUALITY

Philosophy

Quality is important when engineering the product and designing the marketing mix. But quality goes beyond these functions. It also reflects leadership, human resource management, and planning. Quality in this context becomes "total," it permeates all aspects of the organization. This philosophy of building products that satisfy customers affects business from the top to the bottom of the organization. The philosophy of total quality was developed and used successfully by many Japanese industries in the 1980s and has been adopted and adapted in leading companies throughout the world in the 1990s.

The Japanese also have developed specific tools to aid managers in their quality efforts. Sometimes called the "Seven Tools" (Ishikawa, 1986) they reflect the Japanese approach of taking a concept and converting it into a simple but powerful graphical representation of the underling idea. Affinity diagrams, QFD, and the House of Quality are some of the tools. Another of the tools is very similar to the perceptual mapping methods we discussed in chapters 8 to 10. The other tools reflect problem solving methods (e.g., relational matrix, means-ends trees, and functional diagrams) and implementation scheduling techniques like PERT (we discuss this later technique in chapter 18 on the Launch of New Products). Firms customize these techniques to their needs in Japan but almost all firms use some structured method to focus on the critical aspects of total quality control.

Quality in the early 1990s has become a passion for top managers. For the remainder of this book we concentrate on the new-product aspects of quality, but one should always recall that new-product quality is delivered within a wider total quality system. We review customer satisfaction and its relationship to new-product development in chapter 19, Managing through the Life Cycle.

Quality Awards

Early in the Japanese effort to build quality products, an award called the Deming award was established to encourage firms to be serious about quality. Interestingly, Deming was an American whose ideas about quality were adopted in Japan but not initially in the United States. After being badly beaten in the market by Japanese quality products, most European and American companies instituted programs to catch up on the quality dimension. The United States Department of Commerce in 1987 set up the Malcolm Baldrige National Quality Award (Baldrige was not a quality expert but rather a past Secretary of Commerce) to encourage efforts in America (Garvin 1991). This award frames the scope of total quality and is outlined in this section.

In judging applicants for the Baldrige award, seven categories of merit are examined: leadership, information and analysis, strategic quality planning, human resource use, quality assurance of products and services, quality results, and customer satisfaction (see Table 13.5 for definitions). The wide span of quality is evident from these criteria.

Table 13.6 enumerates the subcriteria and weightings for the calculation of the total score. The award is given to the firm that scores the highest in each of various classes of industry (manufacturing, services, small businesses).

TABLE 13.5   Baldrige Awards

Leadership. The senior management's success in creating quality values and in building the values into the way the company operates.

Information and analysis. The effectiveness of the company's collection and analysis of information for quality improvement and planning.

Strategic quality planning. The effectiveness of the company's integration of the customer's quality requirements into its business plans.

Human resource use. The success of the company's efforts to realize the full potential of the work force for quality.

Quality assurance of products and services. The effectiveness of the company's systems for assuring quality control of all its operations and in integrating quality control with continuous quality improvement.

Quality results. The company's improvements in quality and demonstration of quality excellence based upon quantitative measures.

Customer satisfaction. The effectiveness of the company's systems to determine customer requirements and demonstrated success in meeting them.

(Adapted from National Institute of Standards and Technology 1991)

TABLE 13.6 Examination Categories, Items and Point Values

Examination Categories/Items		Maximum Points	
1.0	**Leadership**		100
	Senior executive leadership	40	
	Quality values	15	
	Management for quality	25	
	Public responsibility	20	
2.0	**Information and Analysis**		70
	Scope and management of quality data and information	20	
	Competitive comparisons and benchmarks	30	
	Analysis of quality data and information	20	
3.0	**Strategic Quality Planning**		60
	Strategic quality planning process	35	
	Quality goals and plans	25	
4.0	**Human Resource Use**		150
	Human resource management	20	
	Employee involvement	40	
	Quality education and training	40	
	Employee recognition and performance measurement	25	
	Employee well-being and morale	25	
5.0	**Quality Assurance of Products and Services**		140
	Design and introduction of quality products and services	35	
	Process quality control	20	
	Continuous improvement of processes, products and services	20	
	Quality assessment	15	
	Documentation	10	
	Business process and support service quality	20	
	Supplier quality	20	
6.0	**Quality Results**		180
	Products and service quality results	90	
	Business process, operational, and support service quality results	50	
	Supplier quality results	40	

TABLE 13.6 (*Continued*) Examination Categories, Items and Point Values

Examination Categories/Items		Maximum Points	
7.0	Customer Satisfaction		300
	Determining customer requirements and expectations	30	
	Customer relationship management	50	
	Customer service standards	20	
	Commitment to customers	15	
	Complaint resolution for quality improvement	25	
	Determining customer satisfaction	20	
	Customer satisfaction results	70	
	Customer satisfaction comparison	70	
	TOTAL POINTS		**1000**

(Adapted from National Institute of Standards and Technology 1991)

Interest in the award has been high (over 190,000 requests for information were received in 1991) but few have formally applied for the award (in 1990 about 120 firms actually filed a complete application). The award is exemplary of what total quality means today. It indicates the need for a comprehensive strategy in order to achieve the quality that wins customers patronage. In the 1990s success as a worldwide company will require an effective total quality program.

SUMMARY

The complete new-product design is characterized by

- Target product market and target group of customers
- CBP—Core Benefit Proposition
- Positioning of the product versus its competition
- Well-engineered design that delivers the quality required by the CBP at the primary, secondary, and tertiary levels
- Initial price, advertising, selling, promotion, distribution, and service strategies.

In completing the design care should be taken to understand the relationship between perception, physical features, preference, and choice in the new-product adoption process. Quality is obtained by careful product engineering, creation of advertising and sales copy, and the initial specification of the advertising, selling, price, promotion, distribution, and service levels for the new product. Figure 13.16 reviews our overall approach to the design process.

You should now be aware of a tool kit of methods to support design. You should be comfortable with selecting a set of analyses appropriate to a particular product category and know how to use the output of these analyses to guide a proactive new product design and achieve quality.

To be successful in design, we suggest that you

- Develop an integrated CBP, positioning, product, service strategy, and marketing mix.
- Select advertising, selling, sampling, couponing, rebates, distributions, and so on to support the CBP in a consistent manner.
- Iterate as necessary to understand the customer and modify the product, CBP, and marketing as new information becomes available.

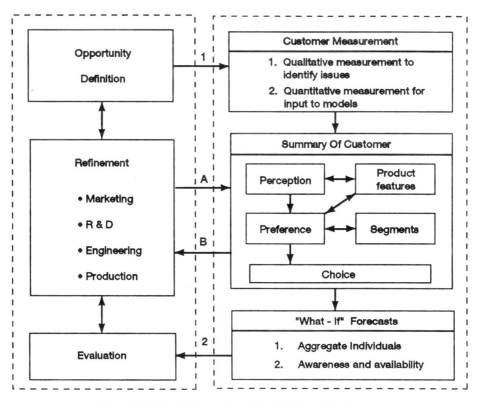

Figure 13.16   Basic Flow of the New Product Design Process

- Work together with marketing, engineering, R&D, production, and other functional areas of the firm as part of a total quality program.
- Blend managerial judgment and creativity with the information developed by market research, manufacturing, engineering, and R&D.

With the completion of the design, the testing phase can begin. In testing, primary emphasis is placed on sales forecasting and on assessing the profitability and return on investment. In testing efforts, more complex models are used and more extensive measures are collected to evaluate and refine the marketing-mix variables. However, before we study the testing phase we provide examples of integrated design to summarize the last eight chapters. The first is a frequently purchased package good and it is described in considerable detail. The durable goods, industrial products and services cases serve to review the salient aspects of the design process and demonstrate how the techniques for design and marketing new products can be tailored for specific situations.

REVIEW QUESTIONS

13.1. Discuss how the House of Quality enhances communication in the new product design process.

13.2. Choose a product with which you are familiar. For example, you might choose a battery charger, a hammer, a deodorant, or a piece of software that you use. Generate a list of customer needs (from your perspective as a customer). Compare that set of needs with sets generated by other members of your class or organization.

13.3. How does an engineering characteristic differ from a product feature? Discuss why the House of Quality links the customer needs to engineering characteristics rather than directly to product features or parts characteristics.

13.4. Consider the marketing mix elements of advertising or sales copy, packaging, name, and point-of-purchase display. How is the diagnostic information generated in the new product design process used to select an appropriate marketing mix?

13.5. What is the inter-relationship between advertising (or selling), distribution, pricing, sampling, couponing, and price-off promotion for the new product? How do each of these affect awareness, availability, trial, and repeat?

13.6. How is the core benefit proposition used in setting the marketing mix?

13.7. What is the purpose of an advertiser's unique selling proposition?

13.8. The marketing department of the Lengvas manufacturing company developed a CBP which they believed had enormous potential. The CBP was:
An extra long-lasting light bulb for situations requiring extensive usage or involving difficult replacement.

The engineering group worked long and hard to come up with a better light bulb. After exhaustive research and the construction of numerous prototypes, the engineering group developed a prototype they felt marketing people would definitely appreciate. This particular prototype not only had a lifetime twice that of average bulbs but had several other remarkable features. With a novel use of gold leaf, the engineers would be able to quadruple brightness while only doubling production costs. Finally, by altering the base of the bulb and adding a special chemical to the shell, the bulb could be dropped from a height of 10 feet without breaking.

The marketing people were overwhelmed by the efforts of engineering. Not only did the bulb meet the CBP but it seemed to be the perfect light bulb. What is your reaction to this chain of events?

13.9. Discuss the basic flow of the design process in Figure 13.16.

13.10. For a new product the following table depicts the classifications of the target market assuming 100% availability, 100% awareness, and no sampling.

Number of Customers	Who Would Try Product	Who Would Not Try the Product without Samples
Who will repeat	400,000	100,000
Who will not repeat	200,000	50,000

    a. Assume sampling is random, all samples are used, 100% availability and 100% awareness. How many repeat purchases will be generated per 100 units employed in sampling?

    b. Now assume awareness without sampling is only 40%. How many repeat purchases would now be generated per 100 units employed in sampling?

    c. Again assume 100% awareness but only 60% of the samples are used. Assume usage is independent of trial probability. How many repeat purchases will be generated per 100 units employed in sampling?

    d. Suppose sampling was not random but could be directed at different segments of the population. Who should receive free samples? How would the effectiveness of the sample change?

14

Integrated Design: Case Examples

We now have completed the opportunity identification and design phases of the new product development process. The new product resulted from a continuous innovation process. In preceding chapters we discussed how to use techniques such as market structure analysis, perceptual mapping, value maps, customer preference analysis, and conjoint analysis to identify a target market, to position a product, and to establish a CBP. Techniques such as the House of Quality coordinate the engineering and production groups within the new product team to assure that the design is well engineered to deliver customer benefits.

While the methods of the previous chapters were presented sequentially, an effective new-product team continues to iterate and improve the target market, the positioning, and the CBP as the engineering and marketing strategies evolve. For example, the team establishes a target position based on an analysis of the existing market, refines that based on customer reaction to concepts, develops a prototype, remeasures customer reaction, modifies the target positioning, redesigns the prototype, modifies the target position again, develops advertising copy, remeasures customer reaction, improves the prototype, reconsiders competition, and so on until all elements of the product and the marketing are coordinated and ready for combined testing. A successful new-product design process involves all of these steps as the product evolves from an idea to a concept to a prototype to a product and marketing strategy. Indeed, as the product evolves many steps are repeated and information is updated. The final result is much more iterative than sequential.

Although the new product process often does not proceed in the orderly flow of Figure 13.16, it is important to consider all the issues raised in the design process. In this chapter we provide some cases to demonstrate the critical aspects of that process. In each case the sequence and emphasis in the design process varies. We want to give you a feeling for the range of issues and methods of attacking them. The laundry detergent case is the most detailed and follows most closely the design process. The medical instrument—"Renaissance Spirometry System"—concentrates on quality and the voice of the customer. The Home Word Processing case is described in less detail but provides examples of the key steps in the design effort and new product strategy. The Industrial CAD/CAM and the HMO cases abstract selected aspects of the process that emphasize the differences and commonalities between services, industrial products, consumer durables, and packaged goods.

CONSUMER PACKAGED GOODS CASE—LAUNDRY DETERGENT

This case describes a hypothetical new laundry detergent, but the data are drawn from a variety of real projects and simplified to illustrate basic points. Thus, when reading this example try to divorce yourself from any specific knowledge you now have of the laundry market—suppose that the information provided is complete rather than a simplification.

Our case concerns a fictitious firm, "Consumer Laboratories, Inc." (CLI). CLI is a major packaged-good manufacturer with previous successes in facial soaps, shampoos, toothpaste, and antacids. CLI uses a proactive strategy based on being first in a market with a major innovation based on both an improved physical product and superior psychological positioning. R&D and marketing have worked closely in designing successful products in the past. At the time of this case, they were investigating a number of potential markets, one of which was the laundry cleaning market.

Market Definition

CLI began with a market profile analysis based on published data. They determined that the global market was large (more than $2 billion annually) and showed a stable growth of 10 percent per year. The entry cost was high (about $40 million), but a moderate share of 2 percent could return this investment in a few years. The $40 million annual sales implied by a 2 percent share exceeded CLI's minimum sales volume criteria of $15 million. The potential rate of return on the investment at this level of sales and expected margins was viewed as good. CLI had experience in related markets and already had a good distribution system for household laundry products in the major European, North American, and Far East markets. The market was highly competitive, but a recent technological breakthrough in CLI's research and development laboratory (tight-packed, homogenized particles) promised a competitive edge in the industry. The market showed high risk because four of the last five new products in the industry were failures, but consumers appeared responsive to a superior quality product with good positioning advantages versus competition. The current number two product was introduced in the last three years and was successful based on a superior cleaning appeal. Those working in the R&D laboratory thought they could modify the product, at an increased cost, to make it safer or stronger, depending on the needed positioning. A new innovation in packaging promised the potential for an environmentally responsible container (recycled paper and decomposable seal). Based on these results, CLI considered the household laundry cleaning market worth further investigation.

Household floor cleaners and hair color markets also were considered, but they were not deemed as desirable in terms of vulnerability, profitability, and match to the company's R&D and marketing capabilities. (The hair color market was CLI's second choice and was identified as the market to consider once the design of a new laundry cleaning product was underway.) CLI's policy was to investigate a major new market each year with a goal of having one successful new product each year. They used a development program that resulted in a new product three to four years after initiation at an average cost of $5 to $6 million. At any given time, four or more new products would be in different phases of design, testing, and introduction.

CLI does not believe in generating ideas until the strategic market opportunity is known. CLI thus began its design effort by performing a hierarchical market definition study to select a specific target market. They wanted to be sure they selected a segment of the market where the greatest opportunity existed. CLI conducted a market research study based on telephone interviews to determine the structure of consideration sets and first-choice/second-choice preferences. Based on this data they established the hierarchical definition shown in Figure 14.1. The first branching was additives versus detergents. These were further divided into liquid versus powder for detergents, and bleach versus softener versus presoaks for additives. Powder detergents were subdivided into hot water and cold water washing products in this analysis.

Opportunity Identification

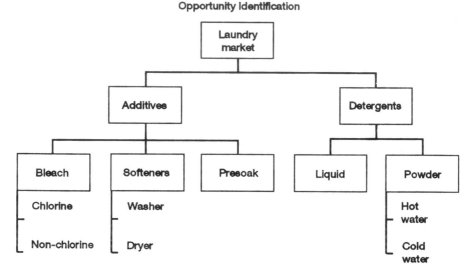

Figure 14.1 Hypothetical Hierarchical Market Definition for Home Laundry Cleaning Products

CLI selected the hot water powder market because it had greater potential. The expected share was highest in this market and a typical new product share was 2.4 percent of the total market or 8 percent of the powdered, hot water detergent market. The new-product team felt no product was positioned in this market as strong yet safe for delicate fabrics, and thus an opportunity existed. Demographically, this market contained a typical cross section of households in the USA, Canada and Europe. In Japan CLI would need a joint venture to compete, so CLI decided to concentrate initially on North America and Europe in its marketing. This represented the biggest part of the detergent market and sales were growing at 9% per year.

Idea Generation

With the target market clearly defined, creative groups were conducted to find innovative product concepts. The groups consisted of marketing, R&D, marketing research, engineering, and production personnel from within the company. Two advertising agency people (the account executive and the creative director), a retailer, and four consumers (representing major global markets) were included in the group.

In support of the idea generation effort, focus groups were conducted and perceptual maps of the existing products were developed from market research studies. Focus groups in Paris, London, Chicago, and New York suggested that "strong" detergents really "get the dirt out," but can "harm synthetic clothes." Complaints were raised about hard-to-handle boxes that often get spilled and about environmental concerns. An important output of the groups was a condensed list of 21 attributes in the consumers' semantics such as "get out dirt," "good for greasy oil," "won't harm synthetics," "safe for lingerie," and "economical."

Based on the focus groups, a questionnaire was developed to measure each laundry detergent in a consumer's evoked set on semantic differential scales which were constructed to measure the 21 attributes (see Figure 14.2 for typical rating questions). The questionnaire was administered to 185 consumers. Figure 14.3 reports the results of the consideration-set measurement indicating that the average number of considered products is small. A sizable introduction campaign may be needed to get consumers to consider the new product.

The perceptual dimensions and market structure were identified with factor analysis of consumer ratings of the considered products. Based on the scree and eigenvalue rules (Figure 14.4) backed by interpretability, two factors were selected. They were labeled "effectiveness" and "mildness" based on the factor loadings in Figure 14.4. Factor scores were then computed for each product and their averages were plotted in Figure 14.5.

Note that the perceptual map indicates a definite gap in this market in

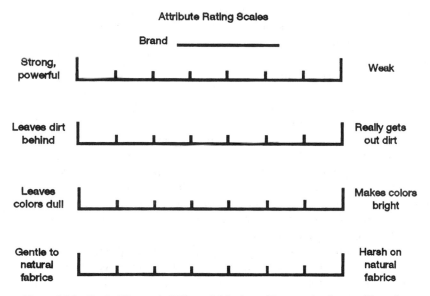

Figure 14.2   Typical Semantic Differential Scales to Measure Attributes of Laundry Detergents

Makeup of Consideration Sets

Size of Consideration Set (Number of Brands in the Consideration Set)		Brand	Number of People	Percent
Brands	People	Cheer	111	60.0
1	10	Tide	129	69.7
2	28	Bold	104	56.2
3	43	Oxydol	79	42.7
4	49	Fab	42	22.7
5	32	Duz	63	34.1
6	12	All (Powder)	40	22.0
7	5	Ajax	39	21.0
8+	6	Others	50	27.0

Figure 14.3 Hypothetical Consideration Sets for Laundry Powders

the upper-right quadrant. To evaluate this positioning opportunity, CLI ran a preference regression to determine the relative importances of the two dimensions. They were .538 for efficacy and .462 for mildness, indicating that movement along both dimensions is important, but with a slight emphasis on effectiveness (see vector in Figure 14.5).

With the background information from the focus groups and the perceptual and preference maps, the creative group set to work. One effort was begun to create a product concept that would position well on effectiveness and mildness. R&D felt they could combine the ingredients used in softening additives within a powder detergent. The new "tightly packed" particles technology would hold the softening ingredients in a matrix of soap and softeners. Marketing felt they could communicate effectively such a product in advertising which portrayed both softness and brighteners. A concept statement was created to represent the Core Benefit Proposition of "a very effective, yet mild laundry powder." A second concept was created to stretch current perceptions. Very round and hard particles were to be used to produce a "pourable powder." It would be packaged like a liquid detergent, but would be powder. The idea was to give the convenience of a liquid to those who are powder users. Other concepts were suggested, but these two were carried to the design evaluation phase. In both concepts a recycled paper container with a milk carton seal was envisioned as a way of adding environmental appeal to the product. Although "environmental responsibility" was not yet a perceptual dimension in the market, designers felt it would be an attractive feature that could be added at low cost, and it was thought that this attribute would become more important in the future.

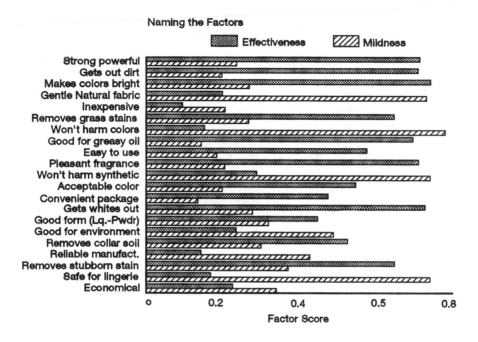

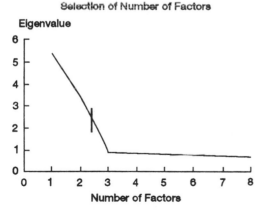

Figure 14.4   Hypothetical Factor Analysis for Laundry Detergents

Concept Evaluation and Refinement

A new survey was conducted to see how the new concepts were positioned. Figure 14.6 shows the results. CLI-1 was the new "gentle and effective" product and did fall in the gap as desired. The pourable powder was

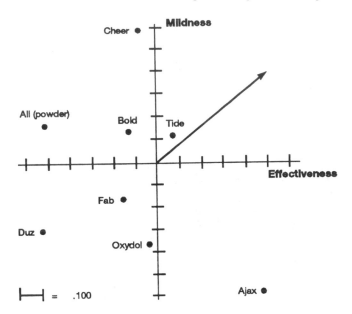

Figure 14.5　Hypothetical Perceptual Map for Selected Laundry Powders

perceived as effective, but was not in the best position. Intent to try was good for CLI-1 (40% definite, 20% probable) and low for CLI-2 (10% definite, 20% probable). Preference data indicated a 42% share of preference for CLI-1 if all consumers were aware and 100% distribution were attained. Definitely, an encouraging result!

Predictions of preference for the other brands indicated that CLI would draw significant share from Cheer and thus could expect a major competitive reaction from Cheer's manufacturer, Procter and Gamble—a dominant packaged-goods firm. In order to preempt a counter product like "new stronger Cheer," CLI decided to try to increase the positioning on effectiveness without a loss in mildness (see Figure 14.6). They thought a stronger claim and improved product for Cheer could not move it very far on the effectiveness dimension. If CLI-3 were able to obtain the improved positioning, it would be less vulnerable to defensive competitive actions. If CLI-3 could fulfill its claims by performance, a major opportunity would be present. Attention then turned to the physical product.

Product Fulfillment and Quality

R&D set out to create the new product. After using the consumer needs (e.g., Figure 14.2) to develop a House of Quality, they were able to link

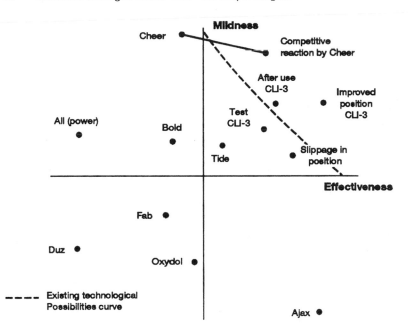

Figure 14.6 Hypothetical Perceptual Map for Alternative Scenarios

engineering capabilities to potential new concepts. Based on the House of Quality they felt they could attain the positioning relative to effectiveness, but the laboratory was uncertain as to the mildness. The engineering tradeoffs between mildness and effectiveness which existed are shown by the dashed line in Figure 14.6. Existing technologies would allow improvement in effectiveness, but only with a loss in mildness. R&D felt, however, that they could advance the state of the art and shift the technology curve upward and to the right if they had six months and $500,000. The new improved position is shown in Figure 14.6.

Marketing felt that stronger claims for effectiveness may reduce perceived mildness (see "slippage in position" in Figure 14.6). They felt that consumers would be skeptical of a product that claimed to be both effective and mild.

The preferences for the improved or slippage products were simulated to assess the relative impacts. The weaker position would yield a 34% share of preference—still strong—and the stronger position would yield a 45% share. Although even with slippage the product is not bad, efforts to achieve the refined positioning were worthwhile.

CLI invested the six months and $500,000. In an integrated effort R&D developed new capabilities and engineering turned these capabilities into a prototype product that was ready to be tested by home placement. Careful experimental design established that the chemical formulation of the product was robust in the sense that it would work well in a variety of home environments and could be manufactured on current machines with minor modifications. New packaging machines were designed for the folding seal and the lower tensile strength of recycled paper. The seals were customer tested to be sure they were easy to open and sealed effectively.

With the prototype ready, marketing established a placement program to evaluate consumer reaction. For example, consumers rated the product on the target consumer needs after they used it in their own home; preference and repurchase intent were also measured. At the conclusion of the home interview, a conjoint study was done to provide information for product improvement. The features varied in the conjoint design were based on the relationships identified by both marketing and engineering.

Based on the home-use ratings the improved product slipped on perceived effectiveness but it did fulfill the mildness claims (see "After use CLI-3" in Figure 14.6). Even though lab tests showed it met the technical effectiveness requirements, consumers did not perceive this. Fortunately, the perceived effectiveness could be improved with the results of the conjoint analysis.

In the conjoint analysis, consumers were shown physical formulations (actual products) that varied by the color of the basic powder, the texture of the basic powder, and whether colored particles were added. The dependent variable was perceived effectiveness. In addition, conjoint analyses were run for mildness to ensure that there would not be slippage along that dimension if features were added to improve effectiveness. The results are shown in Table 14.1.

The conjoint analyses indicated that a coarse, white powder with added blue particles would best enhance perceived effectiveness, but the coarseness of the powder would cause slippage on mildness. Furthermore, a coarse texture adds little to effectiveness, but a fine texture greatly enhances mildness. The white color also enhances mildness, whereas the added particles have only a small negative impact on mildness.

Based on the conjoint analyses, a very fine, white powder with added blue particles was selected as the mix most consistent with a "very effective, yet mild" CBP. This analysis indicated that with the new color and particles, the perceived effectiveness could be raised to the level measured in the lab. The "improved positioning" shown in Figure 14.6 could be achieved. It was also found in the postuse interview the resealable spout was liked, but the product would be further improved if a handle could be attached. Those working on engineering and manufacturing thought they could add a fold out paper handle with a minimum of cost and manufacturing complexity.

TABLE 14.1   Conjoint Analysis to Select Physical Features to Communicate Positioning

Color	Part-Worth	Texture	Effectiveness Part-Worth	Particles	Part-Worth
Green	.5	Coarse	.15	Added blue particles	.8
Blue	.5	Fine	.05	One color	
White	.7				.2

Color	Part-Worth	Texture	Mildness Part-Worth	Particles	Part-Worth
Green	.3	Coarse	.1	Added blue particles	.05
Blue	.4	Fine	.9	One color	
White	.8				.10

With the assurance that the concept was good and the physical product fulfilled it, attention turned to estimating the purchase potential.

Forecasts and Evaluations

In concept and product tests, trial and repeat were measured directly. A logit model was estimated based on the test product so that the alternative positionings could be evaluated in terms of trial and repeat probabilities.

Table 14.2 gives the results for the test product—note that the observed trial (41%) was close to the predicted preference share (45%). The predicted share of 8.3% of powdered, hot water detergent market ($500 million total sales) in North America and Europe would yield a sales volume of $41.5 million for the new brand—enough for CLI to take the product to test market. Financial projections revealed a good rate of return on the investment of $40 million for development and introduction.

TABLE 14.2   Evaluation of Purchase Potential

Trial if aware and available, T	41%
Expected long-run awareness, a_w	75
Expected distribution, a_v	80
$a_v \cdot a_w \cdot T = 24.6\%$ cumulative trial	
Repeat, R_{11}	70.8
Return from competitive brands, R_{EI}	14.8
$R = R_{EI}/(1 + R_{EI} - R_{11}) = 33.6\%$ cumulative repeat	
Share potential = (24.6%)· (33.6%) = 8.3%	

Although the opportunity was exciting, there were risks. How low would the share be if Cheer retaliated? What gains will occur if further product engineering could achieve an improved perceptual positioning which would hold up under home usage tests? The logit model was used to evaluate these scenarios. See Table 14.3. Perceived improvement in effectiveness would increase share to 9.8 percent. Competitive reaction by Cheer would seriously erode the share to 5.8%. But if the "after use" positioning were improved, share would be predicted to be 8.4% even with competitive retaliation. These simulations indicated an exciting opportunity with a manageable competitive situation.

Marketing Mix

Before proceeding to test, the product advertising and promotion strategies were specified. Table 14.4 shows CLI's view of how the marketing mix elements affect sales and market share. Different levels of these variables were simulated to find a good initial specification of the marketing mix.

For example, purchase potential for scenario 3 was based on advertising expenditures of $14 million to produce the 75% awareness estimated in Table 14.2. If awareness could be increased to 90 percent, the share would increase to 10.1 percent, giving a net volume increase of $8.5 million, that is, $(0.101 - 0.084) \times (\$500$ million$)$. Thus, if CLI could attain the additional awareness and production for less than $8.5 million, it would be worth the investment. CLI's advertising agency felt the additional awareness would cost $4 million. Based on this figure and an analysis of production costs, the higher level of advertising was recommended.

Sampling levels were evaluated. For example, suppose we sample 40 percent of the USA households and 87.5 percent of those who receive samples, try the sample. Suppose that repeat (R) is reduced from 35 percent to 30 percent for those sampled. Then the long-run share is 14.4 percent, as computed in Table 14.5. (Note that we use scenario 3 and the increased advertising.) CLI must then weigh this increased revenue ($21.5 million = $[.144 - .101] \cdot [\$500$ million$]$) against (1) the added costs of producing and distributing the sample and (2) the added production costs. If the 40 million

TABLE 14.3 Simulation of Alternative Scenarios

Scenarios	Cumulative Trial	Cumulative Repeat	Forecast Sales
Improved perceived effectiveness	24.6%	40%	9.8%
Competitive reaction by Cheer	23.2	25	5.8
Competitive reaction with improved perceived effect	24.0	35	8.4

TABLE 14.4   CLI's View of the Primary Effects of Marketing Tactics on Sales

Advertising	Causes awareness (consideration), a_w; communicates CBP to encourage trial, T; supports repeat, R, and frequency of use.
Pricing	Influences perception of value hence leads to trial, T; affects long-run value and satisfaction, R. Influenced by competitive environment.
Couponing	Effective price discount to "buy" trial, T; may reduce repeat, R, if product perceived as "cheap."
Sampling	Makes consumers aware of product, a_w; higher chance of trial, T; may reduce repeat, R, if consumers attribute trial to "free."
Distribution	Primary effect is availability, a_v; incentives to trade encourage and end-aisle displays, etc. to enhance trial, T; affects repeat, R.

households were to receive the sample at a delivery cost of 30¢ per sample, it would be profitable to sample if the added production costs were less than $9.5 million. That is, it would be profitable to sample if the increased revenue from sampling ($21.5 million) exceeded sampling delivery ($12 million) and production costs ($9.5 million).

The outcome of a series of such simulations coupled with marketing judgment was the marketing mix of $18 million for advertising in the first year, $12 million for samples, and $10 million in trade promotion.

The brand name was selected to represent the CBP. CLI rejected "Whisper" because "Whisper" implied only mildness and may not fit with the effectiveness appeals. Similarly, "Maxi-clean" missed the mildness appeal. Names like Riptide, Cleanall, Scrubsuds, Ebbtide, Softsilk, and Safewash all miss one part of the CBP. On the other hand, Gentle Power, Soft Strength, and Satinscrub all use the CBP. "Satinbright" was selected for the initial testing.

The advertising strategy was implemented in three copy themes. One stressed the personal recommendation of the product by a neighbor, another used a "scientific" demonstration to show how Satinbright brightened the colors of delicate fabrics but did not harm the fabrics; and the third used graphics to illustrate how the "tight-packing" technology combines "clean-

TABLE 14.5   Computation of the Effects of Sampling

Sampled Consumers ($s = 0.40$)		Unsampled Consumers ($1 - s = .60$)	
		Advanced awareness, a_w	.90
Expected distribution, a_v	.80	Expected distribution, a_v	.80
Try the sample, U_s	.875	Expected trial, T	.40
Repeat if sampled, R_s	.30	Repeat if try, R	.35
$s\, a_v\, U_s\, R_s = 0.084$		$(1 - s)\, a_w\, a_v\, T\, R = .060$	
	Long-run share = 8.4% + 6.0% = 14.4%		

ing" and "protection" particles. These three themes were to be considered as alternatives in the subsequent testing of the product.

The outcome of the design process was

- Target market definition of the hot water, powder detergents
- CBP of an "effective but mild laundry detergent"
- Positioning of more effective than Cheer and milder than Ajax
- Physical product of a very fine, white powder containing softeners and blue particles in a recycled paper package with a handle and resealable spout
- High investment in advertising, sampling, and promotion strategy ($40 million)
- Three advertising themes and a brand name for further testing

Of course the product still needs to be tested further before it can be introduced to the market and a production and distribution plan must be developed. We begin to address these issues in the next chapter where we consider the post design phases of the new-product development process—testing and launch.

PURITAN-BENNETT'S RENAISSANCE SPIROMETRY SYSTEM[1]

The CLI laundry detergent case illustrates how information on consumers helps to define the opportunity, evaluate the opportunity, position the new product vis-à-vis competition, select features to reinforce that position, and set the initial levels of marketing activities. In this case we illustrate how information on customers helps the new-product team design the physical product to meet customer needs. The specific case is the design of a new spirometry system.

Spirometry

Spirometry is a simple medical test that requires a patient to inhale and then exhale as hard, as fast, and as long as possible in one long breath. The spirometer measures lung capacity—the total volume of air in the lungs as well as the amount that can be exhaled in the first second. Some spirometers

---

[1] This vignette is adapted from John R. Hauser (1992), "Puritan-Bennett—the Renaissance Spirometry System: Listening to the Voice of the Customer," MIT Working Paper, Cambridge, Massachusetts, forthcoming Sloan Management Review 1993.

also measure inhaling ability. Measurements are compared to norms for age, height, sex, and so on, and, in the case of prescribed treatment, measurements are compared before and after treatment ("pre/post" measurements).

Spirometry is an important diagnostic tool for a wide variety of illnesses. For example, spirometry is recommended by the National Institute of Health (NIH) as the test to diagnose and follow asthma. Hospitals routinely use spirometry before surgery so that surgeons and anesthesiologists are aware of any lung function impairment before a patient is operated on. General practitioners use spirometers to fine-tune treatments by adjusting the dosage of medication or by changing it entirely. Some insurance companies now require spirometry screening—a requirement that is a new source of revenue for many physicians.

The original spirometers required patients to exhale into a tube which was connected to the bottom of a container. Lung capacity is measured by the amount of volume that is displaced by the exhaled air. Such volume-displacement spirometers are very accurate but are quite large and expensive. Furthermore, to avoid contamination with the expired air, volume-displacement spirometers must be cleaned often.

In 1974 flow spirometers were introduced to address some of the issues with volume-displacement spirometers. In a flow spirometer, the patient exhales into a tube, called a pneumotach. A sensor at the end of the tube measures the pressure and a microprocessor built into the spirometer computes the volume of air that was exhaled. By 1988, most clinics and physicians had adopted the flow devices.

Puritan Bennett

Puritan Bennett's Boston Division was a major player in the spirometry-system market. Their PB900A (Figure 14.7) had earned a 15% market share in 1988. The PB900A was a desktop device with an integrated printer (4¼-inch tape) and a microprocessor capable of pre/post comparisons. A unique feature was a disposable pneumotach that made the spirometer more sanitary and eliminated the need for frequent cleaning and service. It was sold for approximately $4,500.

Competitive Attack

However, in 1989 a major competitor, Welch Allyn introduced a new product, PneumoCheck, at a price less than half that of the PB900A—$1,995 (Figure 14.8). As a result, Puritan Bennett's share slipped to 11% in 1989 and 7% in 1990. Furthermore, because spirometry was the most important prod-

PB900A
DIAGNOSTIC SPIROMETER

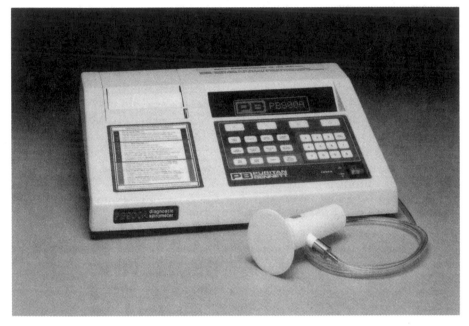

Description

The PB900A Diagnostic Spirometer is the ideal instrument for simple, but complete, screening spirometry. It combines all the necessary pulmonary criteria with flexible programming to meet the specific needs of physician's offices, hospital labs and industrial clinics.

A large fluorescent display, silent thermal printer and modern touch panel keyboard are incorporated into a single compact instrument to make the PB900A today's state-of-the-art automated spirometer.

Like all Puritan-Bennett spirometers, the PB900A Diagnostic Spirometer complies with all published spirometry standards.

Features

* Two disposable pneumotachs eliminate cleaning and minimize the risk of cross-infection for both patients and staff
   — The FS200 is used for expiratory testing only (FVC, MVV, SVC)
   — The BD250 can be used for expiratory and inspiratory testing (FVC, FVL, MVV, SVC)
* Pre- and post-bronchodilator comparisons
* Large "incentigraph" display of patient's effort
* Suggested interpretation of test results
* RS232C serial port
* Unprecedented 5-Year Warranty Program

Figure 14.7   PBs Spirometer

PneumoCheck™
SPEED, ACCURACY, PORTABILITY AND ECONOMY IN A SINGLE UNIT.

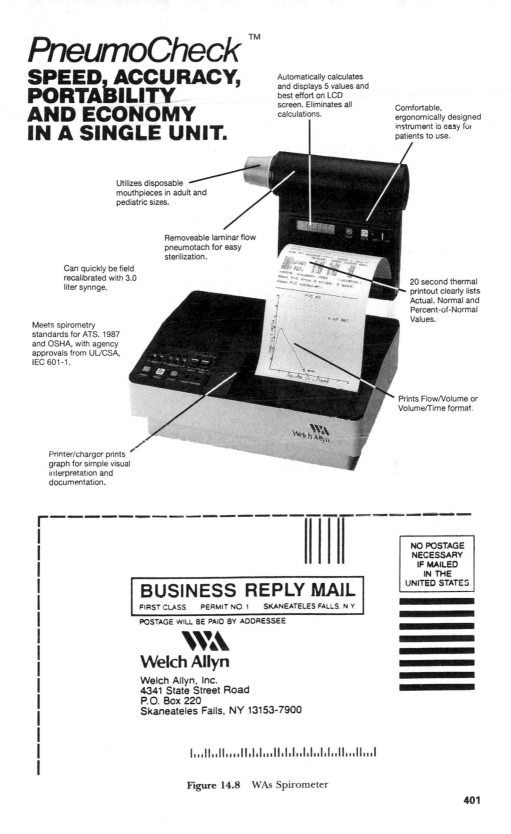

Automatically calculates and displays 5 values and best effort on LCD screen. Eliminates all calculations.

Comfortable, ergonomically designed instrument is easy for patients to use.

Utilizes disposable mouthpieces in adult and pediatric sizes.

Removeable laminar flow pneumotach for easy sterilization.

Can quickly be field recalibrated with 3.0 liter synnge.

20 second thermal printout clearly lists Actual. Normal and Percent-of-Normal Values.

Meets spirometry standards for ATS. 1987 and OSHA, with agency approvals from UL/CSA, IEC 601-1.

Prints Flow/Volume or Volume/Time format.

Printer/charger prints graph for simple visual interpretation and documentation.

Figure 14.8 WAs Spirometer

uct marketed by the Boston office, the Boston office had to respond effectively in order to survive.

Welch Allyn (WA) was a formidable competitor indeed. Although they were new to spirometry, they were well known in the medical-equipment market, had a formidable distribution system, and had the projected staying power to make a commitment to the spirometry market. Furthermore, the WA price of $1,995 meant that WA would penetrate the fastest growing portion of the spirometry market, general practitioners (GPs), a portion of the market that PB had found difficult to attract. Indeed, WAs slogan of "You told us, 'Eliminate the extras,'" placed over a picture of bells and whistles suggested that WA provided a spirometer that fulfilled the basic spirometry functions in a low-cost product.

Response Options

PBs Boston office considered several options.

1. *Provide world-class service to existing customers.* While this option is attractive, PBs sales reps were already calling on 80% of the hospitals and because PB had a well-established distribution system for physicians who did extensive spirometry testing, PB could not grow without penetrating the GP market.
2. *Reduce costs and compete on price.* A concerted effort by R&D could bring down the cost somewhat; however, the best estimates of the Operation's Manager were that, with the present design, a concerted effort would simply hold the line against inflation. It would not achieve the required 60% cost reduction.
3. *Increase marketing activity to maintain sales.* Emergency changes in product marketing, such as the 5-year warranty that was introduced in 1989, could maintain sales, but they were unlikely to reverse the decline in share nor were they likely to achieve the necessary growth in the market.
4. *Develop a new spirometry system to "leap-frog" competition.* This appeared to be the only viable option. But it would require a *dramatic* redesign to deliver the same or improved features (relative to the PB900A) at a cost that was 60% less. Not only that, the window of opportunity was about a year. If the project dragged on, Welch Allyn would secure the market.

Developing the House of Quality

PB engineers had a deep understanding of spirometry, perhaps the best on the market, but to succeed in such a dramatic redesign engineering had to work closely with all the functional areas in the Boston office. Thus, they began by forming an interfunctional product-development team drawn from marketing, customer service, sales, engineering, R&D, manufacturing, and management. This team would stay together throughout the development of a new spirometer and would be involved in all market research, all technical design, and all introductory plans. In this way engineering and R&D personnel would experience first-hand the expressed needs of the customer; marketing, customer service, and sales would understand the technology behind the product, how that technology was used, and what improvements were likely to be feasible in the future; and the product would be designed for cost-effective manufacture and shipping. Any strategic decisions would be made with full knowledge of the customer and the technology and with the support of the team.

Voice of the Customer.   The next step was to build the House of Quality. With the help of Applied Marketing Sciences, Inc., a firm specializing in the voice of the customer, PB collected the data for the voice of the customer. Specifically, they began with focus groups and telephone surveys probing for customer experiences. These interviews were transcribed and analyzed to develop a hierarchical list of customer needs. Table 14.6 lists the secondary needs.

In order to make tradeoffs in the design of a spirometry system, PB determined the priorities that customers assign to each of the 25 customer needs. For example, "product is affordable" is extremely important (100 points) while "effective data handling" is less important for spirometry (48

TABLE 14.6 Customer Needs, Spirometry

• Product is affordable	• Fast to use
• Easy to operate	• Easy to hold
• Easy to clean	• Right size for patient
• Convenient-sized output	• Easy to set up the first time
• Sanitary	• Easy to calibrate
• Quick service response	• Availability machine/ supplies
• Provides accurate readings	• Good training/education
• Eliminates technician variability	• Sleek appearance
• Good printout quality	• Good printer quality
• Reliability	• Low cost of repairs/service
• Diagnostic information meets needs	• Portability
• Easy-to-interpret diagnostic information	• Effective data storage/ retrieval
	• Environmentally safe

points). (These are the importances for one segment of the spirometry market. PB obtained importances for each of the segments in which PB planned to compete.)

Naturally, the priorities that PB assigns to the customer needs depend upon customer priorities, the costs and feasibility of fulfilling the customer needs, and the grades that customers assign to their existing spirometry systems. For example, affordability, accurate readings, and ease of operation are extremely important—a new spirometry system must satisfy these needs. Customers give poor grades (relative to competition) to the PB900A on "good printout quality."[2]

Thus, printout quality also represents an opportunity for improvement.

Engineering Targets.   PB next specified the candidate design characteristics. For example, the words "printout quality" express the customer's concept, but to build a spirometer, these words must be translated into an engineer's vocabulary. In this case, engineering targets are specified in terms of printer resolution, fade resistance, and paper-feed failure rate. Notice that the engineering design attributes are generic descriptions of the spirometry system. They are not solutions such as a 4¼-inch thermal printer or a built-in, letter-quality, 8½- × 11-inch printer. Such solutions may be part of the final design that the team develops, but if such solutions are listed in the first House of Quality, they constrain the range of possible solutions. For example, PB might consider having no printer at all but making it easy for the customer to printout spirometry results on another printer that the customer already has in the office. This more creative solution may not have been identified if the technical problem was defined initially as a choice between a 4¼-inch thermal printer and an 8½- x 11-inch letter-quality printer.

In total, PB specified 56 engineering design attributes as a means to fulfill the twenty-five customer needs. These design attributes are listed at the top of the House of Quality in Figure 14.9. The body of the House indicates which design attributes fulfill which customer needs. For example, printer resolution has a strong relationship to printout quality. Finally, the bottom of the House provides measures of how PB and each competitor performs with respect to the design attributes. Also at the bottom of the House is a measure of "absolute technical importance" which is derived from the importances and the customer-need-design-attribute relationships.

The House of Quality was completed in October 1990. It suggested a number of areas of investigation and provided a means to evaluate potential solutions. Throughout the process, whenever a new design idea or a new

---

[2] The PB900A was given a grade of 75 (out of 100), whereas competitors such as Spirometrics were given better grades. Good printout quality is very important (95 out of 100).

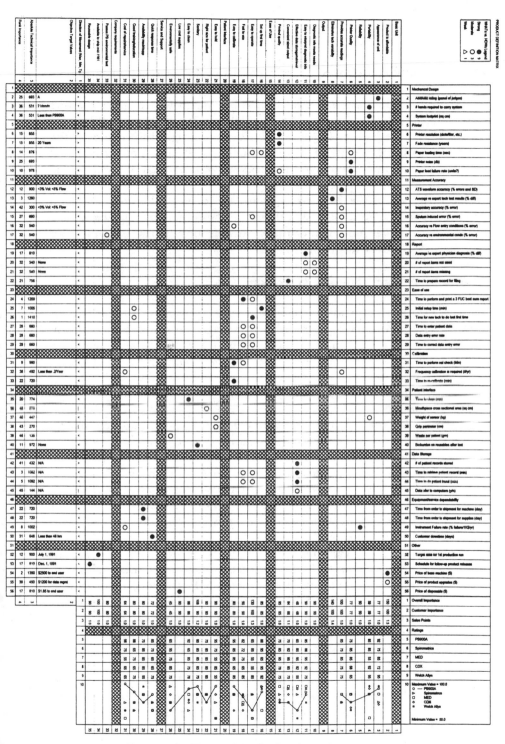

Figure 14.9 House of Quality Developed for Puritan-Bennett

feature was considered, it was "tested" against customer reaction as embodied in the House of Quality. Whenever there were any debates, these debates were resolved by the customer's voice. It is important to recognize that the House of Quality did not substitute for the skill and creativity of the PB design team. However, the House of Quality did provide the right information at the right time. Customer needs suggested potential solutions. The structure of the needs and the importances of the needs suggested which of the potential solutions to develop.

With the aid of the House of Quality, the product-development team developed candidate designs, tested them with customers by showing specifications, then a visual model, and finally working prototypes. By September 1991, the new product was ready.

The Renaissance Spirometry System

The new product, called the Renaissance Spirometry System is illustrated in Figure 14.10. A key design breakthrough was the modular design. Each customer segment could use the Renaissance system to best meet their needs. Larger clinics could place it on a desk or laboratory table; clinics or general practitioners, for whom space was a premium, could attach it to the wall or carry it in their pockets. The spirometer could even fit in a briefcase for visits to patients.

In particular, the Renaissance system consists of a 5- × 7- × 2-inch spirometer that can be run from either an AC adapter or a rechargeable battery. It attaches to a Base Station for recharging the battery and for downloading patient information to a separate printer. (Puritan-Bennett offers brand name printers as options, but the spirometry system also works with most existing office printers.) Data is stored on removable Memory Cards to provide almost unlimited data storage, the ability to do pre/post analyses, and the ability to share data across spirometers.

Because the user can buy only modules as they are needed, an occasional-screening system (spirometer and base station) is priced at $1,590, $405 below Welch-Allyn, but with more functions. However, if the customer wants to enhance the PB system to increase productivity for busy routine testing in three or more examination rooms, the customer can purchase the three spirometers, one base station, two charging stations, two memory cards, and a Canon Bubblejet printer for a total cost of $4,088.

Referring back to Table 14.6, we can see how each of the customer needs are met by the Renaissance system. For example, the modular prices give "affordability" for each segment. "Good printout quality" is achieved by using the customer's existing printers (or reselling a Canon or Citizen printer). "Easy to hold" is achieved with the small spirometer and the PB

The New Age of Spirometry...

The Renaissance™ System

Figure 14.10a   The Renaissance System

RENAISSANCE™

SPIROMETRY SYSTEM

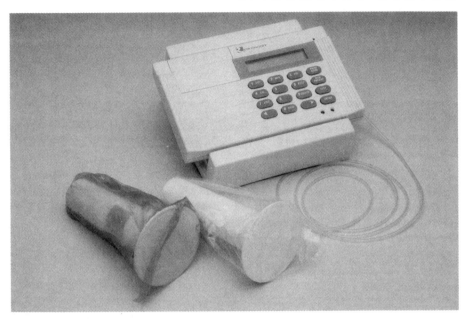

Description

The Renaissance Spirometry System is the simply sophisticated answer to pulmonary function testing. The system features a hand-held spirometer (PB100), offering true portability.

The patient data memory card (PB130) and the rechargeable batteries allow testing of multiple patients away from the office or the pulmonary laboratory.

The base station (PB110) is used for downloading patient information to a choice of two printers available from Puritan-Bennett or to most IBM or Epson-compatible printers. The RS232C port provides the option of sending data to a computer.

A file-size report includes test results compared to a choice of three adult and two pediatric predicted normal values, as well as results from pre- and post-medication testing.

A convenient charging station (PB120) and a wall mount bracket are also available.

The Renaissance spirometer has been validated by an independent laboratory to comply with the 1987 ATS Standards for Spirometry*.

*Independent validation of the American Thoracic Society (ATS) recommendations performed by Robert Crapo, M.D., LDS Hospital, Salt Lake City, Utah. Copy of validation results available from Puritan-Bennett upon request.

Features

- Two disposable pneumotachs eliminate cleaning and minimize the risk of cross-infection for both patients and staff
  - The FS200 is used for expiratory testing only (FVC, MVV)
  - The BD250 is used for expiratory and inspiratory testing (FVC, MVV, FVL)
- Choice of synergistic components for a custom system design
- Rechargeable batteries and hand-held design for true portability
- Integrated miniature memory card allows multiple patient storage
- Audio and visual effort incentive
- Built-in quality assurance program
- 8½" × 11" printout
- Unique 5-year warranty/exchange program

PB PURITAN BENNETT

Figure 14.10b   The Renaissance™ Spirometry System

pneumotachs. The system is clearly "portable," especially with the patient data cards. These cards also deliver "effective data storage and retrieval." The five-year warranty/exchange program, made easier to provide and service by the modular design, provides a "low cost of repair and service" (actually no cost[3]) that signals high "reliability." In the design, the new-product team chose each feature based on the needs expressed in Table 14.6.

Furthermore, the modularity of the Renaissance system makes it easy for future R&D efforts to improve the system with respect to customer needs. ("Reusable design" was one of Puritan-Bennett's company requirements in the House of Quality.) As new printers become popular, PB can add compatibility. Improved software can add new functions, new pneumotach technology can be introduced without major changes in the spirometer, new modules can be designed to add functions or improve existing functions, etc. With careful management and creative engineering solutions Puritan-Bennett can gain market share, enhance its profits and consolidate its position in the market.

On December 12, 1991, the FDA approved the Renaissance system and PB began shipping to customers. Through the next few months they continued to ship all of their production capacity. (The order rate was well above capacity.) Projections of this sales rate suggested a fivefold increase in sales above 1991 levels—in part because PB was now penetrating successfully the general practitioner market.

Summary

This case illustrates how the House of Quality and input on customer needs is used by an interfunctional team to develop a new product. In this case, PB combined their knowledge of the market with their expertise in spirometry to develop a new concept and to implement that concept with state-of-the-art technology. The result was the survival of the Boston division and a major increase in sales and profitability.

CONSUMER DURABLES—HOME WORD PROCESSOR[4]

The Puritan-Bennett case illustrated how the voice of the customer and the House of Quality are used to redesign a product to deliver superior customer

[3] The customer incurs no out-of-pocket cost. PB dispatches a new unit on the same day and pays all shipping costs to and from the customer. The customer need only place the old unit in the box in which the new unit was shipped, affix an enclosed label, and call. PB arranges for pick-up. In other words, customer service programs were also based on the customer needs listed in Table 14.6.

[4] This case adapts and extends material from Urban and Star (1990), pp. 484–503.

benefits at a lower price. We now illustrate how market segmentation and market growth models are used to identify opportunities. To complete the case we indicate how perceptual maps were used to position the product in the market place.

Masamoto Corporation

Masamoto Corporation is a large Japanese manufacturer of telecommunications equipment, computers, consumer electronics products, and office equipment. In 1985, Masamoto introduced three electronic daisy-wheel typewriters ranging from a $150 basic model to a $475 top-of-the-line model with lift-off correction, a 24-character display, and an optional five-page memory. The typewriters were sold through department stores, appliance and electronics "superstores," and typewriter dealers. Even though the line was considered state-of-the-art and was doing well in the market place (15% share), Masamoto sought new products to continue its corporate growth and profitability.

Typewriters, Personal Computers, or Word Processors?

Through its typewriter line, Masamoto has established experience and competency in home word processing, that is, the means by which home users produce printer documents, letters, and reports. However, to build upon this competency in the channel of distribution, in the knowledge of consumer needs, and the technology, Masamoto had to select one of the three emerging (or declining) technologies: typewriters, personal computers, or home word processors.

Typewriters. In 1985 typewriter sales, which had been relatively flat at about 3 million units per year, began to decline. Traditionally the market had been stable being driven by replacement sales (every seven to ten years) and lifestyle change sales such as when students entered high school or college. However, around 1985 personal computers (PCs) were being priced for home use and some consumers were adopting them for word processing. Indeed, 95% of the home-use PC owners cited word processing as one of the functions for which they used their PC. (The next largest were spreadsheets at 40% and education at 20%.) Market research indicated that 85% of the current typewriter owners would consider a PC or other device when it was necessary to replace their typewriter. Clearly, Masamoto had to consider new products outside the typewriter market.

Personal Computers.   In 1985 PCs had just begun to enter the home market, however, with decreased prices and increased functionality driven by new technology, increased competition, and experience curves it was likely that the market would grow rapidly. For example, a simple projection (not modeling the technology and price effects) with a new-product growth model suggested that personal computers would grow rapidly at least until 1995 reaching sales of at least 1.5 million units per year.[5] However, despite this growth the PC market was becoming increasingly competitive with the emergence of strong players such as Packard Bell, IBM (in partnership with Sears), and a variety of mail-order suppliers such as Dell. Masamoto would have to gain competency in these channels.

Home word processors.   About that time a new segment, the home word processor segment seemed to be emerging. A home word processor is a machine that is dedicated to word processing but provides the power of advanced word processing software running on the PC. It has its own keyboard, video display, and printer. It is priced below a PC and is easier to set up and use—the user does not need to learn new operating systems and other overhead associated with PCs. Initial competition included the Magnavox Videowriter by Philips Electronics (priced at $549 to $699), the WP-55 by Brother (competitively priced), and the PWP-14 by Smith-Corona (priced at $799). Although Magnavox was the market pioneer, Brother soon took the lead based on its strong position in the typewriter market, aggressive advertising and pricing, and the superior print quality of its daisy-wheel printer. (Magnavox has chosen a dot-matrix printer.) Sales grew rapidly: 114,000 units shipped in 1988, 166,000 units shipped in 1989, and 240,000 units shipped in 1990. Approximately 60% of these sales were in North America, 35% in Europe, and 5% in other markets.

Although the data were not sufficient for a statistical projection, it was clear that word processors were in their birth and early growth phase. Masamoto made some initial projections guided by the new-product growth models. For example, they felt that initial sales would be greater than that for the home PC market—this meant a larger $P(0)$ in the Bass new-product growth model. They also thought that the products would diffuse more rapidly because they were easier to use and adopt—Q would be larger. As an initial forecast they used a total market size of 25 million.[6] This market size assumes that the sales of home electronic typewriters will decline over the next 10 years as consumers switch to home word processors and PCs. Although these estimates are based on judgment, they do serve to as an initial

---

[5] A Bass model was fit with parameters: $P(0) = 0.002$, $Q = 0.4$, and $M = 25$ million.

[6] The actual values were $P(0) = 0.035$, $Q = 0.55$, and $M = 25$ million.

check on the size of the market. These estimates imply that the market would be in the range of 500,000 units by 1992, 1,000,000 units by 1994 or 1995, and peaking around 2,000,000 units by the end of the 1990s.

Masamoto had goals of becoming number one or two in terms of market share with approximately $125 million in factory sales. They hoped to break even by the end of the fourth year, earn a 15% before-tax profit on sales by the end of five years, and return 7% in real terms on the expected investment of $50 million. If the market grew at the anticipated rate, and if Masamoto could design a quality product for the right consumer segment, these goals were achievable.

Segmentation

There are at least two ways to look at segmentation in this market. One is by products and the other is by psychographics. The product-based segmentation of typewriters, word processors, and PCs seems reasonable to the extent that if shoppers shop for two products, the second most preferred product is more likely to be in the same product segment than would be predicted by market share alone. However, as described above, there does appear to be an evolution as typewriter consumers were switching to PCs or home word processors. By the same token, some PC consumers favored a dedicated word processor as a second computer for the home or for a college-bound young adult.

The psychographic segmentation consisted of three segments: computer literates, computer rejecters, and functional adopters. Review chapter 4 (see Figure 4.6).

- The computer literates feel comfortable with computers, have many uses for computers, have an average of three and one-half years of college education, earn $40,000 per year, shop at computer stores, and prefer brand-name computers.
- The computer rejecters are fearful of computers (with which they have had little experience), feel uncomfortable with change, have less education, earn about $25,000 per year, and shop at discount or department stores.
- The functional adopter is concerned about the difficulty of learning to use computers, needs only word processing, has an average of two years of college education, earns $32,000 per year, and shops at department or discount electronic stores.

This segmentation suggests that the primary target is the functional adopter with some secondary targeting to the computer rejector. It appears that Masamoto can build upon their expertise in the channels of distribution to reach these segments. Furthermore, the full profiles should be used for sales-force training and advertising to the segments.

Technology

The underlying technology is advancing rapidly with expected declines in price from about $500 in 1990 to about $200 in 1995 with a corresponding decrease in weight from about 15 pounds to 5 pounds. Memory (both computer memory, RAM, and hard-disk memory) is expected to be more available and much cheaper. Thus, functionality will increase dramatically. Even the printing function will evolve from daisy wheels, to ink jets, to laser printers providing quieter operation, a wider variety of type faces (fonts), more flexibility, and better print quality.

Developing Core Benefits

To select the target benefits, Masamoto developed perceptual maps based on the three primary needs of power, ease of use, and quality. "Power" meant the ability to do more than word processing, memory capacity, screen size, speed, spreadsheet analysis, use by the whole family, printing quality, printing speed, professional-looking printing, and the correction of spelling mistakes. "Ease of use" meant easy to learn, easy to operate, easy to set up, easy to maintain, convenient size, and portability. "Quality" meant built to last, reliable, made by a reputable manufacturer, attractive design, fast service, good warranty, free of defects at delivery, and the availability of "hot line" assistance.

Figure 14.11 is the value map (coordinates scaled by price) based on these three primary needs. The perceptions were similar across the three psychographic segments. Figure 14.11 also contains the ideal vectors for each of the three segments. The computer rejecters (CR) place greater emphasis on ease of use while the computer literates (CL) place greater emphasis on power. The functional adopters (FA) are in between. All place moderate importance on quality.

To target the functional adopters the new product should be farther out along the FA ideal vector than the competition—the Video Writer, the Brother WP, and the Smith-Corona PWP. This positioning reflects a balance between power and ease of use but certainly more power per dollar than that offered by typewriters and more ease of use per dollar than that offered by PCs (MAC and IBM in Figure 14.11). One such positioning is shown by YWP in Figure 14.11. (Another possibility is a line of two or more products that hit the same "per-dollar" positioning but do so with either less functionality and a lower price or more functionality and a higher price.) Whether the

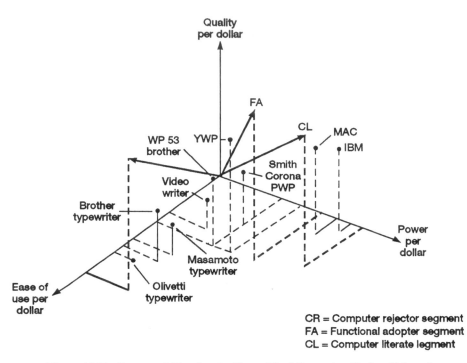

Figure 14.11 Perceptual Map for the Home Word Processing Market (Adapted from Urban and Star 1991, p. 494)

YWP position or the product-line position is chosen, the product must be developed with high quality and distinctive features that provide the benefits to fulfill the consumer needs that make up the three primary needs.

The specific features to fulfill the core benefit proposition were developed based on focus groups with leading-edge users in the target segments. In 1991 the target values of the features were

- Ink-jet printer
- 512 kilobytes (K) of random-access memory (RAM)
- 1 megabyte storage in the form of a hard disk
- 30-line CRT screen
- 12-pound weight (including printer)
- 3 fonts

The projected price was to be $499.

Because the technology is advancing rapidly, new models will need to be introduced two to three years after the YWP. Table 14.7 lists two poten-

TABLE 14.7   Potential 1994 Word-processors

YWP 1000	YWP 2000
Laser printer	Color laser printer
1 megabyte RAM	4 megabytes RAM
10 megabyte hard disk	10 megabyte hard disk
30-line screen	30-line plasma screen
6-pound weight	6-pound weight
6 fonts	12 fonts, graphics
$399	$499

tial models in the product line for 1994. If the market evolves as projected, the two products should be well-positioned to compete effectively in these price-sensitive, feature-sensitive markets. (Although we have listed the features that describe the products, it is clear that Masamoto should not neglect all aspects of the product design that bear on meeting the consumer's needs.)

Although it is difficult to project the market well beyond 1995, it is likely that there will be competition between personal computers and dedicated word processors at the high end of the market. (This is particularly true as operating systems move to graphical user interfaces (GUIs) and easier-to-use software even for the low-end computers.) At the low end of the word-processor market, it is likely that the dedicated word processors will tend to replace typewriters. To prepare for these cases Masamoto must continue to monitor technological trends, consumers needs, and competitive activities and be prepared to react with new and upgraded products.

Marketing Activities

Based on the shopping behavior of the target segments and building upon Masamoto's expertise, the channels of distribution will be department and discount stores for the functional adopter segment. To reach the computer literates who want a home word processor to supplement their PC, Masamoto will attempt to develop the computer-store channel. In both cases demonstration is likely to be an important marketing activity requiring an investment in "self-demonstrators" and sales training.

The advertising will be directed at the target segments. For the functional adopter segment advertising copy should emphasize the easy-to-use positioning combined with the power of entering the world of home word processing. Masamoto plans to spend $10 million on the launch.

Finally, quality can be signaled with a five-year parts and labor guarantee with any repairs done through factory-owned service centers.

Sales Forecast

A preliminary sales forecast was made based on a sample of 300 type-writer owners. They were shown the concept and allowed to try a prototype product. This gave an estimate of trial given awareness. Awareness and shopping behavior was forecast based on the marketing plan. Total market size per year was based on the new-product growth models described earlier. Putting this all together gave forecasts of approximately 50,000 units in 1991, 120,000 units in 1992, 200,000 units in 1993, with continued growth to over 700,000 units in 1998.

When these forecasts were combined with forecasts of price and factory cost, Masamoto projected losses for the first three years, but high returns from 1995 to 1999. The net projected profit was above the 15% return—a go decision.

The outcome was a commitment to develop and test the product and advertising. If these tests confirm the sales and profit projections, then the product will be launched. The design effort was successful—an opportunity was identified and filled to create quality and value for customers.

INDUSTRIAL PRODUCTS—CAD/CAM SOFTWARE

The design process steps for industrial and medical product development is analogous to consumer products. However in industrial products and the spirometer case, more emphasis is on physical performance and personal selling than in consumer products where psychological attributes and advertising are critical to success. Even though industrial buyers may be less emotional and more influenced by product specifications, product performance attributes are seen through the lens of primary perceived needs. Industrial buyers are influenced by a supplier's reputation (perceived quality), perceptions of delivery, reliability, and service, as well as the personal effectiveness of the salesperson. In this section we complete the case study on printed circuit CAD/CAM software and computer support that we began in Chapter 5 (Idea Generation) and 10 (Strategic Product Positioning and Customer Preferences). Our aim here is to highlight the similarities and differences between consumer and industrial products.

Idea Generation

The attractiveness of the CAD/CAM market is high (growing at 35% per year). Earlier in this book we described the generation of an exciting new product idea based on Lead User Analysis in the electronic printed circuit board segment. A technological trend was identified (increasing board density), measures of potential benefit were defined (users build or modify product, innovativeness, dissatisfaction with existing products), lead users identified, and a concept developed based on qualitative research that combined the elements of the lead-user product solutions. The CBP of the concept was a more powerful and easier-to-use system with interfaces to manufacturing. This primary benefit statement was supported at the secondary need level by features of more layers, narrower vias, surface mounting, simulation capabilities, icon driven computer graphics, central data storage, and direct links to numerically controlled production machines.

The design step of forming a Core Benefit Proposition and linking this primary-need level of consideration to the features at the secondary level is evident in both industrial and consumer goods industry. The detergent in the CLI case had a CBP backed by new granules; the word processor generated ease-of-use benefits by dedicating the user interface to a specific set of home use functions. In industrial products more emphasis is upon the technology and customers are more educated and comprehensive than in consumer markets, but the critical user orientation is a common denominator.

Positioning

In the CAD/CAM case perceptual maps (Figure 14.12) were drawn based on attribute ratings collected from lead and non-lead users. As indicated in Chapter 10, the dimensions are (1) "Power/value" (attributes of placement/routing power, value for the dollar, powerful, and high density), (2) "Ease of use" (easy to learn and easy to use), (3) "Manufacturable" (manufacturable and enough layers for my needs), (4) "Integratability" (easy to customize, integrate with manufacturing and other CAD systems), and (5) "Maintenance/upgrading" (easy to maintain, upgrade, and reliable). The new concept is perceived as superior to the user's existing system in power/value, ease of use, and integration, but not manufacturability and ease of maintenance/upgrading. This implies that more design and communication should be directed at these benefit dimensions. In this case, the links to a wide range of automated machines were built and algorithms developed to trade off the number of layers, cost, and the rejection rates that may result when very sophisticated designs are specified. Maintenance was improved by better documentation while upgrading and training was included as an automatic option in the purchase plan.

Because the most important dimensions were power/value, integration, and manufacturability, high priority was placed on the tradeoffs to produce

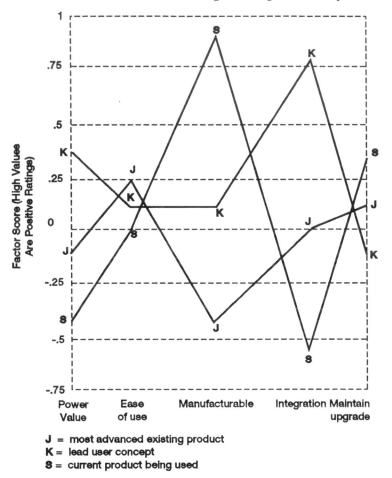

J = most advanced existing product
K = lead user concept
S = current product being used

Figure 14.12   Perception Map for CAD/CAM Software

dense designs that also assured quality manufacturing. This "design for man-ufacturing" was an important differentiating criteria for potential customers of the software.

Evaluation

Since they developed the ideas, we know lead users like the product, but what about the rest of the market? Will the remainder of the market follow? To test this the new-product team measured the preferences of other poten-tial adopters after describing the concept and the future technological frame of reference. Table 14.8 shows the response to the concept by lead and

TABLE 14.8   Concept Preferences of Lead versus Non-lead Users

Concept	Lead Users			Non-lead Users		
	% First Choice	Constant Sum	Probability of Choice	% First Choice	Constant Sum	Probability of Choice
Respondent's current PC-CAD	7.7	2.64	—	11.1	1.56	—
Best system commonly available	0	0.67	12.2	2.8	1.06	34.1
Lead user group concept	92.3	3.20	87.8	80.5	2.37	65.9

non-lead users. Market response for the remaining market was strong. Lead users preferred the concept more, but nonlead users preferred the new product to the most advanced existing product by almost two to one (see constant sum values 2.37/1.06 = 2.24).

As in consumer products preference versus other alternatives is the crucial factor in identifying potential. In this case the potential encouraged improvement of the lead-user design and testing of the product.

Product Fulfillment

The software for better assurance of manufacturability was built in cooperation with one of the lead-user firms. Improved maintenance and training documentation was written. The completed design reflected another technological trend. The software was originally designed to run on a large central computer, but the trend toward workstations was evident at the lead-user engineering departments. This trend alerted the new product team to the need to have PC-based products that could stand alone in a workstation and/or be networked within the engineering/manufacturing information system.

Marketing Mix and Forecasting

The pricing in the software case was critical. Customers were asked their likelihood of purchase at various prices. Figure 14.13 shows the results. The new concept was preferred to the best existing alternative even at twice the price. This indicated a premium price could be established and the revenues could generate the funds to pay back the investment in design, manufacturing, and marketing. Detailed forecasts were developed based on diffusion of innovation models and prices that started at current levels but declined as

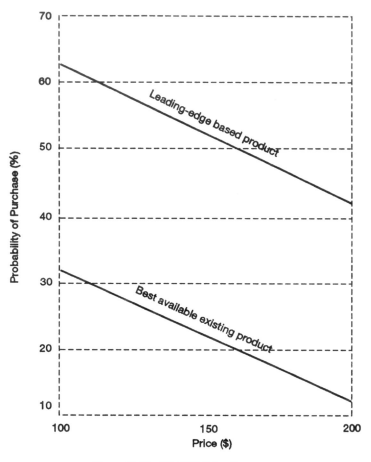

Figure 14.13   PC-CAD Price Response

competition increased and computer productivity increased. The proforma looked good, the product design was completed, and work moved on to the next step in the design process—testing.

Summary

Perceptual maps are useful in both consumer and industrial products to understand the positioning of a new product versus competition. It is common for industrial maps to have more dimensions, but the approach is the same—differentiate and create value through quality products.

In the case of industrial and medical products even more emphasis is often placed on quality and details of design (tertiary needs) because of the increasing complexity of many of these products. But the concept of total quality from CBP to details of design manufacturing, and service are true in both industrial and consumer products.

In both consumer and industrial products the marketing mix is important. In industrial products the key elements are commonly price and selling effort, whereas in consumer goods the top two elements are usually advertising and distribution. In all markets consideration of market response to alternative marketing variable levels is important in completing the design and providing a complete basis for forecasting.

SERVICES—HEALTH MAINTENANCE ORGANIZATIONS

We discussed a case of HMO design in Chapters 9, 11, and 12. We presented the idea of an HMO and positioned it against competitive medical alternatives in a perceptual map (Figure 9.8), derived the importance of these dimensions for various benefit segments (Table 11.1), and generated an enrollment and reenrollment forecast (Table 12.4). This analysis and a revised communication strategy (e.g., better quality perceptions by hospital affiliation and recommendations from HMO members) led to a complete design based on a tested CBP (supply personal, high quality care at lower prices and convenient locations).

These elements of the design process are evident in the consumer and industrial cases cited earlier. Services are delivered through people and more difficult to control, but must be oriented around a CBP and positioned against competitive service options just as in consumer and industrial markets. In all cases customers buy benefits. Whether these are generated through a physical product, service, or a combination of both, the design approach is the same in a customer-driven organization.

CONCLUSION

The cases presented here emphasize that although consumer, medical, industrial and service offerings have differences, there is a basic commonality in the design-process steps. (1) a market segment should be targeted carefully, (2) a CBP must be developed, (3) the competitive position of the CBP should be differentiated and in an area of high customer preference, (4) the relationship between perception, physical features, preference, and choice must be understood so the product can fulfill the CBP within a total quality system, and (5) the initial marketing strategy elements should be set to optimize the organization's profits and enable a go or no decision for further development.

The design should be ready for testing to assure its performance in use, manufacturing quality, and consumer acceptance. The next three chapters consider these issues. Once the new product passes the customer tests, it is *finally* ready to launch. The market determines whether the product is purchased by customers and generates returns for our company.

REVIEW QUESTIONS

14.1 Compare and contrast the cases. What are the greatest differences in terms of new product development process and analytical support? What are the similarities?

14.2. Consider the case of the Home Word Processor and suggest improvements to the design process. Can you suggest how to improve the product itself?

14.3. What makes service development more (or less?) difficult than product development?

14.4. What are the key things to remember when managing the new product design process?

14.5. Consider the concepts of total quality and discuss how they are reflected in each of the cases?

14.6. Review the interaction of engineering, manufacturing, and marketing in each of the cases. What are the relationships implied or discussed in each case?

PART FOUR

Testing and Improving New Products

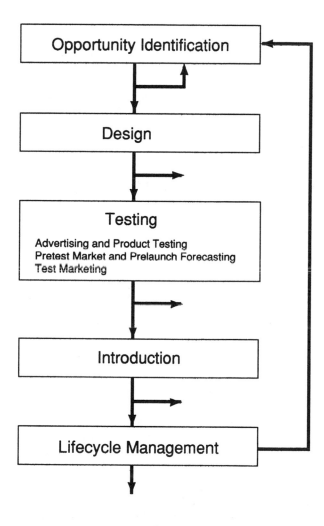

15

Advertising and Product Testing

Your organization has invested time and money in developing a new product from the initial idea to an actual product and marketing strategy. A year or more has been devoted to this design effort, preliminary forecasts of sales potential look good, and there is mounting organizational pressure to go to a full-scale launch. This pressure should be resisted. The design phase was based on models that are reasonable, accurate representations of the market response, but not of reality. Things can go wrong and often do.

A better managerial policy is to test the overall strategy and its components when the consequences of failure are small. Many of the same lessons can be learned for $200,000 or even $50,000 rather than for $50 million. Furthermore, the product can be refined during the test. In chapter 2 we introduced a reactive strategy called "second but better." A firm following this strategy waits for another organization to create a category and then enters with a superior product. If you are first in the market, you want to prevent other organizations from using second-but-better strategies. This means that when you go to market (national or global), you want to go with the best positioning you can achieve. You do this by refining the product through testing.

STRATEGY FOR TESTING NEW PRODUCTS

We can think of a new product in terms of its expected benefit and its risk. All new products have some risk. We can think of a "decision frontier" as the minimum expected benefit that is necessary for a given level of risk, or conversely as the maximum allowable risk for a given expected benefit. This decision frontier is shown conceptually in Figure 15.1. The points represent alternative product and marketing combinations. In this case all of the potential products are below the decision frontier. Suppose we select the starred (*) product for attention. The strategy of testing is to experiment, then improve the product so that it passes the decision frontier. For example, an advertising test might eliminate some uncertainty and identify better copy, thus moving the product along the dotted line. As shown, the risk-benefit position may still be unacceptable. The next step is pretest market (dashed line), and finally test market (solid line). The goal of the testing strategy is to cross the decision frontier in minimum expected cost. To do this, we must be able to reduce risk and increase expected benefit.

Reduction of Risk

Risk is reduced by sequentially testing first the components of the product and then the integrated product design or what we call the "full benefit proposition." The key concept is to delay large testing expenditures (and corresponding risk) until component risks can be minimized. A relatively small expenditure for a pretest-market-laboratory full-proposition test may reduce dramatically the chances of failure in launch. Similarly, product tests

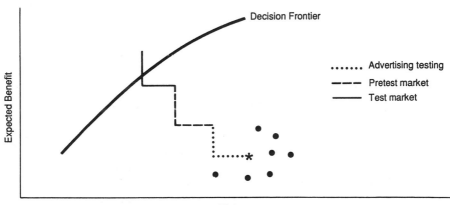

Figure 15.1   One Testing Strategy and the Decision Frontier

can detect flaws that could cause market failure. Testing can cause delays and give competitors a time advantage, so care must be taken to avoid unnecessary delays. In some cases, it may be best to skip a testing stage, but only if pressure to get to market rapidly justifies the risks of doing so.

Uncertainty is always present. Predictions become less uncertain as our tests approximate reality more closely, but costs increase as we approach reality. The testing strategy balances the uncertainty and the cost by careful use of the sequential strategy. After the components are tested, the integrated product is tested, but not yet in a full test market. Rather, laboratory simulations, special consumer panels, and statistical models are used to evaluate the full proposition (product, service, and marketing elements). These pretest market tests eliminate many failures at low cost without revealing the product to competitors. But they are still not full reality. Thus, for many products, the final stage of testing is a test market or phased roll-out. (For high-cost durables such as an auto test markets are not feasible. For many services, pilot programs substitute for test markets.) If the preliminary steps are used, the integrated product should have a high probability of succeeding in test market or roll-out. Test markets are still important when feasible, because, even with a good pretest, unexpected results and serious losses may occur in many cases when investment is large.

Maximization of Expected Benefit

Another goal of testing is to identify the product and marketing variables that maximize the firm's profit at a given level of risk. One way to achieve this is to test all combinations, but trying all combinations is often infeasible and inefficient. The testing strategy should maximize profit by devoting effort to finding ways to improve a product's expected benefit to the organization. In most product tests, results are lower than the desired levels. The testing procedure should produce actionable diagnostics to improve the product. In many cases entrepreneurial spirit is necessary to overcome problems and convert the product into a success based on the diagnostics. Advertising and product testing provide information on the consumer-response process, as well as final buying indications. In pretest market analysis, sales forecasting is the main goal, but perceptual ratings may be collected to improve the final advertising and product to deliver the CBP positioning strategy. Test marketing produces an accurate projection of national sales, but it also produces experimental information on price, advertising, and promotion levels which are critical to improving profit. In fact, this improved marketing mix is a real benefit of test marketing when time penalties due to later entry are not large.

The procedure to achieve the testing goal of reducing risk and maximizing profit is shown in Figure 15.2. First, the components such as advertising and the physical product are tested and improved. Next, the integrated product is tested in a pretest market experiment. This tests the full benefit proposition as customers see it with final product advertising, price, promotion, selling, distribution, and service execution. Failures are eliminated, or sent back to the design phase, and the product and marketing mix is improved. The key idea of pretest market is that it be low-cost and not take an exorbitant amount of time, but yield sufficient accuracy and diagnostics for a Go/No Go decision for further testing or launch. When feasible and justified the product is put to the test of reality in a test market. If the product succeeds in test market, it is introduced to the full market. If not, it is dropped or cycled back to the design phase. Increasingly time-to-market pressures are causing firms to by-pass test market. In these cases the sample size of the premarket study is increased so a more accurate forecast is available and the

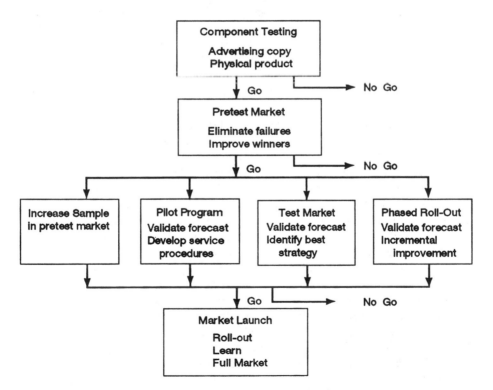

Figure 15.2 Components of the Testing Strategy

launch is carefully monitored to correct problems quickly. In some cases a "roll-out" occurs from a few markets to the total market and learning occurs where the costs of mistakes are lower.

In chapters 15 to 18 we discuss the details of each stage, indicating how to perform the tests, how to interpret the test results, and how to use the tests to reduce risk and maximize benefit. We consider the tradeoffs among cost, time, and benefit to the organization and indicate what testing methods are appropriate for various industries. In Chapter 18, we discuss how to select among the product and marketing combinations beyond the decision frontier (see Figure 16.1) that represent profit opportunities.

ADVERTISING TESTING

Advertising is an important component in the new product design. Good copy creates awareness and communicates the CBP. Advertising testing allows selection of the best ad from the available alternatives, assesses if this ad is sufficient for the new product introduction, and generates diagnostic information to improve the ad. Recall that in our CLI case (see chapter 14) three alternative advertisements were options, so there was a need to test to find the best design. In the YWP word-processing case a story board was created, but it needed further testing before evaluation based on final television execution.

Why test? Managers who have worked closely with the new product have a good feel for the consumer. Each organization has its "experts" in advertising copy and testing techniques can make errors, therefore some firms rely on managerial judgment. Unfortunately, pure judgment has not proven to be much better than random selection. For example, in a study of 24 print advertisements (American Newspaper Publishing Association, 1969) where market results were known, managers' judgments had almost no correlation with the market results ($\rho = 0.06$). The 24 advertisements were rated by 83 middle-management personnel (brand managers, agency account executives, creative agency personnel, and research personnel). Only the account executives had a significant positive correlation ($\rho = 0.10$). A negative correlation ($\rho = -0.13$) was observed for agency creative personnel. Although testing techniques are not perfect, they can usually outperform pure judgment. Certainly managers should bring their opinions to bear on ad copy evaluations, but this should not be the sole measure.

The question is not whether to test but rather which technique should be used and how many advertisements to test. We begin by examining the criteria for evaluating advertising copy.

Criteria for Evaluating Advertising Copy

Consumer Response Hierarchy.   Advertising is effective if it leads to more profitable sales, but to achieve sales, advertising must also achieve a series of intermediate goals (as shown in Figure 15.3). This consumer response hierarchy is important to the evaluation of advertising because it indicates more precisely what is effective about the advertising and what must be improved. In order to use the hierarchy, we must be able to measure the component stages. Figure 15.3 suggests measures for each stage. Some firms use these intermediate measures as the final evaluation of advertising. This is incorrect. These measures only provide clues to effectiveness. Effectiveness is difficult to evaluate without knowing advertising's effect on sales. We advocate using measures for each component, including purchase behavior.

Exposure is the prerequisite for any response and is measured by indicators of whether a consumer is in the audience for a particular media insertion. However, before any response occurs, a consumer must direct some attention to the exposure. Attention is measured by indicators of whether the consumer will see or listen to the ad, and perhaps note its content or read it. Comprehension is the next level of response. It is based on awareness and understanding. Awareness is measured by aided or unaided recall of product name and/or the unique selling proposition. It may be measured immediately, the day after ad exposure, or later. Understand-

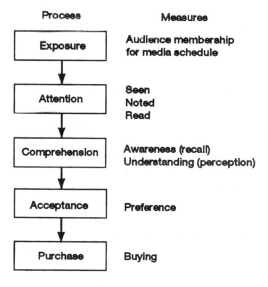

Figure 15.3   A Model for the Response to Advertising Copy

ing is measured by perceptions of the product that the ad evokes. After comprehension comes acceptance which reflects the translation of comprehension into preference. Preference is measured by first choice, a rank order of preference, intent to buy, or purchase in a simulated buying situation. The end result is buying which is measured in market tests or in realistic purchase environments.

Likability, Believability, and Meaningfulness.   In addition to measuring the effects within the hierarchy, it is useful to take measures that determine why these effects occur. Likability, believability, and meaningfulness are three measures found to be correlated with responses in the hierarchy.

Likability improves acceptance. But some researchers believe that advertisements which are disliked can also produce good results. For example, you may recall the abrasive "ring around the collar" and "Tsk, tsk, tsk, wisk, wisk, wisk" appeals for Wisk laundry detergent. Silk (1974) found that an unpleasant "hard sell" radio ad produced better response (brand awareness, recall, preference) than a pleasant "soft sell" ad. But this difference disappeared with repetition over time.

However, the effectiveness of low likability must be evaluated carefully. Advertisements that are disliked may get more attention, but for new products they may score much lower on acceptance once attention is gained. For example for new products, Figure 15.4 shows the correlation of trial in a simulated retail store with ratings of likability. This was based on data from forty new, frequently purchased consumer products. Three hundred women were shown advertisements and interviewed in each of the forty studies. Figure 15.4 suggests strongly that if attention can be achieved for a likable ad, then likability is a desirable feature of that ad. The fraction of consumers that try the product is much higher for likability ratings of 6 or 7 than those below 5.

Believability and meaningfulness also are correlated with trial once attention is gained. For example, Figure 15.5a indicates that high ratings of believability correlate with high trial. But intermediate values (4 and 5) are associated with some response. This could reflect the concept of "curious disbelief," which implies if the consumer is uncertain as to whether to believe claims, they may try the product to find out if they are true. Meaningfulness (personal relevancy) of an ad reflects how meaningful the ad copy is to the respondent's own situation. Figure 15.5b shows high meaningfulness also correlates with higher trial.

Figures 15.4 and 15.5 imply that given attention, good advertisements will get more response if they are liked, believed, and perceived as personally relevant.

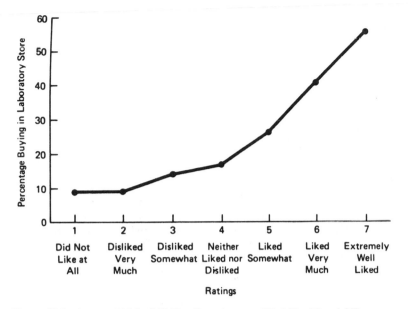

Figure 15.4   Average Trial of 40 New Brands versus Likability After Ad Exposure

Methods Used to Test Advertising Copy

Various organizations may place different emphasis on the criteria for evaluating advertising copy, but each organization should select the method that is best for its needs and resources. Many methods are available; some major methods are shown in Table 15.1.[1] These approaches differ with respect to methods, measures, completeness, accuracy, and cost.

A widely used approach is on-air testing. A test ad is used on a local television station, and after 24 hours, a random sample of the target population is surveyed by telephone to determine whether people saw the ad, recall the key claims, and correctly associate the brand name with the ad. The advantages of on-air testing are that the exposure is natural and that measures of comprehension are collected. Recall, memorability, and name association are important and necessary characteristics. However, they are incomplete measures of the purchase response because they do not consider acceptance.

One approach to measuring acceptance is theater testing. A representative audience is exposed to new television shows, along with commercials

---

[1] We have not included voice analysis which measures involuntary emotional responses given the ad copy or pupil movement methods, which may determine the attention drawing potential of ad components and reading times.

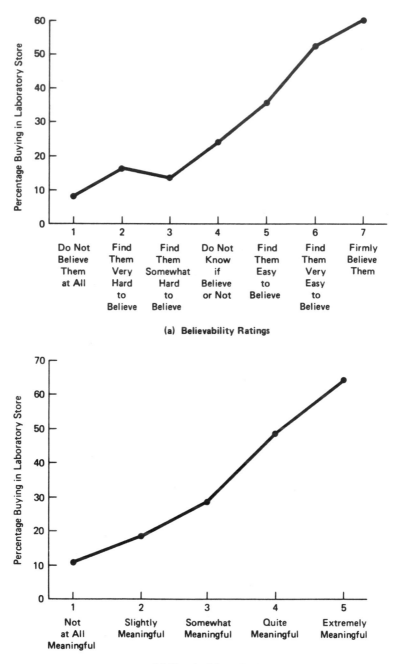

(a) Believability Ratings

(b) Meaningfulness Ratings

Figure 15.5 Average Trial of 40 New Brands versus Believability and Meaningfulness After Ad Exposure

TABLE 15.1 Selected Copy Testing Approaches

Approach	Measure in Hierarchy	Primary Measure
On-air testing	Comprehension	Day after recall
Theater testing	Comprehension and acceptance	Immediate recall, choice of prize
Trailer testing	Acceptance	Coupon redemption in store
Simulated buying	Comprehension and acceptance	Buying in "retail store"
In-market test	Purchase	Panel records of buying

that include the new product ad. Response to the new product is the percentage of people who would select the new product rather than other products for a prize after seeing the programs and advertisements. In the theater setting, measures of interest, believability, and recall are obtained. In some procedures, respondents turn a dial to reflect their interest in the ad, but the acceptance measure is the major output. This is usually compared with past "norms" for similar products.

When the exposure setting is changed by showing advertisements in a trailer outside a store, purchasing of the new product is observed in an actual store by the measuring of how many redeem a new product coupon given the respondent after exposure. Another methodological variant is exposure in a laboratory setting followed by a purchase opportunity in a simulated retail store.

Actual purchase cannot truly be measured in either theaters, trailers, or simulated stores, but each method attempts to make the choice as similar as possible to the real buying situation. The only way to measure actual purchase is through in-market tests. Some services are based on placing the ad on the air and observing purchase behavior through consumer panels and store audit data. The most advanced in-market services are based on targetable television. In these systems each home receives a designated advertisement and a meter determines if they watch. Data collecting UPC scanners in retail outlets report changes in household purchasing behavior. Sophisticated panels link the observed purchase behavior of that family to whether or not a family saw an advertisement.

Selecting a Method

To select the appropriate method, an organization should weigh the reliability and validity of a technique against the cost and the suitability of the technique for the new product under consideration.

Reliability. A testing method is reliable if repeated tests of a given ad give similar results. Suppose that more than one ad is tested. Then the variation among the (true) scores for each ad should be greater than the variation within scores for a given ad. Let σ_b^2 be the variance in the true scores between advertisements and let σ_e^2 be the variance of the error in measuring a given score. The index of reliability, R, is given by

$$R = \left[\frac{\sigma_b^2}{(\sigma_b^2 + \sigma_e^2)} \right]^{\frac{1}{2}} \tag{15.1}$$

Reliabilities in the range of .80 can be expected in a well-designed test (Bultez, Derbaix, and Silk 1976). Clancy and Ostlund (1976) report an overall correlation of 0.67 for 106 pairs of on-air tests, but this dropped to 0.29 after adjusting for statistical problems. Better reliabilities can be achieved for theater, trailer, simulated store, and in-market tests than for on-air testing. This is due to a lack of control of the surrounding television program content, variations in media placement, and lack of effort to match audiences in on-air testing. Furthermore, reliabilities may decrease as the measures get further from actual purchase behavior. For example, in a study of forced advertising exposure tests, Clancy and Ostlund (1976) report reliabilities of .96 for immediate recall, .84 for post-purchase interest ratings, and .64 for the change in buying interest ratings before and after ad exposure.

Thus when selecting a testing method, the new product team should look for high reliability, but must make certain that the reliability is appropriate for the criteria being used to evaluate the copy.

Validity. A testing method is valid if its test scores correlate highly with actual market results (sales or profit). Unfortunately, much less is known about validity than reliability. Various suppliers make claims of high validity, but few of these claims are documented by published research reports since validity measurement requires careful market experimentation. The new product manager should seek high validity, but the validity claims should not be accepted unless they can be well documented.

In general, validity is probably lower than reliability. With careful tests, values of .6 to .8 are reasonable for new product copy testing.[2]

---

[2] Fortunately, validity is usually higher for new product trial than for changes in the share of existing products. For example, Bloom, Jay, and Twyman (1977) found correlations of 0.9 between sales volume and test scores. Kahn and Light (1974) found that "high" scores increased sales 25%, while "low" scores increased sales 9% for the four advertisements they evaluated. On the other hand, Heller (1971) reports a lower correlation of 0.31 between on-air recall and actual coupon redemption.

Expected Revenue Gain.   The purpose of copy testing is to identify and to refine the advertising copy which will result in the most sales, revenue, or profit. To identify accurately the best ad, the test should be both reliable and valid. Some people argue that because reliability and validity are not perfect, advertisements should not be tested. Fortunately, expected revenue gain can be achieved with imperfect tests. To measure expected revenue gain, we use a model developed by Gross (1972).

Intuitively, we would expect the revenue gain to increase with the reliability (R) and the validity (ρ). Furthermore, we would expect that the revenue gain would be greater if there is greater variation between advertisements. (Variability is good because we are choosing the best advertisement, not the average advertisement.[3]) This variation is measured by σ_E, which is the standard deviation of market profitability resulting from the alternative ads. Finally, the revenue gain depends on the number of ads that are tested. Gross shows that the expected gain in revenue, E_n, for testing n ads is given by

$$E_n = e_n\, \sigma_E\, \rho\, R \qquad\qquad (15.2)$$

where e_N is a value that depends only on the number of ads being tested (e_N is the expected value of the largest of n observations sampled from a standardized normal distribution).

To use equation 15.2 to evaluate a testing procedure, we must estimate σ_E and determine ρ and R. We then look up e_n in a standard statistical table[4] and compute E_n for various values of n.

For example, suppose that σ_E equals $2 million. This would mean that for an average profit of $4 million, a profit of $6 million or more could be earned for the top 16% of ads, while a profit of $2 million or less would be earned for the bottom 16% of the ads. Each new product manager must estimate σ_E for their products. If the validity, ρ, were 0.7 and the reliability, R, were 0.8, the gain from testing two ads would be $631,700. (For two ads, e_n is .564. Then $E_n = 0.564 \times \$2,000,000 \times 0.7 \times 0.8$) Even if validity were 0.5 and reliability were .7, the expected gain would be $394,800. These expected gains are weighed against the costs of testing n ads.

Reliability varies by method and sample size. If the sample is increased, reliability and cost increase. A tradeoff between reliability and cost can be made, and each commercial testing service has made a choice. Bultez, Der-

---

[3] For example, suppose you roll a pair of dice. The average outcome is seven points. But suppose you roll the dice 100 times and select the largest single roll. The largest single roll is likely to be 12. Thus, in this case where you choose the best outcome, you prefer the variation of the dice to a low variance process which always gives you 7.

[4] The values of e_n for $n = 1$ to 7 are 0.00, 0.56, 0.85, 1.03, 1.16, 1.27, and 1.35.

baix, and Silk (1976) have estimated the approximate costs, reliability, and validity of various available methods. The costs (in 1976 dollars) and ranges of predictability ($\rho \times R$) are shown in Figure 15.6. As the cost goes up, the predictive ability rises. These are reasonable values to use in calculating expected gains.

Recommendations.   Each manager must evaluate the expected benefits and costs for the new product under consideration, but it is usually worth the cost to test alternative ads. Bultez, Derbaix, and Silk estimate that for most consumer products the best combination would cost in 1990 dollars about $60,000 to $90,000 with a predictability in the range of about .7.

We recommend an on-air *and* simulated store (see later for description of store simulations for premarket forecasting) or an on-air *and* coupon redemption test. Split-cable testing is difficult for a new product because it requires distribution in the test city and substantial costs which would be warranted only as a final selection method during test-market analysis.

The future for copy testing looks bright. With improved procedures, there will be an even more compelling argument to test two, three, or more independent alternative advertisements.

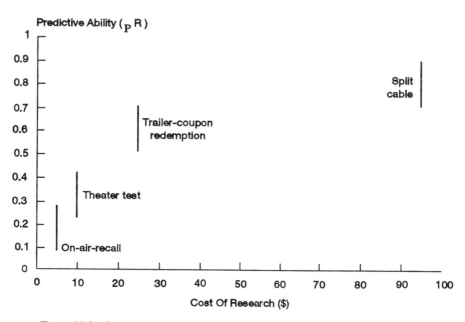

Figure 15.6   Cost versus Predictive Ability for Copy Testing Methods (Adapted by Silk from Bultez, Derbaix, and Silk 1976)

Testing Personal Selling Presentations

While testing of advertisements is common in consumer products, few organizations test their personal selling presentations. In industrial products, these presentations are as important as advertising in consumer products. Alternative presentations could be made to stress particular benefit claims, use various demonstrations, or be based on direct competitive comparisons. These approaches are likely to vary in terms of sales success. If there is a variance, the advertising testing model discussed above is relevant (equation 15.2) for computing testing payoffs.

Such tests can be done by showing video-taped sales presentations to a sample of buyers and making before/after recommendations. Such a laboratory testing procedure could also test industrial advertising in conjunction with the sales presentation. By exposing one subsample to ads and sales presentations and one to only the sales presentation, data would indicate the effect of advertising in improving sales productivity.

Another approach to testing sales messages is through a panel of firms who are exposed experimentally to alternative sales strategies. Longitudinal sales records are then analyzed to determine the impact.

Although the testing is more complex due to multiple participants in the industrial buying process and infrequent purchases, we expect reasonably valid and reliable advertising copy and selling presentation testing methods to be more available in the near future.

PRODUCT QUALITY TESTING

A well-designed product fulfills the core benefit proposition. Earlier, in the design phase, we used perceptual mapping to identify the CBP positioning for the product concept and a prototype. Conjoint analysis was suggested to select features that consumers felt would substantiate the CBP. House of Quality methods were proposed for microdesign aspects to meet feature requirements. Now we determine if the product performs as planned when it is at the production level and if its formulation can be improved. Physical product testing determines whether the product delivers the CBP and generates diagnostic information to improve the product or reduce costs.

Total quality was a major focus in our new product design and product testing plays a critical role in assuring quality before the product is launched. The quality specifications determined at the design stage must be met or exceeded and customers must reconfirm that the actual product has the desired quality level. Some specifications can be met by laboratory testing while others need in-use testing. For example, the durability of a car door can be tested by a machine that opens and closes it 35,000 times, while the "easy to open" dimension may need direct user testing to assure the door is easy to use. The specification for the force in pounds necessary to open the door on a hill may be met, but the perception of ease of operation should also be confirmed. At the level of House-of-Quality analysis, engineering judgments were made about the functional links of engineering attributes to features and perceptions, but at the testing stage the critical perceptual assumptions should be tested.

A new automobile may have a CBP based on comfort and efficiency with adequate power. How low can the horsepower be before it is viewed as "underpowered"? How much padding and carpeting should be added to the interior to provide comfort? In office copiers speed and reliability are important, but increasing speed may also increase jamming under actual office conditions. What tradeoff between speed and reliability should be made? Personal service is important in hospitals. If doctors and nurses greet their patients on a first-name basis, will this enhance personalness without undermining perceived quality?

Physical products can be tested in many ways. The new product manager should try to achieve a test that indicates how the product will perform under actual consumer use situations. Inadequate tests lead to costly mistakes in test market or full-scale launch. Some of the most costly errors have resulted in large-scale auto recalls and aircraft grounding. The following list indicates a variety of things that have gone wrong in products.[5]

- Because packages would not stack, the scouring pads fell off the shelf.
- A dog food package discolored on store shelves.
- In cold weather, baby food separated into a clear liquid and a sludge.
- In hot weather, cigarettes in a new package dried out.
- A pet food produced diarrhea in the animals.
- The electric cord in a powered microscope produced shocks.
- The gas cap on a tractor disengaged due to swelling of tank filler spout in use.
- Mounting bolts on bicycle baby carrier cracked because of stress concentration.
- Sharp edges on vent slots in the inner door of a dishwasher caused injury.
- When it was combined with a price reduction, a product change in a liquid detergent was thought by consumers to be dilution with water.

[5] This list is adapted from Klompmaker, Hughes, and Haley (1976); and Vinson and Heany (1977).

- Excessive settling in a box of tissues caused the box to be one-third empty at purchase.

These product defects are embarrassing and costly. In fact, with the legal product liability that exists in many countries, defects or bad design can create huge losses. Design faults must be eliminated by careful testing. For example childproofing a toy can be assured by design and consumer testing. Sometimes product liability losses occur despite careful design. Asbestos insulation was found to be harmful after many years on the market. As a result Johns Manville Insulation suffered great losses in legal settlements. The Dalcon shield IUD contraceptive was found to cause death by infection in some cases and hundreds of millions of dollars were paid out in claims by the manufacturers. If a product liability risk cannot be eliminated by good design and testing, it must be insured and the price raised accordingly. For example buying a Beechcraft private airplane is expensive, but a major share of the price pays for insurance to protect the manufacturer in case of product liability claims.

There are several approaches for product testing to prevent such problems. Laboratory tests, expert evaluation, and consumer tests can be used. To select the approach or combination of approaches for a particular product, the new product manager must assess the strengths and weaknesses of each approach.

Laboratory Tests

Laboratory tests effectively answer many product performance questions. The efficiency of an automobile engine is measured on a test stand. Alternative designs for engine components such as carburetors and ignition systems are evaluated in the laboratory and on test tracks. A new copy machine is tested at various speeds to determine the relationship between speed and rates of jamming. Betty Crocker kitchens are well equipped to test alternative cake mixes. Credit approval software can be tested under a full range of input demand to be sure there are no "bugs" in the system. Engineering testing practice is well developed and provides valuable insights for product tests.

A disadvantage of laboratory tests is that they may not be completely representative of product use. Few consumers achieve the miles per gallon determined by EPA tests. Copiers may jam more often in the office than in the lab. Automated machine tools may be less reliable "on the line" than laboratory fatigue tests might indicate. Consumers may not be as careful at home with a new cake mix recipe as researchers are in the test kitchens. We suggest that "in-use" tests complement laboratory tests.

Use situations vary across the world, so use testing should not be confined to the manufacturer's home country. For example, although Japanese cars were viewed as very high quality in the early 1980s, drivers in the northeast of the USA found excessive rusting and poor quality in their use environment. Subsequently, the manufacturers used House of Quality procedures to eliminate the rusting problem. Even though some rust conditions occur in Japan, the typical Japanese buyer holds their car only for three years so the problem was not evident. In New England the average buyer holds the car for seven years and the snow, ice, and salt conditions are more severe than in Japan. Realization of the use differences and testing in New England would have prevented the problem.

Another disadvantage of laboratory testing is the tendency of engineers to concentrate on engineering measures. Unfortunately, the consumer rarely does. Engineering measures for a new transit system include travel time, wait time, fare, egress and access time, but not service, quality, safety, convenience, comfort, and privacy. For a new automobile, perceived efficiency may be closely related to engineering tests, but perceived comfort may not have any good engineering surrogates. Comfort may be partially related to the depth of foam in the seats and leg room, but it is also related to the overall "lushness," "quietness," and "softness" of the interior. In many products the CBP is stated in perceptual terms because consumers buy based on perceptions. In such cases, laboratory tests should be enhanced by consumer tests so that the critical assumption linking design to tertiary, secondary, and primary needs can be tested.

For more details on engineering tests and efficient experimental designs see Box, Hunter, and Hunter (1978), Ross (1988), Ryan (1989), and Taguchi (1988).

Expert Evaluation

One way of evaluating perceptual aspects of a product is by "expert" judgment. For example, the "comfort" of new auto interiors may be judged by a panel of styling engineers and marketing executives. Expert tasters are often used for new foods. They may evaluate the "flavor" and "mildness" of different blends of coffee. Some taste tests determine whether a new product fulfills its positioning claims. In others, alternative recipes are evaluated to identify the best or lowest cost combinations. For example, if no difference is detected in flavor and mildness across alternatives, the lower cost formulations could be used.

The advantage of expert evaluation is its relatively low cost. Experts can be trained to carry out intricate comparisons. For example, many paired comparisons may be made to find the effect of each ingredient on taste perceptions. However, these methods rely on the assumption that "experts" accurately reflect consumers' perceptions. If consumers are influenced by their individual past experience or psychological attitudes, the "experts" may most completely represent the buyers reaction to the product.

Customer Tests

To complement laboratory tests and expert evaluation, we turn to the final judge—the customer. Products are tested under conditions close to actual use. Customer perceptions provide key inputs to the evaluation of product performance.

Tests of physical characteristics alone are not sufficient. There is evidence that customers are influenced by more than the physical characteristics of a product. Allison and Uhl (1964) found that when consumers tasted and rated labeled beers, they rated the brand of beer they drank most often significantly higher than other beers. But when they tasted and rated the same beers without labels, there were no significant differences between the ratings of brands. The label and its psychological associations affected the taste evaluation. McConnell (1968) studied the effect of price on the perceived quality of beer. In this study all of the beer was physically the same and only the price level was changed. The taste ratings (undrinkable, poor, fair, good, and very pleasant) were significantly related to price, with the higher-priced beer receiving better ratings. These studies indicate that although physical ingredients are important, past experience and perceptions may affect consumer evaluations.

Psychosocial cues also have an impact on consumer evaluations of durable products. The same physical car may be evaluated differently if it is manufactured by Volkswagen rather than Ford or Mazda. Consumer perceptions of the reliability of a copying machine can depend upon whether the manufacturer is Xerox, Savin, or Philips. Consumer reaction to an organized ride sharing system depends upon whether it is called "community carpooling" or "organized hitchhiking."

Even in industrial products these cues can be important. An air-conditioning system must not only be reliable, but appear and sound reliable. The right face-plate for an electronic component helps communicate that it is "state of the art." Design work should have identified the major cues, but testing should assure that they operate as expected in building customer attitudes.

There are three commonly used procedures for customer tests: single-product evaluation, blind comparisons, and experimental variations. In each procedure it is important that customer attitudes and experience be understood in the evaluation process.

Single-Product Evaluation.   The simplest approach to customer testing is to ask customers to evaluate the new product to see if it is "good." Evaluative ratings are usually on a five- or seven-point overall scale of liking (called the "hedonic scale"). Additional ratings may be collected on various attribute scales to evaluate whether customers like a new product on a specific dimension of the CBP. A sample of consumers may be asked to try a cookie mix at home. A copier may be placed in a sample of offices and perceptions of reliability measured. Prospective auto buyers may be asked to rate the comfort of a new interior. Plant engineers and maintenance engineers may be asked to evaluate the reliability of an air conditioner.

Single product evaluation is useful for uncovering flaws, but because there is no reference value, it is often difficult to interpret the results. For example, how good is a "good" rating? Is "very reliable" rather than "extremely reliable" the best rating that can be achieved? To overcome this problem, organizations have turned to procedures where the comparison is more explicit.

In software it is common to use a "Beta test" where a prototype version of the software is placed with customers and they provide feedback on the defects and needs for improvement. The Beta test is small and set up with cooperating and advanced users who understand that the product is likely to have some bugs at this stage.

If leading-edge-user analysis is used in the design of the product, it should be carried over to the testing stage because the lead users are the most demanding in terms of use requirements. They will cooperate in testing the product because they gain advantages by early use. The manufacturer then has an advanced Beta test and users will not only point out problems but also help solve them.

Blind Tests.   In blind tests the new product is compared to existing products. The manufacturer's identification is suppressed to measure the physical response without the confounding of brand attitudes. If superior mildness is part of the CBP for a new coffee, then the blend should be perceived as milder than existing blends without branding. In many cases brand name or positioning affects the outcomes, so blind testing is replaced by testing with labeled concept statements or other visuals. Blind tests provide useful information, but in some products the manufacturer's image supports the CBP and should be included in the tests. Pharmaceutical testing is often "double blind" so user and experimenter biases can be avoided.

Experimental Variations.   Alternative product formulations are often under consideration, thus tests are often extended by asking consumers to evaluate these alternative formulations. Consumers may be asked to evaluate a few specific blends of coffee or they may be asked to evaluate an experimental design of alternative formulations. In the latter case, functions are estimated linking the physical features to perceptions and preference. For example, Moskowitz (1972) estimated the perceptions of sweetness in a beverage as a function of the sugar content.

In a study of paper towels, consumers were given a rack of towels which contained three different towels. They were asked to use them sequentially. Across the sample, the towels were varied in weight, adhesive content, and plastic reinforcement. Consumers rated the towels on overall preference, "softness," "absorbency," and "durability." Based on these results, a best combination of weight, adhesive, and reinforcement was selected to fulfill the CBP of soft and absorbent while maintaining a competitive cost and acceptable strength.

These procedures, which are well developed for frequently purchased products, are useful for consumer durables and industrial products. A prospective automobile buyer can rate several interiors which are systematically varied in terms of the cost and quality of vinyl materials (plain plastic to simulated leather). An office might use several copiers for one-month periods. Plant engineers can be exposed to several prototype air conditioners. HMOs may vary the color of doctors' coats or size of hospital rooms.

It is not uncommon that some experimental research be done during the design phase. The use of robust design and Taguchi methods for manufacturing/engineering/marketing design coordination is very desirable. See Taguchi (1988) and Ross (1988). Furthermore, when continuous improvement procedures are practiced, the experimental variation and learning persists through the testing and implementation stages. The experiments become more refined and the product and its manufacture is fine tuned. The continuing experimentation also has the advantage of highlighting any changes in the customer use or manufacturing technology. The result should be reduction in risk, improvement in quality, and increased profit potential (see Box, Hunter, and Hunter 1978).

Summary of Product Testing Procedures

A new product is unlikely to succeed if the product is not high quality or if customers do not perceive it as such. But the optimal managerial strategy is not always to produce the best product without regard to cost. To make decisions with respect to ingredients and engineering design, the new product manager must understand how these ingredients and designs affect product performance and consumer perceptions of quality, as well as profit.

Product tests provide the manager with the information with which to make these decisions. Laboratory tests uncover flaws and provide insight on engineering measures, and expert evaluation provides an inexpensive first view of consumer perceptions.

Exposing consumers to alternative formulations allows the most complete measurement of physical and psychological product features. It should be used to supplement engineering laboratory and expert panel evaluations when perceptual attributes are present in the new product and when one cannot be sure "experts" accurately represent buyers and users. The tests should determine the best utility versus cost tradeoffs and result in an optimal quality product.

There is no ideal method that applies to every product. The new product manager must understand the strengths, weaknesses, and complementarities of each procedure and choose the combination of tests that provides sufficient information to select the best product formulation. We now illustrate a product test for one consumer product.

Case: Taste Tests for Squid Chowder

Conventional U.S. seafood supplies such as cod or clams are being depleted and, as a result, prices have risen. For example, the reduced supply of clams coupled with increased popularity has resulted in a tripling of the price of clam chowder. One solution might be to develop new food products which utilize the more plentiful species of fish. One such species, squid, is abundant and nutritious. It is widely accepted in the Orient and the Mediterranean countries, but is not popular in the United States.

Earlier we suggested potential new products to exploit this opportunity. One of these was chowder based on squid and clams. (You may wish to reexamine Figures 3.2 to 3.4.)

The design process was used to develop a CBP; now the physical product and labeling must be carefully developed. Taste tests were undertaken to determine whether consumers would accept squid and whether they would like the taste. FDA regulations require that "squid" be prominent on the label. Tests were required to determine whether the psychological effect of the name "squid" would make the product unacceptable to consumers.

Study Design.   Two hundred consumers were recruited at a shopping mall in a suburb of Boston. The respondents were required to be the household meal planner and to have served fish at home as a main meal item in the last month. Age quotas were used in an attempt to get a representative sample of consumers. Qualified respondents were taken to a room in the mall where they filled out a questionnaire and tasted squid chowder and clam chowder.

They were paid $10.00 as compensation for approximately 45 minutes of their time.

To address the managerial questions, the study was designed to test the effect of squid concentration in the chowder and the effect of squid identification on the label. Clam chowder was used as a reference.

Each consumer tasted the clam chowder and two squid chowders. The first squid chowder, called "Fisherman's Chowder," de-emphasized the presence of squid. It was described as a "delicious blend of seafood" with ingredients of "clams, squid, milk, water, potatoes, onion, and seasonings." The second squid chowder, "Sclam Chowder," emphasized the presence of squid. It was described as a "delicious blend of squid and clams" with ingredients of "squid, clams, milk, water, potatoes, onion, and seasonings." The total weight of the clams and squid was constant in all chowders as were other ingredients. The respondent was presented with a bowl of chowder and a concept board describing the product. For example, the clam chowder concept board said in large letters "Clam Chowder" and in smaller letters "a delicious clam soup." On the bottom, the ingredients were listed in small print as "clams, milk, water, potatoes, onion, and seasonings."

The chowders also varied in terms of the physical concentration of squid. For one half of the respondents "Fisherman's Chowder" was a 90% squid product. For the other half it was a 10% squid product. Similarly, for "Sclam Chowder" one-half of the respondents were given a 90% squid product and half a 10% squid product. The order of presentation was rotated and concentration randomized within the "Fisherman's" and "Sclam" chowder labels.

After each chowder was tasted, a seven-point hedonic scale and a five-point intent-to-buy scale were administered. For each pair, the respondent first identified the preferred item and then specified the degree of preference (slightly better, better, much better). Paired comparisons were made in terms of overall taste, appearance, flavor, texture, and aroma.

Experimental Results. The outcome of this experiment is shown in Table 15.2. The overall preference mean of −.09 is low compared to the scaled value of zero for pure clam chowder. The values for high salience and concentration are lower than those for low salience and concentration, respectively. Although the marginal totals indicate a negative effect for high squid identification and high squid concentration, these effects were not statistically significant (F [2,402] was 0.38 and the t for differences in salience was −.33 and for concentration −.79)]. Overall, there was some penalty for the squid name and concentration, but it was small and not statistically significant.

A more detailed analysis of the data indicated that the significance was much higher for some groups. For those who had previously tasted squid,

TABLE 15.2 Overall Experimental Treatment Means

		Squid Concentration		
		Low (10%)	High (90%)	Total
Salience of squid identification	Low (Fisherman's)	.00	−.11	−.06
	High (Sclam)	−.01	−.24	−.13
	Total	−.01	−.18	−.09

there was a larger negative effect for high concentration, but no salience effect. For those who had not previously tasted squid, there was no significant penalty for squid concentration or salience.

The experiment indicated small negative effects for increasing the concentration of squid in the chowder and labeling the chowder as "Sclam" rather than "Fisherman's Chowder." The greatest penalty was for the high concentration chowder by those who had previously tasted squid.

Managerial Diagnostics. Because some consumers recognize the taste of squid and dislike it, repeat rates for the chowder may be suppressed. One way to increase potential repeat purchase would be to change the recipe by lowering the proportion of squid to say 50 percent. However, such change would reduce the cost advantage of a squid chowder. To search for alternative strategies, we examined the ratings of the squid chowders on flavor, texture, and appearance.

Contrary to expectations, ratings on texture and appearance were better for the squid chowder than the clam chowder. The squid mantels were finely chopped to give a pleasing appearance and the fresh squid carefully cooked to maintain tenderness. The recommended alternative was to increase the clam flavor perception by the use of more clam juice while retaining a high level of squid concentration. Because the overall ratings were most heavily correlated to flavor, improvements in flavor without the loss of texture and appearance should improve the overall taste perceptions and the repeat purchase intents. Further taste testing of revised recipes would be appropriate.

The sensitivity to concentration and flavor also suggests that the maintenance of quality would be important if a squid product were marketed. Most of the previous trial was in restaurants where recipes and quality vary. In a canned chowder, consistency and good quality should be much easier to maintain.

The salience of squid identification had only a small effect on consumers' evaluation. "Sclam" chowder did not produce statistically significantly lower taste evaluations than the same chowder when labeled as "Fisherman's" chowder. It does not appear to be worth a legal battle over the details of labeling. "Sclam" chowder, "a blend of squid and clams" is an honest straightforward identification, and acceptable to consumers.

The experimental data suggest that relative to clam chowder, a squid chowder does not do badly. In the survey, the overall intent to buy the squid chowder after tasting was almost equal to clam chowder. There was a 27.8% definite and 29.8% probable intent for squid chowder versus 28.9% definite and 32.0% probable for clam chowder.

If trial could be obtained by price promotion and advertising to influence prior attitudes, a respectable share of the chowder market could be obtained. A reformulation could further increase the repeat rate and long-run sales. If the supply price of squid remains substantially below clams, a long-range price advantage would further stimulate trial and repeat purchases. The issue of taste and price tradeoffs could be examined further by pretest market procedures.

This case illustrates the use of taste testing in formulating a new product. Our experience indicates paired comparisons are the best way to discriminate among alternative products. Large samples should be collected so that subgroups can be analyzed to find heterogeneity in response and so the power of the statistical tests will be high. If a taste test is to be done, be sure it is carefully designed, and executed, and analyzed. Then, the test can determine if the current formulation is preferred to existing products and how the formulation can be improved.

SUMMARY

Testing strategies reduce risk and maximize expected benefit. This chapter has considered procedures to test advertising copy and physical product characteristics to assure the quality specified in the design phase is delivered to customers. These testing activities are important in assuring that the best advertising has been created and that the product with its manufacturing specifications fulfills requirements and consumer expectations. As well as determining if the product and advertising are good, the procedures improve the product and advertising formulations to reduce costs and better meet consumer preferences. This means testing activity has the potential to further increase the quality of the product.

In the next chapter we present procedures which test the product, advertising, price, promotion, and distribution aspects as a unified entity in a full proposition test.

REVIEW QUESTIONS

15.1. How does a testing strategy reduce risk and increase expected benefit?

15.2. What are the advantages and disadvantages of a sequential testing strategy?

15.3. How does testing improve quality?

15.4. Why is it necessary to have a formal procedure for advertising copy testing? Why not have management merely choose that copy which best conveys the CBP?

15.5. Some advertisements score low on likability yet achieve excellent advertisement and product awareness. Is this enough for a successful new product? Think of an abrasive advertisement. Could you make this advertisement less abrasive yet achieve attention and communicate its unique selling proposition?

15.6. What is the relationship between reliability and validity of advertising testing? Why are both important?

15.7. Consider the expected revenue gain for copy tests as described by the Gross model (equation 15.2). Under which of the following conditions would more testing be advocated? Under which conditions would less testing be advocated? Why?
   a. The reliability of the tests are improved.
   b. The firm is generating some very novel and experimental forms of copy.
   c. The ads generated not only differ in style but actually position the product differently.
   d. One creative specialist is generating the ads rather than a staff of creative people working independently.

15.8. What are the advantages and disadvantages of laboratory tests, expert evaluation, and consumer tests for physical product testing?

15.9. How might you test a new electric turbine?

15.10. What different problems occur in testing consumer durable products as compared to consumer frequently purchased products or services?

16

Pretest Market Forecasting

Once we have refined and tested the design of our product in terms of its component physical features and communication methods, we need to test the integrated new product. Such a "full proposition" test provides an accurate forecast so that risks of failure can be prevented. In this section we indicate the criteria for good premarket methods, review the state-of-the-art of models and measurement methods for packaged goods, consumer durables, industrial, and service innovations, and close with advice on how to use most effectively the model and measurement methodologies.

CRITERIA FOR PRETEST MARKET ANALYSIS

A managerial decision to use a pretest market analysis is justified if: (1) sufficiently accurate predictions can be achieved, (2) the timing of the analysis is before large investment commitments are necessary, (3) useful diagnostics for improvement are generated, and (4) the cost of the analysis is reasonable.

Accuracy

Since the final product environment may change before full-scale launch and measurement error will be present, pretest markets cannot predict perfectly, but they should be sufficiently accurate for a good go/no go market decision. This means that a pretest market should reject poor products with a high probability of being correct. Also, good products should have a high probability of being identified correctly. A reasonable criteria to achieve these managerial goals is that predictions are within 25% of long-run sales 75% of the time. For most consumer brands, this would imply the predicted share should be about two points above the minimum share required for a go decision in order to assure a 75% chance of success in test market. Such accuracy can be obtained as we report below.

Managerial Diagnostics

Many new products (30%–50%) are identified as failures at the pretest stage even after careful design work. One could merely drop these products, but usually there are opportunities to improve the physical product, advertising copy, or marketing mix. A pretest market model and measurement system should provide actionable diagnostics on why the product succeeded or failed, how it could be improved, and what the share implications are of such improvements. When a product is rated as "good" after the pretest analysis, diagnostics generate information to improve the product further. Such improvement is important because the better the product is, the less likely it is to be vulnerable to competitive entries. The diagnostics to improve quality should be many and linked to operational variables that can be changed.

Timeliness

The premarket forecasting must be done early enough before the launch so that major expenditures can be stopped if the analysis indicates the product is likely to be a failure. In packaged goods the big expenditures are for test market (12–18 months before launch) and national launch. For consumer durables there are two significant points—before commitment to production capacity (e.g., in autos 36–48 months before launch) and before committing to specific levels of launch expenditure (e.g., 12 months before launch). In industrial products, the investment in production is the milestone (often one to two years before introduction). In services, the investment points include large fixed costs (e.g., new computers for credit services) or are concentrated at launch time (e.g., a new health service for the very old).

The pretest market should provide results fast enough for managerial action, furthermore, the use of a pretest market should not significantly delay full-scale launch. A good analysis should improve the average time to market by preventing inferior products from getting to launch. Three months is a typical time for a pretest analysis.

Cost

One gains little if the pretest market is very costly in dollars and/or time. The cost of a pretest market should be well below the expected gains (from $50,000 to $100,000 is an attainable cost for pretest market analysis in packaged goods and about 2 or 3 times this amount for consumer durable and industrial products) and should be compared to the value generated.

ALTERNATIVE APPROACHES

The input to a pre-market analysis is the physical product, advertising copy, packaging, price, selling, channels of distribution strategy, service policies, and the advertising and promotion budget. The output is a forecast of sales and diagnostics. To fulfill the preceding criteria, the pretest market must be based on careful measurement and models of consumer response. Table 16.1 lists several alternative approaches. Each approach has its relative strengths and weaknesses; you may wish to combine two or more approaches to enhance accuracy. At least one available model uses such a convergent approach by combining trial/repeat and attitude change models. A final method of early analysis is to use the information acceleration methods introduced in chapter 12.

In this chapter we describe how these approaches have been used in frequently purchased packaged goods, consumer durables, industrial, and service industries. The procedures were invented in the packaged goods in-

TABLE 16.1   Alternative Modeling Approaches to Premarket Analysis

Judgment and past product experience
Trial/repeat measurement
Test-market models
Dynamic stochastic models
Home delivery
Laboratory measurement
Attitude-change models
Convergent approach
Information acceleration

dustry and have diffused into the other marketing domains where the unique aspects of these markets have led to new models and market research approaches.

Packaged Goods

The high failure rates and attendant losses in test markets ($1.5 to $3 million investment) and national launches ($10 to $50 million investment) led innovative packaged goods firms to develop methods to reduce the risks of failure in test scores. As the models developed they used simulated test market measures, models based on trial/repeat behavior, and analyses of attitude change.

Judgment and Past Product Experience

One approach to pretest market forecasting is to examine past experience to determine which measurable characteristics of a new product determines its success. For example, Figure 16.1 suggests one set of critical factors that affects advertising recall, initial purchase, and repeat purchase. These particular factors are used in a model developed by Claycamp and Liddy (1969) some years ago for packaged goods. To develop such a model, one gathers these measures (both the critical factors and consumer response) and uses statistical analysis (regression) of past-product results to estimate the relationships between the critical factors and consumer response. For the new product, the critical factors are measured and the regression equation is used to forecast consumer response.

In many cases, it is infeasible or too expensive to measure directly all of the critical factors for the new product. In such cases some firms substitute managerial judgment or develop a panel of experts. This makes the measurement feasible, but can introduce random error and/or bias depending upon the panel. For example, Table 16.2 suggests one way to obtain measures for the critical factors in Figure 16.1. Note that the measurement may be different for the new product.

The advantage of this approach is that once the regression equation is estimated, the model can produce predictions rapidly and at a low cost. It makes use of previous experience. Because the media and distribution plans appear in the model, alternative plans can be tried and the best one chosen. The approach also has a number of disadvantages. Besides its sensitivity to expert judgment, the model is extremely sensitive to the past products used to estimate the model. Because the model has no underlying theory of the consumer response (beyond a causal diagram), the regressions may not be appropriate for categories that are significantly different from those used to

TABLE 16.2 One Way to Measure the Critical Factors for the Trial Model
in Figure 16.1

Variable	Measure	Source for Past Products	Source for New Products
PP	Judged product positioning	Expert panel	Expert panel
MI	Average number of media impressions/household	Past data	Media plan
CE	Judged quality of advertising copy execution	Expert panel	Expert panel
CP	Coverage of consumer promotion containing advertising messages adjusted for type of promotion	Past data	Expert panel and plan
CI	Index of consumer interest in the product category	Expert panel	Expert panel
DN	Retail distribution, adjusted for shelf space and special displays	Past data	Distribution plan
PK	Judged distinctiveness of package	Expert panel	Expert panel
FB	Known or family brand name	Past data	Plan
CP	Coverage of consumer promotions adjusted for type value of offer	Past data	Expert panel and plan
PSS	Index of consumer satisfaction with new product samples	Past data	Product test data
CU	Percent of households using products in the category	Historical data	Historical data
AR	Percent of housewives able to accurately recall advertising claims at the end of 13 weeks	Test-market data	Predicted by model
IP	Percent of housewives making one or more purchases of the product during the first 13 weeks	Test-market data	Predicted by model

Adapted from Claycamp and Liddy (1969, p. 416).

estimate the model. Finally, because few direct measures are taken from the consumer, the model may miss important consumer concerns.

Figure 16.1 and Table 16.2 are based on the model developed by Claycamp and Liddy (1969). Their model is based on data obtained from 58 new-product introductions that covered 32 different types of package goods. The regressions were run on 35 of those introductions, 50% of which were foods; the other 23 were saved for predictive testing. Two regression equations were estimated, one for advertising recall and one for initial purchase. No results are reported for repeat purchase. The regressions explained more than 70% of the variation in the data and were significant at the 1% level. The

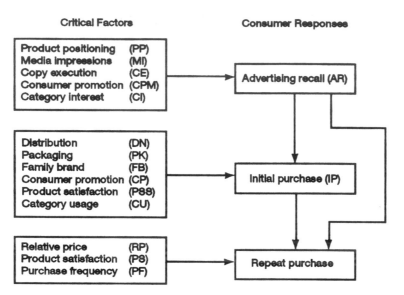

Figure 16.1 Model Based on Past Product Experience (Adapted from Claycamp and Liddy, 1969, p. 415)

largest effects on advertising recall were produced by product positioning (PP), copy and advertising ($\sqrt{MI*CE}$), consumer promotion (CP) and category interest (CI), in that order. Trial was affected most by packaging (PK), family branding (FB), and advertising recall (AR). When the model was tested on 23 new products, 15 of 23 fell within 10 percentage points of observed advertising recall, and 20 of 23 fell within 10 percentage points of the observed trial. The correlations of actual and predicted were .56 for recall and .95 for trial.

This approach is interesting because it indicates that studying past products is useful. But the levels of correlation indicate that past relationships may not be sufficient. The model is limited because no experience with the repeat-purchase sector has been reported. Without a valid repurchase model, the new product share cannot be predicted. The pioneering Claycamp and Liddy model has led to recent research to develop more measures and stronger models to predict market share.

Trial/Repeat Measurement

Long-run sales are based on both trial and repeat. Accurate forecasts of long-run sales can be made if the pretest analysis predicts the percentage of consumers who will try the product (cumulative trial) and the percentage of those who will become repeat users (cumulative repeat). A series of models have been developed which present the new product to consumers in a reasonably realistic setting and take direct consumer measures which are used to forecast trial and repeat purchases. The advantage of this approach is that it is based on direct observation of consumer response to the new product. The disadvantage is that errors are introduced because the direct measures may not be representative of what would happen in a test market or a full-scale launch.

Test-Market Models.   Since premarket analysis for consumer package goods was initially directed at reducing the failure rate in test market, we begin by considering models that were developed for test markets. We adapt them to pretest market forecasts. The approach is to estimate the key trial and repeat parameters based on concept and product tests and then use the test-market model structure to forecast sales. Two examples are NEWS (Pringle, Wilson, and Brody 1982) and SPRINTER (Urban 1970). We discuss these models more completely in the next chapter, but outline the use of the NEWS model here in terms of its premarket forecasting. Figure 16.2 shows the NEWS

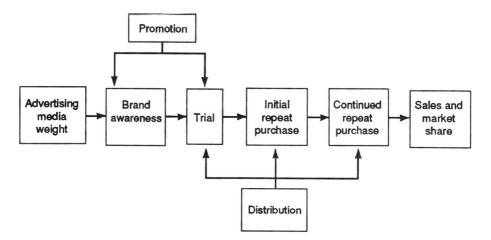

Figure 16.2   The New-Product Introduction Process (adopted from Pringle, Wilson, and Brody 1982)

model logic. The advertising-to-brand-awareness translation is obtained from statistical studies of past brand launches. Promotion and distribution response are similarly based on past experience and the marketing plan for the new brand. NEWS estimates the trial from the "definitely-will-repurchase" intent measure from a home-use test. The research measures plus judgment define the parameters used in the model.

Chapter 12 outlined some of the methods to translate intent to purchase. In premarket analysis, trial and repeat behavior must be estimated. The initial approaches developed "norms" or rules based on experience with past products. In the trial and repeat models two translations are necessary. One transforms stated trial intent (usually on a 5-point scale) into ultimate penetration and the other transforms repeat-intent (also usually on a five point scale) into cumulative repeat. In the NEWS model, the top box, "definitely will buy," is used, but other modelers weigh the top two or three boxes based on their statistical derivation of rules derived from past new product launches and category purchase incidence. The translations represent "norms" to translate stated intent into predicted behavior. These norms depend heavily on the analogy of the new product to past new products. In package goods these analogies are quite close and the norms work surprisingly well.

Dynamic Stochastic Models. In this approach, regressions based on previous purchasing experience are used to identify how the direct measures relate to trial and repeat dynamics. A number of alternative equations are possible. We illustrate the approach by describing parts of one stochastic model developed by Eskin and Malec (1976).

Their equation for cumulative trial is derived from past product trial rates. The cumulative trial after one year (α_1), depends on product class penetration (PCP, percent of households buying at least one item in the product class during one year), the total consumer direct promotional expenditures (SPN) for the new product, and the distribution (DIS, weighted percent of stores stocking the new product). Trial is then given by

$$\alpha_1 = \alpha(PCP)^{b_1}\ (SPN)^{b_2}\ (DIS)^{b_3} \tag{16.1}$$

where α, b_1, b_2, and b_3 are parameters. After taking logs of both sides of this equation, a linear regression is used to estimate b_1, b_2, and b_3 based on past experience from past new products. This equation is similar to Claycamp and Liddy, but it does not include judged variables like the product position, copy effectiveness, or packaging. However, both models fit trial well. The model would be made more useful for diagnostic purposes if more trial variables were included and it was strengthened by direct measures of propensity to try.

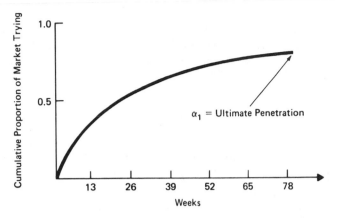

Figure 16.3 Trial Growth

Equation 16.1 gives cumulative trial, but it is important to predict the growth of trial. Figure 16.3 shows the most common form of growth. The stochastic models predict this growth.[1]

Eskin and Malec model first repeat in a similar way except that: (1) the cumulative repeat is estimated from a direct measure of intent to buy after usage and (2) the decay parameter is based on a hypothesis of consumer response and is a function of the frequency of purchase.[2] Similar equations are used for the second repeat purchase, the third, and so on.

To use this model for a new product, penetration is observed for the category, promotion and distribution are obtained from the introduction plan and these values substituted in equation (16.1) to give α_1. Trial over time is given by a curve similar to Figure 16.3. Intent to buy is measured for those who have tried the product and cumulative repeat is determined. Equations predict first repeat, second repeat, third repeat, etc. Total sales comes from summing trial and the various repeat classes (see Eskin and Malec [1976] for details, and Silk and Kalwani [1982] for extensions).

Stochastic models are attractive because of their explicit modeling of trial and repeat dynamics. Using past purchasing data from new product introductions in the model helps achieve good forecasting accuracy.

Home Delivery Measures.   Another approach to forecasting with a trial/repeat model is based on direct measures of trial and repeat in a sample of

[1] The equation used by Eskin and Malec for this curve is $R_t(0) = \alpha_1(1 - \gamma_1{}')$. Where $R_t(0)$ = the percentage of consumers who have tried the new product by time t, α_1 = the cumulative trial given by equation 16.1, γ_1 = a parameter to be estimated ($0 \le \gamma_1 \le 1$).

[2] First repeat, $R_t(1)$, is given by: $R_t(1) = \alpha_2(1 - \gamma_2{}')$.

households served by a home delivery service. The measurement of trial and repeat is done in a panel (1,000 households) which is visited each week by a salesperson. Based on information in a color catalog published each month and a biweekly promotion sheet describing price promotion, the consumer orders from a wide range of frequently purchased consumer products. The products are delivered on the same day and purchase records are computerized.

When a new product is to be tested, an ad is placed in the monthly catalog and trial and repeat purchase is observed. From this data a share of market for the product is forecasted by multiplying cumulative trial times the share of purchases the new brand receives from those who have tried it (Parfitt and Collins, 1968).

The advantage of this approach is that it is based on a home delivery panel that approximates the actual product launch. The direct measures of trial are obtained based on exposure to real advertising, and realistic repeat purchasing environments enhance forecasting accuracy. One disadvantage of this approach is that the panel must be run long enough to get good estimates, probably longer than other pretest market approaches. Therefore, costs are relatively high.

This panel approach has been used both to analyze existing product promotion (Charlton and Pymont 1975; Charlton, Ehrenberg, and Pymont 1972) and to forecast new product sales (Pymont, Reay, and Standen 1976).

Laboratory Measurement.   The success of home delivery measures depends upon the ability of the home delivery service to approximate closely the actual purchase environment. An alternative approach is to use a central location laboratory to approximate the trial purchase environment. Consumers are recruited, exposed to advertisements (television or print), and given the opportunity to buy in a simulated retail store. After buying in the simulated store, the consumer takes the product home and repeat measures are taken with a call-back interview. The basic idea of laboratory measurement is to force exposure to the product and provide a realistic purchase choice environment (a store shelf). The success of the laboratory measurement depends on the ability of the model either to minimize the bias of such a laboratory simulation or to develop procedures to correct for any bias.

The advantages of laboratory measurement are that results are obtained rapidly and at a relatively low cost. The measures of trial and repeat are based on direct consumer response in a realistic purchase environment. Such measures have the potential for producing highly accurate forecasts. The disadvantage of such measurement is that the laboratory abstracts reality. The simulated store is not an actual store, measures are taken shortly after exposure to advertising, and the measurement may influence consumer behavior.

While each of these problems can be overcome, they represent potential systematic biases that must be considered carefully.

One laboratory measurement model was based on a procedure development by Yankelovich, Skelly, and White (1970) called LTM. They adjusted the observed trial and repeat rates based on judgment derived from past experience. For example, the observed trial is reduced by 25% because of "inflation" in the laboratory. Another adjustment is a "clout" factor that varies from .25 to .75 depending on introductory spending. Predictions of market share are made by multiplying trial and repeat by the frequency of purchase where frequency is adjusted based on a judged "frequency factor" which reflects departures of new products from known frequency of purchase patterns. The Yankelovich et al. approach is interesting because it blends direct observation with managerial judgment, but the predictions are very dependent upon the judgmental input.

Another laboratory measurement model is the trial/repeat component of a model developed by Silk and Urban (1978) called ASSESSOR. They use the dynamic stochastic model formulation to estimate market share for the new brand by multiplying the ultimate cumulative trial by the share of purchases from those who have tried.

Trial comes about in one of two ways: direct trial or receipt and use of free samples. The direct trial, given ad exposure and availability, is the proportion of respondents who purchase the new brand in the laboratory on their simulated shopping trip. The predicted awareness from advertisements is based on the planned advertising budget. The predicted availability is based on planned sales force and promotional activity directed at the retail trade. These parameters are obtained from judgment or from regression equations. Direct trial is the product of trial in the lab times awareness and distribution. The amount of trial from free samples depends on the number of samples that will be sent and the observed use in the laboratory simulation. If the probability of a consumer's direct trial is independent of the probability of receipt and use of a sample, the total trial is the sum of both sources of trial less their overlap.

The long-run share for those who have tried is modeled as a stochastic model, similar to the Eskin and Malec structure. Estimates of the repeat purchase probabilities are derived from measurements obtained in the post-usage survey. The proportion of respondents who make a mail order repurchase of the new brand when given the opportunity to do so is taken as an estimate of new product repeat.

The advantages of the Silk and Urban formulation are that it is based on theoretical models of consumer response and that most consumer response estimates come from direct measurement. The disadvantage is that this component of their model is still a laboratory simulation and thus subject to all the criticisms discussed above.

Summary of Trial/Repeat Measurement. Trial and repeat purchase models are the most logical way to represent consumer response to a new frequently purchased brand. Direct measures of trial and repeat are important inputs to forecasting and many of the models discussed above are based firmly in consumer theory. Judgments need to be applied to any model, but direct measures and explicit models promote consistency, methodological rigor, and forecasting accuracy.

Attitude Change Models

In the design phase, forecasts of purchase potential were made based on estimates of consumer preferences for the new product. The advantage of this approach is that preference is predicted more directly and intervening effects such as awareness and availability are incorporated directly in the model. Furthermore, product characteristics or consumer perceptions are readily incorporated in the model through the preference analysis techniques discussed in chapters 10 and 11.

The attitude-based pretest market analysis models use the basic approach of estimating behavior from consumer preferences. Consumer attitudes (preference or beliefs about product attributes) are measured first for existing products. The consumer is then given the new product and, after use, attitudes are measured for the new product.

The advantage of this approach is that the indirect attitude measures avoid some of the laboratory effects inherent in the direct trial and repeat measures. For example, attitudes toward existing products are often measured prior to laboratory exposure and are more representative of the attitudes of the consumer population. This is in contrast to the direct measures of trial which are highly dependent upon the closeness with which the laboratory approximates the real world. The disadvantage of attitude measures is that they are not direct measures. Predictions depend upon the accuracy and completeness of the model used to estimate choice behavior from the measured attitudes.

One early attitude model, called COMP, was developed by Burger (1972). The measurement to support this model is done by an initial interview to measure attitudes and an interview after consumers are exposed to advertisements and products in a simulated store. A call-back interview measures attitudes after use of the new brand.

Burger bases his attitude measures on a direct-measure preference model. That is, he forms a linear preference score from consumer attribute ratings and stated importances of those attributes. Burger's attitude measure is then the relative preference score given by the ratio of preference for the new product divided by the sum of preferences for all products (new and existing).

An alternative attitude model is the second component of the pretest market forecasting model developed by Silk and Urban (1978) using logit modeling procedure. They augment their first component with measures of preference. Their preference measure is developed from a constant sum paired comparison task in which consumers allocate a fixed number of "chips" among each pair of products in their consideration set. A scaling technique developed by Torgerson (1958) transforms the constant sum measures into ratio-scaled preferences. A variation of the logit model is then used to estimate behavior from the preferences. (Review chapter 12.)

To forecast the purchase probability for the new product (brand b), preference measures for the new and existing products are obtained after the consumer has experienced a period of trial usage of the new product. The new product is assumed to be in the consumer's consideration set and the logit model is used to forecast the unadjusted purchase probability for the new product.

The unadjusted purchase probability is forecast assuming the new product will be in the consideration set. To calculate an expected market share for the new brand, Silk and Urban take into account that the new brand will not necessarily become an element of the consideration set of brands for all consumers when it becomes available in the market. To do this, they obtain estimates of the percent of consumers who will consider the new product and multiply the consideration percent times the average unadjusted purchase probability.

For existing brands, the observed consideration levels are used to adjust the logit-based purchase probabilities. (Recall that the purchase probabilities for the existing brands change when the new product is introduced.) These estimates are important to the new product manager because they indicate which established brands are likely to retaliate to defend their share.

Both the Burger and the Silk and Urban models base their estimates on some form of preference measures and both correct for awareness and availability. The predictions in both cases are the probabilities of purchase. The models differ in the specific equations and estimation procedures used. In particular, Silk and Urban should use stronger preference measures (constant sum), behavioral-based statistical techniques (logit), and limit their measurements to the consideration set. Both models assume that the brand enters an established category.

Convergent Measures and Models

Judgment, trial/repeat, and attitude models each have their strengths and their weaknesses. An emerging view on pretest market analyses is to use more than one method in parallel and compare the results. For example, one might use the Eskin and Malec model to develop estimates based on trial and repeat measures and compare this to predictions obtained from Burger's attitude change model. If the models agree, then the product manager has more faith in the predictions. If they disagree, then by comparing and reconciling results, any biases in measurement or structural problems in models can be identified and corrected.

The advantage of such a convergent approach is potentially greater accuracy and more confidence in the resulting forecasts. Furthermore, a combination of approaches gives a more comprehensive indication of how to improve the new product. The disadvantage of a convergent approach is the slightly greater cost. Costs do not double, however, because inputs for more than one model can often be obtained in the same set of consumer measures.

We return to the ASSESSOR model to illustrate the specific measures and analyses used in a convergent approach based on trial/repeat and attitude models.

ASSESSOR is designed to aid management in evaluating new products once a positioning strategy has been developed and executed to the point where the product, packaging, and advertising copy are available and an introductory marketing plan (price, promotion, and advertising) has been formulated. Given these inputs, the system is specifically intended to

1. Predict the new brand's equilibrium of long-run market share and unit sales volume over time.
2. Estimate the sources of the new brand's share—"cannibalization" of the firm's existing brand(s) and "draw" from competitors' brands.
3. Produce actionable diagnostic information for product improvement and develop advertising copy and other creative materials.
4. Permit low cost screening of selected elements of alternative marketing plans (advertising copy, price, and package design).

Figure 16.4 shows the overall structure of the system developed to meet these requirements. The critical task of predicting the brand's market share and sales volume is approached through the trial/repeat and attitude models described earlier. Convergent results strengthen confidence in the prediction while divergent outcomes signal the need for further analyses to identify sources of discrepancies and to provide bases for reconciliation. The measurement inputs required for both models are obtained from a research design involving laboratory and usage tests. The key outputs are a market share prediction plus diagnostic information which is used to make a decision as to the brand's future.

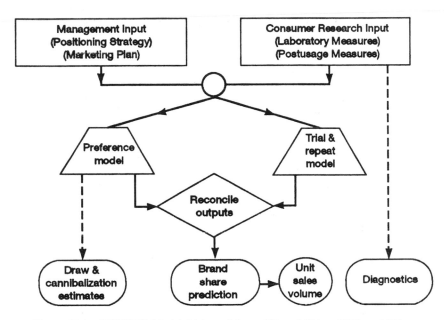

Figure 16.4 ASSESSOR Model (Adapted from Silk and Urban 1978; and Urban and Katz 1983)

Research Design and Measurement.   The measurement inputs required to develop the desired diagnostic information and predictions for ASSESSOR are obtained from a research design structured to parallel the basic stages of the process of consumer response to a new product. Table 16.3 outlines the essential features of the design and identifies the main types of data collected at each step. To simulate the awareness-trial stages of the response process, a laboratory-based experimental procedure is employed wherein a sample of consumers are exposed to advertising for the new product and a small set of the principal competing products already established in the market. Following this, consumers enter a simulated shopping facility where they have the opportunity to purchase quantities of the new or established products. The ability of the new product to attract repeat purchases is assessed by one or more waves of follow-up interviews with the same respondents. These interviews are conducted after sufficient time has passed for consumers to use or consume a significant quantity of the new product at home.

The laboratory phase of the research is executed in a facility located in the immediate vicinity of a shopping center. "Intercept" interviews (O_1) are conducted with shoppers to screen and recruit a sample number of consumers representative of the target market for the new product. Field work is done at several different locations chosen to attain heterogeneity and obtain quotas

TABLE 16.3 ASSESSOR Research Design and Measurement

Design	Procedure	Measurement
0_1	Respondent screening and recruitment (personal interview)	Criteria for target group identification (e.g., product class usage)
0_2	Premeasurement for established brands (self-administered questionnaire)	Composition of "relevant set" of established brands, attribute weights and ratings, and preferences
X_1	Exposure to advertising for established brands *and* new brand	
0_3	Measurement of reactions to the advertising materials (self-administered questionnaire)	Optional, e.g., likability and believability ratings of advertising materials
X_2	Simulated shopping trip and exposure to display of new and established brands	
0_4	Purchase opportunity (choice recorded by research personnel)	Brand(s) purchased
X_3	Home use/consumption of new brand	
0_5	Postusage measurement (telephone interview)	New brand usage rate, satisfaction ratings and repeat purchase Propensity; attribute ratings and preferences for "relevant set" of established brands plus the new brand

0 = Measurement.
X = Advertising or product exposure.

From Silk and Urban (1978, p. 174).

desired in the final sample. Studies typically employ samples of approximately 300 persons.

Upon arriving at the laboratory facility location, respondents are asked to complete a self-administered questionnaire that constitutes the before measurement (0_2). Individually, respondents then proceed to a separate area where they are shown a set of advertising materials (X_1) for the new brand plus the leading established brands. Ordinarily, respondents are exposed to 5 to 6 commercials, one per brand, and the order in which they are presented is rotated to avoid systematic position effects. Measurement of reactions to the advertising materials (0_3) occurs next if such information is desired for diagnostic purposes.

The final stage of the laboratory experiment takes place in a simulated retail store where participants have the opportunity to make a purchase.

When first approached, they are told that they will be given a fixed amount of compensation for their time—typically about ten dollars, but always more than the sum needed to make a purchase. In the lab they are informed that they may use the money to purchase any brand or combination of brands in the product category they choose, with any unexpended cash to be kept by them. They then move to an area where quantities of the full set of competing brands, including the new one, are displayed and available for inspection (X_2). Each brand is priced at a level equal to the average price at which it is being regularly sold in mass retail outlets in the local market area. The brand (or brands) selected by each participant is (are) recorded by one of the research personnel (O_4) at the checkout counter. Although respondents are free to forego buying anything and retain the full ten dollar sum, most do make a purchase. To illustrate, the proportion of participants making a purchase observed in two separate studies of deodorants and antacids were 74% and 64%, respectively. Those who do not purchase the new brand are given a quantity of it free after all buying transactions have been completed. This procedure parallels the common practice of affecting trial usage through the distribution of free samples. A record is maintained for each respondent as to whether the respondent "purchased" or was given the new brand so as to be able to assess whether responses on the postusage survey are differentially affected by trial purchase versus free sampling. (Remember, samples are given to those who do not try based on the advertising.)

The postusage survey (O_5) is administered by telephone after sufficient time has passed for usage experience to have developed. The specific length of the premeasurement-postmeasurement interval is determined by the estimated usage rate for the new product. Respondents are offered an opportunity to make a repurchase of the new brand (to be delivered by mail) and respond to essentially the same set of perception and preference measurements that were utilized in the before or premeasurement step (O_2), except that they now rate the new brand as well as established ones.

Model Structure. As shown in Figure 16.4, ASSESSOR uses both the trial/repeat and an attitude model described earlier. The basic input to estimate the preference model is obtained from measurement O_2. The measurements for prediction are obtained from O_5. The inputs for the trial probability are obtained from O_5. The models are estimated and their outputs are compared.

If the product is entering an established category, the sales volume is obtained by multiplying the share from the preference model times the forecasted total category sales. This is compared to the asymptotic sales from the trial and repeat model. If the brand is creating a completely new category, the preference model cannot be used and the trial/repeat model is used alone to generate the forecast of sales growth and dynamics. In most cases (95% of the applications) brands enter established categories or subsegment an existing category so that both models are useful.

Convergence.   The expression for market share developed from the individual preference-purchase probability model is structurally similar to that defined in terms of trial and repeat purchase levels. In the former case, market share is the product of the relevant set proportion, and the average conditional probability of purchasing the new brand. In the latter case, market share is the product of the cumulative trial proportion and the repeat-purchase share.

The submodels and measures used to arrive at estimates of these conceptually similar quantities are quite distinct. Whereas the trial and repeat proportions are based upon direct observations of these quantities obtained under controlled conditions, the relevant set proportion and the average conditional purchase probability are estimated indirectly from other measures.

Finding that the two models yield outputs that are in close agreement serves to strengthen confidence in the prediction. On the other hand, divergent forecasts trigger a search for and evaluation of possible sources of error or bias that might account for the discrepancy. The first step is to compare the relevant set proportion and trial estimates. Lack of agreement here implies that the assumptions concerning awareness and retail availability are not compatible with those made implicitly or explicitly in estimating the relevant set proportion. After reconciling the trial and relevant set estimates, attention is focused on the values of the conditional purchase probability and the repeat rate. In the end, some judgment may have to be exercised in order to reconcile differences that arise, but that process is facilitated by careful consideration of the structural comparability of the two models.

Predictions and Marketing Plans.   Prediction of a new brand's market share reflects the estimated parameters and the plans for the marketing program to be employed in the future test market or launch. Frequently at this pretest market stage, the new-product team is interested in evaluating variations in the introductory marketing mix for the new brand. The trial/repeat model is used to perform rough simulations of the effects of marketing mix modifications. The changes or alternatives management wishes to consider are approximated by judgmentally altering parameter levels. For example, increasing the level of advertising spending is represented by raising the awareness probability and therefore the estimated trial. Differences in sampling programs are estimated by changing the number of samples or their probability of usage. Other types of changes, such as in advertising copy or price, that affect the conditional first purchase probability are measured by expanding the research design shown in Table 16.3 to observe the differential effects on trial purchases due to alternative price or copy treatments.

After examining the impact of strategic changes in this manner, profitability measures are calculated for the market share estimates. Based on these inputs and the forecasted share, the new-product team can decide whether or not to proceed to test market the new brand.

Summary of Alternative Approaches and Commercial Services

This section has covered a number of generic, alternative approaches for forecasting new package good sales. We have separated the approaches by giving techniques rather than specific models. By understanding the basic approach behind various commercially available models, you can better assess each model and select the model that is most appropriate for your use. Alternatively, if your new product development program is sufficiently large, you can build on these basic ideas and customize a pretest market analysis to best fit the needs of your organization.

The 1980s saw the emergence of many commercial pre-test-market services based on the approaches discussed above. ASSESSOR was initially marketed by Management Decision Systems, Inc. (MDS) and then by Information Resources Inc. (as the result of a merger with MDS) and subsequently by M/A/R/C, Inc. and Macro Strategies, Inc. In this period the model evolved from the original formulation to allow more dynamic forecasting of volume and use of consumer panel and UPC scanner data. Yankalovich, Skelly, and White dropped their LTM model and adopted a new model called LITMUS (Blackburn and Clancy 1980). Probably the largest selling service was marketed by Burke Market Research and was called BASES. This service initially was positioned against ASSESSOR with a full proposition test, but was later modified to produce concept forecasts at a lower cost based on trial and repeat intent norms. Many other services have been developed in the USA and Europe (to name a few: DESIGNER by Novaction, Inc., ESP by NPD, SENSOR by Research International, ENTRO by M/A/R/C, CRITERION by Custom Research, Inc., and a pretest marketing model by Market Simulations Inc). The commercial services could originally be divided into share (preference models) or sales volume (trial and repeat models with intent norms), but now many services use convergent models based on share structures and trial and depth of repeat dynamics.

ACCURACY OF PRETEST MARKET FORECASTING

In this section we review evidence of the accuracy of pretest models as well as suggest guidelines for using pretest forecasts. Although many commercial services have been used, the available published evidence on the predictive accuracy of pretest models is not large and a number of issues make the available evidence difficult to judge. There are commercial services who say "they have never missed" or are "97% correct." Some of the claims are difficult to substantiate. In one case a client sued the supplier for failure to predict sales accurately.

Many services provide lists of "predicted" and "actual" share. However, one must be careful in interpreting them (Tauber 1977). For example, Eskin and Malec report "forecasted" and actual results for their model. The authors clearly state that the model forecast is based not on estimates of repeat (α_2), but the actual value from the test market. Despite this warning, a casual reader may not realize this severely restricts implications of validity from this particular data.

In some cases the "predicted" is not the original prediction, but one adjusted for "differences" between test market and pretest market. For example, after the test, it may have been discovered that advertising spending was less than planned and a new competitor entered the market. Although it is logical to make some adjustments, looking for reasons to make predicted sales agree with actual sales is dangerous. This may occur unintentionally if one only looks at differences and then tries to find reasons why they do not agree. If changes are allowed, they should be pursued with equal vigor in cases where actual and predicted agree as well as when they disagree. Then revision may result in higher or lower differences between predicted and actual. Another bias can occur if the product is tested concurrently with test market rather than prior to test market. It takes a high level of discipline not to be influenced by the concurrent experience. If a service claims an almost perfect record of forecasting, you should examine whether their analysis is biased, either explicitly or implicitly.

Other difficulties occur because "actual" share is itself subject to measurement error and because "actual" long-run share may not stabilize in a 9- to 12-month test market. When we take these cautions into account, we find that many commercial models claim success, but that not all have used rigorous predictive testing procedures.

Published Validation Data

Two sets of data have passed the scrutiny of academic reviews (Pringle, Wilson and Brody 1982; and Urban and Katz 1983). One found a 67% success rate in test market after use of ASSESSOR compared to the success rate of 35.5 percent (Nielsen 1979) for products that did not have a formal pretest market model analysis. On the other side of the error possibilities, 3.8% of the products that failed in ASSESSOR succeeded in test market.

Figure 16.5 shows a plot of actual versus predicted market share for 44 products where validation data was available for ASSESSOR. The correlation is 0.95 and is an encouraging result. Table 16.4 puts the correlation in better perspective. The table shows the original forecasts and the forecast after "adjustment" for differences between the original business plan and the actual execution of advertising, promotion, and distribution in the test market. The average pre-test-market share forecast was 7.77, whereas the average test-market share was 7.16. Thus a positive bias of .61 share point is present and is significant at the 10% level ($t = 2.0$). The average absolute deviation is 1.54 share points and the standard deviation is 1.99 share points.

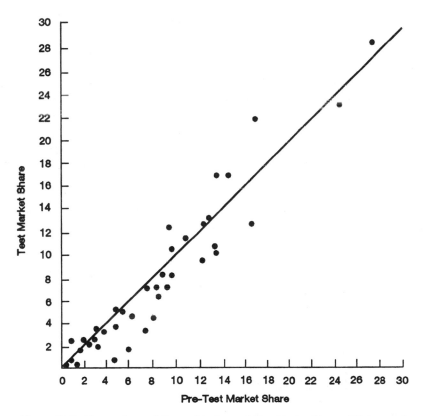

Figure 16.5 Comparison of Pretest-Market and Test-Market Shares (Urban and Katz, 1983, p. 223; reprinted with permission)

TABLE 16.4 Comparison of Pre-Test-Market, Adjusted,
and Test-Market Shares

	Overall (n = 44)	Health and Beauty Aids (n = 13)	Household (n = 11)	Food (n = 20)
Average test market share	7.16	7.35	10.14	5.40
Pre-test versus test-market share				
Mean difference	0.61	0.43	0.61	0.73
Mean absolute difference	1.54	1.66	1.37	1.56
Standard deviation of differences	1.99	2.08	1.71	2.06
Adjusted versus test-market share				
Mean difference	−0.01	−0.29	−0.15	0.25
Mean absolute difference	0.83	0.88	1.04	0.68
Standard deviation of differences	1.12	1.09	1.23	1.02

From Urban and Katz (1983, p. 223; reprinted with permission).

As expected, the comparisons between adjusted and test-market shares show less error—mean deviation of −.01, average absolute deviation of .83, and standard deviation of 1.12. The correlation of the adjusted predictions with test-market shares is .98. Adjustments were made in 36 of the 44 cases. In most of these the adjustments improved the accuracy, but in six of the cases the deviation increased. The systematic over prediction for lower share values shown in Figure 16.5 was reduced substantially by the adjustments.

The validation sample consists of 13 health and beauty aid (HBA) products, 11 household cleaning products, and 20 food products. Table 16.4 reports the individual category results. The absolute differences are small and none of the paired comparisons of means or variances are significantly different at the 10% level. Similar levels of accuracy are observed across these product categories.

Similar predictive results have been reported for NEWS (Pringle, Wilson and Brody, 1982) where it was found, on a pretest unadjusted basis, a mean bias of +1.33 share points and a standard deviation of 1.48.

To put these numbers in perspective, Figure 16.6 represents the distribution of forecast errors with a standard deviation of 2.0 share points and a positive bias of 0.6 share points. These numbers are close to the unadjusted numbers in Table 16.4.

Managerial Use of Validation Data

One way to interpret this predictive accuracy is to consider how the test market decision should be made. If the pretest share forecast is much higher

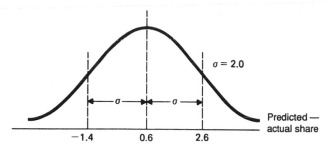

Figure 16.6   Distribution of Errors

than the minimum required share or cut off criteria, a go decision is appropriate. If the predicted share is much less than the required share, a no decision is appropriate. The greater the amount by which the forecast exceeds the required share, the higher is the probability of success in test market.

For example, suppose that the minimum required share were 6.0% and the model predicted 9.1%. Then, accounting for about a .6% bias in the model, the predicted share minus the required share is 1.25 SD above the average model bias. (Number of standard deviations = $(9.1 - 6.0 - 0.6)/2.0 = 1.25$) We use a cumulative normal table to translate the number of standard deviations to a probability of achieving the minimum required share. For example, 1.25 standard deviations translates to a 90% probability of achieving or exceeding the target. Table 16.5 provides the results of these computations for a range of values for the amount by which predicted share exceeds the minimum required share.

TABLE 16.5   Probability of Test Market Success

Amount (Share Points) by Which Predicted Exceeds Required Share	Probability of Success in Test Market
−1.0	21%
−0.5	29
0	38
0.5	48
0.6	50
1.0	58
1.5	67
2.0	76
2.5	83
3.0	89
3.5	93
4.0	96

Now a difficult question is raised. How much risk should be taken in test market? If we require a 95% chance of success, we will need almost a 4 share point margin of forecast over actual. Few products will meet this margin so, although we will have few failures, we will also have few successes. In the final analysis each new-product team must make this tradeoff implicitly or explicitly. The accuracy of forecasts is higher after adjustment (the standard deviation of adjusted and actual share is 1.0 share point rather than 2.0 for initial versus actual), so if management is sure they could execute the test as planned, the risks may be less than indicated in Table 16.5. The accuracy also varies according to the type of product. If the new product fits well into an established category the accuracy is higher. If the product is revolutionary and creates a whole new category, variance is higher. If the brand is going to have a small share (less than 2%), larger samples are needed to achieve the indicated accuracies.

Pretest market forecasts are not perfectly valid, but pretest market analysis can be used by management to control effectively the risk of test-market failure.

Value of Pretest Market Forecasting of Packaged Goods

The value of a pretest market forecast depends upon the costs of failure, the accuracy of the forecast, and the rewards of success. It also depends on the go/no go cutoffs set for both the pretest market analysis and the test market experiment. For example, if the go/no go cutoff is set so low, then everything will pass the pretest market analysis and, hence, it will provide little value. By the same token, if the cutoff is set too high, all products will be eliminated thus eliminating any possibility of success.

There are many means to set cutoffs. One formal method was proposed by Urban and Katz (1983). They use decision analysis (Raiffa and Schlaifer 1961, Rao and Winter 1981) to select the cutoffs that lead to the greatest expected profit. For example, suppose that a typical reward function is:

- A $55 million introductory expense for advertising, promotion, plant, and equipment. A loss that is incurred at a 0.00 share.
- A break-even profit at a 5.75% share.
- A profit of $80 million at a 10% share.
- A profit of $190 million at a 20% share.

Suppose further that the cost of a test market is $1.5 million and the cost of a pretest market analysis is $50,000. From published data for 50 new brands

(*Nielsen Reporter* 1979), the accuracy of a test market is that 50% of the observations of first-year national share are within 10% of the test-market share. (This data is consistent with that of Gold 1964.) If we combine these data with the pretest-market accuracy reported in Table 16.4, then Urban and Katz suggest that the best cutoffs are a cutoff share of 4.5% for pretest market analysis and a cutoff share of 5.5% for a test market experiment. The resulting expected profit is $28.4 million compared to an expected profit with no testing of $16.7 million. The value of testing is $11.7 million!

Of course we can consider other strategies. For example, we might use pretest-market analysis but skip the test-market experiment. In this case it pays to be somewhat more conservative with a cutoff share of 6.0%. The resulting expected profit is $28.0 million. Thus, if the test market is to be skipped, the value of the pretest market analysis is $11.3 million, not a bad return on an investment of $50,000. If we skip the pretest market and use only test markets, then we can achieve an expected profit of $28.1 million with a cutoff of 6% share. Putting it all together we see that both the pretest-market analysis and the test-market experiment provide dramatic returns if used singly or together.

If we plan to test market a product we still gain an incremental expected profit of over $300,000 by using pretest analyses—the $50,000 investment seems to be justified. If we use a pretest-market analysis, the incremental gains from test market are still $400,000. The investment of $1.5 million is justified, but there is risk. If the test market delays introduction without providing useful diagnostic information, some new-product teams may prefer to be more conservative with the pretest-market cutoff and choose to skip test markets.

Naturally, the above calculations are for an average return of an average new-product project in an average category. Each case will be different. The potential for greater losses will raise the screen while the potential for higher rewards will lower the screen. If both are raised, the screen may stay the same. Similarly, if the penalties of delaying are great, there will be justifiable pressure to skip test market although it is unlikely that there will be a justification for skipping both the pretest and test-market analyses.

We suggest that if there is any doubt, the formal analyses be reapplied to your specific situation. However, the following guidelines may help. A test market may not be required if (1) there is a large penalty for reaching the market 12 months later, (2) entry costs are low and losses at small share levels are small, (3) a small market is entered and potential gains and losses are both small, (4) pretest-market sample sizes are large (greater accuracy), accurate awareness and distribution estimates can be made, and the firm's marketing plan will be executed faithfully. Time penalties are increasing and markets are being increasingly subsegmented so it can be expected that test marketing may not be necessary for many consumer packaged goods. For example, in Europe, some markets tend to be small and the associated rewards are small in relation to the fixed cost of test marketing. This is compounded by the difficulty of finding a representative test market city and controlling the marketing execution.

MANAGERIAL USE OF PRETEST MARKET ANALYSES—MINICASES

Pretest market analysis provides accurate forecasts, but the new product team is also interested in how to use the pretest market analyses to improve the product's performance. In this section we describe five minicases to illustrate many of the managerial actions that result from careful pretest market analyses.

Case 1: Laundry Product

The organization introducing this product had several leading brands in the detergent and fabric softener market. It had developed a new fabric conditioner and was poised for a national launch with a share objective of 8%. The organization was so confident of success that test market was to be replaced by a "distribution check." This was a plan to introduce the product for three months in one test city, with advertising, to enable it to achieve the desired retail distribution and self-facings. A pretest market analysis was done to get an early reading on the product and forecast sales.

The results were surprising to the brand manager. Trial was very low in the simulated store. The product was not viewed as new and the advertisements scored poorly on likability and believability. The "new" product was confused with the firm's existing product. The share was forecast at 2%. Faced with these results, the company aborted the national launch. The test market was maintained for nine months and the actual share of 1.8% was close to the prediction.

In this case, the use of a pretest market model prevented a product failure and the $5 million dollar loss such a failure would have entailed. The case emphasizes the danger of becoming overly optimistic and excited about a new product. A pretest-market analysis should often be carried out before test market to reduce the possibility of failure.

Case 2: Household Product

This product used a new applicator to clean and condition wood surfaces more effectively. The frequency of purchase in this category was low (two or three times a year), but concept tests showed the product appealed to many people.

A pretest analysis indicated high-share potential based on good trial and repeat response. However, because of the low frequency of purchase, almost all early sales would be trial; long-run share would depend upon repeat sales. The model indicated that shares of 25% to 30% could occur in months three to six, but the long-run potential would be 18%.

The share dynamics were critical and the prediction was important in production planning and developing a financial plan for the product. The product was subsequently test-marketed. A share of 20% was observed after 16 months in the test cities. In this case, the pretest market confirmed that the product was in the "go" state and generated a forecast to plan production and marketing. Original plans had been laid around an expectation of a revolution in the category and a 30% share. The pre-test showed this was unlikely and plans were revised to achieve target profitability at a share objective of 18%. The test market was then used to find the advertising, couponing, and promotion levels to maximize profits.

Case 3: Deodorant

A new aerosol deodorant was being introduced into a saturated market based on a claim of "goes on dry." The primary goal of the pretest analysis was to forecast share and examine the effects of sampling. The claim of dryness was not portrayed effectively by the ad. In-store trial was low. However, consumer experience with the product was good with respect to the dryness dimension. The share with advertising alone was 5 percent, but if 40 percent of the households were sampled, the model predicted a 10 percent share.

The product was test-marketed and introduced nationally with heavy sampling and achieved a share very close to the predicted 10% in both test market and in national introduction. In this case, the pretest market analysis was used to forecast and predict the effect of introductory marketing strategies.

Case 4: Over-the-Counter Drug

This organization had developed a new over-the-counter pain reliever. The decision to introduce was complex since several other firms were known to be considering introducing similar products. Two studies were run. One with the old market products and one with the set of competitive new products. The new products were represented by advertisements and packaged products for the competitors' products based on how they were expected to appear.

The results indicated that the organization's new product could get 8% of the "old" market, but in the "new" market would achieve only 3% share. The new entries by competitors were viewed as equal to or better than the organization's product. The pretest analysis suggested a NO GO decision.

In this case, the test market was undertaken in spite of the poor prediction. Momentum for the product was so high at the top management level that they felt they would take the risk of failure in test-market rather than miss the possible opportunity to enter the category. After twelve months and $1.5 million, the test-market share achievement was 2%. The project was terminated.

It seems clear from their experience that raw determination can be costly. Organizations should develop a disciplined, new product development process and act upon pretest-market models after they have been institutionalized and validated in the organization. In the preceding case, this was only the second application of the pretest system by the organization and management was not yet sure of its validity.

Case 5: Vitamin Supplement

A large European packaged goods manufacturer had introduced successfully in Europe a vitamin supplement for children. It tested the product in the United States and Canada and predicted 11 percent share in the childrens' vitamin market. They achieved 12.1% share. Japan was the next target, but concerns were raised about the "polite bias" Japanese consumers would have in market research. If they wanted to please the interviewer by saying they would buy the product, a large over-estimate could occur. The design was set up to avoid this bias by placing the new product among other new food products in a full proposition laboratory pretest-market analysis. Even after advertising, only 1% of the consumers picked the new vitamin product from the shelf and those consumers that used the new product would definitely or probably not repeat. A clear failure was avoided by the test. Subsequently no other firm has introduced successfully a nutritional supplement for children in Japan where vitamins are used widely by adults, but for stress relief and not nutritional gains.

Summary of Packaged Goods Pretest-Market Forecasting

The cases demonstrate the impact of pretest market analysis. Test-market failure can be reduced, better introductory market strategies (e.g., advertising, sampling) can be identified, competitive environments can be understood, and improved financial and production plans can be made.

Pretest-market forecasting has been accepted as standard procedure by major packaged-goods firms. Proven techniques are available and if *used correctly* they can generate value, reduce risk, and improve products. We estimate that thousands of premarket model applications were done worldwide in the period from 1972 to 1992.

The number of alternatives is large and they vary by cost and accuracy. See Figure 16.7. The cost goes up when one includes a simulated store, competitive ad exposures, and larger samples, but errors decrease as measured by the standard deviation of difference between actual and predicted sales. Each firm must make its own tradeoff of cost and accuracy, but given that a good design effort has been carried out with preliminary "what-if" forecasts of market potential based on concept tests, it makes sense to do a full proposition test with high accuracy. New technologies such as information acceleration (see chapter 12 and sections below) may reduce the costs for the shopping and ad exposures. This encourages more complete modeling and measurement.

Investing more in pretest eliminates the need for test market when time penalties for delay are high and large introductory budgets are not required.

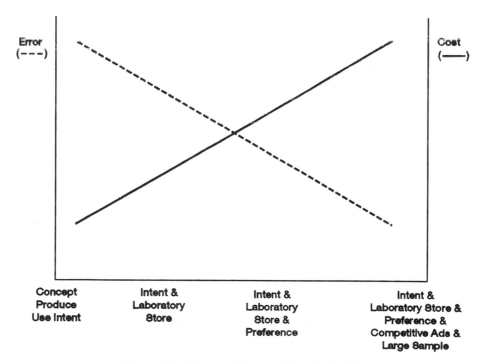

Figure 16.7   Estimated Error and Cost Tradeoffs

In cases where the risk of large losses are present, a test market is appropriate even after a large scale pretest market forecasting analysis. In either case, in package goods, tools are available to produce accurate forecasts and managerial diagnostics on a timely and relatively low cost basis.

DURABLE CONSUMER PRODUCTS[3]

Premarket forecasting models were invented in the consumer package goods field but they have been modified and transferred to the durable goods industry. This has not been easy because durable goods are very different in price and consumers use a different information gathering and decision process. Word-of-mouth communication must be included and norms for translating intent are almost impossible to derive. In this section we use automobile purchasing to demonstrate the durable modeling differences and new measurement and pre-market analysis procedures. Then we discuss applications to other durable goods and describe the state of the art in this area in terms of information acceleration.

The Case of Automobiles (as Representative of Durable Goods)

Automobiles represent a very large market. Sales in the 1988 model year were more than $100 billion in the United States and more than 300 billion world wide. A new car can contribute over one billion dollars per year in sales if it sells a rather modest 100,000 units per year at an average price of $12,000 per car. Major successes generate several times this in sales and associated profits.

These potential rewards encourage firms to allocate large amounts of capital to design, production, and selling of a new model. Ford spent three billion dollars developing the Taurus/Sable line. General Motors routinely spends $1 billion on a new model such as the Buick Electra. Most of this investment occurs before launch; if the car is not a market success, significant losses result.

Rates of failure are not published for the auto industry, but many cars have fallen short of expectations. Most failures are not as dramatic as the Edsel, which was withdrawn from the market, but significant losses occur in two ways. When sales are below forecasts there is excess production capacity and inventories. In this case, capital costs are excessive and prices must be discounted or other marketing actions undertaken to clear inventories. Losses

---

[3] This section is adapted from Urban, Hauser, and Roberts (1990).

also occur when the forecast of sales is below the market demand. In this case not enough cars can be produced, inventories are low, and prices are firm. The car is apparently very profitable, but a large opportunity cost may be incurred. Profits could have been higher if the forecast had been more accurate and more production capacity had been planned.

For those readers unfamiliar with the U.S. automobile industry we describe a few facts that will become important in developing pretest-market models.

Consumer Response

Search and Experience.   In automobiles, consumers reduce risk by searching for information and, in particular, visit showrooms. Typically 75% of buyers test drive one or more cars. The marketing manager's task is to convince the consumer to consider the automobile, get the prospect into the showroom, and facilitate purchasing with test drives and personal selling efforts.

Word-of-Mouth Communication/Magazine Reviews.   One source of information about automobiles is other consumers. Another is independent magazine reviews such as *Consumer Reports* and *Car and Driver*. Given the thousands of dollars involved in buying a car, the impact of these sources is quite large.

Importance of Availability.   Eighty percent of domestic sales are "off the lot" (i.e., purchased from dealer's inventory). Many consumers will consider alternative makes and models if they cannot find a car with the specific features, options, and colors they want.

Managerial Issues

No Test Market.   Building enough cars for test marketing (say, 1,000 cars) requires a full production line that could produce 75,000 units. Once this investment is made, the "bricks and mortar" are in place for a national launch and the major element of risk has been borne. Therefore, test marketing is not done in the auto industry.

Replace Existing Model Car.   Occasionally the auto industry produces an entirely new type of car (for example, Chrysler's introduction of the Minivan), but the predominant managerial issue is a major redesign of a car line such as the introduction of a downsized, front-wheel drive Buick Electra to replace its larger, rear-wheel drive predecessor.

When the management issue is a redesign, the sales history of its predecessor provides important information for forecasting consumer response to the replacement. Even when no direct replacement is planned, say, the introduction of the two-seated Buick Reatta, the sales history of related cars such as the Toyota Supra provide anchors to forecasts.

Production Constraints.   The production capacity level must be set before any actual market sales data can be collected. Once the production line has been built, production is limited to a rather narrow range. The maximum is the plant capacity (e.g., two shifts with the machines in the plant and their maintenance requirements) and the minimum is one 8-hour shift of production unless the plant is shut down completely.

The need to make production commitments early in the new product development process produces a two-stage sequence of decisions. First, a market strategy is developed, advanced engineering specification and designs are created, consumer reaction is gauged, and a go or no go production commitment is made. Because of the long construction times, this usually occurs three or more years before introduction. As market launch nears (18 months or less), the second set of decisions is made. A premarket forecast is generated and a revised marketing plan (e.g., targeting, positioning, advertising copy and expenditure, price, promotion, and dealer training) is formulated. In the first decision, production level is a variable, but in the prelaunch forecasting phase the capacity constraints are taken as given. See chapter 12 (Estimating Sales Potential: "What-If" Analysis) for consideration of the pre-production forecasting.

"Price" Forecasting Problem.   Production capacity is based on the best information available at the time, but as engineering and manufacturing develop the prototype cars, details change as do external conditions in the economy. At the planned price and marketing levels consumers may wish to purchase more or fewer vehicles than will be produced. The number of vehicles that would be sold if there were no production constraints is known as "free expression." Naturally, free expression is pegged to a price and marketing effort.

If the free expression demand at a given level of price and marketing effort is less than the production minimum, the company and its dealers must find a way to sell more cars (e.g., target new markets or change price, promotion, dealer incentives, and advertising). If the forecast is in the range, marketing variables can be used to maximize profit with little constraint. If free expression demand is above the maximum production, then opportunities exist to increase profit by adjusting price, reducing advertising, or by producing cars with many optional features.

Measurement

In keeping with the magnitude of the investment and the potential profit impact of the prelaunch decision, analyses are based on a heavy commitment to measurement to get consumer-based estimates of the relevant inputs. Because norms to translate intent are usually not available, a control group is necessary to calibrate biases. Usually the control group sees the existing car model which is being replaced. The control group does not see the new model car. If the car does not replace an old one, the most similar existing car (or cars) is used for control purposes.

If cost were not an issue one would select a random sample of consumers and gauge their reactions to the test and control vehicles. However, there are a large number of automobiles available (more than 300), the automobile market is highly segmented (luxury, sport, family, etc.), and automobile purchases are infrequent, so stratified sampling is done by grouping consumers by the car model that they purchased previously. Once selected, consumers are contacted via telephone, screened on interest in purchasing an automobile in the next year, and recruited for the study. Consumers who agree to participate are scheduled to come to a central location, a clinic, for a 1-hour interview. They are paid for their participation. If both spouses participate in the decision to buy a new car, both are encouraged to come.

Upon arrival some consumers are assigned randomly to the test car group and some to the control car group. They are next presented with a list of the 300 or so automobile lines available and asked which they would consider seriously. The consideration set commonly consists of about three cars; the median is five cars. In addition, they indicate the cars they feel would be their first, second, and if appropriate, third choices and rate these cars on probability scales and on a constant-sum paired-comparison of preferences. Consumers are shown advertisements and they rate the new car on the same probability and preference scales as the cars they now consider.

In the market, after advertising exposure, some consumers will visit showrooms for more information, others will seek word-of-mouth or magazine evaluations. Thus, as shown in Figure 16.8, the sample is split. For example, one half of each test/control treatment cell might see video tapes which simulate word-of-mouth and evaluations which represent consumer magazine evaluations (e.g., *Consumer Reports*); the other half are allowed to test-drive the car to which they are assigned. The video treatment can be divided into positive and negative exposure cells. Probability and constant-sum paired-comparison preference measures are taken for the stimulus car

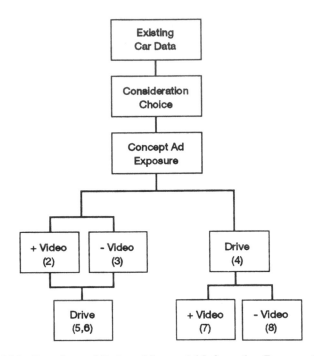

Figure 16.8 Experimental Design of Sequential Information Exposure in Clinic (Urban, Hauser, Roberts 1990, p. 405; reprinted with permission).

and the respondents' top three choices among cars now on the market. The half which saw the videotapes and magazine abstracts now test drives the car; the half which test drove is now exposed to the videotape and magazine information. Again probability and preference measures are taken. (Review chapter 12.)

Flow Models

The experimental condition must now be translated to market response. This means we must predict how many consumers will see advertisements, hear word-of-mouth, visit dealers, etc. One technique to make such forecasts is called flow models. The flow model approach that has been used successfully in the test market and launch analyses of consumer frequently-purchased goods (Urban 1970) and innovative public transportation services (Hauser and Wisniewski 1982). The modeling concept is simple. Each consumer is represented by a behavioral state that describes a level of information about the potential purchase. The behavioral states are chosen to represent consumer behavior as it is affected by the managerial decisions being evaluated.

For example, Buick used the set of behavioral states shown in Figure 16.9 to represent information flow/diffusion theory customized to the automobile market.

In each time period, consumers flow from one state to another. For example, in the third period a consumer, say John Doe, might have been unaware of the new car. If, in the fourth period, he talks to a friend who owns one, but he does not see any advertising, he "flows" to the behavioral state of "aware via word-of-mouth." We call the model a "macro-flow" model because we keep track, probabilistically, of the market. We do not track individual consumers. For details of this modeling technique see chapter 19. The flow probabilities are estimated from the clinic or industry norms, but supplemented by judgment when all else fails. For example, after consumers see the concept boards which simulate advertising, they are asked to indicate how likely they would be to visit a dealer.

In some cases the flow rates (percent of consumers/period) are parameters, say, $X\%$ of those who are aware via advertisements visit dealers in any given period. In other cases, the flows are functions of other variables. For example, the percent of consumers, now unaware, who become aware in a period is clearly a function of advertising expenditures. See, for example, Figure 13.13. For example, consider advertising flows. At zero advertising this

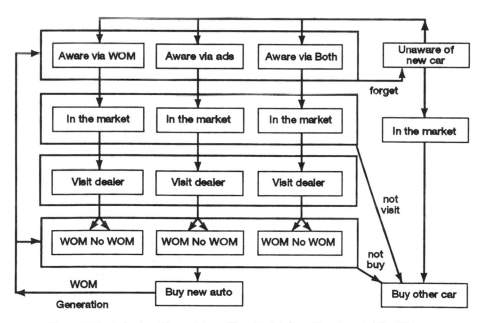

Figure 16.9   Behavioral States Macro-Flow Model for a New Automobile (Urban, Hauser, and Roberts 1990, p. 409; reprinted with permission)

flow from the unaware to the aware state is zero percent; at saturation advertising we expect some upper bound, say α. We also expect this flow to be a concave function of advertising spending. Review chapters 12 and 13. Similarly, word-of-mouth flows will be given by response curves that depend upon the number of consumers who buy the car in each month. For detailed equations see Urban, Hauser and Roberts (1990).

Calibration and Fitting

The models shown in Figure 16.9 incorporate the important managerial phenomena, but the models are complex. Table 16.6 lists the flows in Figure 16.9 and the data sources.

The model is calibrated by interactively selecting parameter values to maximize the fit to the actual sales for the control car. The "fitted" sales are obtained by running the model forward in time with the fitted parameter values.

Figure 16.10 plots the actual and fitted sales for a new Buick model. The macro-flow model fits the data reasonably well with a mean percent error of 5.6% in the 5-month moving average and the model appears to capture the major swings in the data, including the partial seasonal pattern.

Managerial Application of Flow Model

Table 16.7 reports forecasts based on the macro-flow model. The forecasted sales based on the initial marketing strategy were well below goals. The projected shortfall in sales put pressure on management to develop strategies that would improve free expression sales. To improve sales, the new-product team simulated three marketing strategies. The first strategy was a doubling of advertising in an attempt to increase advertising awareness (the model was run with advertising spending doubled). Table 16.7 indicates this would increase sales somewhat, but not enough. Given its cost, this strategy was rejected.

The next strategy considered was a crash effort to improve the advertising copy to encourage more dealer visits. Assuming that such copy would be attainable, the macro-flow analysis was used to simulate 40 percent more dealer visits. (The model was run with dealer-visit flow-parameters multiplied by 1.40 for ad aware conditions.) The forecast was much better and actually achieved the sales goals in year 2. Although a 40 percent increase was viewed as too ambitious, the simulation did highlight the leverage of improved copy that encouraged dealer visits. The new-product team decided to devote resources toward encouraging dealer visits. The advertising agency was directed

TABLE 16.6   New Inputs and Sources

Inputs	Source
Target Group Size	set in plan for number of buyers corpo-
Category Sales (Monthly)	rate econonometrics forecasts
Awareness	
-advertising spending (monthly)	planned levels
-advertising response curve (flow from	fit to past awareness, spending and sales
aware of ad, WOM, or both to unaware)	for control car and modify judgmen-
	tally for changes for new car
In Market	
-fraction of those aware who are in	calculate as category sales divided by tar-
market	get group size for all awareness condi-
	tions
Visit Dealer	
-fraction who visit dealer given ad aware	clinic measured probability of purchase
	after ad exposure
-fraction who visit dealer given ad and	clinic measured probability of purchase
WOM aware	after WOM video tape exposure
-fraction who visit dealer given WOM	judgmentally set given above two
aware	values
Purchase	
-probability of buying new car given	clinic measure probability of purchase
awareness condition:	after ad exposure and test drive
(1) ad aware before visit and no other	clinic measure probability of purchase
awareness	after ad, test drive and WOM exposure
(2) ad aware before visit and WOM	clinic probability of purchase after ad,
	WOM and test drive
(3) ad and WOM aware before visit	judgmentally set
(4) ad aware before and after visit	judgmentally set
(5) WOM aware before and no other	judgmentally set
awareness	
(6) WOM before and after visit	probability of buying new car in clinic
-probability of buying new car if aware	among those respondents who were
of new car and old car	aware of the old car before the clinic
Word of Mouth Communication (WOM)	managerial judgment and fit to past data
-Word-of-mouth response curve	on fraction of awareness due to word of
	mouth and control car sales
-aware of ads and WOM	probability of ad aware times
	probability of WOM aware
Production	planned levels
-levels of production (monthly)	managerial judgment, fit to past data
-production constraints	on control car sales, and past research
	studies
-fraction of buyers who want to buy "off	past studies and judgment
the lot"	

From Urban, Hauser and Roberts (1990, p. 413; reprinted with permission).

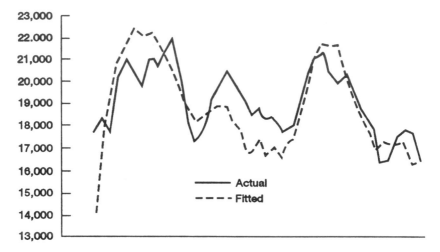

Figure 16.10   Actual versus Fitted Sales of Control Car; Five-Month Moving Average with Production Constrained Macro-Flow (Urban, Hauser, and Roberts 1990, p. 414; reprinted with permission).

to begin work on such copy, especially for the identified segment of women currently driving small cars.

The final decision evaluated was the effect of incentives designed to increase the conversion of potential buyers who visit dealer showrooms. The team simulated a 20% increase in conversation (all dealer-visit flow were parameters multiplied by 1.2). The leverage of this strategy was reasonable but not as high as the improved advertising copy. This simulation coupled with management's realization that an improvement would be difficult to achieve on a national level (competitors could match any incentive program) led management to a more conservative strategy that emphasized dealer training.

The net result of the sales analysis was that management decided to make an effort to improve dealer training *and* advertising copy, but that any

TABLE 16.7   Sales Forecasts and Strategy Simulations (in Units)

Year	Base Case	Advertising Spending Doubled	Advertising Copy Improved 40%	Dealer Incentives Improved 20%
1	281,000	334,000	395,000	340,000
2	334,000	370,000	477,000	406,000
3	282,000	330,000	405,000	345,000
4	195,000	225,000	273,000	234,000

From Urban, Hauser and Roberts (1990, p. 415–416; reprinted with permission).

forecast should be conservative in its assumptions about achieving the 40% and 20% improvements.

The shortfall in projected sales, dealer pressure to retain the popular rear-wheel drive car, and indications that production of the new car would be delayed, caused the new-product team to decide to retain both the old and new cars. Initial thinking was that the total advertising budget would remain the same but be allocated 25/75 between the old and new cars. Evaluation of this strategic scenario required a two-car macro-flow model.

The forecasts for the two-car strategy were done by extending the model flows to include new and old model competition with the above advertising and dealer's incentives tactics shown in Table 16.8. The combined sales were forecast to be higher than a one-car strategy in years 1 and 4, but lower in years 2 and 3. Overall the delayed launch caused a net sales loss of roughly 48,000 units over 4 years. This is not dramatic, especially given potential uncertainty in the forecast. However, the two-car strategy did not achieve the sales goal and made it more difficult to improve advertising copy and dealer training. Once the production decision had been made and the production delays were unavoidable, management was forced to retain the two-car strategy. The macro-flow analysis suggested that it be phased out as soon as was feasible.

This chain of events illustrates the value of a flexible, macro-flow model. The world is not static. Often, unexpected events occur (dramatic sales shortfalls, production delays) that were not anticipated when the initial model was developed.

Validation

Validations of durable-good forecasts face all of the difficulties that are faced by validations of pretest-market predictions. Managers have the incentive to sell cars, not provide a controlled laboratory validation. Not only do they have seek to modify and improve the marketing strategy as the product rolls out, but they often face unexpected production constraints. For example, in the launch of the new automobile model described above, advertising

TABLE 16.8 Sales Forecasts for Two-Car Strategy (in Units)

Year	New Model	Old Model	Combined Sales
1	181,000	103,000	284,000
2	213,000	89,000	301,000
3	174,000	80,000	254,000
4	121,000	84,000	205,000

From Urban, Hauser, and Roberts (1990, p. 416; reprinted with permission).

was adjusted versus the plan, industry sales were above the economic forecasts, there was a special interest-rate incentive program at the end of the first year, and there was a reduced availability of the most popular engine in the first half of the second year.

Once these adjustments were taken into account, Urban, Hauser and Roberts (1990) report that the forecasts agree with the actual sales at a level that is sufficient for strategy formulation. However, unlike pretest markets for frequently purchased packaged goods, we do not yet have sufficient experience with durable-good prelaunch forecasts to determine statistical predictive capabilities such as those in Table 16.4. Based on initial results we believe that such models provide forecasts that are sufficient to evaluate the magnitude of the new-product opportunity and we believe that simulations based on the macro-flow models are sufficiently accurate to set marketing strategies for the roll-out.

Other Auto Applications

Prelaunch forecasting has been used in three other major car introductions. The first was a new downsized "top-of-the-line" luxury car that replaced its larger predecessor. Clinic data indicated that the new car would be preferred by a factor of 1.1 to the old car. The detailed dynamic forecast indicated a 25% improvement in sales volume, but this was less increase than had been desired. Because the clinic data indicated that the old brand buyers liked the new car and were secure, the marketing was oriented through increased advertising spending and copy toward import-buyers who were identified as a high potential group in the clinic responses. Copy was based on building a perception of improved reliability, a weak point identified by market research (e.g., ads showed testing the car in the outback of Australia). After those improvements, the car was launched successfully and sales increased 25% above the old levels.

The next car studied was a full-size luxury two-door sedan that was downsized in an attempt to double sales and meet the corporate fuel economy standards. The clinic data indicated that the old buyers found the car to be small and ordinary, and they would have little interest in buying it. The only group that liked it was import-buyers, but they did not like it as much as other import options. The sales were forecast to be 50% of the old car's level of sales. Advertising and promotion changes were of little help. Unfortunately for the company, the forecast was correct and the first 12 months were 45% of the previous levels. This car should have been repositioned but a subsequent change in the marketing management of the company just after the final forecasts were made caused the bad news to be ignored. The new division director wanted a success and wanted to believe that the car could be "turned around" before the launch.

The final car was a small two-door sports car that subsequently was launched. The clinic data showed that sufficient "free-expression" demand existed to sell 47,600 units over three years. However, production delays of 6 months occurred, advertising spending was reduced 50 percent, dealers "distress" priced the car, and after a relaunch with a convertible model only 20,000 cars in total were sold. The model forecast was close to actual after adjustments, but the car failed due to poor launch execution and delays in relaunch which caused it to miss the market opportunity that was filled by competitors during the time lag.

In each of these cases, the prelaunch forecasts were accurate and representative of the ultimate market. However, these cases also illustrate the dangers inherent when such forecasts are not used correctly by the new-product team.

Other Durable Goods Applications

Prelaunch forecasts have also been applied to cameras, home computers and personal communication devices. Most of the products have not been on the market long enough to carry out the actual versus predicted comparison and in many of those where the experience exists, changes between test and launch conditions cloud the assessment of validity (see the auto cases above). Figure 16.11 provides one case of a new photographic product where the launch was carried out according to plan. In this case there is close agreement on the sales level and the cannibalization from the other products in the line. The forecasts were based on a simulated retail purchase opportunity. Validation conclusions will have to wait for more data, but initial results show some grounds for confidence in the premarket predictions.

Extensions

Categorization and Consideration. One extension to the premarket model described in this section is to include the key behavioral phenomena of categorization and consideration. This involves modifying Figure 16.9 by dividing awareness into categories of awareness. Categories are divided by having customers group cars into similar categories and indicating which ones they would consider. The advantage of this extension is that management can identify with whom they are competing and develop copy to generate the (1) correct categorization, (2) high consideration, and (3) high choice given that

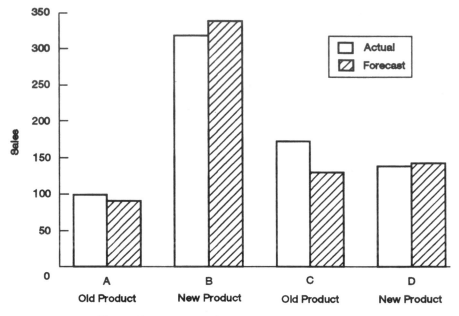

Figure 16.11   Four Product Line Sales after One Year.

a car is considered (see Urban, Hulland, and Weinberg [1993] for more details). Review Figure 4.17, which describes nine categories varying from "foreign high-end sports cars" (e.g., BMW, Mercedes) to "small sporty USA cars" (e.g., Buick Skyhawk, Pontiac Sunbird) and to "Mid price sports cars" (e.g., Nissan 300ZX, Mazda RX7, Chevrolet Camaro). In this case it is important to know if a new two-seat sports car would compete with midprice sports cars as desired or would be classified by customers as foreign high-end sports cars or, worse yet, small sporty U.S. cars.

Information Acceleration.   Another extension is to use the information acceleration methods introduced in chapter 12. In chapter 12 information acceleration was introduced as a design tool to be used before production investments are made. This is particularly important in durables where hundreds of millions of dollars are invested in production capabilities. However, the same measurement methods can be used at 18 to 24 months before launch. At this time the forecast can be updated and marketing targeting and promotion refined for maximum profit. The same interactive search of advertising, magazines, word-of-mouth, and dealer visit could be implemented, but now a preproduction prototype could be driven. The car and advertising and dealer environment would be in final form and a careful targeting of the opportunity could occur.

INDUSTRIAL AND SERVICES PRODUCTS

While premarket forecasting methods have begun to be implemented in durable consumer goods industries, almost no formal premarket models exist for industrial products and services. Some obvious directions for possible application are to pursue the use of information acceleration methods for services and the integration of lead user analysis with flow models for industrial and high technology products.

If a new industrial product is technology-driven and revolutionary, information acceleration methods could be used to "accelerate" the majority of the market to where the lead users now are positioned. This could be done with technical articles and conference papers written for the research study that would represent the likely real articles that would be written after the product was on the market and the technology window was reached. Word-of-mouth communication could be created by filming lead-user comments on the technology and the (hypothetical) new products that would be produced. Sales brochures could be created based on the core benefit proposition and the price and service to be delivered in the market. The product-use experience could be simulated by prototypes. For example, new composites for auto bodies could be supplied from the lab at the specification level of a new production process. Advanced workstations could be simulated by using mainframes to reflect the desktop power that would be available at the time of launch. With these stimuli the future scenario could be represented and measures taken of willingness to buy, preference versus competition, and attribute ratings. The measures would then be input to a flow model of the buying process and forecasts of alternative strategies generated. This is now being attempted, but the path of marketing progress suggests that it might succeed. If it is successful, industrial new product managers would have a tool for effective premarket forecasting.

Services are probably easier to test with an information accelerator than industrial products because it is often easier to represent customer use. For example, telecommunication services can be simulated by expensive means now and provided by low-cost means later. Consider a low-cost Personal Communications Network (PCN) services that provide users a small (1/2- × 2- × 4-inch) personal phone that can be used while walking (but not driving) in a metropolitan area. This use could be simulated by a currently available cellular phone with a filter added to restrict fast moving transmission. Another example is a comprehensive personal investment, legal, and banking service which could be simulated by a trained team of people backed by a workstation and modem at the user's home. In addition to use-experience simulation, the other forms of personal and interpersonal communication would be added to the market research computer system to allow model-based premarket forecasts of market sales volumes.

SUMMARY

Pretest-market models provide a low cost and rapid method to test the combined product, advertising, price, promotion, selling and distribution plan. The "full proposition" analyses are sufficiently accurate to identify most winners and eliminate most losers. They provide an effective way to control the risks of failure and supply actionable managerial diagnostics to improve the product.

Pretest-market models are an accepted practice for most frequently purchased products, relatively new for consumer durables. They have not yet been developed and tested for industrial products and services. Since pretest markets are extremely valuable in reducing risk and increasing the expected benefit of new products, we expect that models will soon be available for all products and services.

Pretest markets provide accurate forecasts and in some cases substitute for market testing because bad products can be eliminated. In cases of large investment risk where test-market products can be produced at low cost, management may still want to refine the potentially successful products in a test market and conduct a final validation. Such test-market analyses are the subject of the next chapter.

REVIEW QUESTIONS

16.1. What are the advantages and disadvantages of pretest market forecasting?

16.2. What are the relative advantages and disadvantages of ASSESSOR?

16.3. Develop a convergent model using the concepts of: (1) judgment and past history, and (2) stochastic models.

16.4. Answer the following questions for the ASSESSOR model:
   a. Suppose that for a particular new product the major source of consumer awareness is store point-of-purchase displays. If these displays are the only source of awareness, what would be the effect on product trial? How would you alter the model to account for this special situation?
   b. Suppose a company using the model carelessly misdefines the market. The company accidentally includes a product which, although popular, does not compete in the new product's product category. What will happen when estimates are made for purchase probabilities?
   c. In the model, the final stage of the laboratory experiment takes place in a simulated retail store where participants have the opportunity to make a

purchase. Those who do not purchase the new brand are given a quantity of it free after all buying transactions have been completed. This procedure parallels the common practice affecting trial usage through the distribution of free samples. How is the procedure similar to distributing free samples and how is it different? Under what conditions would this procedure duplicate the effect of random distribution of free samples by mail?

16.5. How accurate are pretest market models? Is this accurate enough?

16.6. When should test marketing not be done? When should test marketing definitely be done?

16.7. What do you think is the best position for tradeoff of cost and error in Figure 16.7?

16.8. How do pretest markets for durable consumer products, industrial products and services differ from frequently purchased consumer products? What special problems are involved when dealing with these categories?

16.9. Why should a manager accept less than a 100% probability of ultimate success when using pretest markets to screen new products?

16.10. What diagnostic information should a manager expect from pretest market analyses? How is this information used to improve the new product and its marketing mix?

16.11. How would you use pretest market analysis to test the effect of a price change and/or a price-off promotion?

17

Test Marketing

A test market is a major investment to acquire market information. In some cases, the reduction in risk and the improvement in the product and marketing strategy justifies the cost. In other cases it does not. Before an organization commits the resources necessary for test market it should consider carefully the costs and the rewards. Then if the decision is made to test, the organization should plan to achieve the greatest possible return on their investment in the test market. This chapter reviews the advantages and disadvantages of test markets and suggests one approach to making the decision of whether or not to undertake a test market. Next, we outline the basic testing approaches and review the behavioral theory necessary to structure and analyze a test market. We provide the analytic tools, indicate how they can be used to increase profitability, and illustrate this with a case. Finally, we review the procedures on which to base the go/no/no go decision.

DECIDING WHETHER OR NOT TO TEST MARKET

Advantages

The most compelling reason for test marketing is risk reduction. Most managers prefer to lose $1.5 million dollars in test market rather than $20 million in national failure. But the risk is not just monetary. A national failure endangers channel relationships, lowers the morale of the sales force, reduces the confidence of investors, and has a negative effect on customers' perceptions of quality.

A test market not only lowers these risks, it also identifies ways to improve profit. A carefully structured test market can identify how to improve advertising copy, promotion, personal selling, distribution, and price. The production facilities and channel relationships are put to the acid test in launching a new product. In any endeavor things go wrong; the test market provides a format where failure can be identified and corrected before full-scale launch.

Disadvantages

The price of a test market may not be justified. One and one-half million dollars is typical for packaged goods in a one-city test market and some firms spend $3.0 million or more when multiple cities are used. In other organizations a test market costs almost as much as a full-scale launch. For example, auto manufacturers do not test-market new models. The starting costs for making enough cars to sell in a test market is almost as great as a full-scale launch. In some industrial markets, similar costs occur. Making small amounts of a new chemical may require building a pilot plant and millions of dollars of investment. In these cases when a test market is not feasible, the organization relies on pretest market analysis (chapter 16) and careful adaptive control of the launch (chapter 18).

A test market also takes time, typically 9 to 12 months or more, and can mitigate your competitive advantage. In fact, it is not uncommon for a competitor to monitor your test market or run a pretest market analysis on your product while you are in test market. During this time, competitors catch up and perhaps go national at the same time as the initiating firm. As firms try to reduce the time to market, test marketing must be examined closely in light of the need to reach the window of market opportunity before competitors.

Competitors can also disrupt test markets. If the competitor believes the product will be successful, they may reduce prices and increase advertising and promotion to make a good product look bad. For example, in one test market for a new shampoo, the competitor with the leading established brand tripled its advertising and sent a coupon worth $1.00 off on a $1.29 tube to each household in the test city. Alternatively, the competitor may believe your new product is poor. In this case, the competitor may reduce advertising and promotion in order to encourage a national launch of a potential failure.

Considering these risks in test market and considering the proven accuracy of pretest markets, it is not surprising that some organizations skip test markets. In package goods the number of test markets is estimated to have fallen 50% in the last 10 years. At the same time test marketing has become more common in services such as telecommunication. Major test markets have been conducted to test home shopping, on demand movies (order at any time and see them in your home on your television), and extended cellular phone services. These are situations where the risks and investments of full system implementation are great, but limited test market services can be established at reasonable costs.

Making the Decision

The test market decision cannot be totally abstracted from profit considerations. The new product manager must consider seasonal timing, the financial state of the organization, the enthusiasm of top management, the relative channel strength, and a myriad of other factors, but formal decision analysis methods (Raiffa and Schlaifer 1961; Schlaifer 1969; Magee 1964) do provide important guidelines. The technique can be used in specific situations to clarify relative risks. Even if not used formally, it does indicate the general tradeoffs. In this chapter we use a simple form of the analysis to give you a better understanding of when a test market may be bypassed and to demonstrate the underlying representations of the advantages and disadvantages of test marketing.

In decision analysis, the decisions and outcomes are described by a sequential tree such as Figure 17.1a. The square (□) branches represent decisions under the control of the decision maker and the circle (○) branches represent potential outcomes of that decision. We begin at the right and compute the expected value of each potential outcome. Probabilities are given in parentheses below each branch. The branches off the right-most square are compared and a decision made. The actual analysis is shown in Figure 17.1b. The outcomes are in millions of dollars and would represent the best estimates based on earlier testing and analysis. Probabilities come from prior experience and earlier analysis. In this example a 50% chance of "good" test market results and 50% of "bad" test results are shown. If a "good" result is obtained a 90% chance of national success is shown; if a "bad" result is obtained, there is a 90% chance of national failure. If no test is done, a 50%

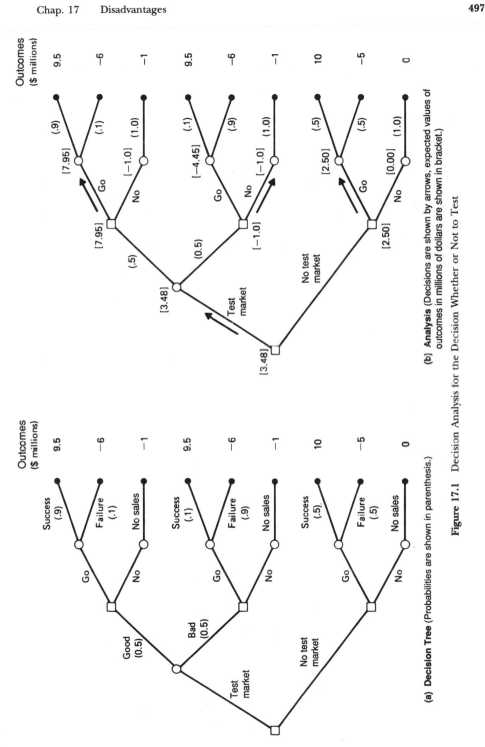

Figure 17.1 Decision Analysis for the Decision Whether or Not to Test

chance of national failure is indicated. For this illustration, we assume the success is worth $10 million if not test marketed and $10.5 million after improvement by test market; a failure loses $5 million; and a test market costs $1 million.

Examine Figure 17.1b. If we do not test then a full-scale launch returns $2.5 million in expected profit [.5 × 10 + .5 × (−5)]. The arrow at the bottom of Figure 17.1b indicates a launch without test is superior to no launch at all. If we test, it is more complicated because the go/no go decision is based on the outcome of the test. A "good" result means that the product has a 90 percent chance of success, while a bad result means a 10 percent chance. Thus, we "go" with a good test, and we "no go" with a bad test. This is indicated by the arrows at the top and middle of the figure. We don't know the outcome of the test before we spend the $1 million, but we can compute probabilities (see Raiffa and Schlaifer, 1961) which in this case are 50-50. Thus, 50% of the time we get to make a decision with a $7.95 million expected outcome [.9 × 9.5 + .1 × (−6)], whereas 50% of the time the best we can achieve is a $1 million loss. Using the decision analysis rules, we compute the expected value of the test market and conditional launch as $3.475 million [.5 × 7.95 + .5 × (−1)]. As illustrated by the arrow in the left of the figure, the best decision is to test yielding $975,000 more in expected profit [3.475 − 2.50].

The real world will never be as clear cut as in Figure 17.1, but this simple example does illustrate the key concepts. As our prior probability of success increases, the value of the test market decreases. For example change the value for success with no test to .80 in Figure 17.1. As the cost of testing increases, the value of testing decreases. For example, change the cost from $1 million to $2 million. As the reliability of the test market increases the value of testing increases. For example, change the probabilities to 95-5 with good results and 5-95 with bad results. As the value added from diagnostic information increases, the value of testing increases. For example, change the post-testing success from $10.5 million to $12 million.

When pretest market analysis is very accurate, the value of test marketing is lessened because the probability of success is high. When the cost of test market is high, as in the auto industry, a test market is not worthwhile even though it would reduce the risk of failure. If competitors retaliate, the reliability of the test drops thus reducing the desirability of test marketing. If the analysis of the test market is done carefully, the reliability and profit improve and thus increase the value of testing. Finally, if the test market increases the time to market and gives competitors a chance to catch up, the profit value of a post-testing success decreases thereby decreasing the value of testing.

The above analysis can be extended to include many more outcomes (not just "success" and "failure") and test results (not just "good" and "bad"). Analysis can also be performed to calculate the amount of money a firm should be willing to invest. Few firms use the formal decision analysis approach, but the analysis and the example given in Figure 17.1 indicate the points to consider in making the strategic decision of whether or not to test. As the figure shows, careful test market analysis increases the expected value of the test market by maximizing the profit from a successful product and reducing the risks.

TEST-MARKET STRATEGIES

The two reasons to test are to obtain an accurate forecast and to obtain diagnostic information that improves profits. Different organizations use different strategies depending upon where the product is located relative to the decision frontier (see Figure 15.1). For example, if the risk before test market is much greater than acceptable, the organization will select a strategy that best reduces risk. Alternatively, if risk is acceptable, but profit is low, a diagnostic strategy will be best.

There are many models to analyze test markets, but each can be viewed as an implementation of one of three basic strategies: replicate national, experimentation, or behavioral-model-based analysis. Each of these strategies places different emphasis on risk reduction and diagnostic information.

Replicate National

The classical approach to test marketing is to attempt to replicate the national environment in two or three "representative" cities and duplicate the national launch plans in them. These cities have typical demographic profiles and are of moderate size, such as Sacramento, California, Peoria, Illinois, and Syracuse, New York.

The planned level of national advertising and promotion is scaled down to the test city level and the product is introduced into the distribution channel. Sales effort is set by specifying the number of calls to be made on each class of retail customer. Media spending is expressed in spending per capita and multiplied by the test city population. The standard scaling measure is "gross rating points" (GRPs) which is defined as the percentage of people reached by the campaign times the number of exposures per person in a specified time period (e.g., 100 GRPs could mean a reach of 50 percent and an average of two exposures per person reached).

As the size of the cities increase, the costs go up. Although some organizations have used very small cities in an attempt to reduce test marketing costs, such mini-test market approaches severely reduce the reliability of fore-casts.

The classical approach emphasizes forecasting national sales. The most common measure for consumer goods is store sales and market share, which is obtained by using commercial services to audit retail store sales. For exam-ple, Information Resources Inc. and A.C. Nielsen monitor retail food and drug store inventories based on scanner data in test cities. If there is not a long distribution pipeline or if such a pipeline inventory is predictable, fac-tory shipments provide another useful measure.

The basic analytic approach is to observe test market share after 9 to 12 months and project it to a national level. The advantage of this approach is its simplicity and the low cost of analysis. One disadvantage is that many anom-alies occur in test market which may make the projections inaccurate. An-other disadvantage is that many opportunities are missed because of the lack of diagnostic information.

Experimentation

As the emphasis of test marketing shifts to profit improvement, exper-imentation on marketing variables gains importance. Early approaches used different strategies in different cities, but this is expensive and allows few variations. Sometimes firms use "controlled store" test marketing where the product is forced in specific stores and only store advertising, promotion, and display are used to build trial. Attention in this case is focused on repeat sales and usage rates. However, one can use "controlled store testing" to vary marketing strategies within cities by sampling or couponing only sections of the market or by varying the price and promotion across retail stores.

Today UPC scanners have made experimentation and measurement easier in frequently purchased consumer goods. Daily store sales as well as trial, repeat, and frequency of use data is collected from a panel of consumers who have their checkout record flagged and stored separately. Information Resources Incorporated conducts electronic test marketing that allows not only store variations, but home advertising variations. In this "targetable tele-vision" method different advertising copy or numbers of exposures are di-rected to individual households so that micro experiments can be used to measure the effects of advertising copy and expenditures on trial and repeat purchases as measured in trial, repeat, and store sales. If in-store video ad-vertising on the shopping cart becomes feasible, experimentation could also be done on advertising and featuring separately in retail outlets.

The advantage of experimentation is that the diagnostic information generates profit improvement opportunities. However, experimentation re-quires substantial analytic capability in the fields of experimental design, measurement, statistical estimation, and decision modeling. Experimentation also is limited to the relatively few alternative strategies possible in a reasonable experimental design and subject to the same projectability problems as a replication test market.

Behavioral Model–Based Analysis

A third approach attempts to compensate for the potential problems inherent in national replication and experimentation. Behavioral model based analysis recognizes that a test market city is different from a national introduction and collects the information necessary to correct for these differences. True experimentation may or may not be done, but in either case, a detailed behavioral model of the consumer is used to analyze the measurements in such a way that forecasts can be made for the effect of modified marketing strategies and profits improved.

Model-based analysis enhances the accuracy of forecasts and provides a wide range of diagnostic information, but such analysis requires good management science capabilities and a willingness to invest considerable time and money. The level of analysis will vary by situation depending upon the resources of the organization and the product's current position relative to the decision frontier.

In the pretest market chapter (Chapter 16) we introduced the NEWS test-market model (Pringle, Wilson, and Brody 1982). This is a behavioral flow model of trial generation and repeat that was designed for test market forecasting but could be used for earlier premarket analysis. We elaborate on this approach here with models based on (1) more complete flows or (2) probabilistic modeling of flows. These models demonstrate the increasing level of complexity that can be accessed to process test market data.

The remainder of the chapter provides the tools necessary to analyze a test market. We begin with the behavioral foundations and then turn to the forecasting models. No manager will use all of these techniques, of course, but to select the technique appropriate for a given situation each manager should understand the basic ideas underlying the techniques.

BEHAVIORAL FOUNDATIONS OF TEST MARKET ANALYSIS

Sales do not reach their long-run level immediately. Many complex phenomena occur during the early stages of a new product introduction. Early promotion is aimed at generating trial, but repeat purchases are necessary for many products. Awareness, opinions, and purchase intent propagates by word of mouth. To properly "read" a test market, we must understand and model these and other phenomena. This topic, called the diffusion of innovations, has received extensive study by sociologists, economists, and marketers. In this section, we summarize their key findings and interpret them in the light of improving forecasts and diagnostic information. (For a more comprehensive survey of the field see Midgley 1977.)

Diffusion Process

One of the underlying concepts of the diffusion process is that different consumers adopt an innovation at different times after it becomes available. These innovators then exert a word-of-mouth influence on others. For purposes of analysis, consumers are classified as innovators, early adopters, early majority, late majority, and laggards, according to when they adopt (Rogers 1962; Rogers and Shoemaker 1971) or their propensity to adopt (Midgley 1977). Figure 17.2 shows a categorization of consumers according to their adoption time. The demarcation lines depend upon the distance in standard deviations (σ) from the mean adoption time (μ).

There are several implications of this diffusion process. As the process moves from innovators to "others," there are several influences on trial rates. All else equal, the "others" are less likely to try, but if the innovators are opinion leaders, the word-of-mouth effect increases the likelihood of trial. However, as more people adopt, there are fewer left to adopt and trial rates decrease. These effects were the basis of Bass's diffusion model (chapter 4). Bass's model and other more complex models can be used to measure and project these diffusion trends. Diffusion also affects repeat purchase. If the product is better suited to the innovators, their repeat sales may be higher than the others. Alternatively, innovators per se may be more vulnerable to competitive new products. In either case, the process should be monitored to

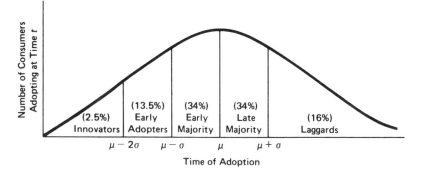

Figure 17.2   Categorization of Consumers According to Time of Adoption

understand and forecast adoption for industrial products, consumer durables, and to forecast trial and repeat for frequently purchased products and services.

As the diffusion process occurs adopters should not be considered mere recipients of the innovation. There is an emerging body of research that indicates early adopters are active in creating products and later adopters are active in improving the product (Rogers 1978; Von Hippel 1990 and review lead user analysis in chapter 5). Reinventions made by users can be substantial improvements in the product. Organizations should carefully monitor how consumers not only adopt, but adapt the innovation. This information may lead to new profit opportunities.

Characteristics of Innovators

Since innovators are crucial to the diffusion process, it is important to understand their characteristics. If innovators can be identified, then media and other promotions can be targeted better. To better understand the characteristics of innovators, Rogers and Stanfield (1968) have classified over 2,400 research studies. Some of the results of these studies are summarized in Table 17.1. In general, this table indicates that an innovator is likely to be educated and knowledgeable with a high income, to have a positive attitude toward change and high aspirations, and to be linked to external information sources of media and change agents.

In industrial markets, the important adopter is the innovative firm. These markets have not been as well studied as consumer markets, but some generalizations have emerged. For example, Webster (1969) argues firms that have a high level of aspiration and can tolerate the risk involved in adoption are likely to be the first to adopt. Mansfield et al. (1971) found, in a study of adoption of numerical control technology in the tool and die industry, that early adopters tended to be larger firms whose presidents were highly educated. Nonusers tended to have low levels of knowledge about numerical controls. Von Hippel's user-active paradigm discussed in our earlier chapter on idea generation (chapter 5), suggests that diffusion is a continuing process of adoption, adaption, and invention by users as well as manufacturers.

Communication Process and Opinion Leadership

Word-of-mouth is an integral component of the diffusion process (Robertson 1971; Midgley 1977). After adopting, innovators communicate their experience to others. Later adopters look to the innovators and early adopters for opinion leadership that will encourage or discourage them from adopting.

A classic study was done on room air conditioners when they were a new

TABLE 17.1 Characteristics of Innovators

Characteristics or Relationships	Number of Generalizations with Each Type of Relationship to Innovativeness (Percent)					Total Number of Generalizations
	Positive	None	Negative	Conditional	Total	
Social Characteristics						
Education	75	16	5	4	100	193
Literacy	70	22	4	4	100	27
Income	80	11	6	3	100	112
Age	32	40	18	10	100	158
Attitudinal Characteristics						
Knowledgeability	79	17	1	3	100	66
General attitude toward change	74	14	8	4	100	159
Achievement motivation	65	23	0	12	100	17
Educational aspirations	83	9	4	4	100	23
Business orientation	60	20	20	0	100	5
Satisfaction with life	29	28	43	0	100	7
Empathy	75	0	25	0	100	4
Mental rigidity	21	25	50	4	100	24
Social Relationships						
Cosmopolitism	81	11	3	5	100	73
Mass media exposure	86	12	0	2	100	49
Contact with change agencies	92	7	0	1	100	136
Deviancy from norms of the social system	54	14	28	4	100	28
Group participation	79	10	6	5	100	156
Interpersonal communication exposure	70	15	15	0	100	40
Opinion leadership	64	22	7	7	100	14

Adapted from Rogers and Stanfield (1968, pp. 240–242).

product. Whyte (1954) observed that air conditioners were being concentrated in clusters of neighboring apartments rather than uniformly spread over the potential housing units. Word-of-mouth from an adopter to neighbors had resulted in additional adoptions in the neighborhood.

Subsequent research has shown the word-of-mouth communication and opinion leadership process to be complex. Figure 17.3 shows a typical influence pattern in a neighborhood group. The primary group (solid boxes) had various degrees of specialization in influence. Subsidiary friendships (broken-line boxes) reinforced and propagated the process.

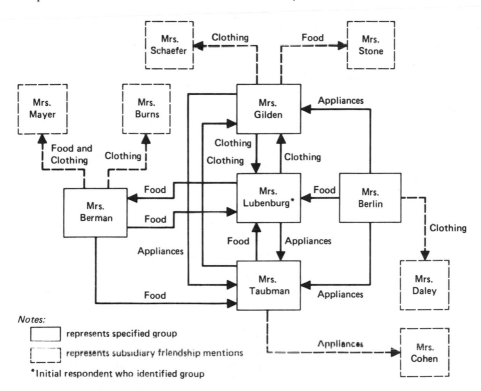

Figure 17.3   Influence Sources for Food, Clothing, and Appliances within a Typical Informal Neighborhood Group (Robertson 1978, p. 217; reprinted with permission)

In today's markets it is not uncommon to find that 50% or more of adopters report receiving and/or providing word-of-mouth communication. The percentage is highest in consumer durable products, but can be very significant in services as well. For example in a cellular telephone study conducted in 1992 by one of the authors, it was found that adopters had talked to, on average, five other people before they bought and that in the 6 months after their purchase they were asked by eight people for their opinion on cellular phones and their cost of usage.

This communication process is not limited to consumer products. Coleman, Katz, and Menzel (1957 and 1966) show that there is social interaction among doctors and that socially integrated doctors adopt new products earlier. Industrial buyers often have informal networks to provide information for them when they buy. With the advent of computer networks and electronic bulletin boards we can expect personal influence to gain in frequency and importance.

It has been difficult to identify the traits of opinion leaders. Although innovators tend to be opinion leaders, all opinion leaders are not innovators. Opinion leadership seems to be specialized by product area (Silk 1966). Opinion leadership is relative—a leader has more information than a follower (Robertson 1978). The concept of opinion leadership is important, but the complexity of this process, the lack of generalized opinion leaders, and importance of the specific personal interaction situation have made this a difficult area to model.

Although the web of personal relationships and communication are complex, they are real and should be recognized as phenomena underlying forecasting of a new product.

Hierarchy of Effects

The diffusion process is important among consumers. The dynamic process for each consumer is also important. In Chapter 12, we introduced the concepts of awareness, availability, trial, and repeat. We expanded this in Chapter 15 to include the details of advertising exposure. That process is exposure, attention, comprehension, acceptance, and purchase. The essence of both models is that the consumer receives and processes information through a hierarchy of steps, then acts on that information to search, find, try and perhaps repeat purchase of the product. Search will not occur without awareness and intent, trial will not occur unless the consumer can obtain the product, and repeat cannot occur without trial. There are alternative ways to model this process including the classic AIDA model (awareness, interest, desire, and action—Strong 1925) and the hierarchy of effects model (unaware, aware, knowledge, liking, preference, conviction, and purchase—Lavidge and Steiner 1961). Each works. The important point is to use some model to represent the dynamic process so that the conditions of purchase can be measured and understood. We have found the simple model in Figure 17.4 to be particularly effective for analyzing test markets.

Figure 17.4   A Useful Hierarchical Model for Test-Market Analysis

Together, the diffusion of innovations among consumers and the dynamic model of information processing provide the behavioral foundations for test market analysis. We turn now to methods which use these ideas to analyze test markets.

METHODS TO ANALYZE TEST MARKETS

If the test market strategy is to replicate national experience, then forecasting is done by simply projecting the test market share to the national level. If the test market strategy is experimentation, then the best marketing mix is the one yielding the greatest profit where the choice is made from the experimental design. If the test market strategy combines either of these approaches with behavioral model based analysis, then more accurate projections and better diagnostic information can be achieved. Whether the new product is a service, an industrial good, or a consumer product, any forecasting procedure must not only include a projection model, but also the capability to adjust the forecast for differences between test and national markets and to project the forecast to alternative marketing strategies.

The behavioral science phenomena identified in the previous section underlie detailed analyses. Some analytic methods explicitly recognize these phenomena, collect data to understand them and make projections based on the diffusion-of-innovation process. Other methods implicitly reflect them in their models.

Data sources include

- UPC scanner records of sales and coupon use
- Telephone surveys of awareness, attitude, trial and repeat purchase, and usage
- Warehouse sales withdrawals
- Electronic consumer panel records of purchasing (UPC or customer hand scanners)
- Factory shipments of product
- Salesperson's call reports
- Tear sheets from retail feature advertising
- Audits of special displays and promotions

A good analysis plan will include data from these various sources to allow accurate forecasting and useful diagnostics (see Narasimhan and Sen 1983).

We begin by discussing panel data and stochastic models that consider trial and repeat phenomena for frequently purchased consumer products. Recursive, macro-flow, and continuous-flow models build from this base to include more behavioral phenomena and provide more managerial insight.

Panel Data Projection Models

The first step toward analyzing a test market is to decompose total sales into trial and repeat as shown in Figure 17.5. These measures are normally obtained from a consumer panel. Trial and repeat measures are used for early projection of results. For example, sales can be higher in months 3 or 4 than 8 or 9 because of high trial purchase. Failure to recognize this has led some firms to cut off the test and go national after a few months based on the "fantastic" sales. Trial and repeat measures are also diagnostic information because they indicate whether the success/failure of the product is due to good promotion (trial) or to a good product (repeat).

Forecasts are made by reexpressing the sales patterns shown in Figure 17.5 as cumulative trial and repeat rates shown in Figure 17.6 (Parfitt and Collins 1968). Based on Figure 17.6 eventual share can be calculated. If no major changes are made in the product, the marketing strategy, or the market itself, then the cumulative trial (percent of market who will ever try the new product) will reach some penetration level, P^*. The repeat rate (share of purchases among those who have tried the product) will level off to some equilibrium share, R^*. The long-run share is estimated by multiplying these two values. In cases of segmented markets, the values are calculated for each group and summed after weighting by a buying-level index. Early forecasts are made by projecting the curves from the panel data obtained for the first few months. Accuracy is often quite good, but only limited diagnostic information is produced.

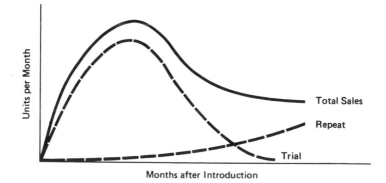

Figure 17.5 Typical Sales Patterns for Trial, Repeat and Total Sales

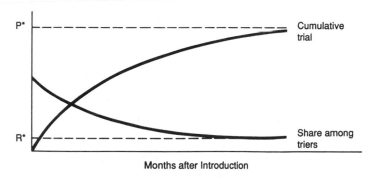

Figure 17.6   Trial—Repeat Model

Often the test market is not totally representative of the national market. In this case, a number of correction factors must be multiplied times the forecast to account for differences in distribution, consumption rates, seasonality, attitudes, and consumer demographics (Ahl 1970). Occasionally, judgmental correction factors are used to account for differences in marketing strategies between test and national.

The basic Parfitt-Collins model provides good estimates of equilibrium share, but stochastic models, such as described for pretest market analysis, provide better estimates of the path to this equilibrium (see Eskin 1973; Eskin and Malec 1976; and chapter 16). These "depth of repeat" models are used in the same way as the stochastic models described in Chapter 16 except that they use more direct observations based on UPC data to determine the proportion of people who repeat after one purchase, after two purchases, and so on.

Recursive Models

Trial and repeat are only two of the components of the dynamic model in Figure 17.4. If the managers want to understand further the acceptance process so that they can better diagnose the test market, then measures must be taken for more components of the dynamic model. In particular, measures are needed with respect to awareness, intent, and search. Further measures may be needed to capture the advertising components of exposure, attention, comprehension, and acceptance.

One approach is based on recursive formulations. In these models, each level of the dynamic model is derived from a regression equation based on the next lower level combined with control variables. For example, the level of awareness depends on the level of advertising and on previous awareness, trial depends upon awareness and previous trial, and so on. The test market is observed for a period long enough to estimate the parameters in the equation and then the regression equations are used to estimate long-run share.

The most recent, completely documented recursive model is called TRACKER (Blattberg and Golanty 1978). In this model, the change in awareness (A_t) depends nonlinearly on the gross rating points (GRPs) and trial results from awareness. The trial in period t, T_r, is given by

$$T_t = T_{t-1} + \alpha_2 (A_t - A_{t-1}) + \beta_2 (A_{t-1} - T_{t-1}) \qquad (17.1)$$

where α_2 and β_2 are again estimated by regression. Note that the fraction of people who recently became aware, A_t-A_{t-1}, can have a different trial rate than those who were previously aware but have not tried, $A_{t-1} - T_{t-1}$. This trial is adjusted by a price elasticity and repeat purchases are represented as the percentage of new triers who are still users at a given point in time. Sales are the sum of the trial and repeat sales.

The advantage of such recursive models is that they are relatively low cost (e.g., $15,000 for data collection and analysis, Blattberg and Golanty 1978) and can accurately predict test market results from three months of test market. They are useful in understanding trial and repeat purchases, and the process by which awareness produces trial and repeat. They are most useful for product categories where data is available from prior new product introductions so parameters can be estimated precisely. In these cases the use of the model can reduce the time in test market and allow a faster launch.

The disadvantage of recursive models is that they measure only part of the dynamic hierarchy. Detailed diagnostic information on the behavioral process is not available and the panel data is not well integrated into the model.

We feel that recursive models are most appropriate for managers who want fast low cost forecasts from actual test market data. If forecasts have already been obtained from pretest market analysis, the manager may wish more diagnostic information. If the test market investment is sufficiently large (say $1 to $1.5 million), the manager may wish to augment the early forecasts with more expensive ($50,000 to $100,000) but more detailed measurement.

Macro-Flow Models

Most managers need more behavioral diagnostic information than the recursive models can provide. A modeling technique to fill this need is macro-flow modeling (Urban 1970). In this approach, the manager and analysts identify the behavioral phenomena that are important to the strategic managerial decisions. These phenomena and other key behavior necessary to interrelate the strategic phenomena are connected in a macro-flow diagram such as Figure 17.7 where the boxes indicate consumer "states" and the

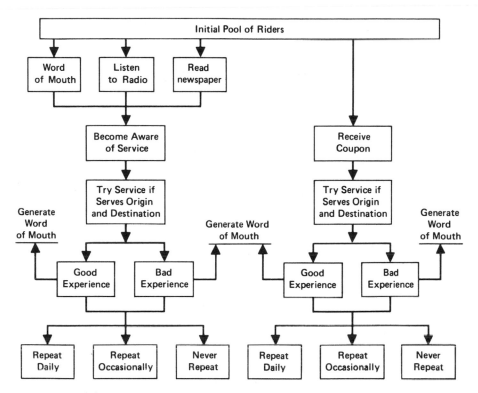

Figure 17.7 Example of a Macro-flow Model for a New Transportation Service
(Hauser and Koppelman 1977, p. 649; reprinted with permission)

arrows represent "flows" from state to state. In this case the flow model
represents the adoption of a new transportation service. The number of states
can vary from 10 in a very simple model to over 500 in a complex model. More
states give greater diagnostic information, but cost more to measure. Panel,
survey, and store audit data are used to measure the number of people in each
state in each time period and to estimate flows between states. Once the flows
are known, the macro-flow model is used to project test market results.

Macro-flow analysis is best illustrated by example. Consider the simple
three-state model in Figure 17.8 which is a macro-flow representation of a
simple depth of repeat model. This model is appropriate for consumer packaged goods (see Figure 16.9 for a macro-flow model of auto purchasing).
Suppose we have observed the test model for a few months and know:

- The target group is 10 million households, and all are potential triers.
- The percent of families who try the new product is 10% in month 1, 5%
  in month 2, 1% in month 3, and zero thereafter.

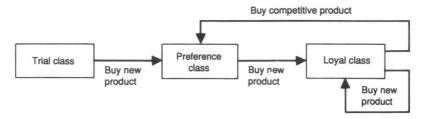

Figure 17.8 Simple Macro-flow Model

- Sixty percent of the preference class will buy our new product when they need to repeat.
- Eighty percent of the loyal class will buy our new product when they need to repeat.
- Every family needs to repeat once per month.

In practice, these flow rates are obtained from panel or survey data.

Now let us use this information to calculate the sales in several periods. In period 1, all states except trial class are empty, thus sales will occur only from trial purchases, in this case, 10 percent of the 10 million in the trial class. This is entered in Table 17.2. Note that the trial class is now reduced in size to 9 million (10 million minus the 1 million that tried). In period 2, 5% of the trial class (450,000 families) and 60 percent of the preference class (600,000 families) will purchase the product for a total of 1.05 million families. We enter these sales in Table 17.2 and adjust the size of each class for period 3.

TABLE 17.2 Calculations for Simple Macro-flow Diagram (Numbers are in thousands).

Period	Trial Class Size	Trial Sales	Prefer- ence Class Size	Prefer- ence Sales	Loyal Class Size	Loyal Sales	Total Sales
1	10,000	1,000	0	0	0	0	1,000
2	9,000	450	1,000	600	0	0	1,050
3	8,550	86	850	510	600	480	1,076
4	8,464	0	546	328	990	792	1,120
5	8,464	0	416	250	1,120	896	1,146
6	8,464	0	390	234	1,146	917	1,151
7	8,464	0	385	231	1,151	920	1,151
8	8,464	0	385	231	1,151	920	1,151
Long run	8,464	0	385	231	1,151	920	1,151

(For example, the preference class started with 1 million families but gained 450,000 from trial purchases and lost 600,000 from the repeat purchase. This gives 1,000,000 + 450,000 - 600,000 = 850,000 families.) We now compute the sales from period 3 and update the class size for period 4. The concept is the same, but the bookkeeping becomes somewhat more complicated. You may wish to do the calculations yourself to reproduce Table 17.2. Remember that those in the loyal class who do not buy the new brand return to the preference class.

The above example illustrates the basic idea of macro-flow. Equilibrium, if it occurs, happens when the flows out of a behavioral state equal the flows into a behavioral state. In Table 17.2, this occurred in the seventh period. This equilibrium is determined by the flow rates and the initial states. As soon as the flow rates stabilize, forecasts can be made. Note that the states are defined such that they are mutually exclusive (no consumer is in more than one state simultaneously) and collectively exhaustive (each consumer is in at least one state). Thus, the number of people in each state always sums to the total number of consumers. Diagnostic information is obtained by examining the flow rates and the number of people in the behavioral states. In Table 17.2, we see that in equilibrium much of the sales come from loyal customers. This is evidence that the product has good performance that encourages repeat purchase, but for some unidentified reason, perhaps poor advertising, only 15.4% of the population has tried the product. One can make similar interpretations from the flow rates.

Usually the manager has many more questions than the simple model in Figure 17.8 can answer. Thus, in practice, macro-flow models are more complex. States are included for advertising, couponing, distribution, and so on. Flows can occur once per time period or more often for such advertising states as exposure, attention, comprehension, and acceptance. Flows can be added for word-of-mouth influence, forgetting of appeals, returns to trial states, etc. Not every consumer will have the same usage rate, thus parallel models may be used for light, medium, and heavy users with transitions among states taking place at different times in different models.

Macro-flow is an extremely flexible concept that enables each manager to customize the analysis model to his test market. If an effect, say coupon response, is important to the marketing strategy, it should be included in the model and measured. But the manager should resist modeling every effect he can think of since the cost of analysis and measurement and the difficulty of interpretation increase as the macro-flow diagram becomes more complex.

Several test market models have been designed based on the macro-flow concept. Midgley (1977) uses innovation theory to derive one relatively complex model, while Assmus (1975) uses a simple eleven-state model, called NewProd, to forecast new product sales. Urban (1970) has designed an extremely flexible model called Sprinter. In Sprinter, the manager can select from three basic models (Mod I, Mod II, and Mod III) and customize the analysis within each model (Urban and Karash 1971). Regression equations are built into the model to link the marketing mix changes to changes in flows between states. Each of the macro-flow models appear to be reasonably accurate and useful to managers. For example, Figure 17.9 provides an example of a Sprinter model which uses a high level of detail to untangle multiple effects in a test market.

Continuous Flow Models

Continuous-flow models combine the detailed dynamic modeling of macro-flow models with the simple regression structure of recursive models. In the spirit of macro-flow models we begin with a flow-diagram in which consumers move from one behavioral state to another. The difference is that rather than detail every transition as in Figure 17.9 we concentrate on product usage. A "flow" by a consumer is then a switch from using one product to using another product.

For example, consider a transportation market (Schaumburg, IL) in which the primary means of transportation are bus, car as a driver (CD), and car as a passenger (CP). A new product called Dial-a-Ride Transportation (DART) is introduced. Before the introduction and after the introduction for those consumers unaware of DART, flows (switches) are among bus, CD, and CP. After the introduction, for those who become aware of DART, flows are among bus, CD, CP, *and* DART. Furthermore, consumers flow from one set of states to another when they become aware of DART. These flows are shown in Figure 17.10a where "A" labels the awareness flow.

So far the analysis is similar to macro-flow modeling, but we introduce two new concepts. First, unlike macro-flow modeling we allow flows to happen continuously. In fact, some consumers may switch from CD to CP back to CD and finally to DART all in one observation period. However, because we take all flows into account in the analysis, for the purposes of calibration we need only know which state the consumer was in at the start of the period and which state the consumer was in at the end of the period.

The second difference is that the flows are considered to be caused by control variables such as consumers perceptions of the new (and existing products) and by advertising, direct mail, word of mouth, and other marketing variables. For example, figure 17.10b lists some of the variables that were used in analyzing the Schaumburg test market. (Convenience, ease of use, safety, and opinions were measured perceptions of the bus, CD, CP, and DART.) To determine how much each marketing action, say direct mail, affects the flow rates, we use a modified linear regression.

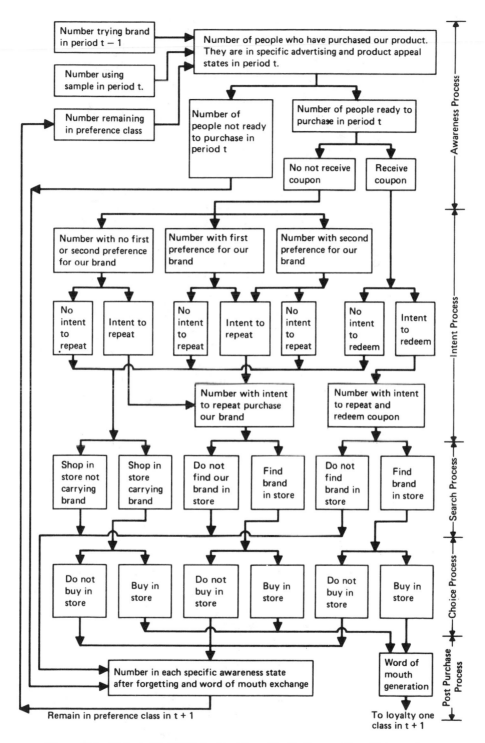

Figure 17.9 Sprinter Mod III Behavioral States for Preference Class (Urban 1970, p. 820; reprinted with permission)

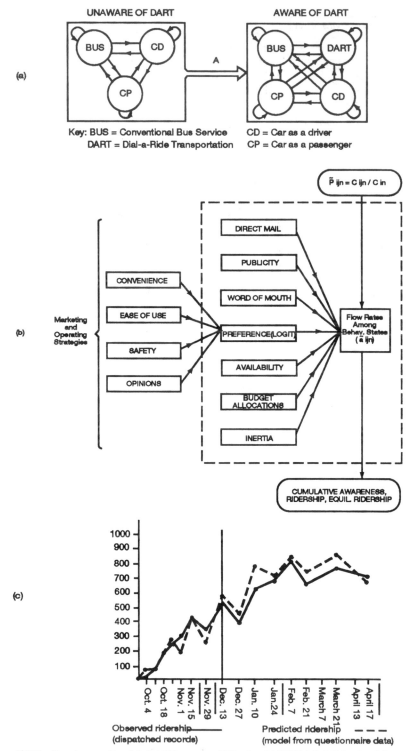

Figure 17.10 Continuous-flow Model (Hauser and Wisniewski 1982b) (a) Behavioral States, (b) Control Variables, (c) Predictions versus Actual Ridership

Conceptually, we measure the number of people, c_{ijn}, who started observation period n in state i, say were riding the bus, and ended in state j, say were riding DART. We change this to a percentage, p_{ijn}, and transform it into flow rates, a_{ijn}. The flow rates are then regressed on the control variables to determine a set of weights. Finally, once we know the control-variable weights, mathematical formulae enable us to forecast trial, repeat, and sales for future periods.[1] Furthermore, by varying the control variables, say twice as many mailings in the third period, we can find the most profitable marketing strategy.

Continuous-flow modeling has proven quite accurate. For example, Figure 17.10c compares the observed ridership on DART to that predicted based on the model. In this case, the model was calibrated based on five measurements in the first 10 weeks of the demonstration period. Based on the analysis and the relative weights of the control variables, the Village of Schaumburg was able to identify a need for more vehicles and extended hours of service. Once this was implemented ridership increased from the 800 or so in Figure 17.10 to approximately 1,300. In this case the detailed diagnostic information was critical to the success of the test market.

Durable and Industrial Products and Services

Most of the previous models can be used for consumer services as well as consumer products. For example, a successful new transit service will be described by high trial ridership and a large volume of repeat usage (see Figure 17.7). A new HMO is tried for one year, but in the long run, year-to-year repeat must be high enough to sustain a successful health plan. Financial and insurance services display similar patterns. In these cases, the macro-flow models outlined in the previous section are utilized to interpret test market, pilot program, or demonstration project results.

The analysis and managerial strategy is somewhat different for consumer durables and many industrial products. For the first few years, sales will depend upon one-time purchases of high-priced items. Replacement sales may not occur for five or ten years. The sales pattern for new durable products tends to appear as an inverted "U" shape, such as that we saw in Figure 17.2. The time to reach the highest levels may be several years after introduction because the diffusion of innovation process takes place much more slowly.

In many industrial and durable products, test markets are not done and

---

[1] The mathematical formulae to transform the percentages into flow rates and the mathematical formulae to compute trial, repeat, and sales are derived in Hauser and Wisniewski (1982a). For example, if P_n is the matrix of the percentages (probabilities), then the matrix of the flows, A_n, is equal to a log-eigenvalue transformation of the probability matrix. For details on the Schaumburg case see Hauser and Wisniewski (1982b).

emphasis shifts to premarket forecasting model (see chapter 16 for examples) and interpreting early national or regional sales data to forecast if the product will succeed. In analyzing these data, it is critical to understand the diffusion process through both primary selling, advertising, and word-of-mouth communication. Furthermore, the test must be run sufficiently long to allow projection of the sales peak. Detailed test market models are not common for durables and industrial products. At present, the best approach seems to be a macro-flow, a continuous-flow, or a single equation diffusion model. In the absence of test markets and models, the innovating organization is forced to use more judgment and bear more risk.

Selecting an Analysis Method

In this section, we have presented a variety of analysis methods ranging from the simple trial/repeat panel projections to the more complete recursive models to the flexible flow models. Recent work has provided new powerful but complex models for forecasting diffusion flow models (Roberts and Urban 1988; and Chatterjee and Eliashberg 1990). The available models vary in complexity and cost as shown in Figure 17.11. All models report good forecasting accuracy; the difference in the models is the degree to which they can provide actionable managerial diagnostics at reasonable costs. We suggest that the new product manager understand the basics of each analysis method and select the model most appropriate for the specific test market analysis and budget.

CASE: HERITAGE PASTRY

To demonstrate the use of a test market model and measurement system, we present the case of a new pastry mix that was developed by a major food manufacturer. There were many cake mixes on the market, but no pastry mixes. The premium cake mix market was growing and analysis indicated a potential for pastry recipes. A line of cream puffs and torts called Heritage Pastry (name disguised) was developed with a core benefit proposition of "elegant and easy to prepare desserts." Advertising fulfilled the CBP by showing the pastry on a crystal dish on a formal dining table. Concept and home use tests were positive and management felt the product was ready for test market. A macro-flow model was used to plan and analyze the test.

Planning the Test Market

Before the product was taken to test market, initial forecasts were made to establish consumer response goals and to provide input to the decision of

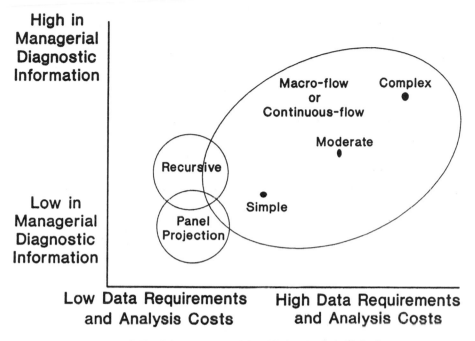

Figure 17.11 Categorization of Test-Market Analysis Methods

whether to proceed with the new product. Early analyses identified the target group as households with income more than $25,000 where the homemaker bakes at least once a month. This was estimated to be 15 million households. Awareness, intent, and availability were projected from concept tests and planned spending levels. Panel data for premium cake mixes was used to estimate the frequency of purchase of this type of mix. The first repeat rate was estimated at 50% (50% of those who tried would repeat at their next purchase opportunity) and the second repeat rate at 88% based on product testing data (88% of those who repeat purchased one time would repeat at their next purchase opportunity).

Based on the above inputs, a macro-flow model was used to estimate trial, repeat, and market share. Financial analysis used these projections to estimate total profit for the first three years of full-scale launch as $5.5 million. This was a sufficient business proposition for management to approve the test market for Heritage Pastry. The forecasts of share and consumer response became the standard for the test market.

The next step was to develop the research plan. Three cities were identified. A sensitivity analysis of the model's inputs showed that frequency of purchase and intent were the most critical parameters. A consumer panel and monthly awareness and intent surveys were commissioned to measure the behavioral states. Because distribution was less in doubt, retail store audits were not purchased and the less expensive warehouse withdrawal and company shipment data were utilized to measure sales. The research data cost $300,000 and model analysis cost $100,000. Advertising, product production, and distribution in the cities cost $1.5 million.

Tracking the Test Market

There was great expectation as the test market began. Would the two years of development be a success? The brand manager in particular felt it *had* to succeed if he was to move ahead rapidly in the organization. After two months, the first month share was available—3%! The goal was one-half of 1 percent. Congratulations all around. There was even talk of aborting the test market and going national. But why had the sales been so high? This question became more important as the second period share became available—1.2% versus the goal of 1.0%. The brand now exceeded the goal for two months and there was evidence that a competitor was ready to introduce a pastry mix. However, the brand manager began to be cautious while others pushed to go national. Months three and four shares were above goal and pressure increased to go national. The brand manager was now actively resisting these pressures. In month five, the share was 4.3% versus the goal of 4.0%. The V.P. of New Products wanted to know why the brand manager did not want to go national. At this time the brand manager forecasted a decline in sales to 2.5% by month nine versus the 5% goal.

The actual share fell to 4.0% in month six, 3.6 percent in month seven, 3 percent in month eight, and 2.5% in month nine (see Figure 17.12). What

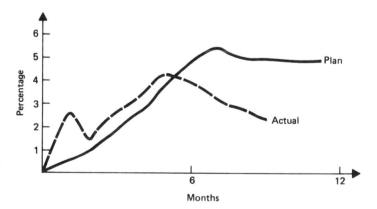

Figure 17.12   Test Market Share

did the brand manager learn in month three that caused him to be cautious and how did he know the share would decline after five months of growth and above goal performance? The answer lies in proper tracking of consumer response—awareness, intent, trial, and repeat.

Figure 17.13 shows trial above the goal while repeat is below the goal. The trial was high for several reasons. The target group was larger than expected because those with income under $15,000 also purchased the prod-

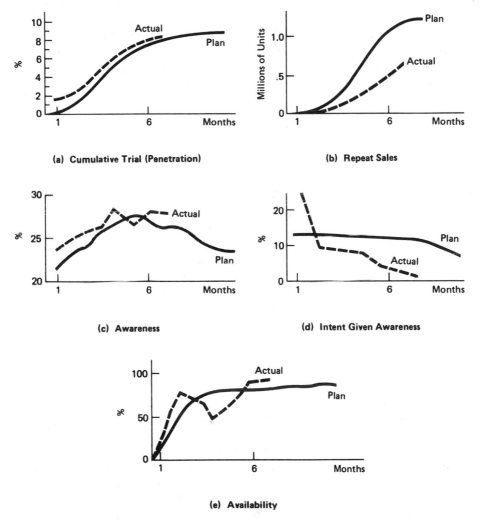

(a) Cumulative Trial (Penetration)

(b) Repeat Sales

(c) Awareness

(d) Intent Given Awareness

(e) Availability

Figure 17.13   Test-Market Results Compared with Prior Forecasts

uct, and awareness was higher than expected (see Figure 17.13c). But intent given awareness was lower after the first month. It was this precipitous drop between months one and two that caused the sobering of the brand manager's expectations and his cautious reaction. Availability was good, but the product was out of stock in months three, four and five due to higher than expected initial sales. Overall trial sales were good, but the falling intent implied a decline in cumulative trial. The survey diagnostics indicated that the pastry mix appealed to innovators, but not to others. Innovative cooks became aware first and purchased quickly, but after the initial adoption, the appeal to the remaining homemakers was low.

The prospect of a real product failure was clearly seen in month 5 as the frequency of purchase and repeat rates were observed to be below standards. This explained the low repeat sales per period. The falling trial, low repeat, and consumer response by month five were used in the model's projecting the share decline to 2.5%.

Forecasting National Sales

A share of 2.5% was well below the forecast 5.0% necessary for the projected profit, but conditions may change in national introduction. Before declaring Heritage Pastries a failure, the brand manager considered changes that would occur between test and national. One change that would improve sales was the fact that the out-of-stock condition would not occur nationally. On the other hand, the same levels of awareness could not be achieved in the national media environment. Forecasted availability was thus increased, awareness decreased, and trial, repeat, and frequency of purchase were set to the observed levels. With these inputs, the model forecast a long-run share of 2% and a loss of $2 million over three years.

Decision: Improve and Go, or Drop

The brand manager was discouraged, but not ready to give up. After two years of development and nine months of testing, the product could not be dropped without an effort to improve it. Fortunately, the test market analyses had identified potential improvements in the marketing mix.

First, the "elegant" positioning hurt the frequency of purchase rates. The pastries were being used for special occasions and not weekly for family dinners. The most popular flavor was chocolate, so a new super chocolate variety could also be developed to improve usage. Diagnostics indicated consumers did not think the filling in the tort was thick enough. Even though it was the authentic European-style tort, American consumers had different preferences. The filling could be made thicker, but only at a higher cost which would be reflected in lower profit or higher prices. New advertising could be developed and more coupons utilized.

The macro-flow model was used to assess the potential impact of these improvements. For example, the new positioning, variety, and advertising were simulated by moving the frequency of purchase distribution to a point half-way between the observed levels and the original premium cake mix distribution. Coupons increased the trial intent and thicker filling increased the repeat rates. In all, more than 500 combinations of marketing strategies were tried. The best result was a 3% long-run share and $500,000 in total profit.

In this case, the managerial diagnostics could increase sales by 50 percent and improve profit by $2.5 million ($500,000 gain rather than a $2 million loss), but it was not enough. The project was terminated. Although the pastry mix had high trial appeal to innovators, its appeal was not wide enough, and the frequency of use was not sufficient to pay back the initial marketing investment.

The brand manager presented these results to the president, vice-president of marketing, and vice-president of New Products. Although they were not pleased by the result, they felt that without the brand manager's careful work, the firm would have gone national and lost $2,000,000 and some good will with the trade. The brand manager was promoted and put in charge of the first major effort to develop low-cholesterol-and-salt-based products for consumer and institution markets.

GO/NO GO ANALYSIS

Not all decisions are as clear-cut as the NO decision for Heritage Pastry. Many times profit is good, but not outstanding, and a balancing of risk versus return must be made relative to the goals of the firm. In this section, we review some analytic approaches to this problem and discuss the emotional reactions that may be involved in such decisions.

Decision Frontier Revisited

In Chapter 15 we introduced the concept of a decision frontier (see Figure 15.1) Test market analysis provided profit forecasts which reduce risk and managerial diagnostics which increase expected benefit. After test market, we must face the managerial decision of whether to go to full-scale launch (GO), drop the product from further consideration (NO GO), or collect further data and attempt to improve the product (ON). We can represent these decisions on the same diagram as the decision frontier (see Figure

17.14). Note that if there is no uncertainty in the forecast, there is one level of minimum expected benefit to divide the GO and NO areas. There is no ON alternative since the uncertainty is zero and more information cannot change it. As risk increases, a greater expected benefit is needed for a GO decision. This is the decision frontier. We have added a lower line which defines the boundary between the NO GO and ON decision areas. It is usually downward sloping as shown. As shown, this line indicates that as risk increases the organization becomes more cautious about dropping a product from further analysis.

If a test market was run, we can assume the product was in the ON region prior to test market. Figure 17.14 shows three possible outcomes. In outcome 1 the test market has produced better forecasts (less uncertainty) and has identified sufficient improvements in the marketing mix to move the product past the decision frontier. Outcome 1 would mean a decision to proceed to full-scale launch. In outcome 2, the test market has reduced uncertainty and improved the marketing mix, but there is still too much risk involved in launching the product. Outcome 2 would mean a consideration of further analysis, but not a GO decision. Finally, in outcome 3, once uncertainty is reduced it is clear the product should be dropped from further consideration.

Figure 17.14 gives the intuitive basis for the GO and NO GO decisions. We can quantify risk and expected benefit to support further the managerial decision. Some managers may wish to use these venture analysis techniques, others may compute expected benefit and judgmentally estimate risk. In either case the GO/ON/NO GO regions provide a useful decision tool.

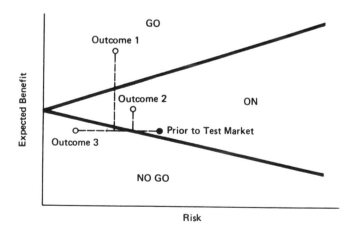

Figure 17.14   Schematic Representation of GO/NO GO Analysis

Quantifying Risk and Expected Benefit

One way to represent expected benefit is by the expected level of profit discounted by the organization's target rate of return. Risk is measured by the standard deviation of the discounted profit. Straight line decision frontiers represent

- GO if the probability of achieving the target ROI is greater than, or equal to, some cutoff level, X, and
- NO GO if the probability of achieving the target ROI is less than, or equal to, another cutoff level, Y.

The slope of the decision frontiers are higher if the probabilities are greater. For example, the straight-line decision frontier may represent the decision criteria of, "We want a 90% chance of achieving a rate of 15% before we will GO national," or the decision criteria of, "We want a 75% probability of making at least $5 million in profit in the first three years." Other measures such as market share or sales which are used to quantify expected benefit produce similar results.

Managing Enthusiasm

Although rational and analytical methods are available, the GO/NO GO decision environment is usually charged with emotion. Some people have invested much time and effort in the project and believe in it. Others may see it as a threat to their organizational domain or take a very conservative approach.

In the extreme, rational methods may be misused to achieve the desired decision. For example, the profit forecast for the product could be arbitrarily raised by the new product advocates. In one large chemical company, this abuse became so frequent that the calculation of risk/return ratios was dropped. Another abuse is to fill in the acceptable bottom line profit first and then make enough assumptions to justify it. For example, a transportation service made revenue estimates by first calculating a politically acceptable subsidy and then subtracting this from expected costs. This revenue was then "justified" by other means.

Enthusiasm is necessary, of course, but a rational forecast must be made in order to protect the stockholders and public interests. One method is to have the new product sponsor's forecast and analysis audited by a corporate marketing or financial service group. The substantive differences would be resolved before top management made a final commitment.

With such resolution, the positive emotion necessary for a successful launch can be maintained, but accurate risks and returns can be presented to top management for a final decision. At this level, the risk/return input must be integrated with a final assessment of the product's contribution to the firm's long-run strategy objectives and its compatibility to the political and social environment top management must face.

SUMMARY

Test markets are an important component in the new product process. While many products cannot or will not be taken to test market, test markets should at least be considered when risk and investment is high. If a test market is used, it should be used intelligently. The proven state of the art of models and measures is well beyond share projections from test markets that replicate national plans. A test market should not only forecast sales, but also generate response data to maximize profits. Data support through experimentation and statistical analysis should be designed carefully to supply the response estimates necessary to track test market performance, adjust for differences between test market and national markets, and maximize profits. Both risk and return should be included in the GO/NO GO decision and procedures should be instituted to prevent biased estimates.

If the product is successfully tested by analysts and accepted by management, a GO decision will be made. The next chapter discusses the issues underlying the launch of a new product. If a NO GO decision is made, the firm will abort the product and allocate its attention to other projects in the design and testing phase, or initiate new projects unless they feel there is enough potential to recycle the product back to the beginning of the design phase.

REVIEW QUESTIONS

17.1. Should new products always be taken to test market? Why or why not?

17.2. Is it ever possible that the best decision will be to launch the new product despite a *bad* test market? If so, under what conditions?

17.3. When management wants to use a decision analysis for the decision as to whether or not to test market, they must assign subjective probabilities to the occurrence of different events. For example, they must quantify the probability the product will be successful. When forming subjective probabilities, the numbers generated must obey different rules. For example, they must all be greater than zero and less than one. Suppose that the probability of the product being successful (as evaluated before test market) is identical to the probability that the test market will be successful. Under this special situation what is the relationship between the following probabilities: (1) the probability of national success given a bad test market, (2) the probability of national success given a good test market, and (3) the before-test-market probability of national success?

17.4. Exotic Games Inc. is launching a new form of video game. To help study its adoption a diffusion of innovation approach was adopted. Innovators were found to be young, educated adults living in large cities. Given this information, what implications does it have for
  a. Media selection
  b. Retail distribution
  c. Packaging

17.5. A company is doing a decision analysis to determine whether to adopt a GO or NO GO decision. After quantifying test market information they find the probability of gaining $2,000,000 is .5 and the probability of losing $1,000,000 is also .5. The company decides to GO. Why could another company facing this same problem decide not to GO?

17.6. What diagnostic information should a manager expect from test market analysis? How can this information be used to improve the new product and marketing mix?

17.7. The following table shows consumer purchases for a consumer panel consisting of eight individuals. Time periods are shown from the first week after the launch of a new brand through the tenth week of the test market. C indicates purchases of a competitive brand; N indicates purchases of the new brand.
Assuming this sample panel is completely representative of the market, forecast the long term market share for the new brand.

					Week after Launch					
	1	2	3	4	5	6	7	8	9	10
Consumer										
1	C	N	N	N	N	N	N	N	N	N
2	C	N	N	N	C	N	N	N	C	N
3	C	C	C	C	C	C	C	C	C	C
4	C	C	C	C	C	C	C	C	C	C
5	C	C	N	N	C	N	N	C	N	C
6	C	C	C	C	C	C	C	C	C	C
7	C	C	C	C	C	C	C	C	C	C
8	C	C	C	C	N	C	N	C	N	C

17.8. Mr. Labas, the vice-president of Growth and Development at Tingus Industries, does not run test markets. When asked to explain this Mr. Labas said, "Why run a test market? Even if the results are bad there is so much enthusiasm after working so hard on the new product that we will launch the new product anyway.'' Comment on this strategy.

17.9. What are the advantages and disadvantages of panel data when monitoring test markets?

17.10. Modify the Blattberg and Golanty recursive model to include other marketing mix variables besides advertising.

PART FIVE

Product Introduction and Profit Management

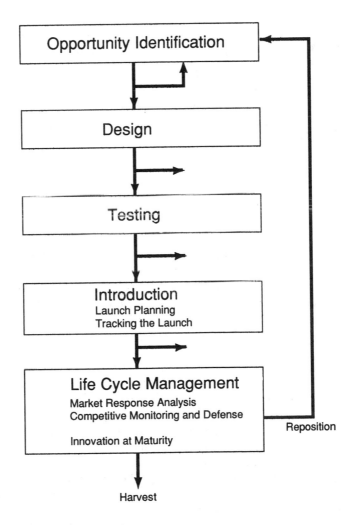

18

Launching the Product

Once a go decision is made, an organization must marshall its resources to plan and implement a full-scale introduction. At this point many of the strategic decisions will have been made and tested. Management has a physical product, advertising copy, personal selling tactics, a promotion plan, price, distribution channels, and service procedures. The key market segments are known. The likelihood of competitive response has been gauged and strategic responses formulated. The product will have a high probability of success since it has passed the testing phase criteria. The management task in full-scale introduction is to achieve the potential success through careful management of the launch.

Although successive testing and development has reduced the risks, a degree of risk still remains. The amount of risk faced at launch depends upon whether the product was test marketed (chapter 17) or not. If test market was bypassed in an effort to reach the market faster and avoid competitive imitation, the risk of failure could be high. There are two ways to deal with this risk. One is to monitor carefully the launch with a fast adaptive control system and the other is to phase the launch. In this later case the launch would be termed a "roll out." A roll out begins in one market and then advances through other markets to span eventually the entire market. In either case the firm must learn from the consumer response and production experience so that it quickly can correct errors and gaps in the planning and react to changes in the competitive market.

At launch time the stakes are high. Physical production investments are made and marketing expenditures are committed. Launch expenditures may be large. For example, Gillette's introduction of the Sensor razor in 1990 reflected more than $50 million in advertising and promotion. In durable goods, the costs of introduction include investment in production as well as in marketing. A new microwave kitchen stove may require $50 million for production line set up and a new model car may require more than $500 million. Industrial products do not require as much introductory marketing expenditure as consumer goods, but may entail more in production. For example, a new line of jets at Boeing requires an investment equal to more than the firm's net worth. Although the magnitudes depend upon the product category, it is clear that by far the largest investment in new product development is in full-scale launch.

This means careful plans for the launch must be made and the introduction must be controlled carefully and tracked to assure that an adequate return on this investment will result.

LAUNCH PLANNING

In planning the launch an organization coordinates the marketing mix and production to assure that quality products are available and that demand requirements and production capacity match. The required tasks are outlined in a critical path analysis to ensure that all components at the introduction are ready in time for the launch. This coordination and timing becomes particularly crucial if competitors also are developing a new product for the target category. The coordination needs also are greater if a global launch in which the product is simultaneously introduced throughout the world is to be conducted. Some firms roll out from one country to another while others launch as if the world were one market to be attacked at the same time. In this section, we first discuss the coordination and timing necessary for launch and then indicate some of the organizational issues in the management of the new product introduction.

Coordination of Marketing and Production

If the launch is to be successful, the advertising, selling, promotion, distribution, and service strategy must be implemented effectively. The sales force is trained and motivated to allocate the planned effort. The channels of distribution are established and combined to stock, display, and service the product. Advertising media are purchased and ad copy manufactured. Samples and coupons are produced and mailed.

While marketing activities are significant, the major pre-launch effort is in production. Machines are purchased and set up in a mass production system. Suppliers must be developed and trained in quality methods. Materials are procured and inventoried at both the original equipment manufacturer (OEM) and supplier location. In some cases new plants must be built and staffed. Increasingly the production facilities are globally distributed (e.g., Singapore, Mexico, Spain) and remote from critical market and the firm's home office. Efficient physical distribution systems must be established. Quality standards are implemented throughout the system. The production facility is tuned to produce consistently the desired product specifications. Service policies are put in place to guarantee the delivery of the promised consumer benefits. Total quality becomes the theme of the launch planning. If the quality is not assured, real risks of national failure will exist. Just as the House of Quality (see Design for Quality, chapter 13) was used to assure that the product was designed to fulfill customer needs, the other "houses" of Quality Function Deployment are used (often during design) to assure that the production process fulfills customer needs.

The marketing and production activities must be closely coordinated. This will be easier if marketing and engineering have worked jointly on the design for manufacturability. One important aspect of launch coordination is the timing of the manufacturing startup. A startup that is too early may create large, expensive inventories and result in product deterioration. If the startup is too late, there may not be enough supply to meet the growing demand and large back orders. Insufficient supplies cause opportunities to be missed and cause goodwill to be lost with consumers and channel members.

In planning the startup date, organizations should consider that full capacity may not be reached immediately. For example, Figure 18.1 illustrates what can happen if production and introduction are begun at the same time, but production capacity grows slowly with experience. In this case, back orders occur resulting in long waits and customer dissatisfaction. If production starts too early, large inventories result.

To manage these problems a joint plan must be developed for marketing and production, which should include the relative timing of production, introduction, and the marketing mix. For example, marketing managers may delay advertising or promotion to avoid too much demand too soon, or manufacturing managers may produce a large inventory so that out-of-stock situations will not leave the company vulnerable to competitive products. This joint planning of the functions has the potential to result in greatly increased profits.

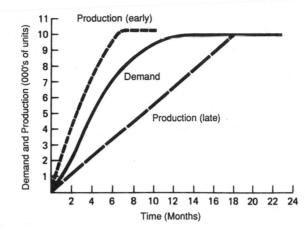

Figure 18.1 Production Startup and Demand Growth (Adapted from Abernathy and Baloff 1972, p. 31)

Joint planning can run into organizational snags. Marketing and production may each have "political muscle" which must be controlled to achieve an effective production plan. To overcome potential difficulties, the plan should represent plans in units that are common to all functions involved (such as sales and net inventory levels at critical dates), offer flexibility once the plan is implemented, control performance with respect to the plan, and be expressed in total quality terms so all functions realize they are striving for the same final goal of customer satisfaction.

Timing of Launch

Besides the relative timing of production and marketing, we must select the specific timing of the launch. Without competitive pressure, most organizations would proceed through introduction planning at a safe but steady pace. An overly cautious approach can delay entry and result in missed opportunities. Usually pressures exist for a fast launch. Competitors may have read your test market and begun their own crash program. You even may find they have just entered the market for your new product. In each case your organization may feel the need to begin its own crash program.

Such pressures for crash programs are compelling, but should be resisted until they can be carefully considered. A crash program may be just the response the competitor wants if it forces you to make a key mistake that may compromise your position. On the other hand, you must take some risk to succeed. This is never an easy decision. The management task is to balance the expected gain and the risk to arrive at a timing for the launch.

The first, and most obvious, consideration is some quantification of the gains to be achieved through early introduction. Among the questions to be considered are: "How much harm can the competitor do if they enter soon after you?" "How firmly entrenched will they be if they enter before you?" To answer these questions, we suggest your organization evaluate the relative strength of the competitive product. If it is inferior, then you lose little by waiting. Usually there is an advantage of being first in a market, but this is not true if the first in does not have a good positioning (see Urban et al. 1985; and chapter 4). A pretest market study (see chapter 16) of your competitor's product can be very useful in assessing the competitive threat if you can define what it is likely to be in terms of its consumer attributes or mock up a prototype.

While revenue may increase for an early launch that allows you to be first in the market, costs also increase. Crash programs usually result in inefficiencies which increase cost. Beyond a certain point costs increase rapidly for small gains in time.

Management also should consider the risks of early launch. One well-known food product manufacturer tried to beat a competitor with an early launch, but did so before lining up a diversified set of suppliers. The supplier of a key ingredient went on strike and the manufacturer had to find alternative suppliers at a high cost. Such risks are inherent in innovation, but should be considered explicitly before rushing the launch.

There are good reasons to launch early, but many organizations miss opportunities by launching too rapidly. The possible loss of revenue must be traded off against the increased costs of a crash program and greater risk of failure. Figure 18.2 shows a hypothetical set of time and cost curves. Costs, risks, and revenue increase, but the gain in revenue probably is not worth the risks and costs involved. Only if the revenue loss by not responding to a competitive threat with a crash effort was large, and the costs low, would it be worth the risk.

In computers Sun Micro Systems in the 1990s built their firm on a strategy of getting to market with the next generation of work stations before their competitors. They were so good at this that they could make public their chips and software to help build standards and still capture the market by being first with the successor generation of computer. In this industry "cycle time" or the time from idea to market introduction is the dimension of competition, so crash programs are the norm. In other industries such as autos where quality is a dominant criteria, rushing to market would be unwise unless one could be assured that in no way would quality be jeopardized. For example, when Saturn autos had many quality problems in readying for their launch, dealers were paid $100,000 each to compensate for cars not being ready for delivery as planned initially.

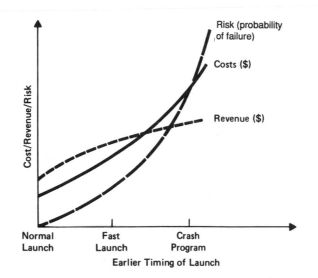

Figure 18.2   Hypothetical Cost, Risk, and Revenue Curves of Launch Timing

Naturally we would most like ultimate speed and quality, but unfortunately there are often tradeoffs between these two performance criteria. These tradeoffs are usually made judgmentally, but formal decision analysis (Keeney and Raiffa 1976) could be applied. It is important to take a rational look at the tradeoffs rather than to panic and rush a premature launch or be overly cautious and miss a market opportunity.

Critical Path Analysis

One method of managing the issues of launch timing and coordination is called critical path analysis (CPA). It structures the sequence of activities and identifies those that are most critical to the success of the timing; it also supplies standards to coordinate the various activities.

When a launch is planned, obviously a wide range of supporting activities must be carried out in the marketing and production areas. Some activities are independent and can proceed simultaneously. For example, the development of advertising copy does not depend upon the negotiations with raw material suppliers. But some activities are sequential. For example, an organization must develop the advertising copy before it begins introductory advertising, or it must begin to stock up on raw materials or arrange for a just-in-time inventory system before it begins production.

To achieve the target dates for launch and to generate time-cost tradeoffs such as shown in Figure 18.2, management must enumerate and schedule all the details of the launch. This is best done by some form of critical path analysis (CPA) such as the program evaluation and review technique (PERT) or the critical path method (CPM).

While the details vary, the concept of CPA is simple. Related tasks are laid out in paths according to the order in which they are to be completed. Figure 18.3 shows the activities that need to be done to reach market with a home word processor.

In the next step in CPA the activities are graphically arrayed to find the longest sequence of activities or "critical path." Independent tasks are indicated by parallel paths while dependent tasks are interconnected by lines that indicate the length of time of each activity. The time required to complete each task is determined; then these times are summed to give the total time for each path. To launch the product early, resources must be directed at shortening the critical path. For example, Figure 18.4 shows one simple critical path network for a new-product launch. The advantages of critical path analysis for new product launch is that it provides information to (1) define the activities and show the interrelationship between tasks, (2) evaluate alternative tactics to get to market faster, (3) establish responsibilities of various functional units, (4) check progress at intervening durations against original schedules, (5) forecast bottlenecks, (6) replan and redesign to avoid bottlenecks, and (7) assure quality while getting to market fast.

Critical path analysis is useful in planning and scheduling, but it is not the only method. Various approaches have been built based on it. For example in PERT, management estimates optimistic, likely, and pessimistic times; decisions are based on both the average times and the variance in times. In the CPM variation, the optimal project duration is identified by trading off the cost of reducing the critical path versus the opportunity cost because of delays in product introduction. Various graphical methods have been used as one of the seven quality management tools in Japan. While the methods vary in their details all of them can work if they generate a dialogue and consensus between all the functional personnel that leads to coordination of the launch activities so that the time to market is short and the quality is high.

Management of the Launch

As the product is moved toward introduction, there may be a shift in management responsibility. In many cases, the design and testing phases will have been handled by a new product team consisting of specialists who can manage and enhance creativity and who know how to gather and act upon consumer information. In launch planning, different skills are needed to plan the details of production and of the marketing mix. The launch demands a

ACTIVITIES	1990					1991										
	Sept	Oct	Nov	Dec	Jan	Feb	Mar	Apr	May	Jun	Jul	Aug	Sept	Oct	Nov	Dec
Production	Set up line and suppliers					Production test				Ship product						
Distribution	Recruit retailers and distributors							Train retail sales staff/ Promotion plan				Point-of-purchase Install				Monitor
Sales	Sell channel								Aid in training and dealer advertising						Support dealers	
Advertising	Final TV copy and print ads						Test ads and buy media				Revise and final copy			National advertising and promotion		
Service	Write service manual						Train dealers				Stock parts		Correct any defects			
Market research	Monitor market							Ad copy test				Set up UPC sample	Telephone survey			
R&D				Work on YWP 2000		Monitor technology										
Global		Global strategy meeting		Tactical plans by country			Review tactics			Coordinate ad/training materials				Share learning		Strategy review

Figure 18.3 Launch Activities For Home Word Processor (Urban and Star 1991, p. 503; reprinted with permission)

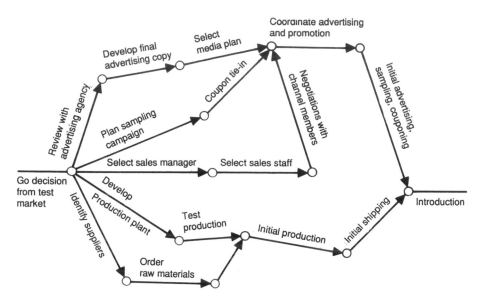

Figure 18.4   Simple Critical Path Analysis Example

large amount of resources which could overwhelm projects in other phases of the new product program. Thus organizations face the difficult problem of how much control to shift from the new-product developers to the product managers.

There are advantages of a shift to a person such as a product manager. Product managers are implementation specialists who can handle the management details of a launch and coordinate a team of critical personnel. Such shifts free the new-product team to devote their skills to other new-product projects. But a shift is not without dangers. Without clear-cut responsibility, the product can fall into "limbo" with no one really committed to it. After all, the new product may not be viewed as the product manager's project and he or she may lack commitment. Furthermore, the product manager may not have the intimate knowledge of the market or of the CBP that is necessary to overcome the hurdles to launch success. Finally, launch may be viewed by the new-product team as a reward for the earlier hard work and risks. They may seek this reward for themselves or may begrudge the reward being given to someone who has not had to bear the risks.

There is no one answer to the very difficult question of transition of management. In some organizations transition is most effective by granting control to the established product group. Others may wish to delay transition until the product has reached a mature state (1 to 2 years after launch). In still others the new-product venture team becomes the management team and stays with the product through its life cycle.

The best system would preserve the knowledge used to develop the product strategy, but add the new skills necessary for large scale implementation. One approach would be to have a hand off to a product manager at launch time. Another would be to have the product manager and production personnel work on the new product team with the product developers and production process planners for the first 12 months of launch and then have them take over responsibility. In all cases, there should be close communication and cooperation among the new-product development group and the introduction management team. Important diagnostic information should be made available to the management team so that they understand how and why the CBP and marketing mix have been developed.

The issues of organization of the new product will be considered more comprehensively in chapter 20. Launch planning is only one aspect of the overall organizational problem, but it is an important aspect of implementing a successful product.

TRACKING THE LAUNCH

Need to Monitor

Unexpected events will take place before and during the launch of a new product. Although the test-market modeling and forecasting prepares you for the sales response and growth, events outside your control are likely to occur.

One set of such events are economic and political changes that may occur between test market and launch, or during the launch. For example, in 1990 the Berlin Wall came down and Iraq invaded Kuwait forcing a U.S. and European military response. In 1991 communism ended in the USSR, the Baltic nations became independent states, Germany reunited, civil war erupted between Croatia and Serbia, while western Europe moved towards wider unification. Few of these changes were predicted and firms launching products globally in 1990/91 had to make major adjustments for material costs (oil), market boundary changes (Eastern Europe), and competition (e.g., Germany invested in Eastern Germany). It is important to monitor the environment between the go decision and the national launch to be sure the environmental assumptions underlying the go decision have not changed.

Consumer preferences may also change. For example, your CBP for a new industrial epoxy glue may be "safe and effective" with an emphasis on effective in joining exotic composites, but during the period prior to launch tastes may shift in the direction of "safe" and environmentally responsible. By recognizing and reacting to this change you can improve profit potential by repositioning the product to emphasize employee safety and less toxic fumes.

Perceived price barriers may change during the launch. In one new-product launch the initial price was fixed just below what management perceived as a $.99 barrier in that category. But inflation pushed competitive products past the barrier, opening up new opportunities for a premium priced product or for a larger size package at $1.09.

Distribution channels may change. If a channel, such as a large retailer, is now carrying a product category formerly carried only by specialty stores, your display strategy may have to be changed. A new mega-retailer may begin operations in a key market or, due to a bargaining failure, a major channel of stores may refuse to carry your brand without a major increase in margin or a subsidy (see Montgomery [1971], and Rao and McLaughlin [1989], for a discussion of intermediaries' decisions to add a product).

During the launch, preference, price, economic, and distribution variables may or may not change, but you can be almost certain that competitors will respond to your introduction. These must be monitored and diagnosed so that appropriate actions can be taken. Competitive reactions are intense, but varied. It is not uncommon to see a competitor increase advertising expenditures substantially to counter a new-product introduction. Although it is doubtful that high spending levels can be maintained indefinitely, they can cause havoc in the launch plan. If the new product is a strong product, competitors may wage the battle by attempting to undermine trial. For example, to counter a strong sampling campaign by "Aim" toothpaste, Procter and Gamble undertook an advertising campaign that appealed to loyal "Crest" users and discouraged them from trying the unnamed sample brought by the postal service.

Other competitors may try to exercise power in the distribution channel by giving channel members incentives to emphasize their product rather than the new product. Such strategies are particularly effective if shelf space is limited in the retail outlet. All these occurrences emphasize the need to monitor the prelaunch and launch environment carefully. The lack of response to a change or an inappropriate response can undermine the profitability and perhaps the success of the product. Each change must be monitored and diagnosed. The revisions must be made to maximize the product's profit.

The final priority is the tracking results when a roll-out strategy is used. In this case not only are we monitoring changes, but we are learning about the basic consumer acceptance of our product. For example, trial may be below goals, frequency of repeat less than desired, word-of-mouth communication negative, customer-use satisfaction below our standards. In all these cases we must recognize the gap between goals and actual achievement on the measure of interest, diagnose why it occurred, and quickly formulate a plan of action to bring the performance back in line with the plans.

In the next sections we outline concepts of a control system to support management of the launch and adaptive control procedures to assure an appropriate and timely response.

Control System

Market intelligence to identify profit opportunities and to formulate responses to unexpected changes is best obtained through an explicit control system. A basic control system is illustrated schematically in Figure 18.5. Plans are set and determine forecasts which are compared to actual results to enable the diagnosis of problems, planning of response, and updating of forecasts.

The basic plan is set by the test or pretest experience. The model that was used to analyze the test (pretest) market provides forecasts of awareness, trial, repeat and, if possible, more-detailed consumer response measures such as word-of-mouth communication and satisfaction. The implementation of the product and marketing mix in the market influences the actual results. Since the marketing mix and production were planned based on this forecast, any deviation of consumer response from forecasts is a signal for analysis. The "actual" and "predicted" results are compared with respect to the behavioral process as well as overall sales. Based on this comparison new plans are developed and new forecasts based on planned changes. New market trends are produced for control of the remainder of the launch. This systematic com-

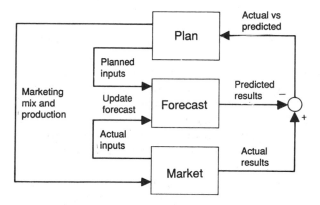

Figure 18.5 Product Launch Information System

parison of actual and predicted results is called "tracking"—this activity continues throughout the launch with periodic updating of the plan and the forecast.

Consumer-response data is important during launch as well as during test market. If a detailed analysis model was used during test market, it should continue to be used during launch. Suppose that a macro-flow model was used to forecast sales and suppose that a monthly awareness survey and store audit data are being collected during the launch to provide data for the model. By comparing actual versus predicted flows through each and every state, management can quickly identify where and why forecast sales differ from actual. Actions can be taken to modify strategy. If a recursive model or if a statistical data projection model was used, each variable in the prediction equations should be remeasured and compared to its forecast value. In either case, the analyses and the strategy identification are performed using the same analytic tools introduced in chapter 17.

Figure 18.6 gives a hypothetical example of predicted and actual results for a new car in terms of customer satisfaction and sales. The sales results could be obtained from sales and product shipment data and the satisfaction measures from continuing monthly surveys of a sample of customers.

The measure here is the percent of customers who overall are "extremely" satisfied with the car and the dealer relative to other cars and dealers they considered (top box on a five point scale); the sales are dealer deliveries of cars to customers. The tracking indicates that satisfaction was below goal and dropping during the first months. Suppose that diagnosis of detailed information on customer-need fulfillment indicates this is due to early production defects in the car and unsatisfactory correction of the problems by the dealer service system. If revisions are made in the production in month three and in the dealer service (faster service, priority handling, and free loaner car during repair) then customer satisfaction returns to target values. These results would be evident in the data as existing owners feel better after the problems are corrected and new customers receive cars with no problems. The sales data might show initial growth and then a drop in sales below goals as the negative experience of early buyers influence sales in months 4, 5, and 6; sales would return to the goal as the defects are corrected and positive word-of-mouth develops. Both the satisfaction and sales data are needed to track the launch problems and quickly correct them. In our next chapter we will have more to say about customer satisfaction in terms of quality ratings and customer expectations, but Figure 18.6 introduces this measure and its use in launch tracking.

The control system shown in Figure 18.5 is a schematic that can readily be implemented through many market models. At the end of this chapter we illustrate a macro-flow model of tracking with a case on family-planning serv-

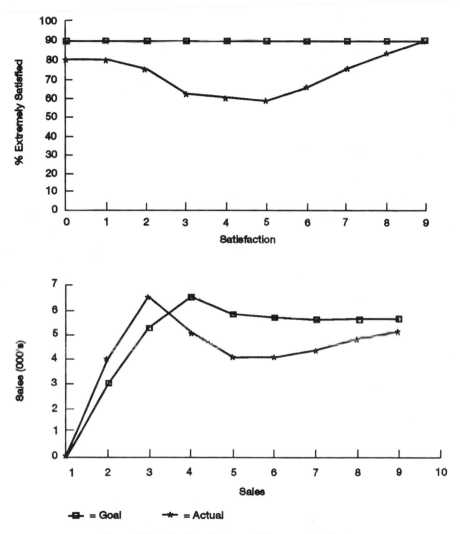

Figure 18.6   Tracking Sales and Customer Satisfaction

ices. We turn now to a formal learning system for adaptive control through experimentation.

It is important to recognize that launch plans should be adaptive in the sense that they are updated continually by market response data. This type of updating makes the plan less susceptible to failures in execution. Any mistake is identified quickly through the feedback mechanism and rectified in the next period. The speed of updating is important, since actions must be taken quickly before the major funds to support the launch have been expended.

The system of control can be used based on market sales or market research measures. These are useful measures in monitoring and forecasting of the diffusion of innovation. However, it also can be implemented by additional response information gained from market experimentation during the launch, growth, or maturity phases of the life cycle. This information is used to improve the setting of price, advertising, and promotion levels.

Adaptive Control and Experimentation

Initial levels of the marketing mix are set based on an analysis of the tradeoffs in the cost of obtaining the sales versus the profit generated. For example, Figure 18.7 illustrates one market response function that could be used to forecast sales from advertising expenditures. If the response functions are accurate and if the environment has not changed dramatically, then actual sales should be close to predicted sales and the launch should proceed as planned. If, on the other hand, the response function shifts, the best level of expenditure will change. Thus it is important to monitor the market response functions throughout the product launch and life cycle.

Suppose we are interested in controlling the market response to advertising. One way to measure this response function might be to increase advertising in all markets by some amount, say 20% over forecast, and observe sales results. This is undesirable for two reasons. First, the increase is a change from the forecast level which was previously identified as the best strategy. It is likely that the advertising change will result in decreased profits, perhaps a larger decrease than the information is worth. Second, the market is not a

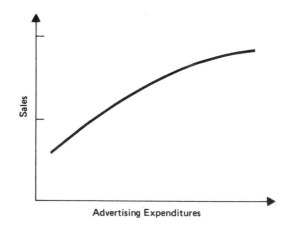

Figure 18.7   Market Response Function

controlled laboratory. Other marketing mix strategies may change, new competitive products may enter, or the basic environment may change. All these effects will influence sales and there may be no way to isolate the effect due to the change in advertising.

Both reasons argue that if experimentation is to be done, it should not be done in all submarkets at the same time. If advertising experimentation is done in only a fraction of the submarkets, then the nonexperimental markets can act as control groups.

Little (1966) has developed a technique, called "adaptive control," to determine both the number of markets in which to experiment and the size (e.g., advertising change) of the experiment. His approach is illustrated in Figure 18.8. The advertising rate is varied by an amount (Δ). It is reduced from its initial level (a_0) to a lower level ($a_0 - \Delta/2$) in some markets and is increased to a high level ($a_0 + \Delta/2$) in others.

In any given time period, t, the best base level, $a_0(t)$, is a function of the current best estimate of market response function and the cost of advertising. That is, without experimentation the manager would select $a_0(t)$ to maximize profit.

Because advertising response is not known with certainty, the profit may not be optimal. There is some potential loss in profit due to this uncertainty. In theory this "expected loss," could be quantified and the value of sample information computed. The manager would then weigh the value of sample information against the expected loss in sales due to experimentation. Based on this comparison, the parameters of the experiment, n and Δ, would be selected to maximize the expected profit in the next period, period $t + 1$.

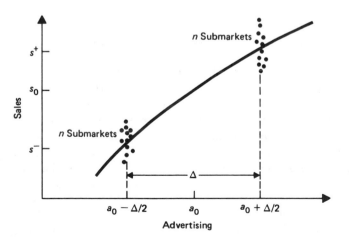

Figure 18.8   Adaptive Control (Little 1966, p. 1080; reprinted with permission)

The computations are straightforward, but tedious. After the parameters of the experiment (n and Δ) are calculated, the optimal advertising in period $t + 1$ is given by Little as:

$$a_0\,(t+1) = a_0(t) + c(ms^+ - ms^- - \Delta) \qquad (18.1)$$

where c is a constant and m is the gross margin on sales; s^+ is the sales rate observed in the markets where advertising was increased, and s^- is the sales rate observed in the markets where advertising was decreased. The first term is the previous expenditure and the second term is the profit due to changing advertising by the amount Δ multiplied by a constant (c). This equation says advertising is revised proportionally to the change in profit. Thus, a manager simply increases (or decreases) the advertising rate by an amount proportional to the observed net profit rate (or loss) due to the advertising change in the experimental markets.

Fortunately, managers do not need to calculate the optimal n and Δ. The method of adaptive control is surprisingly robust and works well even if n and Δ are not chosen optimally. The important idea is that the periodic measurements serve to keep the manager in touch with the market and help the manager learn from experience in an organized way.

We have illustrated adaptive control for advertising response, but the same technique can be used for any element or combination of elements of the marketing mix. Similar equations can be developed for market variables other than advertising and as combinations in the marketing mix. During the launch the models can be extended to a dynamic form (Pekelman and Tse 1980), but the concept of using experimental information to improve the setting of market mix problems is the same.

DURABLE AND INDUSTRIAL PRODUCTS

The full-scale launch of durable and industrial products is similar in many ways to the full-scale launch of frequently purchased products. The marketing mix and production must be coordinated; timing relative to competitors is crucial: Critical path analysis is useful to achieve timing objectives; tracking is important; many of the same behavioral phenomena occur; and the analytic tools of adaptive control are similar. But there are key differences that must be faced when launching a consumer durable or an industrial product. In this section we consider some of the differences that are important in full-scale introduction.

In most durable and industrial products a test market will not have been run due to the expense of a pilot plant or because of the length of time necessary to get a reading on sales. Thus early tracking serves the evaluation and refinement functions that would have been carried out by test market for a frequently purchased product. Adaptive control plays an important role because of the rapid learning that can occur during the launch. For example, in Japan it is common for electronic product manufacturers to put early designs on the market to learn the demand potential and to observe how customers will use the product. Often the early products are sold at high prices. The projections are adjusted for the drop in expected price levels and the expected technological improvements. Continual learning becomes an important aspect of the market launch experience. Sometimes earlier pre-market analysis procedures produce this learning faster and at a lower cost, but if a national launch is to be used for testing, the monitoring and learning methods are very valuable.

Sales in the first few years will result from one time purchases. Repeat purchase occurs later in the life cycle and is dominated by replacement decisions. (The initial products wear out or are replaced by advancing technology.) Customer satisfaction is reflected in the diffusion of innovation because positive word-of-mouth information from a buyer to a prospective customer is critical to success (see Figure 18.6). In durable and industrial products, service is of great importance. For example, FAX and copy machine manufacturers maintain large staffs to service their machines so that product satisfaction is high and positive recommendations are generated.

Another difference between frequently-purchased and durable consumer or industrial products is the role of price. The price of frequently-purchased brands is relatively stable, but the price of new consumer durable or industrial products can fall over time because of economies of scale, industry learning, and competition. These phenomena should be understood and forecast. Furthermore, technology advances so that newer models fulfill customer needs better. For example, the hand-held video cameras represented a great advance and soon sold at a lower price than the larger and older units.

Early Projections of Sales

In Chapter 4 we introduced market growth models as a means to forecast growth for a market. In some durable and industrial products, the new product will establish a new market. In others the new product will enter a rapidly growing, but existing market. In either case a model is useful in forecasting the total market. In the case of an existing market, a model of share similar to those for consumer products will be needed to forecast sales for the innovating organization.

A growth model can be used in two ways during product launch. First, it can be used to establish norms before the launch. These approximate norms are input to the initial planning process. Then, when the product is launched and real-market information becomes available, the parameters of the model are updated to provide information that is necessary to update managerial tactics.

Recall that in the growth model proposed by Bass (see Chapter 4), sales growth depends on the number of initial innovators, $p(0)$, the total number of potential buyers (m), and a parameter to reflect the rate of diffusion, q. In establishing launch norms, each of these three values needs to be estimated. Then they can be substituted into the model (equation 4.3) to produce a sales forecast.

To estimate $p(0)$ we first identify the percentage of the population that are innovators and the likelihood that they will purchase the product; $p(0)$ is then obtained by multiplying these percentages. One could present concept descriptions to a representative sample of potential customers, measure their propensity to purchase through preference and intent scales, and measure situational and demographic characteristics likely to identify innovators.

In the telecommunication case discussed earlier (chapters 8 to 10), innovators were most likely to be scientists and managers whose communication needs are for interactions requiring moderate interaction time (10–30 minutes) and who do not now use visuals, but would like to use visuals. This represented about 4.3 percent of the communication interactions, and this group had a 20.6% chance of trying the new device. The initial innovation probability then was estimated by multiplying 0.043 times 0.206 to give $p(0)$ = 0.009 (Hauser 1978b). Another method of measuring $p(0)$ is by laboratory measurement (see chapter 16). Both these estimation methods serve as initial estimates of initial acceptance.

The next parameter is q, which represents the influence that those consumers who have purchased the product will exert on those who have not yet purchased the product. In Bass's model, q times the percentage who have purchased gives the probability of purchase for a customer who has not yet purchased. This a difficult parameter to obtain prior to launch, thus we suggest that a range be obtained for q rather than a single estimate. This range can then be used in sensitivity analyses. One way to obtain this range is to examine related product categories. For example, one might examine the diffusion rate for home fire alarms to estimate q for home burglar alarms. In the telecommunication study, the diffusion rates for television-related products were used to obtain an estimate of q in the range of .40 to .90. Typical values for past products have been estimated by the study of past innovations (e.g., Sultan, Farley, and Lehmann and Winer 1990; and Montgomery and Srinivasan 1989) and are a good basis for initial estimates.

The final parameter is the market size, m. This is the most difficult parameter to measure if the product is substantially new. Based on reaction to new telecommunication concepts, intent was translated (review Chapter 12) to estimate 11% to 15% as the ultimate penetration for the telecommunications device. Measures of preference and intent establish a range for the initial estimates of the ultimate market size. When measuring m the respondents should be given full information (including word-of-mouth communication) so they can simulate decision making at the mature level of the life cycle. Information acceleration methods are good methods to simulate full information adoption potential measurement (see chapters 12 and 16).

In the telecommunication study the parameters $p(0)$, q, and m are used in the algebraic equations to obtain estimates such as shown in Figure 18.9. Note that we obtain a range of estimates rather than a single estimate. This realistically reflects the uncertainty prior to the launch of the new communication device and enables management to design a flexible plan that can handle the multiple contingencies.

Once the product is introduced, actual sales data becomes available and more accurate estimates of $p(0)$, q, and m, are obtained. The procedures to obtain these estimates are the same procedures (algebraic solution or regression that were used in chapter 4). As data from each new period comes in,

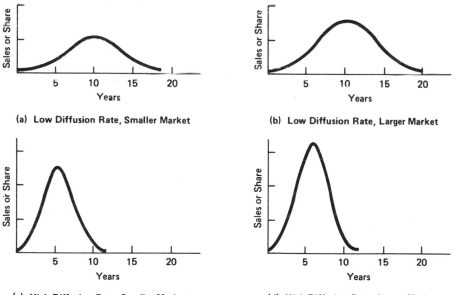

(a) **Low Diffusion Rate, Smaller Market**   (b) **Low Diffusion Rate, Larger Market**

(c) **High Diffusion Rate, Smaller Market**   (d) **High Diffusion Rate, Larger Market**

Figure 18.9   Forecasts to Establish Norms for a New Telecommunication Service

these parameters can be reestimated or updated to provide better forecasts and to refine marketing and production tactics. In this way your organization uses up-to-date market intelligence to control the launch of an industrial product.

Price Dynamics

In many consumer durable and industrial products, we expect that the manufacturer will be able to cut costs because of learning that comes with production experience. Thus as more units are produced, the marginal cost of producing another unit will drop. But if the market is competitive, the price depends on production costs. Prices will drop as more customers purchase the new product. The price drop will in turn accelerate purchases which may then lower costs further.

This experience effect complicates pricing strategies and opens up new managerial considerations. One pricing tactic is to enter with a high price and skim the market, then drop the price as other organizations gain experience. A different tactic is to price low in anticipation of the learning effect to establish good word-of-mouth diffusion and accelerate sales. If this strategy is successful, the firm will become the low-cost producer with a dominant share. This is called "penetration pricing." To identify the appropriate tactic, management needs a forecast of sales and industry price that includes both diffusion phenomena and industry learning.

Integrating learning and diffusion is conceptually easy, but analytically quite difficult. Much marketing science research has been done in this area (some examples are Bass 1980, Dolan and Jeuland 1981, Bass and Bultez 1982, Kalish 1983, Jain and Rao 1990, and Bass and Krishnan 1991). In these approaches the sales life cycle and price declines are predicted to provide tracking criteria. In addition, the implications of changing the variables (price, advertising, and distribution) are calculated to examine ability to affect the life cycle.

The availability of specific models of diffusion and price dynamics for durable and industrial products makes tracking the launch more effective. Better forecasts are made, more effective diagnoses take place, and higher profits are achieved.

SERVICES: FAMILY PLANNING CASE

The above sections emphasize the need for careful tracking and understanding of the dynamics of the launch for consumer and industrial products. This is also true in introducing new services. In this section we describe a case of the introduction of a new health delivery service. It serves as another example of the concept of model-based tracking and control of the early growth phases of an innovation.

Background and Model

Population growth has become a national and worldwide issue as a growing population puts a renewed strain on our natural and economic resources and affects environmental quality. One way to address this problem is by providing people with the contraception, education, and medical services so they can plan their families. This case illustrates the launch of a system of family planning clinics in Atlanta, Georgia. Various clinics existed before this analysis, but the innovation was the deployment of an integrated service.

The Atlanta Area Family Planning Council (AAFPC) developed a macro-flow model to track the growth of family planning in Atlanta. At that time there were three basic service granting agencies: (1) Grady Charity Hospital; (2) Planned Parenthood and World Population; and (3) the Fulton and DeKalb County Health Departments. The purpose of the analysis was to provide forecasts and to integrate plans and budgets for the system.

The analysis began with a simple macro-flow model of patients' clinic visits, acceptance, and continuance. Before long the model was expanded to meet managerial requirements. Because of the flexibility of macro-flow, the model evolved to a basic process (Figure 18.10) with more detailed descrip-

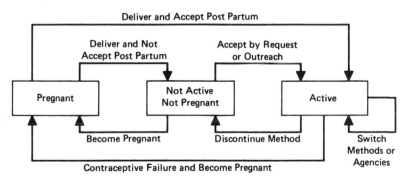

(a) Target Group Sections and Their Interactions

Figure 18.10 Model for the Analysis of Family Planning Programs (Urban 1974, p. 207; reprinted with permission)

tions of consumer flows in post partum (after delivery) hospital clinics and non-postpartum community clinics.

Input and Fitting

The basic source of input was the Centers for Disease Control and its client-record system. This data recorded each patient visit and births in the target population. This data supported trial, repeat, and timing estimation. Outreach workers called on prospective patients. Data were collected on a sample basis to determine the impact of outreach workers on appointments and visits. Tabulations were made to find the response rates.

Initial data estimates were made based on the client record and outreach data of months 1 to 12. After these flow-parameter estimates were put in the model, changes were made so that the model output of "active" and new patients fitted the actual over the first 18 months. "Active" patients were those who accepted family planning on their last visit and were not yet due for their next appointment. The fit for the total number of actives is shown in Figure 18.11. Fitting was also done to assure that the model replicated the real data for each method and for new patients at each agency.

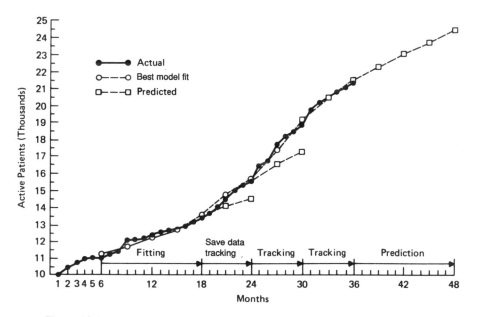

Figure 18.11 Active Family-Planning Patients Using Modern Methods at Major Service Agencies in Atlanta, Georgia

Tracking Results

Although the model fit past data encouragingly well, such fits were the result of considerable massaging of the data. Testing the model was based on comparing actual and predicted patient flows over a six-month period of saved data and over a new twelve-month period. Conditional forecasts were made for months 19 to 24 based on the first 12 months data estimation. This initial prediction is shown in Figure 18.11.

The prediction was lower than the actual figure. This was particularly true at Planned Parenthood, where the prediction was for stable performance and the total active curve increased sharply. The Grady Clinic prediction was also low. The question to be answered was: is the lack of accuracy due to poor input, random error, inadequate model structure, or changes in the real system itself? Answering this question was an exercise in problem finding. In this case, the analysis searched for the reasons for the unexpected success. A detailed analysis of the months 19 to 24 data showed that the number of requests (walk-in appointments) at Planned Parenthood increased from 100 a month to about 250 a month during this time. The initial tracking prediction was based on the past average of 100 per month. Revising the input to reflect the unexpected increase in actual new-patient inflow produced a curve that tracked very well. This implied that the other inputs were probably good and that the structure of the model was reasonably sound. However, the rapid increase of new patients called for diagnosis. There had been an increase in the number of outreach recruitment calls, but very few additional appointments had been made with outreach workers. The hypothesis was that there was an indirect outreach effect in which calls increased appointments and created awareness and interest as demonstrated by clinic visits. Data were collected for new-patient clinic arrivals to see if outreach calls correlated with voluntary requests for appointments.

The lack of correspondence between actual and predicted patient loads at Grady was due to a new volunteer-run clinic which was opened to serve the youth community. It led to an increase of about 50 new patients per month. After these adjustments for new patients at Planned Parenthood and Grady, the active tracking appeared good. Tracking was carried out at the specific method level. This tracking and a new analysis of the months 19 to 24 data indicated a shift in the composition of method selection.

The tracking over the saved-data period (months 19 to 24) was encouraging, but additional tracking over the months 25 to 36 allowed for additional refinements of the model input and understanding of the system structure. The conditional prediction made in month 24 is shown in Figure 18.11. Again the prediction was low. The Planned Parenthood agency increased its new-patient rate to 450 a month, or 200 more than predicted.

Grady referred 50 percent more people per month to the county clinics than expected. New non-postpartum clinic growth added 50 more patients per month. Finally, county-health-department outreach was more effective than anticipated.

The volatility of the system reflected in these changes emphasized the need for tracking and an effective adaptive planning model. With the input updated, the model tracked well. However, diagnosis was necessary to explain the increased new-patient rate. Data indicated the indirect outreach effects were real. Four times as many people contacted by outreach workers came to a clinic without an appointment than came with an appointment. Inputs were revised and new predictions made for months 31 to 36. In month 37, examination of predicted and actual values for months 31 to 36 showed close correspondence. This was encouraging and reflected good predictive performance at the total system level. This was generally true at the agency level except at Planned Parenthood, where actual was less than predicted. Refitting indicated that a decay in continuance rates could explain this. Additional diagnosis showed that the decay was due to an increasing proportion of white college girls. This raised questions of priority between college girls and indigent mothers, because clinic capacity was limited.

In summary, the fitting and tracking of the system growth helped diagnose problems, raised new issues, and provided new insights into the response dynamics.

Managerial Use of the Analysis

The model was used by the Director of AAFPC. She used it to develop an overall system plan and as a tool to aid agencies in their planning of growth of the service system. Special planning sessions were conducted with member agencies so that these managers could understand better their patient response, improve forecasts, and develop goals and plans. Although formal measurement of the impact is difficult, the managers reacted positively and used the model to determine the effects of outreach workers and to predict the number of new patients and the change in the cost per year that would result from undertaking an outreach program. In another agency, the outreach data indicated weakness in the success of outreach workers in making appointments and led to new training sessions based on new communication appeals.

The managerial control process produced some new insights. In particular, the fitting and tracking exercise was valuable because it required a detailed analysis of why predictions were not as good as desired. The indirect effect of outreach workers was one such new insight that resulted from the model use. Another resulted from tracking birth flows. Twenty-five percent of the deliveries from the target group of indigent women were not done at the Grady Hospital, but at private hospitals. Originally, managers had believed that virtually all target-group deliveries were done at Grady on a charity basis. This insight has resulted in a new outreach program to the maternity wards of these private hospitals. The analytic approach fostered by the model led to this new insight and change in the system behavior.

The model proved valuable to managers in generating the forecast for the remainder of the current year so that past funds could be justified and next year's needs could be estimated. It should also be mentioned that the environment surrounding the budgeting is often frantic because of proposal deadlines. The modeling allows rapid simulation and predictions, so that an effective proposal could be formulated on time.

In addition to an orderly forecasting procedure, various strategic alternatives were considered. For example, an outreach program to postpartum non-Grady patients was simulated. With an estimate of the number of calls allocated to this new program and their effect, it was found actives (those who had chosen family planning on their last visit) increased 1 percent over three years and cost per year of protection decreased slightly. The improvements due to strategic analysis were important, but an equal benefit of the analysis has been a better perception of the system dynamics. The discipline of tracking and controlling the launch led to better budgeting and planning for the growth of the family planning system.

SUMMARY

Full-scale launch of a new product is the phase of new-product development that commands the largest commitment of marketing money and managerial resources. No matter how well the product is designed and tested, the launch presents risks to achievement of profit goals—especially if no test market was conducted. Marketing and production must be coordinated, and the timing of the launch planned carefully. Without such planning, profits are jeopardized. Unexpected changes in the consumer, competitive, technological, and economic environments present risks. The need to monitor these events is critical. Appropriate revisions of the launch plan to reflect these changes maintain the desired level of profit and presents opportunities for improvement of plans. A key lesson of this chapter is the need to monitor consumer and competitive response to gain the market intelligence necessary to capitalize on these opportunities. Continuing learning is the key to capitalizing on the new-product potential with quality production and marketing. In con-

sumer, industrial, and service innovations, the control of the launch is equally
as important as any phase in the new-product development process and deserves equal management attention and analytic support.

After the product or service is launched successfully, sales, marketing,
and production will continue to be improved until product maturity occurs.
The next chapter discusses issues concerning long-term profit management
and provides procedures for managing the mature product.

REVIEW QUESTIONS

18.1. Why should management spend the time and money to monitor new products
during national introduction?

18.2. What are the advantages of performing a critical path analysis before product
introduction?

18.3. How does a worldwide launch differ from a national launch followed by a
roll-out to the rest of the world? What activities are similar and which are
different?

18.4. How do consumer-packaged-goods launch procedures differ if a test market
has not been conducted versus a situation where the test market has been
conducted.

18.5. You have spent two years developing a new pie mix, but six months before full-
scale launch your major competitor finds out about your new-product concept
and is rushing to beat you to market. The competitor does not have access to
your technology. Should you begin a crash program to get to market in three,
rather than six, months? What information do you need to make your decision
and how would you go about obtaining the necessary information?

18.6. Why should you compare predicted results to actual results rather than just
monitoring actual results?

18.7. Consider the mathematical implication of Little's control model expressed as
follows:

$$a_0 (t + 1) = a_0(t) + c(ms^+ - ms^- - \Delta)$$

The symbols are defined as indicated by the text. What is the recommended
effect on advertising expenditures of an increase in m, s^+, s^-, or Δ? Why?

18.8. Explain the intuition behind adaptive control? How would adaptive control be
used to set price?

18.9. What special problems does a new-product manager face when monitoring
durable and industrial products? Services?

18.10. Production costs and prices drop rapidly in markets for high-technology products such as calculators and computers. Why? What implications do these decreases have for launching a new high-technology product?

18.11. What diagnostic information should a new product manager look for when monitoring a new-product launch? How is this information obtained?

18.12. Baldai Industries, a manufacturer of large appliances, has developed a new line of European-look dining room furniture called Stalas-Kėdė. Develop a hypothetical plan to help the product manager, Mr. Galva, launch this new line of furniture.

19

Managing through the Life Cycle

Your organization has designed, tested, and introduced a new product. You have a product and marketing strategy that has been successful in either the pretest or test market stages and has been transformed into an effective full-scale introduction. But product management is not finished. There is a significant effort required to realize the profit and reap the rewards of innovation and risk taking. The life cycle of the product must be managed throughout the growth, mature, and decline phases. Marketing and production budgets must be planned and controlled to maximize profits over the life cycle. Advertising, selling, distribution, price, and promotion strategies must be modified in response to changes in competitive situations, economic environment, and consumer tastes. These actions need to be coordinated with the other products in the firm's product line. The product line must be managed by appropriately adding, selectively rejuvenating, or dropping products in the line.

Although profit management is a central task in managing the growth and mature phases of the product history, innovation is still necessary to defend the product against competition and to extend its life by adding product modifications or introducing slightly different brands to tap smaller market segments or carrying the brand name to new categories. These modified products, often called "flankers" and brand "extensions," may be very profitable. In addition, innovation may be needed to improve the efficiency of the production process to reduce costs and increase profits.

Eventually, the product will reach the decline phase of its life cycle. Management then faces the decision of whether to "cash in" and drop the product or to rejuvenate the product through repositioning and redesign for new market needs. Major innovation can launch the product on a new life cycle for continued growth in profits and sales.

In this chapter we consider the growth, mature, and decline phases of a product's life. We examine management changes over the life cycle and emphasize competitive strategy. We use management decision support systems (MDSS) to provide the necessary information and models for profit maximization. We illustrate these concepts through a case application for a major food product. The final sections of the chapter consider competitive strategy, customer satisfaction monitoring, and strategies for product management late in the life cycle.

A THEORETICAL LIFE CYCLE

In theory products tend toward a life cycle of introduction, growth, maturity, and decline stages as illustrated in Figure 19.1. The theory suggests that sales grow slowly during the introduction stage, rapidly during the growth stage, and level off during the maturity stage. In the decline stage, sales and profits

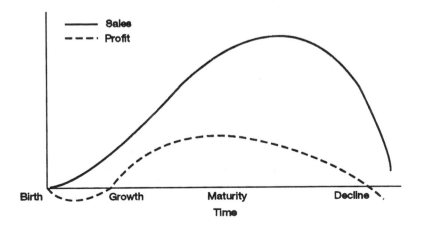

Figure 19.1   Ideal Form of a Product Life Cycle

decline until the firm is forced to withdraw the product from the market-place.

The consequences of ignoring the pressures that lead to deceased sales and profitability can be disastrous. Consider the following examples:

> The replacement of slide rules by electronic calculators was swift and total. (Slide rules are sliding rulers marked with logarithmic scales used by scientists and engineers for making rapid calculations.) In 1972, when Hewlett-Packard introduced the first mass-produced calculator at $395, Keufell & Esser Co. was selling 4,000 of its top-of-the-line slide rules a month at $70 apiece. Four years later, K&E was donating the equipment it used to engrave its slide rules to the Smithsonian Institution. Luckily for K&E, its top executives quickly negotiated an agreement to distribute Texas Instruments' calculators and phased out the slide rules.[1]

> Hoffmann-LaRoche, a Swiss-based pharmaceutical company, which was the world's largest pharmaceutical company until the early 1970s, had slipped into the ninth place by 1983 because of failure to innovate. Made complacent by the success of its two famous tranquilizers—Valium and Librium—the company pursued several research directions but in an unsystematic manner. The success of LaRoche's tranquilizers had created such an impossible benchmark that less spectacular products never made it from the lab to the market. As the patents on the tranquilizers began to expire, profit margins fell sharply and more aggressive competitors surpassed LaRoche's sales and profits.[2]

MONITORING LIFE-CYCLE CAUSES

To manage the life cycle of a product it is necessary to understand some of the forces that lead to the decline phase in the life-cycle phenomena. The life-cycle phenomena is quite complex. We review here some of the key causes including market saturation, new technology, and competition.

Market Saturation

Many products are quite durable. For many products a household or business needs but one (or a few) of the products. For example, in the mid-1970s there was a Citizen-band (CB) radio craze. A CB radio used public airwaves but transmitted over a relatively short distance. Many drivers installed CBs in their cars and many families bought CBs for home use. Furthermore, many of these CBs are still in use today. However, once a driver owned a CB,

---

[1] D. Gates and F. Bruni, "Sliding Toward Oblivion," *Newsweek*, July 23, 1984.
[2] C. Rapoport, "Hoffmann-LaRoche: Struggling to Recover from Success," *Boston Globe*, July 1, 1984, p. A5.

the driver was unlikely to need a second CB. Thus, once the target market was saturated, sales began to decline.

The sales of CB radios through the 1970s are illustrated in Figure 19.2a. Notice the rapid growth from 1972 to 1975. This growth was explained by the rapid diffusion of the technology. (Review chapter 4 for a discussion of this diffusion phenomena and how it might be modeled and forecast. See also chapters 12 and 18.) Around 1976 the market began to saturate and by 1980 the sales in the category had declined. CBs are still sold today, but not nearly in the quantities of the mid-1970s.

In some cases, sales in the total category might stay relatively constant or be subject primarily to general economic conditions. However, if we focus on a subcategory or a particular model, we again see the diffusion/saturation phenomena. For example, Figure 19.2b plots the sales of the Ford Grenada during the same period—the mid-1970s. Notice again, the growth through diffusion and the decline through market saturation.

However, saturation declines are not inevitable and they can be confused with temporary downturns due to other conditions. Both of these considerations are illustrated in Figure 19.3 which plots the sales of color televisions from 1960 to 1985. Notice first the rapid diffusion of console televisions and the decline that began in 1973–74. Although the market saturated there continued to be sufficient replacement sales and/or second-

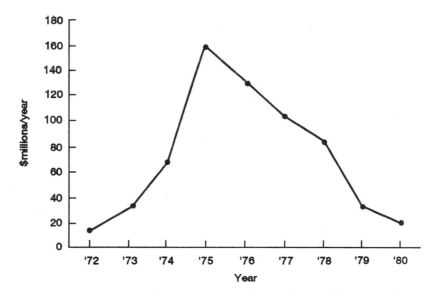

Figure 19.2a   Sales of Citizen Band Radios (*Current Industrial Reports,* MA-36N, Selected Electronic and Associated Products, Bureau of the Census, U.S. Department of Commerce, Washington, D.C.; reprinted with permission)

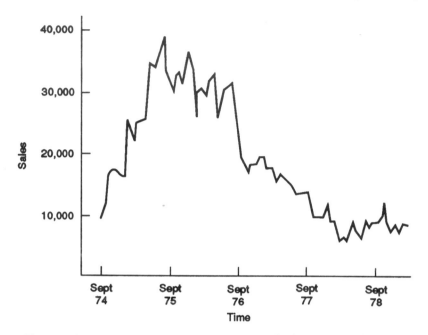

Figure 19.2b Monthly Sales of the Ford Granada 1974–78 (the United States)

television sales to maintain a constant level of shipments. But this was console televisions. At the time that console televisions were declining, a new product form, portable televisions were increasing in popularity. Total television sales began a recycle around 1971 with a peak around 1975. Portable televisions began to decline until 1978 when video games, computers, and other uses caused yet another recycle.

Thus, the product manager should be cognizant of the saturation phenomena and monitor sales in the target market. If, as in the case of CB radios, the category is likely to decline, the product manager can reallocate resources to new products and new categories. If, as in the case of the Ford Grenada, the decline is due to a specific model but the category is stable, the product manager must develop a new model to restart the life cycle. If, as in the case of color television, new product forms or new uses are possible, then the manager can extend the life of the product through creative management.

New Technology

In some ways a portable television was like a new generation of television. In the future we might see more generations with hand-held televisions

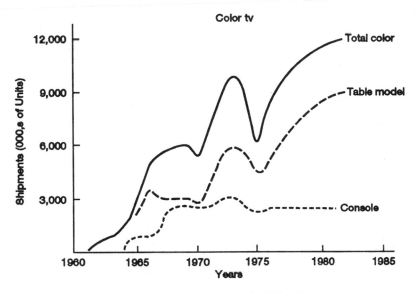

Figure 19.3   Life Cycle of Color Television

or high-definition televisions (HDTV). This generation phenomena is common in many products. For example, early personal computers (at least IBM-compatible computers) relied on the 8086 microprocessor. Soon this was replaced by the advanced technology (AT) 80286 processor that was faster and more powerful. The 80386 processor then made possible 32-bit applications and multitasking and the 80486 processor combined many functions and enabled even greater power and speed. Subsequent generations continue to expand potential. Other cases include software (both applications and operating systems), computer memory (random-access memory, RAM), ignition systems and braking systems for cars, audio media (records, tape cassettes, compact disks, digital audio tape, etc.), and even the sails for sailboats.

For example, Figure 19.4 shows the life cycles for subsequent generations of RAM memory chips. Each generation experienced a rapid growth, a leveling off, and a sharp decline in sales. Over time, the maximum levels for each generation have increased and the life cycle has shortened. In the future we can expect more rapid upgrades and still shorter life cycles. These life cycles have implications for the manufacturers of RAM, but they also impact new products that use RAM (computers, video monitors, etc.) and new products used by the RAM manufacturers (memory testing equipment).

Recently, mathematical models have been developed to model the substitution of subsequent generations (see Norton and Bass 1987 and 1992). For

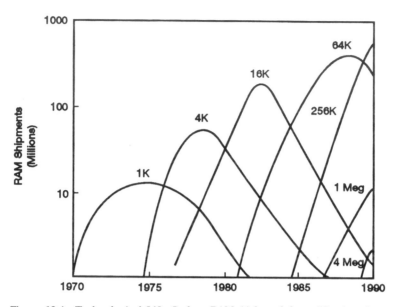

Figure 19.4 Technological Life Cycles—RAM (Adapted from "Semiconductor Memory Chip Peak Sales and Prices," *Fortune*, May 16, 1983, p. 154; "IC Memory Chips Sales Projected 1990," *Electronic Marketing Trends*, April 1982, p. 19; "Solid-State Memory Devices Shipments Projected," *Telephone Engineering & Management*, March 1, 1980, p. 22.)

example, Figure 19.5 shows the actual and fitted values for two successive generations of antihypertensive drugs that are used to prevent heart disease.

Competition

The two vignettes that began this chapter indicated how competition can affect a product life cycle as viewed by the maker of one product competing in a category. For K&E, a new technology, calculators, replaced their core product, slide rules. For Hoffmann-LaRoche, generic competition that resulted when patents expired caused a decline in sales for two of their key products.

This phenomena is true to some extent in many markets. A successful new product attracts imitators. Even if the pioneer chooses the best position in the market, competitors often find benefit segments that are attractive and enter with niche products. Although the pioneer remains the market-share leader, the pioneer's share declines as more and more sales are lost to the niche players.

While there is no way to guarantee that sales are not lost to competitors, a good initial positioning, attention to quality in product design and service

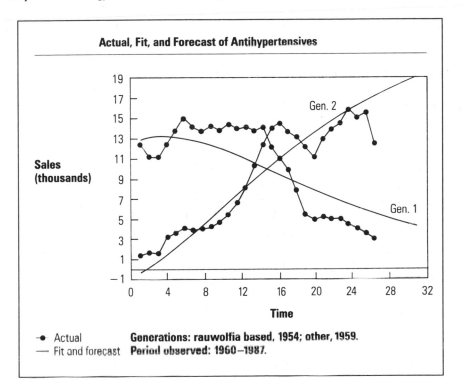

Figure 19.5 Actual and Fitted Values of Antihypertensives Sales (Norton and Bass 1992, p. 71; reprinted with permission)

delivery, pioneering advantages, economies of scale, and other management actions can ensure that a new product remains profitable in the face of competitive pressures.

STRATEGY VARIES OVER THE LIFE CYCLE

While not every product follows the theoretical life cycle in Figure 19.1, there are some general guidelines that apply to each stage of the life cycle. When modified and customized these guidelines help you formulate the most profitable long-term strategy for your product.

Introduction

During the introduction phase it is typical to invest resources in the product. Heavy expenditures for advertising, selling, sampling, promotion, distribution, and/or personal selling facilitate initial purchases stimulating the diffusion of the new product and earning new customers. Customers must be made aware of the product and encouraged to try the product. Continuous improvement and tracking of customer-benefit delivery assures that customer needs are met. Experimentation and innovation in the production process helps reduce costs and improve the product. Competition is monitored and positioning is adjusted to preempt competitive moves. If necessary, the product line is expanded to fill niches and deliver products to benefit segments before competition delivers these benefits.

While cash flows might be negative during the introduction period, these expenditures must be considered investments in future profitability. Forecasts and optimization with macro-flow and continuous-flow models help the firm to modify and improve the introductory marketing.

Pricing is important. It is tempting to skim the market by pricing high. This strategy promises high margins, but slow growth. More importantly, it encourages competition to enter under your price umbrella and, if experience effects or economies of scale are present, prevents you from taking advantage of these cost-reduction strategies. Conversely, a low-price penetration strategy can be risky. When it works, it enables you to reduce costs through accumulated experience and economies of scale and it preempts competition from gaining loyal customers or loyal distributors. Furthermore, a low price may make the category less attractive to competitors thus preventing long-run destructive price competition. However, a penetration strategy has its risks. If you have not forecast demand correctly, then your investment in initial marketing may never be covered. If technology changes too rapidly you may find yourself too committed to the old technology. Or, you may have rushed the product leaving open a second-but-better strategy for followers. Thus, these pricing decisions must be made carefully anticipating demand growth, competitive entry, technological development, risk, and flexibility. If the new-product process has been followed, you have at least some of the forecasts with which to make these decisions.

Growth

As the market grows, the innovator shifts emphasis to holding and building a market of loyal customers and distribution. Techniques such as macro-flow and continuous-flow monitoring and total quality management help improve the product and the marketing mix. Prices drop as costs are reduced. Products are repositioned in light of competitive activity. As more competitors enter or as the innovating firm expands its product line, the market becomes more segmented. As the cash flow approaches break-even and profits begin to accrue, the organization becomes larger and more formal. New uses and new markets, especially a more international focus, presents new opportunities to expand sales and profits.

Maturity

Most of the excitement is in the introduction and growth stages, but the greatest profit potential is in the maturity phase. This is especially true if the maturity phase is managed effectively leading to a long-lasting profitable life of the product. Market growth slows, competition reaches equilibrium levels (potentially quite intense), customer loyalty and satisfaction are important assets as market shares and preferences stabilize.

There are a number of strategies that firms can employ in the maturity phase.

Maintenance.   When there are no threats from competitive activity, technology, or other changing market conditions, the primary management task is maintenance and reinforcement of the product's position in the market. Advertising is maintained and the marketing mix (price, promotion, sales efforts, etc.) are fine-tuned to support the product's profitability. The fine tuning requires a good knowledge of market response, that is, how the market reacts to changes in the marketing mix. We describe later in this chapter a system, called a marketing decision support system (MDSS) that can be used to monitor the product, the competitive activity, and the business environment.

Defense.   New competitors may enter the market or existing competitors may change dramatically their marketing activities. Some competitors identify and target specific benefit segments and erode a mature product's profitability. Others present head-on challenges that must be met aggressively if the firm is to survive. For example, in chapter 11 we described the reaction of McNeil Laboratories when their pain-relief product, Tylenol, was attacked by Bristol-Myers' Datril. Tylenol responded actively with price cuts, national advertising, concentrated sales efforts, and line extensions (Extra Strength Tylenol). The defense was successful as Tylenol not only kept Datril from gaining a major share of the market, but achieved a dominance in the pain-relief category.

An active defense can be formulated by developing and using value maps (chapter 11) and "what-if" forecasting (chapter 12). By adjusting advertising, repositioning the product, making product improvements, modifying price, and altering distribution spending, a firm can maintain the highest level of profitability in light of the competitive attack. For more details and theory see Hauser and Shugan (1983).

Innovation at Maturity.   Some slippage of a product's market position can occur if no actions are taken by product management. While good defensive and maintenance strategies minimize slippage and maintain the best profitability, sometimes innovation is necessary to expand the market, fill customer needs, and preempt competition. Innovation can take a number of forms. (We expand upon innovation at maturity later in this chapter.)

1. *Flankers.* New flavors, colors, sizes, and so on expand the appeal of the core product. By building on the established brand name and assuring quality so that the brand name is not diminished, flankers can enhance profitability with little risk. For example, in 1991 Mars, Inc., expanded their line of M&M candies to include Almond M&M's, peanut butter M&M's, and mint M&M's.

2. *New uses and users.* Arm & Hammer baking soda expanded their traditional market by encouraging people to use baking soda for deodorizing refrigerators and cat litter. Du Pont found new uses for nylon in carpets, sweaters, and tire cord.

3. *Significant product innovation.* If competitive products can cannibalize our sales, why not cannibalize those sales ourselves with significant innovation. For example, most automobile manufacturers and most computer manufacturers continuously introduce new products and new models even if they are likely to cannibalize existing products.

Maintenance, defense, and innovation enable a product to enjoy a long and successful maturity phase. Marketing decision support systems, continuous improvement, and total quality management make the maturity phase more profitable.

Decline

In some cases, despite the best management, the product will decline. If competition becomes too intense, only the firms with unique core competencies (low-cost producer, superior technology, better people, etc.) will survive. Management may find more profitable opportunities or recognize economies of scope that suggest a product should be milked.

Milking the product means that marketing expenditures are reduced. The firm depends upon customer loyalty to maintain margins and sales. Such a harvesting strategy allows the product to die gracefully and profitably by avoiding the temptation to maintain high volumes with excessive marketing spending or prices that are too low to sustain. However, the product manager must be cautious not to make a milking strategy a self-fulfilling forecast—a product may be designated as in decline, expenditures withdrawn, prices raised, and, sure enough, sales decline. As Figure 19.3 indicated, sales may fall and then recover. A milking strategy should only be begun when the product manager is sure that the product is in the decline stage of the life cycle.

In other cases, rejuvenation may be possible. Rejuvenation means finding new uses, new users, or new line extensions. In many cases the product can be recycled back to the opportunity identification or the design phases of the new-product-development process to extend the product's life and begin the life cycle anew. We discuss rejuvenation in more depth later in this chapter.

MARKETING DECISION SUPPORT SYSTEMS

Managing a product over its life cycle requires creativity and skill, the right people, and the right strategies. To select the right strategies managers need information to make decisions on advertising levels, sales efforts, promotions, distribution, quality improvement, and repositioning. With the right data and the right analysis, managers can select the levels of these variables that lead to the best long-term profit. When data and analysis are used on an ongoing basis we call the system an MDSS.

A decision support system consists of data, models, analysis, and display as illustrated in Figure 19.6. The data are a set of summary measures describing the environment. They can consist of special research studies, continuous data tracking, syndicated data sources, and monitoring of the market's response to past decisions. They can be stored in one place, such as on a main-frame computer or a network, or they can be distributed throughout the organization. What matters is that the right people have the right information with which to make decisions.

The data are most effective if they are displayed and summarized in a form that managers can use. With today's database software and computer displays, data are often presented in summary tables and graphs to highlight trends and to identify exceptions to plan. Indeed, the data are often displayed at the level that is most appropriate to the decision. For example, the data might be displayed for every district, every account, and every product in the line as well as the "big picture," that is, the overall sales, the overall advertising responsiveness, and so on.

At the heart of a good MDSS are good analyses—analyses that a manager can use, control, and be comfortable with. We call these analyses *models* because they represent the essence of the environment's complex response to

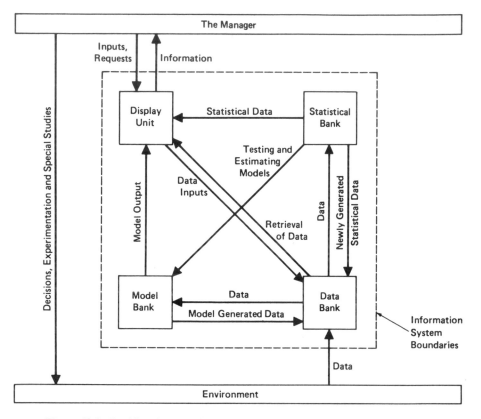

Figure 19.6 Decision Support Structure (Montgomery and Urban 1969, p. 18; reprinted with permission)

marketing actions. Pioneering work in understanding decision support models has been done by J. D. C. Little.[3] The following, in Little's words, are the main characteristics of good decision support models:

1. *Simple.* Simplicity promotes ease of understanding. Important phenomena should be put in the model and unimportant ones left out. Strong pressure often builds up to put more and more detail into a model. This should be resisted, until the users demonstrate they are ready to assimilate it.

---

[3] See J. D. C. Little, "Decision Support Systems for Marketing Managers," *Journal of Marketing* 43 (Summer 1979): 9-27, and J. D. C. Little, "Models and Managers: The Concept of a Decision Calculus," *Management Science* 16 (April 1970): 466–85.

2. *Robust.* Here I mean that a user should find it difficult to make the model give bad answers. This can be done by a structure that inherently constrains answers to a meaningful range of values.

3. *Easy to control.* A user should be able to make the model behave the way he or she wants it to. For example, the user should know how to set inputs to get almost any outputs. This seems to suggest that the user could have a preconceived set of answers and simply fudge the inputs to get them. That sounds bad. Should not the model represent objective truth?

   Wherever objective accuracy is attainable, I feel confident that the vast majority of managers will seize it eagerly. Where it is not, which is most of the time, the view here is that the manager should be left in control. Thus, the goal is to represent the operation as the manager sees it. I rather suspect that if the manager cannot control the model he or she will not use it for fear it will coerce actions he or she does not believe in. However, I do not expect the manager to abuse the capability because he or she is honestly looking for help.

4. *Adaptive.* The model should be capable of being updated as new information becomes available.

5. *Complete on important issues.* Completeness is in conflict with simplicity. Structures must be found that can handle many phenomena without bogging down. An important aid to completeness is the incorporation of subjective judgments. People have a way of making better decisions than their data seem to warrant. Subjective estimates will be valuable for quantities that are currently difficult to measure or which cannot be measured in the time available before a decision must be made.

   One problem posed by the use of subjective inputs is that they personalize the model to the individual or group that makes the judgments. This makes the model, at least superficially, more fragile and less to be trusted by others than, say a totally empirical model. However, the model with subjective estimates may often be a good deal tougher because it is more complete and conforms more realistically to the world.

6. *Easy to communicate with.* The manager should be able to change inputs easily and obtain outputs quickly.

Once a good MDSS consistent with Little's guidelines is developed, it becomes a vital tool for managing the marketing mix of an existing product. Once high-level management-science and computer skills were required to build an MDSS. Such skills are still important, but the task is made easier by the availability of user-friendly decision support software packages and readily available computer hardware. Such systems enable lay users to build decision models using English-like commands or simply by "pointing and clicking."

The advent of powerful personal computers networked to a file server or mainframe and sharing data bases coupled with powerful and easy-to-use software makes the MDSS even more useful and essential.

Marketing-Mix Decisions

To illustrate an MDSS approach to marketing-mix decisions, consider a simple advertising-budgeting model for a mature product. Based on data and judgment, a sales-response model such as that shown in Figure 19.7 is developed by the manager or analyst. Figure 19.7 is a summary of what happens to long-run market share as the manager changes the advertising expenditure. In particular, there is some minimum market share (Min) that will be obtained if the manager cuts all advertising. But this share can be increased with advertising. The amount of the increase depends on the level of advertising. As the manager increases advertising, market share increases, first slowly then more rapidly, until it reaches a maximum level (Max). Beyond this point, no amount of advertising will increase share.

Advertising is not a static phenomenon. A computer MDSS would also represent decays over time, responsiveness to different timings of advertising spending (e.g., pulses, steady advertising, sawtooth shapes), and other phenomena of interest.

Once developed, the advertising response is encoded into a computer. The computer now can simulate how the market would respond to the manager's actions. The manager now has a tool to predict the consequences of actions before, not after, they are tried on the environment. In this way, the manager can "try" a variety of actions and choose the action that satisfies goals best. Other marketing mix decisions can be modeled in an analogous manner. Please review Chapter 13 for consideration of other marketing mix elements, their interactions, and references.

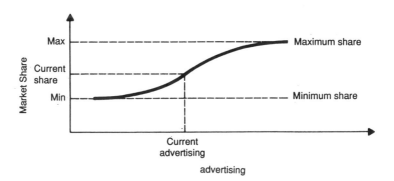

Figure 19.7   Sales Response to Advertising Dollars

Data for Building MDSS Models

Information is obtained from many sources. If data is collected in the design and testing phases, it is updated and used. Beyond that there are many additional sources of information each with its advantages and disadvantages. The best managerial strategy is to be open to, and to utilize, multiple information sources, depending upon their availability and quality. We briefly review three information sources that are useful for response analysis: judgment, experimentation, and statistical analysis of market history.

Managerial Judgment.   Managers make implicit judgments about marketing budgets, prices, advertising, and so on. Therefore, at a minimum, we can use their judgment to obtain response functions. Usually, judgments can be improved if they are obtained in an organized way and from more than one person.

Experimentation.   If better data can be obtained, they are used. One of the best sources of data is market experiments. Explicit market experimentation provides greater detail about market response, but such experiments are difficult and expensive. Newer technologies, such as UPC, supermarket checkout scanners, and addressable television commercials (which can be beamed at specific television sets), and Video carts are making it easier to conduct consumer market experiments. Information acceleration methods are making simulated market experiments feasible in consumer durable, industrial, and services industries.

Statistical Analysis of Market History.   A good marketing information system tracks sales and the levels of the marketing mix variables. The more observations there are over a wider range of strategies, the more useful this tracking data is in determining response functions. Statistical analysis, and in particular, econometrics, is a well-developed field that is valuable for estimating response functions.

Planning and Control

The outcome of analyses with an MDSS is often a one-year plan and a three- to five-year plan for the product. While the most immediate interests are often in the first year's annual plan, effective managers adopt a broader perspective and look at longer-term effects.

Once the plan is established, a control system is instituted to adjust for unexpected events. Figure 19.8 illustrates a planning-and-control system. It begins with plans generated by the models from the decision-information

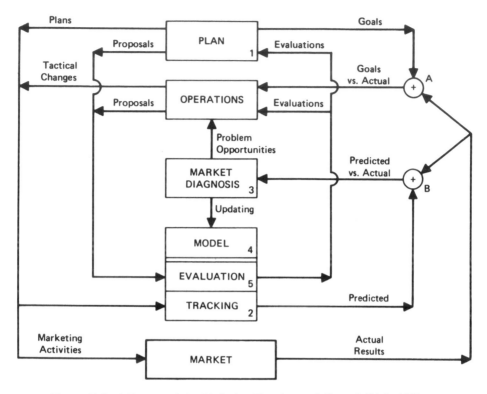

Figure 19.8 A Framework for Marketing Planning and Control (Little 1975, p. 631; reprinted with permission)

system (box 1). Once the basic marketing plan is selected, it is implemented via operations and impacts on the market. The actual results are compared to the goals from planning in circle A and to the predictions based on tracking with management's model of the marketplace (from box 2) in circle B. If the actual results match the predicted results and management's goals, then the plan is continued. If they are not in agreement, a market diagnosis is preformed (in box 3), the model is updated (in box 4), and modifications to the marketing plan are considered and evaluated (in box 5).

By tracking actual, predicted, and desired results, changes can be made to budgets in order to best achieve the plans, or the plan can be revised to best achieve the firm's goals given the changes that may have occurred in the market. Effective management of a mature product requires the development of a marketing decision support system consisting of a planning and a control system. With such systems, the full profit potential for the product is earned.

Case History

We now illustrate the analyses with a case history. The product is a well-established brand of packaged goods sold through grocery stores. For confidentiality, the brand is called GROOVY. Figure 19.9 shows GROOVY sales by month for months 1 to 36. Note the many fluctuations. One question asked was what caused these and how should they be managed?

The MDSS began simply, the analysis was at the national level and the planning period was one month. Advertising, promotion, price, and seasonality were treated in the analysis. The management team, consisting of the brand manager, plus individuals with skills in marketing research, advertising, sales analysis, and management science, met about one-half day per week for a period of three months. The response curves were estimated judgmentally, then checked econometrically. The peaks were the results of special promotions. Both advertising and promotion effects were estimated in the analysis, but management had more confidence in the promotion response function.

The first use of the model was for the annual brand plan. Table 19.1 gives (in coded form) five of the many plans generated. The brand manager presented these and others to upper management along with his recommendation for a plan with an additional promotion, increased advertising, and advertising reallocated to different periods. These changes implied a significant improvement in profit. Since there was some doubt on the advertising response function, the final decision was to approve the promotion, retain the existing advertising level, and begin a field measurement program in advertising.

After the initial plan was developed, tracking began, and the precision of the response function improved. Comparison of actual to predicted sales

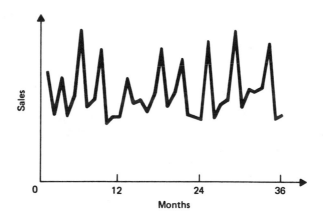

Figure 19.9   GROOVY Sales (Little 1975, p. 663; reprinted with permission)

TABLE 19.1 Alternative Annual Brand Plans

Plan	Advertising	Promotion	Relative Profit
1	30% increase, previous allocation	Jan., June, Nov.	$1,210,000
2	6% increase, previous allocation	June, Nov.	$ 980,000
3	6% increase, previous allocation	None	$ 0
4	30% increase, previous allocation	Jan., June, Nov.	$1,290,000
5	50% increase, new allocation	Jan., June, Nov.	$1,390,000

From Little (1975, p. 664); reprinted with permission.

uncovered a promotion missing in the historical data. Price data was obtained and the price response estimates improved. Figure 19.10 shows the indices developed from the response functions that were multiplied together to produce predicted sales. Figure 19.11 compares actual sales to the sales predicted by the model. The results are good.

The model worked well on past data, but how well did it predict the future? The answer is shown in Figure 19.12a. The model did well in the first months, but then deviated from actual sales. A closer inspection reveals that the model did well until a strike and a new package size disrupted sales.

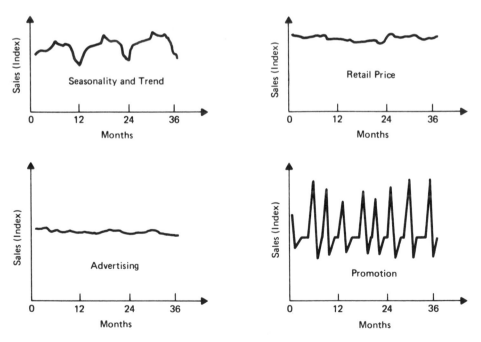

Figure 19.10 The Results of Historical Company Actions as Modeled through the Response Functions (Little 1975, p. 666; reprinted with permission)

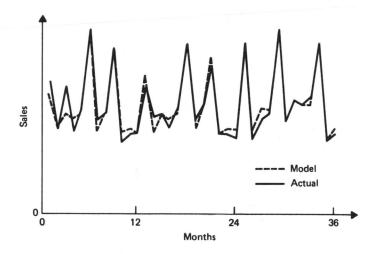

Figure 19.11   Comparison of Predicted Sales with Actual Sales (Little 1975, p. 667; reprinted with permission)

Market research results indicating the response effect of the new package size were entered and the strike effect was fit retrospectively to correspond to the actual results (Figure 19.12b). After adjusting to these unexpected results, the model tracked well. In subsequent years the model tracked well, and has proved useful for price, promotion, and promotion planning.

An example of managerial decision support with the model occurred after the tracking period in month 78. The year-to-date sales were substantially ahead of the previous year, but based on model forecasts and analyses the brand manager announced the brand was in trouble. An additional promotion had been run in month 72 that had not been implemented in month 60. In addition, price had been increased in March. Sales were depressed more than they would have been from a normal price effect, because the change pushed the retail price across a psychological barrier of 50¢. Its effect on sales was masked in part by a large television special and coordinated promotion which featured the brand among others.

Tracking months 72 to 78 and model computations made it clear that, although year-to-date sales were good, much of the annual advertising budget had been spent, the price had been increased, and the sales picture for the rest of the year was bleak. The brand manager proposed an additional promotion. On the strength of his model-supported case, management accepted the recommendation and profits for the year were increased. This is a good illustration of the importance of detailed monitoring of the marketplace. Without prior warning, by the time the losses were detected in actual sales, it would have been difficult to plan and execute the promotion.

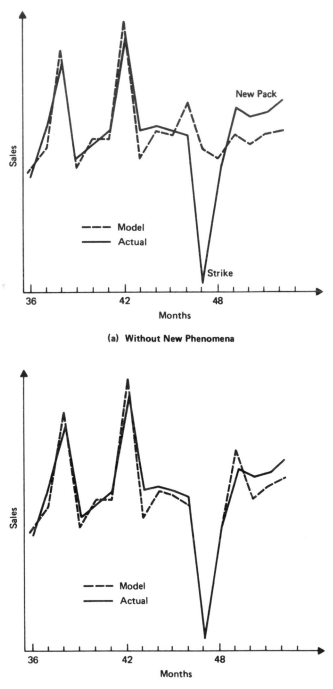

(a) **Without New Phenomena**

(b) **With Strike and Package Effect**

Figure 19.12 Comparison of a Priori Predictions with Actual Sales (Little 1975, pp. 668–669; reprinted with permission)

Summary of the Case and Update

Analysis of Groovy improved annual planning and resulted in increased profits. Response based on statistical and experimental analyses has helped improve the model's ability to predict the sales effects of revision in the marketing mix. The model-based control system has led to a quick and definitive diagnosis of environmental and consumer preference variations. It has provided a tool for effective reaction to those unexpected events so that profit can be managed effectively in the mature phase of the life cycle. In the 1990s planning and control systems for packaged goods use more data than this case describes. Today's comprehensive data suppliers offer detailed UPC-derived data on 20,000 items in 2,000 stores each week! Without a means to simplify this data, it quickly can become overwhelming.

Recent developments have augmented human analysis with expert systems. Such systems carry out appropriate analysis at a very detailed level and report the results only in cases where action is required. Figure 19.13 is an example of a report written by an Artificial Intelligence (AI) system that monitors the marketing plan for a ground coffee. The system, called Cover-Story, generates a report to management automatically based on the protocols in the system that replicate an outstanding analyst who has spent considerable time digging through and analyzing UPC data for the product. Although judgment continues to play a major role in the product-planning process, expert systems increasingly are able to provide meaningful inputs to that process.

COMPETITIVE STRATEGY

With a well-developed MDSS you can select the marketing mix to achieve the largest profit. You do this by modeling the market's response to your decisions and those of your competitors, making some estimates of how competition will respond, using the MDSS to make "what-if" forecasts, and choosing the set of strategies that leads to the greatest profit potential. But suppose that one or more of your competitors has an MDSS. While you are maximizing your profit anticipating their response they are maximizing their profit anticipating your response. However, this may not be the most *strategic* set of actions because your actions can affect competitive actions.

A "Prisoner's Dilemma"

Consider the example in Table 19.2. In this table it is clear that your most profitable promotion is a 10% promotion. For example, if your com-

To: **VP of Marketing**
From: **CoverStory**
Date: **01/03/90**
Subject: **Maxwell House Grnd Caff Summary for Four Weeks Ending January 29, 1989**

Maxwell House Grnd Caff's share points in Total United States was 12.1 in the Total Coffee category for the four weeks ending 1/29/89. This is an increase of .2 points from a year earlier but down .2 from last period (4 Week Ending Jan 1, 89). This reflects volume sales of 9.2 million equiv pounds—up 5.7 percent since last year. Category volume (currently 108.8 million equiv pounds) rose 1.4% from a year earlier.

Maxwell House Grnd Caff's share points is 12.1—up .2 from the same period last year.

Display activity, featuring and unsupported price cuts rose over the past year—unsupported price cuts from 16 points to 32. Price (2.20 dollars) and distribution (99 percent of acv) remained at about the same level as a year earlier.

Components of Maxwell House Grnd Caff Volume

Among components of Maxwell House Grnd Caff, the principal gainers are:

Maxwell House Grnd Caf 13oz: up 5.1 points from last year to 5.1 (but down .1 since last period)
Maxwell House Grnd Caf 39oz: +3.7 to 3.7

The major loser:

Maxwell House Grnd Caf 16oz: −6.1 to .5

Maxwell House Grnd Caf 13oz's share points increase is partly due to 75.1 pts of ACV rise in ACV Wtd Dist vs yr ago.

Competitor Summary

Among Maxwell House Grnd Caff's major competitors, the principal gainer is:

Community Grnd Caff: up .7 points from last year to 1.5

The major losers:

Folgers Grnd Caff: −2.5 to 23.7 (but up .8 since last period)
Chock Full O'Nuts Grnd Caff: −1.0 to 2.4

Chock Full O'Nuts Grnd Caff's share points decrease is associated with 10.4% rise in price versus a year ago.

Market Highlights

Maxwell House Grnd Caff showed significant gains relative to a year ago in:

Denver, Co: up 4.6 points from last year to 9.4. This is partly due to 20.2% fall in price since last year but was counterindicated by 21.5 ACV points rise in display activity versus a year ago.

but posted declines in:

Chicago, Il: −3.1 to 10.9. This follows 19.8 ACV points increase in display activity since last year but occurred in spite of 7.3% decrease in price versus a year ago.

Boston, Ma: −2.1 to 16.4. This occurred in the face of 10.0% decrease in price versus a year ago.

Among competitors to Maxwell House Grnd Caff, major regional changes occurred as follows:

Baltimore, Md: Folgers Grnd Caff is up 8.3 points since last year. This follows 17.7% fall in price since last year.

Dallas, Tx: Maryland Club Grnd Caff fell 8.1 points. This follows 6.2% increase in price versus a year ago. **Hills Brothers Grnd Caff** is up 14.1 points. This follows 75.1 pts of ACV increase in ACV Wtd Dist versus a year ago and 32.4% fall in price vs yr ago. **Folgers Grnd Caff** fell 9.3 points.

San Francisco, Ca: Mjb Grnd Caff fell 8.3 points. This is partly due to 11.6% increase in price since last year.

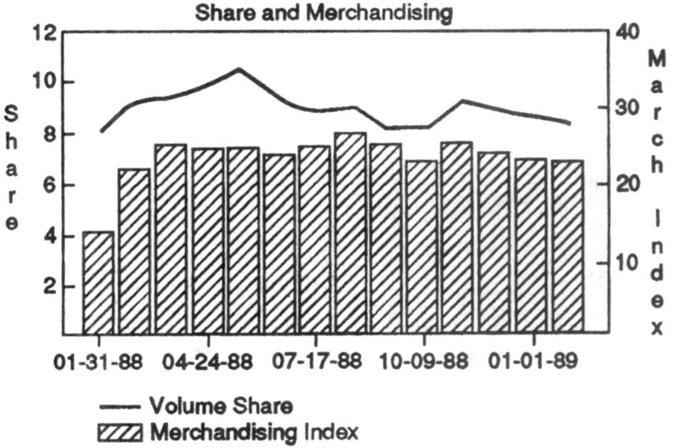

Figure 19.13 Artificial Intelligence System Output Based on UPC Analysis (Personal Communication from John D. C. Little, 1990)

petitor does not promote then you can earn $20 million with no promotion, $27 million with a 5% promotion, and $29 million with a 10% promotion. Clearly if you expect no promotion from your competitor, then 10% maximizes profit. Furthermore, a 10% promotion is best no matter what competition does. It is tempting to set promotion at 10%.

But suppose now that your competitor faces the same market conditions and has the same MDSS. Your competitor will go through the same reasoning and select a 10% promotion. The net result is that you both earn $12 million in profit. This phenomena is known as the "prisoner's dilemma" because it represents the same dilemma faced by a prisoner deciding whether to confess to a crime. If the prisoner remains silent and a partner confesses, the prisoner faces a long prison term. If the prisoner confesses and reports on the partner, the partner gets the long prison term and the prisoner gets a very short term. However, if both the prisoner and the partner remain silent, they get a moderate prison term. As in Table 19.2, both prisoners are tempted to confess and thus both end up with a long prison term.

But suppose that you realize that your actions today will influence the competitor's actions tomorrow. If you set your promotion at 0% this quarter you might influence your competitor to set its promotion at 0% next quarter. If you both do this, then you will earn $3 million this quarter (your promotion at 0% and the competitor's promotion at 10%), but in every subsequent quarter you will earn $20 million (both promotions set at 0%). With any reasonable discount rate, this income stream will be more profitable than the status-quo income stream of $12 million in every quarter. Thus, it might be in your own best interest to "cooperate" by setting your promotion low in the first quarter.

Table 19.2 illustrates the prisoner's dilemma for promotional expenditures, but it applies to price, salesforce spending, advertising spending—any marketing variable that has the potential to gain for you sales at your competitor's expense. For example, Hauser and Wernerfelt (1989) demonstrate that a prisoner's dilemma applies to whether or not a firm automatically anticipates a competitor's response to advertising. If both firms anticipate the

TABLE 19.2 Strategic Promotion Decisions (Profits, in $millions)

Your Promotion	Competitive Promotion				
	0%	5%	10%	15%	20%
0%	20	12	3	-6	-15
5%	27	18	10	1	-8
10%	29	21	12	3	-6
15%	26	18	9	0	-9
20%	15	7	-2	-10	-19

other's spending, then both are better off. But if one firm anticipates and the other does not, then the firm that does *not* anticipate spends more and earns more profit. (The firm that did not anticipate the competitive response spends less.) Clearly, competitive strategy is complex.

Long-run vs. Short-run Strategies

While a rational, long-run strategy is not to overspend,[4] we can cite many examples of price wars, fare wars, advertising wars, and promotion wars. We might wonder if any strategy could encourage "cooperation."

In a set of pioneering studies, Axelrod (1980a, 1980b) asked the top game theorists, political scientists, and economists to enter computer strategies to play a multi-period prisoner's dilemma. Some strategies were aggressive and some quite cooperative, some tried to determine what the competitor was playing and modify their strategy accordingly. However, one of the simplest, called "Tit for Tat," won. "Tit for Tat" begins by cooperating (0% in Table 19.2) and in every subsequent period simply follows the competitive action of the period before. If the competitor was cooperative in one quarter, "Tit for Tat" is cooperative in the next quarter; if the competitor was aggressive in one quarter, "Tit for Tat" is aggressive in the next quarter.

Axelrod's result was interesting and surprising because "Tit for Tat" can never beat a competitor one on one; the best it can do is tie the competitor. Furthermore, "Tit for Tat" was one of the simplest strategies entered—it did not try to learn about the competitor's strategy, it did not randomize to keep the competitor off guard, and it did not experiment. However, what it did do was to encourage cooperative behavior across many markets and, as a result, was the best overall.

Axelrod repeated his experiments and found "Tit for Tat" to be quite robust doing well in competitive environments and in cooperative environments and doing well against sophisticated competitors and against naive competitors. By studying "Tit for Tat" and other strategies Axelrod was able to develop the following generalizable rules.

1. *Nice.* Do not take actions first in an effort to achieve unilateral gains at the expense of competitors.
2. *Forgiving.* After the initial retaliation, do not punish competitors beyond what is appropriate.

---

[4] This result is known in game theory as the "Folk Theorem." That is, almost any reasonable strategy is an equilibrium to the multiperiod game. The challenge is to choose the right set of equilibrium strategies.

3. *Not envious.* Focus on doing well yourself rather on "beating" competition. (For example, in Table 19.2 would you prefer a situation where you make $12 million and your competitor makes $27 million or would you prefer a situation where you make $7 million and your competitor loses $8 million?)

4. *Provocable.* Respond when the competitor takes action so that the competitor is not tempted to exploit you.

5. *Easy to recognize.* The strategy should be sufficiently simple so that the competitor can anticipate how you will respond to the competitive actions. That is, the competitor should be able to understand that you are not exploitable and that you will be responsive to cooperation.

Of course there is no guarantee that the competitor will think like you. In theory, a multiperiod "equilibrium" in this game is cooperation (0% promotion), but in practice the incentives to promote are strong.

In setting strategy with your MDSS you can follow "Tit for Tat" strategies. For example, public statements that "we will match any price reductions by our competitors" sends the signal that you are provocable, but forgiving. Heavy, public investments in capacity send a signal to competitors that you will defend your market and thus discourage destructive price or promotion wars. Trade associations open the lines of communication to humanize competitors leading to fewer self-punishing aggressive actions. Published reports on capacity, prices, market shares, and advertising makes actions and reactions public.

Sometimes firms share technology. Von Hippel (1986) found that, in the steel industry, process engineers often shared production know-how on an informal and reciprocal basis. According to this study, 10 of 11 "mini" steel mills (which process scrap iron into structural shapes) shared their production know-how. Such cooperation is "rational" if the proprietary benefit of the know-how is less than the net benefit from implementing other firms' know-how. In this case, the industry appears to believe that the competitive advantage of proprietary knowledge is outweighed by the common gain (for both the firms and their customers) from the sharing. Similar examples of cooperation are evident in joint R&D contracts and the licensing of technology.

Coalitions

"Tit for Tat" is a good strategy when there are two players, but most markets contain more than two players. When there are three or more players you might face a higher-level dilemma. Consider a three firm market in which you are one of the firms. What if one competitor is cooperative and the other competitor is aggressive? Do you cooperate with the cooperative competitor and allow yourself to be exploited by the aggressive competitor, or do you respond to the aggressor with aggression and thus lead the market into a three-way price (advertising, promotion, etc.) war? Or is there an in-between strategy?

This problem was studied by Fader and Hauser (1988) in a competition that was analogous to that of Axelrod. They invited marketing scientists, game theorists, political scientists, and economists to submit strategies for a three-firm generalized prisoner's dilemma. There was one variable, price, but it could vary in a continuous manner to simulate real markets. In an analogy to Axelrod they found that strategies which were nice, forgiving, provocable, not envious, and easy to recognize did well and were quite robust. However, in order to do well in a three-firm game, the strategies had to recognize implicit coalitions.

An implicit coalition is a simple concept. If one firm is aggressive and the other is cooperative, the best long-run strategy is to seek cooperation with the cooperative firm even though the aggressive firm will earn more profit than you do. The cooperative coalition price is less than would be the case were all three firms to cooperative, but it is well above the three-firm aggressive price.[5] By varying the parameters of the games they were able to show that coalitions are profitable over a variety of conditions and that the strategies that do best are those strategies that signal their intentions to seek a coalition price. Even in markets where it was difficult to determine the coalition price and where the coalition price varied depending on the actions of the third competitor, strategies that signaled their intentions to form implicit coalitions did best. The coalition results appear to generalize to more than three firms.

Relationship to Positioning

In chapter 11 we discussed strategic value positioning. The idea underlying strategic value positioning is that (1) without considering competitive reactions on price and other marketing mix variables there is a temptation for every brand to seek a "central" (perceptual) position in the market but (2) when pricing, advertising, selling, and promotion are considered brands seek to differentiate. The differentiation allows them to serve a "local monopoly" and thus avoid destructive price (advertising, selling, promotion, etc.) competition.

---

[5] For example, in their games the three-firm cooperative price was $1.50 and the aggressive price was $1.40. The two-firm coalition price was $1.44. There was also an "envious" price in which a firm could assure itself of being the market-share leader (but with little profit). The envious price was $1.36.

This concept, that positioning can avoid destructive competition, is important throughout the life cycle. If your firm is sufficiently creative to identify a new market and be one of the first entrants, then it might make sense to seek that part of the market which is central—that is, that part of the market which represents the tastes of the most customers. Of course, if you enter the market, you should seek competitive advantages with respect to cost, advertising, technology, or whatever it takes to tilt the playing field in your direction. If you can identify and sustain such a competitive advantage, then you can defend profitably your position in the market. On the other hand, if you are entering a market with a strong competitor already entrenched and if you have no unique advantage with which to overcome the competitor's inherent first-mover advantage, then your most profitable long-run strategy might be to seek a profitable niche of the market. The niche enables you to provide unique benefits to a segment of customers without attacking the market leader head-on. In such a differentiated niche you can avoid destructive competition with the market leader.

Each and every situation is different and you will have to consider your competitive advantages vis-a-vis the firms already in the market and the firms likely to enter. The perceptual maps, value maps, taste distributions, and forecasting techniques of chapters 8 through 12 give you the tools to build a model-based MDSS to perform the appropriate "what-if" analyses to select the strategy likely to lead to long-run profit.

Other Situations

The prisoner's dilemma competitive situation is perhaps the best known competitive game. However, there are others. For example, Figure 19.14 illustrates a first-mover situation. Here we have two brands, Pirma and Antra. Each can make a decision on whether or not to advertise heavily or lightly. The resulting profits for Pirma are given in the upper right corners of each box and the profits for Antra are given in the lower left corner of each box. If they each advertise heavily then market demand is high and they each get equal shares, but the profit ($1 million) just barely pays for the advertising. On the other hand, if they each advertise lightly then the market demand is moderate as are profits ($4 million). However, if one can enter first and commit to a high level of advertising, then it is in the other firm's best interest to enter at a low level of advertising. In this case the first firm earns $9 million in profit, while the second firm earns $3 million in profit.

To analyze this matrix from a game-theoretic perspective we must compute each firm's unilateral incentives. These are shown as arrows in Figure 19.14. Notice that if the market evolves to either the upper right corner or the lower left corner then there are no unilateral incentives to change advertising

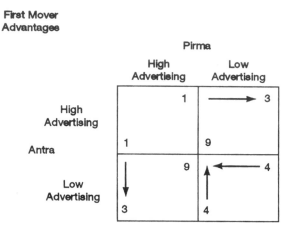

Figure 19.14   First-Mover Advantage Game

levels. These corners are known as equilibria. In either of the other corners there are unilateral incentives to change advertising levels. Neither of the other corners (upper left, lower right) are stable—the market will evolve to one of the equilibria. The equilibria favor either Pirma or Antra depending upon who can move first and credibly.

Table 19.2 (prisoner's dilemma) and Figure 19.14 (first-mover advantage) represent two of the many competitive situations you will face. In many cases you may be able to recognize the appropriate representation of the market. In other cases you may have to make your best guess or analyze all possibilities and act accordingly. The key lesson is that your actions influence and are influenced by competitive actions. You must act accordingly if you are to maximize the long-term profitability of your (now mature) product.

Core Competency

In Figure 19.14 it is clearly better for Pirma to reach the equilibrium in the upper right corner rather than the equilibrium in the lower left corner. Pirma can reach this equilibrium if it moves first with a superior product and then sustains the profitability of that product with substantial advertising. For example, Société Micromécanique et Horlogère (SMH) was able to manufacture a high-quality quartz-analog watch with fewer parts and superior quality control. They introduced this watch as a fashion watch, Swatch, with significant levels of advertising (per potential customer). This advertising gave them a first-mover advantage that competition was unable to match. Thus, by building upon the Swiss watch-making experience and quality reputation, by developing superior manufacturing capability, and by developing a fashion image, Swatch was able to maintain a competitive advantage over several years in the late 1980s and early 1990s.

There are many core competencies—advertising expertise, manufacturing capability, knowledge of customer needs, relationships with suppliers or with the channels of distribution, etc. Whenever you select strategies vs. competition you must look at what you do better than competition and build upon those capabilities. For further discussion see Wernerfelt (1989) and Wernerfelt and Montgomery (1986).

CUSTOMER SATISFACTION AND QUALITY

To play the competitive game effectively we must build upon our assets. One key asset is the satisfied customer.

To understand the value of a satisfied customer consider a new consumer service entering a region before competitors. Suppose that a key benefit of the new service is trust and suppose that search costs are high for a consumer to try this service. In this case, if we can satisfy a consumer's needs, we are likely to retain that consumer for all future transactions. If we net, say $10, on every transaction then the value to us of that consumer's loyalty is the stream of income—$10 now, $10 the next time, $10 the time after that, and so on—from serving that consumer. Of course there is some likelihood the consumer may stop using our service or move from the region, we have to take inflation into account, and we have to discount the cash flow, but it is clear that the value of the stream of income can be substantial. For example, if inflation balances our discount rate and the probability that the consumer will return for every transaction is 90%, then the value to us of that satisfied customer is $100—10 times the value of today's sale.[6] If there are only so many potential consumers in the region we clearly want to attract and retain them before competition can do so.

As important as customer satisfaction is, we must recognize that customer satisfaction is a means to long-run profit not an end in itself. For example, consider low-end copiers—single page copiers usually priced under $1000. To truly satisfy customers we can add features—color copying, collating, stapling, reducing, and so on, we can have a repair person on call 24 hours per day for on-site service, we could provide free paper, and we could guarantee a free replacement or upgrade for the next ten years. However, we are unlikely to make any profit doing so—the cost of these services is well

---

[6] The income stream under these assumptions is $10 + (.90)($10) + (.90)^2($10) + (.90)^3($10) + . . . Adding these terms together gives $100 by the formula, *value* = ($10)/(1 - .90). This formula applies to any transaction value, v, and return rate, r. That is, $v/(1 - r)$.

beyond the price of the copier. Thus, we must pick and choose by understanding the value of that customer to us, the impact of our actions on customer satisfaction, the impact of customer satisfaction on sales and selling price, and the costs of our actions. With these variables in mind, we can take those actions to maximize the long-run profitability of a base of satisfied customers.

But to implement a customer-satisfaction program we must be able to measure customer satisfaction and use those measures to provide information and incentives to product design, customer service, and management strategy. These links are illustrated in Figure 19.15. Notice that the end goal is profit, that customer satisfaction affects share, market volume, price, *and* costs, that many actions including product design, service, and marketing affect customer satisfaction, and that the customer-satisfaction measures are fed back to influence these actions. The system is clearly complex, but if understood and managed it can lead to greater profitability.

A complete description of Figure 19.15 is beyond the scope of this book, however, we can discuss three key features of any customer-satisfaction program: (1) avoiding short-termism, (2) identifying and understanding switch-

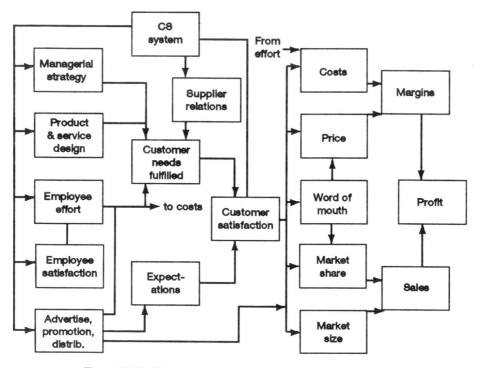

Figure 19.15 The Impact of a Customer Satisfaction (CS) System

ing costs, and (3) providing disaggregate rewards. It is also critical to understand that customer satisfaction must be measured appropriately. If it is measured incorrectly it can provide the wrong incentives and actually reduce profitability. Thus, we close this section with a short review of measurement issues.

Avoids Short-termism

Many firms are under quarterly profit pressure. If profits (or sales) are below target, managers are tempted to take short-term actions. For example, consider our hypothetical example of the consumer service. We might be able to increase our contribution margin from $10 to $15 by decreasing the number of personnel in each office, by spending less time with each customer, and by using lower-cost raw materials. Our quarterly profits might increase because our loyal customers (from the last transaction) will return, but the asset of loyal customers might decrease to more than offset the short-term gain. (While the customers may return this quarter, they might switch to a competitor next quarter.) For example, if our loyalty rate decreases from 90% to 80%, then the value of a customer (new margin, new loyalty rate) drops from $100 to $75.[7] In this case, a fifty-percent increase in the net contribution per transaction is not justified even though the loyalty rate dropped just 10%!

Thus, with the proper attention on customer satisfaction and a reasonable accounting system to take the value of a loyal customer into account, a manager can avoid the bane of short-term thinking that leads to a long-run decrease in the value of the firm.

However, we must avoid short-termism in both directions. A manager might be under short-term pressure to increase sales by lowering the price or by promoting the product. Or, the manager might be rewarded entirely on customer satisfaction. To see the issues suppose that by increasing service we can move the loyalty rate from 90% to 95%. If these actions reduce our margins from $10 to below $5, then the value of the satisfied customer actually decreases. It truly is a balance.

One valuable way to think of customer satisfaction is as a willingness to pay[8] for our service. If the willingness to pay is large, then we are in a better position to make a profitable tradeoff between the price we charge and the number of customers we serve. If the willingness to pay is small, we have fewer options.

---

[7] We now calculate value with $15/(1 - .80)$. This gives us $75.

[8] Willingness to pay is also known as the reservation price, the highest price at which the customer will still purchase our product.

Identifies Potential Switchers

Customer satisfaction endows asymmetric advantages because a satisfied customer is less likely to switch.

Suppose that you are quite familiar with a word-processing system, say WordPerfect or Microsoft Word. You know all the keystrokes or mouse movements and you are able to use the system to produce documents quickly and easily. Even if you believe that a competitive word-processing system is likely to be better, you may not switch because the costs of purchasing and using the new system may not justify the advantages to you of using that new system. The switching costs favor the system you are now using. Now suppose that you become dissatisfied with the system you are now using, perhaps because it will not run under a new operating system or perhaps because the upgrade has changed certain features in way that you do not like. If your dissatisfaction is sufficient, if the switching costs are low enough, and if the other system is significantly better, then you will switch.

Now the switching costs favor the new system—you will not switch back unless the old system improves enough to justify the switch-back costs. In other words, the cost of retaining a satisfied customer is much less than the costs of reattracting a lost customer.

With this in mind, a customer-satisfaction measurement system can be used to identify customers that are about to switch, either customers you are about to lose or competitive customers that you might gain. By focusing on the needs of these customers you can concentrate resources and gain (or retain) customers efficiently.

Rewards at the Proper Levels

Managers and employees are often rewarded based on customer satisfaction. If the measures of customer satisfaction are formulated correctly and incentives structured correctly, then the management decisions and employee actions will be in the interest of the firm. They will maximize long-run, discounted profits. One question that is asked often is, "Why not just reward everyone on the stock price?"

Certainly stock price is an indicator of long-term profits and it certainly makes sense that the chief corporate officers are rewarded on stock prices. However, not every employee or manager can see his or her impact on the stock price of the firm. For example, a telephone representative for a large financial services firm will affect the stock price of the firm by satisfying customers, but the effect that a single representative will have on stock price is negligible. That representative may accrue all the benefit of short-term (less service) actions, but see little of the benefit of the long-term stock-price rewards. Thus, customer-satisfaction-based rewards are one way in which top management can disaggregate the rewards so that the costs and benefits of *individual employee* actions are consistent with top-level concerns.

This phenomena is true for groups of employees as well. At one manufacturing firm the design engineers developed a product improvement that required a packaging change—if the design and packaging were changed together the customer received a much higher-quality product. However, if the design change was made without the packaging change, the customer received a lower-quality product. Initially, the packaging engineers complained—from their perspective they had done nothing wrong but the design engineers had made a change that lowered quality. Furthermore, they would incur significant costs in redesigning the package. In this case top management had to step in and focus both groups on the satisfaction of the ultimate customer by making it clear that the rewards to both would increase if *both* the design and the packaging were changed.

Measurement Issues

Relative to competition.   Customer satisfaction should be a moving target. If we improve our product and service quality, but competition does it at a faster rate, we will lose customers. To some extent this is what happened in the 1970s and 1980s. U.S. automobile manufacturers improved their products, but at a slower rate than the Japanese manufacturers. Customers switched and are now harder to attract back.

Customers *and* potential customers.   The easiest way to maximize a measure of average customer satisfaction is to get rid of dissatisfied customers. Consider a salesperson calling on a new account. Suppose that the potential new customer is particularly difficult to please; even with the best service the new customer will not be as satisfied as the average existing customer. (This is often true during the growth phase of a new product. The easiest to satisfy customers are the customers who try the product first.) Will the salesperson make the sale?

If the salesperson is rewarded entirely on sales, every effort will be made to make the sale. Perhaps too much effort will be expended. If the salesperson is rewarded entirely on the satisfaction of the customers to whom sales are made, there are no incentives to make the sale. The new customer will lower the average satisfaction. Neither extreme gives the salesperson the incentives that are in the best interests of the firm.

However, if we consider the satisfaction of our customers *and* potential customers, then, perhaps, that potential customer is *relatively* more satisfied if we make that sale than if we do not.

To see this measurement effect in a real situation consider Table 19.3. Table 19.3 represents data from a frequently purchased consumer good. The first column is primary-brand share; the second column is a measure of (monadic) satisfaction in which customers were asked only how satisfied consumers were with that brand. (For simplicity we give only the rank orders.) Notice that the monadic satisfaction measure has no statistical correlation with brand share. If fact, the brand with highest satisfaction, brand V, was a niche player with only a few percent of the market. The brand with the largest share, brand Q, was sixth in overall satisfaction, in part because it served about 40% of the market. It was difficult to satisfy everyone, but perhaps these consumers were more satisfied with brand Q than any other brand. The third column lists relative satisfaction—all consumers who heard of a brand were asked how satisfied they were (or expected to be) with that brand relative to other brands on the market. Notice that relative satisfaction is highly correlated with brand share. The market leader has the highest relative satisfaction.

This phenomena is pervasive. By focusing only on the satisfaction of our customers we run the risk of retreating to a niche of the market with easy-to-serve customers. On the other hand, the future survival of the firm may depend upon retaining existing customers *and* attracting new customers.

Room at the Top. A major copier manufacturer set customer-satisfaction targets of 90% in 1990, 94% in 1991, 97% in 1992, and 100% in

TABLE 19.3 Comparison of Monadic Satisfaction, Relative Satisfaction, and Primary-Brand Share

Brand	Primary-Brand Share	Monadic Satisfaction Measure	Relative Satisfaction (Heard of Brand)
Q	1	6	1
R	2	3	3
S	3	8	2
T	4	2	6
U	5	9	7
V	6	1	5
W	7	4	8
X	8	7	4
Y	9	10	9
Z	10	5	10
Rank correlation		0.20	0.83
t-statistic		0.58	4.21

SOURCE: From Griffin and Hauser (1993).

1993, but defined a satisfied customer as a customer that was "somewhat satisfied" or "very satisfied." Although such goals and such definitions focus the firm on customer satisfaction they leave little room for improvement or incentives. Furthermore, if a "perfect" score means that 100% of our customers give us a rating of "somewhat satisfied," then we might be quite vulnerable to a competitor who can provide products and services that more than "somewhat satisfy" our customers.

Not only does the 100% score leave the firm complacent and vulnerable, but it creates unnecessary pressure on the divisions and regions that achieve 100%. Once a division or region is at 100% the movement of even one "satisfied" customer can be traumatic. That division or region might focus its energies on maintaining the 100% rating while allowing the bulk of its customers to slip from "very satisfied" to "somewhat satisfied."

The solution is to select a satisfaction score and a set of targets that can distinguish year-to-year improvements and leave "room at the top" for continued improvement over the near future.

Sufficient Sample

Many firms have a tendency to disaggregate by region, customer segment, and product. While it makes good management sense to have measures and rewards at these levels, management must guard against insufficient sample. Suppose that we collect 10,000 customer-satisfaction ratings per month and that we have 10 regions, 10 customer segments, and are managing 10 products. This gives us only 10 sample points for every region-segment-product combination. If customer satisfaction is at 90%, then these 10 sample points imply a standard deviation of the measure of 9.5%. Thus, we would have to see a movement of almost 20% to be significant—anything else and we are managing against random variation.

This example is extreme, but unfortunately it illustrates one of the pitfalls of current practice. If the sample is not sufficient to the level of detail of the breakouts, then random movements of satisfaction might be misinterpreted as true changes. We have seen examples where, in each quarter, a group is designated as the "best-practice" group and other groups are encouraged to learn their practices. If the "best-practice" group is best only because of random variation, the other groups are chasing an ephemeral target. The lesson is either to gather sufficient sample to justify the breakouts you plan, or to do fewer breakouts.

Relative to Customer Needs

The final measurement issue is quite simple. If you want to develop a system to improve customer satisfaction, then you need to identify how to do so. We suggest that you collect measures not just on overall satisfaction, but on the customer needs as identified in the House of Quality.

INNOVATION IN THE MATURE AND DECLINE PHASE OF THE LIFE CYCLE

If our MDSS is working well, if we plan strategy relative to competition, and if we monitor and maintain customer satisfaction, we should earn substantial profits in the mature phase of the life cycle. But threats exist to our profitability. Increasing competition might cause margins to shrink, sales might decline due to saturation in the market, or new competitive products and technologies might replace our products. In this section we discuss innovation in the mature phases of the life cycle as indicated in Figure 19.16.

Production Innovation

As the product matures, production cost reduction becomes critical to profits. Such cost reduction is possible with explicit programs to improve the

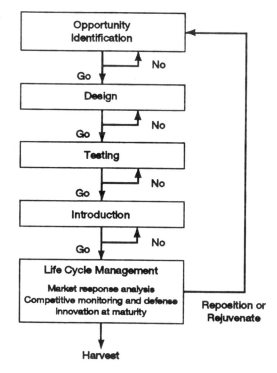

Figure 19.16   Recycling the Declining Product

production process, innovate in materials, and develop more efficient suppliers. The success of these programs often determines the competitive viability of a firm. If our costs and prices do not decline faster than competitors, market share and profits can decline quickly. For example, in the early 1990s Japanese process efficiencies led to the situation in which almost no major consumer electronics producers existed in North America or Europe (Philips being the exception). American firms did offer brands, but they were, for the most part, manufactured in Japan.

Product Line Flankers and Extensions

The increasing homogeneity in the product offerings at the mature phase emphasizes production cost advantages. But there are profit opportunities through management of the product line. For example, Kellogg's cereals, Toyota automobiles, Philips consumer electronics, Citibank financial services are all product lines that have been managed successfully.

A product line is more than a collection of products. It is an entity with an image and composition. For example, the quality image of the line can be raised with a few prestige products or compromised with one or more "bargain" products. Since the line as a whole faces many of the problems faced by a single product, the techniques of this book can be used for the product line. For example, we can view a "line" as a "product" to exploit markets identified in opportunity identification, or we can use idea generation techniques for the line. The line has an image which can be analyzed by perceptual maps and positioning studies. When a single product is tested in a pretest or test market, the information on cannibalization and draw can be used for product-line decisions. Product-line positioning can be addressed through management science models introduced earlier in this text. The success of this endeavor depends on creativity and persistence in translating product specific techniques to product-line problems. Extending the line and careful positioning of the line can create growth opportunity.

Extensions of the product line can be viewed as "flankers." These are new variants in the same product category. These flankers expand the product line to tap specific subsegments and to defend the product line from competitive product elaboration. For example, the product variation may be a "new flavor" or a new "extra strength" variety. Flankers also extend the life cycle by adding more enthusiasm to the advertising and marketing, or by widening the product's appeal. In industrial products and services the original product may be flanked by a stripped down, low-cost product and an enhanced premium-priced version.

Flankers are often tested by pretest market procedures and introduced nationally. Most are not test marketed since the costs and risks are small.

Creative efforts to generate product-line flankers plus a good low-cost screening procedure can lead to lengthening the life cycle.

Product "extensions" represent taking the brand name to a new category of product. For example, the Ivory brand of gentle hand-and-bath soap was extended into liquid laundry detergents and shampoo. Excedrin extended into the ibuprofen pain-reliever market with "Non-aspirin Excedrin." Vuarnet extended into diverse products such as skis, wallets, and watches. American Express extended its brand to travel agencies. Crest toothpaste attempted to extend its brand into mouthwash, chewing gum, and shaving cream. If the core brand is high quality and has a strong perception of benefit delivery, this "brand equity" may be transferred to another product class. The extension must make sense in terms of the attribute perceptions to be transferred. For example if laundry detergents could not benefit from a gentleness carryover, Ivory would not be a good brand extension candidate. The fit of the extension to the new category is important, but sometimes the positive attributes can be selectively transferred with the extension and the negative associations avoided (Aaker and Keller 1990). If the attributes that characterize the core brand can be a benefit in the new category, advertising costs may be lower and growth for the entry in the new category faster. However, on the other side, if the new category entrant fails, it may erode the equity of the core brand. Managers must be careful to balance the risks and rewards of brand extensions. Research is actively being pursued to see when an extension strategy is appropriate and the success in transferring a brand's equity into other markets (e.g., Kardes and Allen 1991; and Sullivan 1990).

Repositioning and Rejuvenation

In some cases, major innovation is possible by recycling the product back to the initial phases of the new-product-development process. Rejuvenation begins by reexamining the current definition of the market to indicate the best opportunities. Ideas for CBP repositioning are generated and translated into concepts and products for evaluation and refinement. If they are successful, testing and introduction would take place.

For example, in the face of rising oil prices, Boeing refused to accept the decline phase of the life cycle, but instead redesigned its products to renew their life cycles. Figure 19.17 shows the results of Boeing's redesign of the 727 in 1970 to achieve greater fuel economy. Sales of the 727 entered a new growth phase, in contrast with the decline of the 747 from 1971–77.

Rejuvenation is a good strategy when the product has a considerable amount of goodwill and if, with a reasonable amount of resources, it can be improved to deliver new benefits to the target market. When the strategy of the rejuvenation is considered, all the phases of the development process

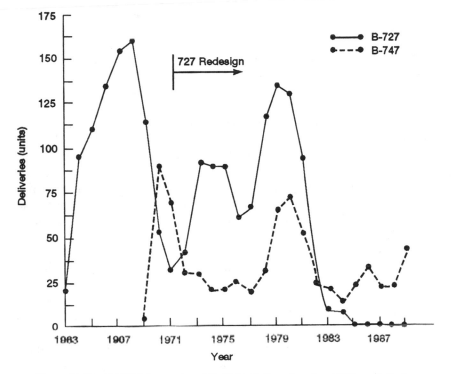

Figure 19.17 B-727 Rejuvenation (*World Jet Airplane Inventory*, 1988, p. 7, Boeing Commercial Airplane Group, The Boeing Co.; reprinted with permission)

begin again. After a strategic review, idea generation and positioning would be undertaken before designing a new quality entrant.

SUMMARY

New-product development is risky and costly, but it is critical to the long-term success of an enterprise. When new-product development is successful, the potential rewards are great. However, to achieve these rewards, the product must be managed profitably throughout its life cycle.

The life-cycle theory of introduction, growth, maturity, and decline provides a template to understand different strategies. In introduction the focus is penetration strategies, in the growth phase on holding and building sales and on determining the most profitable strategies. The mature phase requires maintenance of sales and profit, a careful defense, and continuous innovation. Finally, in the decline phase, if it occurs, the product is milked for maximum salvage value.

We discussed three issues in managing the product through its life cycle: marketing decision support systems (MDSS), competitive strategies, and customer satisfaction.

An MDSS is a tool that provides valuable information with which to set the marketing variables of price, advertising, sales effort, promotion, and distribution. By monitoring the market and understanding how the market responds to changes in these variables, the product manager can select those actions that lead to the best profit. We illustrated one successful use of an MDSS for a food product.

An MDSS tells you how the market will react to your marketing and to that of your competitors. But if the competitor also has an MDSS, then your actions will affect how your competitor responds. By considering the impact of your actions on those of your competitor and by understanding the variation in incentives between short-term exploitive behavior and long-term profitable behavior, you can set more profitable strategies. We illustrated these issues with two games—a prisoner's dilemma and a first-mover game. Although there are other potential competitive scenarios, these games illustrate the types of issues you will face.

Customer satisfaction is a means to balance short-term and long-term incentives to employees and managers. If a satisfied customer is an asset that leads to a continuous stream of profits, then we must avoid actions that sacrifice that profit stream while giving us myopic benefits in this quarter. Customer satisfaction and customer-satisfaction measurement systems provide the metrics with which to account for the long-term asset of a customer and provide incentives that are real to every manager and every employee. However, the measurement is critical. The right measures provide appropriate incentives while the wrong measures are counter-productive. We suggest that customer-satisfaction measures be relative to competition, include the satisfaction of customers *and* potential customers, leave room at the top, be based on sufficient sample sizes, and be relative to customer needs.

Finally, even the best-managed product might enter the decline phase of the life cycle. When this happens the product can be recycled to the opportunity identification and design phases of the new-product development process. With new innovations, product-line flankers and extensions, and repositioning and rejuvenation, there is potential for a long and profitable renewed life cycle.

REVIEW QUESTIONS

19.1. What is different in the life-cycle strategies in the growth versus mature stages? Mature versus decline?

19.2. When is a cooperative strategy the best choice for your firm? When is an aggressive strategy the best?

19.3. What are the sources of a unique competitive advantage?

19.4. What are the criteria for a good decision support model?

19.5. What are the sources of data available for a marketing decision support system? Pick a particular product category, outline the specific data availabilities.

19.6. How does customer satisfaction differ from product quality? What is the role of each in an MDSS?

19.7. What types of problems are encountered when setting the marketing mix for a mature product?

19.8. What is a "flanker" and why can it be very profitable?

19.9. Can flankers be used to reposition the product line?

19.10. What is the difference between a "flanker" and a brand "extension"?

19.11. When should a product be dropped rather than rejuvenated?

19.12. How is the management of a product line different than the management of a single product?

19.13. You are the product manager for a line of office equipment. How would you use the following concepts in managing this line?
   a. CBP
   b. Product-line position
   c. Planning and control system
   d. Prisoner's dilemma
   e. Customer satisfaction measurement

19.14. How does the prisoner's dilemma differ from the first-mover game?

19.15. Why must customer satisfaction be measured relative to competition? Why are potential customers important?

19.16. Explain switching costs and indicate why they are important.

PART SIX

Implementing the Process

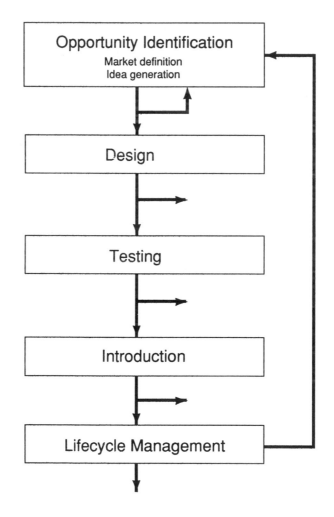

20

Organizing for Innovation

Product development and product management are activities that cut across organizational boundaries. Coordination is critical; people and resources from many areas of the corporation must be brought together if successful products are to be developed and managed throughout their life cycles. In this chapter we highlight organizational issues, that is, managing the people that must develop and manage products.

We begin by reviewing some of the more prevalent organizational structures for product development. Each of these structures has its advantages and disadvantages. The management challenge is to match the organizational structure to the people resources and the development problem.

But some products fail despite the best organizations and some products succeed in spite of a poor organizational structure. There is more to managing people than the formal organizational chart. Somehow, marketing, engineering, production, R&D, finance, strategic management, and other functions must be brought together to get the job done. Someone must have responsibility for product development, someone must become excited about a project, someone must make sure that resources are available and that the project does not get side-tracked, and so on. This coordination challenge and these development roles represent informal organizational efforts that work in parallel with formal organizational efforts. A good product manager recognizes the roles that people must play and encourages people to fill those roles. Thus, following the review of formal organizational structures, we discuss the informal organization—the impact of coordination and the informal roles that people fill.

We close the chapter with a description, diagnosis, and suggested action for twelve common situations in new-product organization. We hope that by these examples you can learn to apply better both the formal and the informal organizational concepts.

FORMAL ORGANIZATION

There are many ways to organize. In any particular company the best organizational structure depends upon the strengths and weaknesses of the firm, the orientation and skills of the officers, and previous organizational history. This section reviews and critiques common organizational forms for new-product development. Any particular firm or any particular project within a firm may require some combination of two or more structures.

Research and Development

One home for new products, especially high technology products, is in the R&D department. The advantage of an R&D department is that the new-product development effort is near the technological research and the product development capability. But the influence of the market, the customer, and intermediate users may be underrepresented if the department has primarily a technology and product outlook.

If management weighs the pros and cons and places new product development within R&D, they must decide whether to organize around underlying scientific groups (basic research) or as specific project groups with assigned new-product responsibility (development). In a study of nineteen R&D laboratories, (Mansfield et al. 1971, pp. 40–42) found that the organizational form depended upon the degree of basic research. If a significant fraction of R&D expense (more than 24%) went to basic research, firms tended to separate basic research from development.

Based on 38 large, long-term projects, (Allen 1977, pp. 211–220) found the functional organizational form produced results that were rated technically as being more successful, but were somewhat more subject to cost overruns. He suggests that for short duration projects or for projects based on technologies that are not changing rapidly, a project organization is best. For assignments that involve rapidly changing knowledge bases or for projects that are of long duration, a functional organization may be best if coordination can be encouraged (see Figure 20.1).

Marketing/Product Managers

Some firms assign the responsibility for new products to the marketing department, which has the advantage of placing a heavy emphasis on customers and markets. However, there are dangers. The time frame of marketing may be too short for truly innovative products. Marketing may emphasize less-risky new products that are minor improvements in existing products; major technological opportunities may be neglected.

The marketing department should not be given the sole responsibility for customer input and market estimation. The viewpoint that says "customers are the driving force of the innovation process and satisfying customers is the ultimate objective" should be shared by all units of the organization. This is an underlying tenant of the total quality movement and should be manifest most in marketing. All employees are in "marketing" in philosophy if not the formal organizational unit.

Because resources from many departments besides marketing are necessary to develop new products, firms have evolved the product manager system to link the various functional areas that underlie a new product's success. The product manager has overall responsibility for a product and must work with the sales, finance, R&D, and production departments to coordinate an organized marketing of the brand. Although the manager does not have authority over these groups, he or she gains cooperation based on expertise, personal influence, and ability to supply valuative information to management about specific managers and departments.

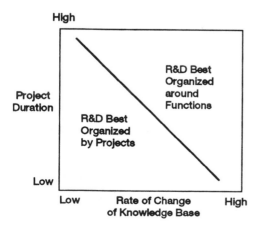

Figure 20.1. Whether R&D Organizes by Function or Project Depends Upon the Duration of the Project and the Rate at Which the Knowledge Base is Changing (Adapted from Allen, 1977, p. 219)

The product manager form of organization is used most commonly for established products, where product managers coordinate price, promotion, advertising, and selling activities to achieve the planned for results. Some firms assign product managers to develop new products. The advantage of this system is that the product manager is already familiar with the complexity of product management and the need to coordinate across functional areas. The disadvantage is that the product manager may be accustomed to short-term results. Product managers are often moved or promoted within a few years and earn bonuses by achieving quarterly profit plans. If the new product is an extra responsibility, it may suffer from neglect. For these reasons product manager systems tend to produce too many product-line flankers rather than major new business opportunities. Product manager systems are most appropriate for incremental growth through product improvement rather than "breakthrough" innovations (in contrast see the venture teams discussion below where the role of the project manager is specifically innovation).

New-Product Department

Because of the long-term, high-risk nature of products, many firms establish a separate department to integrate and coordinate the company's capabilities and bear the responsibility for product innovation. This organizational form has the advantages of establishing innovation as a high priority activity, balancing R&D and marketing, bringing a diverse set of skills together, and freeing itself from the short-run pressures of existing business. Such a group may be called a "growth-and-development department" to emphasize its responsibility to develop major new innovations that build new business areas for the company.

One disadvantage of a new-product department is that instead of linking R&D, marketing, and production, it may be viewed as an interloper by all groups. The R&D, marketing, and production directors are power centers in many companies and they may resent a fourth force based on new products. A clear commitment from the chief executive officer of an organization is needed to make a new products department work. Another problem is that the new-product department may be too structured to facilitate the identification and utilization of entrepreneurial talent. Although it can be an organizational base of major developmental efforts to enter strategic markets, it may not attract people with individual ideas and the ability and determination to pursue them.

Thus, if a new-product department is set up, management must encourage and support coordination techniques such as the House of Quality or QFD. Only by taping the talents of all of the relevant groups can a new-product department marshall the resources to succeed.

Entrepreneurial Division

If a firm does not facilitate internal entrepreneurs, they are likely to leave. Roberts (1991) found that one electronics organization was the source of 39 independent companies which grew to a total sales volume of over twice the parent company. Some firms have attempted to capture this talent by forming an entrepreneurial division. Entrepreneurs are given security and the opportunity to create and develop their ideas in a non-bureaucratic setting. Funds are available to recruit a product team or buy support services from other parts of the company. The outcome can be a new product for the company which the entrepreneur may manage over its life cycle, or spinoff company in which the parent may have a substantial share. If the idea does not develop, the manager can return to their original division. This is an important advantage for the firm. Instead of driving the entrepreneur outside the firm to try their idea and search for a new career if it fails, the entrepreneurial division provides an internal method to retain the valuable employee (see Roberts [1991] for a review of entrepreneurship).

One of the problems in an entrepreneurial division is that the risks and the expected costs of success are high. Because the benefits may be correspondingly high, the firm may find this activity a viable component in its growth and development strategy.

Corporate Structures

Product development is high priority. Some firms use a high-level corporate structure to signal this priority. There are at least three common organizational forms: (1) new-product committee, (2) task force, and (3) small staff reporting to the CEO.

The new-product committee is usually made up of the vice presidents of the major departments and the president. This group may set priorities, and screen ideas, and coordinate the implementation of product ideas. The details of the development effort cannot be handled by the committee, so they must be accomplished in the functional departments and coordinated by the committee. One advantage of this system is that it directs top management's attention toward innovation and gives them involvement and control.

A new-product task force gives more direct responsibility to the corporate group, but task forces are often of limited duration. The advantage of this system is that the firm's top talent is mustered to meet major challenges. For example, Motorola used task forces to successfully penetrate the market for electronic automobile ignition, combustion, and emission controls. The disadvantage is that the task force tends to work on a project rather than a program which may result in the sacrifice of some of the risk spreading and synergies associated with a programmatic effort.

The third form of corporate structure is a small staff that reports directly to the president or the chairman of the board. This group reflects the strategic perspective of top management and attempts to initiate projects in the organization that fill the long-run product/market posture the firm desires. This staff does early market definition and idea generation and, after developing specific projects for departments, monitors the progress of the new product. The advantage of this system is top-level responsibility and continuing effort. But for a staff to work it must be able to coordinate and encourage the follow-up efforts in the departments.

Matrix Organization and Venture Groups

A matrix form of organization has been used effectively by many firms in developing new products. In a matrix organization each person reports to two supervisors. For example, an R&D person in integrated circuits may report to the head of integrated circuits (in R&D) and to the director of a project to develop control circuits for microwave ovens. These dual reporting relationships integrate functional efforts. A matrix "venture group" may be given resources and freedom to meet the responsibility of developing a particular product. A group leader and the original supervisor both make performance evaluations and promotion recommendations.

The advantage of the matrix system is that it allows integration of diverse skills at the working level along with a clear definition of the priority of innovation. It does require flexibility due to the dual reporting relationship, but can be handled effectively by mature management. Its disadvantage is the complexity and the mixture of responsibility that can cause conflict if not managed correctly.

Teamwork is critical in matrix and venture group organizations. The leader must be effective in generating a cohesive sense of purpose, positive interpersonal relations, and a plan of action. Teams have been recognized as critical to organizational success. Studies of technical R&D teams indicate that success is in part based on greater communication outside the group as well as internal team functioning (Allen 1977). Research on new-product team effectiveness is just beginning but some of the early findings suggest that teams that are external looking (e.g. market, customers, environment, technology) and communicate more frequently and in depth with those outside the team are more effective (Ancona and Caldwell 1990; and Ancona and Caldwell 1991). Greater functional diversity encourages this external communication, but there are disadvantages to diversity (Ancona and Caldwell 1992).

Although diversity brings more creativity to the team, it impedes implementation because there is less capability for teamwork compared to homogeneous teams. If heterogeneous teams are used, more time must be allocated to team development and a good leader must function to encourage cooperation and achievement of goals. Tenure diversity in teams impacts internal rather than external functioning and improves group goal setting, priority setting, and overall performance (Ancona and Caldwell 1992).

Innovation is needed in internal venturing and new organizational forms are being proposed (see Zajac, Golden, and Shortell 1991). One kind of multi-discipline team that has been used effectively in some cases is the "skunk works." This is a team that is collected and then geographically separated from the organization. It is freed from the organizational constraints and usually reports to a very high officer in the company. The quarters may be second rate and cramped and the overall budget may be low (thus the name skunk works), but the commitment is high and entrepreneurial attitudes of getting the job done can lead to success. IBM developed their successful PC line in this way. The team was isolated in Florida and given new rights to buy components anywhere. But it had to get a machine to market fast that would meet the competition and be preferred by customers. Although separate, these skunk works groups still have high levels of communication outside their team—especially to those external to the organization.

Multidivisional Groups

Most large firms have many divisions. One approach is to decentralize the new-product activity to the level where the information and the development capabilities exist—the divisional level. But the existence of many divisional-level new-product groups can produce inefficiencies and duplication of effort.

An alternative approach, which overcomes some of the duplication, is to have corporate groups such as R&D, marketing research, advertising, strategic planning, and operations research service the divisional new-product departments. The divisional new-product departments have a small staff, but budget to buy services from the corporate groups (or sometimes outside). This ensures the availability of the required talent for the division, but allows the corporate group to pool projects to prevent duplication. The disadvantage is the need to establish effective communication to ensure that the divisional departments understand the services that are available from the corporate groups.

In some cases, a corporate new-products group might also be given the task of building businesses where no division exists. In this case they may use the venture team approach outlined above. People may be drawn from existing divisions, but be given a charter to create a market in a new area utilizing the firm's core technologies.

Alliances

Not all firms have the resources to organize an internal new-product development effort. Such firms often consider outside alliances. In various points in this book (e.g., chapters 1, 5, and 19) we outlined this concept. In an alliance, a separate organization may be set up as in the case of Semitech (an alliance of firms to develop new micro chip manufacturing technologies). Another example is NUMMI (New United Motor Manufacturing Inc.) for the joint venture of Toyota and GM (see Womack, Jones, and Roos, 1990 for a review of the future of the automotive industry). In the alliance of AT&T and Sun Microsystems, AT&T bought equity in Sun. This is more like the classic Japanese trading group which has interlocking equity among the trading group members as well as its banks. Sometimes a new joint venture project, but not a new corporation is created as in the case of electric battery consortium of Chrysler, GM, and Ford or a distribution and marketing agreement formulated as in the case of Mitsubishi and Chrysler.

These organizational forms do not always function effectively because they are often geographically separated and the team members retain their parent-firm parochial interests. For example, in 1989 DEC announced an alliance with Apple, but it did not yield large dividends. In 1991 Apple formed an alliance with IBM and DEC formed an alliance with Microsoft (IBM's old partner).

Outside alliances are not the only way to supplement the firm's development effort in areas where it is weak. Outside services are numerous and can be another method to fill the holes in the firm's skills and market requirements profile. "Boutiques" create, design, and test the product. Some design firms have strategic alliances with market research firms to assure that the voice of the customer is reflected in the design. Advertising agencies often develop product positioning, specify marketing plans, and run test markets as well as develop advertising copy. Major consulting companies offer technical research and management services for new-product development. Market research firms collect and analyze data, and many offer marketing consulting as well. Valuable support may be obtained from suppliers of raw materials. They may do R&D to create new end uses for their products.

A wide range of outside services exists. They tend to be costly, but may represent a viable alternative for some firms, especially small firms, to acquire creative talent and services for specific projects. Sometimes the total cost of an internal staff is higher than using outside suppliers on an interim basis. The outside supplier provides a new creative stimulus or impartial forecaster of potential.

Top-Management Involvement

One common element in all organizational structures is the need for top-management involvement. Although involvement is needed, too much interaction could be undesirable if it becomes viewed as "meddling" by the staff. Figure 20.2 describes a good balance of involvement and defines the decisions required of top management and the new-product team.

First, a clear policy on innovation should be formulated to describe goals, specify the organizational structure, enumerate constraints, and define the new-product commitment. This is the basic input necessary for the new-product team to design the sequence of steps that comprises its development process and to budget the time and resources necessary to meet the firm's goals. Top management then should review these resource requirements. This is important since the expected time and cost of innovation may be higher than many would suspect (see Chapter 3). Top management must have a realistic expectation of the times and costs involved. With this approval and a clear understanding of top management's corporate product and market strategy, opportunity identification and idea generation are undertaken.

The entry strategy is reviewed for consistency with corporate strategy and budgets are approved for the specific new product development opportunity. Top management should be particularly careful that cross-functional communication and coordination occurs during the design phase so that technology, marketing, and production can produce a superior quality product for the target market. After a CBP is specified, positioned, and fulfilled by a physical product, top management reviews the progress and decides if the testing phase should begin.

After the testing is complete, top management makes the go/no go decision, or recycles the product for more testing and improvement with an on decision.

If a launch is undertaken, top management reviews the launch plan and the subsequent one- and five-year plans. The final involvement is in the decision to rejuvenate or milk the product when it reaches the decline phase of its life cycle.

We have indicated several formal organizational forms for new-product development. All require top management involvement, but they are different in many aspects. Each has its strengths and each has its weaknesses; no one organizational form will serve all needs.

For large firms, current thinking suggests a growth-and-development department with a small staff, supplemented by venture teams drawing mem-

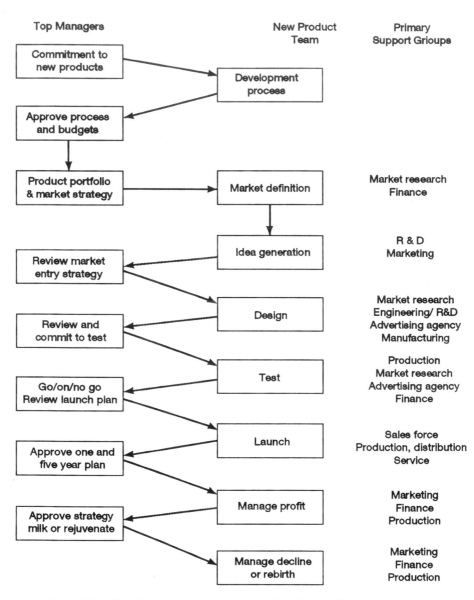

Figure 20.2 Top Management Involvement in New Product Development Process

bers on a project basis from operating functional areas such as R&D and marketing and allied firms. The department would also have funds to buy services from corporate or outside services. Major innovations using new technologies, alliances, or tapping new markets would be addressed by this group, while product-line extensions would be the responsibility of product managers in the marketing department. If such an integrated department is not used, explicit procedures are needed to link marketing, R&D, and production efforts. This could be a technique such as QFD, a merging of people with some marketing people in R&D and vice versa, or a set of informal priorities that establish a culture of cooperation among the three groups. Bringing customer needs and technology together with production is one of the most important functions of the product-development organization.

A portfolio of approaches may exist. A corporate entrepreneurial division could exist to assure that entrepreneurial talent and ideas are utilized to create new businesses. For example, 3M has such a division in addition to extensive new-product efforts within divisions. The large firm could have a complex formal organization based on matrix management concepts with responsibility assigned to a new-product department on a divisional basis, but supported by corporate services and development. For example, the Conference Board (Duerr 1986), in a study of 177 firms, reports that 75% had a new-product function at the corporate level, 75% at the divisional level, and 46% at the group level. Many of these firms reported that the new-product development activities fell under several functional headings including marketing, R&D, and a special commercial development unit. In all there were 28 different managerial titles to which new-product development reports.

The complexity is multiplied when alliances are undertaken on a global scale. Organizations are getting larger but innovation requires that individuals feel motivated or "empowered." This means that more delegation is necessary and organizations must be flatter in the future with fewer levels. The coordination requirements of such organizations will be high, but fortunately the cost of information transfer is coming down and carefully designed computer systems can help (Malone and Rockart 1991).

To select a good organizational form for your situation, you should understand the new-product development process, recognize the strengths and weaknesses of your firm, and use your managerial common sense. In making this decision, do not evaluate only the formal organization; also evaluate how the formal organization encourages or hinders the informal organization, and vice versa.

INFORMAL ORGANIZATION: COORDINATION

One of the challenges of new-product development is that many groups and many individuals within the organization must work together to achieve success. In Chapter 13 we highlighted the fact that even within the same firm there was much more communication within the new-product team for successes than for failures. We used this fact to motivate the need for communication and to suggest a means to achieve that communication.

But why is communication so difficult? One hypothesis, developed by Dougherty (1987) is that different groups within an organization develop different "thoughtworlds" that are characterized by different cultures and even different languages. Engineers speak with the technical vocabulary of their discipline—gear ratios, MIPS, pH balance, etc.; marketing professionals have their specialized language—perceptual maps, CPM, preference vectors, etc.; strategic planning, field service, manufacturing, finance, and other groups within the organization all have developed specialized vocabularies with which they communicate among themselves. Along with the special languages come specialized knowledge, experience, perceived reward structures, self-views, world views, and goals. In some cases engineers at company A may feel more comfortable talking to their counterparts at company B than their own marketing department.

Because these different thoughtworlds raise barriers to communication and cooperation, Dougherty investigated how they communicate in actual new-product projects. In particular, she mapped the communication patterns among the technical groups (R&D, engineering, manufacturing), the business planning groups (strategic planning, finance, top management), and those closest to the customer (marketing and sales).

She found that new product-projects fall naturally into one of four enactment patterns and that only one pattern, which she calls "cut it loose" leads consistently to successes. These enactment patterns are summarized in Figure 20.3.

Leap Before You Look

In the "leap before you look" enactment pattern products are driven by technical design. A business plan is developed before introduction, but in all the cases that Dougherty observed customer inputs came after introduction. The customer input forced redesign which, in turn, called for more customer input continuing until the product was recycled to incorporate inputs from all thoughtworlds.

Plan then Plunge then Plan Again

In the "plan then plunge then plan again" enactment pattern the products began as a plan in opportunity identification but as they entered the design phase, the efforts split into the separate thoughtworlds of technical design and the customers. The products then "plunge" at or near introduction because they fail to function or fail to deliver customer benefits. Only

Plan Then Plunge Then Plan Again

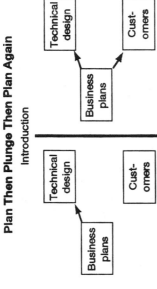

Introduction

Leap Before You Look

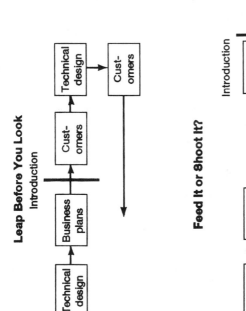

Introduction

Cut It Loose

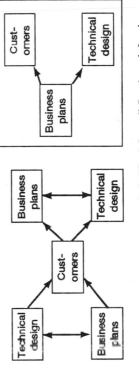

Introduction

Feed It or Shoot It?

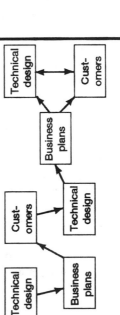

Introduction

Figure 20.3 Four Informal Coordination Structures Observed for New Product Development Projects—Only "Cut it Loose" Consistently Leads to Successes (Adapted from Dougherty 1987)

613

then do they enter a new cycle that may or may not include all the thought-worlds.

Feed it or Shoot it?

In the "feed it or shoot it" enactment pattern the products oscillate between the thoughtworlds of technical design, planning, and the customer. Only as they near introduction do the thoughtworlds coordinate.

Cut it Loose

Finally, in the only enactment pattern with which successes were associated, all thoughtworlds were involved and coordinated early in the development process. There was strong communication among all of the functional areas and, just before introduction, the involvement of the thoughtworlds seemed to merge into one voice.

Clearly, there might be other enactment patterns that Dougherty did not observe and there might be cases where the first three lead to success or "cut it loose" leads to failure, but the concept of thought world coordination is clear. Organizing for new product success calls for more than just the formal organization. Each group, with its specialized goals, language, and knowledge, must work together to assure that the technical design and the business plan deliver the benefits the customer demands.

Workman (1991) built upon this research. He actually lived in a single large computer manufacturer organization for nine months to understand the relationship between marketing, engineering, and "the field" organizations. He found that in each group they had their own "lives." In engineering it was projects, in marketing it was "getting it out the door," and in the field specific customer accounts and sales support. The units held little regard for each other and communication was difficult. For example, engineering and marketing had different time horizons and differing units of analysis. Despite these difficulties among the formal units, much input on customer needs and tradeoffs entered the process. There was no single marketing group, but many—each with its own view on segmenting the market and designing products. These differences were often resolved in group meetings or by resorting to the top-management strategy team.

UP-OVER-DOWN VERSUS ACROSS

Both Workman's on-site observations and Dougherty's site-comparison observations suggest that new-product development is more successful if functional areas such as marketing, production, R&D, and engineering are coordinated in their goals and if good communication occurs across boundaries. In some cases this communication will be the result of architecture—people who work close to one another communicate more, and in some cases this communication will be the result of an inspired leader or a particularly effective team. However, in other cases the new-product process itself can encourage communication.

For example, in Chapter 13 we described one process, QFD, which encouraged communication among marketing, engineering, R&D, and production. Recently, Griffin and Hauser (1992a) compared QFD with a traditional "phase-review" process at a large automobile manufacturer. One development team used QFD; the other used a phased process in which they reviewed development as the project passed certain checkpoints. The teams were chosen to be matched as closely as feasible. Both teams resided in the same organization, developing components of comparable technical complexity, with about the same number of parts, and which serve similar functions in an automobile. Both products are manufactured by outside suppliers, but are designed by the automobile manufacturer (OEM). Both teams report to the same manager two levels up and contain roughly the same number of team members with roughly the same experience. In both cases the team leader was committed to the process being used.

During the 15-week period of observation team members reported on their communications by completing, on a randomly chosen day each week, a one-page form. Figure 20.4 reports the observed communications links on a per-link, per-week basis for each team. Line widths are proportional to measured communication levels between functions while circle sizes are pro-

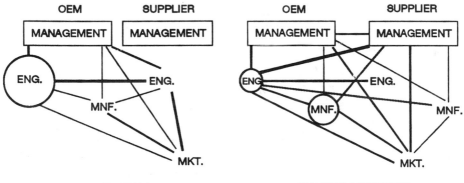

Figure 20.4 Graphical Representation of Communication Patterns (Griffin and Hauser 1992a)

portional to the communication levels within functions. In some cases there was no communication within a function because there was one (or no) person in that function. Notice two qualitative differences. The phase-review team is a more complex diagram with many more links and, in particular, more vertical links to management. On the other hand, the communications of the QFD team are more horizontal, perhaps circumventing the "up-over-down" communication through management for the more-efficient "across" communication within and between functions.

To determine whether patterns of communication were actually changed, Griffin and Hauser defined a "core" new-product team as those members of the team who perform either a marketing, a production, or an engineering/R&D function. Figure 20.5 compares the communication patterns of the core QFD and the core phase-review teams. QFD led to more communication, more communication within functions, and more communication between functions. However, QFD reduced slightly the communication from the core team to management. Figure 20.5 reinforces the

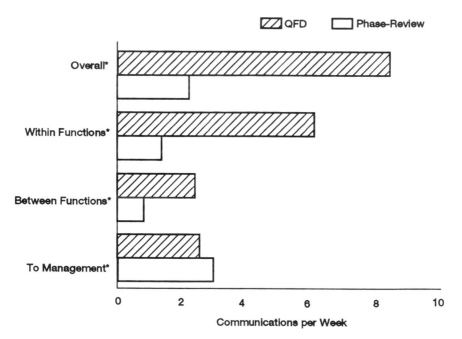

* Significant at the 0.05 level.

Figure 20.5   Communication Comparison (Griffin and Hauser 1991a)

interpretation that QFD leads to more horizontal ("across") communication than the "up-over-down" communication used in the phase-review process. If indeed management was serving primarily as a communication conduit, then this would imply that the QFD pattern of communication was more efficient.

Naturally, Figures 20.4 and 20.5 are based on a single comparison at one manufacturing company. They are consistent with intuition and suggest that QFD may indeed provide a means to enhance communication and, by implication, the success of the new-product development. Griffin and Hauser (1992b) report that these communication gains are typical. It is also possible that other new-product processes can be effective in increasing communication among the functional participants on a new-product team. Attention to the choice of a new-product process indeed can affect communications patterns!

INFORMAL ORGANIZATION: ROLES

If the product is to succeed, the various development tasks must be done by individuals. These tasks will not be accomplished by simply placing names on an organizational chart. They must be assumed by people working together. Interpersonal relationships and personalities of the people in the organization will affect results. The new-product manager and top management must recognize and organize these relationships and encourage their proper functioning. Individuals fill various informal organization roles within the formal structure. We now address the roles that must be filled to encourage communication and new-product success.

Champion

And it is worth noting that nothing is harder to manage, more risky in the undertaking, or more doubtful of success than to set up as the introducer of a new order. Such an innovator has as enemies all the people who were doing well under the old order, and only halfhearted defenders in those who hope to profit from the new.

—Machiavelli

A new product needs an advocate who will champion its cause within the organization. The idea has to be "sold" to many people. Objections must be overcome and energy and enthusiasm to proceed generated. Some of this may be done in formal presentations, but much is done by informal contacts at social or business functions. The champion must believe in the idea and be willing to take career risks to defend it and attract resources to further it.

Protector

An allied role is that of the protector. This is a senior person who can intercede to save the champion when the established power centers of the company fight back. The protector does not overtly advocate the idea, but strongly defends the champion's right to do so. The protector is also a "coach" to the champion. He or she tells the champion of the friendship, power, and interpersonal workings of the organization, and advises the champion on how and when to make the correct contacts and statements to further the project. The protector also provides legitimacy and maturity for the product-development effort.

Auditor/Controller

While the champion pushes on, it is necessary that the organization not be misled by enthusiasm. The auditor balances the enthusiasm of the champion by assuring that the sales forecasts are realistic and accurate. Analytic capabilities are important in this function. The champion is critical and the skills to make this role effective are not common. The auditor helps the organization make sure that the champion is being directed toward the correct product project so his or her capabilities are used effectively. The auditor function may be fulfilled by a member of the new-product team or by an independent person or group outside the development team.

Allied to the audit's role is the controller of the new-product effort. The controller watches the schedules and budgets. Cost overruns are minimized and efforts made to meet time objectives. Most R&D cost overruns occur on projects that are eventual failures (Meadows, 1968). There is a apparently a reluctance to give up on an idea even after it becomes clear that it should be terminated. The controller should be willing to treat past inputs to a project as sunk costs and allocate funds based on future results.

Creator/Inventor

The new-product effort needs creators and inventors to design and market new products successfully. Unfortunately, this creative talent can be vastly underused if the formal structure imposes too may constraints. Creativity does not come automatically by establishing a new-product committee, group, or department. In fact, a rigid structure can stifle creativity. Creative scientists and marketing managers must be identified and involved in the new-product process.

If formal creative procedures are used, the people who demonstrate the most originality should be identified and involved in the design and problem-solving process. In the technological area, creativity also depends on scientific information. Managers should recognize and manage the "gatekeeper" effect in which a few people become the "gate" through which much new information flows (Allen 1977). The creative scientist and the gatekeeper should be nourished and supported. Tapping their skills will be based on a clear understanding of individual capabilities and the problem-solving process in the lab.

The creative talent of a firm may be difficult to pinpoint. Giving a wide variety of people the chance to participate in problem solving helps identify those who have the most creativity. Everyone is creative to some degree if put in the right circumstances. The good manager encourages those circumstances and rewards creativity. For example, a production person was recruited for a creative group as part of a cross-section of managers. When asked to evaluate his own creativity, he said, "I cannot do much with new concepts. I am not a creative type." After three days in a group session he came up with the single most innovative product concept identified during the meeting. In another situation a large midwestern bank found that they were losing their most creative people, partly because these people were not allowed to initiate their own projects.

Leader

New-product development is a team effort that needs a leader. The leader must recruit a staff, mold the talent of this group into a powerful team, and develop effective plans. The leader must motivate, teach, and train members of the team.

In motivating the team, the leader should recognize that the formal reward of pay is not the most effective motivator. Group recognition, career advancement, and the granting of responsibility are more powerful. The simple assignment of interesting tasks is a big motivator—particularly when they are accomplished successfully. Working relationships are also important. Friendly, cooperative functioning within the team that recognizes the needs of individuals on the team builds morale. The team leader must maintain this enthusiasm through the periods when the product future looks bleak. The leader must show strength in pursuing the project through these difficult times and may have to demonstrate courage to kill the project should it clearly prove unwise to continue. Termination of projects that appear likely to fail is critical to maintaining the group's respect.

New-product development requires special skills. The skills necessary for new-product work are often increased on the job and the leader must manage the human resources of the group to develop the capabilities of each person to their maximum level (Schein 1977). This begins by recruiting talent and continues through training. Without talented people the effort is doomed. For example in one organization, those brand managers that could not generate consistent quarterly performance were given a "home" in the new-product department. This does little to create the necessary skill base and level of respect that new-product development must have. The leader has the job of finding talent and instilling respect in the organization.

The leader also provides the interface with other parts of the organization by acting as a translator and an integrator. The new-product idea must be understood clearly by the various thoughtworlds of R&D, marketing, engineering, production, manufacturing, and top management. This communication function is necessary to be sure the idea is correctly perceived by all parties. In the integrator function, the leader collects diverse information from numerous sources in the organization to support decision making and coordinate actions. The leader is important in developing a consensus and integrating different points of view (Souder 1977).

The leader must fulfill many functions and, in most cases, is the person formally heading the new product effort. These have been cases in which the head of new products was the "champion" and the team "leader" was an unrecognized member of the group who earned this position of respect from their peers.

Another level of leadership exists at the top of an organization. If the president or CEO does not demonstrate strong support for product innovation, the new-product effort will probably fail. If the CEO shows real leadership in this area, it can be very successful. Mr. Land at Polaroid is a good example of a man who spearheaded the innovation effort from the top of this organization and introduced a number of successful new instant cameras.

Strategist

It is often easy to become involved with new products for their own sake. To avoid this trap and to keep the firm's strategic goals in the forefront, the new-product development effort needs a strategist with a long-run managerial perspective. For example, Jack Welsch had a strategy at G.E that said a business should be number one or two in its market or he would sell it. If it was one or two in terms of market share he would give it large new-product budgets and major R&D support.

The role of the strategist is to set goals for growth in sales and profit, select marketing priorities, and allocate resources. It is not innovation per se that is important, but innovation as a means to achieve long-range goals. The strategist must select the overall development strategy and set the budget.

We suggest the strategist be a person at a high level in the company (see Figure 20.2). Top management has primary responsibility but the details may be delegated, so this function may fall on the director of new products. The director may undertake market definition studies and request a budget based on strategic analysis instead of waiting for a message from the top. After top management has reacted and revised the director's plan a working strategy can result.

Judge

As new-product development proceeds, honest differences of opinion are certain to occur. People will disagree about whether the product should be introduced or not. Some will feel that the product is reducing their sphere of influence and power or that it will jeopardize some successful ongoing ideas. Conflicts result in these situations.

It is important to have a method of resolving or at least managing this conflict. One role is by a mediator who attempts to find a common ground of agreement and widen this to a working consensus. But in many cases a judicial role must be invoked. The opposing sides should be heard, and then a go or no go decision made on the product. This is particularly important because the judgement must be made before the commitment of the champion and the team make it organizationally impossible to stop the project.

It is healthy to involve top management in resolving major differences since the new-product commitments are large and strategic. This should not be neglected by corporate management. Some top managers like to approve or disapprove only a proposal. Someone below the top level decides which alternatives will be given a go/on/no go review. Other top managers like to see a wide range of alternatives. Some want advocates of each to present them and then to exercise judicial authority in making final commitments. Many styles exist, but the judicial process must be defined clearly.

Relationship between Formal and Informal Roles

Organization is not complete when a chart is drawn. The informal roles of champion, protector, auditor/controller, creator/inventor, leader, strategist, and judge must come into being within the formal organization. Some of these may correspond to the director of new products, but other roles will correspond to other people within the organization.

For example, Figure 20.6 is a map of communication in a R&D laboratory (Allen 1977). It is clear that formal and informal communication is affected by the formal organization sections (A to D). However, the informal gatekeeping function often is present. A statistical analysis of two laboratories indicated that although the formal structure is an important determinant of

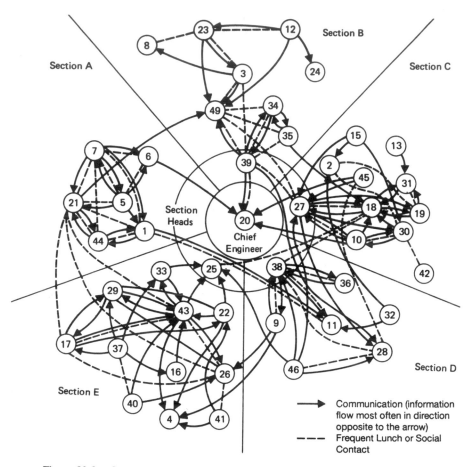

Figure 20.6. Communication Network in a Typical R&D Laboratory Showing the Influence of Formal and Information Organization (Allen 1977, p. 208; reprinted with permission)

communication, the informal organization makes its own independent contributions of nearly equal magnitude.

In considering formal and informal interaction recall the major effects the geography of the office plays (Allen 1977). The closer people are together, the more they communicate. A venture team with adjacent offices will have more interaction than one that is geographically separated and only is in close proximity during meetings. This is particularly important when integrating R&D, engineering, marketing, and production on a global basis. Although it is more expensive, it may be wise for the R&D or engineering people to have two offices—one in R&D and one in the new-product department—so they can be close together on days allocated to the new-product project. The use of office geography is important as a mechanism to improve the organizational functioning of the new-product team. Linking engineering and production also may call for a geographic shift. In some firms the process engineers now live at the factory and have an experimental process facility there. Global separation is becoming an increasing concern as we try to integrate across skills in various parts of the world. Experiments with video conferencing, video "windows" (video screens and voice dialogue between informal areas in distant locations), and electronic networking may simulate proximity and build understanding, coordination, and communication.

Implementing Informal Roles

Some concepts have been proposed, but you must exercise your own judgment in developing an organization. Experimentation is encouraged. The product manager and matrix forms of organization were developed by managers facing difficult problems and not by academics. Evaluation of these formal and informal organizational structures indicate they can be effective. New forms need to be created. In organizing your efforts, do not feel constrained to rigid charts and formal organizational thinking. Try to capture the concepts outlined in the discussion of the formal organization; link R&D, engineering, production, and marketing, assign priority and responsibility, encourage entrepreneurship, integrate top-management perspectives and necessary working-level skills, decentralize development and empower people, encourage communication and teamwork, and do not neglect new-product talent outside the firm. Be creative, receptive, and flexible, recognize people problems, and develop your own managerial style. Encouraging an organization to produce successful innovation is difficult, but the rewards are great.

TYPICAL ORGANIZATIONAL PROBLEMS: SITUATIONS, DIAGNOSIS, AND ACTION

Designing organizations for new-product development is still a developing field, but firms now face and must address many organizational problems. In this section we identify some of these situations, diagnose their possible causes, and indicate actions that might solve them. These are only some of the organizational situations in which you may find yourself, but we hope this discussion makes you more sensitive to the issues and serves as a review of the concepts discussed in this chapter.

Situation 1. At a meeting of the company's executive committee the president summarizes, "I really am not excited about this new-product launch the marketing group is proposing, but it is the only alternative we have to get something to market this year."

Diagnosis: Here the firm is caught by not having generated enough alternatives and developing them into concepts and prototypes. Now they must accept more risk than they should. The new-product work is apparently being done in marketing and the new-product effort is not organized at a large enough scale.

Action: Set up a new-product department and give it top management priority. Budget for a stream of ideas and involve management in the selection before testing. Develop an explicit decision process with go/on/no go elimination steps.

Situation 2. "We spend $100 million per year on R&D and we have not had one major new-product success in five years." Why can't we find a place to sell our technological breakthroughs?

Diagnosis: This firm apparently is relying on R&D to carry out all the new-product development. R&D's perspective is probably too highly oriented towards technology.

Action: Link R&D, engineering, production, and marketing in a new product venture group or department. Use a coordination mechanism such as the House of Quality to develop a CBP. Develop core technologies, but also core markets. Balance filling the needs in the focused market with technological power. You may find an alliance with other firms gives you the capability to be dominant in the strategic market.

Situation 3. The president laments, "Why are we always caught behind our competition in product innovation? Why is it that they get to market faster than we do and when we are first in, we lose our competitive advantage within a year?"

Diagnosis: The competitor apparently has an effective new-product effort. The competitor can both innovate and get to market as well as copy quickly and improve on "first-in" products.

Action: Strengthen the new-product-development effort to be competitive—more people, more funds. Get to market faster by getting the redundant steps out of the process, involving customers sooner to prevent redesign, overlap phases in the new product process, use the most recent technologies for fast design (CAD/CAM), and make an explicit risk return tradeoff on skipping some of the testing phases in the process (see Chapter 3). Stress major innovation. Get more R&D, engineering, and creative talent working to identify breakthroughs, not just "me too's." Do more strategic analysis earlier to define market opportunities and strategic technical market positions. Preempt the competitive second-but-better entry by being sure that the new product is in the best position and has the best delivery of customer benefits in your target segment.

Situation 4. The *director of growth and development* of a U.S. company complains: "We have been trying get into that European category for the past five years and have not yet succeeded."

Diagnosis: Several of reasons can explain the failure to "crack" a category, but one prime reason may be that the firm has artificially constrained itself to a U.S. point of view. Alternatively, the category may be open to innovation, but the firm has not found the opening.

Action: The director of growth and development should develop a global perspective. The world is the market and the question is how to understand needs and create customer benefits in segments of it. Strengthen the strategic decision to enter that category by undertaking a market identification study in each area of the world. Perceptual mapping and value mapping should be done and any gaps (or the lack thereof) should be identified in each area. Understand customer utilities and create a core benefit proposition that reflects the differences in various regions of the world.

Situation 5. *R&D director:* "We send five breakthrough new products to marketing each year and they don't do anything with them!" *Product manager:* "We want a product modified to expand our market and R&D cannot deliver or comes back with an answer too late." *Marketing director:* "Ideas are cheap! What we need is an *action* person who can take an idea to market." *Sales director:* "We get the craziest new products. They divert our effort from already profitable products." *Production manager:* "Engineering just throws the design" over the fence "and expects us to produce it. They do not understand the process, cost tradeoffs, and difficulties and then top management wants to know why we can't build world class quality products."

Diagnosis: Clearly there is little communication and coordination between the groups. R&D is not getting market input. The product manager is thinking of line extensions and the marketing director is portraying a bias toward fast results. The sales director probably already has problems meeting sales goals and is not convinced that new products will help. Production is the end of the line and has not been involved in the design stage of development.

Action: Share developmental goals. Leadership and coordination are needed. Top management could use a task force or product committee to integrate at the upper management levels. A matrix form of development with a person from each area in a venture team could be considered as a supplement to top level coordination. A new-products director who can be a team leader is needed, and a protector should be identified for the director.

Section 6. President: "We have had four new-product directors in the last six years and none of them could deliver sales and profit results."

Diagnosis: A number of reasons could exist for this, but apparently the new-product directors are being judged by results after one year. The expected time to get a product from idea to market is much longer—especially if it is a one-time project rather than an on-going process.

Action: Set evaluation criteria based on progress through the process and successful completion of the opportunity identification, design, testing, and launch phases. Give the new-product director adequate tenure and budget to meet the sales goals. If you want major innovation, pushing for one-year results will prevent it by forcing consideration of minor modifications of products to get to the market fast.

Situation 7. *Founder and chairperson of the board:* "Why can't we grow a business in the same way as I built this company? Start small, work hard, and produce a good product."

Diagnosis: The founder was an entrepreneur. Today's markets are much more complex and highly structured and require more sophistication, but it is still possible to find opportunities by entrepreneurship.

Action: Set up an entrepreneurship division to support people with ideas and determination. Look for entrepreneurs inside and outside the company. Start many projects (50-100) since only a few (2 or 3) will succeed. Major new opportunities may be found in this way that would otherwise have been overlooked. This activity can be used to enhance the efforts of a new-products department. Look for acquisitions to fill the need for new products. If the firm can not be entrepreneurial they may have to buy a start-up at a high but worthwhile price.

Situation 8. *President:* "All our new products look like our existing products. Why can't we come up with some really new ideas?" *Product manager:* "I try, but it is difficult to find breakthrough ideas when I must spend most of my time solving the problems of my existing product line."

Diagnosis: The product manager is too involved with fire-fighting on current products. The product manager does not have the time or is unwilling to take the risk involved in major innovation.

Action: Set up a new product group or department with responsibility for major innovations. Continue to reward product managers for "flankers," but set up a reward system for the new department to encourage careful analysis aiming toward breakthroughs. Give this department sufficient time and resources to undertake the risk of major innovation.

Situation 9. *R&D director:* "Our lab work is good, but we don't do much with it, and either a competitor exploits it or one of our employees leaves and starts a new company."

Diagnosis: The firm's technological capabilities are not being utilized and entrepreneurial talent is being wasted.

Action: If the new technology does not match the priorities of the new-product department, let the inventor take it to the entrepreneurial division and see if he or she can make it work. If it does, a new product is born. If not, the inventor's talent is retained in the firm. Be sure R&D is part of the venture team so that technological opportunities can be utilized in new products. Orient them towards customer benefits.

Section 10. Chairperson of New Product Committee: "This product has been worked on for five years, but if I understand this group, there is a feeling we need to do another pricing study and be sure our guarantee plan is financially stable."

Diagnosis: This is probably a product that should be killed. On-on instead of a go or no go decision is wasting resources.

Action: Pose the go/no go decision and have one person (say the president) make it. The committee is probably trying to be nice to the sponsor when a hard business decision is called for. The new-product effort should concentrate on major winners, not middle-majority ideas that are likely to generate mediocre profits if they do get to market.

Section 11. *President:* "Well, we really failed in the market! What went wrong?" *Market research director:* "We had many negative indicators all along— but no one would listen." *Product manager (champion):* "Market research always tries to come back and say I told you so. If we followed them, we would never introduce a product! If firm X had not cut their prices to cost, we would have had a winner." *Vice-president of growth and development:* "I have never understood those market research models and I have always felt new products is a place where managerial judgment is more critical. We missed, but new products is a risky business."

Diagnosis: Apparently the champion was very effective and marketing research very ineffective in communication. The champion probably could sell anything. The protector (vice-president of growth and development) supported the champion. The models and data were not understood by the vice-president and therefore not heard by top management.

Action: Market-research personnel should be on the venture team. A special new-products research group could be established in the growth-and-development department to ensure effective communication. Market research and the analytic people should be trained to understand and communicate with management. Management should be trained to understand market research and realize when their judgment is needed. Both the quantitative and qualitative skills must be utilized for the implementation of a successful new-product development effort.

Situation 12. *Product manager:* "Why should I spend part of my budget on market research? After all, our firm has survived in this category for almost 10 years without such spending."

Diagnosis: The firm has survived, but has it thrived? Here the product manager is unwilling to invest money and effort on intangible research. This strategy causes opportunities to be missed and, in the long, run causes the firm to be caught with only products that are in decline stages of their life cycles. Markets are getting more complex with global competition and increasing segmentation; market research should help sort out priorities and develop quality products that innovate in the market.

Action: Implement a new-product development process and reward innovation. Set a budget based on expected benefits and quantify the intangible so that it can be balanced against other investment opportunities. Be sure market research is oriented toward decision actions.

Situation 13. _____: Fill in the blanks when you are on the job. This is the situation you will face!

Diagnosis and Action: Be sensitive to organizational issues. Spend time trying to understand what is going on around you. Think of the informal as well as the formal organization. A position is filled by a person and is not merely a job description. People have personal as well as organizational needs. What would you do in their job?

REVIEW QUESTIONS

20.1. What are the major decisions a company must make concerning the organization of the new-product development effort?

20.2. What are the advantages and disadvantages of a product-manager approach to organization?

20.3. In the matrix form of organization, how might channels of authority and responsibility be confused? What rewards would an individual have for cooperating with the innovative effort?

20.4. When choosing a "venture group," how might individuals be chosen? What criteria should be applied?

20.5. What are the advantages of categorizing the informal roles of people influencing the new-product effort? What managerial conclusions can be made based on these classifications?

20.6. How do you judge outside suppliers? What is their role in integration of production and design? What quality standards should we set for them?

20.7. Discuss the role of top management in new-product development. What should they do and what shouldn't they do?

20.8. Discuss how you would encourage and reward people for filling the informal roles necessary for new-product development.

20.9. **Situation 14.** _Vice-president of growth and development:_ "My staff is too technical, all I ever get is numbers and computer printouts." Diagnose the likely situation and prescribe possible actions.

20.10. Situation 15: *Chairman of the board:* "My new-product group is motivated. There is always action and excitement. We have had five new products in the last two years and expect five more products this year. My problem is that while sales are growing, profits are declining." Diagnose, analyze, and suggest actions.

21

Customizing the New-Product Development Process

Every new-product or -service development project has unique elements. The particular customer needs, the local customs, the market niche, the available technology, the competitors, the regulatory pressures, the scale, the time pressure, the material availability, the channels of distribution, the unique characteristics of production, and so on all vary. But there are common issues. The opportunities must be evaluated for long-term profitability, ideas must be generated, the needs of customers must be determined and filled, the product must be perceived to be of higher value (all things considered) than competitive products serving the same market niche. Price may be fixed or negotiated, there may be quantity discounts, or the new product might be on promotion, but in all cases we must consider what the customer "pays" for the product and how this compares to the benefit delivered. There may or may not be advertising, but we must communicate somehow with the customer. There may be no test market, but at some point we must forecast sales for the product. The mix between physical product and human service may vary, but all innovation must have an effective Core Benefit Proposition. Throughout a new-product project, any new-product project, there are managerial responsibilities which have analogs to the generic new-product-development process presented in this text.

The effective new-product team customizes the development process to their specific needs. Naturally we can not anticipate each and every customization need. Instead we give examples of how the process might be customized for variations by scale of the organization, product type (consumer packaged goods, consumer durable, industrial, service, high technology), and strategic emphasis. We close this chapter by considering the tasks that may be found in various industries and organizations when the definition of clientele is viewed widely.

VARIATIONS BY SCALE OF THE ORGANIZATION

Opportunity identification, design, testing, introduction, and profit management are necessary to the development of a new product. All organizations should go through these phases in one way or another. Large organizations with the ability to commit sufficient resources can afford detailed analysis and are well advised to spend resources up front to avoid failure and enhance success. Other organizations may not have the same resources (time, money, personnel), but should still use the key concepts of the development process.

The analysis that precedes the development of good, sound new products ranges in complexity from clear thinking to a formal mathematical models. A useful way of thinking about types of analysis is to organize them into three levels:

- *Strategic* involves a clear structuring of the questions and issues and understanding of interrelationships. Creative alternatives are generated. Inputs of phenomena and outcomes are based on judgment.
- *Tactical* consists of simple analysis to aid in understanding complex interactions. Both judgment and market research inputs go into this analysis. "What-if" analyses are used to explore the implications of strategies.
- *Operational* uses more detailed models and statistics to provide in-depth representation of phenomena. Research data are empirically based and some market experimentation may be done.

All marketing strategy problems demand at least strategic analysis, and most benefit significantly from tactical analysis. Operational analysis requires greater expertise and it may require more data, but it pays off when resources are at risk.

Table 21.1 outlines some of the variations in the process that might result from customization based on scale of the organization. The first column represents the typical large firm like General Electric, Lever Brothers, Kao, Sony, Volkswagon, or IBM. Substantial sums of money are available to do the appropriate research. Such large firms can make use of state-of-the-art analytical techniques because the markets that they are likely to attack justify the up-front investment in "getting it right."

In opportunity identification the large firm would use formal techniques to assure that the market is defined correctly, that the opportunity is of sufficient potential, R&D capabilities and user needs are considered, the best segment is targeted, etc. In the design phase they would invest in market research to identify, structure, and prioritize customer needs and to position the product vis-à-vis competition. The market would be segmented; the House of Quality and QFD analysis might be used to integrate marketing, engineering, and production. Analytical techniques might be used to be sure the potential business justified further investment. A careful marketing plan would be developed to implement the CBP. When the product moves into the testing phase, the firm could afford to test the product carefully in the laboratory and with customers. It could afford large scale pretest or prelaunch analyses. If appropriate it might even consider a test market. With a successful test the launch would be monitored and managed to maximize profit and this would continue throughout the life cycle of the product. In general, the firm could afford to take advantage of the benefits of careful, formal measurement and analysis at all levels.

As indicated in the second column, the smaller business might not have the resources to invest in the more-formal, up-front management techniques. But just because they can not afford the data, does not mean that they should ignore the concepts. For example, in opportunity identification, they might not be able to undertake a formal market-profile analysis, but they might do one more informally. Instead of surveys to collect data for market-structure analyses, they might use focus groups or other qualitative techniques to intuit the market definition. In design, they might not use factor analysis to develop a perceptual map, but, based on talking to customers, they might identify the key strategic benefit-dimensions and attempt to draw a perceptual map or a value map from the less formal customer input. From this they might get a good idea of positioning and of segmentation. The voice of the customer is still key—it must be understood and linked to engineering design. The product will not succeed without a well-developed CBP. A small scale House-of-Quality exercise may be undertaken. Similarly in testing, the smaller business might substitute less formal techniques for the more expensive, formal techniques, but they will still get the job done to assure that the product, the communication, the service, and the marketing mix deliver the CBP. Once

TABLE 21.1 Variations in the New-Product Development Process by the Scale of the Organization

Phase of Development		Scale of the Organization	
	Large Firm or Division	Smaller Business	Entrepreneur
Opportunity identification	Market definition Creative group sessions Market profile analysis Segmentation R & D investment Develop core technology Build world-class manufacturing skill	Informal market definition Focus groups Creative group sessions Segmentation (qualitative) Strategic alliances for new technology and production	Talk to customers Learn about competitors Creative techniques Identify niche Acquire technological ideas and skill
Design	Market reseach to identify consumer needs Perceptual maps, value maps Segmentation Positioning Quality design Engineer product benefits Design for manufacturing Marketing planning Sales forcasting Formal CBP	Customer interviews to identify customer needs Perceptual and value maps by qualitative methods Consider segmentation consider Positioning Quality design Coordinate with engineering and production Concept test Product placement CBP orientation	Talk to customers List customers needs Consider match between voice of the customer and technology Consider niche and competitors' strengths Partner with a customer Beta tests Financial support CBP concept
Testing	Advertising tests Laboratory tests Customer placement test Pretest or prelaunch tests Test market (if appropriate)	Informal communications tests Product tests Customer placement tests Prelaunch forecasts Monitor roll-out and improve	Prototype and beta tests Sell some Revise product Sell more
Introduction	National or International launch Adaptive control and formal monitoring	National (international) penetration Monitor customers	Build business Learn and grow
Life-cycle management	Total quality competitive monitoring and defense Innovation at maturity Continuing learning	Adjust marketing Watch competitors Improve product and service Quality management	Build business Expand capabilities Monitor market and competitors Improve product and service

the product is ready for launch, they may launch it at a smaller scale, but they will continue to monitor customers and the competitive environment.

Finally, as shown in the third column of Table 21.1, the entrepreneur will have even fewer resources to commit prior to selling a few products to generate revenue. This means that he or she must take a greater risk by moving forward without the up-front investment. In a sense, the entrepreneur, who has an idea in which to believe, substitutes the willingness to take a risk for investment. But the entrepreneur must still learn about customers, identify a niche and provide superior value with a creative product. The technology must match the customers' needs and the customers must learn of this. In Table 21.1 we have indicated one means by which an entrepreneur might obtain and use information on customers and competitors. Strategic analysis is used and limited only by the creativity of the entrepreneur. The key point is that the concepts apply and that the concepts of this text can enhance both success rates and profitability.

One key aspect of an entrepreneurial startup is that capital must be generated. One method is venture capital. A good CBP, demonstration that the product will fill a niche, a production plan, and a good marketing plan are key components in obtaining such capital. Another method to generate cash is to sell some products to the customers who need them most—usually based on partnering with a leading-edge customer. If this is the path taken, then the entrepreneur must monitor carefully the delivery of benefits to the customers to improve the product and its marketing to grow the business.

Entrepreneurship is risky. But with the concepts of this book, risk can be managed and the likelihood of success maximized.

VARIATIONS BY PRODUCT TYPE

The basic process of new-product development can be applied to innovations in a wide variety of product types. Only the emphasis shifts. Table 21.2 highlights some of the differences in implementing the process, depending upon whether the product type is a consumer packaged good, a consumer durable, an industrial product, a high-technology product, or a service. Table 21.2 suggests that the new-product development process can be customized to serve best the type innovating organization.

In opportunity identification, the organization should understand market needs and generate innovations in all of the industry types. There are slight variations in the manner in which the organization accomplishes these tasks. For example, as the product type shifts from a consumer good to an industrial good to a high-technology product lead users become more important. Such users are likely to experience greater need and actually modify

TABLE 21.2 Variations in the New-Product Development Process by the Type of Product

Phase of Development	Packaged Goods	Consumer Durable	Product Type Industrial Product	High-Technology Product	Service
Opportunity identification	Market definition Creative groups R & D	Market definition Creative groups R & D Leading-edge users	Market definition Creative groups R & D Leading-edge users	R & D User needs Technological forecast Leading-edge users	Target Market Creative groups Service plans
Design	Consumer needs Product features Positioning Forecasting Marketing mix	Consumer needs Product features Positioning Forecasting Diffusion Intro. strategy	Customer needs Economic value in use Buying process Selling	Customer needs Incremental value Generations Customer relations Selling Diffusion	Customer needs Benefits delivery Communication
Testing	Advertising Product Pretest Test market	Laboratory Consumer placement Prelaunch	Laboratory Joint development In-use tests	Benchmarks Beta tests	Pilot programs
Introduction	Launch Adaptive control	Launch Adaptive control Production monitoring	Launch Work with customers	Launch New development	Launch Adaptive control
Life-cycle management	Response analysis Competition Innovation	Diffusion Continuous improvement	Manage customer relations Continuous improvement	New technology generations	Monitor customers Monitor competition

today's products to meet those needs. By tapping such users new needs and new solutions can be identified early. Similarly as the focus shifts to industrial and high-technology products the role of R&D becomes more important. In fact, in many high-technology industries the firm must be thinking of enhancements to their core technologies as the means by which to fulfill customer needs. If they can not tap into the future, they risk developing products that are obsolete as soon as they reach the market.

In the design phase, a focus on customer needs is first and foremost across all product types. But there are some differences. For consumer durable products and high-technology products there are diffusion phenomena to be considered. Sales will start slow as innovators try the products and tell others. This growth in sales and the subsequent danger of saturation must be managed. In industrial products and high-technology products, the product may not be an end in itself but rather a component in a product that is eventually sold to the end user. In these cases one must consider the economic value in use of the component and think of the needs of the final system, not just the specific product. In high technology, innovations come at a rapid pace. The design phase must consider future generations and upgrades of the product, and choose a position that has staying power over several generations of products.

The marketing mix varies as well. In industrial markets and high technology markets there might be relatively few users rather than millions of consumers. In this case selling takes on a greater role as does the need to understand the buying process.

Testing is undertaken in all areas. Although the methods vary, the purpose is the same—to see that the final product fulfills the CBP at the desired cost, and meets reliability and quality standards. Test marketing is used for packaged goods, but because of high fixed start-up costs, consumer durable and industrial products usually are not test marketed. In these industries much more emphasis is placed on pretest market and prelaunch analyses.

In industrial products the user might be involved in the testing. If the product is sufficiently important to their production process, they might actually become involved in joint development. In high-technology products, especially software, there is the concept of a beta test. In a beta test the user knows that they are working with a product that is still under development. But because the user's needs are so acute, the user is willing to live with some "bugs" and work with the product developer to identify and remove the bugs and to suggest new features.

The next phase of development is the product introduction. If the development process has been followed, the product should have good potential. But no matter how good the product appears things can go wrong. Firms must monitor customers, the market, the environment, and the competitors no matter what product type is being developed. Adaptive control (informal or formal) leads to improvements in strategy that make or break the success of the launch. In consumer-durable products, production quality becomes key in launching a successful product. For all product types, the firm should work with customers to assure that the product (and service) fulfills the core-benefit promises. In high-technology products the firm must continue with new development to survive into the next generation. In all cases quality, as measured by fulfillment of customer's expectation of benefits in use, is a critical success factor.

In the final phase, life-cycle management, the product and its strategy are updated and improved for long-run profitability. This includes response analysis for marketing mix variables, continuous improvement in the production process, the management of customer relations, and the move to new technologies. The firm must continue to monitor customers and competitors and react accordingly.

These are differences in the development processes across product types, but there are many common concepts. These concepts include

- Listening to potential users early
- Evaluating opportunities
- Generating creative ideas
- Developing a CBP
- Integrating marketing, engineering, and production to deliver customer benefits
- Carefully designing communication
- Forecasting and evaluating profit potential for go/no go decisions
- Testing the product and the marketing strategy
- Monitoring customers and competition to assure continued improvement in the delivery of customer satisfaction

The challenge faced by the new-product team is to address these issues with the management and analysis techniques that are right for the product and the situation.

VARIATIONS BY STRATEGIC EMPHASIS

Early in this text we discussed a portfolio of strategies including both reactive and proactive strategies. It is important that each firm recognize the role that each of these strategies plays in new-product development. Not every product is a breakthrough product. Some products fill a niche, others provide incremental benefits relative to existing products, still others are "flankers" that build upon the reputation of a product line or brand extensions that move a firm into a different category. A successfully managed firm may use all of these product strategies.

Flankers and Niche Products

Naturally, the same level of investment is not needed or justified for niche or flanker products as for "clean-sheet" products. Nonetheless, the stages of the new-product process, as indicated in Chapter 3 and reproduced on the left of Figure 21.1a, provide valuable input as they assure that the opportunity is sufficient, that the product is designed to deliver customer benefits, that it does indeed deliver those benefits, that the marketing is appropriate to the CBP, and that the product is managed throughout launch and its subsequent life cycle. The only difference is that the level of analysis for flankers and niche products might be more similar to that for smaller businesses than for proactive, new products. (Review Table 21.1.)

Revolutionary Products

When a new product or technology has the potential to create a new market, the development process and research tools are not the same as when an existing technology is applied to a known market. Figure 21.2 shows four situations varying from known to unknown technologies and markets. Most of the procedures in this book were described in the context of extending known technologies in markets where the needs are known. Many of these procedures can be used in the other situations, but the emphasis is different.

For example if the needs are known, but the technology needed to meet them is unknown, R&D is the critical issue. For example, the customer's need to avoid suffering with the flu is known, but the medical technology is not available. Market research is not needed to direct R&D but rather technology management skills are necessary to assess the possibility of breaking through and solving the problem. A similar situation exists for AIDS, cancer, and heart disease so it is understandable that pharmaceutical companies allocate most of their new-product development to R&D. Research on superconducting materials and nuclear fusion for power generation would also fall in this cell.

If the technology exists but the needs are not known, market research can help. Lead-user analysis of those customers who foreshadow the needs of the market, voice-of-the-customer studies, and information-acceleration meth-

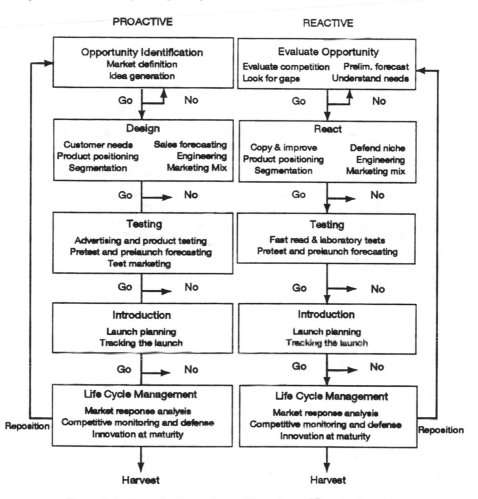

Figure 21.1   Example Comparison of Proactive and Reactive Strategies

ods can be used to reveal and understand the needs. Taking an extension of the known technology and finding a place to sell it is done by a team of R&D personnel who can texture the technology to the needs revealed by the market research.

If neither the needs nor the technology are known, both R&D and marketing skills are needed and the venture would be high risk compared to the other cells in Figure 21.2. Basic research is needed and concept testing of possible benefit propositions accelerated into the future environment may be appropriate.

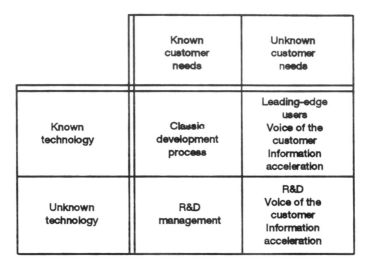

Figure 21.2   Technology-Needs Matrix.

Reactive Strategies

Even the best firm may be surprised by competition. In other cases there may not be sufficient protection for innovations to justify the cost and risk of development. For these and other situations a firm may consider reactive as well as proactive strategies.

We have sketched one potential reactive development process in Figure 21.1. Rather than proactively searching for opportunities, the reactive strategy *evaluates opportunities* as the firm becomes aware of them. For example, if a competitor identifies a market for home-health-care diagnostic devices, then a medical supplier might evaluate that opportunity to determine whether: (1) the product should be copied, (2) the innovator has left some customer-need gaps that can be filled, and (3) taking action now will be profitable.

If a go decision is made on the opportunity, the firm might *react* by copying the innovation (to the extent legally permitted) and improving it to satisfy better the needs of the customers. In some cases the firm might reverse-engineer the product or invent around the patent. Once the second-but-better product is developed, it must still be positioned vis-à-vis competition and engineered to maximize value. Target segments must be identified and the marketing mix set.

Because time is of the essence and because much market information can be gleamed from observing competition, the *testing* phase can be stream-lined. It may be sufficient to test the product in the laboratory and go straight from pretest or rollout to total market launch.

Defensive Innovation

Another form of reaction is defensive innovation. For example, when S. C. Johnson introduced Fiberall, positioned against the market leader, Metamucil, the makers of Metamucil were forced to develop a flanking product that matched the benefits—sugar-free—of the Fiberall attack. In this case, the makers of Metamucil, at the time G. D. Searle, knew the market and, because they also made the number one artificial sweetener, knew the technology. The major emphasis was on defending the niche by setting a marketing strategy to match the technological capabilities of the firm. (Of course they could not ignore customers—there were crucial design decisions to be made on flavors, packaging, density of the product, etc.)

Figure 21.1b gives but one example of how a proactive development process can be modified to become a reactive development process. The important management concept is that the stages can be customized to the situation. Some can be skipped, some can be streamlined, but in the end, the product must provide value to the customers and must do so better than competition. Many of the analysis and management techniques discussed throughout this text provide you with the tools to assure that both proactive and reactive strategies lead to profitable new products.

Acquisition and Licensing

The perspective of this book is that of the innovating organization. The strategic emphasis is toward high use of marketing, R&D, and production. Some firms find their strength lies in other areas and approach growth and development from a financial perspective. Products are acquired on attractive terms, a decentralized organization with a financial control is established, and the product divisions are asked to make the product grow to meet specified financial objectives. Some firms have used this strategy very successfully. Beatrice Foods has become a multibillion dollar company through such an acquisition strategy. Dexter Corporation built billion-dollar-per-year sales through focused acquistions in specialty undustrial materials. Many others have failed and lost substantial sums of money.

For the organization with financial muscle, acquisition may be a viable strategy, but acquisition strategies can be greatly improved through marketing analysis and innovation. For example, the CBP, product features, and advertising for the acquired firm should be examined. Although an acquisition may be attractive from a purely financial viewpoint, higher rewards can be obtained if the products and marketing mix are improved. The acquired firm's position in its market should be examined and new products introduced if opportunities are uncovered. Any innovations should proceed through the development process of design, testing, and introduction. Synergy produces premium returns or investment and the tools developed in this book can assess and build synergy within target markets.

Organizations with little or no excess financial resources, but with a viable patent, may wish to consider the licensing of that patented innovation to other organizations if it cannot utilize an innovation in its product markets or if substantial modifications are necessary to design and sell effective products in other markets. Such arrangements are attractive to the purchasing organization since they save R&D expense, lower risks, and gain access to technology. After a patent is granted, royalties can be collected for seventeen years. Organizations buying, selling, or licensing patent rights should recognize the legal dangers. The laser was patented and licensed in 1959 by Schawlow and Townes and royalties were collected. However, in 1977 a new patent was granted R. Gordon Gould for his work in 1957, which is now legally viewed as the basic patent. In another case it was after more than ten years of legal action that MIT received $10 million in royalties from IBM and other computer manufacturers for Jay Forrester's invention of the magnetic core memory.

Another licensing strategy is to give the license away in order to have your technology established as the standard. Sun Microsystem's open software licensing helped establish their architecture as standard and promote their RISC chip. Matsushita's alliance allowed VHS video format to dominate Sony's Betamax.

Production

Another strategy for product development is based on innovation in production. Costs are reduced and the product improved by production efficiency. The price for the "new" product is reduced and its value improved. This strategy is important for many products such as automobiles and consumer electronics. The advantage of production or process innovations is that they are much more difficult to copy because they are not so readily observed by competition. By becoming the low-cost or high-quality producer, the innovating firm gains market power that can prove quite profitable.

Production innovation capabilities can be leveraged by marketing innovation. Techniques such as the House of Quality, perceptual mapping, value mapping, and conjoint analysis identify those features that are most important to customers. By focusing process innovation on these features the firm can be assured that its improvements are of high value to the customer.

Flexible manufacturing capability also suggests a variation of the new product development process. With flexible manufacturing technology, smaller volumes can be produced at the low costs. For example, Mazda set up a production line that could produce five different models in volumes of 50,000 units per year at costs similar to a 250,000-per-year model run in the old factory. This enabled the Miata to be successful financially with a relatively small sales of 50,000 units per year. In fact Mazda delayed the Miata final development and launch until this new production technology was available. The flexible manufacturing innovation allows more detailed segmentation of markets and encourages wider product lines. In turn, this allows more targeted marketing and refined market research assessment and forecasting techniques.

Summary

The emphasis of marketing, R&D, engineering, finance, and production in an organization's overall strategy depends upon the strength of that organization. There are situations where flanker, revolutionary, reactive, defensive, acquisition, licensing, and production strategies better match an organization's unique capabilities than a strategy of major innovation through up-front investment. The firm should define a sustainable competitive advantage and customize its new-product development strategy to it. However, in each of these cases, many of the analysis techniques and concepts developed by considering up-front strategies are applicable and can improve the overall innovation strategy.

LOCAL INTRODUCTION AND EXPANSION TO NATIONAL AND INTERNATIONAL MARKETS

In this book we have advocated viewing the world as the market, but another strategy is to start small and expand to national and international markets. For example, Procter and Gamble took a brand of coffee, Folger's, that was popular in the western United States and turned it into a national brand by bringing it to the eastern United States. Many of Beatrice Foods' acquisitions were local or regional brands which it then took to national markets. The next step could be to take the brands global.

In regional expansion the emphasis in strategy is somewhat different. The firm has experience with the product which has a proven CBP and advertising strategy. Consumers in new regions are different but can be expected to have somewhat similar tastes. For example, many foods and many brands of beer vary by area to meet local tastes even though the basic product is the same. Some design work and fine-tuning may be necessary, but the emphasis is on testing. The differences between global areas can often be identified with a pretest market laboratory. Once a product is introduced it is important to monitor customer reaction and fine tune the product and its marketing strategy.

In today's economy it is important to look to global marketing. Not only does the firm gain economies of scale in production, but it can spread its risk and gain new knowledge as it moves into new international markets. Language, culture, competitors, distribution channels, media, and regulations often differ among countries, but the core idea of providing value to the customer remains. Throughout the world people buy products that are perceived as having benefits over existing products. The importance of attributes and responses to advertising may vary, but the behavioral process of response is similar. The opportunities for international expansion can be tapped by applying the concepts of the new-product development process with modification based on the constraints of the "new" country.

One important strategic decision is the degree of modification of the product as the product is rolled into new countries. Costs will be low if a standard product is used, but local tastes may not be matched well. The customer's tradeoff between low price and features that match their exact needs will determine the best strategy. The mapping and conjoint procedures outlined earlier in this book are useful in assessing this tradeoff and deciding on the best design. Sometimes the physical product can be standardized and advertising and distribution customized to local tastes. In other cases the product is standardized globally because the market is defined not by country but by psychological and use dimensions. For example the top of the line graphic computer work station for genetic engineers may not vary among Japan, Germany, or the United States, because these groups are homogeneous with respect to the segment needs defined by the use of genetic molecular analysis.

ADAPTING TO EXTERNAL CHALLENGES—OTHER CLIENTELE

When implementing a new-product development effort, an organization may perceive that many constraints limit its freedom. Some of these challenges grow out of the need to use intermediaries to distribute products, others from public interest groups, and of course, government regulation. We highlight briefly some of the aspects of these perceived constraints and consider strategies to deal with them. In each case the clientele is different and communication with respect to each stakeholder group must be considered carefully.

Channels

In many product markets middlemen serve a physical distribution, inventory, selling, or servicing function. These wholesalers, brokers, distributors, or retailers are independent decision makers. For example, a retail food store decides whether it will stock a new product—not the manufacturer. By making the product attractive to the retailer through an adequate margin, special deals, high quality, and consumer advertising the firm can gain shelf space. Some firms directly influence the retail outlet by the use of missionary sales personnel who stock the shelf and install special displays for their brand. In industrial markets, sales effort may be directed both at distributors and customers. In some cases distributors are order takers, while in others they carry out the complete selling function.

The best way to deal with the channel of distribution is to realize that channel members are your customers too. The desires of the channel participant must be considered to assure adequate distribution and selling effort. Some authors have attempted to understand how the channel responds by using explicit models (Stern and El-Ansary 1988; Jeuland and Shugan 1983; Shugan 1985; Coughlan and Wernerfelt 1989). Many of these analyses recognize that there is an issue of channel cooperation. If the channel works together the total channel profits are larger. However, each channel member may have unilateral incentives to deviate from cooperation resulting in less profits for everyone. It is beyond the scope of this text to discuss in-depth how one might form understandings within a channel to encourage cooperation, but the techniques of this text can help you understand the perceived needs of your channel partners and thus arm you to deal with them to achieve coordination. For example, it is reasonable to conduct perception voice-of-the-customer studies with middlemen to see what new-product design and promotion actions would result in the decision to accept the product and sell it aggressively.

Public Interest Groups

Consumer advocacy groups have had an influence on new-product development. Their attacks on issues such as television violence have resulted in some manufacturers withdrawing advertising from some programs. Concern over advertising to children may affect the marketing of new foods. These groups have highlighted product safety and the product liability of manufacturers. The cost of product liability insurance has risen dramatically as claims have increased in volume and the size of awards have grown. Asbestos claims put Johns Manville out of business and the crashes of the Piper Malibu may have the same result on Piper Aircraft Corporation.

The best way to deal with public interest groups is to design the new product to avoid safety problems. If a product is free of design and manufacturing defects and customers are given clear warning of dangers associated with a product's use, then your organization may face fewer liability claims.

When safety is a customer need, and it often is, a good strategy is to design in safety as part of the CBP and promote it.

By testing products rigorously before they are put on the market, you might preempt consumer watchdog groups and the resulting regulatory pressure. By involving customers in the design you can catch and correct problems early before they become a major problem later.

Similarly, environmental complaints by "green" interests may be preempted or even converted into market opportunities by designing environmentally sound products. Recycled paper for packaging may reduce costs and improve the environmental appeal of products. The Nature Company earned considerable market penetration with a line of cosmetics that were not tested on animals. Rather than resisting pollution standards, a firm may be proactive and create a better image with its clientele groups by leading in improving water and air quality.

Government Regulators

Often a new-product-development effort will face government regulations. For example, new pharmaceutical products in the United States must receive approval from the Federal Drug Administration. The approval process can take many years and require extensive support from the potential manufacturer. In automobiles regulations on safety (passive restraints, door reinforcement, etc.), fuel economy, and emissions have resulted in a need for creative design. OSHA regulations in the work place require attention to the production process.

How should a firm deal with these regulations. One approach is to "fight it out" with a large legal staff to defend actions to the letter of the law by drawn out legal battles. A second approach is to modify regulations, if they are perceived as unfair, by lobbying, public relations, and advertising to customer groups. In some cases these tactics are justified.

As with customer advocacy groups, the most mature strategy is to preempt regulations by the careful design of the product and its marketing mix. By recognizing that government regulators are another "customer" group, by understanding the pressures under which they operate, and then designing the product to deliver high value without unnecessary ill effects on the environment, can result in new products that meet or exceed government regulations.

We feel one of the most effective overall responses is through major innovation. Although regulations identify errors of commission, there is a greater error in the omission of innovation. Corporate responsibility should direct the organization to serve society's needs. One of the most beneficial ways of doing so is by creating new products to fill these needs. In return for innovation, society grants the organization profit. It is our view that organizations should concentrate on major innovations where benefits will be perceived widely. For example, the FTC dropped its anti-trust complaints against Quaker Oats in part because of Quaker's record of innovation in products such as "100% Natural Cereal."

Firms should not restrict innovation only to their traditional businesses. Entry into new categories will promote competition and result in new products which serve society better. Although there will be times when specific regulatory actions will have to be dealt with in the courts, a preemptive strategy based on solid innovation is highly desirable.

Employees and Stock Holders

As well as customers, channel members, public interest groups, and government regulators there are two other stakeholders who deserve special consideration while developing new products.

The employees have a large role in determining the quality of products and services. We need them firmly committed to the new product if it is to be a success. For example, Saturn and the Japanese automotive transplants in the United States used their "greenfield" advantage of starting fresh to build employee commitments to quality. These commitments became the cornerstone of their Core Benefit Propositions. New products put demands on employees and they need to understand the strategy and buy into it if the firm expects them to adapt to the new changes and be part of total quality and innovation programs.

Stockholders and financial-support sources also need special communication efforts. Their commitment to the strategy and assessment of potential is necessary to gain capital support. Advertising, personal selling by the CEO and CFO, and persuasive documentation based on market research for the new product can help bring this stakeholder group into the widened new-product team.

SUMMARY

The new-product development process is quite general and can be adapted to a wide variety of situations, but it is not a "cookbook" procedure. The concepts are sound and the analytic tools are powerful, but they need an intelligent manager to use them. Part of this use is a customization of the process to fit the scale of the organization, product type, strategic emphasis, geographic expansion, and external challenges (other customers). This chapter has outlined some of the basic considerations in customization, but the final success depends on your ability to use creatively the ideas presented here in an actual new-product development process.

REVIEW QUESTIONS

21.1. Discuss how the introduction of a new product may vary as the size of the organization varies. As the product type varies. As both vary.

21.2. Suppose you are the manager of a small business and wish to test a possible new product. How would your strategy vary under the following conditions?
  a. You are entering a market dominated by many small businesses.
  b. You are entering a market dominated by one small business.
  c. You are entering a market dominated by several large firms.
  d. You are entering a market composed of large firms, small businesses, and several entrepreneurs.
  e. You are creating your own market.
  f. Your product will compete in two different markets.

21.3. Consider a large firm and a small business each considering launching exactly the same new product. How might they each customize the development process?

21.4. How should a firm allocate its funds between basic research and applied research? How would this allocation depend on the industry, the number of firms in the industry, the size of the research staff, and the size of the company or whether a flanker or revolutionary product strategy is to be used?

21.5. What are the advantages and disadvantages of an "up-front development effort" over a "reactive development effort"? Under which conditions would each strategy be recommended?

21.6. Suppose there are definite worldwide geographic differences in tastes for a new beverage line. How would this situation affect new-product design and testing?

21.7. When launching a new line of 20-speed bicycles, how would you deal with the channel of distribution, potential consumer advocacy groups, and potential government regulations?

22

New-Product Development Revisited

The new-product-development process is a flexible and powerful tool for designing and marketing successful new products. As indicated in the previous chapter it can be customized for a variety of product types including frequently purchased packaged products, durable products such as consumer electronics and automobiles, services such as transportation, health and financial services, industrial (business-to-business) products such as surge protectors, integrated circuit boards, and servo-motors, and high-technology products such as board testers, computers, and software. The process can be further adapted to deal with a variety of external constraints, can be applied differentially to various scales of organizations from the small entrepreneur to the large, multidivisional, international firm, can be used to support global marketing, and can function as an approach to involve effectively diverse clientele groups.

With some customization the parts of the new-product process are extremely useful for a variations by strategic emphasis. If your organization is attempting to be a pioneer in the market you will begin with opportunity identification and apply the process through to life-cycle management, iterating as necessary and picking and choosing the techniques and concepts that are right for your situation. But even if you are forced to react to competition, you can evaluate the opportunity with a modified opportunity identification phase, can use positioning and segmentation methods to identify gaps and produce a second, but better product, and so on to ensure that your reaction is optimized to blunt competition and return profit to your organization. No matter what your strategic emphasis, the concepts of the new-product development process provide indispensable tools for long-run profitability.

In this chapter we review the new-product development process in two ways. We first revisit the correlates of success and the reasons for failure that were introduced in chapter 3. We indicate how each can be addressed within the phases of the process. We then provide a checklist for new-product development. If you can indicate how to respond to each of the challenges on the checklist, avoid the causes for failure, and build on the correlates of success, then you can feel confident of success as you begin the major challenge of new-product development.

CORRELATES OF SUCCESS REVISITED

Table 22.1 revisits the correlates of success that were identified in chapter 3 and indicates how each correlate of success is addressed with one or more phases of the new-product development process. The original list in chapter 3 included only the factors formally studied in the new product literature. But we have revealed three more factors in the exposition of this book: (1) short time to market, (2) worldwide strategy, and (3) quality and customer satisfaction. These are now included in Table 22.1 and reviewed subsequently.

Match to Customer Needs

Matching customer needs is a core concept of the development process. The focus on customer needs in targeted market segments begins when the market is defined and ideas are generated based explicitly on providing the customer with desired benefits. This focus continues through design for quality, perceptual maps, value maps, benefit segmentation, and preference analysis. It is tested and improved in all stages of testing, launch, and life-cycle management.

High Value to the Customer

High value goes hand in hand with providing customer benefits. Ideas are generated with value to the customer in mind. In design, value maps give an explicit indication of value and the price is set with value in mind. This

TABLE 22.1 Correlates of Success Revisited

Correlate of Success	Opportunity Identification		Design			Testing			Introduction	Life-Cycle Management
	Market Definition Strategy	Idea Generation	Positioning Segmentation	Forecasting	Design for Quality	Product Advertising Tests	Pretest Prelaunch	Test Market	Monitor Launch	Monitor Improve Rejuvenate
Match customer needs	✓	✓	✓		✓	✓	✓	✓	✓	✓
High value to the customer	✓	✓	✓		✓		✓	✓		
Innovative		✓	✓		✓					✓
Technical superiority	✓	✓	✓			✓				✓
Screened on growth, analysis, DSS	✓			✓			✓	✓	✓	
Favorable competitive environment	✓		✓						✓	✓
Fit internal company strengths	✓			✓			✓			
Communication among functions		✓	✓		✓					✓
Top-management support	✓				✓		✓			✓
Enthusiastic champion				✓		✓	✓	✓	✓	
New-product organization	✓		✓			✓	✓	✓	✓	✓
Use new-product process	✓	✓	✓	✓		✓	✓	✓	✓	✓
Avoid unnecessary risk				✓		✓		✓	✓	
Short time to market	✓		✓		✓		✓			
Worldwide strategy	✓		✓		✓		✓			
Quality and customer satisfaction	✓	✓					✓	✓	✓	✓

651

value is then tested when customers are exposed to the product and its marketing strategy in pretest/prelaunch forecasting and test market. Only if the product provides high value to the customer will customers buy it (recall the value-priority concept), and only if customers buy the product will it pass these design and testing benchmarks. The value is captured in an explicit core benefit proposition and its fulfillment through product features that satisfy detailed needs.

Innovative

For products to be innovative they must provide new benefits or provide old benefits in new ways. Idea generation is the first step toward this goal, but positioning and segmentation continue the quest for innovativeness by identifying key benefits and what is required to exceed competitive offerings. Innovation should be reflected in the benefit propostion, product performance, and quality.

Technical Superiority

Technical superiority requires either good R&D, prior technological expertise, or acquisition of technology. To some extent this is addressed in opportunity identification when ideas are generated based on available or to-be-developed technology. The firm should have core technical competencies that can be matched to targeted markets to deliver benefits to customers with product technologies that represent a unique competitive advantage. Technical superiority is also a critical ingredient in the design of quality through procedures like QFD or House of Quality that assure that the R&D, engineering, production, and marketing groups are working together with a focus on the voice of the customer. Technical superiority can never be taken for granted and without it the chances of success are not high. The assumption of technical superiority is tested in the R&D lab as well as with customers and is continually improved throughout the life cycle of the product.

Screening, Analysis, and Decision Support Systems

Opportunities are screened formally in market definition; this screening includes concepts of growth, vulnerability, competitive response, margins, etc. These criteria are checked throughout the process in forecasting, pretest/prelaunch testing, and test markets (if appropriate). Analysis is the key to reducing risk and obtaining customer feedback to improve product design, position, and targeting. Decision support systems are important in tracking the launch and managing adaptively the life cycle to earn profits on a global basis.

Favorable Competitive Environment

One can never assure that competitive response will be favorable. After all, competitors are seeking profitable new products as well. However, competitive response is considered when identifying markets, products are positioned with competitors in mind, and segments are chosen to avoid unnecessary competition.

In the mature phase the firm should consider cooperative strategies to avoid price wars and develop sustainable competitive advantages.

Fit Internal Company Strengths

Internal company strengths are explicit criteria in target market definition. They are reviewed throughout the process, especially in pretest/prelaunch testing and test market (if appropriate).

Communication among Functions

It's not just communication among functions that matters, but the amount and type of communication. In this book we have emphasized the need to use techniques which encourage and enhance communication among the functions of marketing, manufacturing, R&D, engineering, and general management. Communication also is addressed early in the process by involving multiple functions in screening markets and identifying ideas with which to enter those markets.

Top-Management Support

Top-management support is a necessary condition for success in new products. Careful attention to reviewing tactics and strategy throughout the process provide the information necessary for top management to evaluate progress and provide their support when the support is justified. Review Figure 20.2. We have indicated this involvement in Table 22.1 by the review checkpoints in market definition, completing design, pretest/prelaunch testing, and test market (if appropriate).

Enthusiastic Champion

No process can ensure that a champion will emerge, but this role is present in almost every successful new-product effort. By involving multiple functions, encouraging top management support, and providing information on customer needs, the new-product process makes the situation ripe for such a champion to thrive. It gives the champion the information and power to back up the emotional commitment to move the project ahead. The champion plays an important role in all phases, but especially at the go/no go decision points.

New-Product Organization

The effective formal and informal organizational functioning is necessary for a coordinated and effective new product development program. Many functions must be involved and committed. This means good communication, incentives, and people must be in place (review chapter 20). The people in the organization in all functions must be empowered to make decisions without a rigid hierarchical review. This is necessary throughout the process.

Use New-Product Process

The process must be disciplined, but at the same time encourage creativity. It must exert a force to meet deadlines, but also be flexible enough to adapt to unexpected difficulties that are bound to emerge.

Avoid Unnecessary Risk

By screening opportunities, by using "what-if" forecasting and the formal testing techniques, and by monitoring and reacting to the product launch, an organization balances risk and reward. New products are risky and the risk can never by eliminated, but careful use of these phases of the new-product process lets an organization take those risks with confidence that the risks are justified.

Short Time to Market

The time from strategic commitment to launch should be short. The threat of a competitor getting to market first or the danger of missing a technology or market window of opportunity means success can be obtained only if there is a short cycle time to form ideas to develop and launch. This has to be addressed in the design of the process (e.g., overlapping of phases in the process, skipping steps), getting customer input early, use of advanced design and manufacturing technology (e.g., CAD/CAM and flexible manufacturing) and effective organization functioning.

Worldwide Strategy

To be successful a firm's new-product development program should have a global focus. Market definition should consider the world to be a market with various segments. Production is likely to be dispersed and, increasingly, technical alliances are occurring worldwide. Selection of segments may be by demographic or psychological basis rather than countries and the design should reflect the needs in those segments. Forecasting may be based on a global "roll-out" and managing the life cycle leads to continued learning about the global opportunities.

Quality and Customer Satisfaction

Quality should be reflected in all phases of the process of strategy, design, and implementation. It should be evident as a driving force in all functions and at all levels of management. Testing confirms that the quality is delivered and adaptive control of the launch and life cycle assures that the customer is satisfied with the delivery of the benefit proposition.

REASONS FOR FAILURE REVISITED

Table 22.2 revisits the reasons for failure in new-product development. Each of these reasons can be avoided by techniques and concepts in one or more of the phases of the new-product development process.

Market Too Small

This issue is addressed from the start when markets are screened in the market definition phase. In design, market size is considered explicitly when positioning the product vis-à-vis competition and vis-à-vis a target segment of customers. The size of the market is checked and go/no go decisions are made during "what-if" forecasting, and pretest/prelaunch/test-market testing. All told, the process does not proceed unless the market is of sufficient size in terms of volume and potential profitability.

Poor Match for the Company

Markets are identified that match a company's strengths whether they be in production, technology, marketing, distribution, or finance. These markets and the resulting product/marketing strategy are testing in pretest/prelaunch/test-market testing. Throughout the process go/no go review

TABLE 22.2 Reasons for Failure Revisited

Reason for Failure	Opportunity Identification			Design			Testing		Introduction	Life Cycle Management
	Market Definition	Idea Generation	Position Segment	Forecasting	Design for Quality	Product, Adv. Tests	Pretest Prelaunch	Test Market	Monitor Launch	Monitor Improve Rejuvinate
Market too small	✓		✓	✓			✓	✓		
Poor match for company	✓						✓	✓		
Not new/not different		✓	✓							
No real benefit			✓			✓	✓			
Poor positioning versus competition			✓			✓				
Inadequate support from the channel of distribution	✓				✓			✓	✓	
Forecasting error	✓			✓			✓	✓	✓	
Poor timing	✓		✓		✓		✓		✓	✓
Competitive response	✓		✓	✓	✓			✓	✓	✓
Shifts in technology		✓			✓				✓	✓
Changes in customers' tastes			✓		✓			✓	✓	✓
Changes in environmental constraints	✓				✓			✓	✓	✓
Poor repeat purchase or no diffusion of sales	✓			✓			✓	✓	✓	
Poor after-sales service					✓			✓		✓
Insufficient return of investment	✓			✓	✓		✓	✓	✓	✓
Lack of coordination in functions	✓	✓	✓					✓		
Organizational problems	✓		✓						✓	✓

points assure top management that the product and market fit the strengths and avoid the weaknesses of the firm.

Not New/Not Different

Parity products are not sufficient. Successful products provide customer benefits in ways that are not otherwise available. In the new-product process we use idea-generation techniques to generate creative solutions to customer needs. By understanding the structure and priorities of customer needs we position our product to provide unique benefits. Product tests with customers check whether or not these benefits are delivered.

No Real Benefit

Providing benefits is the key concept underlying the new-product development process. The quality design procedures, perceptual maps, value maps, preference analysis, and benefit segmentation all address this issue by highlighting to the new-product team customer benefits and by linking the voice of the customer to the engineering characteristics that deliver the benefits. These benefits are tested explicitly in product tests and in pretest/prelaunch/test-market testing.

Poor Positioning versus Competition

Perceptual maps and value maps identify the benefits that competitive products provide and preference analysis identifies the tradeoffs that customers are willing to make with respect to those benefits in target market segments. An integrated new-product design effort uses these tools to position the product vis-à-vis competition and understand how they should react to competitive counter actions.

Inadequate Support from the Channel of Distribution

Understanding channel structures and their likely response helps the new-product team identify target markets. A completed design considers channel functions and plans based on the recognition that channels are customers too. Channel response is tested by personal interviews and with test markets when they are feasible. They are monitored during launch whether test markets are feasible or not

Forecasting Error

Forecasting is given attention throughout the process. Informally in the opportunity identification and early design phases and formally during "what-if" forecasting. These forecasts are refined and further diagnostic information is obtained during the testing phases of pretest/prelaunch forecasting and test market (when appropriate). These checkpoints are designed to assure that key negative findings are not ignored and provide precise and timely sales forecasts for go/no go decisions.

Poor Timing

By monitoring competition and technology, by selecting a competitive positioning to pre-empt or out-maneuver competition, and by using quality techniques to reduce cycle time, a firm can assure that they enter the market at the appropriate time.

Competitive Response

Competitors will respond. You cannot avoid it, but you can plan for it and limit competitive impacts. Careful attention to the selection of a market with competitive vulnerability and with characteristics that make it feasible to defend can give you a head start on competitive response. You can position your product and choose a segment to minimize the impact of competitive response and you can check that potential impact during "what-if" forecasting. A good marketing mix including advertising, promotion, channel selection, sales force messages, and so on strengthen your position to withstand competitive response. You can plan further in pretest/prelaunch testing, check competitive response in test market, and monitor and react during launch and life-cycle management.

Major Shifts in Technology

Products succeed because they fulfill customer needs better (and at a better price) than competition. In order to be in the best position to deliver benefits most effectively and efficiently, it is important to monitor technology when developing ideas and when designing the product. By monitoring during launch and life-cycle management, the product can be improved continuously based on new technology.

Changes in Customers' Tastes

Because customers' tastes (needs and benefit priorities) are measured and monitored throughout the process, you can react if they change. The key concept here is that customers' tastes can change—continual monitoring before every go/no go point in the process is necessary to avoid the pitfall of changing tastes.

Changes in Environmental Constraints

One way to avoid this pitfall is to be set to react quickly to changes, another way is to anticipate potential changes and plan accordingly. Thus, we avoid the pitfall of changes in environmental constraints by anticipating them in market definition and monitoring them at every go/no go checkpoint. Political, social, and economic changes will occur at some point in the development cycle so explicit contingency actions should be considered when the changes are evident.

Poor Repeat Purchase or No Diffusion of Sales

Careful attention throughout the process to quality, benefits delivery, and customer needs helps the new-product team design and market a product that customers find useful and are willing to purchase. Thus, a well-designed product does not just generate one-time purchase but generates repeat sales and/or diffusion of sales. These issues are addressed explicitly in market definition, in "what-if" forecasting, in pretest/prelaunch/test-market testing, and in the monitoring of the new-product launch. Customer satisfaction is the key to rapid diffusion and good repeat purchase.

Poor After-Sales Service

A quality product is not just the physical product but the marketing mix and the after-sales service that goes with the product. A complete design considers service. Service procedures are tested, monitored, and improved in testing, introduction, and throughout the life cycle of the product. By "getting it all right" the new-product team ensures success and continued, long-run profitability. The customer needs to get quality delivered in a manner that perceived as meeting or exceeding expectations.

Insufficient Return on Investment

Long-run profitability is the ultimate indicator of success. A product may be a sales success, but if it is not profitable it is a failure. Careful attention to profit and related criteria (margin, scale, vulnerability, etc.) in market definition set the stage for profitability. "What-if" forecasts check potential profitability and all aspects of completing the design keep this focus. The go/no go checkpoints as well as diagnostic improvements during testing, introduction, and life-cycle management continue to improve the product and its marketing strategy for maximum profit.

Lack of Coordination in Functions

Coordination is an explicit goal in the design process and cross-functional communication techniques related to quality provide the means. Coordination is also encouraged in the opportunity identification steps of market definition and idea generation. If the functions are involved early, they are less likely to quarrel later.

Organizational Problems

The new-product process cannot avoid organizational problems, but its focus on integration and on providing the right information to the right people at the right time in the development process helps mitigate organizational problems. The go/no go checkpoints encourage critical review so that there are no misunderstandings that later lead to problems. Initial process design should include careful thought to formal structure and informal roles necessary for success.

CHECKLIST FOR NEW-PRODUCT DEVELOPMENT

We have revisited the correlates of success and potential reasons for failure by indicating how the new-product process addresses both. In this section we present a proactive checklist for new-product development as a third review perspective. If you know how to address each of these questions, you have learned the basics of new-product development. You are now ready to apply the concepts, ideas, and techniques presented in this textbook. You are ready to manage new-product development for success and profitability.

1. *Does our development strategy reflect the best long-term interest of our organization?* It is easy to concentrate on short-term results by making small enhancements to products. The long term should be reflected in a balance of proactive and reactive strategies that focus on customer needs and deliver the benefits that fulfill these needs in a manner that exceeds the benefits offered by competitive products. The right market, idea, position, focused target segment, product, service, and marketing mix are all key to successful new-product development. These can be achieved by careful attention to detail, continued customer input, inte-

gration of R&D, engineering, and marketing and disciplined management through the various go/no go checkpoints.

2. *Are we allocating enough time, money, and talent to the up-front phases of new-product development?* Early efforts pay off in lower expected risks and costs of successful innovation. Although the up-front investment may appear to add cost and extra steps to the process, it enables the identification of profitable innovations, minimizes the risk of failure, maximizes creativity, and leads to the best possible new-product introduction. Up-front development enables the new-product team to take the most risks when the least investment is at stake. It provides the information necessary to refine the product and its marketing so that once it is launched, it is likely to succeed. It can prevent delays in time to market by getting the design right in the beginning and focusing the team's design strategy on the most important need dimensions.

3. *Are we targeting the right market?* By considering the product/market strategy early in the process you can avoid later problems. A fantastic technological product idea will not be sufficient if it does not address customer needs in a market that can provide adequate return on the new-product investment. A great need identification will be of little value unless the firm can employ its skills to create a competitive advantage through technology, production, or marketing. Market definition identifies markets that match your firm's capabilities, have potential growth and scale, are vulnerable to your entry, and are defensible. If a good market is found, idea generation creates concepts with which to enter the market. Later, benefit segmentation refines the target market to build upon your strengths and avoid competitors' strengths.

4. *Are R&D, engineering, production, and marketing working together?* Each of these functions has its strengths, but each function represents a different thoughtworld with different goals and different languages. It is difficult to coordinate these functions but the evidence is clear that when they are coordinated, new products are more successful. By using techniques that link the voice of the customer to the engineering and technological characteristics of the product you ensure that the product delivers customer benefits. By using techniques such as QFD you encourage communication and by involving all of these functions from the start you avoid later problems.

5. *Are we fully using our creative skills?* People and organizations have tremendous creative potential, but if that potential is not tapped, new products may not be successful. Concentrating too much on mature products that are generating cash and devoting too much time to "fire-fighting" all sap an organization's creative energies. Many ideas can

result by organizing to free up time for creativity and, if necessary, using formal creative idea-generation techniques. Throughout the process it is productive to achieve a balance among the analytic and the creative. For example, perceptual maps and value maps are analytical tools, but they can provide the spark for a creative positioning of the new product. But do not forget the people. Recruiting should be based on creative skills and a track record of producing creative designs.

6. *Have we developed a good CBP for our product?* Customers buy products that provide them with the benefits they need. These benefits can be direct or they can be derived by the value of the product in use. But in either case you must identify the benefits customers desire and understand their priorities with respect to those benefits. The CBP states the benefits—unique and not so unique—that your product provides relative to competitive offerings. The CBP also includes a statement of value that reflects the relationship of the product's benefits to its price.

7. *Do our products fulfill their CBP?* It is not just enough to identify an opportunity. The product must be designed to fulfill the core benefits. This means a coordination of R&D, engineering, production, and marketing to design the product. It means as well testing the product with customers and developing a marketing mix that communicates the core benefits. Customers will be happy when their needs are met.

8. *Are we using pretest market or prelaunch forecasting techniques?* For frequently purchased packaged goods, pretest market simulators provide accurate forecasts and useful diagnostic information at a relatively low level of investment. For durable goods, where the product cannot be produced for a test market, prelaunch forecasting, and information-acceleration laboratory techniques provide forecasts of volume or what it will take to sell the planned volume that will be produced. Services, high tech, and industrial product environments can be simulated in market research procedures as well. After accelerating the relevant information to customers, measures of acceptance can be obtained for sales and diffusion forecasting.

9. *When test markets are appropriate, are we using the full potential of the information that we could obtain?* In some cases producing enough product for a test market requires a major investment in a production facility and in other cases time-to-market pressures are high. In these cases prelaunch forecasting rather than test marketing is the most appropriate activity. But in cases where enough product can be made for a test market without an investment approaching that of a full-scale launch and when risks are large, test markets can provide valuable information. Test markets do more than simply replicate a national or international plan.

Experiments and customer response measures supply data for behavioral models that help diagnose improvements, maximize profit, and make conditional forecasts. Good test market models identify the best positioning and marketing mix for a full-scale launch.

10. *Have we implemented a control system for the launch of the new product?* The advantages of development efforts do not stop when the product is launched. Environments change, customer tastes shift, competitors respond, channels change, and so on. With a control system you can identify the unexpected events, make a timely response, and improve performance and profitability. There may be as many opportunities to earn profit in the revision of a launch plan as in revisions of a product plan based on earlier phases of the development process. Continuing learning and adaptive control are important in launch success.

11. *Are we maximizing the profit potential from our maturing products?* Profit, as a reward for risk taking and creativity, comes as the product matures. A monitoring system maximizes these rewards through response analyses. There are opportunities to revise the marketing mix, reduce cost through process innovation, add flankers, or reposition the product to increase profits. A decision support system is valuable in today's markets. Innovation at the end of a life cycle can lead to another profitable life cycle or, at minimum, extend a product's life long enough to support more innovation to replace the product. Good defensive strategy throughout a product's life cycle ensures the best continuing stream of profits. Continued product improvement can be a good defense and set the stage for a rejuvenation of the life cycle.

12. *Do we have the best people managing and working on our new products?* People make a process real. Success comes when each functional group and outside partner makes its contribution and when that contribution is coordinated with all other groups. The right organization enhances creativity while controlling risk. Confidence and competence backed by energy, drive, commitment, and effective formal and informal organization structures are needed to succeed.

13. *Is our process up to date with respect to the latest techniques and concepts of new-product development?* Many proven techniques have been presented in this book and more will be developed in the future. You can use the techniques intelligently if you know what they can and cannot do, and when they are appropriate and when they are not. You should know their strengths and their pitfalls and make sure they reflect your organization's needs. A successful new-product team is neither enthralled with the elegance of a technique nor intimidated by its seeming complexity. The formal and informal techniques presented in this textbook

for each phase of the development process are powerful and useful, but they can be misused. We hope that we armed you with the knowledge that is necessary to get the maximum benefit from each phase of new-product development. We hope that our presentation has been sufficiently generic that you can adapt as new techniques are developed.

FUTURE OF NEW-PRODUCT DEVELOPMENT

New-product development is exciting. It combines the thrill of technical, marketing, and production creativity with the challenge of global competition and the satisfaction of providing benefits to customers. To succeed one must be both imaginative and realistic. The potential rewards are great, but so is the risk.

The successful new-product team represents a wide range of managerial functions including marketing, R&D, engineering, finance, production, and administration. The team keeps a long-term managerial perspective, but balances it against the short-term organizational needs for profit performance and the need to get to market. Most importantly, the team channels creativity with a disciplined process and a set of effective, proven concepts and techniques. The team matches corporate strategy with innovation tactics to develop products that earn substantial profits and investment returns by delivering benefits to customers.

The critical success factors that have characterized new-product development have changed in emphasis over time. In the 1970s the five most talked about concepts were (1) market and benefit segmentation; (2) product positioning and perceptual mapping; (3) stochastic forecasting models; (4) creative group methods (e.g., Synectics); and (5) idea screening. In the 1980s these concepts became standard components in new-product development, and new ideas and emphasis became prominent. In the 1980s the critical factors were described as (1) portfolio theory (popularized by the Boston Consulting Group this portfolio was a matrix of market share and sales growth that defined "cash cows," "stars," "dogs," and "?"); (2) premarket forecasting and conjoint analysis; (3) decision support systems and UPC scanner data; (4) technology/marketing integration and lead users; and (5) competitive strategy and sustainable competitive advantage. In the 1990s the five most popular issues are (1) total quality; (2) customer satisfaction; (3) time to market; (4) manufacturing integration with R&D and marketing; and (5) worldwide strategy and alliances. In the future the most salient concepts will again change, but the cumulative effect of this history will be a growing and powerful set of concepts, strategies, and tools that are proven in use to be effective methods of creating successful new products.

As we enter the 21st century the challenges will be even greater as technology advances more rapidly, international competition becomes more fierce, customer needs become more refined and subject to change, and as startling social, political and organizational change occurs. New approaches and techniques will be developed and existing concepts will have to be improved. The environment will be changing rapidly so the new-product team must learn to adapt and evolve to thrive under new challenges and new goals.

As organizations justify their role in society and our changing environment, one of the important rationales for their existence will become evident. The success of the firm will be based increasingly on innovation to fulfill societal and customer needs. Profit will be justified as the reward for taking risks and innovating. Major new products that increase the physical, economic, psychological, social, environmental, and aesthetic well-being of people will be a major method for organizations to fulfill their social responsibilities, earn a return on the investment of stockholders, provide for the well being for their employees, and contribute to economic and social progress.

We hope that this textbook has helped equip you with the managerial perspective and set of tools to meet this responsibility to design and market new products.

REVIEW QUESTIONS

22.1. Review opportunity identification, design, testing, introduction, and life-cycle management indicating specifically how each can be used to enhance success and minimize failure in new-product development.

22.2. Discuss the checklist for new-product development. How can you address each question for frequently purchased products? For durable products? For industrial products? For high-technology products? For services?

22.3. Discuss the organizational issues involved for each question in the checklist.

22.4. Discuss the future, as you see it, for new-product development. What will be the five most talked about concepts of new product development in the 21st century?

Bibliography

AAKER, D., and J. MEYERS, *Advertising Management* (Englewood Cliffs, NJ: Prentice Hall, 1975).

―――, and K. L. KELLER, "Consumer Evaluations of Brand Extensions," *Journal of Marketing*, 54 (1), (1990), 27–41.

―――, and D. M. STAYMAN, "Measuring Audience Perceptions of Commercials and Relating Them to Ad Impact," *Journal of Advertising Research*, 30(4), (August/September 1990), 7–18.

ABERNATHY, W. J., and N. BALOFF, "Interfunctional Planning for New Product Introduction," *Sloan Management Review*, 14 (2), (Winter 1972–73), 25–44.

―――, and K. WAYNE, "Limits of the Learning Curve," *Harvard Business Review*, 52, no. 5 (September–October 1974), 109–19.

ADDELMAN, S., "Orthogonal Main-Effect Plans for Asymmetrical Factorial Experiments," *Technometrics*, 4 (1) (February 1962), 21–57.

ADLER, L., "Time Lag in New Product Development," *Journal of Marketing Research* (January 1966), 17–21.

ADLER P. S., and K. B. CLARK, "Behind the Learning Curve: A Sketch of the Learning Process," *Management Science*, 37 (3), (March 1991), 267–81.

―――, and D. A. HELLELOID, "Effective Implementation of Integrated CAD/CAM: A

667

Model," *IEEE Transactions on Engineering Management,* EM-34, (2), (May 1987), 101–107.

AHL, D. H., "New Product Forecasting Using Consumer Panels," *Journal of Marketing Research,* 7 (2), (May 1970), 159–67.

ALBERS, S., "PROPOPP: A Program Package for Optimal Positioning in an Attribute Space," *Journal of Marketing Research,* 19 (November 1982), 606–608.

ALLAIRE, Y., "A Model for the Evaluation of Risk and Additional Information in New Product Decisions," INFOR, 13 (1), (February 1975), 36–47.

ALLEN, T. J., "Studies of the Problem-Solving Process in Engineering Design," *IEEE Transactions on Engineering Management,* EM-13, (2) (June 1966), 72–83.

———, "Communication Networks in R&D Laboratories, *"R and D Management,* 1, (1) (1970), 14–21.

———, *Managing the Flow of Technology, Technology Transfer and the Dissemination of Technological Information within the R&D Organization.* (Cambridge, MA: MIT Press, 1977, first MIT Press paperback printing 1984).

———, J. M. UTTERBACK, M. S. SIRBU, N. A. ASHFORD, and J. H. HOLLOMAN, "Government Influence on the Process of Innovation in Europe and Japan," *Research Policy,* 7, 1978.

ALLISON, R. E., and K. P. UHL, "Influence of Beer Brand Identification on Taste Perception," *Journal of Marketing Research,* 1 (3), (August 1964), 36–39.

AMERICAN NEWSPAPER PUBLISHERS ASSOCIATION, Bureau of Advertising, "What Can One Newspaper Ad Do? An Experimental Study of Newspaper Advertising Communication and Results" (1969).

ANCONA, D. G. and D. CALDWELL, "Beyond Boundary Spanning: Managing External Dependence in Product Development Teams," *The Journal of High Technology Management Research,* 1 (2), (1990), 119–135.

———, "Bridging the Boundary: External Process and Performance in Organizational Teams" (MIT Sloan School of Management Working Paper No. BPS-3305-91), (June 1991).

———, "Demography and Design: Predictors of New Product Team Performance," forthcoming in *Organization Science,* 1992.

ANGELUS, T. L., "Why Do Most New Products Fail?" *Advertising Age,* 40 (March 24, 1969), 85–86.

ANSOFF, H. I., "Strategies for Diversification," *Harvard Business Review,* 35 (September-October 1957), 113–24.

ARNOLD, J. E., "Useful Creative Techniques," Source Book for Creative Thinking, eds. S. J. Parnes and H. F. Harding (New York: Charles Scribner's Sons, 1962).

ARTHUR D. LITTLE, Inc., *Patterns and Problems of Technical Innovation in American Industry,* Report C65344 to the National Science Foundation (Cambridge, MA: Arthur D. Little, Inc., 1959).

ASSMUS, G., "Newprod: The Design and Implementation of a New Product Model," *Journal of Marketing,* 39, (1) (January 1975), 16–23.

ASSOCIATON OF NATIONAL ADVERTISERS, *Prescription for New Product Success,* (New York: Association of National Advertisers, Inc., 1984).

AXELROD, J. N., "Attitude Measures that Predict Purchase," *Journal of Advertising Research,* 8 (1), (March 1968), 3–18.

Axelrod, R., "Effective Choice in the Prisoners-Dilemma," *Journal of Conflict Resolution,* 24 (1) (1980a), 3–25.

———, "More Effective Choice in the Prisoners-Dilemma," *Journal of Conflict Resolution,* 24 (3) (1980b), 379–403.

AYERS, R. U., *Technological Forecasting and Long Range Planning* (New York: McGraw-Hill Book Company, 1969).

BAKER, N. R., "R&D Project Selection Models: An Assessment," *IEEE Transactions on Engineering Management,* Vol. EM-21, (4), (November 1974), 165–71.

———, W. E. SOUDER, D. R. SHUMWAY, P. M. MAHER, and A. H. RUBENSTEIN, "A Budget Allocation Model for Large Hierarchical R&D Organizations," *Management Science,* 23 (1), (September 1976), 59–70.

BARABBA, V. P., and G. ZALTMAN, *Hearing the Voice of the Market Competitive Advantage through Creative Use of Market Information* (Boston, MA: Harvard Business School Press, 1991).

BARKEN, P., "Strategic and Tactical Benefits of Simultaneous Engineering," (Department of Mechanical Engineering, Stanford University working paper, 1991).

BARTHOL, R. P., and R. G. BRIDGE, "Echo Multi-Response Method for Surveying Value and Influence Patterns in Groups," *Psychological Reports,* 22 (3) (1968), 2.

BASS, F. M., "A New Product Growth Model for Consumer Durables," *Management Science,* 15, (5) (January 1969), 215–27.

———, "The Relationships between Diffusion Rates, Experience Curves, and Demand Elasticities for Consumer Durable Technological Innovations," presented at *Interfaces Between Marketing and Economics* (Rochester, NY: University of Rochester, April 1978) and forthcoming, *Journal of Business* (1980).

———, and A. B. BULTEZ, "A Note on Optimal Strategic Pricing of Technological Innovations," *Management Science,* 1, (1982), 371–78.

———, A. JEULAND, and G. P. WRIGHT, "Equilibrium Stochastic Choice and Market Penetration Theories: Derivations and Comparisons," *Management Science,* 22 (10), (June 1976), 1051–63.

———, and T. V. KRISHNAN, "A Generalization of the Bass Model: Decision Variable Considerations," (University of Texas at Dallas Working Paper No. 49-10-91), 1991.

BASU, S., and R. G. SCHROEDER, "Incorporating Judgments in Sales Forecasts: Application of the Delphi Method at American Horst and Derrick," *Interfaces,* 7 (3), (May 1977), 18–27.

BECKWITH, N. E., and D. R. LEHMANN, "Halo Effects in Multiattribute Attitude Models: An Appraisal of Some Unresolved Issues," *Journal of Marketing Research,* 13 (November 1976), 418–21.

BELK, R. W., "Situational Variables and Consumer Behavior," *Journal of Consumer Research,* 2 (December 1975), 157–64.

BEN-AKIVA, M. E., "Structure of Passenger Travel Demand Model," Ph.D. thesis, MIT Department of Civil Engineering (1973).

————, and S. LERMAN, *Discrete Choice Analysis: Theory and Application to Travel Demand* (Cambridge, MA: MIT Press, 1985).

BETTMAN, J. R., "Information Processing Models of Consumer Behaviour," *Journal of Marketing Research,* 7 (1970), 370–76.

————, "The Structure of Consumer Choice Processes," *Journal of Marketing Research,* 8 (November 1971), 465–71.

BIGGADIKE, R. E., *Entry Strategy and Performance* (Cambridge, MA: Harvard University Press, 1976).

BLACKBURN, J. D., and K. J. CLANCY, "LITMUS: A New Product Planning Model," in *Proceedings: Market Measurement and Analysis,* Robert P. Leone (ed.), The Institute of Management Sciences, Providence, R.I. (1980), 182–93.

BLATTBERG, R., T. BUESING, and S. SEN, "Segmentation Strategies for New National Brands," *Journal of Marketing,* 44 (Fall 1980), 59–67.

————, and J. GOLANTY, "TRACKER: An Early Test Market Forecasting and Diagnostic Model for New Product Planning," *Journal of Marketing Research,* 15 (2), (May 1978), 192–202.

BLOOM, D., A. JAY, and T. TWYMAN, "The Validity of Advertising Pretests," *Journal of Advertising Research,* 17 (2), (April 1977), 14.

————, and S. A. NESLIN, *Sales Promotion: Concepts, Methods and Strategies* (Englewood Cliffs, NJ: Prentice Hall, 1990).

BOEING COMPANY, THE, Boeing Commercial Airplane Group, *World Jet Airplane Inventory,* 1988.

BOOZ, ALLEN, and HAMILTON, *Management of New Products* (New York: Booz, Allen, and Hamilton, Inc., 1971).

————, *New Product Management for the 1980's* (New York: Booz, Allen, and Hamilton, 1982).

BOSTON CONSULTING GROUP, *Perspectives on Experience,* (Boston, MA: Boston Consulting Group, 1970).

BOUCHARD, T. J., and M. HARE, "Size, Performance, and Potential in Brainstorming Groups," *Journal of Applied Psychology,* 54 (1), (January 1970), 51–55.

BOUWMAN, M. J., P. A. FRISHKOFF, and P. FRISHKOFF, "How Do Financial Analysts Make Decisions? A Process Model of the Investment Screening Decision," *Accounting, Organizations and Society,* 12 (1987), 1–29.

BOX, G. E. P., W. G. HUNTER, and J. S. HUNTER, *Statistics For Experimenters* (New York: John Wiley and Sons, 1978).

————, and G. M. JENKINS, *Times Series Analysis Forecasting and Control* (San Francisco: Holden-Day, Inc., 1970).

————, G. E. P., S. BISGAARD, and C. FUNG, "An Explanation and Critique of Taguchi's Contributions to Quality Engineering," *Quality and Reliability Engineering International* (May 1988).

BREALEY, R., and S. MYERS, *Principles of Corporate Finance*, 4th ed. (New York: McGraw-Hill, 1991).

BRISCOE, G., "Some Observations on New Industrial Product Failures," *Industrial Marketing Management*, 2 (February 1973), 151–62.

BROWNOSKI, J., *Scientific American*, special issue distributed to subscribers (1987), 1.

BRUCKS, M., "Search Monitor: An Approach for Computer-Controlled Experiments Involving Consumer Information Search," *Journal of Consumer Research*, 15 (1988), 117–21.

BRUNSWICK, E., *The Conceptual Framework of Psychology* (Chicago: University of Chicago Press, 1952).

BUCKLIN, R. E., and V. SRINIVASAN, "Determining Inter-Brand Substitutability Through Survey Measurement of Consumer Preference Structures," Marketing Science Institute Report Number 91–102 (January 1991).

BULTEZ, A., C. DERBAIX, and A. J. SILK, "Developing Advertising Alternatives: Is the Magic Number One, or Could It Be Four?" Working Paper, MIT, Sloan School of Management (1976).

BURGER, P., "COMP: A New Product Forecasting System," Working Paper # 123–72, Graduate School of Management, Northwestern University (1972).

BURKE, R. R., A. RANGASWAMY, J. WIND, and J. ELIASHBERG, "A Knowledge-Based System for Advertising Design," *Marketing Science*, 9 (3), (Summer 1990), 212–29.

———, B. E. KAHN, L. M. LODISH, and B. HARLAM, "Comparing Dynamic Consumer Decision Processes in Real and Computer-Simulated Environments," Working Paper, Marketing Science Institute, Cambridge, MA (1991).

Business Week, June 8, 1976.

Business Week, June 15, 1989, Special Issue: "Innovation in America."

Business Week, July 8, 1991, p. 35.

Business Week, October 25, 1991, Special Issue.

BUZZELL, R. D., and B. T. GALE, "*The PIMS Principles* (New York: The Free Press), 1987.

———, ———, and R. C. M. SULTAN, "Market Share—A Key to Profitability," *Harvard Business Review*, 53(1) (January–February 1975), 97–106.

———, and R. E. M. NOURSE, *Product Innovation in Food Processing, 1954–1964* (Boston: Division of Research, Graduate School of Business Administration, Harvard University, 1967).

CADBURY, N. D., "When, Where, and How to Test Market," *Harvard Business Review*, 53 (3), (May–June 1975), 96–105.

CALDER, B. J., "Focus Groups and the Nature of Qualitative Marketing Research," *Journal of Marketing Research*, 14 (August 1977), 353–64.

CAMPBELL, D. T., and D. W. FISKE, "Convergent and Discriminant Validation by the Multitrait-Multimethod Matrix," *Psychological Bulletin*, 56, (2) (March 1959).

CARPENTER, G. S., and K. NAKAMOTO, "Consumer Preference Formation and Pioneering Advantages," *Journal of Marketing Research*, 26 (3) (August 1989), 285–98.

CARTER, C. F., and B. R. WILLIAMS, *Industry and Technical Progress: Factors Governing the Speed of Application of Science* (London: Oxford University Press, 1957).

CATTIN, P., and D. R. WITTINK, "A Monte Carlo Study of Metric and Nonmetric Estimation Methods for Multiattribute Models," Research Paper No. 341, Graduate School of Business, Stanford University (November 1976).

———, and ———, "Commercial Use of Conjoint Analysis: A Survey," *Journal of Marketing*, 46 (1982) 44–53.

CHAKRAVATI, D., A. MITCHELL, and R. STAELIN, "Judgment Based Marketing Decision Models: An Experimental Investigation of the Decision Calculus Approach," *Management Science*, 25 (3), (March 1979), 251–63.

CHARLTON, P., A. S. C. EHRENBERG, and B. PYMONT, Buyer Behavior under Mini-Test Conditions," *Journal of the Market Research Society*, 14 (3) (July 1972), 171–83.

———, and B. PYMONT, "Evaluating Marketing Alternatives," *Journal of the Market Research Society*, 17 (2), (April 1975), 90–103.

CHATTERJEE, R., and J. ELIASHBERG, "The Innovation Diffusion Process in a Heteroogeneous Population: A Micromodeling Approach," *Management Science*, 36 (9), (September 1990), 1057–79.

CHOFFRAY, J. M., and G. L. LILIEN, "The Market for Solar Cooling: Perceptions, Response, and Strategy Implications," *Studies in the Management Sciences*, 10 (1978), 209–26.

CHOW, G. C., "Tests of Equality Between Sets of Coefficients on Two Linear Regressions," *Econometrica*, 28 (3), (July 1960).

CHURCHILL, G. A., Jr., *Basic Marketing Research*, 2nd ed. (Hinsdale, IL: The Dryden Press, 1991).

CHURCHMAN, L. W., and A. K., Shainblatt, "The Researcher and the Manager: A Dialectic of Implementation," *Management Science*, 11 (4) (February 1965), B69-B87.

CLANCY, K., and L. E. OSTLUND, "Commercial Effectiveness Measures," *Journal of Advertising Research*, 16 (1), (February 1976), 29–34.

CLARK, K. B., "What Strategy Can Do For Technology," *Harvard Business Review*, 67 (6), (November-December, 1989), 94–98.

———, and T. FUJIMOTO, *Product Development Performance: Strategy, Organization, and Management in the World Auto Industry* (Boston, MA: Harvard Business School Press, 1991).

CLARKE, D. G., "Strategic Advertising Planning," *Management Science*, 24 (16), (December 1978), 1687–99.

———, "*Marketing Analysis and Decision Making: Text and Cases With Lotus 123*" (Redwood City, CA: The Scientific Press, 1987), 180–211.

CLAYCAMP, H., and L. E. LIDDY, "Prediction of New Product Performance: An Analytical Approach," *Journal of Marketing Research*, 6 (3), (November 1969), 414–20.

COCHRAN, W. G., and G. M. Cox, *Experimental Designs*, 2nd ed. (New York: John Wiley and Sons, 1957).

Coleman, J. C., E. Katz, and H. Menzel, *Medical Innovation: A Diffusion Study*, (Indianapolis, IN: Bobbs-Merrill, 1966).

———, "The Diffusion of an Innovation among Physicians," *Sociometry*, 20 (4), (December 1957), 253–70.

COOLEY, W. W., and P. R. LOHNES, *Multivariate Data Analysis* (New York: John Wiley and Sons, 1971).

COOPER, R. G., "Why New Industrial Products Fail," *Industrial Marketing Management,* 4 (2), (December 1975), 315–26.

———, "How New Product Strategies Impact on Performance," *Journal of Product Innovation,* 1 (1), (1984a) 5–18.

———, "New Product Strategies—What Distinguishes the Top Performers," *Journal of Product Innovation* 1 (3), (1984b), 151–64.

———, and E. J. KLEINSCHMIDT, "An Investigation Into the New Product Process—Steps, Deficiencies, and Impact," *Journal of Product Innovation,* 3 (2), (1986), 71–85.

———, "New Products: What Separates Winners from Losers?," *Journal of Product Innovation Management,* 4, (1987), 169–184.

COUGHLAN, A. T., and B. WERNERFELT, "Credible Delegation by Oligopolists: An Example from Distribution Channel Management," *Management Science,* 35 (2), (February 1989), 226–39.

COX, W. E., "Product Life Cycles as Marketing Models," *Journal of Business* (October 1967), 375–84.

Crawford, C. M., "New Product Failure Rates—Facts and Fallacies," *Research Management* (September 1979), 9–13.

———, "Marketing Research and the New Product Failure Rates," *Journal of Marketing,* 41 (April 1977), 51–61

———, "Unsolicited Product Ideas—Handle with Care," *Research Management,* 18 (January 1975), 19–24.

DALKEY, N. C., "The Delphi Method: An Experimental Study of Group Opinion," Rand Report RM-5888-PR, The Rand Corporation, Santa Monica, CA (1969).

DAVIDSON, J. H., "Why Most New Consumer Brands Fail," *Harvard Business Review,* 54 (March-April 1976), 117–21.

DAVIS, K., and F. Webster, *Sales Force Management* (New York: The Ronald Press, 1968).

DAY, G. S., "Diagnosing the Product Portfolio," *Journal of Marketing* (April 1977), 29–38.

———, *Analysis for Strategic Market Decisions,* (St. Paul, MN: West Publishing, 1986).

———, A. D. SHOCKER, and R. K. SRIVASTAVA, "Consumer Oriented Approaches to Identifying Product Markets," *Journal of Marketing,* 43 (4), (Fall 1979), 8–19.

———, and D. B. MONTGOMERY, "Diagnosing the Experience Curve," *Journal of Marketing,* 47 (Spring 1983), 44–58.

DE BONO, E., *Lateral Thinking: Creativity Step by Step* (New York: Harper Colphon Books, Harper & Row, 1973)

DE BRENTANI, U., "Success and Failure in New Industrial Services," *Journal of Product Innovation,* 6 (4) (1989), 239–58.

DESARBO, W. S., and V. R. RAO, "GENFOLD2: A New Constrained Unfolding Model for Product Positioning," *Marketing Science,* 5 (1986), 1–19.

DEVINNEY, T. M., "Entry and Learning," *Management Science,* 33 (6) (June 1987), 706–24.

DOBSON, G., and S. KALISH, "Positioning and Pricing a Product Line," *Marketing Science,* 7 (Spring 1988), 107–25.

DODSON, J. A., and E. MULLER, "Models of New Product Diffusion through Advertising and Word of Mouth," *Management Science,* 15 (November 1978), 1568–78.

DOLAN, R. J., AND A. P. JEULAND, "Experience Curves and Dynamic Demand Models: Implications for Optimal Pricing Strategies," *Journal of Marketing,* 45 (Winter 1981), 52–62.

DOUGHERTY, D., "New Products in Old Firms: The Myth of the Better Mousetrap in Search of a Beaten Path" (Cambridge, MA: Ph.D. thesis, MIT, Sloan School of Management, 1987).

————, "Interpretive Barriers to Successful Product Innovation in Large Firms," (Cambridge, MA: Marketing Science Institute Report No. 89–114, 1989)

DRUCKER, P. F., "The Discipline of Innovation," *Harvard Business Review,* 63 (May-June 1985), 67–72.

DUERR, M. G., *The Commercial Development of New Products* (New York: Conference Board, 1986).

EHRENBERG, A. S. C., "Predicting the Performance of New Brands," *Journal of Advertising Research,* 11 (December 1971), 3–10.

————, and G. J. GOODHARDT, "Repeat Buying of a New Brand," *British Journal of Marketing,* 2 (Autumn 1968), 200–205.

EINHORN, H. J., and R. M. HOGARTH, "Unit Weighting Schemes for Decision Making" *Organizational Behavior and Human Performance,* 13 (1975), 171–92.

ELIASHBERG, J., and A. P. JEULAND, "The Impact of Competitive Entry in a Developing Market upon Dynamic Pricing Strategies," *Marketing Science* 5 (1), (Winter 1986), 20–36.

ELROD, T., "Choice Map: Inferring a Product-Market Map from Panel Data," *Marketing Science,* 7 (1), (Winter 1988), 21–41.

————, and A. P. KELMAN, "Reliability of New Product Evaluation as of 1968 and 1981," Working Paper, Owen Graduate School of Management, Vanderbilt University (1987) p. 23.

ENOS, J. L., *The Rate and Direction of Inventive Activity: Economic and Social Factors,* ed. R. R. Nelson (Princeton, NJ: Princeton University Press, 1962), 299–322.

ESKIN, G. J., "Dynamic Forecasts of New Product Demand Using a Depth of Repeat Model," *Journal of Marketing Research,* 10 (2), (May 1973), 115–29.

————, and J. MALEC, "A Model for Estimating Sales Potential Prior to the Test Market," *Proceedings of the American Marketing Association 1976 Fall Educators' Conference,* (Chicago, IL: American Marketing Association, 1976), 230–33.

FADER, P. T., and J. R. HAUSER, "Implicit Coalitions in a Generalized Prisoners-Dilemma," *Journal of Conflict Resolution,* 32 (3), (1988), 553–82.

FELDMAN, L. P., and A. L. PAGE, "Principles vs. Practice in New Product Planning," *Journal of Product Innovation,* 1 (1), (1984) 43–55.

————, and ————, "Harvesting: The Misunderstood Market Exit Strategy," *Journal of Business Strategy,* 5 (Spring 1985), 79–85.

FERN, E. F., "The Use of Focus Groups for Idea Generation: The Effect of Group Size, Acquaintanceship, and Moderator on Response Quantity and Quality," *Journal of Marketing Research*, 19 (February 1982), 1–13.

FISHER, F. M., "Tests of Equality between Sets of Coefficients in Two Linear Regressions: An Expository Note," *Econometrica*, 38 (2), (March 1970), 361–66.

FRANK, R. E., W. F. MASSY, and Y. WIND, *Market Segmentation* (Englewood Cliffs, NJ: Prentice Hall, 1972).

FRASER, C. and J. W. BRADFORD, "Competitive Market Structure Analysis: Principal Partitioning of Revealed Substitutabilities," *Journal of Consumer Research*, 10 (June 1983), 15–30.

———, "Competitive Market Structure Analysis: A Reply," *Journal of Consumer Research*, 11 (December 1984), 842–847.

FREIMER, M., and L. SIMON, "The Evaluation of Potential New Product Alternatives," *Management Science*, 13 (February 1967), 279–92.

FULGA, M., "Competitive Pricing and Positioning in the Dating Service Industry," (Ph.D. thesis, M.I.T., Sloan School of Management, 1986).

GAGNON, R. J. and S. J. MANTEL, "Strategies and Performance Improvement for Computer-Assisted Design," *IEEE Transactions on Engineering Management*, EM-34 (4), (November 1987), 223–235.

GARVIN, D. A., "How the Baldridge Award Really Works," *Harvard Business Review*, (November-December 1991), 80–95.

GATIGNON, H., J. ELIASHBERG, and T. S. ROBERTSON, "Modeling Multinational Diffusion Patterns: An Efficient Methodology," *Marketing Science*, 8 (3), (Summer 1989), 231–47.

———, B. WEITZ, and P. BANSAL, "Brand Introduction Strategies and Competitive Environments," *Journal of Marketing Research*, 27 (November 1990), 390–401.

GENSCH, D., and W. W. RECKER, "The Multinomial, Multiattribute Logit Choice Model," *Journal of Marketing Research*, 16 (February 1979), 124–32.

GEORGE, V. P., and T. J. ALLEN, "Netgraphs: A Graphic Representation of Adjacency Matrices As a Tool for Network Analysis", MIT Sloan School of Management, Working Paper No. 3194-90-BPS, (November 1989).

GERSTENFELD, A., *Effective Management of Research and Development* (Reading, MA: Addison-Wesley, 1970).

GILLETTE COMPANY, *A Word About Ideas* (Boston, MA: The Gillette Co., 1972).

GOLD, J. A., "Testing Test Market Predictions," *Journal of Marketing Research* (August 1964), 8–16.

GOLDBERGER, P. N. "Competitive Marketing Strategy in the Running Shoe Industry," (unpublished Ph.D. thesis, MIT, Sloan School of Management, 1985).

GOMORY, R. E., "From the 'Ladder of Science' to the Product Development Cycle," *Harvard Business Review*, 67 (6), (November-December, 1989) 99–105.

GORDON, W. J. J., *Synectics: The Development of Creative Capacity* (New York: Harper & Row, 1961).

GREEN, P. E., *Analyzing Multivariate Data* (Hinsdale, IL: The Dryden Press, 1978).

————, "Hybrid Models for Conjoint Analysis: An Expository Review," *Journal of Marketing Research*, 21 (1984) 155–69.

————, and F. J. CARMONE, *Multidimensional Scaling and Related Techniques in Marketing Analysis* (Boston: Allyn and Bacon, 1970).

————, and A. M. KRIEGER, "A Simple Heuristic for Selecting 'Good' Products in Conjoint Analysis," *Advances in Management Science*, 5 (1987).

————, "Recent Contributions to Optimal Product Positioning and Buyer Segmentation," *European Journal of Operational Research*, 41 (1989) 127–141.

————, "An Application of a Product Positioning Model to Pharmaceutical Products," *Marketing Science*, 11 (2), (Spring 1992), 117.

————, "Product Design Strategies for Target-Market Positioning," *The Jounal of Product Innovation Management*, 8 (3), (September 1991), 189–202.

————, and J. D. CARROLL, "Conjoint Analysis and Multidimensional Scaling: A Complementary Approach," *Journal of Advertising Research*, 27 (October/November, 1987), 21–27.

————, and V. R. RAO, *Applied Multidimensional Scaling* (New York: Holt, Rinehart and Winston, 1972).

————, and V. SRINIVASAN, "Conjoint Analysis in Consumer Research: Issues and Outlook," *Journal of Consumer Research*, 5 (2), (September 1978), 103–23.

————, "Conjoint Analysis in Marketing Research: New Developments and Directions," *Journal of Marketing*, 54 (4), (October 1990), 3–19.

————, D. S. TULL, and G. ALBAUM, *Research for Marketing Decisions*, 5th ed. (Englewood Cliffs, NJ: Prentice Hall, 1988).

————, and J. WIND, *Multiattribute Decisions in Marketing* (Hinsdale, IL: The Dryden Press, 1973).

————, "New Way to Measure Consumer's Judgments," *Harvard Business Review* (July-August 1975), 107–17.

GRIFFIN, A. J., "Evaluating QFDs Use in U.S. Firms as a Process for Developing Products," *Journal of Product Innovation Management*, 9 (3), (1992c).

————, and J. R. HAUSER, "Patterns of Communication among Marketing, Engineering and Manufacturing—A Comparison Between Two New Product Teams," *Management Science*, 38 (3), (March 1992a), 360–73.

————, "The Marketing and R&D Interface," ICRMOT Working Paper, Sloan School of Management, M.I.T., Cambridge, MA, (November 1992b).

————, "The Voice of the Customer" *Marketing Science*, 12 (1), (1993).

GROSS, I., "The Creative Aspects of Advertising," *Sloan Management Review*, 14 (1), (Fall 1972), 83–109.

GRUBER, A., "Purchase Intent and Purchase Probability," *Journal of Advertising Research*, 10 (1970), 23–28.

GUPTA, A. C., "The Personal Computer Industry: Economic and Market Influences on Product Development Strategies" (MIT, Sloan School of Management thesis, 1986).

GUPTA, A. K., and D. WILEMON, "The Credibility-Corporation Connection at the R&D Marketing Interface," *Journal of Product Innovation*, 5 (1), (1988), 20–31.

―――, S. P. RAJ, and D. WILEMON, "A Model for Studying R&D—Marketing Interface in the Product Innovation Process," *Journal of Marketing*, 50 (1986), 7–17.

GUTMAN, JONATHAN, "A Means-End Chain Model Based on Consumer Categorization Processes," *Journal of Marketing*, 46 (Spring 1982), 60–72.

HAGERTY, M. R., "Improving the Predictive Power of Conjoint Analysis: The Use of Factor Analysis and Cluster Analysis," *Journal of Marketing Research*, 22 (May 1985), 168–84.

―――, "The Cost of Simplifying Preference Models," *Marketing Science*, 5 (4), (Fall 1986), 298–319.

HALEY, R. I., "Benefit Segmentation: A Decision Oriented Research Tool," *Journal of Marketing*, 32 (July 1968), 30–35.

HAMBERG, D., "Invention in the Industrial Research Laboratory," *The Journal of Political Economy*, 71 (April 1963), 95.

HANSSENS, D. M., L. J. PARSONS, and R. L. SCHULTZ, *Market Response Models: Econometric and Time Series Analysis* (Boston, MA: Kluwer Academic Publishers, 1990).

HARMAN, H. H., *Modern Factor Analysis*, 3rd ed. (Chicago, IL: University of Chicago Press, 1976).

HAUSER, J. R., "Testing and Accuracy, Usefulness, and Significance of Probabilistic Models: An Information Theoretic Approach," *Operations Research*, 26 (3), (May-June 1978), 406–21.

―――, "Consumer Research to Focus R&D Projects," *Journal of Product Innovation Management*, 1 (2), (January 1984), 70–84.

―――, "Agendas and Consumer Choice," *Journal of Marketing Research*, 23 (2), (August 1986a), 199–212.

―――, "Theory and Application of Defensive Marketing Strategy," *The Economics of Strategic Planning*, ed. L. G. Thomas (Lexington, MA: Lexington Books, 1986b), pp. 113–139.

―――, "Competitive Price and Positioning Strategies," *Marketing Science*, 7 (1), (Winter 1988), 76–91.

―――, "Puritan-Bennett, The Renaissance Spirometry System: Listening to the Voice of the Customer," *Sloan Management Review*, 34, (1993).

―――, "Comparison of Importance Measurement Methodologies and Their Relationship to Consumer Satisfaction" (MIT Working Paper, Sloan School of Management, Cambridge, MA, January 1991).

―――, and D. CLAUSING, "The House of Quality," *Harvard Business Review*, 66 (3), (1988) 63–73.

―――, and S. GASKIN, "Application of the 'DEFENDER' Consumer Model," *Marketing Science*, 3 (4), (Fall 1984), 327–351.

―――, and F. S. KOPPELMAN, "Designing Transportation Services: A Marketing Approach," *Transportation Research Forum*, 18 (1) (October 1977), 628–52.

———, and S. M. SHUGAN, "Intensity Measures of Consumer Preferences," *Operations Research* 28 (2), (March-April, 1980), 278–320.

———, "Defensive Marketing Strategies," *Marketing Science*, 2, (Fall 1983), 319–60.

———, and P. SIMMIE, "Profit Maximizing Perceptual Positioning: An Integrated Theory for the Selection of Product Features and Price," *Management Science*, 27 (2), (January 1981), 33–56.

———, A. M. TYBOUT, and F. S. KOPPELMAN, "Consumer-Oriented Transportation Service Planning: Consumer Analysis and Strategies," *Applications of Management Science*, ed. R. Schultz (Jai Press, 1979), vol. 1, 1098–1138.

———, and G. L. URBAN, "A Normative Methodology for Modeling Consumer Response to Innovation," *Operations Research*, 25 (4), (July-August 1977), 579–619.

———, "The Value Priority Hypotheses for Consumer Budget Plans", *Journal of Consumer Research*, 12 (4), (March 1986), 446–462.

———, ———, and B. WEINBERG, "Time Flies When You're Having Fun: How Consumers Allocate Their Time When Evaluating Products," (Cambridge, MA: Working Paper No. 68–92, International Center for Research on the Management of Technology, MIT, 1992).

———, and B. WERNERFELT, "The Competitive Implications of Relevant-Set/Response Analysis," *Journal of Marketing Research*, 26 (4), (November 1989), 391–405.

———, "An Evaluation Cost Model of Consideration Sets," *Journal of Consumer Research*, 16 (4) (March 1990), 393–408.

———, and K. WISNIEWSKI, "Consumer Analysis for General Travel Destinations," Technical Report, Transportation Center, Northwestern University, Evanston, IL (March 1979).

———, "Dynamic Analysis of Consumer Response to Marketing Strategies," *Management Science*, 28 (5), (May 1982), 455–86.

HAYES, R., and R. J., "Manufacturing Crisis—New Technologies, Obsolete Organizations," *Harvard Business Review*, 66 (5), 1988, 77–85.

HELLER, H. B., "The Ostrich and the Copy Researcher: A Comparative Analysis," paper presented at the December 1971 Meeting of the Advertising Effectiveness Research Group, New York Chapter, American Marketing Association.

HENDERSON, R., "Underinvestment and Incompetence as Responses to Radical Innovation: Evidence From the Photolithographic Alignment Equipment Industry" (Working Paper, MIT, Sloan School of Management, May 1990), 3163–90.

———, and K. B. CLARK, "Architectural Innovation: The Reconfiguration of Existing Product Technologies and the Failure of Established Firms," *Administrative Science Quarterly*, ASQ 35, (March 1990), 9–30.

HERNITER, J., "A Comparison of the Entropy and the Hendry Model," *Journal of Marketing Research*, 11 (February 1974), 21–29.

HISE, R. T., L. O'NEAL, J. U. MCNEAL and A. PARASURAMAN, "The Effect of Product Design Activities on Commercial Success Levels of New Industrial Products," *Journal of Product Innovation*, 6 (1) (1989), 43–50.

HOLAK, S. L., M. E. PARRY, and X. M. SONG, "The Relationship of R&D Sales to Firm

Experience: An Investigation of Marketing Contingencies," *The Journal of Product Innovation Management,* 8 (4), (December, 1991), 267–282.

HORSKY, D., "A Diffusion Model Incorporating Product Benefits, Price, Income and Information," *Marketing Science,* 9 (4), (Fall 1990), 342.

HOWARD, J. A., and W. M. MORGENROTH, Information Processing Model of Executive Decisions," *Management Science,* 14 (March 1968), 416–28.

HUBER, J., and D. SHELUGA, "The Analysis of Graded Paired Comparisons in Marketing Research" (Working paper, Purdue University, May 1977).

ILLINOIS INSTITUTE of TECHNOLOGY RESEARCH INSTITUTE, *Technology in Retrospect and Critical Events in Science,* Report to the National Science Foundation Chicago, IL (1968).

INFOSINO, WILLIAM J., "Forecasting New Product Sales from Likelihood of Purchase Ratings", *Marketing Science,* 5 (4) (Fall 1986), 372–84.

ISAACS, DANIEL B., "Competitive Price and Positioning Strategy in the Imported Beer Market" (unpublished thesis, MIT Sloan School of Management, 1986).

ISENSON, R., "Project Hindsight: An Empirical Study of the Sources of Ideas Utilized in Operational Weapon Systems," *Factors in the Transfer of Technology,* ed. W. Gruber and D. Marquis. (Cambridge, MA: MIT Press, 1969), 157.

ISHIKAWA, KAORU, ed., Special Issue: "Seven Management Tools for QC," *Reports of Statistical Application Research, Union of Japanese Scientists and Engineers,"* 323 (2), (June 1986).

JACOBSON, R. "Distinguishing among Competing Theories of the Market Share Effect," *Journal of Marketing,* 52 (1988), 66–80.

————, and D. A. AAKER, "Is Market Share All That It's Cracked Up to Be?" *Journal of Marketing,* 49 (1985), 11–22.

JAIN A. K., and RAM C. RAO, "Effect of Price on the Demand for Durables: Modelling, Estimation, and Findings," *Journal of Business & Economic Statistics,* 1990, 8, 163–170.

JAMIESON, LINDA F. and FRANK M. BASS, "Adjusting Stated Intention Measures to Predict Trial Purchase of New Products: a Comparison of Models and Methods," *Journal of Marketing Research,* 26 (August 1989), 336–45.

JEULAND, A. P. and S. M. SHUGAN, "Managing Channel Profits When Channel Members Form Conjectures", *Marketing Science,* 2 (3), 1983, 239.

JEWKES, J., D. SAWERS, and R. STILLERMAN, *The Sources of Invention* (London: W. W. Norton, 1970).

JOHNSON, ERIC J., JOHN W. PAYNE, and JAMES R. BETTMAN, "Information Displays and Preference Reversals," *Organizational Behavior and Human Decision Processes,* 42 (1988) 1–21.

————, ————, DAVID A. SCHKADE, and ————, "Monitoring Information Processing and Decisions: The Mouselab System" (Durham, NC: W.P. Center for Decision Science, Fuqua School of Business, Duke University, 1986).

————, and DAVID A. SCHKADE, "Heuristics and Bias in Utility Assessment: Further Evidence and Explanations," *Management Science,* 35 (1989), 406–424.

JOHNSON, R. M., "Multiple Discriminant Analysis Applications to Marketing Research," Market Facts, Inc. (January 1970).

———, "Tradeoff Analysis of Consumer Values," *Journal of Marketing Research* (May 1974), 121–27.

JOHNSTON, J., *Econometric Methods* (New York: McGraw-Hill Book Company, 1972). *Journal of Advertising Research*, "Special Issue: Marketing Research Made in Japan", 30 (2), (April/May 1990).

JUSTER, F. T., "Consumer Buying Intentions and Purchase Probability: An Experiment in Survey Design," *Journal of American Statistical Association*, 61 (1966), 658–96.

KAHN, F., and L. LIGHT, "Copytesting—Communication vs. Persuasion," *Advances in Consumer Research*, ed. M. J. Schlinger, *Proceedings*, 2 (November 1974), Conference of the Association for Consumer Research), 595–605.

KALISH, S., "Monopolistic Pricing with Dynamic Demand and Production Cost," *Marketing Science*, 2 (1983), 135–160.

KALYANARAM, G. and G. L. URBAN, "Dynamic Effects of the Order of Entry on Market Share, Trial Penetration, and Repeat Purchases for Frequently Purchased Consumer Goods," *Marketing Science*, 11 (3), (Summer 1992).

KAMAKURA, W. A., "A Least Squares Procedure for Benefit Segmentation with Conjoint Experiments," *Journal of Marketing Research*, 25 (May 1988), 157–167.

KANNO, M. "Effects on Communication Between Labs and Plants of the Transfer of R&D Personnel," unpublished Master's thesis, MIT, Sloan School of Management, Cambridge, MA (May 1968).

KARDES, F. R., and C. T. ALLEN, "Perceived Variability and Inferences about Brand Extensions," *Advertising Consumer*, 18 (1991), 392–98.

KATAHIRA, H., "Perceptual Mapping Using Ordered Logit Analysis," *Marketing Science*, 9 (1), (Winter 1989), 1–17.

KEENEY, R. L., and H. RAIFFA, *Decision Analysis with Multiple Objectives* (New York: John Wiley and Sons, 1976).

KELLY, G. A., *The Psychology of Personal Constructs*, 1 (New York, NY: W. W. Norton, 1955).

KING, B., *Better Designs in Half the Time: Implementing Quality Function Deployment (QFD) in America*, (Methuen, MA: G.O.A.L., Inc., 1987).

KLOMPMAKER, J. E., G. D. HUGHES and R. I. HALEY, "Test Marketing in New Product Development," *Harvard Business Review*, 54 (3), (1976), 128–138.

KOHLI, R., and R. KRISHNAMURTHI, "A Heuristic Approach to Product Design", *Management Science*, 33 (December 1987), 1523–33.

KOPPELMAN, F., and J. R. HAUSER, "Destination Choice Behavior for Non-grocery Shopping Trips," *Transportation Research Record*, No. 673, Transportation Research Board, Washington, D.C. (1979), pp. 157–65.

KOTABE, M., "Corporate Product Policy and Innovative Behavior of European and Japanese Multinationals: An Empirical Investigation," *Journal of Marketing*, 54 (2), (April 1990), 19–33.

KOTLER, P., "Harvesting Strategies for Weak Products," *Business Horizons*, 19 (August 1978), 15–22.

————, and R. Singh, "Marketing Warfare in the 1980s," *Journal of Business Strategy*, 3 (Winter, 1981), 30–41.

Krishnan, S., "Making More Effective Use of Market Information," Conference Summary of Marketing Science Institute Conference, April 12–14, 1989, Report No. 89–113 (Cambridge, MA: Marketing Science Institute, September 1989), p. 10.

Kruskal, J. B., "Analysis of Factorial Experiments by Estimating Monotone Transformations of the Data," *Journal of Royal Statistical Society*, Series B, 27 (1965), 251–63.

Kuga, M.," Kao's Marketing Strategy and Marketing Intelligence System," *Journal of Advertising Research*, 30 (2) (April/May 1990), 20.

Langrish, J., "Technology Transfer: Some British Data," *R&D Management*, 1 (133), (June 1971).

Lavidge, R. J., and G. A. Steiner, "A Model for Predictive Measurements of Advertising Effectiveness," *Journal of Marketing*, 25 (6), (October 1961), 59–62.

Lehmann, D. R., *Market Research and Analysis*, 3rd ed. (Homewood, IL: Richard D. Irwin, Inc., 1988).

————, and Russell S. Winer, *Analysis for Marketing Planning*, 2nd ed. (Homewood, IL: Irwin Press, 1990).

Lenk, P. and A. G. Rao, "New Models from Old: Forecasting Product Adoption by Hierarchical Bayes Procedures", *Marketing Science*, 9 (1), (Winter 1990), 42–53.

Levitt, T., "Exploit the Product Life Cycle," *Harvard Business Review*, 43 (6), (November-December 1965), 81–94.

Lewis, A. C., T. L. Sadosky, and T. Connolly, "The Effectiveness of Group Brainstorming in Engineering Problem Solving," *IEEE Transactions on Engineering Management*, EM-22 (3), (August 1975), 119–24.

Lieberman, M. B., and D. B. Montgomery, "First-Mover Advantages," *Strategic Management Journal*, 9, (1988), 41–58.

Lilien, G. L., and J. D. C. Little, "The Advisor Project: A Study of Industrial Marketing Budgets," *Sloan Management Review*, 17 (3), (Spring 1976), 17–31.

Little, J. D. C. "A Proof for the Queuing Formula: $L = \lambda W$," *Operating Research*, 9, (May 1961) 383–387.

————, "A Model of Adaptive Control of Promotional Spending," *Operations Research*, 14 (6), (November-December 1966), 1075–98.

————, "Models and Managers: The Concept of a Decision Calculus," *Management Science*, 16 (8), (April 1970), 466–85.

————, "Brandaid: A Marketing Mix Model, Structure, Implementation, Calibration, and Case Study," *Operations Research*, 23 (4), (July/August 1975), 628–73.

————, "Aggregate Advertising Models: The State of the Art," *Operations Research*, 27, (4), (July-August, 1979), 629–67.

————, "Information Technology in Marketing," (Cambridge, MA: MIT Sloan School Working Paper No. 1860–87, revised September 1990).

————, and L. M. Lodish, "A Media Planning Calculus," *Operations Research*, 17 (1), (January-February 1969), 1–35.

LODISH, LEONARD M., "Callplan: An Interactive Salesman's Calling Planning System," *Management Science*, 18 (4), Part 11 (December 1971), 25–40.

———, *The Advertising and Promotion Challenge, Vaguely Right or Precisely Wrong?* (New York: Oxford Press, 1986).

LOUVIERE, J. J., and G. WOODWORTH, "Design and Analysis of Simulated Consumer Choice or Allocation Experiments: An Approach Based on Aggregate Data," *Journal of Marketing Research*, 20 (November 1983), 350–67.

MACKAY, D. B., and J. L. ZINNES, "A Probabilistic Model for the Multidimensional Scaling of Proximity and Preference Data," *Marketing Science*, 5 (4) (Fall 1986), pp. 325–44.

MAGEE, J. F., "Decision Trees for Decision Making," *Harvard Business Review*, 42 (4) (July-August 1964), 126–39.

MAHAJAN, V. and E. MULLER, "Timing, Diffusion and Substitution of Successive Generations of Durable Technological Innovations: The IBM Mainframe Case," Working paper, University of Texas (November 1990), to be published.

———, ——— and F. M. BASS, "New Product Diffusion Models in Marketing: A Review and Directions for Research," *Journal of Marketing* 54 (1), (January 1990), pp. 1–26.

———, and J. WIND "New Product Forecasting Models, Directions for Research and Implementation," *International Journal of Forecasting*, 4 (1988), 341–58.

MALONE, T. W. and J. F. ROCKART, "Computers, Networks and the Corporation," *Scientific American*, 265 (3), (September 1991), 128.

MANSFIELD, E., *Industrial Research and Technological Innovation* (New York: W. W. NORTON, 1968).

———, and J. RAPOPORT, "The Costs of Industrial Product Innovation," *Management Science*, 21 (12), (August 1975), 1380–86.

———, J. SCHNEE, S. WAGNER, and M. HAMBERGER, *Research and Innovation in the Modern Corporation* (New York: W. W. Norton, 1971).

———, and S. WAGNER, "Organizational and Strategic Factors Associated with Probabilities of Success in Industrial R&D," *Journal of Business* (April 1975).

MARKET FACTS, INC., "High Efficiency Electric Motors: Focus Group Results," *Contract Job Report No. 9312.* (Washington, D.C.: Department of Energy, August 1978).

MARQUIS, D. G., "The Anatomy of Successful Innovation," *Innovation*, 1 (7), (1969), 28–37.

MARSCHAK, T., T. K. GLENNAN, and R. SUMMERS, *Strategy for R&D: Studies in Microeconomics of Development* (New York: Springer-Verlag, 1967).

MARSHALL, A. W., and W. H. MECKLING, "Predictability of Costs, Time, and Success of Development," *The Rate and Direction of Inventive Activity: Economic and Social Factors*, ed. National Bureau of Economic Research, (Princeton, NJ: Princeton University Press, 1962), 461–76.

MASON, C. H., "New Product Entries and Product Class Demand," *Marketing Science*, 9 (1), (Winter 1990), 58–73.

MCBRIDE, R. D., and F. S. ZUFRYDEN, "An Integer Programming Approach to Optimal Product Line Selection," *Marketing Science*, 7 (Spring 1988), 126–140.

MCCONNELL, J. D., "The Price-Quality Relationship in an Experimental Setting," *Journal of Marketing Research*, 5 (3), (August 1968), 300–303.

MCFADDEN, D., "Conditional Logit Analysis of Qualitative Choice Behavior," *Frontiers in Econometrics*, ed. P. Zarembka (New York: Academic Press, 1970), pp. 105–42.

MEADOWS, D. L., "Estimate Accuracy and Project Selection Models in Industrial Research," *Industrial Management Review*, 9 (3), (Spring 1968), 105–19.

MEYER, R. J., and A. SATHI, "A Multiattribute Model of Consumer Choice During Product Learning," *Marketing Science*, 4 (1), (Winter 1985), 41–61.

MIDGLEY, D. F., *Innovation and New Product Marketing* (London: Croom Helm, 1977).

MILLER, J. E., *Innovation, Organization, and Environment* (Sherbrooke, Quebec, Canada: University of Sherbrooke, 1971).

MONTGOMERY, D. B., "Consumer Characteristics Associated with Dealing: An Empirical Example," *Journal of Marketing Research*, 8 (1), (February 1971), 118–20.

———, "New Product Distribution—An Analysis of Supermarket Buyer Decision," *Journal of Marketing Research*, 12 (3), (August 1975), 255–64.

———, and V. SRINIVASAN, "An Improved Method for Meta Analysis: With Application to New Product Diffusion Models," (Stanford, CA: Working Paper, Stanford University Graduate School of Business, 1989).

———, and G. L. URBAN, *Management Science in Marketing* (Englewood Cliffs, NJ: Prentice Hall, 1969).

MOOD, A. M., and F. A. GRAYBILL, *Introduction to the Theory of Statistics* (New York: McGraw-Hill Book Company, 1963).

MOORE, W. L., "New Product Development Practices of Industrial Marketers," *Journal of Product Innovation*, 4 (1) (1987), pp. 6–20.

MORRISON, D. G., "Purchase Intentions and Purchase Behavior," *Journal of Marketing*, 43, (2) (Spring 1979a), 65–74.

MOSKOWITZ, H. R., "Subjective Ideals and Sensory Optimization in Evaluating Perceptual Dimensions in Food," *Journal of Applied Psychology*, 56 (1), (1972), 60–66.

MUELLER, W. F., in *The Rate and Direction of Inventive Activity: Economic and Social Factors*, ed. R. R. NELSON (Princeton, NJ: Princeton University Press, 1962), 299–322.

MYERS, J. H., "Benefit Structure Analysis: A New Tool for Product Planning," *Journal of Marketing*, 40 (4), (October 1976), 23–33.

MYERS, S., and D. G. MARQUIS, *Successful Industrial Innovation: A Study of Factors Underlying Innovation in Selected Firms*," NSF 69–17 (Washington, D.C.: National Science Foundation, 1969).

NAERT, P. A., and P. S. M. LEEFLANG, *Building Implementable Models* (Boston, MA: Martinus Nijhoff/Leiden, 1978).

NARASIMHAN, C., "Incorporation Consumer Price Expectations in Diffusion Models," *Marketing Science*, 8 (4) (Fall 1989), 343–357.

———, and S. K. SEN, "New Product Models for Test Market Data," *Journal of Marketing*, 47 (Winter 1983), 11–24.

NARVER, J. C., and S. F. SLATER, "The Effect of a Market Orientation on Business Profitability", *Journal of Marketing*, 54 (4), (October 1990), 20–28.

NATIONAL INSTITUTE OF STANDARDS AND TECHNOLOGY, Malcolm Baldridge National Quality Award, 1991 Application Guidelines.

NELSON, C. R., *Applied Time Series Analysis for Managerial Forecasting* (San Francisco: Holden-Day, Inc., 1973).

NESLIN, S. A., "A Market Response Model for Coupon Promotions," *Marketing Science,* 9 (2), (Spring 1990), 125–145.

NEVERS, J. V., "Extensions of a New Product Growth Model," *Sloan Management Review,* 13 (2), (Winter 1972), 77–90.

NIELSEN MARKETING SERVICE, "New Product Success Ratios," *Nielsen Researcher* (1979), 5, 2–9.

———, *Preview (Northbrook),* (Northbrook, IL: Nielsen Market Research 1982).

NORRIS, K. P., "The Accuracy of Project Cost and Duration Estimates in R&D," *R and D Management,* 2 (1), (October 1971), 25–36.

NORTON, J. A., and F. M. BASS, "Evolution of Technological Generations: The Law of Capture", *Sloan Management Review,* 33 (2), (Winter 1992), 66–77.

———, "A Diffusion-Theory Model of Adoption and Substitution for Successive Generations of High-Technology Products," *Management Science,* 33 (9), (September, 1987) 1069–1086.

NORUSIS, M. J., *SPSS Guide to Data Analysis for SPSS-PC Plus,* (SPSS Inc., Staff, ed. LC88-80966, 1988).

NOYCE, R. N., "Microelectronics," *Scientific American,* 237 (3), (September 1977), 63–69.

OGAWA, K., "An Approach to Simultaneous Estimation and Segmentation in Conjoint Analysis", *Marketing Science,* 6 (1), (Winter 1987), 66–81.

OHMAE, K., *The Mind of the Strategist,* (New York: McGraw-Hill, 1982).

OLIVER, R. M., "A Bayesian Model to Predict Saturation and Logistic Growth," *Journal of Operational Research Society,* 38 (1), (1987) 49.

O'MEARA, J. T., "Selecting Profitable Products," *Harvard Business Review,* 39 (1), (January-February 1961), 83–89.

OPPENHEIM, A. N., *Questionnaire Design and Attitude Measurement* (New York: Basic Books, 1966).

OSBORN, A. J., *Applied Imagination,* (New York, NY: Charles Scribner's Sons, 1963).

PAINTON, S., and J. W. GENTRY, "Another Look at the Impact of Information Presentation Format," *Journal of Consumer Research,* 12 (2), (September 1985), 240–44.

PARFITT, J. H., and B. J. K. COLLINS, "Use of Consumer Panels for Brand Share Prediction, "*Journal of Marketing Research,* 5 (2), (May 1968), 131–46.

PAYNE, S. L., *The Art of Asking Questions* (Princeton, NJ: Princeton University Press, 1951).

PC Magazine, May 12, 1992, p. 36.

PEKELMAN, D., and E. TSE, "Experimentation and Control in Advertising: An Adaptive Control Approach," *Operations Research,* 28 (2), (March-April 1980).

PESSEMIER, E. A., *New Product Decision: An Analytical Approach* (New York, NY: McGraw Hill Book Company, 1966).

PORTER, M. E., *Competitive Strategy: Techniques of Analyzing Industries and Competitors,* (New York, NY: The Free Press, 1980).

PRATT, J. W., H. RAIFFA, and R. SCHLAIFER, *Introduction to Statistical Decision Theory* (New York: McGraw-Hill Book Company, 1965).

PRINCE, G. M., *The Practice of Creativity* (New York: Collier Books, 1970, reprinted 1972).

PRINGLE, L. G., R. D. WILSON, and E. I. BRODY, "NEWS: A Decision-Oriented Model for New Product Analysis and Forecasting," *Marketing Science,* 1 (Winter 1982), pp. 1–30.

PUNJ, G. N., and R. STAELIN, "The Choice Process for Graduate Business Schools," *Journal of Marketing Research,* 15 (November 1978), 588–98.

PYMONT, B. C., D. REAY, and P. G. M. STANDEN, "Towards the Elimination of Risk from Investment in New Products: Experience with Micro-Market Testing," paper presented at the 1976 ESOMAR Congress, Venice, Italy (September 1976).

QUELCH, J. A., *Sales Promotion Management* (Englewood Cliffs, NJ: Prentice Hall, 1989).

QUINN, J. B., "Technology Forecasting," *Harvard Business Review,* 45 (2), (March-April 1967), 73–90.

———, "Managing Innovation: Controlled Chaos," *Harvard Business Review,* 63 (May-June 1985), 73–84.

RAIFFA, H., "Assessments of Probabilities," unpublished manuscript (January 1969).

———, *Decision Analysis: Introductory Lectures on Choices Under Uncertainty* (Reading, MA: Addison-Wesley, 1968).

———, and R. SCHLAIFER, *Applied Statistical Decision Theory* (Boston, MA: Harvard University Press, 1961).

RAO, V. R., and E. W. MCLAUGHLIN, "Modeling the Decision to Add New Products by Channel Intermediaries," *Journal of Marketing* (January 1989), 53, (1), 80–88.

———, and F. W. WINTER, "A Bayesian Approach to Test Market Selection," *Management Science,* 12 (December 1981), 1351–68.

REIBSTEIN, D., J. E. G. BATESON, and KENNETH BOULDING, "Conjoint Analysis Reliability: Empirical Findings," *Marketing Science,* 7 (1988), 271–286.

REYNOLDS, T. J., and J. GUTMAN, "Laddering Theory, Method, Analysis, and Interpretation," *Journal of Advertising Research,* 28 (1), (1988), 11–31.

ROBERTS, E. B., "A Simple Model of R&D Project Dynamics," *R and D Management,* 5 (1), (October 1974), 1–15.

———, "Exploratory and Normative Technological Forecasting: A Critical Appraisal," *Technological Forecasting,* 1 (1969), 113–27.

———, "Resolving 'The Innovation Dilemma': Corporate Development of New Technology-based Product-lines and Businesses," Proceedings of the First International Forum on Technology Management, (1990a), 146–68.

———, "Evolving Toward Product and Market Orientation: The Early Years of Technology Based Firms" (Working Paper No. 27–90, MIT, Sloan School of Management, Cambridge, MA 1990b).

————, "Strategic Transformation and the Success of High Technology Companies" (Working Paper 2–90, MIT, Sloan School of Management, Cambridge, MA 1989).

————, "Entrepreneurs in High Technology, Lessons From MIT and Beyond" (New York, New York: Oxford University Press, 1991).

————, and C. A. BERRY, "Entering New Businesses: Selecting Strategies for Success," *Sloan Management Review*, 26 (3), (Spring 1985), 3–17.

————, and MARC H. MEYER, "Product Strategy and Corporate Success" (Working Paper No. 30–91, MIT, Sloan School of Management, Cambridge, MA, 1991).

————, and H. A. Wainer, "New Enterprises on Route 128" *Science Journal*, 4 (12), (December 1968), 78–83.

ROBERTS, J. H., and J. M. LATTIN, "Developing and Testing of a Model of Consideration Set Composition" *Journal of Marketing Research*, 28, 3 (November 1991), 429–40.

————, and G. L. URBAN, "Modeling Multiattribute Utility, Risk and Belief Dynamics for New Consumer Durable Brand Choice," *Management Science*, (February 1988), 34 (2), 167–85.

ROBERTSON, A. B., B. ACHILLADELIS, and P. JERVIS, *Success and Failure in Industrial Innovation: Report on Project Sappho* (London: Centre for the Study of Industrial Innovation, 1972).

ROBERTSON, T. S., "Diffusion Theory and the Concept of Personal Influence," *Behavioral and Management Science in Marketing*, ed. H. L. Davis and A. J. Silk (New York, NY: John Wiley and Sons, 1978), 214–36.

————, *Innovative Behavior and Communication* (New York: Holt, Rinehart, and Winston, 1971).

ROBINSON, W. T. "Sources of Market Pioneer Advantages: The Case of Industrial Goods Industries," *Journal of Marketing Research*, 25 (February 1988a), 87–94.

————, "Marketing Mix Reactions to Entry," *Marketing Science*, 7 (4), (Fall, 1988b), 368–85.

————, and C. FORNELL, "The Sources of Market Pioneer Advantages in Consumer Goods Industries," *Journal of Marketing Research*, 22 (2), (August 1985), pp. 297–304.

ROGERS, E. M., "Re-inventing During the Innovation Process" (Working Paper, Stanford University, Palo Alto, CA, Institute for Communication Research, 1978).

————, *The Diffusion of Innovations* (New York: The Free Press, 1962).

————, and F. F. SHOEMAKER, *Communications of Innovations: A Cross-Cultural Approach* (New York: The Free Press, 1971).

————, and J. D. STANFIELD, "Adoption and Diffusion of New Products: Emerging Generalizations and Hypotheses," *Applications of the Sciences in Marketing Management*, ed. F. Bass et al. (New York: John Wiley and Sons, 1968), pp. 227–50.

ROSCH, E. "Principles of Categorization," *Cognition and Categorization*, ed. E. Rosch and B. Lloyd, (Hillsdale, NJ: Lawrence Earlbaum, 1981).

ROSENBLOOM, R. S., and M. A. CUSUMANO, "Techological Pioneering and Competitive Advantage: The Birth of the VCR Industry," *California Management Review*, 29 (4), (Summer 1987) 51–76.

Ross, P. J., *Taguchi Techniques for Quality Engineering* (New York, NY: McGraw-Hill, 1988).

Rothwell, R., et al, "Sappho Updated Project Sappho Phase 11," *Research Policy,* 3 (1974), 258–91.

———, "Hungarian Sappho—Some Comments and Comparisons," *Research Policy,* 3 (1) (1974), 50.

Rubenstein, A. H., and H. Schroder, "Management Differences in Assessing Probabilities of Technical Success for R&D Projects," *Management Science,* 24 (2), (October 1977), 137–48.

Ruiz, D., and D. Jain, "Designing and Developing New Products: The Subproblem Decomposition Approach", Working Paper, Northwestern University, Department of Marketing (June 7, 1991).

Rummel, R. J., *Applied Factor Analysis* (Evanston, IL: Northwestern University Press, 1970).

Ryan, T. P., *Statistical Methods for Quality Improvement* (New York, NY: John Wiley and Sons, 1989).

Schein, E. H., "Increasing Organizational Effectiveness through Better Human Resource Planning and Development," *Sloan Management Review,* 19 (1), (Fall 1977), 1–20.

Schlaifer, R, *Analysis of Decisions Under Uncertainty* (New York, NY: McGraw-Hill Book Company, 1969).

Schmalensee, R., "Product Differentiation Advantages of Pioneering Brands," *American Economic Review,* 27, (1982) 349–65.

Schmidt, M. S., and L. C. Meile, "Taguchi Designs and Linear Programming Speed New Product Formulation", *Interfaces,* 19 (5), (September–October 1989), 49–56.

Schmittlein, D. C., and V. Mahajan, "Maximum Likelihood Estimation for an Innovation Diffusion Model of New Product Acceptance," *Marketing Science,* 1, (1982), 57–78.

Scott, C. A., "The Effects of Trial and Incentives on Repeat Purchase Behavior," *Journal of Marketing Research,* 13 (3), (August 1976), 263–69.

Scott Morton, M. S., *The Corporation of the 1990s, Information Technology and Organizational Transformation,* (New York: Oxford University Press, 1991).

Sheriff, A. M., "Product Development in the Automobile Industry: Corporate Strategies and Project Performance", (Cambridge, MA: MIT Sloan School of Management, unpublished master's thesis, 1988).

Shield, R., "Competitive Pricing and Positioning In a Chemical Analysis Instrumentation Market" (unpublished thesis, MIT, Sloan School of Management, 1986).

Shocker, A. D., and V. Srinivasan, "Multiattribute Approaches to Product Concept Evaluation and Generation: A Critical Review," *Journal of Marketing Research,* 16 (May 1979), 159–80.

———, D. W. Stewart, and A. J. Zahorik, "Determining the Competitive Structure of Product-Markets: Practices, Issues, and Suggestions," *Journal of Managerial Issues,* 2 (Summer 1990), 127–59.

SHUGAN, S. M., "Implicit Understandings in Channels of Distribution," *Management Science*, 31 (4), (1985), 435–60.

———, "Estimating Brand Positioning Maps Using Supermarket Scanning Data," *Journal of Marketing Research*, 24 (February 1986), 1–19.

SIGFORD, J. V., and R. H. PARVIN, "Project PATTERN: A Normative Methodology for Determining Relevance in Complex Decision Making," *IEEE Transactions on Engineering Management*, Vol. EM-12, No. 1 (March 1965), 2–7.

SILK, A. J., "Overlap Among Self-Designated Opinion Leaders: A Study of Selected Dental Products and Services," *Journal of Marketing Research*, 3 (3), (August 1966), 255–59.

———, "The Influence of Advertising's Affective Qualities on Consumer Response," in *Buyer/Consume Information Processing*, ed. G. D. Hughes and M. L. Ray (Chapel Hill, NC: University of North Carolina Press, 1974), 157–86.

———, and M. KALWANI, "Measuring Influence in Organization Purchase Decisions," *Journal of Marketing Research*, 19, (1982), 165–181.

———, and G. L. URBAN, "Pre-Test-Market Evaluation of New Packaged Goods: A Model and Measurement Methodology," *Journal of Marketing Research*, 15 (2) (May 1978), 171–91.

SILVER, J. A. and J. C. THOMPSON, Jr., "Understanding Customer Needs: A Systematic Approach to the 'Voice of the Customer,' " (Cambridge, MA: Master's Thesis, Sloan School of Mangement, MIT, 1991).

SIMMIE, P., "Alternative Perceptual Models: Reproducibility, Validity, and Data Integrity," *Proceedings of American Marketing Association Educators Conference* (Chicago, IL, American Marketing Association, 1978), 12–16.

SINGH, J., R. D. HOWELL, and G. K. RHOADS, "Adaptive Designs for Likert-Type Data: An Approach for Implementing Marketing Surveys," *Journal of Marketing Research*, 27 (August 1990), 304–21.

SONQUIST, J. A., E. L. BAKER, and J. N. MORGAN, *Searching for Structure*, Survey Research Center, Institute for Social Research, University of Michigan, Ann Arbor, MI (1973).

SOUDER, W. E., "Effectiveness of Nominal and Interacting Group Decision Processes for Integrating R&D and Marketing," *Management Science*, 23 (6), (February 1977), 595–605.

———, "Managing Relations Between R&D and Marketing in New Product Development Projects," *Journal of Product Innovation*, 5 (1), (1988) 6–19.

———, *Managing New Product Innovations* (Lexington MA: Lexington Books, 1987)

SRINIVASAN, V., "A Theoretical Comparison of the Predictive Power of the Multiple Regression and Unit Weighting Procedures," paper presented at the Joint National Meeting of the Operations Research Society of America/The Institute of Management Science, Atlanta, GA (November 7–9, 1977).

———, and C. H. MASON, "Nonlinear Least Squares Estimation of New Product Diffusion Models", *Marketing Science*, 5 (1986), 169–178.

———, and A. D. SHOCKER, "Estimating the Weights for Multiple Attributes in a Composite Criterion Using Pairwise Judgments," *Psychometrika,* 38 (4), (December 1973), 473–93.

———, "Linear Programming Techniques for Multidimensional Analysis of Preferences," *Psychometrika,* 38 (3), (September 1973), 337–69.

SRIVASTAVA, R. K., R. P. LEONE and A. D. SHOCKER "Market Structure Analysis: Hierarchical Clustering of Products Based on Substitution-in-Use," *Journal of Marketing,* 45 (Summer 1981), 38–48.

STANTON, F., "What Is Wrong with Test Marketing?" *Journal of Marketing,* 31 (2), (April 1967), 43–47.

STEFFLRE, V., "Some Applications of Multidimensional Scaling to Social Science Problems, in *Multidimensional Scaling: Theory and Applications in the Behavioral Sciences,* vol. 2, ed. A. K. Romney, R. N. Shepard, and S. B. Nerlove (New York: Seminar Press, 1972).

STERN, L. W., and A. I. EL-ANSARY, *Marketing Channels,* 3rd ed. (Englewood Cliffs, NJ: Prentice Hall, 1988).

STOBAUGH, R. B., and P. O. TOWNSEND, "Price Forecasting and Strategic Planning—Case of Petrochemicals," *Journal of Marketing Research,* 12 (1), (1975), 19–29.

STRONG, E. K., *The Psychology of Selling* (New York: McGraw-Hill Book Company, 1925).

SUDHARSHAN, J. H. MAY, and T. GRUCA, "DIFFSTRAT: An Analytical Procedure for Generating Optimal New Product Concepts for a Differentiated-Type Strategy," *European Journal of Operational Research,* 36 (1988), 50–65.

———, and A. SHOCKER, "A Simulation Comparison of Methods for New Product Location," *Marketing Science,* 6 (Spring 1987), 182–201.

SULLIVAN, M., "Measuring Image Spillovers in Umbrella-Branded Products," *Journal of Business,* 63 (3) (1990), 309–29.

SULTAN, F. J. FARLEY, and D. LEHMANN, "A Meta-Analysis of Applications of Diffusion Models," *Journal of Marketing Research,* 2 (1990), 70–77.

TAGUCHI, G., *Introduction to Quality Engineering: Designing Quality into Products and Processes,* (Dearborn, MI: American Supplier Institute, Inc.), (1983).

———, *System of Experimental Design: Engineering Methods to Optimize Quality and Minimize Costs,* (Dearborn MI: American Supplier Institute, 1988).

———, and D. CLAUSING, "Robust Quality," *Harvard Business Review,* (1), (January-February 1990), 65–75.

TANNENBAUM, M., et al., *Report of the Ad Hoc Committee on Principles of Research/Engineering Interaction,* report No. MAB 222-M, National Academy of Sciences-National Research Council Material Advisory Board, Washington, D.C. (1966).

TAUBER, E. M., "Predictive-Validity in Consumer Research," *Journal of Advertising Research,* (1975), 15 (5), 59–64.

———, "Forecasting Sales Prior to Test Market," *Journal of Marketing,* 41, (1) (January 1977), 80–84.

TORGERSON, W. S., *Theory and Method of Scaling* (New York: John Wiley & Sons, 1958).

TVERSKY, A and S. SATTATH, "Preference Trees," *Psychological Review,* 86 (6), (19■■), 542–73.

TYBOUT, A. M. and J. R. HAUSER, "A Marketing Audit Using a Conceptual Model of Consumer Behavior: Application and Evaluation," *Journal of Marketing*, 45 (3), (Summer 1981) 81–101.

URBAN, GLEN L., "A Model for Managing a Family-Planning System," *Operations Research*, 22 (2), (March-April 1974), 205–33.

———, "A New Product Analysis and Decision Model," *Management Science*, 14 (8), (April 1968), 490–517.

———, "PERCEPTOR: A Model for Product Positioning," *Management Science*, 21 (8), (April 1975a), 858–71.

———, "Allocating Ad Budgets Geographically," *Journal of Advertising Research*, 15, No. 6 (December 1975b), 7–18.

———, "Building Models for Decision Makers," *Interfaces*, 4 (3), (May 1974), 1–11.

———, "SPRINTER mod III: A Model for the Analysis of New Frequently Purchased Consumer Products," *Operations Research*, 18 (5) (September-October 1970), 805–53.

———, J. R. HAUSER, and J. H. ROBERTS, "Prelaunch Forecasting of New Automobiles: Models and Implementation", *Management Science*, 36 (4), (April 1990), 401–21.

———, and N. DHOLAKIA, *Essentials of New Product Management*, (Englewood Cliffs, NJ: Prentice Hall, 1987).

———, P. JOHNSON and R. BRUDNICK, "Market Entry Strategy Formulation: A Hierarchical Model and Consumer Measurement Approach" (Working paper, MIT, Sloan School of Management, Cambridge, MA, 1981).

———, and J. R. HAUSER, "Testing Competitive Market Structures," *Marketing Science*, 3 (Spring 1984), 83–112.

———, and R. KARASH, "Evolutionary Model Building," *Journal of Marketing Research*, 8 (1), (February 1971), 62–66.

———, and G. M. KATZ, "Pre-test-Market Models: Validation and Managerial Implications," *Journal of Marketing Research*, 20 (August 1983), 221–34.

———, and E. VON HIPPEL, "Lead User Analysis for the Development of New Industrial Products," *Management Science*, 34 (5), (May 1988), 569–82.

———, and S. STAR, *Advanced Marketing Strategy: Phenomena, Analysis, and Decisions.* (Englewood Cliffs, NJ: Prentice Hall, 1991).

———, T. CARTER, S. GASKIN, and Z. MUCHA, "Market Share Rewards to Pioneering Brands: An Empirical Analysis and Strategic Implications," *Management Science*, 32 (6), (June 1986), 645–59.

———, J. S. HULLAND, and B. D. WEINBERG, "Premarket Forecasting of New Consumer Durables: Modeling Categorization, Elimination, and Consideration Phenomena," *Journal of Marketing*, 57, (April 1993).

URBANY, J. E. "An Experimental Examination of the Economics of Information," *Journal of Consumer Research*, 13, (September 1986), 257–271.

U.S. DEPARTMENT OF TRANSPORTATION, Feasibility Study of Shared-Ride Auto Transit," report IT-06-0144-77-1, Urban Mass Transportation Administration, Service and Methods Demonstration Program (September 1977).

UTTERBACK, J. M., "Innovation in Industry and the Diffusion of Technology," *Science,* 183 (February 15, 1974), 620–26.

——, "The Process of Innovation: A Study of the Origination and Development of Ideas for New Scientific Instruments," *IEEE Transactions on Engineering Management,* Vol. EM-18 (4), (November 1971), 124–31.

VINSON, W. D., and D. F. HEANY, "Is Quality Out of Control?" *Harvard Business Review,* 55 (6), (1977) 114–122.

VON HIPPEL, E., "Successful Industrial Products from Consumers' Ideas," *Journal of Marketing,* 42 (1), (January 1978), 39–49.

——, *The Sources of Innovation,* (New York: Oxford University Press 1988).

——, "Lead Users: A Source of Novel Product Concepts," *Management Science,* 32 (1986) 791–805.

——, "The Impact of 'Sticky Data' on Innovation and Problem-Solving" (Working Paper No. 3147-90-BPS, MIT, Sloan School of Management, Cambridge, MA, April 1990).

VON OECH, ROGER, *A Whack on the Side of the Head: How You Can Be More Creative* (New York: Warner Books, 1990).

WEBSTER, F. E., "New Product Adoption in Industrial Markets: A Framework for Analysis," *Journal of Marketing,* 33 (3), (July 1969), 35–39.

WELLS, W. D., "Psychographics: A Critical Review," *Journal of Marketing Science,* 12 (May 1975) 916–213.

WERNER, NANCY C., "Competitive Pricing and Positioning in the Integrated Office Automation Systems Market", (unpublished thesis, MIT, Sloan School of Management, Cambridge, MA, 1986).

WERNERFELT, B., "From Critical Resources to Corporate Strategy," *Journal of General Management,*" 14 (3) (Spring 1989), 4–12.

——, and C. A. MONTGOMERY, "What is an Attractive Industry?" *Management Science,* 32 (10), (October 1986), 1223–30.

WHYTE, W. H., "The Web of Word-of-Mouth," *Fortune,* 50 (5), (November 1954), 140–43.

WILEY, JAMES B., and JAMES T. LOW, "A Monte Carlo Simulation Study of Two Approaches for Aggregating Conjoint Data," *Journal of Marketing Research,* 20 (November 1983), 405–16.

WILSON, R. D., and L. G. PRINGLE, "Modeling New Product Performance: A Comparison of News, Sprinter and Tracker," *Analytic Approaches to Product and Marketing Planning The Second Conference,* ed. R. K. SRIVASTAVA and A. D. SHOCKER (Cambridge, MA: Marketing Science Institute, 1982), 294–311.

WIND, J., V. MAHAJAN, and J. L. BAYLESS, "The Role of New Product Models in Supporting and Improving the New Product Development Process: Some Preliminary Results" (Cambridge, MA: The Marketing Science Institute, 1990).

WIND, Y., *Product Policy* (Reading, MA: Addison-Wesley, 1982).

——, and V. MAHAJAN, "Designing Product and Business Portfolios," *Harvard Business Review,* 59 (January–February 1981), 155–65.

———, ———, and R. N. CARDOZO, eds. *New Product Forecasting* (Lexington, MA: Lexington Books, 1981).

———, T. ROBERTSON, and C. FRASER, "Industrial Product Diffusion by Market Segment," *Industrial Marketing Management*, 11, (1982), 1–8.

WOMACK, J. P., D. T. JONES, and D. ROOS, *The Machine That Changed the World* (New York: Rawson Associates, Division of MacMillan, 1990).

WORKMAN, J. P., "Racing to Market: An Ethnogaphy of New Product Development in the Computer Industry" (Ph.D. thesis, MIT, Sloan School of Management, September 1991).

YANKELOVICH, S. and WHITE, *LTM Estimating Procedures* (New York: Yankelovich, Skelly and White, Inc., 1970).

ZAJAC, E. J., B. R. GOLDEN, and S. M. SHORTELL, "New Organizational Forms for Enhancing Innovation: The Case of Internal Corporate Joint Ventures," *Management Science*, 37 (2), (February 1991), 170–84.

ZIRGER, B. J. O., and M. A. MAIDIQUE, "Model of New Product Development: Empirical Test," *Management Science*, 36 (7), (July 1990), 867–83.

ZUFRYDEN, F. S., "ZIPMAP-A Zero-One Integer Programming Model for Market Segmentation and Product Positioning," *Journal of the Operational Research Society*, 30 (1979), 63–76.

———, "A Conjoint-Measurement-Based Approach for Optimal New Product Design and Product Positioning," *Analytical Approaches to Product and Market Planning*, ed. A. D. Shocker (Cambridge, MA: Marketing Science Institute, 1977), 100–14.

Concepts and Techniques Index